TAKING SIDES

Clashing Views on Controversial

Educational Issues

TWELFTH EDITION

Selected, Edited, and with Introductions by

James Wm. Noll
University of Maryland

McGraw-Hill/Dushkin
A Division of The McGraw-Hill Companies

For Stephanie and Sonja

Photo Acknowledgment
Cover image: © 2003 by PhotoDisc, Inc.

Cover Art Acknowledgment
Charles Vitelli

Library of Congress Cataloging-in-Publication Data
Main entry under title:
Taking sides: clashing views on controversial educational issues/selected, edited, and with introductions by James Wm. Noll.—12th ed.
Includes bibliographical references and index.
1. Education—United States. I. Noll, James Wm., *comp.*
370.973
0-07-293303-8
ISSN: 1091-8817

Printed on Recycled Paper

Preface

Controversy is the basis of change and often of improvement. Its lack signifies the presence of complacency, the authoritarian limitation of viewpoint expression, or the absence of realistic alternatives to the existing circumstances. An articulate presentation of a point of view on a controversial matter breathes new life into abiding human and social concerns. Controversy prompts reexamination and perhaps renewal.

Education is controversial. Arguments over the most appropriate aims, the most propitious means, and the most effective control have raged over the centuries. Particularly in the United States, where the systematic effort to provide education has been more democratically dispersed and more varied than elsewhere, educational issues have been contentiously debated. Philosophers, psychologists, sociologists, professional educators, lobbyists, government officials, school boards, local pressure groups, taxpayers, parents, and students have all voiced their views.

This book presents opposing or sharply varying viewpoints on educational issues of current concern. Part 1 offers for consideration five topics that have endured through history and are still debated today: the purposes of education, curriculum content and its imposition on the young, the motivational atmosphere in which learning takes place, the problem of church-state separation, and compulsory school attendance. Part 2 features issues that are fundamental to understanding the present circumstances that shape American education: the resurgence of moral education, the push toward a multicultural curriculum, federal initiatives in school reform, standards and testing, and the assessment of the effectiveness of public schooling. Part 3 examines more specific issues currently being debated: vouchers and choice plans, charter schools, religion in public schools, mainstreaming and inclusion policies, reduction of class size and school size, bilingual education, violence prevention, the plight of inner-city schools, computers in education, community service, and alternative teacher certification.

I have made every effort to select views from a wide range of thinkers—philosophers, psychologists, sociologists, professional educators, political leaders, historians, researchers, and gadflies.

Each issue is accompanied by an *introduction*, which sets the stage for the debate, and each issue concludes with a *postscript* that considers other views on the issue and suggests additional readings. I have also provided relevant Internet site addresses (URLs) on the *On the Internet* page that accompanies each part opener. By combining the material in this volume with the informational background provided by a good introductory textbook, the student should be prepared to address the problems confronting schools today.

My hope is that students will find challenges in the material presented here—provocations that will inspire them to better understand the roots of educational controversy, to attain a greater awareness of possible alternatives in dealing with the various issues, and to stretch their personal powers of creative thinking in the search for more promising resolutions of the problems.

Changes to this edition This 12th edition offers three completely new issues: *Can Federal Initiatives Rescue Failing Schools?* (Issue 8); *Is Size Crucial to School Improvement?* (Issue 15); and *Should Alternative Teacher Training Be Encouraged?* (Issue 21). In addition, new selections have been placed in Issue 5 on compulsory attendance, Issue 11 on school vouchers, Issue 12 on charter schools, Issue 19 on computer technology, and Issue 20 on community service. In all, there are 14 new selections.

A word to the instructor An *Instructor's Manual With Test Questions* (multiple-choice and essay) is available through the publisher for the instructor using *Taking Sides* in the classroom. A general guidebook, called *Using Taking Sides in the Classroom,* which discusses methods and techniques for integrating the pro-con approach into any classroom setting, is also available. An online version of *Using Taking Sides in the Classroom* and a correspondence service for Taking Sides adopters can be found at http://www.dushkin.com/usingts/.

    Taking Sides: Clashing Views on Controversial Educational Issues is only one title in the Taking Sides series. If you are interested in seeing the table of contents for any of the other titles, please visit the Taking Sides Web site at http://www.dushkin.com/takingsides/.

Acknowledgments I am thankful for the kind and efficient assistance given to me by Theodore Knight, list manager for the Taking Sides series, and the staff at McGraw-Hill/Dushkin.

James Wm. Noll
University of Maryland

Contents In Brief

Contents

Preface   i

Introduction: Ways of Thinking About Educational Issues   x

Professor emeritus of education R. Freeman Butts warns that current efforts to redefine the relationship between religion and schooling are eroding the Constitution's intent. Professor of political science Robert L. Cord
argues that none of the school practices currently being allowed violate
the First Amendment's establishment clause.

Horace Mann, a leader of the common school movement in the nineteenth
century, presents the basic arguments for publicly funded education in
which all citizens could participate and lays the groundwork for compulsory
attendance laws. Writer-editor Daniel H. Pink declares compulsory mass
schooling an aberration and finds hope in the home schooling revolution
and the ultimate demise of high school.

PART 2   CURRENT FUNDAMENTAL ISSUES   91

Developmental psychologist Thomas Lickona, a leading exponent of the
new character education, charts a course of action to deal with the moral
decline of American youth. Writer-lecturer Alfie Kohn sees character education as mainly a collection of exhortations and extrinsic inducements
that avoid more penetrating efforts at social and moral development.

Professor of language, literacy, and culture Sonia Nieto examines the realities of diversity in American society that underlie an effective approach
to multicultural education. Former English instructor Thomas J. Famularo
contends that the multiculturalism movement, rather than representing diversity, is centered on the themes of race and gender and the debunking
of Western culture.

Gary Rosen, a *Commentary* editor, counters what he feels are cynical criticisms leveled by anti-voucher forces and makes the case for expanding
voucher programs. The National Education Association, a major voucher
foe, offers an array of research studies and reports to substantiate its
position.

Former assistant secretaries of education Chester E. Finn, Jr., and Bruno
V. Manno, along with Gregg Vanourek, vice president of the Charter
School Division of the K12 education program, provide an update on the
charter school movement, which, they contend, is reinventing public education. School superintendent Marc F. Bernstein sees increasing racial
and social class segregation, church-state issues, and financial harm as
outgrowths of the charter school movement.

Edd Doerr, executive director of Americans for Religious Liberty, asserts
that a fair balance between free exercise rights and the obligation of neutrality has been achieved in the public schools. Warren A. Nord, a professor
of the philosophy of religion, contends that the schools are still too secular
and that a place in the curriculum must be found for religion.

Attorney Jean B. Arnold and school superintendent Harold W. Dodge discuss the federal Individuals with Disabilities Education Act and argue that
its implementation can benefit all students. Assistant professor of education Karen Agne argues that legislation to include students with all sorts of
disabilities has had mostly negative effects.

Education dean Patricia A. Wasley contends that schools and classrooms must be small if they are to be places where students' personal and learning needs are met. Policy analyst Kirk A. Johnson, of the Heritage Foundation, argues that while small scale is a popular concept when it comes to class size, the cost is not justified by research findings.

Rosalie Pedalino Porter, director of the Research in English Acquisition and Development Institute, contends that there is no consistent support for transitional bilingual education programs. Richard Rothstein, a research associate of the Economic Policy Institute, reviews the history of bilingual education and argues that, although many problems currently exist, there is no compelling reason to abandon these programs.

Albert Shanker, president of the American Federation of Teachers (AFT), advocates a "get tough" policy for dealing with violent and disruptive students. Professor of education Pedro A. Noguera maintains that the AFT's zero-tolerance stance and other "armed camp" attitudes fail to deal with the heart of the problem and do not build an atmosphere of trust.

Deborah Meier, a leading urban educator, contends that decaying public schools in large cities can be rejuvenated by the proliferation of self-governing exemplary schools. High school principal Emeral A. Crosby maintains that only a powerful political force and a massive infusion of funds can halt the downward spiral of urban school quality.

Introduction

Ways of Thinking About Educational Issues

James Wm. Noll

Concern about the quality of education has been expressed by philosophers, politicians, and parents for centuries. There has been a perpetual and unresolved debate regarding the definition of education, the relationship between school and society, the distribution of decision-making power in educational matters, and the means for improving all aspects of the educational enterprise.

In recent decades the growing influence of thinking drawn from the humanities and the behavioral and social sciences has brought about the development of interpretive, normative, and critical perspectives, which have sharpened the focus on educational concerns. These perspectives have allowed scholars and researchers to closely examine the contextual variables, value orientations, and philosophical and political assumptions that shape both the status quo and reform efforts.

The study of education involves the application of many perspectives to the analysis of "what is and how it got that way" and "what can be and how we can get there." Central to such study are the prevailing philosophical assumptions, theories, and visions that find their way into real-life educational situations. The application situation, with its attendant political pressures, sociocultural differences, community expectations, parental influence, and professional problems, provides a testing ground for contending theories and ideals.

This "testing ground" image applies only insofar as the status quo is malleable enough to allow the examination and trial of alternative views. Historically, institutionalized education has been characteristically rigid. As a testing ground of ideas, it has often lacked an orientation encouraging innovation and futuristic thinking. Its political grounding has usually been conservative.

As social psychologist Allen Wheelis points out in *The Quest for Identity* (1958), social institutions by definition tend toward solidification and protectionism. His depiction of the dialectical development of civilizations centers on the tension between the security and authoritarianism of "institutional processes" and the dynamism and change-orientation of "instrumental processes."

The field of education seems to graphically illustrate this observation. Educational practices are primarily tradition bound. The twentieth-century reform movement, spurred by the ideas of John Dewey, A. S. Neill, and a host of critics who campaigned for change in the 1960s, challenged the structural rigidity of schooling. In more recent decades, reformers have either attempted to restore uniformity in the curriculum and in assessment of results or campaigned for the support of alternatives to the public school monopoly. The latter group comes from both the right and the left of the political spectrum.

We are left with the abiding questions: What is an "educated" person? What should be the primary purpose of organized education? Who should control the decisions influencing the educational process? Should the schools follow society or lead it toward change? Should schooling be compulsory?

Long-standing forces have molded a wide variety of responses to these fundamental questions. The religious impetus, nationalistic fervor, philosophical ideas, the march of science and technology, varied interpretations of "societal needs," and the desire to use the schools as a means for social reform have been historically influential. In recent times other factors have emerged to contribute to the complexity of the search for answers—social class differences, demographic shifts, increasing bureaucratization, the growth of the textbook industry, the changing financial base for schooling, teacher unionization, and strengthening of parental and community pressure groups.

The struggle to find the most appropriate answers to these questions now involves, as in the past, an interplay of societal aims, educational purposes, and individual intentions. Moral development, the quest for wisdom, citizenship training, socioeconomic improvement, mental discipline, the rational control of life, job preparation, liberation of the individual, freedom of inquiry—these and many others continue to be topics of discourse on education.

A detailed historical perspective on these questions and topics may be gained by reading the interpretations of noted scholars in the field. R. Freeman Butts has written a brief but effective summary portrayal in "Search for Freedom—The Story of American Education," *NEA Journal* (March 1960). A partial listing of other sources includes R. Freeman Butts and Lawrence Cremin, *A History of Education in American Culture*; S. E. Frost, Jr., *Historical and Philosophical Foundations of Western Education*; Harry Good and Edwin Teller, *A History of Education*; Adolphe Meyer, *An Educational History of the American People*; Robert L. Church and Michael W. Sedlak, *Education in the United States: An Interpretive History*; Merle Curti, *The Social Ideas of American Educators*; Henry J. Perkinson, *The Imperfect Panacea: American Faith in Education, 1865-1965*; Clarence Karier, *Man, Society, and Education*; V. T. Thayer, *Formative Ideas in American Education*; H. Warren Button and Eugene F. Provenzo, Jr., *History of Education and Culture in America*; David Tyack and Elisabeth Hansot, *Managers of Virtue: Public School Leadership in America, 1820-1980*; Joel Spring, *The American School, 1642-1990*; S. Alexander Rippa, *Education in a Free Society: An American History*; John D. Pulliam, *History of Education in America*; Edward Stevens and George H. Wood, *Justice, Ideology, and Education*; and Walter Feinberg and Jonas F. Soltis, *School and Society*.

These and other historical accounts of the development of schooling demonstrate the continuing need to address educational questions in terms of cultural and social dynamics. A careful analysis of contemporary education demands attention not only to the historical interpretation of developmental influences but also to the philosophical forces that define formal education and the social and cultural factors that form the basis of informal education.

Examining Viewpoints

In his book *A New Public Education* (1976), Seymour Itzkoff examines the interplay between informal and formal education, concluding that economic and technological expansion have pulled people away from the informal culture by placing a premium on success in formal education. This has brought about a reactive search for less artificial educational contexts within the informal cultural community, which recognizes the impact of individual personality in shaping educational experiences.

This search for a reconstructed philosophical base for education has produced a barrage of critical commentary. Those who seek radical change in education characterize the present schools as mindless, manipulative, factory-like, bureaucratic institutions that offer little sense of community, pay scant attention to personal meaning, fail to achieve curricular integration, and maintain a psychological atmosphere of competitiveness, tension, fear, and alienation. Others deplore the ideological movement away from the formal organization of education, fearing an abandonment of standards, a dilution of the curriculum, an erosion of intellectual and behavioral discipline, and a decline in adult and institutional authority.

Students of education (whether prospective teachers, practicing professionals, or interested laypeople) must examine closely the assumptions and values underlying alternative positions in order to clarify their own viewpoints. This tri-level task may best be organized around the basic themes of purpose, power, and reform. These themes offer access to the theoretical grounding of actions in the field of education, to the political grounding of such actions, and to the future orientation of action decisions.

A general model for the examination of positions on educational issues includes the following dimensions: identification of the viewpoint, recognition of the stated or implied assumptions underlying the viewpoint, analysis of the validity of the supporting argument, and evaluation of the conclusions and action-suggestions of the originator of the position. The stated or implied assumptions may be derived from a philosophical or religious orientation, from scientific theory, from social or personal values, or from accumulated experience. Acceptance by the reader of an author's assumptions opens the way for a receptive attitude regarding the specific viewpoint expressed and its implications for action. The argument offered in justification of the viewpoint may be based on logic, common experience, controlled experiments, information and data, legal precedents, emotional appeals, and/or a host of other persuasive devices.

Holding the basic model in mind, readers of the positions presented in this volume (or anywhere else, for that matter) can examine the constituent elements of arguments—basic assumptions, viewpoint statements, supporting evidence, conclusions, and suggestions for action. The careful reader will accept or reject the individual elements of the total position. One might see reasonableness in a viewpoint and its justification but be unable to accept the assumptions on which it is based. Or one might accept the flow of argument from assumptions to viewpoint to evidence but find illogic or impracticality in the stated conclusions and suggestions for action. In any event, the reader's personal view is tested and honed through the process of analyzing the views of others.

Philosophical Considerations

Historically, organized education has been initiated and instituted to serve many purposes—spiritual salvation, political socialization, moral uplift, societal stability, social mobility, mental discipline, vocational efficiency, and social reform, among others. The various purposes have usually reflected the dominant philosophical conception of human nature and the prevailing assumptions about the relationship between the individual and society. At any given time, competing conceptions may vie for dominance—social conceptions, economic conceptions, conceptions that emphasize spirituality, or conceptions that stress the uniqueness and dignity of the individual, for example.

These considerations of human nature and individual-society relationships are grounded in philosophical assumptions, and these assumptions find their way to such practical domains as schooling. In Western civilization there has been an identifiable (but far from consistent and clear-cut) historical trend in the basic assumptions about reality, knowledge, values, and the human condition. This trend, made manifest in the philosophical positions of idealism, realism, pragmatism, and existentialism, has involved a shift in emphasis from the spiritual world to nature to human behavior to the social individual to the free individual, and from eternal ideas to fixed natural laws to social interaction to the inner person.

The idealist tradition, which dominated much of philosophical and educational thought until the eighteenth and nineteenth centuries, separates the changing, imperfect, material world and the permanent, perfect, spiritual or mental world. As Plato saw it, for example, human beings and all other physical entities are particular manifestations of an ideal reality that in material existence humans can never fully know. The purpose of education is to bring us closer to the absolute ideals, pure forms, and universal standards that exist spiritually, by awakening and strengthening our rational powers. For Plato, a curriculum based on mathematics, logic, and music would serve this purpose, especially in the training of leaders whose rationality must exert control over emotionality and baser instincts.

Against this tradition, which shaped the liberal arts curriculum in schools for centuries, the realism of Aristotle, with its finding of the "forms" of things *within* the material world, brought an emphasis on scientific investigation and on environmental factors in the development of human potential. This fundamental view has influenced two philosophical movements in education: naturalism, based on following or gently assisting nature (as in the approaches of

John Amos Comenius, Jean-Jacques Rousseau, and Johann Heinrich Pestalozzi), and scientific realism, based on uncovering the natural laws of human behavior and shaping the educational environment to maximize their effectiveness (as in the approaches of John Locke, Johann Friedrich Herbart, and Edward Thorndike).

In the twentieth century, two philosophical forces (pragmatism and existentialism) have challenged these traditions. Each has moved primary attention away from fixed spiritual or natural influences and toward the individual as shaper of knowledge and values. The pragmatic position, articulated in America by Charles Sanders Peirce, William James, and John Dewey, turns from metaphysical abstractions toward concrete results of action. In a world of change and relativity, human beings must forge their own truths and values as they interact with their environments and each other. The European-based philosophy of existentialism, emerging from such thinkers as Gabriel Marcel, Martin Buber, Martin Heidegger, and Jean-Paul Sartre, has more recently influenced education here. Existentialism places the burdens of freedom, choice, and responsibility squarely on the individual, viewing the current encroachment of external forces and the tendency of people to "escape from freedom" as a serious diminishment of our human possibilities.

These many theoretical slants contend for recognition and acceptance as we continue the search for broad purposes in education and as we attempt to create curricula, methodologies, and learning environments that fulfill our stated purposes. This is carried out, of course, in the real world of the public schools in which social, political, and economic forces often predominate.

Power and Control

Plato, in the fourth century B.C., found existing education manipulative and confining and, in the *Republic,* described a meritocratic approach designed to nurture intellectual powers so as to form and sustain a rational society. Reform-oriented as Plato's suggestions were, he nevertheless insisted on certain restrictions and controls so that his particular version of the ideal could be met.

The ways and means of education have been fertile grounds for power struggles throughout history. Many educational efforts have been initiated by religious bodies, often creating a conflict situation when secular authorities have moved into the field. Schools have usually been seen as repositories of culture and social values and, as such, have been overseen by the more conservative forces in society. To others, bent on social reform, the schools have been treated as a spawning ground for change. Given these basic political forces, conflict is inevitable.

When one speaks of the control of education, the range of influence is indeed wide. Political influences, governmental actions, court decisions, professional militancy, parental power, and student assertion all contribute to the phenomenon of control. And the domain of control is equally broad—school finances, curriculum, instructional means and objectives, teacher certification, accountability, student discipline, censorship of school materials, determination of access and opportunity, and determination of inclusion and exclusion.

The general topic of power and control leads to a multitude of questions: Who should make policy decisions? Must the schools be puppets of the government? Can the schools function in the vanguard of social change? Can cultural indoctrination be avoided? Can the schools lead the way to full social integration? Can the effects of social class be eradicated? Can and should the schools teach values? Dealing with such questions is complicated by the increasing power of the federal government in educational matters. Congressional legislation has broadened substantially from the early land grants and aid to agricultural and vocational programs to more recent laws covering aid to federally impacted areas, school construction aid, student loans and fellowships, support for several academic areas of the curriculum, work-study programs, compensatory education, employment opportunities for youth, adult education, aid to libraries, teacher preparation, educational research, career education, education of the handicapped, and equal opportunity for females. This proliferation of areas of influence has caused the federal administrative bureaucracy to blossom from its meager beginnings in 1867 into a cabinet-level Department of Education in 1979.

State legislatures and state departments of education have also grown in power, handling greater percentages of school appropriations and controlling basic curricular decisions, attendance laws, accreditation, research, and so on. Local school boards, once the sole authorities in policy making, now share the role with higher governmental echelons as the financial support sources shift away from the local scene. Simultaneously, strengthened teacher organizations and increasingly vocal pressure groups at the local, state, and national levels have forced a widening of the base for policy decisions.

Some Concluding Remarks

The schools often seem to be either facing backward or completely absorbed in the tribulations of the present, lacking a vision of possible futures that might guide current decisions. The present is inescapable, obviously, and certainly the historical and philosophical underpinnings of the present situation must be understood, but true improvement often requires a break with conventionality —a surge toward a desired future.

The radical reform critique of government-sponsored compulsory schooling has depicted organized education as a form of cultural or political imprisonment that traps young people in an artificial and mainly irrelevant environment and rewards conformity and docility while inhibiting curiosity and creativity. Constructive reform ideas that have come from this critique include the creation of open classrooms, the de-emphasis of external motivators, the diversification of educational experience, and the building of a true sense of community within the instructional environment.

Starting with Francis Wayland Parker's schools in Quincy, Massachusetts, and John Dewey's laboratory school at the University of Chicago around the turn of the twentieth century, the campaign to make schools into more productive and humane places has been relentless. The duplication of A. S. Neill's Summerhill model in the free school movement in the 1960s, the open classroom/

open space experiments, the several curricular variations, and the emergence of schools without walls, charter schools, privatization of management, and home schooling across the country testify to the desire to reform the present system or to build alternatives to it.

The progressive education movement, the development of "life adjust-ment" goals and curricula, and the "whole person" theories of educational psychology moved the schools toward an expanded concept of schooling that embraced new subject matters and new approaches to discipline during the first half of this century. Since the 1950s, however, pressure for a return to a narrower concept of schooling as intellectual training has sparked new waves of debate. Out of this situation have come attempts by educators and academicians to design new curricular approaches in the basic subject matter areas, efforts by private foundations to stimulate organizational innovations and to improve the training of teachers, and federal government support of educational technol-ogy. Yet criticism of the schools abounds. The schools, according to many who use their services, remain too factorylike, too age-segregated, and too custo-dial. Alternative paths are still sought—paths that would allow action-learning, work-study, and a diversity of ways to achieve success.

H. G. Wells has told us that human history becomes more and more a race between education and catastrophe. What is needed in order to win this race is the generation of new ideas regarding cultural change, human relationships, ethical norms, the uses of technology, and the quality of life. These new ideas, of course, may be old ideas newly applied. One could do worse, in thinking through the problem of improving the quality of education, than to turn to the third-century philosopher Plotinus, who called for an education directed to "the outer, the inner, and the whole." For Plotinus, "the outer" represented the public person, or the socioeconomic dimension of the total human being; "the inner" reflected the subjective dimension, the uniquely experiencing in-dividual, or the "I"; and "the whole" signified the universe of meaning and relatedness, or the realm of human, natural, and spiritual connectedness. It would seem that education must address all of these dimensions if it is to truly help people in the lifelong struggle to shape a meaningful existence. If educa-tional experiences can be improved in these directions, the end result might be people who are not just filling space, filling time, or filling a social role, but who are capable of saying something worthwhile with their lives.

On the Internet ...

The Center for Dewey Studies

The Center for Dewey Studies offers a wealth of source materials for the study of America's quintessential philosopher-educator, John Dewey.

http://www.siu.edu/~deweyctr/index2.html

The National Paideia Center

The National Paideia Center promotes and supports the efforts of educators who are implementing the long-term systemic school reform known as the Paideia Program.

http://www.paideia.org

Coalition of Essential Schools

This site offers facts and ideas on this national curriculum movement.

http://www.essentialschools.org

The Association for Humanistic Psychology

This site features the theories of Carl Rogers, Abraham Maslow, Rollo May, and others.

http://ahpweb.org/aboutahp/whatis.html

Learn in Freedom!

This site offers resources for unschoolers, home schoolers, and all learners with or without school.

http://www.learninfreedom.org

Americans United for Separation of Church and State

Since 1947, Americans United for Separation of Church and State has worked to protect the constitutional principle of church-state separation.

http://www.au.org

J. M. Dawson Institute of Church-State Studies

This site of the J. M. Dawson Institute of Church-State Studies at Baylor University provides articles and links to other sites.

http://www3.baylor.edu/Church_State

PART 1

Enduring Issues

*W*hat is the basic purpose of education? How should the curriculum be organized? What is the best way to teach and motivate students to learn? Does religion have any place in public education? Does the government have the right to compel school attendance? These questions have been discussed since the beginnings of organized schooling, and they continue to be debated today. In this section, the views of seven influential figures in American education—Horace Mann, John Dewey, Robert M. Hutchins, Mortimer J. Adler, John Holt, B. F. Skinner, and Carl R. Rogers—and three scholars in the field of education—R. Freeman Butts, Robert L. Cord, and Daniel H. Pink—are used to address these enduring questions.

- Should Schooling Be Based on Social Experiences?

- Should the Curriculum Be Standardized for All?

- Should Behaviorism Shape Educational Practices?

- Should Church-State Separation Be Maintained?

- Should School Attendance Be Compelled?

ISSUE 1

Should Schooling Be Based on Social Experiences?

YES: John Dewey, from *Experience and Education* (Macmillan, 1938)

NO: Robert M. Hutchins, from *The Conflict in Education in a Democratic Society* (Harper & Row, 1953)

ISSUE SUMMARY

YES: Philosopher John Dewey suggests a reconsideration of traditional approaches to schooling, giving fuller attention to the social development of the learner and the quality of his or her total experience.

NO: Robert M. Hutchins, noted educator and one-time chancellor of the University of Chicago, argues for a liberal arts education geared to the development of intellectual powers.

Throughout history, organized education has served many purposes—the transmission of tradition, knowledge, and skills; the acculturation and socialization of the young; the building and preserving of political-economic systems; the provision of opportunity for social mobility; the enhancement of the quality of life; and the cultivation of individual potential, among others. At any given time, schools pursue a number of such goals, but the elucidation of a primary or overriding goal, which gives focus to all others, has been a source of continuous contention.

Schooling in America has been extended in the last 100 years to vast numbers of young people, and during this time the argument over aims has gained momentum. At the turn of the century, John Dewey was raising serious questions about the efficacy of the prevailing approach to schooling. He believed that schooling was often arid, pedantic, and detached from the real lives of children and youths. In establishing his laboratory school at the University of Chicago, Dewey hoped to demonstrate that experiences provided by schools could be meaningful extensions of the normal social activities of learners, having as their primary aim the full experiential growth of the individual.

In order to accomplish this, Dewey sought to bring the learner into an active and intimate relationship with the subject matter. The problem-solving, or inquiry, approach that he and his colleagues at Columbia University in New York City devised became the cornerstone of the "new education"—the progressive education movement.

In 1938 Dewey himself (as expressed in the selection that follows) sounded a note of caution to progressive educators who may have abandoned too completely the traditional disciplines in their attempt to link schooling with the needs and interests of the learners. Having spawned an educational revolution, Dewey, in his later years, emerges as more of a compromiser.

In that same year, William C. Bagley, in "An Essentialists' Platform for the Advancement of American Education," harshly criticized what he felt were anti-intellectual excesses promulgated by progressivism. In the 1950s and 1960s this theme was elaborated on by other academics, among them Robert M. Hutchins, Hyman Rickover, Arthur Bestor, and Max Rafferty, who demanded a return to intellectual discipline, higher standards, and moral guidance.

Hutchins's critique of Dewey's pragmatic philosophy was perhaps the best reasoned. He felt that the emphasis on immediate needs and desires of students and the focus on change and relativism detracted from the development of the intellectual skills needed for the realization of human potential.

A renewal of scholarly interest in the philosophical and educational ideas of both Dewey and Hutchins has resulted in a number of books, among which are *Hutchins' University: A Memoir of the University of Chicago* by William H. O'Neill (1991); *Robert M. Hutchins: Portrait of an Educator* by Mary Ann Dzuback (1991); *John Dewey and American Democracy* by Robert B. Westbrook (1991); *The End of Epistemology: Dewey and His Allies on the Spectator Theory of Knowledge* by Christopher B. Kulp (1992); and *The Promise of Pragmatism* by John Patrick Diggins (1994). Their continuing influence is charted by Rene Vincente Arcilla in "Metaphysics in Education After Hutchins and Dewey," *Teachers College Record* (Winter 1991).

More recent articles on the legacies of Dewey's progressivism and the traditionalism of Hutchins include "Education and the Pursuit of Happiness: John Dewey's Sympathetic Character," by Sam Stack, *Journal of Thought* (Summer 1996); "A Conversation Between John Dewey and Rudolph Steiner," by Jacques Ensign, *Educational Theory* (Spring 1996); "Toward a Theory of Progressive Education?" by Jurgen Herbst, *History of Education Quarterly* (Spring 1997); "Why Traditional Education Is More Progressive," by E. D. Hirsch, Jr., *The American Enterprise* (March 1997); "The Plight of Children Is Our Plight," by William H. Schubert, *Educational Horizons* (Winter 1998); and Diana Schaub's "Can Liberal Education Survive Liberal Democracy?" *The Public Interest* (Spring 2002).

In the following selections, Dewey charts what he considers a necessary shift from the abstractness and isolation of traditional schooling to the concreteness and vitality of the newer concept. Hutchins dissects the assumptions underlying Dewey's position and puts forth his own theory based on the premise that human nature is constant and functions the same in every society.

3

Experience and Education

Mankind likes to think in terms of extreme opposites. It is given to formulating its beliefs in terms of *Either-Ors,* between which it recognizes no intermediate possibilities. When forced to recognize that the extremes cannot be acted upon, it is still inclined to hold that they are all right in theory but that when it comes to practical matters circumstances compel us to compromise. Educational philosophy is no exception. The history of educational theory is marked by opposition between the idea that education is development from within and that it is formation from without; that it is based upon natural endowments and that education is a process of overcoming natural inclination and substituting in its place habits acquired under external pressure.

At present, the opposition, so far as practical affairs of the school are concerned, tends to take the form of contrast between traditional and progressive education. If the underlying ideas of the former are formulated broadly, without the qualifications required for accurate statement, they are found to be about as follows: The subject-matter of education consists of bodies of information and of skills that have been worked out in the past; therefore, the chief business of the school is to transmit them to the new generation. In the past, there have also been developed standards and rules of conduct; moral training consists of forming habits of action in conformity with these rules and standards. Finally, the general pattern of school organization (by which I mean the relations of pupils to one another and to the teachers) constitutes the school as a kind of institution sharply marked off from other social institutions. Call up in imagination the ordinary schoolroom, its time schedules, schemes of classification, of examination and promotion, of rules of order, and I think you will grasp what is meant by "pattern of organization." If then you contrast this scene with what goes on in the family, for example, you will appreciate what is meant by the school being a kind of institution sharply marked off from any other form of social organization.

The three characteristics just mentioned fix the aims and methods of instruction and discipline. The main purpose or objective is to prepare the young for future responsibilities and for success in life, by means of acquisition of the organized bodies of information and prepared forms of skill which comprehend the material of instruction. Since the subject-matter as well as standards of proper conduct are handed down from the past, the attitude of pupils must, upon the whole, be one of docility, receptivity, and obedience. Books, especially textbooks, are the chief representatives of the lore and wisdom of the past, while teachers are the organs through which pupils are brought into effective connection with the material. Teachers are the agents through which knowledge and skills are communicated and rules of conduct enforced.

I have not made this brief summary for the purpose of criticizing the underlying philosophy. The rise of what is called new education and progressive schools is of itself a product of discontent with traditional education. In effect it is a criticism of the latter. When the implied criticism is made explicit it reads somewhat as follows: The traditional scheme is, in essence, one of imposition from above and from outside. It imposes adult standards, subject-matter, and methods upon those who are only growing slowly toward maturity. The gap is so great that the required subject-matter, the methods of learning and of behaving are foreign to the existing capacities of the young. They are beyond the reach of the experience the young learners already possess. Consequently, they must be imposed; even though good teachers will use devices of art to cover up the imposition so as to relieve it of obviously brutal features.

But the gulf between the mature or adult products and the experience and abilities of the young is so wide that the very situation forbids much active participation by pupils in the development of what is taught. Theirs is to do —and learn, as it was the part of the six hundred to do and die. Learning here means acquisition of what already is incorporated in books and in the heads of the elders. Moreover, that which is taught is thought of as essentially static. It is taught as a finished product, with little regard either to the ways in which it was originally built up or to changes that will surely occur in the future. It is to a large extent the cultural product of societies that assumed the future would be much like the past, and yet it is used as educational food in a society where change is the rule, not the exception.

If one attempts to formulate the philosophy of education implicit in the practices of the new education, we may, I think, discover certain common principles amid the variety of progressive schools now existing. To imposition from above is opposed expression and cultivation of individuality; to external discipline is opposed free activity; to learning from texts and teachers, learning through experience; to acquisition of isolated skills and techniques by drill, is opposed acquisition of them as means of attaining ends which make direct vital appeal; to preparation for a more or less remote future is opposed making the most of the opportunities of present life; to static aims and materials is opposed acquaintance with a changing world.

Now, all principles by themselves are abstract. They become concrete only in the consequences which result from their application. Just because the principles set forth are so fundamental and far-reaching, everything depends upon the interpretation given them as they are put into practice in the school and the home. It is at this point that the reference made earlier to *Either-Or* philosophies becomes peculiarly pertinent. The general philosophy of the new education may be sound, and yet the difference in abstract principles will not decide the way in which the moral and intellectual preference involved shall be worked

out in practice. There is always the danger in a new movement that in rejecting the aims and methods of that which it would supplant, it may develop its
principles negatively rather than positively and constructively. Then it takes its
clew in practice from that which is rejected instead of from the constructive
development its own philosophy.

I take it that the fundamental unity of the newer philosophy is found in
the idea that there is an intimate and necessary relation between the processes
of actual experience and education. If this be true, then a positive and constructive development of its own basic idea depends upon having a correct idea
of experience. Take, for example, the question of organized subject-matter....
The problem for progressive education is: What is the place and meaning of
subject-matter and of organization *within* experience? How does subject-matter
function? Is there anything inherent in experience which tends towards progressive organization of its contents? What results follow when the materials
of experience are not progressively organized? A philosophy which proceeds
on the basis of rejection, of sheer opposition, will neglect these questions. It
will tend to suppose that because the old education was based on ready-made
organization, therefore it suffices to reject the principle of organization *in toto*,
instead of striving to discover what it means and how it is to be attained on the
basis of experience. We might go through all the points of difference between
the new and the old education and reach similar conclusions. When external
control is rejected, the problem becomes that of finding the factors of control
that are inherent within experience. When external authority is rejected, it does
not follow that all authority should be rejected, but rather that there is need to
search for a more effective source of authority. Because the older education
imposed the knowledge, methods, and the rules of conduct of the mature person upon the young, it does not follow, except upon the basis of the extreme
Either-Or philosophy, that the knowledge and skill of the mature person has no
directive value for the experience of the immature. On the contrary, basing education upon personal experience may mean more multiplied and more intimate
contacts between the mature and the immature than ever existed in the traditional school, and consequently more, rather than less, guidance by others. The
problem, then, is: how these contacts can be established without violating the
principle of learning through personal experience. The solution of this problem
requires a well thought-out philosophy of the social factors that operate in the
constitution of individual experience.

What is indicated in the foregoing remarks is that the general principles of
the new education do not of themselves solve any of the problems of the actual
or practical conduct and management of progressive schools. Rather, they set
new problems which have to be worked out on the basis of a new philosophy
of experience. The problems are not even recognized, to say nothing of being
solved, when it is assumed that it suffices to reject the ideas and practices of
the old education and then go to the opposite extreme. Yet I am sure that you
will appreciate what is meant when I say that many of the newer schools tend
to make little or nothing of organized subject-matter of study; to proceed as
if any form of direction and guidance by adults were an invasion of individual freedom, and as if the idea that education should be concerned with the

present and future meant that acquaintance with the past has little or no role to play in education. Without pressing these defects to the point of exaggeration, they at least illustrate what is meant by a theory and practice of education which proceeds negatively or by reaction against what has been current in education rather than by a positive and constructive development of purposes, methods, and subject-matter on the foundation of a theory of experience and its educational potentialities.

It is not too much to say that an educational philosophy which professes to be based on the idea of freedom may become as dogmatic as ever was the traditional education which is reacted against. For any theory and set of practices is dogmatic which is not based upon critical examination of its own underlying principles. Let us say that the new education emphasizes the freedom of the learner. Very well. A problem is now set. What does freedom mean and what are the conditions under which it is capable of realization? Let us say that the kind of external imposition which was so common in the traditional school limited rather than promoted the intellectual and moral development of the young. Again, very well. Recognition of this serious defect sets a problem. Just what is the role of the teacher and of books in promoting the educational development of the immature? Admit that traditional education employed as the subject-matter for study facts and ideas so bound up with the past as to give little help in dealing with the issues of the present and future. Very well. Now we have the problem of discovering the connection which actually exists *within* experience between the achievements of the past and the issues of the present. We have the problem of ascertaining how acquaintance with the past may be translated into a potent instrumentality for dealing effectively with the future. We may reject knowledge of the past as the *end* of education and thereby only emphasize its importance as a *means*. When we do that we have a problem that is new in the story of education: How shall the young become acquainted with the past in such a way that the acquaintance is a potent agent in appreciation of the living present? . . .

In short, the point I am making is that rejection of the philosophy and practice of traditional education sets a new type of difficult educational problem for those who believe in the new type of education. We shall operate blindly and in confusion until we recognize this fact; until we thoroughly appreciate that departure from the old solves no problems. What is said in the following pages is, accordingly, intended to indicate some of the main problems with which the newer education is confronted and to suggest the main lines along which their solution is to be sought. I assume that amid all uncertainties there is one permanent frame of reference: namely, the organic connection between education and personal experience; or, that the new philosophy of education is committed to some kind of empirical and experimental philosophy. But experience and experiment are not self-explanatory ideas. Rather, their meaning is part of the problem to be explored. To know the meaning of empiricism we need to understand what experience is.

The belief that all genuine education comes about through experience does not mean that all experiences are genuinely or equally educative. Experience and education cannot be directly equated to each other. For some experiences are miseducative. Any experience is miseducative that has the effect of arresting or distorting the growth of further experience. An experience may be such as to engender callousness; it may produce lack of sensitivity and of responsiveness. Then the possibilities of having richer experience in the future are restricted. Again, a given experience may increase a person's automatic skill in a particular direction and yet tend to land him in a groove or rut; the effect again is to narrow the field of further experience. An experience may be immediately enjoyable and yet promote the formation of a slack and careless attitude; this attitude then operates to modify the quality of subsequent experiences so as to prevent a person from getting out of them what they have to give. Again, experiences may be so disconnected from one another that, while each is agreeable or even exciting in itself, they are not linked cumulatively to one another. Energy is then dissipated and a person becomes scatter-brained. Each experience may be lively, vivid, and "interesting," and yet their disconnectedness may artificially generate dispersive, disintegrated, centrifugal habits. The consequence of formation of such habits is inability to control future experiences. They are then taken, either by way of enjoyment or of discontent and revolt, just as they come. Under such circumstances, it is idle to talk of self-control.

Traditional education offers a plethora of examples of experiences of the kinds just mentioned. It is a great mistake to suppose, even tacitly, that the traditional schoolroom was not a place in which pupils had experiences. Yet this is tacitly assumed when progressive education as a plan of learning by experience is placed in sharp opposition to the old. The proper line of attack is that the experiences which were had, by pupils and teachers alike, were largely of a wrong kind. How many students, for example, were rendered callous to ideas, and how many lost the impetus to learn because of the way in which learning was experienced by them? How many acquired special skills by means of automatic drill so that their power of judgment and capacity to act intelligently in new situations was limited? How many came to associate the learning process with ennui and boredom? How many found what they did learn so foreign to the situations of life outside the school as to give them no power of control over the latter? How many came to associate books with dull drudgery, so that they were "conditioned" to all but flashy reading matter?

If I ask these questions, it is not for the sake of wholesale condemnation of the old education. It is for quite another purpose. It is to emphasize the fact, first, that young people in traditional schools do have experiences; and, secondly, that the trouble is not the absence of experiences, but their defective and wrong character—wrong and defective from the standpoint of connection with further experience. The positive side of this point is even more important in connection with progressive education. It is not enough to insist upon the necessity of experience, nor even of activity in experience. Everything depends upon the *quality* of the experience which is had. The quality of an experience has two aspects. There is an immediate aspect of agreeableness or disagreeableness, and there is its influence upon later experiences. The first is obvious and easy to judge. The *effect* of an experience is not borne on its face. It sets a problem to the educator. It is his business to arrange for the kind of experiences which, while they do not repel the student, but rather engage his activities are, nevertheless, more than immediately enjoyable since they promote having desirable future experiences. Just as no man lives or dies to himself, so no experience lives or dies to itself. Wholly independent of desire or intent, every experience lives on in further experiences. Hence the central problem of an education based upon experience is to select the kind of present experiences that live fruitfully and creatively in subsequent experiences.

... Here I wish simply to emphasize the importance of this principle [of the continuity of experience] for the philosophy of educative experience. A philosophy of education, like my theory, has to be stated in words, in symbols. But so far as it is more than verbal it is a plan for conducting education. Like any plan, it must be framed with reference to what is to be done and how it is to be done. The more definitely and sincerely it is held that education is a development within, by, and for experience, the more important it is that there shall be clear conceptions of what experience is. Unless experience is so conceived that the result is a plan for deciding upon subject-matter, upon methods of instruction and discipline, and upon material equipment and social organization of the school, it is wholly in the air. It is reduced to a form of words which may be emotionally stirring but for which any other set of words might equally well be substituted unless they indicate operations to be initiated and executed. Just because traditional education was a matter of routine in which the plans and programs were handed down from the past, it does not follow that progressive education is a matter of planless improvisation.

The traditional school could get along without any consistently developed philosophy of education. About all it required in that line was a set of abstract words like culture, discipline, our great cultural heritage, etc., actual guidance being derived not from them but from custom and established routines. Just because progressive schools cannot rely upon established traditions and institutional habits, they must either proceed more or less haphazardly or be directed by ideas which, when they are made articulate and coherent, form a philosophy of education. Revolt against the kind of organization characteristic of the traditional school constitutes a demand for a kind of organization based upon ideas. I think that only slight acquaintance with the history of education is needed to prove that educational reformers and innovators alone have felt the need for a philosophy of education. Those who adhered to the established system needed merely a few fine-sounding words to justify existing practices. The real work was done by habits which were so fixed as to be institutional. The lesson for progressive education is that it requires in an urgent degree, a degree more pressing than was incumbent upon former innovators, a philosophy of education based upon a philosophy of experience.

I remarked incidentally that the philosophy in question is, to paraphrase the saying of Lincoln about democracy, one of education of, by, and for experience. No one of these words, *of, by,* or *for,* names anything which is self-evident. Each of them is a challenge to discover and put into operation a principle of order and organization which follows from understanding what education experience signifies.

It is, accordingly, a much more difficult task to work out the kinds of materials, of methods, and of social relationships that are appropriate to the new education than is the case with traditional education. I think many of the difficulties experienced in the conduct of progressive schools and many of the criticisms leveled against them arise from this source. The difficulties are aggravated and the criticisms are increased when it is supposed that the new education is somehow easier than the old. This belief is, I imagine, more or less current. Perhaps it illustrates again the *Either-Or* philosophy, springing from the idea that about all which is required is *not* to do what is done in traditional schools.

I admit gladly that the new education is *simpler* in principle than the old. It is in harmony with principles of growth, while there is very much which is artificial in the old selection and arrangement of subjects and methods, and artificiality always leads to unnecessary complexity. But the easy and the simple are not identical. To discover what is really simple and to act upon the discovery is an exceedingly difficult task. After the artificial and complex is once institutionally established and ingrained in custom and routine, it is easier to walk in the paths that have been beaten than it is, after taking a new point of view, to work out what is practically involved in the new point of view. The old Ptolemaic astronomical system was more complicated with its cycles and epicycles than the Copernican system. But until organization of actual astronomical phenomena on the ground of the latter principle had been effected the easiest course was to follow the line of least resistance provided by the old intellectual habit. So we come back to the idea that a coherent *theory* of experience, affording positive direction to selection and organization of appropriate educational methods and materials, is required by the attempt to give new direction to the work of the schools. The process is a slow and arduous one. It is a matter of growth, and there are many obstacles which tend to obstruct growth and to deflect it into wrong lines.

... [W]e must escape from the tendency to think of organization in terms of the *kind* of organization, whether of content (or subject-matter), or of methods and social relations, that mark traditional education. I think that a good deal of the current opposition to the idea of organization is due to the fact that it is so hard to get away from the picture of the studies of the old school. The moment "organization" is mentioned imagination goes almost automatically to the kind of organization that is familiar, and in revolting against that we are led to shrink from the very idea of any organization. On the other hand, educational reactionaries, who are now gathering force, use the absence of adequate intellectual and moral organization in the newer type of school as proof not only of the need of organization, but to identify any and every kind of organization with that instituted before the rise of experimental science. Failure to develop a conception of organization upon the empirical and experimental basis gives reactionaries a too easy victory. But the fact that the empirical sciences now offer the best type of intellectual organization which can be found in any field shows that there is no reason why we, who call ourselves empiricists, should be "pushovers" in the matter of order and organization.

NO

The Basis of Education

The obvious failures of the doctrines of adaptation, immediate needs, social reform, and of the doctrine that we need no doctrine at all may suggest to us that we require a better definition of education. Let us concede that every society must have some system that attempts to adapt the young to their social and political environment. If the society is bad, in the sense, for example, in which the Nazi state was bad, the system will aim at the same bad ends. To the extent that it makes men bad in order that they may be tractable subjects of a bad state, the system may help to achieve the social ideals of the society. It may be what the society wants; it may even be what the society needs, if it is to perpetuate its form and accomplish its aims. In pragmatic terms, in terms of success in the society, it may be a "good" system.

But it seems to me clearer to say that, though it may be a system of training, or instruction, or adaptation, or meeting immediate needs, it is not a system of education. It seems clearer to say that the purpose of education is to improve men. Any system that tries to make them bad is not education, but something else. If, for example, democracy is the best form of society, a system that adapts the young to it will be an educational system. If despotism is a bad form of society, a system that adapts the young to it will not be an educational system, and the better it succeeds in adapting them the less educational it will be.

Every man has a function as a man. The function of a citizen or a subject may vary from society to society, and the system of training, or adaptation, or instruction, or meeting immediate needs may vary with it. But the function of a man as man is the same in every age and in every society, since it results from his nature as a man. The aim of an educational system is the same in every age and in every society where such a system can exist: it is to improve man as man.

If we are going to talk about improving men and societies, we have to believe that there is some difference between good and bad. This difference must not be, as the positivists think it is, merely conventional. We cannot tell this difference by any examination of the effectiveness of a given program as the pragmatists propose; the time required to estimate these effects is usually too long and the complexity of society is always too great for us to say that the consequences of a given program are altogether clear. We cannot discover the

From Robert M. Hutchins, *The Conflict in Education in a Democratic Society* (Harper & Row, 1953). Copyright © 1953 by Harper & Row Publishers, Inc.; renewed 1981 by Vesta S. Hutchins. Reprinted by permission of HarperCollins Publishers, Inc.

difference between good and bad by going to the laboratory, for men and societies are not laboratory animals. If we believe that there is no truth, there is no knowledge, and there are no values except those which are validated by laboratory experiment, we cannot talk about the improvement of men and societies, for we can have no standard of judging anything that takes place among men or in societies.

Society is to be improved, not by forcing a program of social reform down its throat, through the schools, or otherwise, but by the improvement of the individuals who compose it. As Plato said, "Governments reflect human nature. States are not made out of stone or wood, but out of the characters of their citizens: these turn the scale and draw everything after them." The individual is the heart of society....

Man is by nature free, and he is by nature social. To use his freedom rightly he needs discipline. To live in society he needs the moral virtues. Good moral and intellectual habits are required for the fullest development of the nature of man.

To develop fully as a social, political animal man needs participation in his own government. A benevolent despotism will not do. You cannot expect the slave to show the virtues of the free man unless you first set him free. Only democracy, in which all men rule and are ruled in turn for the good life of the whole community, can be an absolutely good form of government....

Education deals with the development of the intellectual powers of men. Their moral and spiritual powers are the sphere of the family and the church. All three agencies must work in harmony; for, though a man has three aspects, he is still one man. But the schools cannot take over the role of the family and the church without promoting the atrophy of those institutions and failing in the task that is proper to the schools.

We cannot talk about the intellectual powers of men, though we can talk about training them, or amusing them, or adapting them, and meeting their immediate needs, unless our philosophy in general tells us that there is knowledge and that there is a difference between true and false. We must believe, too, that there are other means of obtaining knowledge than scientific experimentation. If knowledge can be sought only in the laboratory, many fields in which we thought we had knowledge will offer us nothing but opinion or superstition, and we shall be forced to conclude that we cannot know anything about the most important aspects of man and society. If we are to set about developing the intellectual powers of man through having them acquire knowledge of the most important subjects, we have to begin with the proposition that experimentation and empirical data will be of only limited use to us, contrary to the convictions of many American social scientists, and that philosophy, history, literature, and art give us knowledge, and significant knowledge, on the most significant issues.

If the object of education is the improvement of men, then any system of education that is without values is a contradiction in terms. A system that seeks bad values is bad. A system that denies the existence of values denies the possibility of education. Relativism, scientism, skepticism, and anti-intellectualism, the four horsemen of the philosophical apocalypse, have produced that chaos in education which will end in the disintegration of the West.

The prime object of education is to know what is good for man. It is to know the goods in their order. There is a hierarchy of values. The task of education is to help us understand it, establish it, and live by it. This Aristotle had in mind when he said: "It is not the possessions but the desires of men that must be equalized, and this is impossible unless they have a sufficient education according to the nature of things."

Such an education is far removed from the triviality of that produced by the doctrines of adaptation, of immediate needs, of social reform, or of the doctrine of no doctrine at all. Such an education will not adapt the young to a bad environment, but it will encourage them to make it good. It will not overlook immediate needs, but it will place these needs in their proper relationship to more distant, less tangible, and more important goods. It will be the only effective means of reforming society.

This is the education appropriate to free men. It is liberal education. If all men are to be free, all men must have this education. It makes no difference how they are to earn their living or what their special interests or aptitudes may be. They can learn to make a living, and they can develop their special interests and aptitudes, after they have laid the foundation of free and responsible manhood through liberal education. It will not do to say that they are incapable of such education. This claim is made by those who are too indolent or unconvinced to make the effort to give such education to the masses.

Nor will it do to say that there is not enough time to give everybody a liberal education before he becomes a specialist. In America, at least, the waste and frivolity of the educational system are so great that it would be possible through getting rid of them to give every citizen a liberal education and make him a qualified specialist, too, in less time than is now consumed in turning out uneducated specialists.

A liberal education aims to develop the powers of understanding and judgment. It is impossible that too many people can be educated in this sense, because there cannot be too many people with understanding and judgment. We hear a great deal today about the dangers that will come upon us through the frustration of educated people who have got educated in the expectation that education will get them a better job, and who then fail to get it. But surely this depends on the representations that are made to the young about what education is. If we allow them to believe that education will get them better jobs and encourage them to get educated with this end in view, they are entitled to a sense of frustration if, when they have got the education, they do not get the jobs. But, if we say that they should be educated in order to be men, and that everybody, whether he is ditch-digger or a bank president, should have this education because he is a man, then the ditch-digger may still feel frustrated, but not because of his education.

Nor is it possible for a person to have too much liberal education, because it is impossible to have too much understanding and judgment. But it is possible to undertake too much in the name of liberal education in youth. The object of liberal education in youth is not to teach the young all they will ever need to know. It is to give them the habits, ideas, and techniques that they need to continue to educate themselves. Thus the object of formal institutional liberal education in youth is to prepare the young to educate themselves throughout their lives.

I would remind you of the impossibility of learning to understand and judge many of the most important things in youth. The judgment and understanding of practical affairs can amount to little in the absence of experience with practical affairs. Subjects that cannot be understood without experience should not be taught to those who are without experience. Or, if these subjects are taught to those who are without experience, it should be clear that these subjects can be taught only by way of introduction and that their value to the student depends on his continuing to study them as he acquires experience. The tragedy in America is that economics, ethics, politics, history, and literature are studied in youth, and seldom studied again. Therefore the graduates of American universities seldom understand them.

This pedagogical principle, that subjects requiring experience can be learned only by the experienced, leads to the conclusion that the most important branch of education is the education of adults. We sometimes seem to think of education as something like the mumps, measles, whooping cough, or chicken pox. If a person has had education in childhood, he need not, in fact he cannot, have it again. But the pedagogical principle that the most important things can be learned only in mature life is supported by a sound philosophy in general. Men are rational animals. They achieve their terrestrial felicity by the use of reason. And this means that they have to use it for their entire lives. To say that they should learn only in childhood would mean that they were human only in childhood.

And it would mean that they were unfit to be citizens of a republic. A republic, a true *res publica*, can maintain justice, peace, freedom, and order only by the exercise of intelligence. When we speak of the consent of the governed, we mean, since men are not angels who seek the truth intuitively and do not have to learn it, that every act of assent on the part of the governed is a product of learning. A republic is really a common educational life in process. So Montesquieu said that, whereas the principle of a monarchy was honor, and the principle of a tyranny was fear, the principle of a republic was education.

Hence the ideal republic is the republic of learning. It is the utopia by which all actual political republics are measured. The goal toward which we started with the Athenians twenty-five centuries ago is an unlimited republic of learning and a worldwide political republic mutually supporting each other.

All men are capable of learning. Learning does not stop as long as a man lives, unless his learning power atrophies because he does not use it. Political freedom cannot endure unless it is accompanied by provision for the unlimited acquisition of knowledge. Truth is not long retained in human affairs without continual learning and relearning. Peace is unlikely unless there are continuous, unlimited opportunities for learning and unless men continuously avail themselves of them. The world of law and justice for which we yearn, the worldwide political republic, cannot be realized without the worldwide republic of learning. The civilization we seek will be achieved when all men are citizens of the world republic of law and justice and of the republic of learning all their lives long.

POSTSCRIPT

Should Schooling Be Based on Social Experiences?

Intellectual training versus social-emotional-mental growth—the argument between Dewey and Hutchins reflects a historical debate that flows from the ideas of Plato and Aristotle and that continues today. Psychologists, sociologists, curriculum and instruction specialists, and popular critics have joined philosophers in commenting on this central concern.

Followers of Dewey contend that training the mental powers cannot be isolated from other factors of development and, indeed, can be enhanced by attention to the concrete social situations in which learning occurs. Critics of Dewey worry that the expansion of effort into the social and emotional realm only detracts from the intellectual mission that is schooling's unique province.

Was the progressive education movement ruinous, or did it lay the foundation for the education of the future? A reasonably even-handed appraisal can be found in Lawrence Cremin's *The Transformation of the School* (1961). The free school movement of the 1960s, at least partly derived from progressivism, is analyzed in Allen Graubard's *Free the Children* (1973) and Jonathan Kozol's *Free Schools* (1972). Diane Ravitch's *Troubled Crusade* (1983) and Mary Eberstadt's "The Schools They Deserve," *Policy Review* (October/November 1999) offer effective critiques of progressivism.

Among the best general explorations of philosophical alternatives are Gerald L. Gutek's *Philosophical and Ideological Perspectives on Education* (1988); Edward J. Power's *Philosophy of Education: Studies in Philosophies, Schooling, and Educational Policies* (1990); and *Philosophical Foundations of Education* by Howard Ozmon and Samuel Craver (1990).

Also worth perusing are Philip W. Jackson's "Dewey's *Experience and Education* Revisited," *The Educational Forum* (Summer 1996); Jerome Bruner's 1996 book *The Culture of Education* (particularly chapter 3, "The Complexity of Educational Aims"); Robert Orrill's *Education and Democracy: Re-imaging Liberal Learning in America* (1997); Christine McCarthy's "Dewey's Ethics: Philosophy or Science?" *Education Theory* (Summer 1999); Debra J. Anderson and Robert L. Major, "Dewey, Democracy, and Citizenship," *The Clearing House* (November/December 2001); and Julie Webber, "Why Can't We Be Deweyan Citizens?" *Educational Theory* (Spring 2001).

Questions that must be addressed include: Can the "either/or" polarities of this basic argument be overcome? Is the articulation of overarching general aims essential to the charting of a worthwhile educational experience? And how can the classroom teacher relate to general philosophical aims?

ISSUE 2

Should the Curriculum Be Standardized for All?

YES: Mortimer J. Adler, from "The Paideia Proposal: Rediscovering the Essence of Education," *American School Board Journal* (July 1982)

NO: John Holt, from *Escape From Childhood* (E. P. Dutton, 1974)

ISSUE SUMMARY

YES: Philosopher Mortimer J. Adler contends that democracy is best served by a public school system that establishes uniform curricular objectives for all students.

NO: Educator John Holt argues that an imposed curriculum damages the individual and usurps a basic human right to select one's own path of development.

Controversy over the content of education has been particularly keen since the 1950s. The pendulum has swung from learner-centered progressive education to an emphasis on structured intellectual discipline to calls for radical reform in the direction of "openness" to the recent rally to go "back to basics."

The conservative viewpoint, articulated by such writers as Robert M. Hutchins, Clifton Fadiman, Jacques Barzun, Arthur Bestor, and Mortimer J. Adler, arises from concerns about the drift toward informalism and the decline in academic achievement in recent decades. Taking philosophical cues from Plato's contention that certain subject matters have universal qualities that prompt mental and characterological development, the "basics" advocates argue against incidental learning, student choice, and diminution of structure and standards. Barzun summarizes the viewpoint succinctly: "Nonsense is at the heart of those proposals that would replace definable subject matters with vague activities copied from 'life' or with courses organized around 'problems' or 'attitudes.'"

The reform viewpoint, represented by John Holt, Paul Goodman, Ivan Illich, Charles Silberman, Edgar Friedenberg, and others, portrays the typical traditional school as a mindless, indifferent, social institution dedicated to producing fear, docility, and conformity. In such an atmosphere, the viewpoint holds, learners either become alienated from the established curriculum or learn to play the school "game" and thus achieve a hollow success. Taking cues from the ideas of John Dewey and A. S. Neill, the "radical reformers" have given rise to a flurry of alternatives to regular schooling during recent decades. Among these are free schools, which follow the Summerhill model; urban storefront schools, which attempt to develop a true sense of "community"; "schools without walls," which follow the Philadelphia Parkway Program model; "commonwealth" schools, in which students, parents, and teachers share responsibility; and various "humanistic education" projects within regular school systems, which emphasize students' self-concept development and choice-making ability.

The utilitarian tradition that has descended from Benjamin Franklin, Horace Mann, and Herbert Spencer, Dewey's theory of active experiencing, and Neill's insistence on free and natural development support the reform position. The ideology rejects the factory model of schooling with its rigidly set curriculum, its neglect of individual differences, its social engineering function, and its pervasive formalism. "Basics" advocates, on the other hand, express deep concern over the erosion of authority and the watering down of demands upon students that result from the reform ideology.

Arguments for a more standardized curriculum have been embodied most recently in Theodore R. Sizer's Coalition of Essential Schools and the Core Knowledge Schools of E. D. Hirsch, Jr., whose 1996 book *The Schools We Need and Why We Don't Have Them* summarizes the basic points of this view. An interview with Hirsch by Mark F. Goldberg titled "Doing What Works" appeared in the September 1997 issue of *Phi Delta Kappan*. A thorough critique of Hirsch's position is presented by Kristen L. Buras in "Questioning Core Assumptions," *Harvard Educational Review* (Spring 1999). In 1998 Terry Roberts and the staff of the National Paideia Center at the University of North Carolina released *The Power of Paideia Schools: Defining Lives Through Learning.*

A broad spectrum of ideas on the curriculum may be found in John I. Goodlad's *A Place Called School* (1984), Maxine Green's *The Dialectic of Freedom* (1987), Theodore R. Sizer's *Horace* trilogy, and Ernest L. Boyer's *The Basic School* (1995).

In the following selections, Mortimer J. Adler outlines his "Paideia Proposal," which calls for a uniform and unified curriculum and methodological approach—a common schooling for the development of a truly democratic society. In opposition, John Holt goes beyond his earlier concerns about the oppressiveness of the school curriculum to propose complete freedom for the learner to determine all aspects of his or her educational development.

Mortimer J. Adler

 **YES**

The Paideia Proposal: Rediscovering the Essence of Education

In the first 80 years of this century, we have met the obligation imposed on us by the principle of equal educational opportunity, but only in a quantitative sense. Now as we approach the end of the century, we must achieve equality in qualitative terms.

This means a completely on-track system of schooling. It means, at the basic level, giving all the young the same kind of schooling, whether or not they are college bound.

We are aware that children, although equal in their common humanity and fundamental human rights, are unequal as individuals, differing in their capacity to learn. In addition, the homes and environments from which they come to school are unequal—either predisposing the child for schooling or doing the opposite.

Consequently, the Paideia Proposal, faithful to the principle of equal educational opportunity, includes the suggestion that inequalities due to environmental factors must be overcome by some form of preschool preparation—at least one year for all and two or even three for some. We know that to make such preschool tutelage compulsory at the public expense would be tantamount to increasing the duration of compulsory schooling from 12 years to 13, 14, or 15 years. Nevertheless, we think that this preschool adjunct to the 12 years of compulsory basic schooling is so important that some way must be found to make it available for all and to see that all use it to advantage.

The Essentials of Basic Schooling

The objectives of basic schooling should be the same for the whole school population. In our current two-track or multitrack system, the learning objectives are not the same for all. And even when the objectives aimed at those on the upper track are correct, the course of study now provided does not adequately realize these correct objectives. On all tracks in our current system, we fail to cultivate proficiency in the common tasks of learning, and we especially fail to develop sufficiently the indispensable skills of learning.

The uniform objectives of basic schooling should be threefold. They should correspond to three aspects of the common future to which all the children are destined: (1) Our society provides all children ample opportunity for personal development. Given such opportunity, each individual is under a moral obligation to make the most of himself and his life. Basic schooling must facilitate this accomplishment. (2) All the children will become, when of age, full-fledged citizens with suffrage and other political responsibilities. Basic schooling must do everything it can to make them good citizens, able to perform the duties of citizenship with all the trained intelligence that each is able to achieve. (3) When they are grown, all (or certainly most) of the children will engage in some form of work to earn a living. Basic schooling must prepare them for earning a living, but not by training them for this or that specific job while they are still in school.

To achieve these three objectives, the character of basic schooling must be general and liberal. It should have a single, required, 12-year course of study for all, with no electives except one—an elective choice with regard to a second language, to be selected from such modern languages as French, German, Italian, Spanish, Russian, and Chinese. The elimination of all electives, with this one exception, excludes what *should* be excluded—all forms of specialization, including particularized job training.

In its final form, the Paideia Proposal will detail this required course of study, but I will summarize the curriculum here in its bare outline. It consists of three main columns of teaching and learning, running through the 12 years and progressing, of course, from the simple to the more complex, from the less difficult to the more difficult, as the students grow older. Understand: The three columns (see Table 1) represent three distinct modes of teaching and learning. They do not represent a series of courses. A specific course or class may employ more than one mode of teaching and learning, but all three modes are essential to the overall course of study.

The first column is devoted to acquiring knowledge in three subject areas: (A) language, literature, and the fine arts; (B) mathematics and natural science; (C) history, geography, and social studies.

The second column is devoted to developing the intellectual skills of learning. These include all the language skills necessary for thought and communication—the skills of reading, writing, speaking, listening. They also include mathematical and scientific skills; the skills of observing, measuring, estimating, and calculating; and skills in the use of the computer and of other scientific instruments. Together, these skills make it possible to think clearly and critically. They once were called the liberal arts—the intellectual skills indispensable to being competent as a learner.

The third column is devoted to enlarging the understanding of ideas and values. The materials of the third column are books (*not* textbooks), and other products of human artistry. These materials include books of every variety—historical, scientific, and philosophical as well as poems, stories, and essays—and also individual pieces of music, visual art, dramatic productions, dance productions, film or television productions. Music and works of visual art can be used in seminars in which ideas are discussed; but as with poetry and fiction,

Table 1

The Paideia Curriculum

	Column One	Column Two	Column Three
Goals	Acquisition of Organized Knowledge	Development of Intellectual Skills and Skills of Learning	Improved Understanding of Ideas and Values
	by means of	*by means of*	*by means of*
Means	Didactic Instruction, Lecturing, and Textbooks	Coaching, Exercises, Supervised Practice	Maieutic or Socratic Questioning and Active Participation
	in these three subject areas	*in these operations*	*in these activities*
Subject Areas, Operations, and Activities	Language, Literature, and Fine Arts; Mathematics and Natural Science; History, Geography, and Social Studies	Reading, Writing, Speaking, Listening, Calculating, Problem Solving, Observing, Measuring, Estimating, Exercising Critical Judgment	Discussion of Books (Not Textbooks) and Other Works of Art; Involvement in Music, Drama, and Visual Arts

The three columns do not correspond to separate courses, nor is one kind of teaching and learning necessarily confined to any one class.

---

they also are to be experienced aesthetically, to be enjoyed and admired for their excellence. In this connection, exercises in the composition of poetry, music, and visual works and in the production of dramatic works should be used to develop the appreciation of excellence.

The three columns represent three different kinds of learning on the part of the student and three different kinds of instruction on the part of teachers.

In the first column, the students are engaged in acquiring information and organized knowledge about nature, man, and human society. The method of instruction here, using textbooks and manuals, is didactic. The teacher lectures, invites responses from the students, monitors the acquisition of knowledge, and tests that acquisition in various ways.

In the second column, the students are engaged in developing habits of performance, which is all that is involved in the development of an art or skill. Art, skill, or technique is nothing more than a cultivated, habitual ability to do a certain kind of thing well, whether that is swimming and dancing, or reading and writing. Here, students are acquiring linguistic, mathematical, scientific, and historical *know-how* in contrast to what they acquire in the first column, which is *know-that* with respect to language, literature, and the fine arts, mathematics and science, history, geography, and social studies. Here, the method of instruction cannot be didactic or monitorial; it cannot be dependent on textbooks. It must be coaching, the same kind used in the gym to develop bodily skills; only here it is used by a different kind of coach in the classroom to develop intellectual skills.

In the third column, students are engaged in a process of enlightenment, the process whereby they develop their understanding of the basic and controlling ideas in all fields of subject matter and come to appreciate better all the human values embodied in works of art. Here, students move progressively from understanding less to understanding more—understanding better what they already know and appreciating more what they already have experienced. Here, the method of instruction cannot be either didactic or coaching. It must be the Socratic, or maieutic, method of questioning and discussing. It should not occur in any ordinary classroom with the students sitting in rows and the teacher in front of the class, but in a seminar room, with the students sitting around a table and the teacher sitting with them as an equal, even though a little older and wiser.

Of these three main elements in the required curriculum, the third column is completely innovative. Nothing like this is done in our schools, and because it is completely absent from the ordinary curriculum of basic schooling, the students never have the experience of having their minds addressed in a challenging way or of being asked to think about the important ideas, to express their thoughts, to defend their opinions in a reasonable fashion.

The only thing that is innovative about the second column is the insistence that the method of instruction here must be coaching carried on either with one student at a time or with very small groups of students. Nothing else can be effective in the development of a skill, be it bodily or intellectual. The absence of such individualized coaching in our schools explains why most of the students cannot read well, write well, speak well, listen well, or perform well any of the other basic intellectual operations.

The three columns are closely interconnected and integrated, but the middle column—the one concerned with linguistic, mathematical, and scientific skills—is central. It both supports and is supported by the other two columns. All the intellectual skills with which it is concerned must be exercised in the study of the three basic subject-matters and in acquiring knowledge about them, and these intellectual skills must be exercised in the seminars devoted to the discussion of books and other things.

In addition to the three main columns in the curriculum, ascending through the 12 years of basic schooling, there are three adjuncts: One is 12 years of physical training, accompanied by instruction in bodily care and hygiene. The second, running through something less than 12 years, is the development of basic manual skills, such as cooking, sewing, carpentry, and the operation of all kinds of machines. The third, reserved for the last year or two, is an introduction to the whole world of work—the range of occupations in which human beings earn their livings. This is not particularized job training. It is the very opposite. It aims at a broad understanding of what is involved in working for a living and of the various ways in which that can be done. If, at the end of 12 years, students wish training for specific jobs, they should get that in two-year community or junior colleges, or on the job itself, or in technical institutes of one sort or another.

Everything that has not been specifically mentioned as occupying the time of the school day should be reserved for after-hours and have the status of extra-curricular activities.

Please, note: The required course of study just described is as important for what it *displaces* as for what it introduces. It displaces a multitude of elective courses, especially those offered in our secondary schools, most of which make little or no contribution to general, liberal education. It eliminates all narrowly specialized job training, which now abounds in our schools. It throws out of the curriculum and into the category of optional extracurricular activities a variety of things that have little or no educational value.

If it did not call for all these displacements, there would not be enough time in the school day or year to accomplish everything that is essential to the general, liberal learning that must be the content of basic schooling.

The Quintessential Element

So far, I have set forth the bare essentials of the Paideia Proposal with regard to basic schooling. I have not yet mentioned the quintessential element—the *sine qua non*—without which nothing else can possibly come to fruition, no matter how sound it might be in principle. The heart of the matter is the quality of learning and the quality of teaching that occupies the school day, not to mention the quality of the homework after school.

First, the learning must be active. It must use the whole mind, not just the memory. It must be learning by discovery, in which the student, never the teacher, is the primary agent. Learning by discovery, which is the only genuine learning, may be either unaided or aided. It is unaided only for geniuses. For most students, discovery must be aided.

Here is where teachers come in—as aids in the process of learning by discovery not as knowers who attempt to put the knowledge they have into the minds of their students. The quality of the teaching, in short, depends crucially upon how the teacher conceives his role in the process of learning, and that must be as an aid to the student's process of discovery.

I am prepared for the questions that must be agitating you by now: How and where will we get the teachers who can perform as teachers should? How will we be able to staff the program with teachers so trained that they will be competent to provide the quality of instruction required for the quality of learning desired?

The first part of our answer to these questions is negative: We *cannot* get the teachers we need for the Paideia program from schools of education as *they are now constituted*. As teachers are now trained for teaching, they simply will not do. The ideal—an impracticable ideal—would be to ask for teachers who are, themselves, truly educated human beings. But truly educated human beings are too rare. Even if we could draft all who are now alive, there still would be far too few to staff our schools.

Well, then, what can we look for? Look for teachers who are actively engaged in the process of *becoming* educated human beings, who are themselves deeply motivated to develop their own minds. Assuming this is not too much to ask for the present, how should teachers be schooled and trained in the future? First, they should have the same kind of basic schooling that is recommended in the Paideia Proposal. Second, they should have additional schooling, at the college and even the university level, in which the same kind of general, liberal learning is carried on at advanced levels—more deeply, broadly, and intensively than it can be done in the first 12 years of schooling. Third, they must be given something analogous to the clinical experience in the training of physicians. They must engage in practice-teaching under supervision, which is another way of saying that they must be *coached* in the arts of teaching, not just given didactic instruction in educational psychology and in pedagogy. Finally, and most important of all, they must learn how to teach well by being exposed to the performances of those who are masters of the arts involved in teaching.

It is by watching a good teacher at work that they will be able to perceive what is involved in the process of assisting others to learn by discovery. Perceiving it, they must then try to emulate what they observe, and through this process, they slowly will become good teachers themselves.

The Paideia Proposal recognizes the need for three different kinds of institutions at the collegiate level: The two-year community or junior college should offer a wide choice of electives that give students some training in one or another specialized field, mainly those fields of study that have something to do with earning a living. The four-year college also should offer a wide variety of electives, to be chosen by students who aim at the various professional or technical occupations that require advanced study. Those elective majors chosen by students should be accompanied, for all students, by one required minor, in which the kind of general and liberal learning that was begun at the level of basic schooling is continued at a higher level in the four years of college. And we should have still a third type of collegiate institution—a four-year college in which general, liberal learning at a higher level constitutes a required course of study that is to be taken by all students. *It is this third type of college, by the way, that should be attended by all who plan to become teachers in our basic schools.*

At the university level, there should be a continuation of general, liberal learning at a still higher level to accompany intensive specialization in this or that field of science or scholarship, this or that learned profession. Our insistence on the continuation of general, liberal learning at all the higher levels of schooling stems from our concern with the worst cultural disease that is rampant in our society—*the barbarism of specialization.*

There is no question that our technologically advanced industrial society needs specialists of all sorts. There is no question that the advancement of knowledge in all fields of science and scholarship, and in all the learned professions, needs intense specialization. But for the sake of preserving and enhancing our cultural traditions, as well as for the health of science and scholarship, we need specialists who also are generalists—generally cultivated human beings, not just good plumbers. We need truly educated human beings who can perform their special tasks better precisely because they have general cultivation as well as intensely specialized training.

Changes indeed are needed in higher education, but those improvements cannot reasonably be expected unless improvement in basic schooling makes that possible.

The Future of Our Free Institutions

I already have declared as emphatically as I know how that the quality of human life in our society depends on the quality of the schooling we give our young people, both basic and advanced. But a marked elevation in the quality of human life is not the only reason improving the quality of schooling is so necessary—not the only reason we must move heaven and earth to stop the deterioration of our schools and turn them in the opposite direction. The other reason is to safeguard the future of our free institutions.

They cannot prosper, they may not even survive, unless we do something to rescue our schools from their current deplorable deterioration. Democracy, in the full sense of that term, came into existence only in this century and only in a few countries on earth, among which the United States is an outstanding example. But democracy came into existence in this century, only in its initial conditions, all of which hold out promises for the future that remain to be fulfilled. Unless we do something about improving the quality of basic schooling for all and the quality of advanced schooling for some, there is little chance that those promises ever will be fulfilled. And if they are not, our free institutions are doomed to decay and wither away.

We face many insistently urgent problems. Our prosperity and even our survival depend on the solution of those problems—the threat of nuclear war, the exhaustion of essential resources and of supplies of energy, the pollution or spoilage of the environment, the spiraling of inflation accompanied by the spread of unemployment.

To solve these problems, we need resourceful and innovative leadership. For that to arise and be effective, an educated populace is needed. Trained intelligence—not only on the part of leaders, but also on the part of followers—holds the key to the solution of the problems our society faces. Achieving peace, prosperity and plenty could put us on the threshold of an early paradise. But a much better educational system than now exists also is needed, for that alone can carry us across the threshold. Without it, a poorly schooled population will not be able to put to good use the opportunities afforded by the achievement of the general welfare. Those who are not schooled to enjoy society can only despoil its institutions and corrupt themselves.

NO

John Holt

Escape From Childhood

Young people should have the right to control and direct their own learning, that is, to decide what they want to learn, and when, where, how, how much, how fast, and with what help they want to learn it. To be still more specific, I want them to have the right to decide if, when, how much, and by whom they want to be *taught* and the right to decide whether they want to learn in a school and if so which one and for how much of the time.

No human right, except the right to life itself, is more fundamental than this. A person's freedom of learning is part of his freedom of thought, even more basic than his freedom of speech. If we take from someone his right to decide what he will be curious about, we destroy his freedom of thought. We say, in effect, you must think not about what interests and concerns *you*, but about what interests and concerns *us*.

We might call this the right of curiosity, the right to ask whatever questions are most important to us. As adults, we assume that we have the right to decide what does or does not interest us, what we will look into and what we will leave alone. We take this right for granted, cannot imagine that it might be taken away from us. Indeed, as far as I know, it has never been written into any body of law. Even the writers of our Constitution did not mention it. They thought it was enough to guarantee citizens the freedom of speech and the freedom to spread their ideas as widely as they wished and could. It did not occur to them that even the most tyrannical government would try to control people's minds, what they thought and knew. That idea was to come later, under the benevolent guise of compulsory universal education.

This right to each of us to control our own learning is now in danger. When we put into our laws the highly authoritarian notion that someone should and could decide what all young people were to learn and, beyond that, could do whatever might seem necessary (which now includes dosing them with drugs) to compel them to learn it, we took a long step down a very steep and dangerous path. The requirement that a child go to school, for about six hours a day, 180 days a year, for about ten years, whether or not he learns anything there, whether or not he already knows it or could learn it faster or better somewhere else, is such gross violation of civil liberties that few adults would

stand for it. But the child who resists is treated as a criminal. With this requirement we created an industry, an army of people whose whole work was to tell
young people what they had to learn and to try to make them learn it. Some
of these people, wanting to exercise even more power over others, to be even
more "helpful," or simply because the industry is not growing fast enough to
hold all the people who want to get into it, are now beginning to say, "If it is
good for children for us to decide what they shall learn and to make them learn
it, why wouldn't it be good for everyone? If compulsory education is a good
thing, how can there be too much of it? Why should we allow anyone, of any
age, to decide that he has had enough of it? Why should we allow older people,
any more than young, not to know what we know when their ignorance may
have bad consequences for all of us? Why should we not *make* them know what
they *ought* to know?"

They are beginning to talk, as one man did on a nationwide TV show,
about "womb-to-tomb" schooling. If hours of homework every night are good
for the young, why wouldn't they be good for us all—they would keep us away
from the TV set and other frivolous pursuits. Some group of experts, somewhere, would be glad to decide what we all ought to know and then every so
often check up on us to make sure we knew it—with, of course, appropriate
penalties if we did not.

I am very serious in saying that I think this is coming unless we prepare
against it and take steps to prevent it. The right I ask for the young is a right
that I want to preserve for the rest of us, the right *to decide what goes into our
minds*. This is much more than the right to decide whether or when or how
much to go to school or what school you want to go to. That right is important,
but it is only part of a much larger and more fundamental right, which I might
call the right to Learn, as opposed to being Educated, *i.e.*, made to learn what
someone else thinks would be good for you. It is not just compulsory schooling
but compulsory Education that I oppose and want to do away with.

That children might have the control of their own learning, including the
right to decide if, when, how much, and where they wanted to go to school,
frightens and angers many people. They ask me, "Are you saying that if the
parents wanted the child to go to school, and the child didn't want to go, that
he wouldn't have to go? Are you saying that if the parents wanted the child to
go to one school, and the child wanted to go to another, that the child would
have the right to decide?" Yes, that is what I say. Some people ask, "If school
wasn't compulsory, wouldn't many parents take their children out of school
to exploit their labors in one way or another?" Such questions are often both
snobbish and hypocritical. The questioner assumes and implies (though rarely
says) that these bad parents are people poorer and less schooled than he. Also,
though he appears to be defending the right of children to go to school, what
he really is defending is the right of the state to compel them to go whether they
want to or not. What he wants, in short, is that children should be in school,
not that they should have any choice about going.

But saying that children should have the right to choose to go or not to
go to school does not mean that the ideas and wishes of the parents would
have no weight. Unless he is estranged from his parents and rebelling against

them, a child cares very much about what they think and want. Most of the time, he doesn't want to anger or worry or disappoint them. Right now, in families where the parents feel that they have some choice about their children's schooling, there is much bargaining about schools. Such parents, when their children are little, often ask them whether they want to go to nursery school or kindergarten. Or they may take them to school for a while to try it out. Or, if they have a choice of schools, they may take them to several to see which they think they will like the best. Later, they care whether the child likes his school. If he does not, they try to do something about it, get him out of it, find a school he will like.

I know some parents who for years had a running bargain with their children. "If on a given day you just can't stand the thought of school, you don't feel well, you are afraid of something that may happen, you have something of your own that you very much want to do—well, you can stay home." Needless to say, the schools, with their supporting experts, fight it with all their might— Don't Give in to Your Child, Make Him Go to School, He's Got to Learn. Some parents, when their own plans make it possible for them to take an interesting trip, take their children with them. They don't ask the schools' permission, they just go. If the child doesn't want to make the trip and would rather stay in school, they work out a way for him to do that. Some parents, when their child is frightened, unhappy, and suffering in school, as many children are, just take him out. Hal Bennett, in his excellent book *No More Public School*, talks about ways to do this.

A friend of mine told me that when her boy was in third grade, he had a bad teacher, bullying, contemptuous, sarcastic, cruel. Many of the class switched to another section, but this eight-year-old, being tough, defiant, and stubborn, hung on. One day—his parents did not learn this until about two years later—having had enough of the teacher's meanness, he just got up from his desk and without saying a word, walked out of the room and went home. But for all his toughness and resiliency of spirit, the experience was hard on him. He grew more timid and quarrelsome, less outgoing and confident. He lost his ordinary good humor. Even his handwriting began to go to pieces—it was much worse in the spring of the school year than in the previous fall. One spring day he sat at breakfast, eating his cereal. After a while he stopped eating and sat silently thinking about the day ahead. His eyes filled up with tears, and two big ones slowly rolled down his cheeks. His mother, who ordinarily stays out of the school life of her children, saw this and knew what it was about. "Listen," she said to him, "we don't have to go on with this. If you've had enough of that teacher, if she's making school so bad for you that you don't want to go any more, I'll be perfectly happy just to pull you right out. We can manage it. Just say the word." He was horrified and indignant. "No!" he said, "I couldn't do that." "Okay," she said, "whatever you want is fine. Just let me know." And so they left it. He had decided that he was going to tough it out, and he did. But I am sure knowing that he had the support of his mother and the chance to give it up if it got too much for him gave him the strength he needed to go on.

To say that children should have the right to control and direct their own learning, to go to school or not as they choose, does not mean that the law would forbid the parents to express an opinion or wish or strong desire on the matter. It only means that if their natural authority is not strong enough the parents can't call in the cops to make the child do what they are not able to persuade him to do. And the law may say that there is no limit to the amount of pressure or coercion the parents can apply to the child to deny him a choice that he has a legal right to make.

When I urge that children should control their learning, there is one argument that people bring up so often that I feel I must anticipate and meet it here. It says that schools are a place where children can for a while be protected against the bad influences of the world outside, particularly from its greed, dishonesty, and commercialism. It says that in school children may have a glimpse of a higher way of life, of people acting from other and better motives than greed and fear. People say, "We know that society is bad enough as it is and that if children go out into the larger world as soon as they wanted, they would be tempted and corrupted just that much sooner."

They seem to believe that schools are better, more honorable places than the world outside—what a friend of mine at Harvard once called "museums of virtue." Or that people in school, both children and adults, act from higher and better motives than people outside. In this they are mistaken. There are, of course, some good schools. But on the whole, far from being the opposite of, or an antidote to, the world outside, with all its envy, fear, greed, and obsessive competitiveness, the schools are very much like it. If anything, they are worse, a terrible, abstract, simplified caricature of it. In the world outside the school, some work, at least, is done honestly and well, for its own sake, not just to get ahead of others; people are not everywhere and always being set in competition against each other; people are not (or not yet) in every minute of their lives subject to the arbitrary, irrevocable orders and judgement of others. But in most schools, a student is every minute doing what others tell him, subject to their judgement, in situations in which he can only win at the expense of other students.

This is a harsh judgement. Let me say again, as I have before, that schools are worse than most of the people in them and that many of these people do many harmful things they would rather not do, and a great many other harmful things that they do not even see as harmful. The whole of school is much worse than the sum of its parts. There are very few people in the U.S. today (or perhaps anywhere, any time) in *any* occupation, who could be trusted with the kind of power that schools give most teachers over their students. Schools seem to me among the most anti-democratic, most authoritarian, most destructive, and most dangerous institutions of modern society. No other institution does more harm or more lasting harm to more people or destroys so much of their curiosity, independence, trust, dignity, and sense of identity and worth. Even quite kindly schools are inhibited and corrupted by the knowledge of children and teachers alike that they are *performing* for the judgement and approval of others—the children for the teachers; the teachers for the parents, supervisors, school board, or the state. No one is ever free from feeling that he is being judged all the time, or soon may be. Even after the best class experiences teachers must ask themselves, "Were we right to do that? Can we prove we were right? Will it get us in trouble?"

What corrupts the school, and makes it so much worse than most of the people in it, or than they would like it to be, is its power—just as their powerlessness corrupts the students. The school is corrupted by the endless anxious demand of the parents to know how their child is doing—meaning is he ahead of the other kids—and their demand that he be kept ahead. Schools do not protect children from the badness of the world outside. They are at least as bad as the world outside, and the harm they do to the children in their power creates much of the badness of the world outside. The sickness of the modern world is in many ways a school-induced sickness. It is in school that most people learn to expect and accept that some expert can always place them in some sort of rank or hierarchy. It is in school that we meet, become used to, and learn to believe in the totally controlled society. We do not learn much science, but we learn to worship "scientists" and to believe that anything we might conceivably need or want can only come, and someday will come, from them. The school is the closest we have yet been able to come to Huxley's *Brave New World*, with its alphas and betas, deltas and epsilons—and now it even has its soma. Everyone, including children, should have the right to say "No!" to it.

POSTSCRIPT

Should the Curriculum Be Standardized for All?

The free/open school movement values small, personalized educational settings in which students engage in activities that have personal meaning. One of the movement's ideological assumptions, emanating from the philosophy of Jean-Jacques Rousseau, is that given a reasonably unrestrictive atmosphere, the learner will pursue avenues of creative and intellectual self-development. This confidence in self-motivation is the cornerstone of Holt's advocacy of freedom for the learner, a position he elaborates upon in his books *Instead of Education* (1988) and *Teach Your Own* (1982). The argument has gained some potency with recent developments in home-based computer-assisted instruction.

Adler's proposal for a unified curricular and methodological approach, released in 1982 by the Institute for Philosophical Research, was fashioned by a group of distinguished scholars and practitioners and has its roots in such earlier works as Arthur Bestor's *Educational Wastelands* (1953), Mortimer Smith's *The Diminished Mind* (1954), and Paul Copperman's *The Literacy Hoax* (1978). The proposal has been widely discussed since its release, and it has been implemented in a number of school systems. See, for example, "Launching Paideia in Chattanooga," by Cynthia M. Gettys and Anne Wheelock, *Educational Leadership* (September 1994). The essentialist position articulated by Adler is echoed in a number of recent calls for a more standardized and challenging curriculum by such thinkers as E. D. Hirsch, Jr., Allen Bloom, William Bennett, Diane Ravitch, and Lynne Cheney.

Holt's plea for freedom from an imposed curriculum has a champion in John Taylor Gatto, New York City and New York State Teacher of the Year. Gatto has produced two provocative books, *Dumbing Us Down: The Hidden Curriculum of Compulsory Schooling* (1992) and *Confederacy of Dunces: The Tyranny of Compulsory Schooling* (1992). Two other works that build upon Holt's basic views are Lewis J. Perelman's *School's Out: The New Technology and the End of Education* (1992) and George Leonard's "Notes: The End of School," *The Atlantic Monthly* (May 1992). A less ideological appraisal can be found in Paul Gagnon's "What Should Children Learn?" *The Atlantic Monthly* (December 1995). Theodore R. Sizer offers a plea for individualized instruction in "No Two Are Quite Alike," *Educational Leadership* (September 1999).

Among recent provocative books and articles dealing with the topic are Susan Ohanian, *Caught in the Middle: Nonstandard Kids and a Killing Curriculum* (2001): John Berlau, "What Happened to the Great Ideas?" *Insight on the News* (August 27, 2001); and Elliott W. Eisner, "The Kind of Schools We Need," *Phi Delta Kappan* (April 2002), which is a balanced and thoughtful presentation of needed alterations.

ISSUE 3

Should Behaviorism Shape Educational Practices?

YES: B. F. Skinner, from *Beyond Freedom and Dignity* (Alfred A. Knopf, 1971)

NO: Carl R. Rogers, from *Freedom to Learn for the Eighties* (Merrill, 1983)

ISSUE SUMMARY

YES: B. F. Skinner, an influential proponent of behaviorism and professor of psychology, critiques the concept of "inner freedom" and links learning and motivation to the influence of external forces.

NO: Professor of psychology and psychiatry Carl R. Rogers offers the "humanistic" alternative to behaviorism, insisting on the reality of subjective forces in human motivation.

Intimately enmeshed with considerations of aims and purposes and determination of curricular elements are the psychological base that affects the total setting in which learning takes place and the basic means of motivating learners. Historically, the atmosphere of schooling has often been characterized by harsh discipline, regimentation, and restriction. The prison metaphor often used by critics in describing school conditions rings true all too often.

Although calls to make schools pleasant have been sounded frequently, they have seldomly been heeded. Roman rhetorician Marcus Fabius Quintilian (ca. A.D. 35–100) advocated a constructive and enjoyable learning atmosphere. John Amos Comenius in the seventeenth century suggested a gardening metaphor in which learners were given kindly nurturance. Johann Heinrich Pestalozzi established a model school in the nineteenth century that replaced authoritarianism with love and respect.

Yet school as an institution retains the stigma of authoritarian control —attendance is compelled, social and psychological punishment is meted out, and the decision-making freedom of students is limited and often curtailed. These practices lead to rather obvious conclusions: the prevailing belief is either that young people are naturally evil and wild and therefore must be tamed in a restricting environment or that schooling as such is so unpalatable that people must be forced and cajoled to reap its benefits—or both.

Certainly, philosopher John Dewey (1895–1952) was concerned about this circumstance, citing at one time the superintendent of his native Burlington, Vermont, school district as admitting that the schools were a source of "grief and mortification" and were "unworthy of patronage." Dewey rejected both the need for "taming" and the defeatist attitude that the school environment must remain unappealing. He hoped to create a motivational atmosphere that would engage learners in real problem-solving activities, thereby sustaining curiosity, creativity, and attachment. The rewards were to flow from the sense of accomplishment and freedom, which was to be achieved through the disciplined actions necessary to solve the problem at hand.

More recent treatment of the allied issues of freedom, control, and motivation has come from the two major camps in the field of educational psychology: the behaviorists (rooted in the early-twentieth-century theories of Ivan Pavlov, Edward L. Thorndike, and John B. Watson) and the humanists (emanating from the Gestalt and field theory psychologies developed in Europe and America earlier in the twentieth century).

B. F. Skinner has been the dominant force in translating behaviorism into recommendations for school practices. He and his disciples, often referred to as "neobehaviorists," have contributed to widely used innovations such as behavioral objectives in instruction and testing, competency-based education, mastery learning, assertive discipline, and outcome-based education. The humanistic viewpoint has been championed by Carl R. Rogers, Abraham Maslow, Fritz Perls, Rollo May, and Erich Fromm, most of whom ground their psychological theories in the philosophical assumptions of existentialism and phenomenology.

Skinner believes that "inner" states are merely convenient myths, that motives and behaviors are shaped by environmental factors. These shaping forces, however, need not be negative, nor must they operate in an uncontrolled manner. Our present understanding of human behavior allows us the freedom to shape the environmental forces, which in turn shape us. With this power, Skinner contends, we can replace aversive controls in schooling with positive reinforcements that heighten the students' motivation level and make learning more efficient.

Recent manifestations of the continuing interest in Skinner's behaviorism and the humanistic psychology of Rogers include Virginia Richardson's "From Behaviorism to Constructivism in Teacher Education," *Teacher Education and Special Education* (Summer 1996) and Tobin Hart's "From Category to Contact: Epistemology and the Enlivening and Deadening of Spirit in Education," *Journal of Humanistic Education and Development* (September 1997).

Skinner deals with the problem of freedom and control in the selection that follows. In the second selection, Carl R. Rogers critiques Skinner's behaviorist approach and sets forth his argument supporting the reality of freedom as an inner human state that is the wellspring of responsibility, will, and commitment.

35

B. F. Skinner  **YES**

Beyond Freedom and Dignity

Almost all living things act to free themselves from harmful contacts. A kind of freedom is achieved by the relatively simple forms of behavior called reflexes. A person sneezes and frees his respiratory passages from irritating substances. He vomits and frees his stomach from indigestible or poisonous food. He pulls back his hand and frees it from a sharp or hot object. More elaborate forms of behavior have similar effects. When confined, people struggle ("in rage") and break free. When in danger they flee from or attack its source. Behavior of this kind presumably evolved because of its survival value; it is as much a part of what we call the human genetic endowment as breathing, sweating, or digesting food. And through conditioning similar behavior may be acquired with respect to novel objects which could have played no role in evolution. These are no doubt minor instances of the struggle to be free, but they are significant. We do not attribute them to any love of freedom; they are simply forms of behavior which have proved useful in reducing various threats to the individual and hence to the species in the course of evolution.

A much more important role is played by behavior which weakens harmful stimuli in another way. It is not acquired in the form of conditioned reflexes, but as the product of a different process called operant conditioning. When a bit of behavior is followed by a certain kind of consequence, it is more likely to occur again, and a consequence having this effect is called a reinforcer. Food, for example, is a reinforcer to a hungry organism; anything the organism does that is followed by the receipt of food is more likely to be done again whenever the organism is hungry. Some stimuli are called negative reinforcers; any response which reduces the intensity of such a stimulus—or ends it—is more likely to be emitted when the stimulus recurs. Thus, if a person escapes from a hot sun when he moves under cover, he is more likely to move under cover when the sun is again hot. The reduction in temperature reinforces the behavior it is "contingent upon"—that is, the behavior it follows. Operant conditioning also occurs when a person simply avoids a hot sun—when, roughly speaking, he escapes from the *threat* of a hot sun.

Negative reinforcers are called aversive in the sense that they are the things organisms "turn away from." The term suggests a spatial separation—moving or running away from something—but the essential relation is temporal. In a standard apparatus used to study the process in the laboratory, an arbitrary response simply weakens an aversive stimulus or brings it to an end. A great deal of physical technology is the result of this kind of struggle for freedom. Over the centuries, in erratic ways, men have constructed a world in which they are relatively free of many kinds of threatening or harmful stimuli—extremes of temperature, sources of infection, hard labor, danger, and even those minor aversive stimuli called discomfort.

Escape and avoidance play a much more important role in the struggle for freedom when the aversive conditions are generated by other people. Other people can be aversive without, so to speak, trying; they can be rude, dangerous, contagious, or annoying, and one escapes from them or avoids them accordingly. They may also be "intentionally" aversive—that is, they may treat other people aversively because of what follows. Thus, a slave driver induces a slave to work by whipping him when he stops; by resuming work the slave escapes from the whipping (and incidentally reinforces the slave driver's behavior in using the whip). A parent nags a child until the child performs a task; by performing the task the child escapes nagging (and reinforces the parent's behavior). The blackmailer threatens exposure unless the victim pays; by paying, the victim escapes from the threat (and reinforces the practice). A teacher threatens corporal punishment or failure until his students pay attention; by paying attention the students escape from the threat of punishment (and reinforce the teacher for threatening it). In one form or another intentional aversive control is the pattern of most social coordination—in ethics, religion, government, economics, education, psychotherapy, and family life.

A person escapes from or avoids aversive treatment by behaving in ways which reinforce those who treated him aversively until he did so, but he may escape in other ways. For example, he may simply move out of range. A person may escape from slavery, emigrate or defect from a government, desert from an army, become an apostate from a religion, play truant, leave home, or drop out of a culture as a hobo, hermit, or hippie. Such behavior is as much a product of the aversive conditions as the behavior the conditions were designed to evoke. The latter can be guaranteed only by sharpening the contingencies or by using stronger aversive stimuli.

Another anomalous mode of escape is to attack those who arrange aversive conditions and weaken or destroy their power. We may attack those who crowd us or annoy us, as we attack the weeds in our garden, but again the struggle for freedom is mainly directed toward intentional controllers—toward those who treat others aversively in order to induce them to behave in particular ways. Thus, a child may stand up to his parents, a citizen may overthrow a government, a communicant may reform a religion, a student may attack a teacher or vandalize a school, and a dropout may work to destroy a culture.

It is possible that man's genetic endowment supports this kind of struggle for freedom: when treated aversively people tend to act aggressively or to be reinforced by signs of having worked aggressive damage. Both tendencies should have had evolutionary advantages, and they can easily be demonstrated. If two organisms which have been coexisting peacefully receive painful shocks, they immediately exhibit characteristic patterns of aggression toward each other.

The aggressive behavior is not necessarily directed toward the actual source of stimulation; it may be "displaced" toward any convenient person or object. Vandalism and riots are often forms of undirected or misdirected aggression. An organism which has received a painful shock will also, if possible, act to gain access to another organism toward which it can act aggressively. The extent to which human aggression exemplifies innate tendencies is not clear, and many of the ways in which people attack and thus weaken or destroy the power of intentional controllers are quite obviously learned.

What we may call the "literature of freedom" has been designed to induce people to escape from or attack those who act to control them aversively. The content of the literature is the philosophy of freedom, but philosophies are among those inner causes which need to be scrutinized. We say that a person behaves in a given way because he possesses a philosophy, but we infer the philosophy from the behavior and therefore cannot use it in any satisfactory way as an explanation, at least until it is in turn explained. The literature of freedom, on the other hand, has a simple objective status. It consists of books, pamphlets, manifestoes, speeches, and other verbal products, designed to induce people to act to free themselves from various kinds of intentional control. It does not impart a philosophy of freedom; it induces people to act.

The literature often emphasizes the aversive conditions under which people live, perhaps by contrasting them with conditions in a freer world. It thus makes the conditions more aversive, "increasing the misery" of those it is trying to rescue. It also identifies those from whom one is to escape or those whose power is to be weakened through attack. Characteristic villains of the literature are tyrants, priests, generals, capitalists, martinet teachers, and domineering parents.

The literature also prescribes modes of action. It has not been much concerned with escape, possibly because advice has not been needed; instead, it has emphasized how controlling power may be weakened or destroyed. Tyrants are to be overthrown, ostracized, or assassinated. The legitimacy of a government is to be questioned. The ability of a religious agency to mediate supernatural sanctions is to be challenged. Strikes and boycotts are to be organized to weaken the economic power which supports aversive practices. The argument is strengthened by exhorting people to act, describing likely results, reviewing successful instances on the model of the advertising testimonial, and so on.

The would-be controllers do not, of course, remain inactive. Governments make escape impossible by banning travel or severely punishing or incarcerating defectors. They keep weapons and other sources of power out of the hands of revolutionaries. They destroy the written literature of freedom and imprison or kill those who carry it orally. If the struggle for freedom is to succeed, it must then be intensified.

The importance of the literature of freedom can scarcely be questioned. Without help or guidance people submit to aversive conditions in the most surprising way. This is true even when the aversive conditions are part of the natural environment. Darwin observed, for example, that the Fuegians seemed to make no effort to protect themselves from the cold; they wore only scant clothing and made little use of it against the weather. And one of the most striking things about the struggle for freedom from intentional control is how often it has been lacking. Many people have submitted to the most obvious religious, governmental, and economic controls for centuries, striking for freedom only sporadically, if at all. The literature of freedom has made an essential contribution to the elimination of many aversive practices in government, religion, education, family life, and the production of goods.

The contributions of the literature of freedom, however, are not usually described in these terms. Some traditional theories could conceivably be said to define freedom as the absence of aversive control, but the emphasis has been on how the condition *feels*. Other traditional theories could conceivably be said to define freedom as a person's condition when he is behaving under nonaversive control, but the emphasis has been upon a state of mind associated with doing what one wants. According to John Stuart Mill, "Liberty consists in doing what one desires." The literature of freedom has been important in changing practice (it has changed practices whenever it has had any effect whatsoever), but it has nevertheless defined its task as the changing of states of mind and feelings. Freedom is a "possession." A person escapes from or destroys the power of a controller in order to feel free, and once he feels free and can do what he desires, no further action is recommended and none is prescribed by the literature of freedom, except perhaps eternal vigilance lest control be resumed.

The feeling of freedom becomes an unreliable guide to action as soon as would-be controllers turn to nonaversive measures, as they are likely to do to avoid the problems raised when the controllee escapes or attacks. Nonaversive measures are not as conspicuous as aversive and are likely to be acquired more slowly, but they have obvious advantages which promote their use. Productive labor, for example, was once the result of punishment: the slave worked to avoid the consequences of not working. Wages exemplify a different principle; a person is paid when he behaves in a given way so that he will continue to behave in that way. Although it has long been recognized that rewards have useful effects, wage systems have evolved slowly. In the nineteenth century it was believed that an industrial society required a hungry labor force; wages would be effective only if the hungry worker could exchange them for food. By making labor less aversive—for instance, by shortening hours and improving conditions—it has been possible to get men to work for lesser rewards. Until recently teaching was almost entirely aversive: the student studies to escape the consequences of not studying, but nonaversive techniques are gradually being discovered and used. The skillful parent learns to reward a child for good behavior rather than punish him for bad. Religious agencies move from the threat of hellfire to an emphasis on God's love, and governments turn from aversive sanctions to various kinds of inducements.... What the layman calls a reward is a "positive reinforcer," the effects of which have been exhaustively studied in the experimental analysis of operant behavior. The effects are not as easily recognized as those of aversive contingencies because they tend to be deferred, and applications have therefore been delayed, but techniques as powerful as the older aversive techniques are now available....

The literature of freedom has never come to grips with techniques of control which do not generate escape or counterattack because it has dealt with the problem in terms of states of mind and feelings. In his book *Sovereignty,* Bertrand de Jouvenel quotes two important figures in that literature. According to Leibnitz, "Liberty consists in the power to do what one wants to do," and according to Voltaire, "When I can do what I want to do, there is my liberty for me." But both writers add a concluding phrase: Leibnitz, " . . . or in the power to want what can be got," and Voltaire, more candidly, " . . . but I can't help wanting what I do want." Jouvenel relegates these comments to a footnote, saying that the power to want is a matter of "interior liberty" (the freedom of the inner man!) which falls outside the "gambit of freedom."

A person wants something if he acts to get it when the occasion arises. A person who says "I want something to eat" will presumably eat when something becomes available. If he says "I want to get warm," he will presumably move into a warm place when he can. These acts have been reinforced in the past by whatever was wanted. What a person *feels* when he feels himself wanting something depends upon the circumstances. Food is reinforcing only in a state of deprivation, and a person who wants something to eat may feel parts of that state—for example, hunger pangs. A person who wants to get warm presumably feels cold. Conditions associated with a high probability of responding may also be felt, together with aspects of the present occasion which are similar to those of past occasions upon which behavior has been reinforced. Wanting is not, however, a feeling, nor is a feeling the reason a person acts to get what he wants. Certain contingencies have raised the probability of behavior and at the same time have created conditions which may be felt. Freedom is a matter of contingencies of reinforcement, not of the feelings the contingencies generate. The distinction is particularly important when the contingencies do not generate escape or counterattack. . . .

The literature of freedom has encouraged escape from or attack upon all controllers. It has done so by making any indication of control aversive. Those who manipulate human behavior are said to be evil men, necessarily bent on exploitation. Control is clearly the opposite of freedom, and if freedom is good, control must be bad. What is overlooked is control which does not have aversive consequences at any time. Many social practices essential to the welfare of the species involve the control of one person by another, and no one can suppress them who has any concern for human achievements. . . . [I]n order to maintain the position that all control is wrong, it has been necessary to disguise or conceal the nature of useful practices, to prefer weak practices just because they can be disguised or concealed, and—a most extraordinary result indeed!— to perpetuate punitive measures.

The problem is to be free men, not from control, but from certain kinds of control, and it can be solved only if our analysis takes all consequences into account. How people feel about control, before or after the literature of freedom has worked on their feelings, does not lead to useful distinctions.

Were it not for the unwarranted generalization that all control is wrong, we should deal with the social environment as simply as we deal with the nonsocial. Although technology has freed men from certain aversive features of the environment, it has not freed them from the environment. We accept the fact that we depend upon the world around us, and we simply change the nature of the dependency. In the same way, to make the social environment as free as possible of aversive stimuli, we do not need to destroy that environment or escape from it; we need to redesign it.

Man's struggle for freedom is not due to a will to be free, but to certain behavioral processes characteristic of the human organism, the chief effect of which is the avoidance of or escape from so-called "aversive" features of the environment. Physical and biological technologies have been mainly concerned with natural aversive stimuli; the struggle for freedom is concerned with stimuli intentionally arranged by other people. The literature of freedom has identified the other people and has proposed ways of escaping from them or weakening or destroying their power. It has been successful in reducing the aversive stimuli used in intentional control, but it has made the mistake of defining freedom in terms of states of mind or feelings, and it has therefore not been able to deal effectively with techniques of control which do not breed escape or revolt but nevertheless have aversive consequences. It has been forced to brand all control as wrong and to misrepresent many of the advantages to be gained from a social environment. It is unprepared for the next step, which is not to free men from control but to analyze and change the kinds of control to which they are exposed.

Carl R. Rogers

 **NO**

Freedom to Learn

One of the deepest issues in modern life, in modern man, is the question as to whether the concept of personal freedom has any meaning whatsoever in our present-day scientific world. The growing ability of the behavioral scientist to predict and to control behavior has brought the issue sharply to the fore. If we accept the logical positivism and strictly behavioristic emphases which are predominant in the American psychological scene, there is not even room for discussion....

But if we step outside the narrowness of the behavioral sciences, this question is not only *an* issue, it is one of the primary issues which define modern man. Friedman in his book (1963, p. 251) makes his topic "the problematic of modern man—the alienation, the divided nature, the unresolved tension between personal freedom and psychological compulsion which follows on 'the death of God'." The issues of personal freedom and personal commitment have become very sharp indeed in a world in which man feels unsupported by a supernatural religion, and experiences keenly the division between his awareness and those elements of his dynamic functioning of which he is unaware. If he is to wrest any meaning from a universe which for all he knows may be indifferent, he must arrive at some stance which he can hold in regard to these timeless uncertainties.

So, writing as both a behavioral scientist and as one profoundly concerned with the human, the personal, the phenomenological and the intangible, I should like to contribute what I can to this continuing dialogue regarding the meaning of and the possibility of freedom.

Man Is Unfree

... In the minds of most behavioral scientists, man is not free, nor can he as a free man commit himself to some purpose, since he is controlled by factors outside of himself. Therefore, neither freedom nor commitment is even a possible concept to modern behavioral science as it is usually understood.

From Carl R. Rogers, *Freedom to Learn for the Eighties* (Merrill, 1983). Copyright © 1983 by Carl R. Rogers. Adapted by permission of Prentice Hall, Inc., Upper Saddle River, NJ.

To show that I am not exaggerating, let me quote a statement from Dr. B. F. Skinner of Harvard, who is one of the most consistent advocates of a strictly behavioristic psychology. He says,

The hypothesis that man is not free is essential to the application of scientific method to the study of human behavior. The free inner man who is held responsible for his behavior is only a prescientific substitute for the kinds of causes which are discovered in the course of scientific analysis. All these alternative causes lie *outside* the individual (1953, p. 477).

This view is shared by many psychologists and others who feel, as does Dr. Skinner, that all the effective causes of behavior lie outside of the individual and that it is only through the external stimulus that behavior takes place. The scientific description of behavior avoids anything that partakes in any way of freedom. For example, Dr. Skinner (1964, pp. 90–91) describes an experiment in which a pigeon was conditioned to turn in a clockwise direction. The behavior of the pigeon was "shaped up" by rewarding any movement that approximated a clockwise turn until, increasingly, the bird was turning round and round in a steady movement. This is what is known as operant conditioning. Students who had watched the demonstration were asked to write an account of what they had seen. Their responses included the following ideas: that the pigeon was conditioned to *expect* reinforcement for the right kind of behavior; that the pigeon *hoped* that something would bring the food back again; that the pigeon *observed* that a certain behavior seemed to produce a particular result; that the pigeon *felt* that food would be given it because of its action; that the bird came to *associate* his action with the clock of the food dispenser. Skinner ridicules these statements because they all go beyond the observed behavior in using such words as *expect, hope, observe, felt,* and *associate.* The whole explanation from his point of view is that the bird was reinforced when it emitted a given kind of behavior; the pigeon walked around until the food container again appeared; a certain behavior produced a given result; food was given to the pigeon when it acted in a given way; the click of the food dispenser was related in time to the bird's action. These statements describe the pigeon's behavior from a scientific point of view.

Skinner goes on to point out that the students were undoubtedly reporting what they would have expected, felt and hoped under similar circumstances. But he then makes the case that there is no more reality to such ideas in the human being than there is in the pigeon, that it is only because such words have been reinforced by the verbal community in which the individual has developed, that such terms are used. He discusses the fact that the verbal community which conditioned them to use such terms saw no more of their behavior than they had seen of the pigeon's. In other words the internal events, if they indeed exist, have no scientific significance.

As to the methods used for changing the behavior of the pigeon, many people besides Dr. Skinner feel that through such positive reinforcement human behavior as well as animal behavior can be "shaped up" and controlled. In his book *Walden Two*, Skinner says,

> Now that we know how positive reinforcement works and how negative doesn't, we can be more deliberate and hence more successful in our cultural design. We can achieve a sort of control under which the controlled, though they are following a code much more scrupulously than was ever the case under the old system, nevertheless *feel free*. They are doing what they want to do, not what they are forced to do. That's the source of the tremendous power of positive reinforcement—there is no restraint and no revolt. By a careful cultural design we control not the final behavior but the *inclination* to behave—the motives, the desires, the wishes. The curious thing is that in that case *the question of freedom never arises* (1948, p. 218).

... I think it is clear from all of this that man is a machine—a complex machine, to be sure, but one which is increasingly subject to scientific control. Whether behavior will be managed through operant conditioning as in *Walden Two* or whether we will be "shaped up" by the unplanned forms of conditioning implied in social pressure, or whether we will be controlled by electrodes in the brain, it seems quite clear that science is making out of man an object and that the purpose of such science is not only understanding and prediction but control. Thus it would seem to be quite clear that there could be no concept so foreign to the facts as that man is free. Man is a machine, man is unfree, man cannot commit himself in any meaningful sense; he is simply controlled by planned or unplanned forces outside of himself.

Man Is Free

I am impressed by the scientific advances illustrated in the examples I have given. I regard them as a great tribute to the ingenuity, insight, and persistence of the individuals making the investigations. They have added enormously to our knowledge. Yet for me they leave something very important unsaid. Let me try to illustrate this, first from my experience in therapy.

I think of a young man classed as schizophrenic with whom I had been working for a long time in a state hospital. He was a very inarticulate man, and during one hour he made a few remarks about individuals who had recently left the hospital; then he remained silent for almost forty minutes. When he got up to go, he mumbled almost under his breath, "If some of *them* can do it, maybe I can too." That was all—not a dramatic statement, not uttered with force and vigor, yet a statement of choice by this young man to work toward his own improvement and eventual release from the hospital. It is not too surprising that about eight months after that statement he was out of the hospital. I believe this experience of responsible choice is one of the deepest aspects of psychotherapy and one of the elements which most solidly underlies personality change.

I think of another young person, this time a young woman graduate student, who was deeply disturbed and on the borderline of a psychotic break. Yet after a number of interviews in which she talked very critically about all of the people who had failed to give her what she needed, she finally concluded: "Well, with that sort of a foundation, it's really up to *me*. I mean it seems to be really apparent to me that I can't depend on someone else to *give* me an education." And then she added very softly: "I'll really have to get it myself." She goes on to explore this experience of important and responsible choice. She finds it a frightening experience, and yet one which gives her a feeling of strength. A force seems to surge up within her which is big and strong, and yet she also feels very much alone and sort of cut off from support. She adds: "I am going to begin to do more things that I know I should do." And she did.

I could add many other examples. One young fellow talking about the way in which his whole life had been distorted and spoiled by his parents finally comes to the conclusion that, "Maybe now that I *see* that, it's up to *me*." . . .

For those of you [who] have seen the film *David and Lisa*—and I hope that you have had that rich experience—I can illustrate exactly what I have been discussing. David, the adolescent schizophrenic, goes into a panic if he is touched by anyone. He feels that "touching kills," and he is deathly afraid of it, and afraid of the closeness in human relationships which touching implies. Yet toward the close of the film he makes a bold and positive choice of the kind I have been describing. He has been trying to be of help to Lisa, the girl who is out of touch with reality. He tries to help at first in an intellectually contemptuous way, then increasingly in a warmer and more personal way. Finally, in a highly dramatic movement, he says to her, "Lisa, take my hand." He *chooses*, with obvious conflict and fear, to leave behind the safety of his untouchableness, and to venture into the world of real human relationships where he is literally and figuratively in *touch* with another. You are an unusual person if the film does not grow a bit misty at this point.

Perhaps a behaviorist could try to account for the reaching out of his hand by saying that it was the result of intermittent reinforcement of partial movements. I find such an explanation both inaccurate and inadequate. It is the *meaning* of the *decision* which is essential to understanding the act.

What I am trying to suggest in all of this is that I would be at a loss to explain the positive change which can occur in psychotherapy if I had to omit the importance of the sense of free and responsible choice on the part of my clients. I believe that this experience of freedom to choose is one of the deepest elements underlying change.

The Meaning of Freedom

Considering the scientific advances which I have mentioned, how can we even speak of freedom? In what sense is a client free? In what sense are any of us free? What possible definition of freedom can there be in the modern world? Let me attempt such a definition.

In the first place, the freedom that I am talking about is essentially an inner thing, something which exists in the living person quite aside from any of the outward choices of alternatives which we so often think of as constituting freedom. I am speaking of the kind of freedom which Viktor Frankl vividly describes in his experience of the concentration camp, when everything—possessions, status, identity—was taken from the prisoners. But even months and years in such an environment showed only "that everything can be taken from a man but one thing: the last of the human freedoms—to choose one's own attitude in any given set of circumstances, to choose one's own way" (1959, p. 65). It is this inner, subjective, existential freedom which I have observed. It is the realization that "I can live myself, here and now, by my own choice." It is the quality of courage which enables a person to step into the uncertainty of the unknown as he chooses himself. It is the discovery of meaning from within oneself, meaning which comes from listening, sensitively and openly to the complexities of what one is experiencing. It is the burden of being responsible for the self one chooses to be. It is the recognition of a person that he is an emerging process, not a static end product. The individual who is thus deeply and courageously thinking his own thoughts, becoming his own uniqueness, responsibly choosing himself, may be fortunate in having hundreds of objective outer alternatives from which to choose, or he may be unfortunate in having none. But his freedom exists regardless. So we are first of all speaking of something which exists within the individual, something phenomenological rather than external, but nonetheless to be prized.

The second point in defining this experience of freedom is that it exists not as a contradiction of the picture of the psychological universe as a sequence of cause and effect, but as a complement to such a universe. Freedom rightly understood is a fulfillment by the person of the ordered sequence of his life. The free man moves out voluntarily, freely, responsibly, to play his significant part in a world whose determined events move through him and through his spontaneous choice and will.

I see this freedom of which I am speaking, then, as existing in a different *dimension* than the determined sequence of cause and effect. I regard it as a freedom which exists in the subjective person, a freedom which he courageously uses to live his potentialities. The fact that this type of freedom seems completely irreconcilable with the behaviorist's picture of man is something which I will discuss a bit later....

The Emergence of Commitment

I have spoken thus far primarily about freedom. What about commitment? Certainly the disease of our age is lack of purpose, lack of meaning, lack of commitment on the part of individuals. Is there anything which I can say in regard to this?

It is clear to me that in therapy, as indicated in the examples that I have given, commitment to purpose and to meaning in life is one of the significant elements of change. It is only when the person decides, "I am someone; I am someone worth being: I am committed to being myself," that change becomes possible.

At a very interesting symposium at Rice University recently, Dr. Sigmund Koch sketched the revolution which is taking place in science, literature and the arts, in which a sense of commitment is again becoming evident after a long period in which that emphasis has been absent.

Part of what he meant by that may be illustrated by talking about Dr. Michael Polanyi, the philosopher of science, formerly a physicist, who has been presenting his notions about what science basically is. In his book, *Personal Knowledge*, Polanyi makes it clear that even scientific knowledge is personal knowledge, committed knowledge. We cannot rest comfortably on the belief that scientific knowledge is impersonal and "out there," that it has nothing to do with the individual who has discovered it. Instead, every aspect of science is pervaded by disciplined personal commitment, and Polanyi makes the case very persuasively that the whole attempt to divorce science from the person is a completely unrealistic one. I think I am stating his belief correctly when I say that in his judgment logical positivism and all the current structure of science cannot save us from the fact that all knowing is uncertain, involves risk, and is grasped and comprehended only through the deep, personal commitment of a disciplined search.

Perhaps a brief quotation will give something of the flavor of his thinking. Speaking of great scientists, he says:

> So we see that both Kepler and Einstein approached nature with intellectual passions and with beliefs inherent in these passions, which led them to their triumphs and misguided them to their errors. These passions and beliefs were theirs, personally, even universally. I believe that they were competent to follow these impulses, even though they risked being misled by them. And again, what I accept of their work today, I accept personally, guided by passions and beliefs similar to theirs, holding in my turn that my impulses are valid, universally, even though I must admit the possibility that they may be mistaken (1959, p. 145).

Thus we see that a modern philosopher of science believes that deep personal commitment is the only possible basis on which science can firmly stand. This is a far cry indeed from the logical positivism of twenty or thirty years ago, which placed knowledge far out in impersonal space.

Let me say a bit more about what I mean by commitment in the psychological sense. I think it is easy to give this word a much too shallow meaning, indicating that the individual has, simply by conscious choice, committed himself to one course of action or another. I think the meaning goes far deeper than that. Commitment is a total organismic direction involving not only the conscious mind but the whole direction of the organism as well.

In my judgment, commitment is something that one *discovers* within oneself. It is a trust of one's total reaction rather than of one's mind only. It has much to do with creativity. Einstein's explanation of how he moved toward his formulation of relativity without any clear knowledge of his goal is an excellent example of what I mean by the sense of commitment based on a total organismic reaction. He says:

> "During all those years there was a feeling of direction, of going straight toward something concrete. It is, of course, very hard to express that feeling in words but it was decidedly the case and clearly to be distinguished from later considerations about the rational form of the solution" (quoted in Wertheimer, 1945, p. 183–184).

Thus commitment is more than a decision. It is the functioning of an individual who is searching for the directions which are emerging within himself. Kierkegaard has said, "The truth exists only in the process of becoming, in the process of appropriation" (1941, p. 72). It is this individual creation of a tentative personal truth through action which is the essence of commitment.

Man is most successful in such a commitment when he is functioning as an integrated, whole, unified individual. The more that he is functioning in this total manner the more confidence he has in the directions which he unconsciously chooses. He feels a trust in his experiencing, of which, even if he is fortunate, he has only partial glimpses in his awareness.

Thought of in the sense in which I am describing it, it is clear that commitment is an achievement. It is the kind of purposeful and meaningful direction which is only gradually achieved by the individual who has come increasingly to live closely in relationship with his own experiencing—a relationship in which his unconscious tendencies are as much respected as are his conscious choices. This is the kind of commitment toward which I believe individuals can move. It is an important aspect of living in a fully functioning way.

The Irreconcilable Contradiction

I trust it will be very clear that I have given two sharply divergent and irreconcilably contradictory points of view. On the one hand, modern psychological science and many other forces in modern life as well, hold the view that man is unfree, that he is controlled, that words such as purpose, choice, commitment have no significant meaning, that man is nothing but an object which we can more fully understand and more fully control. Enormous strides have been and are being made in implementing this perspective. It would seem heretical indeed to question this view.

Yet, as Polanyi has pointed out in another of his writings (1957), the dogmas of science can be in error. He says:

> In the days when an idea could be silenced by showing that it was contrary to religion, theology was the greatest single source of fallacies. Today, when any human thought can be discredited by branding it as unscientific, the power previously exercised by theology has passed over to science; hence science has become in its turn the greatest single source of error.

So I am emboldened to say that over against this view of man as unfree, as an object, is the evidence from therapy, from subjective living, and from objective research as well, that personal freedom and responsibility have a crucial significance, that one cannot live a complete life without such personal freedom and responsibility, and that self-understanding and responsible choice make a sharp and measurable difference in the behavior of the individual. In this context, commitment does have meaning. Commitment is the emerging and changing total direction of the individual, based on a close and acceptant relationship between the person and all of the trends in his life, conscious and unconscious. Unless, as individuals and as a society, we can make constructive use of this capacity for freedom and commitment, mankind, it seems to me, is set on a collision course with fate. . . .

A part of modern living is to face the paradox that, viewed from one perspective, man is a complex machine. We are every day moving toward a more precise understanding and a more precise control of this objective mechanism which we call man. On the other hand, in another significant dimension of his existence, man is subjectively free; his personal choice and responsibility account for the shape of his life; he is in fact the architect of himself. A truly crucial part of his existence is the discovery of his own meaningful commitment to life with all of his being.

POSTSCRIPT

Should Behaviorism Shape Educational Practices?

The freedom-determinism or freedom-control argument has raged in philosophical, political, and psychological circles down through the ages. Is freedom of choice and action a central, perhaps *the* central, characteristic of being human? Or is freedom only an illusion, a refusal to acknowledge the external shaping of all human actions?

Moving the debate into the field of education, John Dewey depicted a developmental freedom that is acquired through improving one's ability to cope with problems. A. S. Neill (*Summerhill: A Radical Approach to Child Rearing,* 1984), who advanced the ideas of early-twentieth-century progressive educators and the establishment of free schools, sees a more natural inborn freedom in human beings, which must be protected and allowed to flourish. Skinner refuses to recognize this "inner autonomous man" but sees freedom resulting from the scientific reshaping of the environment that influences us.

Just as Skinner has struggled to remove the stigma from the word *control,* arguing that it is the true gateway to freedom, John Holt, in *Freedom and Beyond* (1972), contends that freedom and free activities are not "unstructured" —indeed, that the structure of an open classroom is vastly more complicated than the structure of a traditional classroom.

If both of these views have validity, then we are in a position, as Dewey counselled, to go beyond either-or polemics on these matters and build a more constructive educational atmosphere. Jerome S. Bruner has consistently suggested ways in which free inquiry and subject matter structure can be effectively blended. Arthur W. Combs, in a report titled *Humanistic Education: Objectives and Assessment* (1978), helped to bridge the ideological gap between humanists and behaviorists by demonstrating that subjective outcomes can be assessed by direct or modified behavioral techniques.

Skinner's death in 1990 prompted a number of evaluations, among them "Skinner's Stimulus: The Legacy of Behaviorism's Grand Designer," by Jeff Meade, *Teacher* (November/December 1990); "The Life and Contributions of Burrhus Frederic Skinner," by Robert P. Hawkins, *Education and Treatment of Children* (August 1990); and Carson M. Bennett, "A Skinnerian View of Human Freedom," *The Humanist* (July/August 1990).

Other perspectives on the learning atmosphere in schools may be found in *In Search of Understanding: The Case for Constructivist Classrooms* by Jacqueline G. Brooks and Martin G. Brooks (1993); Dave Perkins, "The Many Faces of Constructivism," *Educational Leadership* (November 1999); Robert J. Sternberg, "Ability and Expertise," *American Educator* (Spring 1999); Howard Gardner, *Intelligence Reframed: Multiple Intelligences for the Twenty-First Century* (1999); and John Steadman Rice, "The Therapeutic School," *Society* (January/February 2002), which is a critique of Rogers and other humanistic psychologists.

ISSUE 4

Should Church-State Separation Be Maintained?

YES: R. Freeman Butts, from "A History and Civics Lesson for All of Us," *Educational Leadership* (May 1987)

NO: Robert L. Cord, from "Church-State Separation and the Public Schools: A Re-evaluation," *Educational Leadership* (May 1987)

ISSUE SUMMARY

YES: Professor emeritus of education R. Freeman Butts warns that current efforts to redefine the relationship between religion and schooling are eroding the Constitution's intent.

NO: Professor of political science Robert L. Cord offers a more accommodating interpretation of this intent, one that allows for the school practices that Butts condemns as unconstitutional.

The religious grounding of early schooling in America certainly cannot be denied. Nor can the history of religious influences on the conduct of America's governmental functions and school practices. In the nineteenth century, however, protests against the prevailing Protestant influence in the public schools were lodged by Catholics, Jews, nonbelievers, and other groups, giving rise to a number of issues that revolve around interpretations of the "establishment of religion" and the "free exercise of religion" clauses of the Constitution.

Twentieth-century U.S. Supreme Court cases such as *Cochran* (1930), *Everson* (1947), *McCollum* (1948), *Zorach* (1952), *Engel* (1962), and *Murray* (1963) attempted to clarify the relationship between religion and schooling. Most of these decisions bolstered the separation of church and state position. Only recently has a countermovement, led in some quarters by the Christian Coalition organization of Pat Robertson, sought to sway public and legal opinion toward an emphasis on the "free exercise" clause and toward viewing the influence of secular humanism in the schools as "an establishment of religion."

At both the legislative and judicial levels, attempts were made in the 1980s to secure an official place in public education for voluntary prayer, moments of silent meditation, and creationism in the science curriculum. Censorship of textbooks and other school materials, access to facilities by religious groups, and the right of parents to withdraw their children from instruction deemed to be morally offensive and damaging have also been promoted. Humanists (who may be either religious or nonreligious) find a good deal of distortion in these recent attacks on the "secularization" of schooling, and they argue that the materials used in the schools are consistent with the historical goals of character development while also being in tune with the realities of the present times.

John Buchanan of People for the American Way argues that public schools are places where young people of differing backgrounds and beliefs can come together and learn tolerance. He and others worry that parental veto power will undermine decision making and impair school effectiveness. Bill Keith of the Creation Science Legal Defense Fund contends that a parent's liberty with regard to a child's education is a fundamental right, an enduring American tradition.

In the 1990s congressional attempts to pass a constitutional amendment allowing voluntary prayer in public schools were stymied, and two U.S. Supreme Court rulings came down on the side of church-state separation, although not without ambiguity. In the 1992 graduation prayer case *Lee v. Weisman,* which originated in Rhode Island, the 5–4 decision held that clergy-led devotionals at commencement exercises violated the establishment clause because of the coercive effect of the practice. In 1996, reviewing *Moore v. Ingrebretsen,* the Court rejected an appeal by Mississippi officials who sought to allow student-led prayer in public schools. State lawmakers had stipulated that "invocations, benedictions, or nonsectarian, non-proselytizing student-initiated voluntary prayer shall be permitted." The appellate court had upheld the suspension of enforcement of that law (except in cases of voluntary, student-led prayer at graduation ceremonies). A detailed examination of this aspect of the church-state separation issue can be found in Martha M. Mc-Carthy's "Public School Prayer Continues to Spark Controversy and Possibly a Constitutional Amendment," *Educational Horizons* (Winter 1996).

Resolution of the philosophical questions regarding the content and conduct of public education has become increasingly politicized. Who should control the school curriculum and its materials—school boards, professional educators, community groups, the federal or state governments, parents, or students? Should censorship boards operate at the local, state, or national level —or none of the above? Where does the line get drawn between benevolent intervention and thought control? Can schools be value-neutral?

In the following selections, R. Freeman Butts makes the case that legal and historical scholarship points to the broader, separatist, and secular meaning of the First Amendment, which controls the answers to many of these questions. Robert L. Cord bases his argument for a more accommodating interpretation on his findings in primary historical sources and on the actions of the framers of the Constitution.

R. Freeman Butts  **YES**

A History and Civics Lesson for All of Us

As chairman of the Commission on the Bicentennial of the U.S. Constitution, former Chief Justice Warren E. Burger urges that the occasion provide "a history and civics lesson for all of us." I heartily agree, but the lesson will depend on which version of history you read—and believe.

From May 1982, when President Reagan advocated adoption of a constitutional amendment to permit organized prayer in public schools, Congress has been bitterly divided during the repeated efforts to pass legislation aimed either at amending the Constitution or stripping the Supreme Court and other federal courts of jurisdiction to decide cases about prayers in the public schools. Similar controversies have arisen over efforts of the Reagan administration to promote vouchers and tuition tax credits to give financial aid to parents choosing to send their children to private religious schools.

School/Religion Controversies

I would like to remind educators that the present controversies have a long history, and the way we understand that history makes a difference in our policy judgments. A watershed debate occurred, for example, in 1947 when the Supreme Court spelled out the meaning of the part of the First Amendment which reads, "Congress shall make no law respecting an establishment of religion." The occasion was a challenge to a New Jersey law giving tax money to Catholic parents to send their children by bus to parochial schools. The Court split 5-4 in that case, *Everson* v. *Board of Education,* on whether this practice was, in effect, "an establishment of religion" and thus unconstitutional, but there was no disagreement on the principle. Justice Hugo Black wrote for the majority.

> The "establishment of religion" clause of the First Amendment means at least this: Neither a state nor the Federal Government can pass laws which aid one religion, aid all religions, or prefer one religion over another.... No tax in any amount, large or small, can be levied to support any religious activities or institutions, whatever they may be called, or whatever form they may adopt to teach or practice religion.... In the words of Jefferson,

From R. Freeman Butts, "A History and Civics Lesson for All of Us," *Educational Leadership,* vol. 44, no. 8 (May 1987), pp. 21–25. Copyright © 1987 by The Association for Supervision and Curriculum Development. Reprinted by permission of The Association for Supervision and Curriculum Development; permission conveyed via Copyright Clearance Center, Inc.

the clause against establishment of religion by law was intended to erect "a wall of separation between Church and State."[1]

The *Everson* majority accepted this broad principle, but decided, nevertheless, that bus fares were merely welfare aid to parents and children and not aid to the religious schools themselves. The 1948 *McCollum* case prohibited released time for religious instruction in the public schools of Champaign, Illinois, because it violated the *Everson* principle.

These two cases set off a thunderous denunciation of the Supreme Court and calls for impeachment of the justices. They also sent historians of education scurrying to original sources to see how valid this broad and liberal interpretation was.

Establishment Principle

The two books at that time that gave most attention to the establishment principle as it related to education were James M. O'Neill's *Religion and Education Under the Constitution*[2] and my own, *The American Tradition in Religion and Education.*[3] O'Neill found the Court's interpretation appalling; I found it basically true to Madison and the majority of the framers of the First Amendment. My book was cited in 1971 in the concurring opinions of Justices Brennan, Douglas, and Black in *Lemon* v. *Kurtzman.*[4] Chief Justice Burger summarized for a unanimous court the accumulated precedents since *Everson* and listed three tests of constitutional state action in education: a secular purpose; neither advancement nor inhibition of religion; and no excessive government entanglement with religion.

With that decision, I concluded that my views of the framers' intentions had been pretty well accepted: namely, that "an establishment of religion" in the 1780s was "a multiple establishment" whereby public aid could go to several churches, and that this is what the majority of framers, particularly Madison, intended to prohibit in the First Amendment.

Indeed, single religious establishments had existed in nine of the early colonies, but by 1789 when the First Congress drafted the First Amendment, religious diversity had become such a powerful political force that seven states, which included the vast majority of Americans, had either disestablished their churches or had never established any. Only six state constitutions still permitted "an establishment of religion," and all six provided tax funds for several churches, not just one.[5] Naturally, some representatives and senators from those states did not want their multiple establishment threatened by a Bill of Rights in the new federal government. But Madison did.

Madison had prevented just such a multiple establishment in Virginia in 1785 and 1786 and managed instead the passage of Jefferson's powerful Statute for Religious Freedom. In his speech of 8 June 1789, when he introduced his Bill of Rights proposals in the House, he made a double-barreled approach to religious freedom. He proposed (1) to prohibit Congress from establishing religion on a national basis, and (2) to prohibit the states from infringing "equal rights of conscience."

After considerable discussion and some changes of language, the House of Representatives approved both of Madison's proposals and sent them to the Senate. The Senate, however, did not approve the prohibition on the states. Furthermore, a minority in the Senate made three attempts to narrow the wording of the First Amendment to prohibit Congress from establishing a single church or giving preference to one religious sect or denomination. The majority, however, rejected all such attempts to narrow Madison's proposal, and the Senate finally accepted the wording of Madison's conference committee. This was then finally adopted by both houses. Madison's broad and liberal interpretation of the establishment clause as applied to Congress had won.[6]

Neither Madison nor the majority of framers intended for government to disdain religion. They intended that republican government guarantee equal rights of conscience to all persons, but it took some 150 years before Madison's views were applied specifically to the states through the Fourteenth Amendment. That is what the Supreme Court did in *Everson*.

Framers' Intentions Redefined

But today, "a jurisprudence of original intention" has revived the debates of the 1940s and 1950s, expounding much the same views as those of O'Neill namely that "the framers" intended only to prohibit Congress from establishing a single national church, but would permit aid to all religions on a nonpreferential basis and would even permit the states to establish a single church if they wished. These arguments are now being resurrected or reincarnated (to use the secular meaning of those terms) with even more sophisticated scholarship by such authors as Walter Berns of Georgetown University, Michael Malbin of the American Enterprise Institute, and Robert L. Cord of Northeastern University.[7]

Their works have been cited in legal briefs in several state actions and in at least one federal district court decision, while an increasingly vigorous campaign has been launched by conservative members of Congress and the Reagan administration to appeal to the history of "original intention."

These efforts reached a crescendo of confrontation in summer and fall of 1985, following two Supreme Court decisions. In *Wallace* v. *Jaffree* on 4 June 1985, the Court reversed Federal Judge W. Brevard Hand's decision that Alabama's laws providing for prayer in the public schools were, indeed, permissible and did not violate the First Amendment's prohibition against "an establishment of religion." Relying in part on Cord's version of history, Judge Hand argued that the Supreme Court had long erred in its reading of the original intention of the framers of the First Amendment. He said that they intended solely to prevent the federal government from establishing a single national church such as the Church of England; therefore, the Congress could aid all churches if it did not give preference to any one; that a state was free to establish a state religion if it chose to do so and, thus, could require or permit prayers in its public schools.

The Supreme Court reversed this decision (6-3), and Justice John Paul Stevens, writing for the Court, rebuked Judge Hand by referring to his "newly discovered historical evidence" as a "remarkable conclusion" wholly at odds with the firmly established constitutional provision that "the several States have no greater power to restrain the individual freedoms protected by the First Amendment than does the Congress of the United States." Justice Stevens emphasized that the Court had confirmed and endorsed time and time again the principle of incorporation, by which the Fourteenth Amendment imposes the same limitations on the states that it imposes on Congress regarding protection of civil liberties guaranteed by the First Amendment and the original Bill of Rights.[8]

However, the confrontations between these views of history were not over. In his long dissenting opinion in *Jaffree,* Associate Justice William H. Rehnquist, now Chief Justice, reasserted an "accommodationist" view of church and state relations. Relying on O'Neill's and Cord's version of history, he argued that the "wall of separation between church and state" is a metaphor based on bad history and that the *Everson* principle "should be frankly and explicitly abandoned." Justice Byron R. White's dissent also supported such "a basic reconsideration of our precedents."

Soon after, on 1 July 1985, the Supreme Court ruled in *Aguilar* v. *Fenton* (5-4) that the practices of New York City and Grand Rapids, Michigan, in sending public school teachers to private religious schools to teach remedial and enhancement programs for disadvantaged children, were also unconstitutional. Justice William J. Brennan, delivering the Court's opinion, cited the *Everson* principle that the state should remain neutral and not become entangled with churches in administering schools. Dissents were written by the Chief Justice and Justices Sandra Day O'Connor, White, and Rehnquist.[9]

These Supreme Court decisions were greeted with some surprise and considerable elation by liberals and with dismay by conservatives. Attorney General Edwin Meese III quickly and forcefully responded on 10 July 1985 in a speech before the American Bar Association. He explicitly criticized the Court's decisions on religion and education as a misreading of history and commended Justice Rehnquist's call for overruling *Everson.* Secretary of Education William Bennett echoed the complaint that the Supreme Court was misreading history. And, then, in October 1985 Justices Brennan and Stevens both gave speeches sharply criticizing the Attorney General's campaign for a "jurisprudence of original intention."

In addition, the White House, the Attorney General, the Justice Department, the Secretary of Education, the former Republican majority of the Senate Judiciary Committee, the new Chief Justice, and the conservative justices of the Supreme Court, by public statements are now ranged against the liberal and centrist members of the Supreme Court and such notable constitutional scholars as Laurence Tribe of Harvard, Herman Schwartz of American University, A. E. Dick Howard of the University of Virginia, and Leonard W. Levy of the Claremont Graduate School. They all appeal to history, but whose version of history do you read—and believe?

All in all, I think it fair to say that the predominant stream of constitutional, legal, and historical scholarship points to the broader, separatist, and secular meaning of the First Amendment against the narrower, cooperationist, or accommodationist meaning. A nonspecialist cannot encompass the vast literature on this subject, but a valuable and readily available source of evidence is the recently published book by Leonard Levy, professor of humanities and chairman of the Claremont University Graduate Faculty of History. He is editor of the *Encyclopedia of the American Constitution* and the author of a dozen books devoted mostly to the Bill of Rights.

In his book on the First Amendment's establishment clause Levy concludes, and I fully agree, that the meaning of "an establishment of religion" is as follows:

> After the American Revolution seven of the fourteen states that comprised the Union in 1791 authorized establishments of religion by law. Not one state maintained a single or preferential establishment of religion. An establishment of religion meant to those who framed and ratified the First Amendment what it meant in those seven states, and in all seven it meant public support of religion on a nonpreferential basis. It was specifically this support on a nonpreferential basis that the establishment clause of the First Amendment sought to forbid.[10]

Acceptance of a narrow, accommodationist view of the history of the establishment clause must not be allowed to be turned into public policies that serve to increase public support for religious schools in any form: vouchers, tax credits, or aid for extremes of "parental choice." They must not be allowed to increase the role of religion in public schools by organized prayer, teaching of Creationism, censorship of textbooks on the basis of their "secular humanism," or "opting out" of required studies in citizenship on the grounds that they offend any sincerely held religious belief, as ruled by Federal District Judge Thomas Hull in Greeneville, Tennessee, in October 1986.[11]

These practices not only violate good public policy, but they also vitiate the thrust toward separation of church and state which, with minor exceptions, marked the entire careers of Madison and Jefferson. William Lee Miller, professor of religious studies at the University of Virginia, wrote the following succinct summary of their views:

> Did "religious freedom" for Jefferson and Madison extend to atheists? Yes. To agnostics, unbelievers, and pagans? Yes. To heretics and blasphemers and the sacrilegious? Yes. To the Jew and the Gentile, the Christian and Mohametan, the Hindoo, and infidel of every denomination? Yes. To people who want freedom *from* religion? Yes. To people who want freedom *against* religion? Yes. . . .
>
> Did this liberty of belief for Jefferson and Madison entail separation of church and state? Yes. A ban on tax aid to religion? Yes. On state help to religion? Yes. Even religion-in-general? Yes. Even if it were extended without any favoritism among religious groups? Yes. The completely voluntary way in religion? Yes.
>
> Did all the founders agree with Jefferson and Madison? Certainly not. Otherwise there wouldn't have been a fight.[12]

The fight not only continues, but seems to be intensifying on many fronts. So, it behooves educators to study these issues in depth, to consider the best historical scholarship available, and to judge present issues of religion and education accordingly.

Notes

1. *Everson* v. *Board of Education,* 330 U.S. 1 (1947). Black was joined by Chief Justice Vinson and Justices Douglas, Murphy, and Reed. .

2. James M. O'Neill, *Religion and Education Under the Constitution* (New York: Harper, 1949). O'Neill was chairman of the department of speech at Queens College, New York. See also Wilfrid Parsons, S.J., *The First Freedom: Considerations on Church and State in the United States* (New York: Declan X. McMullen, 1948).

3. R. Freeman Butts, *The American Tradition in Religion and Education* (Boston: Beacon Press, 1950). I was professor of education at Teachers College, Columbia University, teaching courses in the history of education. See O'Neill's review of my book in *America,* 9 September 1950, pp. 579–583. See also Leo Pfeffer, *Church, State, and Freedom* (Boston: Beacon Press, 1953) for views similar to mine.

4. *Lemon* v. *Kurtzman,* 403 U.S. 602 (1971). The law struck down in Pennsylvania would have paid part of the salaries of private school teachers of nonreligious subjects.

5. Those six states were Massachusetts, Connecticut, New Hampshire, Maryland, South Carolina, and Georgia.

6. R. Freeman Butts, *Religion, Education, and the First Amendment: The Appeal to History* (Washington, D.C.: People for the American Way, 1985), 35. R. Freeman Butts, "James Madison, the Bill of Rights, and Education," *Teachers College Record* 60, 3 (December 1958): 123–128.

7. Walter Berns, *The First Amendment and the Future of American Democracy* (New York: Basic Books, 1976). Michael J. Malbin, *Religion and Politics: The Intentions of the Authors of the First Amendment* (Washington, D.C.: American Enterprise Institute, 1978). Robert L. Cord, *Separation of Church and State: Historical Fact and Current Fiction* (New York: Lambeth Press, 1982) with a Foreword by William F. Buckley, Jr.

8. *Wallace* v. *Jaffree,* 105 S.Ct. 2479 (1985).

9. *Aguilar* v. *Felton,* 105 S.Ct. 3232 (1985).

10. Leonard W. Levy, *The Establishment Clause: Religion and the First Amendment* (New York: Macmillan, 1986), p. xvi.

11. *Mozert* v. *Hawkins,* U.S. District Court for Eastern District of Tennessee, 24 October 1986.

12. *The Washington Post National Weekly Edition,* 13 October 1986, pp. 23–24.

Robert L. Cord

 **NO**

Church-State Separation and the Public Schools: A Re-evaluation

For four decades—since the *Everson* v. *Board of Education*[1] decision in 1947 —a volatile national debate has raged about the meaning and scope of the First Amendment's establishment clause that mandates separation of church and state. Many of the U.S. Supreme Court's decisions about this matter involve education; therefore, their importance is great to school administrators and teachers who establish and execute policy.

Because of the vagueness of Supreme Court decision making in this important area of constitutional law, public school educators have been accused of violating the First Amendment by allowing or disallowing, for example, the posting of the Ten Commandments, a meeting on school property of a student religious club, or a moment of silent meditation and/or prayer. Today even the very textbooks that students read have become a subject of litigation by parents against a school system, a controversy most likely to end before the Supreme Court.

As this national debate rages, most scholars generally agree that the Founding Fathers' intentions regarding church-state separation are still extremely relevant and important. While the framers of the Constitution and the First Amendment could not foresee many twentieth century problems—especially those growing from advanced technology—many church-state concerns that they addressed in 1787 and 1789 are similar to those we face today.

Constitution's Words Not Trivial

Further, if a nation, such as the United States, proclaims that its written Constitution protects individual liberties and truly provides legal restrictions on the actions of government, the words of that organic law—and the principles derived from them—cannot be treated as irrelevant trivia by those who temporarily govern. That is the surest single way to undo constitutional government, for constitutional government requires that the general power of government be defined and limited by law *in fact* as well as in theory.[2]

From Robert L. Cord, "Church-State Separation and the Public Schools: A Re-evaluation," *Educational Leadership*, vol. 44, no. 8 (May 1987), pp 26–32. Copyright © 1987 by The Association for Supervision and Curriculum Development. Reprinted by permission of The Association for Supervision and Curriculum Development; permission conveyed via Copyright Clearance Center, Inc.

Published in 1979 to the praise of many respected constitutional scholars, the encyclopedic *Congressional Quarterly's Guide to the U.S. Supreme Court* provided the following meaning of the establishment clause.

> The two men most responsible for its inclusion in the Bill of Rights construed the clause *absolutely.* Thomas Jefferson and James Madison thought that the prohibition of establishment meant that a presidential proclamation of Thanksgiving Day was just as improper as a tax exemption for churches.[3]

Despite this authoritative statement, the historical facts are that, as President, James Madison issued at least four Thanksgiving Day proclamations— 9 July 1812, 23 July 1813, 16 November 1814, and 4 March 1815.[4] If Madison interpreted the establishment clause absolutely, he violated both his oath of office and the very instruments of government that he helped write and labored to have ratified.[5]

Similarly, if President Thomas Jefferson construed the establishment clause absolutely, he also violated his oath of office, his principles, and the Constitution when, in 1802, he signed into federal law tax exemption for the churches in Alexandria County, Virginia.[6]

Since Jefferson and Madison held the concept of separation of church and state most dear, in my judgment, neither man—as president or in any other public office under the federal Constitution—was an absolutist and neither violated his understanding of the First Amendment's establishment clause. For me, it therefore logically follows that President Madison did not think issuing Thanksgiving Day Proclamations violated the constitutional doctrine of church-state separation, and that President Jefferson held the same view about tax exemption for churches.

Whoever wrote the paragraph quoted from the prestigious *Guide to the U.S. Supreme Court,* I assume, did not intend to deceive, but evidently did not check primary historical sources, was ignorant of Madison's and Jefferson's actions when each was president, and mistakenly relied on inadequate secondary historical writings considered authoritative, as no doubt the paragraph from the *Guide* is, too. This indicates that much misunderstanding and/or misinformation exists about the meaning of the constitutional concept of separation of church and state.

In that context, I examine ideas critical of my writing published in a monograph—*Religion, Education, and the First Amendment: The Appeal to History* —by the eminent scholar, R. Freeman Butts. There he characterized my book, *Separation of Church and State: Historical Fact and Current Fiction,* as a manifestation of some "conservative counterreformation," the purpose of which is "to attack once again the [U.S. Supreme] Court's adherence to the principle of separation between church and state" by characterizing that principle as a "myth" or a "fiction" or merely "rhetoric."[7] The very first paragraph of my book refutes this erroneous characterization.

> Separation of Church and State is probably the most distinctive concept that the American constitutional system has contributed to the body of political ideas. In 1791, when the First Amendment's prohibition that "Congress shall make no law respecting an establishment of religion" was added to

the United States Constitution, no other country had provided so carefully to prevent the combination of the power of religion with the power of the national government.[8]

While primary historical sources exist that substantiate the Founding Fathers' commitment to church-state separation, other primary sources convince me that much of what the United States Supreme Court and noted scholars have written about it is historically untenable and, in many instances, sheer fiction at odds with the words and actions of the statesmen who placed that very principle in our Constitution.

Absolute Separation v. "No Preference" Doctrine

In the 40-year-old *Everson* case the Supreme Court justices, while splitting 5-4 over the immediate issue, were unanimous in proclaiming that the purpose of the establishment clause—and the intention of its framers in the First Congress —was to create a "high and impregnable" wall of separation between church and state.[9]

Unlike the *Everson* Court, Professor Butts, and all "absolute separationist" scholars, I think the full weight of historical evidence—especially the documented public words and deeds of the First Amendment's framers, including James Madison and our early presidents and Congresses—indicates that they embraced a far narrower concept of church-state separation. In my judgment, they interpreted the First Amendment as prohibiting Congress from (1) creating a national religion or establishment, and (2) placing any one religion, religious sect, or religious tradition in a legally preferred position.[10]

Simply put, the framers of the establishment clause sought to preclude discriminatory government religious partisanship, not nondiscriminatory government accommodation or, in some instances, government collaboration with religion. When this "no religious preference" interpretation of the establishment clause is substituted for the Supreme Court's "high and impregnable wall" interpretation, it is easier to understand many historical documents at odds with the absolutists' position. They substantiate that all our early Congresses, including the one that proposed to the states what subsequently became the First Amendment, and all our early presidents, including Jefferson and Madison, in one way or another used sectarian means to achieve constitutional secular ends.

Everson Case

In the *Everson* case, writing the Court's opinion, Justice Black sought to bolster his "high and impregnable wall" dictum with appeals to some carefully chosen actions of Madison, Jefferson, the Virginia Legislature of 1786, and the framers of the First Amendment. Omitted from all of the *Everson* opinions are any historical facts that run counter to that theory. In his writings, I think Professor Butts employs a similar technique of "history by omission." By this I mean that he fails to address indisputable historical facts that are irreconcilable with his absolute separationist views. A few examples will substantiate this extremely important point.

Mentioning Madison's successful Virginia battle against the "Bill Establishing a Provision for Teachers of the Christian Religion" and "Jefferson's historic statute for religious freedom in 1786,"[11] Professor Butts does not explain away Jefferson's Virginia "Bill for Punishing Disturbers of Religious Worship and Sabbath Breakers," which was introduced by Madison in the Virginia Assembly in 1785 and became law in 1786.[12] Further, while he emphasizes Madison's role in introducing and guiding the Bill of Rights through the First Congress,[13] Professor Butts does not explain why the "absolutist" Madison served as one of six members of a Congressional Committee which, without recorded dissent, recommended the establishment of a Congressional Chaplain System. Adopting the Committee's recommendation, the First Congress voted a $500 annual salary from public funds for a Senate chaplain and a like amount for a House chaplain, both of whom were to offer public prayers in Congress.[14]

Nor does Professor Butts explain why, as an absolute separationist, James Madison would, as president, issue discretionary proclamations of Thanksgiving, calling for a day "to be set apart for the devout purposes of rendering the Sovereign of the Universe and the Benefactor of Man [identified earlier in the proclamation by Madison as "Almighty God"] the public homage due to His holy attributes...."[15]

Unexplained also is why Professor Butts' absolute separationist version of Thomas Jefferson would, as president, conclude a treaty with Kaskaskia Indians which, in part, called for the United States to build them a Roman Catholic Church and pay their priest, and subsequently would urge Congress to appropriate public funds to carry out the terms of the treaty.[16] An understanding of what the framers of our Constitution thought about church-state separation would also be furthered if we had explanations of why Presidents Washington, John Adams, and Jefferson apparently did not think they were breaching the "high and impregnable" wall when they signed into law Congressional bills that, in effect, purchased with enormous grants of federal land, in controlling trusts, the services of the "Society of the United Brethren for propagating the Gospel among the Heathen" to minister to the needs of Christian and other Indians in the Ohio Territory.[17] Like the majority of the Supreme Court, Professor Butts does not comment on these historical documents and events.

When all the historical evidence is considered, I think it relatively clear that the establishment clause was designed to prevent Congress from either establishing a national religion or from putting any one religion, religious sect, or religious tradition into a legally preferred position. In *Everson*, the Supreme Court interpreted the Fourteenth Amendment as prohibiting state legislatures, or their instrumentalities such as school boards, from doing likewise. As a result, the interpretation of the establishment clause by Supreme Court decisions governs the permissible range of both state and federal legislative authority.

Professor Butts thinks my definition of an "establishment of religion" too narrow, and the prohibition which I think the framers intended "plausible but false."[18] Plausible because in the sixteenth and seventeenth centuries, establishments in Europe and in the early American colonies usually meant the establishment of a single church. False because Professor Butts contends that, by the end of the eighteenth century, in America the term "establishment of religion" had taken on a different meaning.

His argument is that "the idea of a single church as constituting 'an establishment of religion' was no longer embedded in the legal framework of any American state when the First Amendment was being debated in Congress in the summer of 1789." Adding that in all of the states that still retained establishments, "multiple establishments were the rule," Professor Butts concludes that "the founders and the framers could not have been ignorant of this fact; they knew very well that this is what the majority in the First Congress intended to prohibit at the federal level."[19]

Butts' Argument Untenable

This argument is simply untenable when considered with the primary historical record. Professor Butts virtually ignored the documents most crucial to an understanding of what the religion clauses were designed to prohibit at the federal level—the suggested constitutional amendments from the various State Ratifying Conventions. Those documents show that they feared, among other things, that important individual rights might be infringed by the powerful new national legislature authorized by the adoption of the federal Constitution.

Their amendments indicate that the states feared interference with the individual's right of conscience and an exclusive religious establishment, *not a multiple national establishment,* as Professor Butts wants us to believe. Typical was the Maryland Ratifying Convention's proposed amendment stating "that there will be no national religion established by law; but that all persons be equally entitled to protection in their religious liberty."[20]

The Virginia Ratifying Convention proposed a "Declaration of Bill of Rights" as amendments to the Constitution that was echoed by North Carolina, Rhode Island, and New York Conventions. Virginia's Article Twenty, adopted 27 June 1788, stated:

> That religion, or the duty which we owe to our Creator, and the manner of discharging it, can be directed only by reason and conviction, not by force or violence; and therefore all men have an equal, natural, and unalienable right to the free exercise of religion, according to the dictates of conscience, and that no particular religious sect or society ought to be favored or established, by law, in preference to others.[21]

States Wanted Nonpreference

In short, when it came to religious establishments, the State Ratifying Conventions proposed "nonpreference" amendments.

With these proposals in mind, it is easier to understand the wording of Madison's original religion amendment: "The Civil rights of none shall be abridged on account of religious belief or worship, nor shall any national religion be established, nor shall the full and equal rights of Conscience be in any manner, or on any pretext, infringed."[22] Madison wanted the Constitution to forbid the federal government from interfering with the rights of conscience or establish an exclusive national religion—not religions—and the record said so.

The "nonpreference" interpretation is further bolstered by Madison's original wording of his own establishment clause and his later interpretation on the floor of the House of Representatives of the intended prohibitions of the amendment. On 15 August 1789, using virtually the same words employed by the petitioning State Ratifying Conventions,

> Mr. Madison said, he apprehended the meaning of the words to be, that Congress should not establish a religion, and enforce the legal observation of it by law, nor compel men to worship God in any manner contrary to their conscience. Whether the words are necessary or not, he did not mean to say, but . . . he thought it as well expressed as the nature of the language would admit.[23]

Further, the House record indicates that Madison said that "he believed that the people feared one sect might obtain a preeminence, or two combine together, and establish a religion to which they would compel others to conform."[24] Certainly Madison's statements from the record of the First Congress and the other primary documents mentioned here run contrary to the "multiple establishment" thesis.

Implications for the Public Schools

Professionals in education may wonder appropriately what the impact would be on public education should the U.S. Supreme Court now choose to reverse some of its major rulings and adopt the narrower interpretation of church-state separation which I believe was intended and embraced by the First Amendment's framers.

First, the establishment clause would continue to prohibit Congress and individual states from creating, in Madison's words, "a national religion."

Second, in keeping with the framers' intent, the establishment clause's "no preference" doctrine, applied directly to the federal government and to the states by the Fourteenth Amendment, would constitutionally preclude all governmental entities from placing any one religion, religious sect, or religious tradition into a preferred legal status. As a consequence, in public schools, the recitation of the Lord's Prayer or readings taken solely from the New Testament would continue to be unconstitutional because they place the Christian religion in a preferred position.

Similarly, the posting of the Ten Commandments only or reading only from the Old Testament would place the Judeo-Christian tradition in an unconstitutionally favored religious status. However, unendorsed readings or postings from many writings considered sacred by various religions, such as the Book of Mormon, the interpretative writings of Mary Baker Eddy, the Bible, the Koran, the Analects of Confucius, would be constitutional. A decision to teach only "creationism" or Genesis would be unconstitutional, while a course in cosmology, exploring a full range of beliefs about the origin of life or the nature of the universe—religious, areligious, or nonreligious—would not violate the First Amendment any more than would a course on comparative religions without teacher endorsement.

In all circumstances where the state is pursuing a valid educational goal, and is religiously nonpartisan in doing so, the professional leadership of the educational unit would decide, as in any other policy, whether such an activity was educationally appropriate or desirable. This would be the case whether the educational unit was a school, a school district, or an entire state educational system. Consequently, adherence to the "no preference" doctrine would return many policy decisions to the appropriate educational authorities, elected or appointed, and reduce the all too frequent present pattern of government by judiciary.

Third, although the First Amendment's free exercise of religion clause would not be contracted by the "no preference" principle, that interpretation would, in some instances, expand the individual's free exercise of religion and other First Amendment rights. This would happen where "equal access" is currently denied public school students.

Equal Access Act

The Equal Access Act of 1984 (Public Law 98-377) prohibits public high schools receiving federal aid from preventing voluntary student groups, including religious ones, from meeting in school facilities before and after class hours or during a club period, if other extracurricular groups have access.[25] The constitutionality of refusing "equal access" to voluntary student religious organizations was litigated in the lower courts[26] before reaching the U.S. Supreme Court in *Bender* v. *Williamsport* in March 1986.[27]

In deciding equal access cases, the lower federal courts applied the Supreme Court's "three part *Lemon*" test to determine whether the establishment clause had been violated. Under this test, first described in *Lemon* v. *Kurtzman,* the Supreme Court held that in order to pass constitutional muster under the establishment clause, the challenged governmental policy or activity must (1) have a secular purpose, (2) be one that has a principal or primary effect which neither advances nor inhibits religion, and (3) not foster an excessive government entanglement with religion.[28]

The "no preference" doctrine, on the other hand, would provide a relatively clearer and easier-to-apply test. Alleged violations would be measured by two simple questions: (1) Is the governmental action within the constitutional power of the acting public body? and (2) Does the governmental action elevate any one religion, religious sect, or religious tradition into a preferred legal status? Either a "no" to the first question or a "yes" to the second would make the policy unconstitutional.

Unlike the *Lemon* interpretation, the "no preference" interpretation poses less danger to a student's individual First and Fourteenth Amendment liberty. The Third U.S. Circuit Court's decision in *Bender* v. *Williamsport* illustrates this point. There the court held that it was constitutional for a school board to refuse to permit a student-initiated nondenominational prayer club to meet during the regularly scheduled activity period in a public school room.[29] As I see it, that decision subordinated three First Amendment freedoms—free exercise of religion, freedom of speech, and voluntary assembly—to one misinterpreted First Amendment guarantee. Under the "no preference" doctrine, equal access would be guaranteed to *all* religious or, for that matter, irreligious student groups under the same conditions that apply to any other voluntary student group.

Application of the "no preference" interpretation also avoids enormous dangers to an "open society" possible under the *Lemon* test. Can we not see that a court which can hold today that a classroom could not be used by a voluntary religious student group because that use may have as its primary effect the advancement of religion, can tomorrow, by the same logic, bar meeting rooms to students who want to discuss atheism or a book negative about religion, such as Bertrand Russell's *Why I Am Not a Christian,* because the primary effect there might be said to inhibit religion? By the use of *Lemon's* "primary effect" test, books about religion or those said to be irreligious can be removed from public school libraries. Is C. S. Lewis' *The Screwtape Letters* safe? And what about *Inherit the Wind,* or Darwin's *Origin of the Species?* Are we so frightened of ourselves that we are willing to disallow, in our institutions of learning, scrutinization of ultimate issues and values because of fear about where an open marketplace of ideas may eventually take the nation?

Finally, while some actions such as an uncoerced moment of silence for meditation and/or prayer in a public schoolroom[30] or the teaching of educationally deprived students from low-income families for several hours each week in a parochial school by public school teachers, recently held unconstitutional,[31] would be constitutional under the "no preference" interpretation, that does not mean they would automatically become educational policy. In all public educational entities, large or small, what would become policy would be up to the legally empowered decision makers in each of those entities.

Notes

1. 330 U.S. 1 (1947).
2. Charles H. McIlwain, *Constitutionalism: Ancient and Modern,* rev. ed. (Ithaca, N.Y.: Great Seal Books, 1958), 19-22.
3. *Congressional Quarterly's Guide to the United States Supreme Court* (Washington, D.C.: Congressional Quarterly, Inc., 1979), 461. Emphasis added. The First Amendment has two religion clauses, the "establishment" clause and the "free exercise" clause. U.S. Constitution Amendment I: "Congress shall make no law respecting an establishment of religion, or prohibiting the free exercise thereof...."
4. These proclamations, in their entirety, are published in James D. Richardson, *A Contemplation of the Messages and Papers of the Presidents, 1789-1897,* vol. I (Washington, D.C.: Bureau of National Literature and Art, 1901), 34-35; and Robert L. Cord, *Separation of Church and State: Historical Fact and Current Fiction* (Grand Rapids, Michigan: Baker Book House, 1988), 257-260.
5. After he had left the presidency, and toward the end of his life, Madison wrote a document commonly known as the "Detached Memoranda," which was first published as recently as 1946 in *William and Mary Quarterly* 3 (1946): 534. In it Madison *does* say that Thanksgiving Day proclamations are unconstitutional,

as are chaplains in Congress. In light of his actions in public office, these were obviously not his views as a congressman and president. For a fuller discussion of Madison's "Detached Memoranda," see Cord, *Separation,* 29-36.

6. *2 Statutes at Large* 194, Seventh Congress, Sess. 1, Chap. 52. Jefferson *did* believe Thanksgiving Proclamation violated the First Amendment and, unlike Washington, John Adams, and James Madison, declined to issue them.

7. R. Freeman Butts, *Religion, Education, and the First Amendment: The Appeal to History* (Washington, D.C.: People for the American Way, 1986), 9. Butts, an educational historian, is William F. Russell Professor Emeritus, Teachers College, Columbia University; Senior Fellow of the Kettering Foundation; and Visiting Scholar at the Hoover Institution, Stanford University.

8. Cord, *Separation,* XIII.

9. For an extensive critique of the *Everson* case and its interpretation of the establishment clause, see Cord, *Separation,* 103-133.

10. For in-depth study of the "no preference" principle, see Robert L. Cord, "Church-State Separation: Restoring the 'No Preference' Doctrine of the First Amendment," *Harvard Journal of Law & Public Policy* 9 (1986): 129.

11. Butts, *Religion,* 18.

12. Cord, *Separation,* 215-218.

13. Butts, *Religion,* 18-21.

14. Cord, *Separation,* 22-26.

15. Quoted from President Madison's "Proclamation" of "the 9th day of July A.D. 1812." This proclamation is republished in its entirety in Cord, *Separation,* 257.

16. For the entire text of the treaty, see Ibid., 261-263.

17. The full texts of these laws are republished in Cord, 263-270.

18. Butts, *Religion,* 16.

19. Ibid., 18.

20. Jonathan Elliott, *Debates on the Federal Constitution,* vol. II (Philadelphia: J.B. Lippincott Co., 1901), 553.

21. Ibid., vol. III, 659.

22. *Annals of the Congress of the United States, The Debates and Proceedings in the Congress of the United States,* vol. I, Compiled from Authentic Materials, by Joseph Gales, Senior (Washington, D.C.: Gales and Seaton, 1834), 434.

23. Ibid., 730.

24. Ibid., 731.

25. *Congressional Quarterly Weekly Report,* vols. 42, p. 1545, 1854; 43, p. 1807.

26. *Brandon v. Board of Education,* 635 F. 2d 971 (2d Cir. 1980); *cert. denied,* 454 U.S. 1123 (1981); *Lubbock Civil Liberties Union* v. *Lubbock Independent School District,* 669 F. 2d 1038 (5th Cir. 1982), *cert. denied,* 459 U.S. 1155 (1983).

27. *Bender* v. *Williamsport,* 475 U.S. 534, 89 L.Ed. 2d 501 (1986). While the Third Circuit Court dealt with the "equal access" question, the Supreme Court did not reach that constitutional issue because one of the parties to the suit in the Circuit Court lacked standing and, therefore, that Court should have dismissed the case for want of jurisdiction. Ibid., 516.

28. *Lemon* v. *Kurtzman,* 403 U.S. 602, 612, 613 (1971).

29. *Bender* v. *Williamsport,* 741 F. 2d 538, 541 (3rd Cir. 1984).

30. In *Wallace* v. *Jaffree,* 105 S. Ct. 2479 (1985), the U.S. Supreme Court held such a law unconstitutional.

31. In *Grand Rapids* v. *Ball,* 473 U.S. 373, 87 L.Ed. 2d 267 (1985) and *Aguilar* v. *Felton,* 473 U.S. 402, 87 L.Ed. 2d 290 (1985), the Supreme Court held similar programs unconstitutional.

POSTSCRIPT

Should Church-State Separation Be Maintained?

If the Constitution indeed attempts to guarantee the protection of minority opinions from a possibly oppressive majority, can it be applied equally to all parties in any value-laden dispute such as those involving the relationship of church and state? An exhaustive review of historical cases dealing with manifestations of this basic problem may be found in Martha McCarthy's article "Religion and Public Schools" in the August 1985 issue of the *Harvard Educational Review*.

A wide variety of articles is available on this volatile area of concern, including "Textbook Censorship and Secular Humanism in Perspective," by Franklin Parker, *Religion and Public Education* (Summer 1988); Rod Farmer's "Toward a Definition of Secular Humanism," *Contemporary Education* (Spring 1987); Mel and Norma Gabler's "Moral Relativism on the Ropes," *Communication Education* (October 1987); and Donald Vandenberg's "Education and the Religious," *Teachers College Record* (Fall 1987).

Other excellent sources are Warren A. Nord, "The Place of Religion in the World of Public School Textbooks," and Mark G. Yudof, "Religion, Textbooks, and the Public Schools," both in *The Educational Forum* (Spring 1990); James Davison Hunter's "Modern Pluralism and the First Amendment," *The Brookings Review* (Spring 1990); "Taking a Few Bricks Off the Wall: The Effect of Three Recent Cases on the Separation of Church and State," *Journal of Law and Education* (Spring 1995); Elliott A. Wright, "Religion in American Education: A Historical View," *Phi Delta Kappan* (September 1999); Michael H. Romanowski and Keith M. Talbert, "Addressing the Influence of Religion and Faith in American History," *The Clearing House* (January/February 2000); Alan Singer, "Separation of Church and State Protects Both Secular and Religious Worlds," *Phi Delta Kappan* (February 2000); and Elliott A. Wright, "Religion in American Education: A Historical View," *Phi Delta Kappan* (September 1999).

Books that explore aspects of the issue include *The Rights of Religious Persons in Public Education* by John W. Whitehead (1991); *Religious Fundamentalism and American Education: The Battle for the Public Schools* by Eugene F. Provenzo, Jr. (1990); *A Standard for Repair: The Establishment of Religion Clause of the U.S. Constitution* by Jeremy Gunn (1992); and *Why We Still Need Public Schools: Church/State Relations and Visions of Democracy* edited by Art Must, Jr. (1992).

In the end, the main problem is one of finding an appropriate balance between the two First Amendment clauses within the context of public schooling and making that balance palatable and realizable at the local school level.

ISSUE 5

Should School Attendance Be Compelled?

YES: Horace Mann, from *Tenth Annual Report* and *Twelfth Annual Report* (1846 and 1848)

NO: Daniel H. Pink, from "School's Out," *Reason* (October 2001)

ISSUE SUMMARY

YES: Horace Mann, a leader of the common school movement in the nineteenth century, presents the basic arguments for publicly funded education in which all citizens could participate and lays the groundwork for compulsory attendance laws.

NO: Writer-editor Daniel H. Pink declares compulsory mass schooling an aberration and finds hope in the home schooling revolution and the ultimate demise of high school.

The common school crusade, led by Massachusetts education leader Horace Mann (1796–1859) and other activists, built on the growing sentiment among citizens and business leaders that public schools were needed to deal with the increase in immigration, urbanization, and industrialism, as well as to bind together the American population and to prepare everyone for participatory democracy.

As the free public school movement got underway, however, it became clear that quite a few parents were reluctant to send their children to school because many of them contributed to the economic well-being of the family. Mann, who had observed first-hand the effectiveness of compulsory school attendance in Prussia, pushed for such legislation in Massachusetts. In 1852 an Act Concerning the Attendance of Children at School was passed, compelling all children from age 8 to 14 to attend school (public or private) for at least 12 weeks each year. Between that time and 1918 all of the states passed similar laws with expanded periods of attendance and stiff penalties for noncompliance.

For the most part, the right of the government to compel school attendance went unchallenged. In the 1920s there were even efforts to eliminate all alternatives to public schooling as a means of compliance. Such an effort in

Oregon was challenged in court, and the U.S. Supreme Court ultimately ruled, in *Pierce v. Society of Sisters* (1925), that such legislation unreasonably interferes with parental rights. While this ruling preserved the private school option, it did not alter the governmental prerogative to compel school attendance.

Beginning in the 1950s an increasing number of activists and scholars produced sharp criticisms of this governmental authority, and this barrage has continued to the present day. Among the more widely discussed of these works are Paul Goodman's *Compulsory Mis-education* (1964), Ivan Illich's *Deschooling Society* (1971), Carl Bereiter's *Must We Educate?* (1973), John Holt's *Instead of Education* (1976), Roger White's *Absent With Cause* (1980), and John Taylor Gatto's *Dumbing Us Down: The Hidden Curriculum of Compulsory Schooling* (1992).

Goodman felt that attendance should only be compelled during the elementary school years and that adolescents need more freedom and support to fashion their own education and training. Illich campaigned for the abolition of all compulsory education, contending that only in a "deschooled" society could meaningful education occur. He argued that the present laws led to an artificial system of sifting and rewarding that is unfair and unproductive. More recently, Gatto has attacked the historical basis of compulsory schooling. For him, Mann's admiration of the Prussian approach guaranteed the evolution of a system that emphasizes obedience and subordination rather than the unleashing of the intellectual and creative powers of the individual.

Jackson Toby, in "Obsessive Compulsion," *National Review* (June 28, 1999), condemns the folly of mandatory high school attendance. Toby cites three myths undergirding present policies: (1) adolescents can be educated whether they like it or not; (2) the students who will leave school as soon as they can will generate a crime wave; and (3) those who do not complete high school are doomed to live an economically and culturally impoverished life.

The home schooling movement, which has expanded during the past three decades, is another manifestation of parental concern over the manipulativeness of a governmentally mandated system. Almost all states have accommodated parents who select this alternative while still maintaining varying degrees of control over the process. The National Education Association, however, believes that home schooling programs cannot provide a comprehensive educational experience. According to Howard Klepper, in "Mandatory Rights and Compulsory Education," *Law and Philosophy* (May 1996), the public has a right to an educated citizenry in order to ensure the collective good. "The best way we know to protect this public right," he states, "is to compel schooling." The justification of compulsory education involves not individual benefit but societal benefit.

In the following selections, Horace Mann's original argument for a system of common schools to bind together the diverse people of the new nation is presented, while home schooling advocate Daniel H. Pink puts forth the case that compelled attendance is no longer appropriate in America's evolving "free agency" culture.

The Education of Free Men

I believe in the existence of a great, immutable principle of natural law, or natural ethics,—a principle antecedent to all human institutions and incapable of being abrogated by any ordinances of man,—a principle of divine origin, clearly legible in the ways of Providence as those ways are manifested in the order of nature and in the history of the race,—which proves the *absolute right* of every human being that comes into the world to an education; and which, of course, proves the correlative duty of every government to see that the means of that education are provided for all.

In regard to the application of this principle of natural law,—that is, in regard to the extent of the education to be provided for all, at the public expense, —some differences of opinion may fairly exist, under different political organizations; but under a republican government, it seems clear that the minimum of this education can never be less than such as is sufficient to qualify each citizen for the civil and social duties he will be called to discharge;—such an education as teaches the individual the great laws of bodily health; as qualifies for the fulfillment of parental duties; as is indispensable for the civil functions of a witness or a juror; as is necessary for the voter in municipal affairs; and finally, for the faithful and conscientious discharge of all those duties which devolve upon the inheritor of a portion of the sovereignty of this great republic....

In obedience to the laws of God and to the laws of all civilized communities, society is bound to protect the natural life; and the natural life cannot be protected without the appropriation and use of a portion of the property which society possesses. We prohibit infanticide under penalty of death. We practise a refinement in this particular. The life of an infant is inviolable even before he is born; and he who feloniously takes it, even before birth, is as subject to the extreme penalty of the law, as though he had struck down manhood in its vigor, or taken away a mother by violence from the sanctuary of home, where she blesses her offspring. But why preserve the natural life of a child, why preserve unborn embryos of life, if we do not intend to watch over and to protect them, and to expand their subsequent existence into usefulness and happiness? As individuals, or as an organized community, we have no natural right; we can derive no authority or countenance from reason; we can cite no attribute or purpose of the divine nature, for giving birth to any human being,

From Horace Mann, *Tenth Annual Report* and *Twelfth Annual Report* (1846, 1848).

and then inflicting upon that being the curse of ignorance, of poverty and of vice, with all their attendant calamities. We are brought then to this startling but inevitable alternative. The natural life of an infant should be extinguished as soon as it is born, or the means should be provided to save that life from being a curse to its possessor; and therefore every State is bound to enact a code of laws legalizing and enforcing Infanticide, or a code of laws establishing Free Schools! . . .

⋯❦⋯

Under the Providence of God, our means of education are the grand machinery by which the "raw material" of human nature can be worked up into inventors and discoverers, into skilled artisans and scientific farmers, into scholars and jurists, into the founders of benevolent institutions, and the great expounders of ethical and theological science. By means of early education, those embryos of talent may be quickened, which will solve the difficult problems of political and economical law; and by them, too, the genius may be kindled which will blaze forth in the Poets of Humanity. Our schools, far more than they have done, may supply the Presidents and Professors of Colleges, and Superintendents of Public Instruction, all over the land; and send, not only into our sister states, but across the Atlantic, the men of practical science, to superintend the construction of the great works of art. Here, too, may those judicial powers be developed and invigorated, which will make legal principles so clear and convincing as to prevent appeals to force; and, should the clouds of war ever lower over our country, some hero may be found,—the nursling of our schools, and ready to become the leader of our armies,—that best of all heroes, who will secure the glories of a peace, unstained by the magnificient murders of the battle-field. . . .

Without undervaluing any other human agency, it may be safely affirmed that the Common School, improved and energized, as it can easily be, may become the most effective and benignant of all the forces of civilization. Two reasons sustain this position. In the first place, there is a universality in its operation, which can be affirmed of no other institution whatever. If administered in the spirit of justice and conciliation, all the rising generation may be brought within the circle of its reformatory and elevating influences. And, in the second place, the materials upon which it operates are so pliant and ductile as to be susceptible of assuming a greater variety of forms than any other earthly work of the Creator. The inflexibility and ruggedness of the oak, when compared with the lithe sapling or the tender germ, are but feeble emblems to typify the docility of childhood, when contrasted with the obduracy and intractableness of man. It is these inherent advantages of the Common School, which, in our own State, have produced results so striking, from a system so imperfect, and an administration so feeble. In teaching the blind, and the deaf and dumb, in kindling the latent spark of intelligence that lurks in an idiot's mind, and in the more holy work of reforming abandoned and outcast children, education has proved what it can do, by glorious experiments. These wonders, it has done in its infancy, and with the lights of a limited experience; but, when its faculties shall be fully developed, when it shall be trained to wield its mighty energies for the protection of society against the giant vices which now invade and torment it;—against intemperance, avarice, war, slavery, bigotry, the woes of want and the wickedness of waste,—then, there will not be a height to which these enemies of the race can escape, which it will not scale, nor a Titan among them all, whom it will not slay....

Now, surely, nothing but Universal Education can counter-work this tendency to the domination of capital and the servility of labor. If one class possesses all the wealth and the education, while the residue of society is ignorant and poor, it matters not by what name the relation between them may be called; the latter, in fact and in truth, will be the servile dependants and subjects of the former. But if education be equably diffused, it will draw property after it, by the strongest of all attractions; for such a thing never did happen, and never can happen, as that an intelligent and practical body of men should be permanently poor. Property and labor, in different classes, are essentially antagonistic; but property and labor, in the same class, are essentially fraternal. The people of Massachusetts have, in some degree, appreciated the truth, that the unexampled prosperity of the State,—its comfort, its competence, its general intelligence and virtue,—is attributable to the education, more or less perfect, which all its people have received; but are they sensible of a fact equally important?—namely, that it is to this same education that two thirds of the people are indebted for not being, to-day, the vassals of as severe a tyranny, in the form of capital, as the lower classes of Europe are bound to in the form of brute force.

Education, then, beyond all other devices of human origin, is the great equalizer of the conditions of men—the balance-wheel of the social machinery. I do not here mean that it so elevates the moral nature as to make men disdain and abhor the oppression of their fellow-men. This idea pertains to another of its attributes. But I mean that it gives each man the independence and the means, by which he can resist the selfishness of other men. It does better than to disarm the poor of their hostility towards the rich; it prevents being poor. Agrarianism is the revenge of poverty against wealth. The wanton destruction of the property of others,—the burning of hay-ricks and corn-ricks, the demolition of machinery, because it supersedes hand-labor, the sprinkling of vitriol on rich dresses,—is only agrarianism run mad. Education prevents both the revenge and the madness. On the other hand, a fellow-feeling for one's class or caste is the common instinct of hearts not wholly sunk in selfish regards for person, or for family. The spread of education, by enlarging the cultivated class or caste, will open a wider area over which the social feelings will expand; and, if this education should be universal and complete, it would do more than all things else to obliterate factitious distinctions in society....

But to all doubters, disbelievers, or despairers, in human progress, it may still be said, there is one experiment which has never yet been tried. It is an experiment which, even before its inception, offers the highest authority for its ultimate success. Its formula is intelligible to all; and it is as legible as though written in starry letters on an azure sky. It is expressed in these few and simple words:—"*Train up a child in the way he should go, and when he is old he will not depart from it.*" This declaration is positive. If the conditions are complied with, it makes no provision for a failure. Though pertaining to morals, yet, if the terms of the direction are observed, there is no more reason to doubt the result, than there would be in an optical or a chemical experiment.

But this experiment has never yet been tried. Education has never yet been brought to bear with one hundredth part of its potential force, upon the natures of children, and, through them, upon the character of men, and of the race. In all the attempts to reform mankind which have hitherto been made, whether by changing the frame of government, by aggravating or softening the severity of the penal code, or by substituting a government-created, for a God-created religion;—in all these attempts, the infantile and youthful mind, its amenability to influences, and the enduring and self-operating character of the influences it receives, have been almost wholly unrecognized. Here, then, is a new agency, whose powers are but just beginning to be understood, and whose mighty energies, hitherto, have been but feebly invoked; and yet, from our experience, limited and imperfect as it is, we do know that, far beyond any other earthly instrumentality, it is comprehensive and decisive....

If, then, a government would recognize and protect the rights of religious freedom, it must abstain from subjugating the capacities of its children to any legal standard of religious faith, with as great fidelity as it abstains from controlling the opinions of men. It must meet the unquestionable fact, that the old spirit of religious domination is adopting new measures to accomplish its work, —measures, which, if successful, will be as fatal to the liberties of mankind, as those which were practised in by-gone days of violence and terror. These new measures are aimed at children instead of men. They propose to supersede the necessity of subduing free thought, *in the mind of the adult,* by forestalling the development of any capacity of free thought, *in the mind of the child.* They expect to find it easier to subdue the free agency of children, by binding them in fetters of bigotry, than to subdue the free agency of men, by binding them in fetters of iron. For this purpose, some are attempting to deprive children of their right to labor, and, of course, of their daily bread, unless they will attend a government school, and receive its sectarian instruction. Some are attempting to withhold all means, even of secular education, from the poor, and thus punish them with ignorance, unless, with the secular knowledge which they desire, they will accept theological knowledge which they condemn. Others, still, are striving to break down all free Public School systems, where they exist, and to prevent their establishment, where they do not exist, in the hope, that on the downfall of these, their system will succeed. The sovereign antidote against these machinations, is, Free Schools for all, and the right of every parent to determine the religious education of his children.

Daniel H. Pink

 **NO**

School's Out

Here's a riddle of the New Economy: Whenever students around the world take those tests that measure which country's children know the most, American kids invariably score near the bottom. No matter the subject, when the international rankings come out, European and Asian nations finish first while the U.S. pulls up the rear. This, we all know, isn't good. Yet by almost every measure, the American economy outperforms those very same nations of Asia and Europe. We create greater wealth, deliver more and better goods and services, and positively kick butt on innovation. This, we all know, *is* good.

Now the riddle: If we're so dumb, how come we're so rich? How can we fare so poorly on international measures of education yet perform so well in an economy that depends on brainpower? The answer is complex, but within it are clues about the future of education—and how "free agency" may rock the school house as profoundly as it has upended the business organization.

We are living in the founding of what I call "free agent nation." Over the past decade, in nearly every industry and region, work has been undergoing perhaps its most significant transformation since Americans left the farm for the factory a century ago. Legions of Americans, and increasingly citizens of other countries as well, are abandoning one of the Industrial Revolution's most enduring legacies—the "job"—and forging new ways to work. They're becoming self-employed knowledge workers, proprietors of home-based businesses, temps and permatemps, freelancers and e-lancers, independent contractors and independent professionals, micropreneurs and infopreneurs, part-time consultants, interim executives, on-call troubleshooters, and full-time soloists.

In the U.S. today, more than 30 million workers—nearly one-fourth of the American workforce—are free agents. And many others who hold what are still nominally "jobs" are doing so under terms closer in spirit to free agency than to traditional employment. They're telecommuting. They're hopping from company to company. They're forming ventures that are legally their employers', but whose prospects depend largely on their own individual efforts.

In boom times, many free agents—fed up with bad bosses and dysfunctional workplaces and yearning for freedom—leapt into this new world. In leaner times, other people—clobbered by layoffs, mergers, and downturns—have been pushed. But these new independent workers are transforming the nation's social and economic future. Soon they will transform the nation's education system as well.

The Homogenizing Hopper

Whenever I walk into a public school, I'm nearly toppled by a wave of nostalgia. Most schools I've visited in the 21st century look and feel exactly like the public schools I attended in the 1970s. The classrooms are the same size. The desks stand in those same rows. Bulletin boards preview the next national holiday. The hallways even *smell* the same. Sure, some classrooms might have a computer or two. But in most respects, the schools American children attend today seem indistinguishable from the ones their parents and grandparents attended.

At first, such déjà vu warmed my soul. But then I thought about it. How many other places look and feel exactly as they did 20, 30, or 40 years ago? Banks don't. Hospitals don't. Grocery stores don't. Maybe the sweet nostalgia I sniffed on those classroom visits was really the odor of stagnation. Since most other institutions in American society have changed dramatically in the past half-century, the stasis of schools is strange. And it's doubly peculiar because school itself is a modern invention, not something we inherited from antiquity.

Through most of history, people learned from tutors or their close relatives. In 19th-century America, says education historian David Tyack, "the school was a voluntary and incidental institution." Not until the early 20th century did public schools as we know them—places where students segregated by age learn from government-certified professionals—become widespread. And not until the 1920s did attending one become compulsory. Think about that last fact a moment. Compared with much of the world, America is a remarkably hands-off land. We don't force people to vote, or to work, or to serve in the military. But we do compel parents to relinquish their kids to this institution for a dozen years, and threaten to jail those who resist.

Compulsory mass schooling is an aberration in both history and modern society. Yet it was the ideal preparation for the Organization Man economy, a highly structured world dominated by large, bureaucratic corporations that routinized the workplace. Compulsory mass schooling equipped generations of future factory workers and middle managers with the basic skills and knowledge they needed on the job. The broader lessons it conveyed were equally crucial. Kids learned how to obey rules, follow orders, and respect authority—and the penalties that came with refusal.

This was just the sort of training the old economy demanded. Schools had bells; factories had whistles. Schools had report card grades; offices had pay grades. Pleasing your teacher prepared you for pleasing your boss. And in either place, if you achieved a minimal level of performance, you were promoted. Taylorism—the management philosophy, named for efficiency expert Frederick Winslow Taylor, that there was One Best Way of doing things that could and should be applied in all circumstances—didn't spend all its time on the job. It also went to class. In the school, as in the workplace, the reigning theory was One Best Way. Kids learned the same things at the same time in the same manner in the same place. Marshall McLuhan once described schools as "the homogenizing hopper into which we toss our integral tots for processing." And schools made factory-style processing practically a religion—through standardized testing, standardized curricula, and standardized clusters of children. (Question: When was the last time *you* spent all day in a room filled exclusively with people almost exactly your own age?)

So when we step into the typical school today, we're stepping into the past —a place whose architect is Frederick Winslow Taylor and whose tenant is the Organization Man. The one American institution that has least accommodated itself to the free agent economy is the one Americans claim they value most. But it's hard to imagine that this arrangement can last much longer—a One Size Fits All education system cranking out workers for a My Size Fits Me economy. Maybe the answer to the riddle I posed at the beginning is that we're succeeding *in spite of* our education system. But how long can that continue? And imagine how we'd prosper if we began educating our children more like we earn our livings. Nearly 20 years ago, a landmark government report, *A Nation at Risk*, declared that American education was "being eroded by a rising tide of mediocrity." That may no longer be true. Instead, American schools are awash in a rising tide of irrelevance.

Don't get me wrong. In innumerable ways, mass public schooling has been a stirring success. Like Taylorism, it has accomplished some remarkable things—teaching immigrants both English and the American way, expanding literacy, equipping many Americans to succeed beyond their parents' imaginings. In a very large sense, America's schools have been a breathtaking democratic achievement.

But that doesn't mean they ought to be the same as they were when we were kids. Parents and politicians have sensed the need for reform, and have pushed education to the top of the national agenda. Unfortunately, few of the conventional remedies—standardized testing, character training, recertifying teachers—will do much to cure what ails American schools, and may even make things worse. Free agency, though, will force the necessary changes. Look for free agency to accelerate and deepen three incipient movements in education—home schooling, alternatives to traditional high school, and new approaches to adult learning. These changes will prove as pathbreaking as mass public schooling was a century ago.

The Home-Schooling Revolution

"School is like starting life with a 12-year jail sentence in which bad habits are the only curriculum truly learned." Those are the words of John Taylor Gatto, who was named New York state's Teacher of the Year in 1991. Today he is one of the most forceful voices for one of the most powerful movements in American education—home schooling. In home schooling, kids opt out of traditional school to take control of their own education and to learn with the help of parents, tutors, and peers. Home schooling is free agency for the under-18 set. And it's about to break through the surface of our national life.

As recently as 1980, home schooling was illegal in most states. In the early 1980s, no more than 15,000 students learned this way. But Christian conservatives, unhappy with schools they considered God-free zones and eager to teach their kids themselves, pressed for changes. Laws fell, and home schooling surged. By 1990, there were as many as 300,000 American home-schoolers. By 1993, home schooling was legal in all 50 states. Since then, home schooling has swum into the mainstream—paddled there by secular parents dissatisfied with low-quality, and even dangerous, schools. In the first half of the 1990s, the home-schooling population more than doubled. Today some 1.7 million children are home-schoolers, their ranks growing as much as 15 percent each year. Factor in turnover, and one in 10 American kids under 18 has gotten part of his or her schooling at home.

Home schooling has become perhaps the largest and most successful education reform movement of the last two decades:

- While barely 3 percent of American schoolchildren are now home-schoolers, that represents a surprisingly large dent in the public school monopoly—especially compared with private schools. For every four kids in private school, there's one youngster learning at home. The home-schooling population is roughly equal to all the school-age children in Pennsylvania.
- According to *The Wall Street Journal*, "Evidence is mounting that home-schooling, once confined to the political and religious fringe, has achieved results not only on par with public education, but in some ways surpassing it." Home-schooled children consistently score higher than traditional students on standardized achievement tests, placing on average in the 80th percentile in all subjects.
- Home-schooled children also perform extremely well on nearly all measures of socialization. One of the great misconceptions about home schooling is that it turns kids into isolated loners. In fact, these children spend more time with adults, more time in their community, and more time with children of varying ages than their traditional-school counterparts. Says one researcher, "The conventionally schooled tended to be considerably more aggressive, loud, and competitive than the home educated."

"Home schooling," though, is a bit of a misnomer. Parents don't re-create the classroom in the living room any more than free agents re-create the cubicle in their basement offices. Instead, home schooling makes it easier for children to pursue their own interests in their own way—a My Size Fits Me approach to learning. In part for this reason, some adherents—particularly those who have opted out of traditional schools for reasons other than religion—prefer the term "unschooling."

The similarities to free agency—having an "unjob"—are many. Free agents are independent workers; home-schoolers are independent learners. Free agents maintain robust networks and tight connections through informal groups and professional associations; home-schoolers have assembled powerful groups—

like the 3,000-family Family Unschoolers Network—to share teaching strategies and materials and to offer advice and support. Free agents often challenge the idea of separating work and family; home-schoolers take the same approach to the boundary between school and family.

Perhaps most important, home schooling is almost perfectly consonant with the four animating values of free agency: having freedom, being authentic, putting yourself on the line, and defining your own success. Take freedom. In the typical school, children often aren't permitted to move unless a bell rings or an adult grants them permission. And except for a limited menu of offerings in high school, they generally can't choose what to study or when to study it. Home-schoolers have far greater freedom. They learn more like, well, children. We don't teach little kids how to talk or walk or understand the world. We simply put them in nurturing situations and let them learn on their own. Sure, we impose certain restrictions. ("Don't walk in the middle of the street.") But we don't go crazy. ("Please practice talking for 45 minutes until a bell rings.") It's the same for home-schoolers. Kids can become agents of their own education rather than merely recipients of someone else's noble intentions.

Imagine a 5-year-old child whose current passion is building with Legos. Every day she spends up to an hour, maybe more, absorbed in complex construction projects, creating farms, zoos, airplanes, spaceships. Often her friends come over and they work together. No one assigns her this project. No one tells her when and how to do it. And no one will give her creation a grade. Is she learning? Of course. This is how many home-schoolers explore their subjects.

Now suppose some well-intentioned adults step in to teach the child a thing or two about Lego building. Let's say they assign her a daily 45-minute Lego period, give her a grade at the end of each session, maybe even offer a reward for an A+ building. And why not bring in some more 5-year-olds to teach them the same things about Legos? Why not have them all build their own 45-minute Lego buildings at the same time, then give them each a letter grade, with a prize for the best one? My guess: Pretty soon our 5-year-old Lego lover would lose her passion. Her buildings would likely become less creative, her learning curve flatter. This is how many conventional schools work—or, I guess, *don't work*.

The well-meaning adults have squelched the child's freedom to play and learn and discover on her own. She's no longer in control. She's no longer having fun. Countless studies, particularly those by University of Rochester psychologist Edward L. Deci, have shown that kids and adults alike—in school, at work, at home—lose the intrinsic motivation and the pure joy derived from learning and working when somebody takes away their sense of autonomy and instead imposes some external system of reward and punishment. Freedom isn't a detour from learning. It's the best pathway toward it.

Stay with our Lego lass a moment and think about authenticity—the basic desire people have to be who they are rather than conform to someone else's standard. Our young builder has lost the sense that she is acting according to her own true self. Instead, she has gotten the message. You build Legos for the same reason your traditionally employed father does his work assignments: because an authority figure tells you to.

Or take accountability. The child is no longer fully accountable for her own Lego creating. Whatever she has produced is by assignment. Her creations are no longer truly hers. And what about those Lego grades? That A+ may motivate our girl to keep building, but not on her own terms. Maybe she liked the B− building better than the A+ creation. Oh well. Now she'll probably bury that feeling and work to measure up—to someone else's standards. Should she take a chance—try building that space shuttle she's been dreaming about? Probably not. Why take that risk when, chances are, it won't make the grade? Self-defined success has no place in this regime. But for many home-schoolers, success is something they can define themselves. (This is true even though, as I mentioned, home-schoolers score off the charts on conventional measures of success—standardized tests in academic subjects.)

To be sure, some things most kids should learn are not intrinsically fun. There are times in life when we must eat our Brussels sprouts. For those subjects, the punishment-and-reward approach of traditional schooling may be in order. But too often, the sheer thrill of learning a new fact or mastering a tough equation is muted when schools take away a student's sense of control. In home schooling, kids have greater freedom to pursue their passions, less pressure to conform to the wishes of teachers and peers—and can put themselves on the line, take risks, and define success on their own terms. As more parents realize that the underlying ethic of home schooling closely resembles the animating values of free agency, home schooling will continue to soar in popularity.

Free Agent Teaching

Several other forces will combine to power home schooling into greater prominence. One is simply the movement's initial prominence. As more families choose this option, they will make it more socially acceptable—thereby encouraging other families to take this once-unconventional route. The home-schooling population has already begun to look like the rest of America. While some 90 percent of home-schoolers are white, the population is becoming more diverse, and may be growing fastest among African Americans. And the median income for a home-school family is roughly equal to the median income for the rest of the country; about 87 percent have annual household incomes under $75,000.

Recent policy changes—in state legislatures and principals' offices—will further clear the way. Not only is home schooling now legal in every state, but many public schools have begun letting home-schoolers take certain classes or play on school teams. About two-thirds of American colleges now accept transcripts prepared by parents, or portfolios assembled by students, in lieu of an accredited diploma.

Another force is free agency itself. Thanks to flexible schedules and personal control, it's easier for free agents than for traditional employees to home-school their children. Free agents will also become the professionals in this new world of learning. A carpenter might hire herself out to teach carpentry skills to home-schoolers. A writer might become a tutor or editor to several home-schoolers interested in producing their own literary journal. What's more, the huge cadre of teachers hired to teach the baby boom will soon hit retirement age. However, perhaps instead of fully retiring, many will hire themselves out as itinerant tutors to home-schoolers—and begin part-time careers as free agent educators. For many parents, of course, the responsibility and time commitment of home schooling will be daunting. But the wide availability of teachers and tutors might help some parents overcome the concern that they won't be able to handle this awesome undertaking by themselves.

The Internet makes home schooling easier, too. Indeed, home-schoolers figured out the Internet well before most Americans. For example, my first Internet connection was a DOS-based Compuserve account I acquired in 1993. Before the wide acceptance of the Internet and the advent of the World Wide Web, the most active discussion groups on Compuserve were those devoted to home schooling. Using the Web, home-schoolers can do research and find tutors anywhere in the world. There are now even online ventures—for instance, the Christa McAuliffe Academy (www.cmacademy.org) in Washington state and ChildU.com in Florida—that sell online courses and provide e-teachers for home-schoolers. Physical infrastructure might also accelerate this trend. Almost three-fourths of America's public school buildings were built before 1969. School administrations might be more likely to encourage some amount of home schooling if that means less strain on their crowded classrooms and creaky buildings.

I don't want to overstate the case. Home schooling, like free agency, won't be for everyone. Many parents won't have the time or the desire for this approach. And home schooling won't be for all time. Many students will spend a few years in a conventional school and a few years learning at home—just as some workers will migrate between being a free agent and holding a job. But home schooling is perhaps the most robust expression of the free agent way outside the workplace, making its continued rise inevitable.

The End of High School

One other consequence of the move toward home schooling will be something many of us wished for as teenagers: the demise of high school. It wasn't until the 1920s that high school replaced work as the thing most Americans did in their teens. "American high school is obsolete," says Bard College president Leon Botstein, one of the first to call for its end. He says today's adolescents would be better off pursuing a college degree, jumping directly into the job market, engaging in public service, or taking on a vocational apprenticeship. Even the National Association of Secondary School Principals, which has blasted home schooling, concedes that "high schools continue to go about their business in ways that sometimes bear startling resemblance to the flawed practices of the past."

In the future, expect teens and their families to force an end to high school as we know it. Look for some of these changes to replace and augment traditional high schools with free-agent-style learning—and to unschool the American teenager:

- A *renaissance of apprenticeships*. For centuries, young people learned a craft or profession under the guidance of an experienced master. This method will revive and expand to include skills like computer programming and graphic design. Imagine a 14-year-old taking two or three academic courses each week, and spending the rest of her time apprenticing as a commercial artist. Traditional high schools tend to separate learning and doing. Free agency makes them indistinguishable.
- A *flowering of teenage entrepreneurship*. Young people may become free agents even before they get their driver's licenses—and teen entrepreneurs will become more common. Indeed, most teens have the two crucial traits of a successful entrepreneur: a fresh way of looking at the world and a passionate intensity for what they do. In San Diego County, 8 percent of high school students already run their own online business. That will increasingly become the norm and perhaps even become a teenage rite of passage.
- A *greater diversity of academic courses*. Only 16 states offer basic economics in high school. That's hardly a sound foundation for the free agent workplace. Expect a surge of new kinds of "home economics" courses that teach numeracy, accounting, and basic business.
- A *boom in national service*. Some teenagers will seek greater direction than others and may want to spend a few years serving in the military or participating in a domestic service program. Today, many young people don't consider these choices because of the pressure to go directly to college. Getting people out of high school earlier might get them into service sooner.
- A *backlash against standards*. A high school diploma was once the gold standard of American education. No more. Yet politicians seem determined to make the diploma meaningful again by erecting all sorts of hurdles kids must leap to attain one—standardized subjects each student must study, standardized tests each student must pass. In some schools, students are already staging sit-ins to protest these tests. This could be American youth's new cause célèbre. ("Hey hey, ho ho. Standardized testing's got to go.")

Most politicians think the answer to the problems of high schools is to exert more control. But the real answer is *less* control. In the free agent future, our teens will learn by less schooling and more doing.

The Unschooling of Adults

For much of the 20th century, the U.S. depended on what I call the Thanksgiving turkey model of education. We placed kids in the oven of formal education for 12 years, and then served them up to employers. (A select minority got a final, four-year basting at a place called college.) But this model doesn't work in a world of accelerated cycle times, shrinking company half-lives, and the rapid obsolescence of knowledge and skills. In a free agent economy, our education system must allow people to learn throughout their lives.

Home schooling and alternatives to high school will create a nation of self-educators, free agent learners, if you will. Adults who were home-schooled youths will know how to learn and expect to continue the habit throughout their lives.

For example, how did anybody learn the Web? In 1993, it barely existed. By 1995, it was the foundation of dozens of new industries and an explosion of wealth. There weren't any college classes in Web programming, HTML coding, or Web page design in those early years. Yet somehow hundreds of thousands of people managed to learn. How? They taught themselves—working with colleagues, trying new things, and making mistakes. That was the secret to the Web's success. The Web flourished almost entirely through the ethic and practice of self-teaching. This is not a radical concept. Until the first part of this century, most Americans learned on their own—by reading. Literacy and access to books were an individual's ticket to knowledge. Even today, according to my own online survey of 1,143 independent workers, "reading" was the most prevalent way free agents said they stay up-to-date in their field.

In the 21st century, access to the Internet and to a network of smart colleagues will be the ticket to adult learning. Expect more of us to punch those tickets throughout our lives. Look for these early signs:

- *The devaluation of degrees.* As the shelf life of a degree shortens, more students will go to college to acquire particular skills than to bring home a sheepskin. People's need for knowledge doesn't respect semesters. They'll want higher education just in time—and if that means leaving the classroom before earning a degree, so be it. Remember: Larry Ellison, Steve Jobs, and Steven Spielberg never finished college.
- *Older students.* Forty percent of college students are now older than 25. According to *The Wall Street Journal*, "By some projections, the number of students age 35 and older will exceed those 18 and 19 within a few years." Young adults who do forgo a diploma in their early 20s may find a need and desire for college courses in their 40s.
- *Free agent teaching.* Distance learning (private ventures like the University of Phoenix, Unext, Ninth House Network, and Hungry Minds University) will help along this self-teaching trend. Today, some 5,000 companies are in the online education business. Their $2 billion of revenues is expected to hit $11 billion by 2003. And nontraditional teaching arrangements will abound. One lament of independent scholars—genre-straddling writers like Judith Rich Harris and Anne Hollander—is that they don't have students. Here's a ready supply. More free agent teachers and more free agent students will create tremendous liquidity in the learning market—with the Internet serving as the matchmaker for this new marketplace of learning.

- *Big trouble for elite colleges*. All this means big trouble in Ivy City. Attending a fancy college serves three purposes in contemporary life: to prolong adolescence, to award a credential that's modestly useful early in one's working life, and to give people a network of friends. Elite colleges have moved slowly to keep up with the emerging free agent economy. In 1998, 78 percent of public four-year colleges offered distance-learning programs, compared with only 19 percent of private schools. Private college costs have soared, faster even than health care costs, for the past 20 years. But have these colleges improved at the same rate? Have they improved at all? What's more, the students who make it to elite colleges are generally those who've proved most adroit at conventional (read: outdated) schooling. That could become a liability rather than an advantage. In his bestseller, *The Millionaire Mind*, Thomas J. Stanley found a disproportionately large number of millionaires were free agents—but that the higher somebody's SAT scores, the *less* likely he or she was to be a financial risk-taker and therefore to become a free agent.
- *Learning groupies*. The conference industry, already hot, will continue to catch fire as more people seek gatherings of like-minded souls to make new connections and learn new things. Conferences allow attendees to become part of a sort of Socratic institution. They can choose the mentor they will pay attention to for an hour, or two hours, or a day—whatever. In addition, many independent workers have formed small groups that meet regularly and allow members to exchange business advice and offer personal support. These Free Agent Nation Clubs, as I call them, also provide an important staging ground for self-education. At F.A.N. Club meetings, members discuss books and articles and share their particular expertise with the others. This type of learning—similarly alive in book clubs and Bible study groups— represents a rich American tradition. One of the earliest self-organized clusters of free agents was Benjamin Franklin's Junto, formed in 1727, which created a subscription library for its members, which in turn became the first public library in America.

The next few decades will be a fascinating, and perhaps revolutionary, time for learning in America. The specifics will surprise us and may defy even my soundest predictions. But the bottom line of the future of education in Free Agent Nation is glaringly clear: School's out.

POSTSCRIPT

Should School Attendance Be Compelled?

One of the most recent serious critiques of compulsory attendance laws was provided by Len Botstein, the long-time president of Bard College, in his book *Jefferson's Children: Education and the Promise of American Culture* (1997). Botstein argues that it is time to abolish compulsoriness at the secondary school level in recognition of the biological, sociological, and psychological changes in modern adolescents. "The American high school is obsolete," he contends, "and no amount of testing or mere imposition of national standards will make the difference." This attack on holding adolescents in school, along with the success of home schooling at the elementary level, adds pressure for further change and accommodation.

Some other sources of opinion on the issue of compulsory schooling are "Mandatory Schooling: A Teacher's Eye View," *Reason* (January 1997); "End Compulsory Schooling," by Sheldon Richman and David B. Kopel, Independence Issue Paper (January 10, 1996); Matt Hern, ed., *Deschooling Our Lives* (1995); Barry McGhan, "Choice and Compulsion: The End of an Era," *Phi Delta Kappan* (April 1998); *The Parents' Guide to Alternatives in Education* by Ronald E. Koetzsch (1997); *The Teenage Liberation Handbook,* rev. ed., by Grace Llewellyn (1998); Mitchell L. Stevens, *Kingdom of Children: Culture and Controversy in the Home Schooling Movement* (2001); George E. Pawlas, "Clearing the Air About Home Schooling," *Kappa Delta Pi Record* (Winter 2001); Sarah Deschenes, Larry Cuban, and David Tyack, "Mismatch: Historical Perspectives on Schools and Students Who Don't Fit Them," *Teachers College Record* (August 2001); and Michael H. Romanowski, "Common Arguments About the Strengths and Limitations of Home Schooling," *The Clearing House* (November/December 2001).

One of the arguments against compulsoriness is that the law forces young people who do not want to be in school to be there, thereby setting the scene for disruption of the learning of those who do want to be there. This is probably the central factor in current calls for reconsideration of compulsory attendance laws. But would alteration of the present laws merely shift the problem from the school to the street?

Compulsory education is often justified in terms of the individual's right to education. But does it make sense to compel someone to exercise a right? On the other hand, would the demolition of attendance laws set young people adrift without appropriate guidance and resources in the most crucial years of their lives and condemn many of them to low levels of employment and personal development?

The Character Education Partnership

This is an advocacy site that offers principles and resources for development of character education in public schools.

        http://www.character.org

National Association for Multicultural Education

This site offers position papers and other resources on multiculturalism and related topics.

        http://www.nameorg.org

Eighth Floor: Multicultural Education

This New Horizons for Learning site features articles, reading lists, and Internet links on multiculturalism.

    http://www.newhorizons.org/multicultural.html

No Child Left Behind

This U.S. Department of Education site examines the implementation of the new Elementary and Secondary Education Act and links to a No Child Left Behind Web site for parents.

        http://www.ed.gov/offices/OESE/esea/

Education World

This site examines the effects of high-stakes testing and related issues.

    http://www.educationworld.com/a_issues/issues093.shtml

Standards, Testing & Accountability

This Thomas B. Fordham Foundation site is dedicated to examining reform issues.

    http://www.edexcellence.net/topics/standards.html

Ten Public School "Signposts of Failure"

This Libertarian Rock site condemns public education for 10 specific failures.

    http://www.libertarianrock.com/topics/school/
    ten_posts_of_failure.html

PART 2

Current Fundamental Issues

*T*he issues discussed in this section cover basic social, cultural, and political problems currently under consideration by education experts, social scientists, and politicians, as well as by parents and the media. Positions on these issues are expressed by Thomas Lickona, Alfie Kohn, Sonia Nieto, Thomas J. Famularo, Andrew Rotherham, Lisa Snell, Nina Hurwitz, Sol Hurwitz, Martin G. Brooks, Jacqueline Grennon Brooks, William J. Bennett and his colleagues, and Forrest J. Troy.

- Can "Character Education" Reverse Moral Decline?

- Should Multiculturalism Permeate the Curriculum?

- Can Federal Initiatives Rescue Failing Schools?

- Do High-Stakes Assessments Improve Learning?

- Have Public Schools Failed Society?

ISSUE 6

Can "Character Education" Reverse Moral Decline?

YES: Thomas Lickona, from "The Return of Character Education," *Educational Leadership* (November 1993)

NO: Alfie Kohn, from "How Not to Teach Values: A Critical Look at Character Education," *Phi Delta Kappan* (February 1997)

ISSUE SUMMARY

YES: Developmental psychologist Thomas Lickona, a leading exponent of the new character education, details the rationale behind the movement and charts a course of action to deal with the moral decline of American youth.

NO: Writer-lecturer Alfie Kohn sees current attempts at character education as mainly a collection of exhortations and extrinsic inducements that avoid more penetrating efforts at social and moral development.

Do schools have a moral purpose? Can virtue be taught? Should the shaping of character be as important as the training of the intellect? Should value-charged issues be discussed in the classroom?

Much of the history of education chronicles the ways in which philosophers, theorists, educators, politicians, and the general public have responded to these and similar questions. In almost all countries (and certainly in early America), the didactic teaching of moral values, often those of a particular religious interpretation, was central to the process of schooling. Although the direct connection between religion and public education in the United States has faded, the image of the teacher as a value model persists, and the ethical dimension of everyday activities and human relations insinuates itself into the school atmosphere. Normative discourse inundates the educational environment; school is often a world of "rights" and "wrongs" and "oughts" and "don'ts."

Problems emerge when the attempt is made to delineate the school's proper role in setting value guidelines: Can school efforts supplement the efforts of home and church? Can the schools avoid representing a "middle-class morality" that disregards the cultural base of minority group values? Should the schools do battle against the value-manipulating forces of the mass media and the popular culture?

During the 1960s and 1970s a number of psychology-based approaches supplanted the traditional didacticism. Psychologist Lawrence Kohlberg fashioned strategies that link ethical growth to levels of cognitive maturity, moving the student through a range of stages that demand increasingly sophisticated types of moral reasoning. Another approach popularized during this period was "values clarification," developed and refined by Louis Raths, Merrill Harmin, Sidney Simon, and Howard Kirschenbaum. This moral education program attempted to assist learners in understanding their own attitudes, preferences, and values, as well as those of others, and placed central emphasis on feelings, emotions, sensitivity, and shared perceptions.

The current concern that many people have about the moral condition of American society and its young people in particular is prompting a reevaluation of the school's role in teaching values. "The schools are failing to provide the moral education they once did; they have abandoned moral teaching," says William Kilpatrick, author of *Why Johnny Can't Tell Right From Wrong* (1992). "If we want our children to possess the traits of character we most admire, we need to teach them what those traits are and why they deserve both admiration and allegiance," says William J. Bennett in the introduction to his best-selling book *The Book of Virtues* (1993). Both of these thinkers reject the moral relativism associated with values clarification and with similar approaches, and they call for a character-development strategy based upon time-tested materials that contribute to "moral literacy."

Evidence that character education continues to be a hot topic can be seen in books such as Gertrude Himmelfarb's *The De-Moralization of Society: From Victorian Virtues to Modern Values* (1995), *The Moral Intelligence of Children* by Robert Coles (1997), Ivor A. Pritchard's *Good Education: The Virtues of Learning* (1998), *The Students Are Watching: Schools and the Moral Contract* by Theodore R. Sizer and Nancy Faust Sizer (1999), and *Building Character in Schools* by Kevin A. Ryan and Karen E. Bohlin (1999).

The following articles are also recommended: "The Missing Ingredient in Character Education," by Thomas J. Lasley II, *Phi Delta Kappan* (April 1997); "Should Morals Be Taught in the Classroom?" (a debate), *NEA Today* (May 1997); "Education and Character: A Conservative View," by Denis P. Doyle, *Phi Delta Kappan* (February 1997); "The Death of Character Education," by Timothy Rusnak and Frank Ribich, *Educational Horizons* (Fall 1997); and "Character Education: Reclaiming the Social," by Barbara J. Duncan, *Educational Theory* (Winter 1997).

In the selections that follow, Thomas Lickona makes the case for a new character education movement and charts the course that this effort must take in order to have a pronounced effect on the moral life of students. Alfie Kohn contends that character educators such as Lickona should scrutinize their programs in terms of their ultimate goals, their view of human nature, and the meaning of the values that they attempt to instill.

Thomas Lickona  **YES**

The Return of Character Education

To educate a person in mind and not in morals is to educate a menace to society.

— Theodore Roosevelt

Increasing numbers of people across the ideological spectrum believe that our society is in deep moral trouble. The disheartening signs are everywhere: the breakdown of the family; the deterioration of civility in everyday life; rampant greed at a time when one in five children is poor; an omnipresent sexual culture that fills our television and movie screens with sleaze, beckoning the young toward sexual activity at ever earlier ages; the enormous betrayal of children through sexual abuse; and the 1992 report of the National Research Council that says the United States is now *the* most violent of all industrialized nations.

As we become more aware of this societal crisis, the feeling grows that schools cannot be ethical bystanders. As a result, character education is making a comeback in American schools.

Early Character Education

Character education is as old as education itself. Down through history, education has had two great goals: to help people become smart and to help them become good.

Acting on that belief, schools in the earliest days of our republic tackled character education head on—through discipline, the teacher's example, and the daily school curriculum. The Bible was the public school's sourcebook for both moral and religious instruction. When struggles eventually arose over whose Bible to use and which doctrines to teach, William McGuffey stepped onto the stage in 1836 to offer his McGuffey Readers, ultimately to sell more than 100 million copies.

McGuffey retained many favorite Biblical stories but added poems, exhortations, and heroic tales. While children practiced their reading or arithmetic,

From Thomas Lickona, "The Return of Character Education," *Educational Leadership,* vol. 51, no. 3 (November 1993), pp. 6–11. Copyright © 1993 by The Association for Supervision and Curriculum Development. Reprinted by permission of The Association for Supervision and Curriculum Development; permission conveyed via Copyright Clearance Center, Inc.

they also learned lessons about honesty, love of neighbor, kindness to animals, hard work, thriftiness, patriotism, and courage.

Why Character Education Declined

In the 20th century, the consensus supporting character education began to crumble under the blows of several powerful forces.

Darwinism introduced a new metaphor—evolution—that led people to see all things, including morality, as being in flux.

The philosophy of logical positivism, arriving at American universities from Europe, asserted a radical distinction between *facts* (which could be scientifically proven) and *values* (which positivism held were mere expressions of feeling, not objective truth). As a result of positivism, morality was relativized and privatized—made to seem a matter of personal "value judgment," not a subject for public debate and transmission through the schools.

In the 1960s, a worldwide rise in personalism celebrated the worth, autonomy, and subjectivity of the person, emphasizing individual rights and freedom over responsibility. Personalism rightly protested societal oppression and injustice, but it also delegitimized moral authority, eroded belief in objective moral norms, turned people inward toward self-fulfillment, weakened social commitments (for example, to marriage and parenting), and fueled the socially destabilizing sexual revolution.

Finally, the rapidly intensifying pluralism of American society (Whose values should we teach?) and the increasing secularization of the public arena (Won't moral education violate the separation of church and state?), became two more barriers to achieving the moral consensus indispensable for character education in the public schools. Public schools retreated from their once central role as moral and character educators.

The 1970s saw a return of values education, but in new forms: values clarification and Kohlberg's moral dilemma discussions. In different ways, both expressed the individualist spirit of the age. Values clarification said, don't impose values; help students choose their values freely. Kohlberg said, develop students' powers of moral reasoning so they can judge which values are better than others.

Each approach made contributions, but each had problems. Values clarification, though rich in methodology, failed to distinguish between personal preferences (truly a matter of free choice) and moral values (a matter of obligation). Kohlberg focused on moral reasoning, which is necessary but not sufficient for good character, and underestimated the school's role as a moral socializer.

The New Character Education

In the 1990s we are seeing the beginnings of a new character education movement, one which restores "good character" to its historical place as the central desirable outcome of the school's moral enterprise. No one knows yet how broad or deep this movement is; we have no studies to tell us what percentage of schools are making what kind of effort. But something significant is afoot.

In July 1992, the Josephson Institute of Ethics called together more than 30 educational leaders representing state school boards, teachers' unions, universities, ethics centers, youth organizations, and religious groups. This diverse assemblage drafted the Aspen Declaration on Character Education, setting forth eight principles of character education.[1]

The Character Education Partnership was launched in March 1993, as a national coalition committed to putting character development at the top of the nation's educational agenda. Members include representatives from business, labor, government, youth, parents, faith communities, and the media.

The last two years have seen the publication of a spate of books—such as *Moral, Character, and Civic Education in the Elementary School, Why Johnny Can't Tell Right From Wrong,* and *Reclaiming Our Schools: A Handbook on Teaching Character, Academics, and Discipline*—that make the case for character education and describe promising programs around the country. A new periodical, the *Journal of Character Education,* is devoted entirely to covering the field.[2]

Why Character Education Now?

Why this groundswell of interest in character education? There are at least three causes:

1. The decline of the family.   The family, traditionally a child's primary moral teacher, is for vast numbers of children today failing to perform that role, thus creating a moral vacuum. In her recent book *When the Bough Breaks: The Cost of Neglecting Our Children,* economist Sylvia Hewlett documents that American children, rich and poor, suffer a level of neglect unique among developed nations (1991). Overall, child well-being has declined despite a decrease in the number of children per family, an increase in the educational level of parents, and historically high levels of public spending in education.

In "Dan Quayle Was Right," (April 1993) Barbara Dafoe Whitehead synthesizes the social science research on the decline of the two biological-parent family in America:

> If current trends continue, less than half of children born today will live continuously with their own mother and father throughout childhood.... An increasing number of children will experience family break-up two or even three times during childhood.

Children of marriages that end in divorce and children of single mothers are more likely to be poor, have emotional and behavioral problems, fail to achieve academically, get pregnant, abuse drugs and alcohol, get in trouble with the law, and be sexually and physically abused. Children in stepfamilies are generally worse off (more likely to be sexually abused, for example) than children in single-parent homes.

No one has felt the impact of family disruption more than schools. White-head writes:

> Across the nation, principals report a dramatic rise in the aggressive, acting-out behavior characteristic of children, especially boys, who are living in single-parent families. Moreover, teachers find that many children are so upset and preoccupied by the explosive drama of their own family lives that they are unable to concentrate on such mundane matters as multiplication tables.

Family disintegration, then, drives the character education movement in two ways: schools have to teach the values kids aren't learning at home; and schools, in order to conduct teaching and learning, must become caring moral communities that help children from unhappy homes focus on their work, control their anger, feel cared about, and become responsible students.

2. Troubling trends in youth character.   A second impetus for renewed character education is the sense that young people in general, not just those from frac-tured families, have been adversely affected by poor parenting (in intact as well as broken families); the wrong kind of adult role models; the sex, violence, and materialism portrayed in the mass media; and the pressures of the peer group. Evidence that this hostile moral environment is taking a toll on youth character can be found in 10 troubling trends: rising youth violence; increasing dis-honesty (lying, cheating, and stealing); growing disrespect for authority; peer cruelty; a resurgence of bigotry on school campuses, from preschool through higher education; a decline in the work ethic; sexual precocity; a growing self-centeredness and declining civil responsibility; an increase in self-destructive behavior; and ethical illiteracy.

The statistics supporting these trends are overwhelming.[3] For example, the U.S. homicide rate for 15- to 24-year-old males is 7 times higher than Canada's and 40 times higher than Japan's. The U.S. has one of the highest teenage preg-nancy rates, the highest teen abortion rate, and the highest level of drug use among young people in the developed world. Youth suicide has tripled in the past 25 years, and a survey of more than 2,000 Rhode Island students, grades six through nine, found that two out of three boys and one of two girls thought it "acceptable for a man to force sex on a woman" if they had been dating for six months or more (Kikuchi 1988).

3. A recovery of shared, objectively important ethical values.   Moral decline in society has gotten bad enough to jolt us out of the privatism and relativism dominant in recent decades. We are recovering the wisdom that we do share a basic morality, essential for our survival; that adults must promote this morality by teaching the young, directly and indirectly, such values as respect, respon-sibility, trustworthiness, fairness, caring, and civil virtue; and that these values are not merely subjective preferences but that they have objective worth and a claim on our collective conscience.

Such values affirm our human dignity, promote the good of the indi-vidual and the common good, and protect our human rights. They meet the classic ethical tests of reversibility (Would you want to be treated this way?) and universalizability (Would you want all persons to act this way in a similar situation?). They define our responsibilities in a democracy, and they are recognized by all civilized people and taught by all enlightened creeds. *Not* to teach children these core ethical values is grave moral failure.

What Character Education Must Do

In the face of a deteriorating social fabric, what must character education do to develop good character in the young?

First, it must have an adequate theory of what good character is, one which gives schools a clear idea of their goals. Character must be broadly conceived to encompass the cognitive, affective, and behavioral aspects of morality. Good character consists of knowing the good, desiring the good, and doing the good. Schools must help children *understand* the core values, *adopt* or commit to them, and then *act upon* them in their own lives.

The cognitive side of character includes at least six specific moral qualities: awareness of the moral dimensions of the situation at hand, knowing moral values and what they require of us in concrete cases, perspective-taking, moral reasoning, thoughtful decision making, and moral self-knowledge. All these powers of rational moral thought are required for full moral maturity and citizenship in a democratic society.

People can be very smart about matters of right and wrong, however, and still choose the wrong. Moral education that is merely intellectual misses the crucial emotional side of character, which serves as the bridge between judgment and action. The emotional side includes at least the following qualities: conscience (the felt obligation to do what one judges to be right), self-respect, empathy, loving the good, self-control, and humility (a willingness to both recognize and correct our moral failings).

At times, we know what we should do, feel strongly that we should do it, yet still fail to translate moral judgment and feeling into effective moral behavior. Moral action, the third part of character, draws upon three additional moral qualities: competence (skills such as listening, communicating, and cooperating), will (which mobilizes our judgment and energy), and moral habit (a reliable inner disposition to respond to situations in a morally good way).

Developing Character

Once we have a comprehensive concept of character, we need a comprehensive approach to developing it. This approach tells schools to look at themselves through a moral lens and consider how virtually everything that goes on there affects the values and character of students. Then, plan how to use all phases of classroom and school life as deliberate tools of character development.

If schools wish to maximize their moral clout, make a lasting difference in students' character, and engage and develop all three parts of character (knowing, feeling, and behavior), they need a comprehensive, holistic approach. Having a comprehensive approach includes asking, Do present school practices support, neglect, or contradict the school's professed values and character education aims?

In classroom practice, a comprehensive approach to character education calls upon the individual teacher to:

- *Act as caregiver, model, and mentor,* treating students with love and respect, setting a good example, supporting positive social behavior, and correcting hurtful actions through one-on-one guidance and whole-class discussion;
- *Create a moral community,* helping students know one another as persons, respect and care about one another, and feel valued membership in, and responsibility to, the group;
- *Practice moral discipline,* using the creation and enforcement of rules as opportunities to foster moral reasoning, voluntary compliance with rules, and a respect for others;
- *Create a democratic classroom environment,* involving students in decision making and the responsibility for making the classroom a good place to be and learn;
- *Teach values through the curriculum,* using the ethically rich content of academic subjects (such as literature, history, and science), as well as outstanding programs (such as *Facing History and Ourselves*[4] and *The Heartwood Ethics Curriculum for Children*[5]), as vehicles for teaching values and examining moral questions;
- *Use cooperative learning* to develop students' appreciation of others, perspective taking, and ability to work with others toward common goals;
- *Develop the "conscience of craft"* by fostering students' appreciation of learning, capacity for hard work, commitment to excellence, and sense of work as affecting the lives of others;
- *Encourage moral reflection* through reading, research, essay writing, journal keeping, discussion, and debate;
- *Teach conflict resolution,* so that students acquire the essential moral skills of solving conflicts fairly and without force.

Besides making full use of the moral life of classrooms, a comprehensive approach calls upon the school *as a whole* to:

- *Foster caring beyond the classroom,* using positive role models to inspire altruistic behavior and providing opportunities at every grade level to perform school and community service;
- *Create a positive moral culture in the school,* developing a schoolwide ethos (through the leadership of the principal, discipline, a schoolwide sense of community, meaningful student government, a moral community among adults, and making time for moral concerns) that supports and amplifies the values taught in classrooms;

- *Recruit parents and the community as partners in character education,* letting parents know that the school considers them their child's first and most important moral teacher, giving parents specific ways they can reinforce the values the school is trying to teach, and seeking the help of the community, churches, businesses, local government, and the media in promoting the core ethical values.

The Challenges Ahead

Whether character education will take hold in American schools remains to be seen. Among the factors that will determine the movement's long-range success are:

- *Support for schools.* Can schools recruit the help they need from the other key formative institutions that shape the values of the young —including families, faith communities, and the media? Will public policy act to strengthen and support families, and will parents make the stability of their families and the needs of their children their highest priority?
- *The role of religion.* Both liberal and conservative groups are asking, How can students be sensitively engaged in considering the role of religion in the origins and moral development of our nation? How can students be encouraged to use their intellectual and moral resources, including their faith traditions, when confronting social issues (For example, what is my obligation to the poor?) and making personal moral decisions (For example, should I have sex before marriage?)?
- *Moral leadership.* Many schools lack a positive, cohesive moral culture. Especially at the building level, it is absolutely essential to have moral leadership that sets, models, and consistently enforces high standards of respect and responsibility. Without a positive schoolwide ethos, teachers will feel demoralized in their individual efforts to teach good values.
- *Teacher education.* Character education is far more complex than teaching math or reading; it requires personal growth as well as skills development. Yet teachers typically receive almost no preservice or inservice training in the moral aspects of their craft. Many teachers do not feel comfortable or competent in the values domain. How will teacher education colleges and school staff development programs meet this need?

"Character is destiny," wrote the ancient Greek philosopher Heraclitus. As we confront the causes of our deepest societal problems, whether in our intimate relationships or public institutions, questions of character loom large. As we close out a turbulent century and ready our schools for the next, educating for character is a moral imperative if we care about the future of our society and our children.

Notes

1. For a copy of the Aspen Declaration and the issue of *Ethics* magazine reporting on the conference, write the Josephson Institute of Ethics, 310 Washington Blvd., Suite 104, Marina del Rey, CA 90292.

2. For information write Mark Kann, Editor, *The Journal of Character Education,* Jefferson Center for Character Education, 202 S. Lake Ave., Suite 240, Pasadena, CA 91101.

3. For documentation of these youth trends, see T. Lickona, (1991), *Educating for Character: How Our Schools Can Teach Respect and Responsibility* (New York: Bantam Books).

4. *Facing History and Ourselves* is an 8-week Holocaust curriculum for 8th graders. Write Facing History and Ourselves National Foundation, 25 Kennard Rd., Brookline, MA 02146.

5. *The Heartwood Ethics Curriculum for Children* uses multicultural children's literature to teach universal values. Write The Heartwood Institute, 12300 Perry Highway, Wexford, PA 15090.

References

Benninga, J. S., ed. (1991). *Moral, Character, and Civic Education in the Elementary School.* New York: Teachers College Press.

Hewlett, S. (1991). *When the Bough Breaks: The Cost of Neglecting Our Children.* New York: Basic Books.

Kikuchi, J. (Fall 1988). "Rhode Island Develops Successful Intervention Program for Adolescents." *National Coalition Against Sexual Assault Newsletter.*

National Research Council. (1992). *Understanding and Preventing Violence.* Washington, D.C.: National Research Council.

Whitehead, B. D. (April 1993) "Dan Quayle Was Right." *The Atlantic* 271: 47–84.

Wynne, E. A., and K. Ryan. (1992). *Reclaiming Our Schools: A Handbook on Teaching Character, Academics, and Discipline.* New York: Merrill.

Alfie Kohn  **NO**

How Not to Teach Values

Were you to stand somewhere in the continental United States and announce, "I'm going to Hawaii," it would be understood that you were heading for those islands in the Pacific that collectively constitute the 50th state. Were you to stand in Honolulu and make the same statement, however, you would probably be talking about one specific island in the chain—namely, the big one to your southeast. The word *Hawaii* would seem to have two meanings, a broad one and a narrow one; we depend on context to tell them apart.

The phrase *character education* also has two meanings. In the broad sense, it refers to almost anything that schools might try to provide outside of academics, especially when the purpose is to help children grow into good people. In the narrow sense, it denotes a particular style of moral training, one that reflects particular values as well as particular assumptions about the nature of children and how they learn.

Unfortunately, the two meanings of the term have become blurred, with the narrow version of character education dominating the field to the point that it is frequently mistaken for the broader concept. Thus educators who are keen to support children's social and moral development may turn, by default, to a program with a certain set of methods and a specific agenda that, on reflection, they might very well find objectionable.

My purpose in this article is to subject these programs to careful scrutiny and, in so doing, to highlight the possibility that there are other ways to achieve our broader objectives. I address myself not so much to those readers who are avid proponents of character education (in the narrow sense) but to those who simply want to help children become decent human beings and may not have thought carefully about what they are being offered.

Let me get straight to the point. What goes by the name of character education nowadays is, for the most part, a collection of exhortations and extrinsic inducements designed to make children work harder and do what they're told. Even when other values are also promoted—caring or fairness, say—the preferred method of instruction is tantamount to indoctrination. The point is to drill students in specific behaviors rather than to engage them in deep, critical reflection about certain ways of being. This is the impression one gets from reading articles and books by contemporary proponents of character education

From Alfie Kohn, "How Not to Teach Values: A Critical Look at Character Education," *Phi Delta Kappan* (February 1997). Copyright © 1997 by Alfie Kohn. Reprinted by permission of the author.

as well as the curriculum materials sold by the leading national programs. The impression is only strengthened by visiting schools that have been singled out for their commitment to character education. To wit:

> A huge, multiethnic elementary school in Southern California uses a framework created by the Jefferson Center for Character Education. Classes that the principal declares "well behaved" are awarded Bonus Bucks, which can eventually be redeemed for an ice cream party. On an enormous wall near the cafeteria, professionally painted Peanuts characters instruct children: "Never talk in line." A visitor is led to a fifth-grade classroom to observe an exemplary lesson on the current character education topic. The teacher is telling students to write down the name of the person they regard as the "toughest worker" in school. The teacher then asks them, "How many of you are going to be tough workers?" (Hands go up.) "Can you be a tough worker at home, too?" (Yes.)

> A small, almost entirely African American School in Chicago uses a framework created by the Character Education Institute. Periodic motivational assemblies are used to "give children a good pep talk," as the principal puts it, and to reinforce the values that determine who will be picked as Student of the Month. Rule number one posted on the wall of a kindergarten room is "We will obey the teachers." Today, students in this class are listening to the story of "Lazy Lion," who orders each of the other animals to build him a house, only to find each effort unacceptable. At the end, the teacher drives home the lesson: "Did you ever hear Lion say thank you?" (No.) "Did you ever hear Lion say please?" (No.) "It's good to always say ... what?" (Please.) The reason for using these words, she points out, is that by doing so we are more likely to get what we want.

> A charter school near Boston has been established specifically to offer an intensive, homegrown character education curriculum to its overwhelmingly white, middle-class student body. At weekly public ceremonies, certain children receive a leaf that will then be hung in the Forest of Virtue. The virtues themselves are "not open to debate," the headmaster insists, since moral precepts in his view enjoy the same status as mathematical truths. In a first-grade classroom, a teacher is observing that "it's very hard to be obedient when you want something. I want you to ask yourself, 'Can I have it—and why not?'" She proceeds to ask the students, "What kinds of things show obedience?" and, after collecting a few suggestions, announces that she's "not going to call on anyone else now. We could go on forever, but we have to have a moment of silence and then a spelling test."

Some of the most popular schoolwide strategies for improving students' character seem dubious on their face. When President Clinton mentioned the importance of character education in his 1996 State of the Union address, the only specific practice he recommended was requiring students to wear uniforms. The premises here are first, that children's character can be improved by forcing them to dress alike, and second, that if adults object to students' clothing, the best solution is not to invite them to reflect together about how this problem might be solved, but instead to compel them all to wear the same thing.

A second strategy, also consistent with the dominant philosophy of character education, is an exercise that might be called "If It's Tuesday, This Must Be Honesty." Here, one value after another is targeted, with each assigned its own day, week, or month. This seriatim approach is unlikely to result in a lasting commitment to any of these values, much less a feeling for how they may be related. Nevertheless, such programs are taken very seriously by some of the same people who are quick to dismiss other educational programs, such as those intended to promote self-esteem, as silly and ineffective.

Then there is the strategy of offering students rewards when they are "caught" being good, an approach favored by right-wing religious groups[1] and orthodox behaviorists but also by leaders of—and curriculum suppliers for—the character education movement.[2] Because of its popularity and because a sizable body of psychological evidence germane to the topic is available, it is worth lingering on this particular practice for a moment.

In general terms, what the evidence suggests is this: the more we reward people for doing something, the more likely they are to lose interest in whatever they had to do to get the reward. Extrinsic motivation, in other words, is not only quite different from intrinsic motivation but actually tends to erode it.[3] This effect has been demonstrated under many different circumstances and with respect to many different attitudes and behaviors. Most relevant to character education is a series of studies showing that individuals who have been rewarded for doing something nice become less likely to think of themselves as caring or helpful people and more likely to attribute their behavior to the reward.

"Extrinsic incentives can, by undermining self-perceived altruism, decrease intrinsic motivation to help others," one group of researchers concluded on the basis of several studies. "A person's kindness, it seems, cannot be bought."[4] The same applies to a person's sense of responsibility, fairness, perseverance, and so on. The lesson a child learns from Skinnerian tactics is that the point of being good is to get rewards. No wonder researchers have found that children who are frequently rewarded—or, in another study, children who receive positive reinforcement for caring, sharing, and helping—are less likely than other children to keep doing those things.[5]

In short, it makes no sense to dangle goodies in front of children for being virtuous. But even worse than rewards are awards—certificates, plaques, trophies, and other tokens of recognition whose numbers have been artificially limited so only a few can get them. When some children are singled out as "winners," the central message that every child learns is this: "Other people are potential obstacles to my success."[6] Thus the likely result of making students beat out their peers for the distinction of being the most virtuous is not only less intrinsic commitment to virtue but also a disruption of relationships and, ironically, of the experience of community that is so vital to the development of children's character.

Unhappily, the problems with character education (in the narrow sense, which is how I'll be using the term unless otherwise indicated) are not restricted to such strategies as enforcing sartorial uniformity, scheduling a value of the week, or offering students a "doggie biscuit" for being good. More deeply troubling are the fundamental assumptions, both explicit and implicit, that inform character education programs. Let us consider five basic questions that might be asked of any such program: At what level are problems addressed? What is the underlying theory of human nature? What is the ultimate goal? Which values are promoted? And finally, How is learning thought to take place?

At What Level Are Problems Addressed?

One of the major purveyors of materials in this field, the Jefferson Center for Character Education in Pasadena, California, has produced a video that begins with some arresting images—quite literally. Young people are shown being led away in handcuffs, the point being that crime can be explained on the basis of an "erosion of American core values," as the narrator intones ominously. The idea that social problems can be explained by the fact that traditional virtues are no longer taken seriously is offered by many proponents of character education as though it were just plain common sense.

But if people steal or rape or kill solely because they possess bad values—that is, because of their personal characteristics—the implication is that political and economic realities are irrelevant and need not be addressed. Never mind staggering levels of unemployment in the inner cities or a system in which more and more of the nation's wealth is concentrated in fewer and fewer hands; just place the blame on individuals whose characters are deficient. A key tenet of the "Character Counts!" Coalition, which bills itself as a nonpartisan umbrella group devoid of any political agenda, is the highly debatable proposition that "negative social influences can [be] and usually are overcome by the exercise of free will and character."[7] What is presented as common sense is, in fact, conservative ideology.

Let's put politics aside, though. If a program proceeds by trying to "fix the kids"—as do almost all brands of character education—it ignores the accumulated evidence from the field of social psychology demonstrating that much of how we act and who we are reflects the situations in which we find ourselves. Virtually all the landmark studies in this discipline have been variations on this theme. Set up children in an extended team competition at summer camp and you will elicit unprecedented levels of aggression. Assign adults to the roles of prisoners or guards in a mock jail, and they will start to become their roles. Move people to a small town, and they will be more likely to rescue a stranger in need. In fact, so common is the tendency to attribute to an individual's personality or character what is actually a function of the social environment that social psychologists have dubbed this the "fundamental attribution error."

A similar lesson comes to us from the movement concerned with Total Quality Management associated with the ideas of the late W. Edwards Deming. At the heart of Deming's teaching is the notion that the "system" of an organization largely determines the results. The problems experienced in a corporation, therefore, are almost always due to systemic flaws rather than to a lack of effort or ability on the part of individuals in that organization. Thus, if we are troubled by the way students are acting, Deming, along with most social psychologists, would presumably have us transform the structure of the classroom rather than try to remake the students themselves—precisely the opposite of the character education approach.

What Is the View of Human Nature?

Character education's "fix-the-kids" orientation follows logically from the belief that kids need fixing. Indeed, the movement seems to be driven by a stunningly dark view of children—and, for that matter, of people in general. A "comprehensive approach [to character education] is based on a somewhat dim view of human nature," acknowledges William Kilpatrick, whose book *Why Johnny Can't Tell Right from Wrong* contains such assertions as: "Most behavior problems are the result of sheer 'willfulness' on the part of children."[8]

Despite—or more likely because of—statements like that, Kilpatrick has frequently been invited to speak at character education conferences.[9] But that shouldn't be surprising in light of how many prominent proponents of character education share his views. Edward Wynne says his own work is grounded in a tradition of thought that takes a "somewhat pessimistic view of human nature."[10] The idea of character development "sees children as self-centered," in the opinion of Kevin Ryan, who directs the Center for the Advancement of Ethics and Character at Boston University as well as heading up the character education network of the Association for Supervision and Curriculum Development.[11] Yet another writer approvingly traces the whole field back to the bleak world view of Thomas Hobbes: it is "an obvious assumption of character education," writes Louis Goldman, that people lack the instinct to work together. Without laws to compel us to get along, "our natural egoism would lead us into 'a condition of warre one against another.' "[12] This sentiment is echoed by F. Washington Jarvis, headmaster of the Roxbury Latin School in Boston, one of Ryan's favorite examples of what character education should look like in practice. Jarvis sees human nature as "mean, nasty, brutish, selfish, and capable of great cruelty and meanness. We have to hold a mirror up to the students and say, 'This is who you are. Stop it.' "[13]

Even when proponents of character education don't express such sentiments explicitly, they give themselves away by framing their mission as a campaign for self-control. Amitai Etzioni, for example, does not merely include this attribute on a list of good character traits; he *defines* character principally in terms of the capacity "to control impulses and defer gratification."[14] This is noteworthy because the virtue of self-restraint—or at least the decision to give special emphasis to it—has historically been preached by those, from St. Augustine to the present, who see people as basically sinful.

In fact, at least three assumptions seem to be at work when the need for self-control is stressed: first, that we are all at war not only with others but with ourselves, torn between our desires and our reason (or social norms); second, that these desires are fundamentally selfish, aggressive, or otherwise unpleasant; and third, that these desires are very strong, constantly threatening to overpower us if we don't rein them in. Collectively, these statements describe religious dogma, not scientific fact. Indeed, the evidence from several disciplines converges to cast doubt on this sour view of human beings and, instead, supports the idea that it is as "natural" for children to help as to hurt. I will not rehearse that evidence here, partly because I have done so elsewhere at some length.[15] Suffice it to say that even the most hard-headed empiricist might well conclude that the promotion of prosocial values consists to some extent of supporting (rather than restraining or controlling) many facets of the self. Any educator who adopts this more balanced position might think twice before joining an educational movement that is finally inseparable from the doctrine of original sin.

What Is the Ultimate Goal?

It may seem odd even to inquire about someone's reasons for trying to improve children's character. But it is worth mentioning that the whole enterprise —not merely the particular values that are favored—is often animated by a profoundly conservative, if not reactionary, agenda. Character education based on "acculturating students to conventional norms of 'good' behavior . . . resonates with neoconservative concerns for social stability," observed David Purpel.[16] The movement has been described by another critic as a "yearning for some halcyon days of moral niceties and social tranquillity."[17] But it is not merely a *social* order that some are anxious to preserve (or recover): character education is vital, according to one vocal proponent, because "the development of character is the backbone of the economic system" now in place.[18]

Character education, or any kind of education, would look very different if we began with other objectives—if, for example, we were principally concerned with helping children become active participants in a democratic society (or agents for transforming a society *into* one that is authentically democratic). It would look different if our top priority were to help students develop into principled and caring members of a community or advocates for social justice. To be sure, these objectives are not inconsistent with the desire to preserve certain traditions, but the point would then be to help children decide which traditions are worth preserving and why, based on these other considerations. That is not at all the same as endorsing anything that is traditional or making the preservation of tradition our primary concern. In short, we want to ask character education proponents what goals they emphasize—and ponder whether their broad vision is compatible with our own.

Which Values?

Should we allow values to be taught in school? The question is about as sensible as asking whether our bodies should be allowed to contain bacteria. Just as humans are teeming with microorganisms, so schools are teeming with values. We can't see the former because they're too small; we don't notice the latter because they're too similar to the values of the culture at large. Whether or not we deliberately adopt a character or moral education program, we are always teaching values. Even people who insist that they are opposed to values in school usually mean that they are opposed to values other than their own.[19]

And that raises the inevitable question: Which values, or whose, should we teach? It has already become a cliché to reply that this question should not trouble us because, while there may be disagreement on certain issues, such as abortion, all of us can agree on a list of basic values that children ought to have. Therefore, schools can vigorously and unapologetically set about teaching all of those values.

But not so fast. Look at the way character education programs have been designed and you will discover, alongside such unobjectionable items as "fairness" or "honesty," an emphasis on values that are, again, distinctly conservative—and, to that extent, potentially controversial. To begin with, the famous Protestant work ethic is prominent: children should learn to "work hard and complete their tasks well and promptly, even when they do not want to," says Ryan.[20] Here the Latin question *Cui bono?* comes to mind. Who benefits when people are trained not to question the value of what they have been told to do but simply to toil away at it—and to regard this as virtuous?[21] Similarly, when Wynne defines the moral individual as someone who is not only honest but also "diligent, obedient, and patriotic,"[22] readers may find themselves wondering whether these traits really qualify as *moral*—as well as reflecting on the virtues that are missing from this list.

Character education curricula also stress the importance of things like "respect," "responsibility," and "citizenship." But these are slippery terms, frequently used as euphemisms for uncritical deference to authority. Under the headline "The Return of the 'Fourth R'"—referring to "respect, responsibility, or rules"—a news magazine recently described the growing popularity of such practices as requiring uniforms, paddling disobedient students, rewarding those who are compliant, and "throwing disruptive kids out of the classroom."[23] Indeed, William Glasser observed some time ago that many educators "teach thoughtless conformity to school rules and call the conforming child 'responsible.'"[24] I once taught at a high school where the principal frequently exhorted students to "take responsibility." By this he meant specifically that they should turn in their friends who used drugs.

Exhorting students to be "respectful" or rewarding them if they are caught being "good" may likewise mean nothing more than getting them to do whatever the adults demand. Following a lengthy article about character education in the *New York Times Magazine,* a reader mused, "Do you suppose that if Germany had had character education at the time, it would have encouraged children to fight Nazism or to support it?"[25] The more time I spend in schools that are enthusiastically implementing character education programs, the more I am haunted by that question.

In place of the traditional attributes associated with character education, Deborah Meier and Paul Schwarz of the Central Park East Secondary School in New York nominated two core values that a school might try to promote: "empathy and skepticism: the ability to see a situation from the eyes of another and the tendency to wonder about the validity of what we encountered."[26] Anyone who brushes away the question "Which values should be taught?" might speculate on the concrete differences between a school dedicated to turning out students who are empathic and skeptical and a school dedicated to turning out students who are loyal, patriotic, obedient, and so on.

Meanwhile, in place of such personal qualities as punctuality or perseverance, we might emphasize the cultivation of autonomy so that children come to experience themselves as "origins" rather than "pawns," as one researcher put it.[27] We might, in other words, stress self-determination at least as much as self-control. With such an agenda, it would be crucial to give students the chance to participate in making decisions about their learning and about how they want their classroom to be.[28] This stands in sharp contrast to a philosophy of character education like Wynne's, which decrees that "it is specious to talk about student choices" and offers students no real power except for when we give "some students authority over other students (for example, hall guard, class monitor)."[29]

Even with values that are widely shared, a superficial consensus may dissolve when we take a closer look. Educators across the spectrum are concerned about excessive attention to self-interest and are committed to helping students transcend a preoccupation with their own needs. But how does this concern play out in practice? For some of us, it takes the form of an emphasis on *compassion*; for the dominant character education approach, the alternative value to be stressed is *loyalty*, which is, of course, altogether different.[30] Moreover, as John Dewey remarked at the turn of the century, anyone seriously troubled about rampant individualism among children would promptly target for extinction the "drill-and-skill" approach to instruction: "The mere absorbing of facts and truths is so exclusively individual an affair that it tends very naturally to pass into selfishness."[31] Yet conservative champions of character education are often among the most outspoken supporters of a model of teaching that emphasizes rote memorization and the sequential acquisition of decontextualized skills.

Or take another example: all of us may say we endorse the idea of "cooperation," but what do we make of the practice of setting groups against one another in a quest for triumph, such that cooperation becomes the means and victory is the end? On the one hand, we might find this even more objectionable than individual competition. (Indeed, we might regard a "We're Number One!" ethic as a reason for schools to undertake something like character education in the first place.) On the other hand, "school-to-school, class-to-class, or row-to-row academic competitions" actually have been endorsed as part of a character education program,[32] along with contests that lead to awards for things like good citizenship.

The point, once again, is that it is entirely appropriate to ask which values a character education program is attempting to foster, notwithstanding the ostensible lack of controversy about a list of core values. It is equally appropriate to put such a discussion in context—specifically, in the context of which values are *currently* promoted in schools. The fact is that schools are already powerful socializers of traditional values—although, as noted above, we may fail to appreciate the extent to which this is true because we have come to take these values for granted. In most schools, for example, students are taught—indeed, compelled—to follow the rules regardless of whether the rules are reasonable and to respect authority regardless of whether that respect has been earned. (This process isn't always successful, of course, but that is a different matter.) Students are led to accept competition as natural and desirable, and to see themselves more as discrete individuals than as members of a community. Children in American schools are even expected to begin each day by reciting a loyalty oath to the Fatherland, although we call it by a different name. In short, the question is not whether to adopt the conservative values offered by most character education programs, but whether we want to consolidate the conservative values that are already in place.

What Is the Theory of Learning?

We come now to what may be the most significant, and yet the least remarked on, feature of character education: the way values are taught and the way learning is thought to take place.

> The character education coordinator for the small Chicago elementary school also teaches second grade. In her classroom, where one boy has been forced to sit by himself for the last two weeks ("He's kind of pesty"), she is asking the children to define tolerance. When the teacher gets the specific answers she is fishing for, she exclaims, "Say that again," and writes down only those responses. Later comes the moral: "If somebody doesn't think the way you think, should you turn them off?" (No.)
>
> Down the hall, the first-grade teacher is fishing for answers on a different subject. "When we play games, we try to understand the—what?" (Rules.) A moment later, the children scramble to get into place so she will pick them to tell a visitor their carefully rehearsed stories about conflict resolution. Almost every child's account, narrated with considerable prompting by the teacher, concerns name-calling or some other unpleasant incident that was "correctly" resolved by finding an adult. The teacher never asks the children how they felt about what happened or invites them to reflect on what else might have been done. She wraps up the activity by telling the children, "What we need to do all the time is clarify—make it clear—to the adult what you did."

The schools with character education programs that I have visited are engaged largely in exhortation and directed recitation. At first one might assume this is due to poor implementation of the programs on the part of individual educators. But the programs themselves—and the theorists who promote them —really do seem to regard teaching as a matter of telling and compelling. For example, the broad-based "Character Counts!" Coalition offers a framework of six core character traits and then asserts that "young people should be specifically and repeatedly told what is expected of them." The leading providers of curriculum materials walk teachers through highly structured lessons in which character-related concepts are described and then students are drilled until they can produce the right answers.

Teachers are encouraged to praise children who respond correctly, and some programs actually include multiple-choice tests to ensure that students have learned their values. For example, here are two sample test questions prepared for teachers by the Character Education Institute, based in San Antonio, Texas: "Having to obey rules and regulations (a) gives everyone the same right to be an individual, (b) forces everyone to do the same thing at all times, (c) prevents persons from expressing their individually [sic]"; and "One reason why parents might not allow their children freedom of choice is (a) children are always happier when they are told what to do and when to do it, (b) parents aren't given a freedom of choice; therefore, children should not be given a choice either, (c) children do not always demonstrate that they are responsible enough to be given a choice." The correct answers, according to the answer key, are (a) and (c) respectively.

The Character Education Institute recommends "engaging the students in discussions," but only discussions of a particular sort: "Since the lessons have been designed to logically guide the students to the right answers, the teacher should allow the students to draw their own conclusions. However, if the students draw the wrong conclusion, the teacher is instructed to tell them why their conclusion is *wrong.*"[33]

Students are told what to think and do, not only by their teachers but by highly didactic stories, such as those in the Character Education Institute's "Happy Life" series, which end with characters saying things like "I am glad that I did not cheat," or "Next time I will be helpful," or "I will never be selfish again." Most character education programs also deliver homilies by way of posters and banners and murals displayed throughout the school. Children who do as they are told are presented with all manner of rewards, typically in front of their peers.

Does all of this amount to indoctrination? Absolutely, says Wynne, who declares that "school is and should and must be inherently indoctrinative."[34] Even when character education proponents tiptoe around that word, their model of instruction is clear: good character and values are *instilled in* or *transmitted to* students. We are "planting the ideas of virtue, of good traits in the young," says William Bennett.[35] The virtues or values in question are fully formed, and, in the minds of many character education proponents, divinely ordained. The children are—pick your favorite metaphor—so many passive receptacles to be filled, lumps of clay to be molded, pets to be trained, or computers to be programmed.

Thus, when we see Citizen-of-the-Month certificates and "Be a good sport!" posters, when we find teachers assigning preachy stories and principals telling students what to wear, it is important that we understand what is going on. These techniques may appear merely innocuous or gimmicky; they may strike us as evidence of a scattershot, let's-try-anything approach. But the truth is that these are elements of a systematic pedagogical philosophy. They are manifestations of a model that sees children as objects to be manipulated rather than as learners to be engaged.

Ironically, some people who accept character education without a second thought are quite articulate about the bankruptcy of this model when it comes to teaching academic subjects. Plenty of teachers have abandoned the use of worksheets, textbooks, and lectures that fill children full of disconnected facts and skills. Plenty of administrators are working to create schools where students can actively construct meaning around scientific and historical and literary concepts. Plenty of educators, in short, realize that memorizing right answers and algorithms doesn't help anyone to arrive at a deep understanding of ideas.

And so we are left scratching our heads. Why would all these people, who know that the "transmission" model fails to facilitate intellectual development, uncritically accept the very same model to promote ethical development? How could they understand that mathematical truths cannot be shoved down students' throats but then participate in a program that essentially tries to shove moral truths down the same throats? In the case of individual educators, the simple answer may be that they missed the connection. Perhaps they just failed to recognize that "a classroom cannot foster the development of autonomy in the intellectual realm while suppressing it in the social and moral realms," as Constance Kamii and her colleagues put it not long ago.[36]

In the case of the proponents of character education, I believe the answer to this riddle is quite different. The reason they are promoting techniques that seem strikingly ineffective at fostering autonomy or ethical development is that, as a rule, they are not *trying* to foster autonomy or ethical development. The goal is not to support or facilitate children's social and moral growth, but simply to "demand good behavior from students," in Ryan's words.[37] The idea is to get compliance, to *make* children act the way we want them to.

Indeed, if these are the goals, then the methods make perfect sense— the lectures and pseudo-discussions, the slogans and the stories that conk students on the head with their morals. David Brooks, who heads the Jefferson Center for Character Education, frankly states, "We're in the advertising business." The way you get people to do something, whether it's buying Rice Krispies or becoming trustworthy, is to "encourage conformity through repeated messages."[38] The idea of selling virtues like cereal nearly reaches the point of self-parody in the Jefferson Center's curriculum, which includes the following activity: "There's a new product on the market! It's Considerate Cereal. Eating it can make a person more considerate. Design a label for the box. Tell why someone should buy and eat this cereal. Then list the ingredients."[39]

If "repeated messages" don't work, then you simply force students to conform: "Sometimes compulsion is what is needed to get a habit started," says William Kilpatrick.[40] We may recoil from the word "compulsion," but it is the premise of that sentence that really ought to give us pause. When education is construed as the process of inculcating *habits*—which is to say, unreflective actions—then it scarcely deserves to be called education at all. It is really, as Alan

Lockwood saw, an attempt to get "mindless conformity to externally imposed standards of conduct."[41]

Notice how naturally this goal follows from a dark view of human nature. If you begin with the premise that "good conduct is not our natural first choice," then the best you can hope for is "the development of good habits"[42] —that is, a system that gets people to act unthinkingly in the manner that someone else has deemed appropriate. This connection recently became clear to Ann Medlock, whose Giraffe Project was designed to evoke "students' own courage and compassion" in thinking about altruism, but which, in some schools, was being turned into a traditional, authoritarian program in which students were simply told how to act and what to believe. Medlock recalls suddenly realizing what was going on with these educators: "Oh, *I* see where you're coming from. You believe kids are no damn good!"[43]

The character education movement's emphasis on habit, then, is consistent with its view of children. Likewise, its process matches its product. The transmission model, along with the use of rewards and punishments to secure compliance, seems entirely appropriate if the values you are trying to transmit are things like obedience and loyalty and respect for authority. But this approach overlooks an important distinction between product and process. When we argue about which traits to emphasize—compassion or loyalty, cooperation or competition, skepticism or obedience—we are trafficking in value judgments. When we talk about how best to teach these things, however, we are being descriptive rather than just prescriptive. Even if you like the sort of virtues that appear in character education programs, and even if you regard the need to implement those virtues as urgent, the attempt to transmit or instill them dooms the project because that is just not consistent with the best theory and research on how people learn. (Of course, if you have reservations about many of the values that the character educators wish to instill, you may be *relieved* that their favored method is unlikely to be successful.)

I don't wish to be misunderstood. The techniques of character education may succeed in temporarily buying a particular behavior. But they are unlikely to leave children with a *commitment* to that behavior, a reason to continue acting that way in the future. You can turn out automatons who utter the desired words or maybe even "emit" (to use the curious verb favored by behaviorists) the desired actions. But the words and actions are unlikely to continue—much less transfer to new situations—because the child has not been invited to integrate them into his or her value structure. As Dewey observed, "The required beliefs cannot be hammered in; the needed attitudes cannot be plastered on."[44] Yet watch a character education lesson in any part of the country and you will almost surely be observing a strenuous exercise in hammering and plastering.

For traditional moralists, the constructivist approach is a waste of time. If values and traditions and the stories that embody them already exist, then surely "we don't have to reinvent the wheel," remarks Bennett.[45] Likewise an exasperated Wynne: "Must each generation try to completely reinvent society?"[46] The answer is no—and yes. It is not as though everything that now exists must be discarded and entirely new values fashioned from scratch. But the process of learning does indeed require that meaning, ethical or otherwise, be actively invented and reinvented, from the inside out. It requires that children be given the opportunity to make sense of such concepts as fairness or courage, regardless of how long the concepts themselves have been around. Children must be invited to reflect on complex issues, to recast them in light of their own experiences and questions, to figure out for themselves—and with one another—what kind of person one ought to be, which traditions are worth keeping, and how to proceed when two basic values seem to be in conflict.[47]

In this sense, reinvention is necessary if we want to help children become moral people, as opposed to people who merely do what they are told—or reflexively rebel against what they are told.

Notes

1. See, for example, Linda Page, "A Conservative Christian View on Values," *School Administrator,* September 1995, p. 22.

2. See, for example, Kevin Ryan, "The Ten Commandments of Character Education," *School Administrator,* September 1995, p. 19; and program materials from the Character Education Institute and the Jefferson Center for Character Education.

3. See Alfie Kohn, *Punished by Rewards: The Trouble with Gold Stars, Incentive Plans, A's, Praise, and Other Bribes* (Boston: Houghton Mifflin, 1993); and Edward L. Deci and Richard M. Ryan, *Intrinsic Motivation and Self-Determination in Human Behavior* (New York: Plenum, 1985).

4. See C. Daniel Batson et al., "Buying Kindness: Effect on an Extrinsic Incentive for Helping on Perceived Altruism," *Personality and Social Psychology Bulletin,* vol 4, 1978, p. 90; Cathleen L. Smith et al., "Children's Causal Attributions Regarding Help Giving," *Child Development,* vol. 59, 1979, pp. 203–10; and William Edward Upton III, "Altruism, Attribution, and Intrinsic Motivation in the Recruitment of Blood Donors," *Dissertation Abstracts International* 34B, vol 12, 1974, p. 6260.

5. Richard A. Fabes et al., "Effects of Rewards on Children's Prosocial Motivation: A Socialization Study," *Developmental Psychology,* vol. 25, 1989, pp. 509–15; and Joan Grusec, "Socializing Concern for Others in the Home," *Develomental Psychology,* vol. 27, 1991, pp. 338–42.

6. See Alfie Kohn, *No Contest: The Case Against Competition,* rev. ed. (Boston: Houghton Mifflin, 1992).

7. This statement is taken from an eight-page brochure produced by the "Character Counts!" Coalition, a project of the Josephson Institute of Ethics. Members of the coalition include the American Federation of Teachers, the National Association of Secondary School Principals, the American Red Cross, the YMCA, and many other organizations.

8. William Kilpatrick, *Why Johnny Can't Tell Right from Wrong* (New York: Simon & Schuster, 1992), pp. 96, 249.

9. For example, Kilpatrick was selected in 1995 to keynote the first in a series of summer institutes on character education sponsored by Thomas Lickona.

10. Edward Wynne, "Transmitting Traditional Values in Contemporary Schools," in Larry P. Nucci, ed., *Moral Development and Character Education: A Dialogue* (Berkeley, Calif.: McCutchan, 1989), p. 25.

11. Kevin Ryan, "In Defense of Character Education," in Nucci, p. 16.

12. Louis Goldman, "Mind, Character, and the Deferral of Gratification," *Educational Forum,* vol. 60, 1996, p. 136. As part of "educational reconstruction," he goes on to say, we must "connect the lower social classes to the middle classes who may provide role models for self-discipline" (p. 139).

13. Jarvis is quoted in Wray Herbert, "The Moral Child," *U.S. News & World Report,* 3 June 1996, p. 58.

14. Amitai Etzioni, *The Spirit of Community: The Reinvention of American Society* (New York: Simon & Schuster, 1993), p. 91.

15. See Alfie Kohn, *The Brighter Side of Human Nature: Altruism and Empathy in Everyday Life* (New York: Basic Books, 1990); and "Caring Kids: The Role of the Schools," *Phi Delta Kappan,* March 1991, pp. 496–506.

16. David E. Purpel, "Moral Education: An Idea Whose Time Has Gone," *The Clearing House,* vol. 64, 1991, p. 311.

17. This description of the character education movement is offered by Alan L. Lockwood in "Character Education: The Ten Percent Solution," *Social Education,* April/May 1991, p. 246. It is a particularly apt characterization of a book like *Why Johnny Can't Tell Right from Wrong,* which invokes an age of "chivalry" and sexual abstinence, a time when moral truths were uncomplicated and unchallenged. The author's tone, however, is not so much wistful about the past as angry about the present: he denounces everything from rock music (which occupies an entire chapter in a book about morality) and feminism to the "multiculturalists" who dare to remove "homosexuality from the universe of moral judgment" (p. 126).

18. Kevin Walsh of the University of Alabama is quoted in Eric N. Berg, "Argument Grows That Teaching of Values Should Rank with Lessons," *New York Times,* 1 January 1992, p. 32.

19. I am reminded of a woman in a Houston audience who heatedly informed me that she doesn't send her child to school "to learn to be nice." That, she declared, would be "social engineering." But a moment later this woman added that her child ought to be "taught to respect authority." Since this would seem to be at least as apposite an example of social engineering, one is led to conclude that the woman's real objection was to the teaching of *particular* topics or values.

20. Kevin Ryan, "Mining the Values in the Curriculum," *Educational Leadership,* November 1993, p. 16.

21. Telling students to "try hard" and "do their best" begs the important questions. *How,* exactly, do they do their best? Surely it is not just a matter of blind effort. And *why* should they do so, particularly if the task is not engaging or meaningful to them, or if it has simply been imposed on them? Research has found that the attitudes students take toward learning are heavily influenced by whether they have been led to attribute their success (or failure) to innate ability, to effort, or to other factors—and that traditional classroom practices such as grading and competition lead them to explain the results in terms of ability (or its absence) and to minimize effort whenever possible. What looks like "laziness" or insufficient perseverance, in other words, often turns out to be a rational decision to avoid challenge; it is rational because this route proves most expedient for performing well or maintaining an image of oneself as smart. These systemic factors, of course, are complex and often threatening for educators to address; it is much easier just to impress on children the importance of doing their best and then blame them for lacking perseverance if they seem not to do so.

22. Edward A. Wynne, "The Great Tradition in Education: Transmitting Moral Values," *Educational Leadership,* December 1985/January 1986, p. 6.

23. Mary Lord, "The Return of the 'Fourth R,' " *U.S. News & World Report,* 11 September 1995, p. 58.

24. William Glasser, *Schools Without Failure* (New York: Harper & Row, 1969), p. 22.

25. Mare Desmond's letter appeared in the *New York Times Magazine*, 21 May 1995, p. 14. The same point was made by Robert Primack, "No Substitute for Critical Thinking: A Response to Wynne," *Educational Leadership*, December 1985/January 1986, p. 12.

26. Deborah Meier and Paul Schwarz, "Central Park East Secondary School," in Michael W. Apple and James A. Beane, eds., *Democratic Schools* (Alexandria, Va.: Association for Supervision and Curriculum Development, 1995), pp. 29–30.

27. See Richard de Charms, *Personal Causation: The Internal Affective Determinants of Behavior* (Hillsdale, N.J.: Erlbaum, 1983). See also the many publications of Edward Deci and Richard Ryan.

28. See, for example, Alfie Kohn, "Choices for Children: Why and How to Let Students Decide," *Phi Delta Kappan*, September 1993, pp. 8–20; and Child Development Project, *Ways We Want Our Class to Be: Class Meetings That Build Commitment to Kindness and Learning* (Oakland, Calif.: Developmental Studies Center, 1996).

29. The quotations are from Wynne, "The Great Tradition," p. 9; and Edward A. Wynne and Herbert J. Walberg, "The Complementary Goals of Character Development and Academic Excellence," *Educational Leadership*, December 1985/January 1986, p. 17. William Kilpatrick is equally averse to including students in decision making; he speaks longingly of the days when "schools were unapologetically authoritarian," declaring that "schools can learn a lot from the Army," which is a "hierarchial [sic], authoritarian, and undemocratic institution" (see *Why Johnny Can't*, p. 228).

30. The sort of compassion I have in mind is akin to what the psychologist Ervin Staub described as a "prosocial orientation" (see his *Positive Social Behavior and Morality*, vols. 1 and 2 [New York: Academic Press, 1978 and 1979])—a generalized inclination to care, share, and help across different situations and with different people, including those we don't know, don't like, and don't look like. Loyally lending a hand to a close friend is one thing; going out of one's way for a stranger is something else.

31. John Dewey, *The School and Society* (Chicago: University of Chicago Press, 1900; reprint, 1990), p. 15.

32. Wynne and Walberg, p. 17. For another endorsement of competition among students, see Kevin Ryan, "In Defense," p. 15.

33. This passage is taken from page 21 of an undated 28-page "Character Education Curriculum" produced by the Character Education Institute. Emphasis in original.

34. Wynne, "Great Tradition," p. 9. Wynne and other figures in the character education movement acknowledge their debt to the French social scientist Emile Durkheim, who believed that "all education is a continuous effort to impose on the child ways of seeing, feeling, and acting which he could not have arrived at spontaneously.... We exert pressure upon him in order that he may learn proper consideration for others, respect for customs and conventions, the need for work, etc." (See Durkheim, *The Rules of Sociological Method* [New York: Free Press, 1938], p. 6.)

35. This is from Bennett's introduction to *The Book of Virtues* (New York: Simon & Schuster, 1993), pp. 12–13.

36. Constance Kamii, Faye B. Clark, and Ann Dominick, "The Six National Goals: A Road to Disappointment," *Phi Delta Kappan*, May 1994, p. 677.

37. Kevin Ryan, "Character and Coffee Mugs," *Education Week*, 17 May 1995, p. 48.

38. The second quotation is a reporter's paraphrase of Brooks. Both it and the direct quotation preceding it appear in Philip Cohen, "The Content of Their Character: Educators Find New Ways to Tackle Values and Morality," *ASCD Curriculum Update*, Spring 1995, p. 4.

39. See B. David Brooks, *Young People's Lessons in Character: Student Activity Workbook* (San Diego: Young People's Press, 1996), p. 12.

40. Kilpatrick, p. 231.

41. To advocate this sort of enterprise, he adds, is to "caricature the moral life." See Alan L. Lockwood, "Keeping Them in the Courtyard: A Response to Wynne," *Educational Leadership,* December 1985/January 1986, p. 10.

42. Kilpatrick, p. 97.

43. Personal communication with Ann Medlock, May 1996.

44. John Dewey, *Democracy and Education* (New York: Free Press, 1916; reprint, 1966), p. 11.

45. Bennett, p. 11.

46. Wynne, "Character and Academics," p. 142.

47. For a discussion of how traditional character education fails to offer guidance when values come into conflict, see Lockwood, "Character Education."

POSTSCRIPT

Can "Character Education" Reverse Moral Decline?

Former secretary of education William J. Bennett has stated that we must not permit disputes over political and theological matters to suffocate the obligation we have to instruct our young in the importance of good character (see "Moral Literacy and the Formation of Character," *NASSP Bulletin,* December 1988). Yet in the public domain, questions of whose values should be presented and whether or not religion-based values can be proffered take on a political cast that is hard to dismiss. Two books that address specific aspects of this dilemma are *The Moral Life of Schools* by Philip W. Jackson, Robert E. Boostrom, and David T. Hansen (1993) and *Reclaiming Our Schools* by Edward A. Wynne and Kevin Ryan (1993).

For a full perspective on the issue of values and moral education, review John Dewey, *Moral Principles in Education* (1911); Abraham Maslow, *New Knowledge in Human Values* (1959); Milton Rokeach, *The Nature of Human Values* (1973); and Robert Coles, *The Moral Life of Children* (1986).

Alternative approaches to moral education can be explored in Howard Kirschenbaum, "A Comprehensive Model of Values Education and Moral Education," *Phi Delta Kappan* (June 1992); *The Moral Self: Building a Better Paradigm* edited by Gil Noam and Thomas Wren (1993); "The Three Rs of Moral Education," by M. Jean Bouas, and "Education and Family Values," by John Martin Rich, *The Educational Forum* (Winter 1993); "Restoring Our Moral Voice," by Amitai Etzioni, *The Public Interest* (Summer 1994); Arthur Dobrin, "Finding Universal Values in a Time of Relativism," *The Educational Forum* (Spring 2001); and R. E. Myers, "Taking a Common-Sense Approach to Moral Education," *The Clearing House* (March–April 2001).

A number of journals have produced issues around the theme of character education that can be valuable sources of information. Among them are *The Clearing House* (May–June 1991), featuring articles by Maxine Greene, Nel Noddings, John Martin Rich, Kevin Ryan, and Henry A. Giroux; *The Journal of Education* (Spring 1993), particularly an article by Edwin J. Delattre and William E. Russell titled "Schooling, Moral Principles, and the Formation of Character"; and *Educational Leadership* (November 1993), which contains over 20 articles on the subject of character education. For an elaboration of Lickona's theories and opinions, see his 1991 book *Education for Character: How Our Schools Can Teach Respect and Responsibility.* Multiple articles on the issue can be found in *The Educational Forum* (Winter 1996), *Journal of Education* (nos. 2 and 3, 1997), *Phi Delta Kappan* (February 1998), *The School Administrator* (May 1998), *NASSP Bulletin* (October 1999), and *Kappa Delta Pi Record* (Summer 2000).

ISSUE 7

Should Multiculturalism Permeate the Curriculum?

YES: Sonia Nieto, from "What Does It Mean to Affirm Diversity?" *The School Administrator* (May 1999)

NO: Thomas J. Famularo, from "The Intellectual Bankruptcy of Multiculturalism," *USA Today Magazine,* a publication of the Society for the Advancement of Education (May 1996)

ISSUE SUMMARY

YES: Professor of language, literacy, and culture Sonia Nieto examines the realities of diversity in American society that underlie an effective approach to multicultural education.

NO: Former English instructor Thomas J. Famularo contends that the multiculturalism movement, rather than representing diversity, is centered on the themes of race and gender and the debunking of Western culture.

During the past 20 years or so, American public schools have been encouraged to embrace multiculturalism as a curricular focus. The "No One American" statement, issued by the American Association of Colleges of Teacher Education in 1972, set the tone for the movement by calling for an effort to support cultural diversity and global understanding. In the 1980s a number of influential writers, such as Allan Bloom, E. D. Hirsch, Jr., Arthur M. Schlesinger, Jr., William J. Bennett, and Nathan Glazer, warned of the divisive nature of multiculturalism and called for a renewed curricular focus on cultural commonalities shaped by the Western tradition.

Thus was launched the so-called culture wars, which have persisted on an educational battlefield that extends from kindergarten to graduate school. Several books, including Bennett's *To Reclaim a Legacy* (1984), Lynne Cheney's *American Memory: A Report on the Humanities in the Nation's Public Schools* (1988), and Dinesh D'Souza's *Illiberal Education: The Politics of Race and Sex on Campus* (1991), stirred much of the public's concern over what many felt was an encroachment by the multiculturalists upon the traditional canon and the subsequent diminishment of cultural literacy. In defense of multiculturalism, Ira Shor, in his book *Culture Wars: School and Society in the Conservative Restoration* (1987), argues that the underlying motivation of the cultural literacy "backlash" was to restore conservative themes and "right words" that establish "raw authority at the top" while discrediting the liberalism of the 1960s. Also supportive of a multicultural curriculum is Asa G. Hilliard III, who contends that the traditional Eurocentric curriculum is warped and restrictive; that the primary goal of multiculturalism is to present a truthful and meaningful rendition of the whole of human experience; and that a pluralistic curriculum is not a matter of ethnic quotas for "balance," as some conservatives contend.

A number of prominent scholars have joined the fray. Harold Bloom, in *The Western Canon* (1994), deplores multiculturalism and other "isms" that politicize choice. Thomas Sowell devotes chapters of *Inside American Education: The Decline, the Deception, the Dogmas* (1993) to what he considers misconceptions put forth by multiculturalists and bilingual education advocates. Richard Bernstein, in *Dictatorship of Virtue: Multiculturalism and the Battle for America's Future* (1994), expresses fear that there is a pulling away from certain cultural norms, adherence to which has traditionally enabled Americans "to board the great engine of upward social mobility." Also noteworthy are the many books and articles of James A. Banks, a leader in the multicultural education movement, and Nathan Glazer's *We Are All Multiculturalists Now* (1997). Recent articles of note include "Multiculturalism Is Driving Us Apart," by Linda Chavez, *USA Today Magazine* (May 1996); "Multicultural Education as a Moral Responsibility," by Michael R. Hillis, *The Educational Forum* (Winter 1996); "Multiculturalism, Diversity, and Cultural Pluralism," by Vanessa J. Lawrence, *Journal of Black Studies* (January 1997); and Dennis Wrong's "Adversarial Identities and Multiculturalism," *Society* (January/February 2000).

Two social realities undergird the multiculturalist effort to reform the curriculum at all levels: the traditional curriculum has neglected the contributions made by minority groups to the American culture, and the economy is becoming more and more globalized. Given these conditions, the multicultural approach may be seen as serving to give a new and expanded definition to the "American experience." What effect a multicultural curriculum will have on American traditions and social institutions remains to be seen. Serious questions continue to be debated—questions involving the future path of cultural development in American society, and sociological questions about the relationships between the institutionally dominant majority culture and the minority cultures, the populations of which are increasing.

In the following opposing selections, Sonia Nieto, author of *Affirming Diversity*, 3rd ed. (2000) and *The Light in Their Eyes* (1999), pleads for greater attention to and respect for ethnic minorities and poor children in their quest for social justice. Thomas J. Famularo argues that multiculturalism, which began as an attempt to increase awareness of ethnic and minority contributions to history and culture, has evolved into an approach that makes diversity and difference the prime movers of the curriculum.

Sonia Nieto  **YES**

What Does It Mean to Affirm Diversity?

About 15 years ago, I was interviewing a young woman for admission to our multicultural teacher education program and I asked her why she had chosen to apply for this particular program. (At the time, we had a number of undergraduate teacher preparation programs from which students to choose.)

The young woman, let's call her Nancy, mentioned that she was doing a prepracticum at Marks Meadow School, the laboratory school of our School of Education at the University of Massachusetts. Marks Meadow is an extraordinarily diverse place with children from every corner of the globe representing multiple languages and various social and economic backgrounds.

When the children in her 1st-grade classroom were doing self-portraits, one of them asked Nancy for a brown crayon. She was momentarily confounded by his request, thinking *Why brown?* It never before had occurred to her that children would make their faces anything other than the color of the white paper they used. "I decided then and there that I needed this program," she confessed.

As naive as her reaction was, it was the beginning of Nancy's awakening to diversity. It was also a courageous disclosure of her own ignorance.

Ill-Prepared for Diversity

It is by now a truism that our country's public schools are undergoing a dramatic shift that reflects the growing diversity of our population. Yet many educators and the schools in which they work seem no better prepared for this change than was Nancy a decade and a half ago. Most educators nationwide are very much like Nancy: white, middle-class, monolingual English-speaking women and men who have had little direct experience with cultural, ethnic, linguistic or other kinds of diversity, but they are teaching students who are phenomenally diverse in every way.

Given this scenario, what do educators—teachers, aides, curriculum developers, principals, superintendents and school board members—need to know to create effective schools for students of all backgrounds, and how can they learn it? Let me suggest five realities that educators need to appreciate and understand if this is to happen:

Affirming diversity is above all about social justice.

Contrary to what the pundits who oppose multicultural education might say, multicultural education is *not* about political correctness, sensitivity training or ethnic cheerleading. It is primarily about social justice. Given the vastly unequal educational outcomes among students of different backgrounds, equalizing conditions for student learning needs to be at the core of a concern for diversity.

If this is the case, "celebrating diversity" through special assembly programs, multicultural dinners or ethnic celebrations are hollow activities if they do not also confront the structural inequalities that exist in schools.

A concern for social justice means looking critically at why and how our schools are unjust for some students. It means that we need to analyze school policies and practices that devalue the identities of some students while overvaluing others: the curriculum, testing, textbooks and materials, instructional strategies, tracking, the recruitment and hiring of staff and parent involvement strategies. All of these need to be viewed with an eye toward making them more equitable for all students, not just those students who happen to be white, middle class and English speaking.

Students of color and poor students bear the brunt of structural inequality.

Schools inevitably reflect society, and the evidence that our society is becoming more unequal is growing every day. We have all read the headlines: The United States has one of the highest income disparities in the world, and the combined wealth of the top 1 percent of U.S. families is about the same as the entire bottom 80 percent.

Growing societal inequities are mirrored in numerous ways in schools, from highly disparate financing of schools in rich and poor communities, to academic tracking that favors white above black and brown students, to SAT scores that correlate perfectly with income rather than with intelligence or ability. Although it is a worthy goal, equality is far from a reality in most of our schools, and those who bear the burden of inequality are our children, particularly poor children of all backgrounds and many children of Latino, Native American, Asian American and African American backgrounds. The result is schools that are racist and classist, if not by intention, at least by result.

Inequality is a fact of life, but many educators refuse to believe or accept it, and they persist in blaming children, their families, their cultural and linguistic backgrounds, laziness or genetic inferiority as the culprits. Once educators accept the fact that inequality is alive and thriving in our schools, they can proceed to do something about it. Until they do, little will change.

Positive Acculturation

Diversity is a valuable resource.

I went to elementary school in Brooklyn, N.Y., during the 1950s. My class-mates were enormously diverse in ethnicity, race, language, social class and family structure.

But even then, we were taught as if we were all cut from the same cloth. Our mothers were urged to speak to us in English at home (fortunately, my mother never paid attention, and it is because of this that I am fluent in Spanish today), and we were given the clear message that anything having to do with our home cultures was not welcome in school. To succeed in school, we needed to learn English, forget our native language and behave like the kids we read about in our basal readers.

Of course, learning English and learning it well is absolutely essential for academic and future life success, but the assumption that one must discard one's identity along the way needs to be challenged. There is nothing shameful in knowing a language other than English. In fact, becoming bilingual can benefit individuals and our country in general.

As educators, we no longer can afford to behave as if diversity were a dirty word. Every day, more research underscores the positive influence that cultural and linguistic diversity has on student learning. Immigrant students who maintain a positive ethnic identity as they acculturate and who become fluent bilinguals are more likely to have better mental health, do well academ-ically and graduate from high school than those who completely assimilate. Yet we insist on erasing cultural and linguistic differences as if they were a burden rather than an asset.

Effectively teaching students of all backgrounds means respecting and affirm-ing who they are.

To become effective teachers of all students, educators must undergo a profound shift in their beliefs, attitudes and values about difference.

In many U.S. classrooms, cultural, linguistic and other differences are commonly viewed as temporary, if troublesome, barriers to learning. Conse-quently, students of diverse backgrounds are treated as walking sets of deficien-cies, as if they had nothing to bring to the educational enterprise.

Anybody who has walked into a classroom knows that teaching and learn-ing are above all about relationships, and these relationships can have a pro-found impact on students' futures. But significant relationships with students are difficult to develop when teachers have little understanding of the stu-dents' families and communities. The identities of nonmainstream students frequently are dismissed by schools and teachers as immaterial to academic achievement.

When this is the case, it is unlikely that students will form positive re-lationships with their teachers or, as a result, with learning. It is only when educators and schools accept and respect who their students are and what they know that they can begin to build positive connections with them.

Affirming diversity means becoming a multicultural person.

Over the years, I have found that educators believe they are affirming di-versity simply because they say they are. But mouthing the words is not enough. Children sense instantly when support for diversity is superficial.

Because most educators in the United States have not had the benefit of firsthand experiences with diversity, it is a frightening concept for many of them. If we think of teaching as a life-long journey of personal transformation, becoming a multicultural person is part of the journey. It is different for each person.

For Nancy, it began with recognition of her own ignorance. For others, it means learning a second language or working collaboratively with colleagues to design more effective strategies of reaching all students. However we begin the journey, until we take those tentative first steps, what we say about diversity is severely limited by our actions.

Comfort With Differences

Taking these realities to heart means we no longer can think of some students as void of any dignity and worth simply because they do not confirm to our conventional image. All students of all backgrounds bring talents and strengths to their learning and as educators we need to find ways to build on these.

Acknowledging and affirming diversity is to everyone's interest, includ-ing middle-class white students. Understanding people of other backgrounds, speaking languages other than English and learning to respect and appreciate differences are skills that benefit all students and our nation as a whole. We do all our students a disservice when we prepare them to live in a society that no longer exists.

Given the tremendous diversity in our society, it makes eminent good sense to educate all our students to be comfortable with differences.

Thomas J. Famularo  **NO**

The Intellectual Bankruptcy of Multiculturalism

It is along ideological lines that the debate over multiculturalism has assumed its current form and substance. Thomas Sowell, in *Inside American Education,* states that the "ideological components of multiculturalism can be summarized as a cultural relativism which finds the prominence of Western civilization in the world or in the schools intolerable." Recently, this anti-West aspect of multiculturalism was evidenced at Yale University, where a $20,000,000 grant by Texas billionaire Lee M. Bass, exclusively for the development of programs and courses in Western culture, met highly politicized faculty opposition, with the result that Yale returned the money.

John O'Sullivan, editor of *National Review,* decries the multiculturalist assertion that America is an "idea rather than a nation [possessing] a distinctive but encompassing American identity." Peter W. Cookson, Jr., author of *School Choice: The Struggle for the Soul of American Education,* offers the insight that multiculturalism's hostility to the West and repudiation of an identifiable American culture is augmented by a radically new definition of community, one that swerves from the traditional emphasis on "family, neighborhood, church, lodge, and school to race, gender, occupation, and sexual preference."

These ideological divisions within U.S. society threaten to rend the nation into hostile factions. For example, Richard Bernstein, in *Dictatorship of Virtue: Multiculturalism and the Battle for America's Future,* brands ideological multiculturalists as "radical-left inhabitants of a political dreamland." Its critics maintain that multiculturalism is not—and never can be—a viable educational principle.

A few points of clarification regarding multiculturalism's recent evolution might be helpful. What began during the early part of this century as a shift towards increased awareness of ethnic and minority contributions to American history has evolved into a pedagogy that makes diversity and difference the prime movers of the curriculum.

In response to the New York State Department of Education's *A Curriculum of Inclusion* (1989), Diane Ravitch, writing in *The American Scholar* (Summer 1990), argued that current manifestations of multiculturalism extend far beyond the kind of pluralism that "seeks a richer common culture" to "multicultural particularism," which denies that a "common culture is possible or desirable."

According to the authors of *A Curriculum of Inclusion*, including controversial City University of New York (CUNY) former Black Studies chairman Leonard Jeffries, multiculturalism no longer should be construed to mean "adding marginal examples of 'other' cultures to an assumed dominant culture." On the contrary, multiculturalists adamantly gainsay the idea of an identifiable and definable American culture that might form the basis of a core curriculum. "The old curriculum is essentially based on the premise that America has one cultural heritage augmented by minor contributions from other peoples who by and large have presented 'problems' to the primary culture. To combat teaching and learning based on this premise, a radical, new approach to building a curriculum is needed," *A Curriculum of Inclusion* claims. Multicultural particularism, counters Ravitch, "is a bad idea whose time has come. It is also a fashion spreading like wildfire through the education system."

As multiculturalism is infused into mainstream American public education, I am reminded of a question asked by a former Brooklyn College colleague which captures the ultimate unfeasibility of multicultural education: "What comes out?" Although learning should be lifelong, schooling is a finite process. Inevitably, additions to the curriculum made in the name of diversity and inclusion render the necessity of displacement. A curriculum can contain just so much, and because education succeeds only when it includes prolonged and in-depth consideration of specific books, authors, ideas, and historical events, more in education often is less.

As far back as 1984, the Committee of Correspondence, a St. Louis-based international network of educational reformers, offered both a definition and defense of multicultural education: Knowledge of "diverse intellectual and cultural traditions," they wrote, should be a primary objective of a democratic curriculum, and this knowledge must include "not only the familiar academic disciplines and traditions of high culture, but the great multiplicity of cultures, perspectives and ways of knowing of the western and non-western world."

The committee faltered, however, in regard to the possible implementation of multicultural education by allowing that "There are difficult dilemmas in how to realize [this] in everyday schools and curriculum practice." These dilemmas must be "negotiated out of the conflicting values and interests of the students, teachers, and members of the local community." The key question, which the committee did not entertain, is whether or not this process of negotiation can result in anything other than what one educator has described as "dens of babble."

Multicultural education is undermined by two fatal flaws. The first is that the more the curriculum represents a multicultural test based upon "exposure to diversity," the more shallow and superficial learning becomes. By disavowing the "difficult dilemma" of choosing what comes out, multiculturalism ultimately reduces education to its shallowest possibilities—the mere glossing over of diverse subject matter—and renders the kind of understanding that comes from intensive, prolonged study of selected material impossible to attain.

Multiculturalism's second fatal flaw is that it necessarily precludes the single most important requirement for successful education—coherent means to a discernible end. By denying the existence of desirability of a distinctive American culture, thereby repudiating the need for public education to assist in the process of assimilation, multicultural education is both aimless and rudderless. Multicultural curricula careen to and fro, touching fleetingly upon cultural tidbits of theoretically limitlessly diverse groups.

The culture wars that have ravaged American society for more than 30 years have forced America's public schools to capitulate to the relativism inherent in multiculturalism and to abandon education based upon desired ends for the cafeteria-style taste-test type of learning which does not work. Ravitch reasons that the final results of this "fractionation" are high school graduates who can "no longer be said to share a common body of knowledge, not to mention a common culture."

In an attempt to validate multiculturalism's emphasis on particularism and its concomitant subversion of cultural commonality, knowledge and facts in multicultural education consistently are subordinated to so-called "critical thinking skills." I say "so-called" because my experience with hundreds of college freshmen invariably revealed young adults who were as oblivious to real critical thinking concepts such as induction, deduction, syllogism, appeal to authority, point-counterpoint, comparison, and contrast as they were to rudimentary historical facts and dates. The dismal truth is that, more often than not, critical thinking in the classroom means little more than subjective questioning and unsubstantiated, unreasoned, personal opinion. Attempts to structure student opinion according to classical logical models often are met by multiculturalist accusations of Eurocentricity and pro-Western prejudices.

As an instructor of English at Brooklyn and Lehman Colleges of CUNY during the 1980s, I never had to look far for the results of education that substitutes critical thinking skills for the teaching of selected factual knowledge. The defining characteristic of my freshman students transcended race, sex, and ethnic heritage. Although predominantly intelligent, they essentially were empty vessels devoid of quantifiable academic information.

Contrary to the assertions of proponents of multiculturalism that limitless pluralism enriches education, the de-emphasizing of specific core material and factual knowledge in high school resulted in what it inevitably must have —a plague of ignorance. Multiculturalism's subordination of facts and knowledge to critical thinking skills demonstrates its educational bankruptcy, for any critical opinion worthy of a passing grade must evolve out of knowledge and be grounded in objective facts.

Anyone familiar with the nation's campus culture clashes knows what the call for diversity in education too often really is—a red herring for a radical agenda. When Stanford University, for instance, recommends only three subjects of study in the music segment of its required Culture, Ideas, Values course —Reggae lyrics, Rastafarian poetry, and Andean music—it answers the question "What comes out?" with a list that includes Bach, Mozart, and Beethoven. It constructs, as well, a curriculum which, far from being representatively diverse, is unified around a theme of race and sex and the debunking of Western culture.

Ironically, many multiculturalists, either consciously or instinctively, recognize the intellectual bankruptcy of the cultural particularism they ostensibly espouse. Multicultural curricula, overtly committed to diversity and difference, almost invariably are focused on underlying, latent, and often dogmatic themes.

In what direction is multiculturalism headed? Although educators such as Thomas Sowell have written of "the multiple evidences of declining educational quality during the period when multiculturalism and other non-academic preoccupations have taken up more and more of the curriculum," educational leaders attempted to plunge ahead into the multicultural morass with the ill-conceived National Standards for United States History, a part of the Clinton Administration's Goals 2000 Act.

As is inevitable with a multicultural curriculum, in order to make room for diverse additions, the National Education Standards and Improvement Council needed to make equivalent quantitative subtractions. Omitted from this proposed curriculum—in the name of respect for diversity—were, among other touchstones of traditional American history, the First Continental Congress, Robert E. Lee, Alexander Graham Bell, Thomas Edison, Albert Einstein, Jonas Salk, and the Wright brothers. Ultimately, students educated within the vague parameters of this multicultural curriculum will learn the hard truth —that any "critical" opinion of the birth of our nation without knowledge of the First Continental Congress or of the Civil War without considering Robert E. Lee is not based on sufficient factual knowledge and, therefore, has little or no value in the marketplace of ideas.

Goals 2000 risks continued educational decline. Its emphasis on multicultural diversity within the curriculum is not America's only choice. Educators should continue to explore other possibilities such as more diversity *of* schools and less diversity *within* schools.

A Success Story

One example worthy of study is Mortimer J. Adler's Chattanooga, Tenn.-based Paideia schools, founded on his prescription of "one required course of study for all." Syndicated columnist William Raspberry visited the Paideia schools in 1994 and was impressed with the high quality of teaching and learning that goes on there. "Parents of rich children and poor, black and white, camp out as long as a week in advance of registration to secure a place in these new schools," he wrote. He described a district that once was an "academic basket case," but where students now regularly achieve at the honor student level and for which the college acceptance rate approaches 98%.

In the same article, Raspberry juxtaposed the Paideia success story with the "disservice" of the old Georgia Tech "multicultural education" that urged minority students to take light course loads, shun the more difficult subjects such as science, and sign up for the "special multi-cultural tutoring program." The Paideia program, Raspberry indicated, proves that all students, regardless of race or cultural heritage, are capable of rising to the highest of expectations and that to think otherwise is "borderline racist."

In contradistinction to Goals 2000, Adler warns against a national curriculum that would be "unpardonably presumptuous in a country, such as ours, which is radically pluralistic." Within each individual school, he argues, a "single track" of connected courses should lead to a definable end. Unlike the multiculturalists who seek limitless curricular inclusion, Adler advocates the elimination of all material that might dilute, confuse, or clutter up the curriculum.

In the final book of his Paideia trilogy, *The Paideia Program: An Educational Syllabus,* Adler addresses the assumption that a focused curriculum breeds provincialism and narrowness of mind—"that learning about the United States only, or even about Western civilization, is not enough":

"What is meant by Oriental? Is it Chinese, and if so, Northern or Southern or Mandarin? Is it Japanese or Korean? Is it Javanese or Cambodian? Is it Indian (Hindu) or Pakistani (Moslem)? One could go on asking and each new name would point to a notably different culture. In short, what we face is several lifetimes of work to master diverse histories, each remote from that of New England or Texas, between which we ourselves see enough differences to require special effort in the teaching of a unified American history.

"What may we conclude? Are American school children to remain 'provincial' in the sense of knowing only the history of the West? Two answers suggest themselves. First, 'world history' is a term that can apply to information that varies in depth—deeper 'at home' (wherever home may be) than elsewhere. It is still a kind of knowledge of the world to know that something exists or took place, and even something of what it amounted to, without presuming to say how it was and is regarded by those in whose country it occurred. Every educated mind shows this variation in depth and range: natural limitations make encyclopedic knowledge an impossibility."

Adler's Paideia proposal is realistic and grounded in sound pedagogy. It evolves out of a distinction that the multiculturalists either fail to grasp or refuse to make. While the Paideia schools are *select* schools, they are neither exclusionary nor elitist. Their emphasis is on Western culture. Their selectivity is justifiable because it is not grounded in irrational bigotry, but in cultural choice (which is what multiculturalism is supposed to be, but never is, about).

This rationale for school choice has begun to trickle into mainstream public opinion. E. R. Shipp, a New York-based journalist, has demanded a public school curriculum that "places ancient Africa at the center of education for our 20th century African-American children." In doing so, she eloquently makes the case for another Paideia school.

Multiculturalism, writes *National Review*'s O'Sullivan, is "liberalism deconstructing itself." He very well may be right. It will not be until the educational bankruptcy of multiculturalism is exposed fully that the deconstruction of American public education will be halted successfully.

POSTSCRIPT

Should Multiculturalism Permeate the Curriculum?

The issue of multicultural education is complex and difficult to resolve because it reverberates to the core of the American democratic experience. Is the nation strengthened and its minority populations empowered by the process of assimilation into a culture with primarily Western European origins? Or is the United States—which is an immigrant nation—constantly redefined by the cultural influences that come to its shores?

Further research will reveal a wealth of theories and opinions that illuminate the basic problem and its many aspects. Recommended sources include "Dimensions of Multicultural Education," by Carlos F. Diaz, *National Forum* (Winter 1994); "Self-Esteem and Multiculturalism in the Public Schools," by Kay S. Hymowitz, *Dissent* (Winter 1992); "Multicultural Education: Five Views," by Christine E. Sleeter, *Kappa Delta Pi Record* (Fall 1992); Valerie Ooka Pang, John Rivera, and Jill Kerper Mora, "The Ethic of Caring," *Educational Forum* (Fall 1999); and Peter Skerry, "Do We Really Want Immigrants to Assimilate?" *Society* (March/April 2000).

The political perspective on this topic is examined in Henry A. Giroux, "Curriculum, Multiculturalism, and the Politics of Identity," *NASSP Bulletin* (December 1992); Christine Canning, "Preparing for Diversity: A Social Technology for Multicultural Community Building," *The Educational Forum* (Summer 1993); and Francis J. Ryan, "Will Multiculturalism Undercut Student Individuality?" *Educational Horizons* (Spring 1993).

Some theme issues of journals to explore are "Polarizing American Culture," *Society* (July/August 1993); "Multicultural Education," *Phi Delta Kappan* (September 1993); "Critical Perspectives on Diversity," *The Educational Forum* (Summer 1993); two issues of *National Forum* that focus on "Immigration and the Changing Face of America" (Summer 1994) and "Multiculturalism and Diversity" (Winter 1994); and "Diversity in a New America," *The Brookings Review* (Winter 2002).

Articles of note include a provocative defense of Western culture by Bernard Lewis, "Eurocentrism Revisited," *Commentary* (December 1994) and Carl A. Grant, "Challenging the Myths About Multicultural Education," *Multicultural Education* (Winter 1994). Further ideas can be found in Todd Gitlin's *The Twilight of Common Dreams* (1995); David A. Hollinger's *Postethnic America* (1995); Michael Lind's *The Next American Nation* (1995); Lawrence W. Levine's *The Opening of the American Mind* (1996); Roger Clegg's "The Perversity of 'Diversity,'" *The Chronicle of Higher Education* (July 14, 2000); and "Will Multicultural Education Survive the Standards Movement?" by Anita Perna Bohn and Christine E. Sleeter, *The Education Digest* (January 2001).

ISSUE 8

Can Federal Initiatives Rescue Failing Schools?

YES: Andrew Rotherham, from "A New Partnership," *Education Next* (Spring 2002)

NO: Lisa Snell, from "Schoolhouse Crock," *Reason* (August/September 2001)

ISSUE SUMMARY

YES: Education policy expert Andrew Rotherham argues that new federally imposed accountability standards will enhance opportunity and overhaul failing schools.

NO: Lisa Snell, of the Reason Public Policy Institute, describes why President George W. Bush's education plans will not help disadvantaged students in public schools.

W hile schooling in the United States has always been and remains primarily a state and local function, the federal government has played a significant role in initiating programs to meet specific needs and charting general goals. Beginning with the 1862 Morrill Act creating a land grant program to fund state agricultural and mechanical colleges, the legislative and executive branches of the federal government have provided support for vocational education (1917); educational assistance for veterans (1944); funds for strengthening instruction in science, math, and foreign languages (1958); funds to support school desegregation (1964 and 1972); mandates and partial funding for meeting the needs of children with disabilities (1975 and 1990); and assistance for drug abuse prevention (1986). President George Bush and the nation's governors set goals for American schools in 1989, and the Clinton administration continued this effort in 1994 with the Goals 2000: Educate America Act, which set standards and provided aid for state reforms.

In 1965 Congress passed the Elementary and Secondary Education Act (ESEA), a wide-ranging program emphasizing aid for disadvantaged students. Reauthorization of this law in 2002 under the George W. Bush administration as the No Child Left Behind Act has prompted a good deal of debate. Is the new

ESEA a welcome increase in federal attention to school reform, or is it an expansion of bureaucratic red tape and a usurpation of state and local perogatives? While there is much agreement on the goals to be met, there is philosophical division over the means of achieving these goals. In the words of historian Diane Ravitch, "The most important national priority must be to redesign policies and programs so that education funding is used to educate children, not to preserve the system."

The new ESEA, a 1,080-page document authorizing $26.5 billion in fiscal year 2002 alone, sets standards and accountability measures aimed at closing the achievement gap over a period of 12 years. Richard F. Elmore, in "Unwarranted Intrusion," *Education Next* (Spring 2002), finds it ironic that Republicans have sponsored the single largest expansion of federal power over the nation's education system in history. While the most discussed portions of the new law are those dealing with mandates for annual statewide assessments in reading and mathematics (and later in science) and the requirements for yearly progress reports toward 100 percent proficiency, the law covers many more areas, among which are school and district report cards, bilingual education, teacher and principal quality, public charter schools, and military recruitment. Summaries of the law may be found at http://www.edweek.com and http://www.aft.org/ESEA.

Thomas Toch, in "Bush's Big Test," *The Washington Monthly* (November 2001), regrets that the federal administration has "punted the decision to the states," allowing states to set the passing grades on tests that will be used to parcel out rewards and sanctions. Another flaw Toch identifies is the plan's dependence on the U.S. Department of Education to police the testing efforts of the states. He feels that without a uniform test of achievement in reading and mathematics, the legislation will fail to meet its goals.

In the following selections, Andrew Rotherham offers a justification for federal enforcement of an accountability system to rescue disadvantaged students, while Lisa Snell provides reasons why she believes that the Bush plan will do little or nothing to improve education for the average student.

Andrew Rotherham  **YES**

A New Partnership

The issue of whether the federal government should outline and enforce an accountability system for states, school districts, and schools was essentially settled the day that George W. Bush took office as president. Bush had made "accountability" a cornerstone of his education platform, using his stated goal of ensuring equity for poor and minority children as a way of bolstering his credentials as a moderate. New Democrats, led by Democratic senators Joseph Lieberman and Evan Bayh, were also committed to the idea of accountability. They had made a results-based approach to federal education programs a major component of their "Three R's" proposal—on which much of the Bush plan and the final ESEA [Elementary and Secondary Education Act] legislation were based.

The legislation would build on the accountability measures first introduced during the 1994 reauthorization. That legislation required the states to develop academic standards and tests linked to the standards, but its accountability language was too vague and porous. For example, under the 1994 legislation, states were required to define "adequate yearly progress" in a way that resulted in "continuous and substantial yearly improvement" by schools and school districts toward the goal of getting all students to the proficient level. With states defining the annual yearly progress standard and with no concrete timeline in place, practices varied widely from state to state. This led to great differences in results at the state level. Michigan and Arkansas identified 76 percent and 64 percent, respectively, of their Title I schools as low performing, while Connecticut and Maryland identified only 6 percent each. Regardless, the low-performing label is sadly almost meaningless: 41 percent of principals in these schools reported not even being aware of the designation. And for schools that were identified as low performing there was little in the way of sustained assistance. According to a Department of Education analysis, only 40 percent of schools identified as needing improvement received assistance from the state or their school district. This dismal statistic climbs to only 50 percent for schools that have been identified as low performing for three or more years.

In this system, what passed for accountability was the ability to provide detailed reports of planned and actual spending of federal funds—in other words, a system of accounting, not of accountability. In addition, the federal

From Andrew Rotherham, "A New Partnership," *Education Next* (Spring 2002). Copyright © 2002 by The Board of Trustees of Leland Stanford Junior University. Reprinted by permission.

government was quite lax in enforcing the accountability provisions that were in the law. As a result, as of this writing only 16 states had fully complied with the requirements of the 1994 ESEA reauthorization.

Critics have seized on the states' seeming inability to comply with the previous law as evidence of the folly of proceeding down the accountability route. In fact, critics warn, these federal efforts to demand results-based accountability are at best futile and at worst drive all sorts of perverse and unintended consequences, jeopardizing recent accomplishments at the state and local level. These arguments are the dullest yet most common arrows in the quivers of those fighting change. And they fall apart under close scrutiny. The critics' alternative to the accountability plan is to keep the federal dollars flowing regardless of the results. They have little to offer beyond tired bromides about needing more money for capacity building, innovative partnerships, and a host of other buzzwords that make no difference in the lives of children who attend failing schools.

Why Federal Accountability?

The states' haphazard results in complying with the 1994 requirements and improving low-performing schools overall are precisely why the law's accountability provisions ought to be strengthened and clarified. In a host of policy areas inside and outside of education, history shows that clear federal prescriptions accompanied by real consequences bring results. That's why, for example, you can't buy an alcoholic drink almost anywhere in the country if you're under 21. It's why our cars and airplanes are increasingly safe. And it's why the vestiges of discrimination are being eradicated from our schools and society, through laws like the Civil Rights Act and the Americans with Disabilities Act. Federal policymakers did not wait for states to address these issues on their own. Nor did they lament the states' incapacity to do so. Rather, they mandated clear standards and demanded results.

Increasing the rigor and specificity of the accountability provisions in ESEA doesn't mean imposing the same system on every state, or a "one size fits all" approach in the political jargon. It means establishing clear criteria for improvement, specific indicators of success, and common goals. Such a system need not be incompatible with a variety of approaches at the state level, but it is at odds with the notion that wildly divergent results for students of various races, ethnic groups, and incomes are somehow acceptable.

Obviously there is a world of difference between a standard that says all cars must contain passenger-side airbags by a certain date and one that defines what it means to be academically proficient. Complicated issues of how to measure success or failure vex the process of education policymaking. Still, complicated doesn't mean futile. It doesn't mean we should just throw up our hands in collective frustration, because in the end it is simply irresponsible to continue pouring resources into systems that we know are failing without establishing clear benchmarks for their improvement and consequences if they do not reach them. To do otherwise essentially makes Washington the enabler in a terribly dysfunctional relationship that victimizes poor and minority children.

It is ironic that many of the same interest groups and individuals that so readily look to Washington to address various ills suddenly resist federal intrusion in this particular area. Are they satisfied with a situation where African-American and Hispanic 12th graders read and do math as well as white 8th graders? Where, according to an analysis by Jay Greene of the Manhattan Institute, only 56 percent of African-American students and 54 percent of Hispanics graduate from high school?

Perhaps it's because white students score higher on achievement tests and graduate at substantially higher rates that many of the loudest voices in this debate aren't troubled by asking for patience and time to get things exactly right before proceeding. These critics can represent a powerful bloc. Consider that in states like Massachusetts, Virginia, and New York, resistance to the accountability system has come predominantly from affluent white suburbs. Call it the Scarsdale Syndrome. In Massachusetts, writes Georgia Alexakis in the *Washington Monthly*, the paradox of these reform efforts is, "The schools most likely to do poorly on the MCAS [the state test in Massachusetts] have also been most likely to embrace it, while those districts whose scores are already quite high are fighting hardest to get rid of it." The relative political strengths in such a fight are sadly obvious; this is one more reason why accountability can't be left solely to the states.

Listening to the critics' complaints, one is left wondering, What are the wondrous accomplishments that more rigorous accountability will place in jeopardy? It is clear that we have failed to successfully educate poor and minority students on a large-scale basis. It is also clear that despite their best intentions many teachers, principals, superintendents, and professors at schools of education do not know how to address these shortcomings on a meaningful scale. Federal requirements driving states to address these problems would be much more troubling if they were interfering with a variety of successful state and local approaches, but that is simply not the case. In fact, based on what we know, federal accountability provisions will complement the most successful state practices.

States Show Results

Will there be unintended consequences from the new federal accountability provisions? Undoubtedly. Will they all be perverse? No one knows, and unintended consequences that prove positive are certainly not unheard of. We do, however, know something of the intended consequences policymakers hope for. There is evidence that accountability systems with concrete goals change the behavior of school systems, at a minimum by refocusing efforts on disadvantaged students. Consider the experiences of Massachusetts, Virginia, and Texas. In Massachusetts and Virginia, where students are tested in key grades and will soon need to pass exit exams to graduate from high school, Cassandras predicted all kinds of pernicious results. They haven't materialized. In fact, although much work remains, test scores are steadily rising in both states.

During the past four years, the share of Virginia students passing the Algebra I and Algebra II Standards of Learning (SOL) assessments has risen by 34 and 43 percent, respectively. The pass rates for African-American students have gone from 20 percent to 59 percent in Algebra I and 13 percent to 58 percent in Algebra II since 1998. Virginia still needs to address a substantial achievement gap, but its minority students' scores have clearly improved.

In Massachusetts, test-score performance improved, once graduation requirements were imposed. In 2001, 75 percent of 10th graders passed the math portion of the state's MCAS test, and 82 percent passed the language-arts test. This is up from 55 percent and 66 percent, respectively, the previous year. The Massachusetts example is particularly encouraging in light of Achieve, Inc.'s recent finding that "The grade 10 tests are rigorous yet reasonable—and are, in fact, the most challenging of the exit-level tests Achieve has yet reviewed." Achieve also lauded Massachusetts for its work to align its standards, curriculum, and assessments, which has provided a model for other states.

In Texas, where the TAAS test is widely considered to be less rigorous than the SOLs or MCAS tests (although the state is revising the TAAS), minority students nonetheless have shown gains that are corroborated by the National Assessment of Educational Progress. There is considerable evidence that during the past decade in Texas the needs of minority students have received increased attention as a result of an accountability system that demands that a school show not only overall progress, but also progress among its most disadvantaged charges.

Accountability systems are no panacea, and there are certainly problems in Texas and elsewhere. But these results at least indicate that accountability systems can help to focus attention on poor and minority students whose needs have been ignored or neglected. These results also seem to prove the point that states, if left to their own devices, will take action. It's true that the accountability movement has been state-led, to a large extent. Yet most states have yet to meet the requirements of the 1994 law, and it's clear that some won't move forward in any aggressive way without federal action.

What Must Be Done

Obviously, designing an accountability system of this nature is complex. Any workable proposal must be clear to practitioners; fair in the sense of not holding educators accountable for things they can't control; technically sound; and supported and enforced. It also should not squelch promising approaches that the states are developing.

Perhaps the most contentious issue in this debate is the use of standardized tests to measure school performance. Much of the hostility to accountability is actually just hostility toward testing. While standardized tests are certainly not perfect (in fact, they're primitive from a technological point of view), they're still the best objective way to measure progress. They lay bare discrepancies in educational quality in a quantifiable way. Sure, too many state assessment systems are lacking in quality or rigor. Yet this is a case for improvement, not abandonment.

There are legitimate complaints about the ways in which states are using the results of standardized tests. As Thomas Kane and Douglas Staiger point

out . . ., test scores bounce up and down from year-to-year for a variety of reasons that are unrelated to actual school performance. Thus no system should
rely solely on the snapshot of a single year's test scores in making decisions
about incentives or consequences. Accountability systems also need to include
safeguards against the statistical unreliability of small classes and demographic
groups that may include only a few students at a particular school.

Because some states are experimenting with value-added approaches to
measuring school progress, it's important that federal accountability standards
allow for this type of innovation. And while it may be desirable to have a
purely technocratic system that makes no allowances for political and human
impulses, it is not feasible. Because schools are human institutions shaped by
a variety of forces and influences that may or may not be within their control, some "give" is required to address exceptional circumstances that will
inevitably arise. States should have discretion to undertake and prioritize interventions and consequences. But such discretion (or "safe harbor" provisions)
need not equal the vague 1994 language or allow states to use measures that are
divorced from academic results or are purely subjective and porous. During the
debate over the federal "annual yearly progress" standard, many of the proposals that would have included other indicators as measures of a school's annual
yearly progress were simply thinly disguised attempts to eradicate any rigor
from the system. There were proposals to, among other things, hold schools
accountable only for the progress of the lowest-performing students in the bottom quintile; not disaggregate data by race and ethnicity; require states to deal
only with the lowest-performing schools; or ignore test results altogether as an
accountability tool.

The new law appears to have addressed all of these issues in a workable
manner. In the end, it may well turn out that the president's mandate that states
annually test all children in grades 3 through 8 will prove to be much more
burdensome and troubling for states than the new accountability provisions.
It's also entirely possible that the annual yearly progress provisions will cause
trouble, as more and more schools wind up on lists of the low performing and
politicians take the heat. Nonetheless, there is reason for cautious optimism.

What Washington must avoid is simply demanding accountability and
then walking away. The New Democratic Lieberman-Bayh approach on education was predicated not only on more accountability, but also on more investment, more flexibility for states and localities, and a strategic federal role aimed
at helping states and localities solve these problems, serving almost as a consultant to states and localities. This argues for a more active but less programmatic
federal role in education.

States are increasingly failing to reach their revenue targets as a result
of the slowing economy. The reforms of the ESEA legislation, especially the
testing requirements, will require an expenditure of state resources on issues
that aren't tied directly to the day-to-day provision of education. In a tight
fiscal climate, testing and accountability initiatives will be curtailed or put on
hold before direct services. It's up to Washington to help see that states aren't
forced to make this choice. It is also essential that funding for interventions in
low-performing schools accompany the new requirements. President Clinton

inaugurated an accountability fund as part of Title I as a way to focus resources specifically on this purpose. However, more money will not provide a solution without enforcing clear goals for results.

There must also be a greater emphasis on getting these new resources to underserved communities. Funds must be concentrated rather than spread as far and wide as possible for political advantage. Democratic senator Mary Landrieu, a cosponsor of the "Three R's" bill, worked tirelessly, and against considerable opposition from members of both political parties, to increase the targeting of federal education dollars to low-income communities and schools in an effort to better support their school reform efforts.

Unfortunately, this legislation does not do enough to define the federal role in terms of consolidating programs and increasing local flexibility to meet diverse circumstances. The law includes flexibility provisions and some stream-lining that are improvements. However, if raising overall test-score performance and addressing the achievement gap are to be the main focus of federal policy, it is foolish to have a panoply of programs that direct state and local officials toward a host of other priorities, distracting them from their core mission.

Someone must enforce the new rules if they are to be workable. Washington will encounter resistance at both the federal and state levels. As Senator Bayh of Indiana aptly told the *Los Angeles Times* in the midst of the debate, "Everyone is for accountability until it actually gets put into place and applies to them." Washington has a dismal record of enforcing its dictates in education. Of course, considering some of those dictates, sometimes this is a blessing. But one lesson of the 1994 reforms is that without enforcement states will simply ignore or delay parts of federal education laws they don't like. Tightening and clarifying the accountability provisions and then failing to enforce them only means states will be ignoring a new set of requirements. That's not much of an improvement on the status quo.

It's worth remembering that an army of naysayers predicting adverse consequences, or at best futility, has accompanied every major federal policy shift in education. However, the positive impact of accountability systems, particularly for the poor and minority students who traditionally have been excluded from educational opportunities, outweighs the risks. Mistakes will be made, lessons will be learned, policies will be fine-tuned. But we shouldn't delay the good while waiting for the perfect.

Schoolhouse Crock

My son Jacob will be 5 years old this summer, and I have had to face every parent's nightmare of discovering where and how to register him for kindergarten. As the director of an education policy program at a national think tank, I imagined that I had an advantage over the average parent. After all, my job is to evaluate charter schools and tax credits, public school choice and private school voucher programs, homeschooling efforts and privatized school management. Additionally, I am a member of a Los Angeles urban school improvement committee. Finding an acceptable school for my child, I assumed, shouldn't be difficult.

But my confidence began to wane when I started to explore the Web site for our neighborhood school, El Cerrito Elementary, in Corona, California. My heart sank as I reviewed test results and realized that the school to which my son is assigned does not have a Stanford 9 score above the 50th percentile. The Stanford 9 is a standardized test widely used by schools across the country to track educational achievement. El Cerrito Elementary's score is not that low by California's standards, but who wants to send her child to a below-average school?

I still held out the hope that I would be able to exercise some limited degree of school choice by enrolling my son in a quality public school. The school district had allowed the developer of a middle-class housing tract down the hill and across the freeway from my home to erect a brand new school. By doing so, the developer bypassed the normal per-dwelling school tax and finished building this state-of-the-art facility in less than one year. The new school, Woodrow Wilson Elementary, is even a little closer to my house (I live in a semi-rural area of Riverside County) than the "neighborhood" school that requires my son to ride the bus for 45 minutes each way.

Armed with this knowledge, I naively contacted the Corona-Norco Unified School District's "central registration" office to request an intra-district school transfer. A procedure I expected to be simple and direct turned out to be almost impossible. Presumably to discourage requests like mine, the district only accepts transfer applications one week per year, from the 1st to the 7th of December. The polite voice at the other end of the phone informed me that I would be welcome to apply in December for the following year.

Like millions of other parents stuck with low-performing public schools, my only options are relocation, home-schooling, or, given the decisive failure of the California school choice initiative last fall, investment of a small fortune in private school tuition.

What's more depressing is that there is no relief in sight. President Bush's widely touted education reform plan—which has earned him kudos on the right and attacks on the left—will have minimal impact on American schools and will do little or nothing to improve education for the average kid. That's because the Bush plan deals almost exclusively with Title I, the major federal education program, which is designed to improve schooling for at-risk students. On paper, zeroing in on Title I, widely considered a colossal failure, makes sense. Ninety percent of America's school districts—some 23,000 schools nationwide—receive grants under the program. But the Bush plan's focus is misguided and diverts attention from more sweeping education reform that would help more parents provide their children with a quality education.

What Is Title I?

In 1965, President Lyndon Johnson established Title I of the Elementary and Secondary Education Act as part of his Great Society program. The lofty goal of Title I has been to improve the basic and advanced skills of students who are at risk of failing in school. In particular, the program is designed to assist low-achieving children living in low-income areas where school funding is deemed to be inadequate. At $9 billion a year, Title I is the largest program of federal aid for elementary and secondary education. The money is used mostly to provide intensive math and reading instruction.

In Title I's 36-year history, the U.S. Department of Education has released two major longitudinal studies on the program's effectiveness: *Sustaining Effects* in 1984 and *Prospects* in 1997. The *Sustaining Effects* study demonstrated that the $40 billion spent on the program to that point had done little to improve the achievement of the children it was designed to help. Although the elementary school students showed slight gains over their peers, "By the time students reached junior high school, there was no evidence of sustained or delayed effects of Title I," wrote Launer R. Carter, director of the study, in *Educational Researcher*.

Thirteen years later, the most recent longitudinal study of the program found that even after the federal government spent another $78 billion (from 1984 to 1997), bringing the total spent on Title I to $118 billion, little had changed. "After controlling for student, family, and school differences between participants and non-participants, we still find that participants score lower than non-participants and that this gap in achievement is not closed over time," the authors of the *Prospects* study wrote.

Researchers could not discern any long-term achievement gains directly linked to the Title I program. The program tries to identify and serve the children who need the most help, but according to the study, "The services appear to be insufficient to allow them to overcome the relatively large differences between them and their more-advantaged classmates." Similarly, Wayne Riddle, an education analyst at the federal government's Congressional Research Service, analyzed the two federal longitudinal studies and five other Title I studies. His conclusion: "Title I participants tend to increase their achievement levels at the same rate as non-disadvantaged pupils, so gaps in achievement do not significantly change."

In 1999, the U.S. Department of Education released a congressionally mandated evaluation of Title I that seemed to show, based on results from the 1998 National Assessment of Educational Progress (NAEP), that the 1994 reauthorization of Title I had led to some increases in student achievement due to program reforms. The NAEP tests a sample of fourth-graders, eighth-graders, and 12th-graders from 40 states in writing, science, math, and reading. The test is considered the "nation's school report card" and is widely viewed as an independent measurement of public school achievement. The 1998 NAEP results initially appeared to show significant improvements in fourth-grade reading scores in nine states since 1994.

The progress reported in this study was largely fictitious, however. A skeptical parent in Kentucky, Richard Innes, discovered a problem with the 1998 NAEP reading scores. According to the official results, Kentucky was one of the most improved states in fourth-grade reading. But using data gleaned from the Internet, Innes discovered that the gains in some states, including Kentucky, resulted from the exclusion of students considered to be slow learners and those with learning disabilities. Innes asked this critical question: Can a state's scores be accurate when they don't include large numbers of low-scoring students? An analysis by the U.S. Department of Education confirmed that several states had inflated average reading scores by excluding greater numbers of special-education students from testing in 1998 than in 1994. The federal analysis established that more than half of the 36 states where the NAEP is administered had excluded significantly larger numbers of special-education students in 1998. Five states excluded substantially more non-English-speaking students than they had in 1994.

For example, Kentucky dumped test results for 10 percent of the students who were selected for its 1998 sample, compared with 4 percent in 1994. Louisiana ignored 13 percent in 1998, up from 6 percent in 1994. And Connecticut, the nation's highest-scoring state, removed 10 percent of the students selected to participate, compared with 6 percent in 1994. Not surprisingly, states with larger increases in total exclusions also tended to have larger score increases. When the test scores were compared on a realistic basis, Kentucky gained nothing.

Despite these flaws, the Department of Education's 1999 report showing student improvement from 1994 was widely cited in the education press and the general media. Incredibly, the Department of Education's own investigation into special education exclusions was never made public. I only discovered it accidentally when researching congressional testimony regarding the effectiveness of Title I.

The most recent results of the 2000 NAEP tests for fourth-grade reading paint a bleak picture for Title I: 63 percent of black fourth-graders, 58 percent of Hispanics, 47 percent of urban students, and 60 percent of poor children scored below "basic" in reading—which for all practical purposes means they cannot read.

Why Bush's Plan Won't Work

President Bush has proposed to increase the Department of Education's budget by 11 percent, to $44.5 billion. Assuming his budget is passed as is, Title I, which continues to be the largest single item in the federal education budget, would spend approximately $10 billion for a program that has consistently failed to produce any measurable results for close to four decades. (Democrats are pushing to boost Title I spending to $18 billion.) By comparison, charter schools in Bush's budget would receive around $175 million for start-up and facility costs.

The central component of the Bush plan would overhaul the Title I program for disadvantaged students by requiring states to develop systems of rewards and penalties to hold districts and students accountable for academic progress. Specifically, states would be required to test all students in grades three through eight in reading and mathematics every year, as a condition of receiving federal Title I aid. In a nod to federalism, Bush would not institute a national curriculum and would allow individual states to design their own diagnostic tests.

A voucher sanction in Bush's original plan has evolved, through the legislative process, into a $600 tutoring credit. It would allow parents at failing schools that do not make "adequate yearly progress" for three consecutive years to pay for extra reading and math instruction for their child.

That's not much help. But there's a bigger problem with the Bush plan: The current focus on failing Title I schools ignores the grim reality that many schools that have not been designated as failures are still not the kinds of places that most parents want to send their children. To fully appreciate this phenomenon, it is important to consider exactly how dysfunctional a school must become before it is designated a "failure."

Individual states vary widely in how they define what constitutes a "failing" school. Many states have set standards that deem a school's performance adequate even if less than half of its students meet state standards for proficiency. At least eight states have set their standard at or around the 40th percentile, and a few have set the standard even lower. In Alabama, for example, more than half of a school's students must score below the 38th percentile for the school to be put on an intervention track, and more than half must score below the 23rd percentile to immediately target a school for improvement efforts.

To appreciate how most schools escape the "failure" label, one must understand the notion of "adequate yearly progress" (AYP) and how it is measured. AYP is determined at the state level and is tied to meeting performance goals and state standards.

Some states require schools to meet an absolute target or performance threshold. In the president's home state of Texas, for example, a rating of "acceptable" means that at least 50 percent of students at a given school must pass the state assessment in reading, writing, and math. The 50 percent standard doesn't address the obvious: Do the parents of the 50 percent of students who did not pass the Texas Assessment of Academic Skills find this level of achievement to be "acceptable"? Such a low standard means that less than 1 percent of Title I schools in Texas are labeled as failures.

California schools must improve every year by 5 percent of the difference between their academic performance index and the state's performance target of 800. The formula is complex and is based on student scores on the Stanford 9 test. The bottom line is that in order to show AYP, my local school must gain a few percentage points each year on a standardized test.

Assuming that the school can actually achieve the mandated minimums each year, it could be two decades before my local school meets the state target score of 800. In effect, the state and the school district are willing to sacrifice the minds of the children who will be forced to attend this school over the course of the next 20 years while the school struggles to meet minimum AYP standards.

The real failures of El Cerrito Elementary, which can stand in for many schools across the country, become increasingly apparent when actual improvements in reading scores on the Stanford 9 test are considered. In 1998, the average second-grade test scores at El Cerrito Elementary were at the 36th percentile. By 2000, average second-grade reading scores jumped to the 38th percentile. A similar small improvement in achievement has occurred for the other grades at El Cerrito Elementary.

As a parent, perhaps I should be proud of the progress my local school is making. Instead, I am shocked that the school's accepted rate of yearly academic progress could mean that my son will spend his six years of elementary school at an institution that will not come close to meeting California's statewide target goal of 800 by the end of his tenure there.

Why Vouchers Hardly Mattered

Even if the voucher component of Bush's plan had not died in Congress, it would have had little impact on parents who are stuck with low-performing schools. President Bush's plan mirrored Florida Gov. Jeb Bush's A-Plus education program, so the Florida plan is instructive as a model of how the president's plan would likely work over time. By offering vouchers to students at failing schools, the Florida plan is intended to motivate those schools to improve their academic performance. Each public school in Florida is assigned a grade, from A through F, based on the proportion of its students earning a passing grade on the Florida Comprehensive Assessment Test (FCAT). Students attending schools that receive two F grades in four years are eligible to attend a private school or to transfer to another public school.

In practice, few Florida students have actually received the promised vouchers. In the first year that students were eligible to receive vouchers under the program, a total of 53 students from two schools statewide got tickets to go elsewhere. In 1999, there were 78 public schools that received a failing grade based on their FCAT scores. If those schools got the same grades in 2000, they would have been sanctioned with vouchers. Miraculously, by year two of the A-Plus program, every school in Florida (including the 78 schools that had a failing grade the year before) managed to pull test scores up enough to avoid the voucher sanction.

Apparently, the public school establishment in Florida sensed an end to their monopoly and reacted accordingly. Dr. Jay P. Greene, an education researcher at the Manhattan Institute, recently analyzed FCAT test scores covering the initial two years of the A-Plus program. He found that "schools that received F grades in 1998–1999 experienced increases in test scores that were more than twice as large as those experienced by schools with higher state grades."

All of this suggests that the public school establishment will react to the threat of a club, particularly the voucher sanction. But, beyond the minimal threshold of sanction, inertia seems to set in. The never-mentioned tragedy is the fact that, despite improvement, hundreds of thousands of students are still attending inferior schools.

Imagine the frustration of Florida parents with children in those mediocre schools who are now denied the opportunity of a real education for their children simply because an 18-point improvement earned a formerly failing school a D grade? The average failing school did improve but still showed an average score of only 272 out of a possible 500 points. That is the effective equivalent of a doctor being wrong in her diagnosis almost as often as she is correct. Will it soothe those parents to know that President Bush plans to continue with Title I spending of $10 billion a year to ensure that their failing local school, and others like it around the nation, will improve from 50 percent of students failing a standardized test to 47 percent failing the same standardized test? Will they rest easy knowing that average reading test scores will possibly improve from the 39th percentile to the 42nd? Will such results persuade inner-city parents, and all parents for that matter, that truly robust school choice is not a necessary option in the United States?

Failing History

President Bush's proposed program is just the latest attempt to fix Title I. The program has been reformed several times over the last 30 years. Completely absent from the reform debate are the Department of Education's own Title I program evaluations, which demonstrate that after spending more than $150 billion, the program has not improved achievement for disadvantaged students.

Aside from that, education reform is so focused on poorly performing schools and students that education for average and above-average students doesn't even make it to the radar screen. Even if the purest form of Bush's education plan was implemented and the sanctions were enforced, most schools will still be mediocre and most parents will still have few options between their state-mandated public school or paying private school tuition on top of public school taxes.

Real education reform would give parents a way to find a better quality education *now*, instead of waiting years for their failing or simply mediocre public school to improve. Until the federal government allows real education reforms—such as universal tax credits or actual vouchers that are at least equal to the federal portion of per-pupil spending—it will have little impact on the educational experience of students who need better schools while they're still in school.

Meanwhile, the rest of us are supposed to settle for the status quo because El Cerrito Elementary School and others like it around the nation can claim they have made adequate yearly progress (second-grade reading scores average in the 42nd percentile instead of the 38th!). My son Jacob would still be forced to attend a school that is not considered failing even though reading scores average well below the 50th percentile. For most parents and students, whether eligible for Title I or not, the Bush plan is, at best, too little, too late.

POSTSCRIPT

Can Federal Initiatives Rescue Failing Schools?

> The history of struggles over schooling suggests that to make individual learning a subject of political conflict weakens the participation of individuals in their own education, reduces the professionalism of teaching, and undermines intellectual and cultural diversity.

So said Stephen Arons in his article "Constitutional Implications of National Curriculum Standards," *The Educational Forum* (Summer 1994). Similarly, James Moffett argued in his book *The Universal Schoolhouse* (1994) that political and economic considerations are obscuring practical knowledge about how to improve learning in the schools. These sentiments also flow through some of the concern over President George W. Bush's ideas on education reform. Some critics see a future progression from strict accountability to nationwide voucher plans to diversion of public funds to private schools. Michael C. Milam, in "G. W., the Privatization of Education, and American Values," *The Humanist* (May/June 2001), for example, states that "the implications of an expanded or even totally private educational system are awesome and contradict the spirit of the fundamental ideals upon which the U.S. was founded. Public schools dedicated to equal opportunity, where children study free of denominational bias and corporate influence and among fellow students representing a variety of religious and ethnic backgrounds, are essential for a democratic society based upon pluralism and tolerance."

Further questions about the federal role in school improvement are expressed in Stephen Metcalf, "Numbers Racket: W. and the Uses of Testing," *The New Republic* (February 12, 2001); Thomas Toch, "An Education Plan With the Right Goal, Wrong Yardstick," *The Washington Post* (November 18, 2001); Beverly Falk, "Standards-Based Reforms: Problems and Possibilities," *Phi Delta Kappan* (April 2002); and Juan Necochea and Zulmara Cline, "School Reform Without a Heart," *Kappa Delta Pi Record* (Spring 2002). A somewhat different take on the issue is presented by education reporter Jay Matthews in "The Best Thing About Reform: It Won't Matter," *The Washington Post* (February 17, 2002).

In light of all the concern over wasted federal money, underfunded mandates, and anxiety-producing state testing programs, perhaps Rosetta Marantz Cohen has a good idea. In "Schools Our Teachers Deserve: A Proposal for Teacher-Centered Reform," *Phi Delta Kappan* (March 2002), she suggests putting teacher morale first in any reform efforts, offering sabbaticals, involving teachers in the evaluation process, making tenure mean something, and reallocating the use of time.

ISSUE 9

Do High-Stakes Assessments Improve Learning?

YES: Nina Hurwitz and Sol Hurwitz, from "Tests That Count," *American School Board Journal* (January 2000)

NO: Martin G. Brooks and Jacqueline Grennon Brooks, from "The Courage to Be Constructivist," *Educational Leadership* (November 1999)

ISSUE SUMMARY

YES: High school teacher Nina Hurwitz and education consultant Sol Hurwitz assemble evidence from states that are leading the movement to set high standards of educational performance and cautiously conclude that it could stimulate long-overdue renewal.

NO: High school superintendent Martin G. Brooks and associate professor of education Jacqueline Grennon Brooks contend that the push for standardized state assessments constricts student learning and prevents implementation of constructivism.

In the 1980s a number of national reports found America's public schools to be seriously lacking in the production of students who were qualified to compete successfully in the emerging global economy. Among these reports were the National Commission on Excellence in Education's *A Nation at Risk,* the Education Commission of the States' *Action for Excellence,* the Twentieth Century Fund's *Making the Grade,* and the National Science Foundation's *Educating Americans for the Twenty-First Century.* In response to these calls for higher standards, the Bush administration adopted the following national goals in its "America 2000" plan: all children starting school prepared to learn, at least 90 percent of students graduating from high school, all students being able to cope with challenging subject matter (particularly math and science), all adults being literate and responsible citizens, and all graduates being able to compete in a global economy.

To move toward these goals the Republican administration emphasized more choice and competition, more influence from business leaders, and the development of nationwide curriculum standards and testing programs. The Clinton administration adopted the goals, renaming them "Goals 2000: Educate America," but downplayed the role of the private sector and placed responsibility for assessing student progress on the individual states. The George W. Bush administration, while backing away from privatization and voucher issues, has strengthened the call for accountability and rigorous testing.

To date, many states have risen to the challenge, imposing statewide standardized tests of subject matter and mental skills. In some cases, states have set up procedures for taking over the administration of chronically underperforming local schools. In others, schools that dramatically increase student performance are rewarded in some tangible way.

Peter Sacks, in *Standardized Minds: The High Price of America's Testing Culture and What We Can Do to Change It* (1999), contends that "the case against standardized testing is as intellectually and ethically rigorous as any argument about social policy . . . and yet such testing continues to dominate the education system, carving further inroads into the employment arena as well." He further warns that "when thinking becomes standardized people are easily objectified, their skills and talents translated into the language and mechanisms of commercial enterprise." This sentiment is shared by Alfie Kohn, who, in "Unlearning How We Learn," *Principal* (March 2000), says that "raising standards has come to mean little more than higher scores on poorly-designed standardized tests," leading to abandonment of the best kind of teaching and learning.

This central concern about the direct impact of test mania on the nature of the learning process has been widely voiced by educators who advocate instructional approaches based on the theory of constructivism. Drawn from the thinking of John Dewey, Jean Piaget, Lev Vygotsky, Howard Gardner, and others, constructivism views learning as an active, group-oriented process in which students "construct" an understanding of knowledge utilized in problem-solving situations. Such sense-making activities can be time-consuming and therefore can get in the way of teachers and schools whose primary focus is on test performance. Applications of the theory are explained in Mark Windschitl's "The Challenges of Sustaining a Constructivist Classroom Culture," *Phi Delta Kappan* (June 1999).

Those who see the standards and testing movement as the clearest path to school improvement include Joan L. Herman, "The State of Performance Assessments," *The School Administrator* (December 1998); Jerry Jesness, "Why Johnny Can't Fail: How the 'Floating Standard' Has Destroyed Public Education," *Reason* (July 1999); and Mike Schmoker, "The Results We Want," *Educational Leadership* (February 2000). These and other advocates feel that a standardized testing program ensures acquisition of basic skills, holds schools accountable for results, and identifies problem areas.

In the following selections, Nina Hurwitz and Sol Hurwitz examine experiences with high-stakes testing in Texas, Chicago, and New York in order to identify crucial elements of successful implementation, while Martin G. Brooks and Jacqueline Grennon Brooks argue that the central aim of improving student learning on a long-term basis is not well served by high-stakes accountability pressures.

Nina Hurwitz and Sol Hurwitz  **YES**

Tests That Count

They are tests that count, high-stakes tests that can deny promotion or graduation to students with failing scores. Schools with too many low-performing students can be exposed to the glare of publicity, placed on probation, or closed. A widening coalition of governors, business leaders, parents, and teachers—appalled that youngsters can advance through school, receive a diploma, and seek further education or a job without mastering basic skills—is promoting the use of these tests as a means of boosting standards and improving accountability in public education.

The movement is gaining national momentum. Forty-nine states have adopted performance standards for elementary and secondary education; 26 have high school exit exams in place or in process; 19 publicly identify failing schools. President Clinton is in the vanguard, calling for higher standards and a crackdown on social promotion. Last fall he urged the nation's governors, "Look dead in the eye some child who has been held back [and say], 'We'll be hurting you worse if we tell you you're learning something when you're not.' "

High Standards, High Stakes

High-stakes testing is forcing the debate over a fundamental question in American education—whether it is possible to achieve both excellence and equity. On one side are those who claim that tests with consequences are the only sure route to higher standards and stricter accountability. On the other are those who contend that high-stakes tests are a command-and-control instrument for "standardizing" education and punishing disadvantaged and minority children. But a more pragmatic middle position is evolving based on the experience of front-line practitioners: High-stakes testing can work with clear but limited goals, flexibility in meeting those goals, and the will to address head-on the problems of students at risk of failure.

Texas, Chicago, and New York City and state, discussed below, are being carefully watched by educators and decision makers nationwide for both positive and negative lessons. The states are driving the high-stakes movement: Kentucky, Maryland, Massachusetts, North Carolina, and Virginia are running noteworthy programs as well.

Even as states and school districts attempt to raise standards and impose high-stakes tests, they are confronted with excessive numbers of their urban, minority, and disadvantaged students who are failing these tests. In urban districts, large-scale failure is inevitable, says *Education Week*'s Ron Wolk, given the shoddy education these students are receiving. "For tens of thousands of urban youngsters, it's a kind of double jeopardy," Wolk declares. "The system failed to educate them adequately, and now it punishes them for not being educated." Schools and school districts might face punishment as well: Low scores could result in the reorganization of schools or a shift of resources to charter schools or private-school vouchers.

Parent advocacy and civil rights groups are challenging the tests on racial and equity grounds. The penalties, they claim, fall disproportionately on minority and at-risk students, who have been shortchanged in their education. Meanwhile, teachers and researchers are beginning to question the tests' educational validity: Do they, in fact, improve learning?

Educators are unanimous that high-stakes tests should be aligned with curriculum and instruction—they should measure what students have been taught and are expected to know—and that teachers should be involved in the process. But only gradually are states and school districts committing sufficient resources and time to achieve proper alignment with full teacher participation. The time lag, educators argue, makes it risky to impose consequences prematurely.

Disagreement between states and urban school districts over which test to use means students in the same grade might have to take two tests—in the same subject. Learning suffers, educators say, when teachers spend time preparing students for too many tests. "The first thing to go in a school or district where these tests matter," says education expert Alfie Kohn, "is a more vibrant, integrated, active, and effective kind of instruction." [See "Raising the Scores, Ruining the Schools," *ASBJ*, October 1999.] A fifth-grade teacher in Virginia concurs: "Sometimes, when I wish I could stay longer on a subject, I have to move on to prepare my kids for the tests."

A 1999 study titled *High Stakes* by the prestigious National Research Council sharply criticized the practice of relying solely on tests to determine promotion or graduation. Such decisions, the council argued, "should be buttressed by other relevant information about the student's knowledge and skills, such as grades, teacher recommendations, and extenuating circumstances." Many educators question the value of holding kids back *period*—but certainly not without a highly structured, and often costly, intervention and remediation strategy.

The growing public demand for standards with accountability has made high-stakes testing a tempting political issue. The public is fed up with low standards and courses that lack content—they want American students to be able to compete favorably with kids in other countries. Test scores provide an aura of businesslike accountability for superintendents, principals, and teachers and a stimulus for students. Initially, at least, testing seems easy and inexpensive compared with more deep-seated reforms such as hiring and training competent teachers, reducing class size, or repairing crumbling school buildings. But achieving accountability is neither simple nor cheap.

The states and school districts that have had the most success with high-stakes testing share several common characteristics. They have maintained bipartisan political support and the backing of a broad coalition of interest groups, including the business community, over a sustained period. High-stakes tests have not only raised standards but have stimulated systemwide reform. Most important, there has been a heavy investment in addressing the academic performance of the weakest students.

Turnaround in Texas

Texas is a dramatic case in point. Once considered one of the nation's educational backwaters, the Texas public school system, according to the *New York Times,* is now viewed by educators as "a model of equity, progress and accountability." The state's education reforms have spanned the administrations of former Democratic governor Ann W. Richards and current Republican governor and presidential hopeful George W. Bush. In a system of 3.7 million students that is half African American and Hispanic, the scores of African-American and Hispanic students on national assessments in reading and mathematics in 1996 and 1998 outranked those of most other states, and scores on state assessments for all students have risen for the fourth straight year.

A unique feature of the Texas system is the Texas Assessment of Academic Skills (TAAS), the state's high-stakes exam program, introduced in 1990. The tests combine clearly stated educational standards with a detailed reporting of results by ethnicity and class. Scores are sorted according to white, African-American, Hispanic, and economically disadvantaged groups. Along with attendance and dropout rates, TAAS scores are used to identify a school as failing if any one of its four demographic cohorts falls below standard. "Disaggregation of scores has focused the schools' attention on kids that were once ignored," according to University of Texas professor Uri Treisman, who is director of the Charles A. Dana Center in Austin. Texas is gradually raising the passing bar to 50 percent for each cohort from the original 20 percent.

Until recently, the high stakes associated with the TAAS have consisted almost entirely of public disclosure of school-by-school test results, a process Gov. Bush calls "shining a spotlight of shame on failure." The ratings, published on the web, identify schools as exemplary, recognized, acceptable, or low-performing and provide strong incentives to improve for adults and students alike. For example, superintendents, principals, and teachers find it hard to get jobs if they come from failing schools. Although low-performing schools are bolstered by additional financial support, they are rarely closed. "There are no great ideas on what to do with really problematical schools," says Treisman.

Elementary and middle-school students are tested in grades three through eight on various combinations of reading, writing, and mathematics, with science and social studies added in the eighth grade. In response to political pressure, Texas will move to end social promotion by 2003. Hoping to avoid widespread retention, the state has instituted the Student Success Initiative, an early-intervention program, starting with the current year's kindergarten class. A skeptic on retention, Treisman cautions that research on the dropout problem indicates that "being overage in your class has the single highest correlation for dropping out and is twice as high as for any other factor, including race." Also, as pressure mounts to pass the TAAS, state officials have become increasingly concerned over outbreaks of alleged cheating.

There is wide agreement that Texas high schools have not shown as much improvement as elementary schools. However, the state plans to beef up the content of the 10th-grade exit exam and move it to the 11th grade and to allow substitution of end-of-course exams in core subjects. The present 10th-grade exam is the subject of a lawsuit by the Mexican-American Legal Defense Fund in the U.S. District Court in San Antonio, which claims the test discriminates against minority students. Gov. Bush counters this claim: "Some say it is a racist test," he told the *New York Times* [recently]. "I strongly say it is racist not to test because by not testing we don't know, and by not knowing we are just moving children through the system." The outcome is sure to have an impact on other states, researchers agree.

Remarkably, the state's educational resurgence has occurred while expenditures remained below the national average: In 1998–99, Texas spent $5,488 per student compared with the national average of $6,407. Striking, too, is the autonomy that Texas gives its principals and teachers as long as test results remain positive. Bilingual education, for example, is a local option. However, scores for Spanish-speaking and special education students must now be included in overall ratings to ensure more accurate results.

Success in Chicago

Just as Texas has drawn raves for educational attainment at the state level, Chicago, with an enrollment of 431,000 students, has become the promised land for city reformers. Mayors, superintendents, and educators have flocked there to study the remarkable turnaround orchestrated by chief executive officer Paul Vallas, formerly budget director under Mayor Richard M. Daley. With no previous experience in education, Vallas has performed what many consider an educational miracle in a school district that U.S. Secretary of Education William J. Bennett in 1987 called "the worst in the country." Vallas achieved credibility largely through the selective but determined application of high-stakes testing. Scores on Chicago's performance benchmark, the Iowa Test of Basic Skills in Reading and Mathematics, have risen for the fourth straight year.

When Vallas took charge in 1995, an earlier reform effort, which stressed decision making by local school councils, had virtually hit bottom. With high truancy, low standards, and rampant grade inflation, Vallas declared, "there was wide agreement that the earlier reform initiative had failed." Vallas exploited public dissatisfaction with the previous reform, while drawing grassroots support from a network of parents, community groups, foundations, and universities to fashion a new strategy.

Fundamental to his success was the solid backing of Mayor Daley and Gery Chico, president of the Chicago School Reform Board (successor to the former elected school board), whose members were all mayoral appointees. Vallas forged a close working relationship with Tom Reece, who heads both the

Chicago Teachers Union and the Illinois Federation of Teachers, and together they have succeeded in avoiding strikes and confrontations by building communication and trust. In addition, he won points with the public for his skills as a financial manager by stamping out waste, ending deficits, and securing state funds for building and renovating schools.

Three years ago, Chicago gained national attention as the first big-city school system to end social promotion. Students who don't meet minimum standards on the Iowa Tests are at risk of retention, but the passing bar was set low at first to avoid massive failure and is only gradually being raised.

Chicago's promotion gates kick in for students in grades three, six, and eight. For those who fail, the city's mandatory Summer Bridge Program, staffed with experienced teachers, provides a scripted curriculum from the central administration with hour-by-hour guidelines. University of Chicago professor Melissa Roderick, a member of the Consortium on Chicago School Research, believes the program goads parents, students, and teachers to work harder to avoid retention. "Students love Summer Bridge," says Roderick, because they know it helps them. Of the estimated 25,000 students who attended summer school last year, two-thirds moved to the next grade. Chicagoans call the policy "retention plus" because it comes front-loaded with ample resources for intervention and remediation. "Retention is a last resort," Vallas maintains.

Chicago also provides tutoring during school, and in an after-school Lighthouse Program (with supper included), for students who fail. Cozette Buckney, the system's chief education officer, shares the prevailing view of education experts that students should not merely repeat the same curriculum once they are held back. "You must teach them differently, use different materials—give them a different experience," she says.

Finally, if students have not passed the eighth-grade test by age 15, they move to "academic prep centers" that offer small transitional classes and intensive test preparation, where expenditures per pupil are one-and-a-half times those for high schools. Most students move on to high school after one year, although some teachers believe the centers accentuate problems of self-esteem and increase the tendency to drop out.

So dazzling is Chicago's success in the lower grades that outside observers have hardly noticed that real achievement stops at the high school door. "In the high schools, we have been at a loss," Buckney admits. Standards remain low, and there is widespread disengagement of students, a weak curriculum, and meager support services. Half of the city's ninth-graders fail two or more courses.

The Chicago Academic Standards Exams (CASE), which are end-of-semester high school tests in core subjects, are currently being upgraded. Teachers now receive detailed content guides from the administration but complain about the rigidity that the guides impose on their teaching. Although most teachers allow the exams to count for only 15 percent of the semester grade, a biology teacher contends that "the tests shape what I teach, what order I teach in, and how long I spend on each subject."

High school teachers have been more resistant to control from the central office than elementary school teachers, according to Vallas. "They view themselves as college professors—they're more set in their ways," he complains. Last year George Schmidt, an activist teacher, published parts of the CASE tests in protest, and students at top-rated Whitney Young High School boycotted the tests. Vallas dismisses such opposition, saying, "There is enough to be irritating but not enough to delay reform."

Recent efforts to close down and reconstitute Chicago's worst high schools have proved unsuccessful, and discharging low-performing administrators and teachers has been difficult. "The burden of proof [on the school administration] in removing failing teachers is pretty strong," Vallas admits.

Vallas is seeking to garner support for Chicago's high-stakes tests by allowing waivers and retesting. He is also identifying at-risk students early and conducting special programs for pregnant teens and teen mothers. "Good attendance, behavior, and grades" can help students get promoted, he says. The time will come, he predicts, when tests will become a diminishing factor in promotion decisions.

Disappointment in New York

Chicago's success in strengthening standards and ending social promotion in the early grades contrasts sharply with New York City's recent dismal experience with high-stakes testing. New York's gigantic scale—it is the nation's largest school system with 1.1 million students—and the fractured relationship between the schools chancellor and the mayor have vastly complicated attempts to impose high stakes on state and city tests. Unlike Chicago, where Paul Vallas and Mayor Daley work in blissful harmony, New York City's Schools Chancellor Rudy Crew has recently been at loggerheads with Mayor Rudolph W. Giuliani.

High-stakes testing [has been brought] to the boiling point. After months of cramming and intense pressure on students, teachers, and parents, the news came in May [1999] that 67 percent of New York City students had failed the state's new and more demanding fourth-grade language arts test. The test was given over three days and included passages to be read for comprehension and answered in essay form. Stunned by the low test scores, the mayor proposed the removal of principals from the bottom third of all city elementary schools and called for a major management shake-up. State Education Commissioner Richard P. Mills recommended summer school for all students who failed the test.

Then came the disappointing results on year-end city tests, administered and graded by CTB/McGraw-Hill, which showed only 44.6 percent of students reading at grade level, a five-point decline from the previous year. Mathematics scores were even lower, falling 10 percent. After this second dose of bad news, the mayor prescribed even stronger medicine. Impressed by Chicago's example, he called for abolishing the semi-independent board of education and placing the schools under his own control.

After constant badgering from the mayor, Crew responded in mid-June with a hastily arranged mandatory summer-school program starting in July for 37,000 third-, sixth-, and eighth-graders who had scored at or below the 15th percentile on the city's standardized reading test and the 10th percentile on the mathematics test, both taken in the spring. Students failing the tests a second time would be held back.

The summer-school program was plagued with problems. For six weeks the schools were forced to cope with thousands of youngsters who needed to pass the city tests to avoid retention. Many teachers were handicapped by a lack of student records and by inadequate course materials, and school buildings were stifling from a record-setting heat wave. Although paid at a lower rate than their school-year salaries, many teachers had to buy their own materials and bring fans from home. In some instances, students who were supposed to take only the mathematics test were drilled mainly for the reading test.

Chancellor Crew's pride in announcing that 64 percent of the students passed the tests was soon dampened when scoring errors by CTB/McGraw-Hill revealed that more than 8,600 students were sent to summer school by mistake. Lack of accurate summer-school attendance figures cast further doubt on the number of students who would be retained. The Puerto Rican Legal Defense Fund and Advocates for Children, a nonprofit legal services organization, have threatened court challenges, citing late warning of the new requirement to attend summer school and the use of a single test to determine promotion.

New York City's problems are likely to be exacerbated by Commissioner Mills' determined belief in high-stakes testing as a means of raising standards for the state's high schools. In a program that is unique in the nation, Mills and the State Board of Regents are requiring that by 2003, all students will have to receive a passing grade of at least 65 percent on the state's tough new Regents examinations in five subjects—English, mathematics, science, global studies, and American history—before they can graduate. Currently less than a quarter of New York City students qualify for a Regents diploma.

Turning aside his critics, Mills contended in a [recent] *New York Times* interview that without high standards, "You simply decide in advance that some students don't have access to the good life. They don't have access to jobs, they don't have access to enriched curriculum and everything that goes with it."

Mills understood the need for a structured program of remediation and support for those who fail the Regents tests. To this end, he proposed a $900 million program targeted toward poor districts, but Gov. George E. Pataki's budget came nowhere near to providing that amount. . . . [S]tate lawmakers—under pressure from parents, teachers, and school administrators who feared widespread failure on the Regents tests—argued for scaling down requirements. In October a consortium of parents and educators at 35 New York City alternative high schools asked legislators to compel the Regents to exempt its students from the new English Regents exams. With public opposition rising, it is doubtful the Regents will have enough public support to sustain such an extensive testing program with such high stakes over the long term.

As the results of [the] more rigorous six-hour, two-day English Regents tests were being released, accusations of deceptive scoring on the essay questions began to surface. According to a Harlem high-school teacher, "I never would have given points in a regular class for the kind of answers we were getting on those essays."

Many teachers had never seen the state's new standards; nor had they been trained to teach courses to the level of the Regents' demands. "No business or military organization would do that kind of campaign without adequate training," Thomas Sobol, former state education commissioner, asserted at a meeting in Purchase, N.Y.... For New York City's students, the stakes are overwhelming and probably unrealistic.

Making High-Stakes Testing Work

High-stakes tests are transforming the education landscape, and lawmakers and educators are learning to navigate in uncharted terrain. Conditions and requirements vary state-by-state, and progress in meeting the new standards requires patience. But some early lessons can be drawn from states and school districts that are beginning to achieve success:

Make sure that learning—not testing—is the goal   "Are we teaching for testing or teaching for knowledge?" a senior administrator asks. Tests can be important in identifying weaknesses. But too much testing in too many subjects overwhelms teachers, drains resources from enriched educational programs, stifles creativity, and increases cheating.

Give disadvantaged students special assistance   High-stakes tests can be a powerful tool for raising standards for at-risk students, but only if resources are reallocated to schools that serve them. And the testing program must be held accountable for ensuring that the tests are reliable, fair, and free of cultural bias.

Set failure rates at a realistic level   Most schools lack the resources and capacity to absorb masses of failing students in after-school and summer-school remediation programs and to conduct programs for students who repeatedly fail. But setting failure rates too low damages credibility in the system's standards. The right balance will vary according to circumstances, but finding it is crucial.

Invest in a wide range of educational reforms—not just tests   Tests don't work in a vacuum but in an environment that supports systemwide reform. Tests should be part of a program that encourages early childhood education; the recruitment, training, and development of capable teachers; smaller class size; and safer buildings.

Make retention a last resort   Most studies show that retention does more harm than good. Frequent failure erodes self-confidence, and students who are retained have a higher probability of dropping out. If retention helps at all, it does so only when students are supported by innovative learning strategies. Decisions to deny promotion should not be based on a single test and should involve the teacher.

Use publicity to force improvement   School rankings draw attention to the weakest schools and can be used to drive decisions regarding school reform, reorganization, or closure. School officials have an obligation to interpret test results to the public consistently and accurately and to be forthright about problems in the system.

Focus on urban high schools   Tests can be effective in raising standards but only if problems of school climate are addressed. Expect high school exit exams to be challenged in the courts by minority groups. Excessive testing narrows curriculum choice, and the need for remediation may lead to de facto tracking and high dropout rates.

Prepare for the long haul   It is the rare state or school district that gets high-stakes testing right the first time. Success takes time and requires experimentation. Be ready to adapt, adjust, and compromise in order to achieve long-term success.

On balance, high-stakes tests that are well-designed and carefully administered appear to be working, at least in the lower grades. But if their benefits are oversold and their dangers ignored, disenchantment could lead to diminished support for public education. If, on the other hand, they call attention to failure and encourage strategies to ensure success, they could stimulate a long-overdue educational renewal for the nation's neediest students.

NO

**Martin G. Brooks and
Jacqueline Grennon Brooks**

The Courage to Be Constructivist

For years, the term *constructivism* appeared only in journals read primarily by philosophers, epistemologists, and psychologists. Nowadays, *constructivism* regularly appears in the teachers' manuals of textbook series, state education department curriculum frameworks, education reform literature, and education journals. Constructivism now has a face and a name in education.

A theory of learning that describes the central role that learners' ever-transforming mental schemes play in their cognitive growth, constructivism powerfully informs educational practice. Education, however, has deep roots in other theories of learning. This history constrains our capacity to embrace the central role of the learner in his or her own education. We must rethink the very foundations of schooling if we are to base our practice on our understandings of learners' needs.

One such foundational notion is that students will learn on demand. This bedrock belief is manifested in the traditional scope and sequence of a typical course of study and, more recently, in the new educational standards and assessments. This approach to schooling is grounded in the conviction that all students can and will learn the same material at the same time. For some students, this approach does indeed lead to the construction of knowledge. For others, however, it does not.

The people working directly with students are the ones who must adapt and adjust lessons on the basis of evolving needs. Constructivist educational practice cannot be realized without the classroom teacher's autonomous, on-going, professional judgment. State education departments could and should support good educational practice. But too often they do not.

Their major flaw is their focus on high-stakes accountability systems and the ramifications of that focus on teachers and students. Rather than set standards for professional practice and the development of local capacity to enhance student learning, many state education departments have placed even greater weight on the same managerial equation that has failed repeatedly in the past: State Standards = State Tests; State Test Results = Student Achievement; Student Achievement = Rewards and Punishments.

We are not suggesting that educators should not be held accountable for their students' learning. We believe that they should. Unfortunately, we are not holding our profession accountable for learning, only for achievement on high-stakes tests. As we have learned from years of National Assessment of Educational Progress research, equating lasting student learning with test results is folly.

The Emerging Research From Standards-Driven States

In recent years, many states have initiated comprehensive educational reform efforts. The systemic thinking that frames most standards-based reform efforts is delectably logical: Develop high standards for all students; align curriculum and instruction to these standards; construct assessments to measure whether all students are meeting the standards; equate test results with student learning; and reward schools whose students score well on the assessments and sanction schools whose students don't.

Predictably, this simple and linear approach to educational reform is sinking under the weight of its own flaws. It is too similar to earlier reform approaches, and it misses the point. Educational improvement is not accomplished through administrative or legislative mandate. It is accomplished through attention to the complicated, idiosyncratic, often paradoxical, and difficult to measure nature of learning.

A useful body of research is emerging from the states. With minor variations, the research indicates the following:

- Test scores are generally low on the first assessment relating to new standards. Virginia is an extreme example of this phenomenon: More than 95 percent of schools failed the state's first test. In New York, more than 50 percent of the state's 4th graders were deemed at risk of not graduating in 2007 after taking that state's new English language arts test in 1999.

- Failure, or the fear of failure, breeds success on subsequent tests. After the first administration of most state assessments, schools' scores rise because educators align curriculum closely with the assessments, and they focus classroom instruction directly on test-taking strategies.

- To increase the percentages of students passing the state assessments—and to keep schools off the states' lists of failing schools—local district spending on student remediation, student test-taking skills, and faculty preparation for the new assessments increases.

- Despite rising test scores in subsequent years, there is little or no evidence of increased student learning. A recent study by Kentucky's Office of Educational Accountability (Hambleton et al., 1995) suggests that test-score gains in that state are a function of students' increasing skills as test takers rather than evidence of increased learning.

When Tests Constrict Learning

Learning is a complex process through which learners constantly change their internally constructed understandings of how their worlds function. New information either transforms their current beliefs—or doesn't. The efficacy of the learning environment is a function of many complex factors, including curriculum, instructional methodology, student motivation, and student developmental readiness. Trying to capture this complexity on paper-and-pencil assessments severely limits knowledge and expression.

Inevitably, schools reduce the curriculum to only that which is covered on tests, and this constriction limits student learning. So, too, does the undeviating, one-size-fits-all approach to teaching and assessment in many states that have crowned accountability king. Requiring all students to take the same courses and pass the same tests may hold political capital for legislators and state-level educational policymakers, but it contravenes what years of painstaking research tells us about student learning. In discussing the inordinate amount of time and energy devoted to preparing students to take and pass high-stakes tests, Angaran (1999) writes

> Ironically, all this activity prepares them for hours of passivity. This extended amount of seat time flies in the face of what we know about how children learn. Unfortunately, it does not seem to matter. It is, after all, the Information Age. The quest for more information drives us forward. (P. 72)

We are not saying that student success on state assessments and classroom practices designed to foster understanding are inherently contradictory. Teaching in ways that nurture students' quests to resolve cognitive conflict and conquer academic challenges fosters the creative problem solving that most states seek. However, classroom practices designed to prepare students for tests clearly do not foster deep learning that students apply to new situations. Instead, these practices train students to mimic learning on tests.

Many school districts question the philosophical underpinnings of the dominant test-teach-test model of education and are searching for broader ways for students to demonstrate their knowledge. However, the accountability component of the standards movement has caused many districts to abandon performance-based assessment practices and refocus instead on preparing students for paper-and-pencil tests. The consequences for districts and their students are too great if they don't.

Constructivism in the Classroom

Learners control their learning. This simple truth lies at the heart of the constructivist approach to education.

As educators, we develop classroom practices and negotiate the curriculum to enhance the likelihood of student learning. But controlling what students learn is virtually impossible. The search for meaning takes a different route for each student. Even when educators structure classroom lessons and curriculums to ensure that all students learn the same concepts at the same time, each student still constructs his or her own unique meaning through his or her own cognitive processes. In other words, as educators we have great control over what we teach, but far less control over what students learn.

Shifting our priorities from ensuring that all students learn the same concepts to ensuring that we carefully analyze students' understandings to customize our teaching approaches is an essential step in educational reform that results in increased learning. Again, we must set standards for our own professional practice and free students from the anti-intellectual training that occurs under the banner of test preparation.

The search for understanding motivates students to learn. When students want to know more about an idea, a topic, or an entire discipline, they put more cognitive energy into classroom investigations and discussions and study more on their own. We have identified five central tenets of constructivism (Grennon Brooks & Brooks, 1993).

- First, constructivist teachers seek and value students' points of view. Knowing what students think about concepts helps teachers formulate classroom lessons and differentiate instruction on the basis of students' needs and interests.
- Second, constructivist teachers structure lessons to challenge students' suppositions. All students, whether they are 6 or 16 or 60, come to the classroom with life experiences that shape their views about how their worlds work. When educators permit students to construct knowledge that challenges their current suppositions, learning occurs. Only through asking students what they think they know and why they think they know it are we and they able to confront their suppositions.
- Third, constructivist teachers recognize that students must attach relevance to the curriculum. As students see relevance in their daily activities, their interest in learning grows.
- Fourth, constructivist teachers structure lessons around big ideas, not small bits of information. Exposing students to wholes first helps them determine the relevant parts as they refine their understandings of the wholes.
- Finally, constructivist teachers assess student learning in the context of daily classroom investigations, not as separate events. Students demonstrate their knowledge every day in a variety of ways. Defining understanding as only that which is capable of being measured by paper-and-pencil assessments administered under strict security perpetuates false and counterproductive myths about academia, intelligence, creativity, accountability, and knowledge.

Opportunities for Constructing Meaning

Recently, we visited a classroom in which a teacher asked 7th graders to reflect on a poem. The teacher began the lesson by asking the students to interpret the first two lines. One student volunteered that the lines evoked an image of a dream. "No," he was told, "that's not what the author meant." Another student said that the poem reminded her of a voyage at sea. The teacher reminded the student that she was supposed to be thinking about the first two lines of the poem, not the whole poem, and then told her that the poem was not about the sea. Looking out at the class, the teacher asked, "Anyone else?" No other student raised a hand.

In another classroom, a teacher asked 9th graders to ponder the effect of temperature on muscle movement. Students had ice, buckets of water, gauges for measuring finger-grip strength, and other items to help them consider the relationship. The teacher asked a few framing questions, stated rules for handling materials safely, and then gave the students time to design their experiments. He posed different questions to different groups of students, depending on their activities and the conclusions that they seemed to be drawing. He continually asked students to elaborate or posed contradictions to their responses, even when they were correct.

As the end of the period neared, the students shared initial findings about their investigations and offered working hypotheses about the relationship between muscle movement and temperature. Several students asked to return later that day to continue working on their experiments.

Let's consider these two lessons. In one case, the lesson was not conducive to students' constructing deeper meaning. In the other case, it was. The 7th grade teacher communicated to her students that there is one interpretation of the poem's meaning, that she knew it, and that only that interpretation was an acceptable response. The students' primary quest, then, was to figure out what the teacher thought of the poem.

The teacher spoke to her students in respectful tones, acknowledging each one by name and encouraging their responses. However, she politely and calmly rejected their ideas when they failed to conform to her views. She rejected one student's response as a misinterpretation. She dismissed another student's response because of a procedural error: The response focused on the whole poem, not on just the designated two lines.

After the teacher told these two students that they were wrong, none of the other students volunteered interpretations, even though the teacher encouraged more responses. The teacher then proceeded with the lesson by telling the students what the poet really meant. Because only two students offered comments during the lesson, the teacher told us that a separate test would inform her whether the other students understood the poem.

In the second lesson, the teacher withheld his thoughts intentionally to challenge students to develop their own hypotheses. Even when students' initial responses were correct, the teacher challenged their thinking, causing many students to question the correctness of their initial responses and to investigate the issue more deeply.

Very few students had awakened that morning thinking about the relationship between muscle movement and temperature. But, as the teacher helped students focus their emerging, somewhat disjointed musings into a structured investigation, their engagement grew. The teacher provoked the students to search for relevance in a relationship they hadn't yet considered by framing the investigation around one big concept, providing appropriate materials and general questions, and helping the students think through their own questions. Moreover, the teacher sought and valued his students' points of view and used their comments to assess their learning. No separate testing event was required.

What Constructivism Is and Isn't

As constructivism has gained support as an educational approach, two main criticisms have emerged. One critique of constructivism is that it is overly permissive. This critique suggests that constructivist teachers often abandon their curriculums to pursue the whims of their students. If, for example, most of the students in the aforementioned 9th grade science class wished to discuss the relationship between physical exercise and muscle movement rather than pursue the planned lesson, so be it. In math and science, critics are particularly concerned that teachers jettison basic information to permit students to think in overly broad mathematical and scientific terms.

The other critique of constructivist approaches to education is that they lack rigor. The concern here is that teachers cast aside the information, facts, and basic skills embedded in the curriculum—and necessary to pass high-stakes tests—in the pursuit of more capricious ideas. Critics would be concerned that in the 7th grade English lesson described previously, the importance of having students understand the one true main idea of the poem would fall prey to a discussion of their individual interpretations.

Both of these critiques are silly caricatures of what an evolving body of research tells us about learning. Battista (1999), speaking specifically of mathematics education, writes,

> Many... conceive of constructivism as a pedagogical stance that entails a type of non-rigorous, intellectual anarchy that lets students pursue whatever interests them and invent and use any mathematical methods they wish, whether those methods are correct or not. Others take constructivism to be synonymous with "discovery learning" from the era of "new math," and still others see it as a way of teaching that focuses on using manipulatives or cooperative learning. None of these conceptions is correct. (P. 429)

Organizing a constructivist classroom is difficult work for the teacher and requires the rigorous intellectual commitment and perseverance of students. Constructivist teachers recognize that students bring their prior experiences with them to each school activity and that it is crucial to connect lessons to their students' experiential repertoires. Initial relevance and interest are largely a function of the learner's experiences, not of the teacher's planning. Therefore, it is educationally counterproductive to ignore students' suppositions and points of view. The 7th grade English lesson is largely nonintellectual. The 9th grade science lesson, modeled on how scientists make state-of-the-art science advancements, is much more intellectually rigorous.

Moreover, constructivist teachers keep relevant facts, information, and skills at the forefront of their lesson planning. They usually do this within the context of discussions about bigger ideas. For example, the dates, battles, and names associated with the U.S. Civil War have much more meaning for students when introduced within larger investigations of slavery, territorial expansion, and economics than when presented for memorization without a larger context.

State and local curriculums address *what* students learn. Constructivism, as an approach to education, addresses *how* students learn. The constructivist teacher, in mediating students' learning, blends the *what* with the *how*. As a 3rd grader in another classroom we visited wrote to his teacher, "You are like the North Star for the class. You don't tell us where to go, but you help us find our way." Constructivist classrooms demand far more from teachers and students than lockstep obeisance to prepackaged lessons.

The Effects of High-Stakes Accountability

As we stated earlier, the standards movement has a grand flaw at the nexus of standards, accountability, and instructional practice. Instructional practices designed to help students construct meaning are being crowded out of the curriculum by practices designed to prepare students to score well on state assessments. The push for accountability is eclipsing the intent of standards and sound educational practice.

Let's look at the effects of high-stakes accountability systems. Originally, many states identified higher-order thinking as a goal of reform and promoted constructivist teaching practices to achieve this goal. In most states, however, policymakers dropped this goal or subsumed it into other goals because it was deemed too difficult to assess and quantify. Rich evidence relating to higher-order thinking is available daily in classrooms, but this evidence is not necessarily translatable to paper-and-pencil assessments. High-stakes accountability systems, therefore, tend to warp the original visions of reform.

Education is a holistic endeavor. Students' learning encompasses emerging understandings about themselves, their relationships, and their relative places in the world. In addition to academic achievement, students develop these understandings through nonacademic aspects of schooling, such as clubs, sports, community service, music, arts, and theater. However, only that which is academic and easily measurable gets assessed, and only that which is assessed is subject to rewards and punishments. Jones and Whitford (1997) point out that Kentucky's original educational renewal initiative included student self-sufficiency and responsible group membership as goals, but these goals were dropped because they were deemed too difficult to assess and not sufficiently academic.

Schools operating in high-stakes accountability systems typically move attention away from principles of learning, student-centered curriculum, and constructivist teaching practices. They focus instead on obtaining higher test scores, despite research showing that higher test scores are not necessarily indicative of increased student learning.

Historically, many educators have considered multiple-choice tests to be the most valid and reliable form of assessment—and also the narrowest form of assessment. Therefore, despite the initial commitment of many states to performance assessment, which was to have been the cornerstone of state assessment efforts aligned with broader curriculum and constructivist instructional practices, multiple-choice questions have instead remained the coin of the realm. As Jones and Whitford (1997) write about Kentucky,

> The logic is clear. The more open and performance based an assessment is, the more variety in the responses; the more variety in the responses, the more judgment is needed in scoring; the more judgment in scoring, the lower the reliability.... At this point, multiple-choice items have been reintroduced, performance events discontinued. (P. 278)

Ironically, as state departments of education and local newspapers hold schools increasingly accountable for their test results, local school officials press state education departments for greater guidance about material to be included on the states' tests. This phenomenon emboldens state education departments to take an even greater role in curriculum development, as well as in other decisions typically handled at the local level, such as granting high school diplomas, determining professional development requirements for teachers, making special education placements, and intervening academically for at-risk students. According to Jones and Whitford (1997),

> [In Kentucky] there has been a rebound effect. Pressure generated by the state test for high stakes accountability has led school-based educators to pressure the state to be more explicit about content that will be tested. This in turn constrains local school decision making about curriculum. This dialectical process works to increase the state control of local curriculum. (P. 278)

Toward Educational Reform

Serious educational reform targets cognitive changes in students' thinking. Perceived educational reform targets numerical changes in students' test scores. Our obsession with the perception of reform, what Ohanian (1999) calls "the mirage theory of education," is undermining the possibility of serious reform.

History tells us that it is likely that students' scores on state assessments will rise steadily over the next decade and that meaningful indexes of student learning generally will remain flat. It is also likely that teachers, especially those teaching in the grades in which high-stakes assessments are administered, will continue to narrow their curriculum to match what is covered on the assessments and to use instructional practices designed to place testing information directly in their students' heads.

We counsel advocacy for children. And vision. And courage.

Focus on student learning. When we design instructional practices to help students construct knowledge, students learn. This is our calling as educators.

Keep the curriculum conceptual. Narrowing curriculum to match what is covered on state assessments results in an overemphasis on the rote memorization of discrete bits of information and pushes aside big ideas and intellectual curiosity. Keep essential principles and recurring concepts at the center.

Assess student learning within the context of daily instruction. Use students' daily work, points of view, suppositions, projects, and demonstrations to assess what they know and don't know, and use these assessments to guide teaching.

Initiate discussions among administrators, teachers, parents, school boards, and students about the relationship among the state's standards, the state's assessments, and your district's mission. Ask questions about what the assessments actually assess, the instructional practices advocated by your district, and the ways to teach a conceptual curriculum while preparing students for the assessments. These are discussions worth having.

Understand the purposes of accountability. Who wants it, and why? Who is being held accountable, and for what? How are data being used or misused? What are the consequences of accountability for all students, especially for specific groups, such as special education students and English language learners?

Students must be permitted the freedom to think, to question, to reflect, and to interact with ideas, objects, and others—in other words, to construct meaning. In school, being wrong has always carried negative consequences for students. Sadly, in this climate of increasing accountability, being wrong carries even more severe consequences. But being wrong is often the first step on the path to greater understanding.

We observed a 5th grade teacher return a test from the previous day. Question 3 was, "There are 7 blue chips and 3 green chips in a bag. If you place your hand in the bag and pull out 1 chip, what is the probability that you will get a green chip?" One student wrote,"You probably won't get one." She was "right" —and also "wrong." She received no credit for the question.

References

Angaran, J. (1999, March). Reflection in an age of assessment. *Educational Leadership, 56,* 71–72.

Battista, M. T. (1999, February). The mathematical miseducation of America's youth: Ignoring research and scientific study in education. *Phi Delta Kappan, 80*(6), 424–433.

Grennon Brooks, J., & Brooks, M. G. (1993). *In search of understanding: The case for constructivist classrooms.* Alexandria, VA: ASCD.

Hambleton, R., Jaeger, R. M., Koretz, D., Linn, R. L., Millman, J., & Phillips, S. E. (1995). *Review of the measurement quality of the Kentucky instructional results information system 1991–1994.* (Report prepared for the Kentucky General Assembly.) Frankfort, KY: Office of Educational Accountability.

Jones, K., & Whitford, B. L. (1997, December). Kentucky's conflicting reform principles: High stakes accountability and student performance assessment. *Phi Delta Kappan, 78*(4), 276–281.

Ohanian, S. (1999). *One size fits few.* Portsmouth, NH: Heinemann.

POSTSCRIPT

Do High-Stakes Assessments Improve Learning?

Whether standardized tests are a crucial tool in improving overall student performance or whether they rob teachers of the autonomy and creativity needed for lasting improvement of learning is among the most hotly debated topics on the current scene. Is Jerry Jesness correct in condemning "floating" standards that shield the status quo and guarantee the reign of mediocrity, or is Susan Ohanian right in demolishing high-stakes testing in her book *One Size Fits Few: The Folly of Educational Standards* (1999)?

Here are some further sources to tilt your thinking one way or the other: Mary E. Diez, "Assessment as a Lever in Education Reform," *National Forum* (Winter 1997); Elliot W. Eisner, "Standards for American Schools: Help or Hindrance?" *Phi Delta Kappan* (June 1995); Jack Kaufhold, "What's Wrong With Teaching for the Test?" *The School Administrator* (December 1998); Donald C. Orlich, "Education Reform and Limits to Student Achievement," *Phi Delta Kappan* (February 2000); David Campbell, "Authentic Assessment and Authentic Standards," *Phi Delta Kappan* (January 2000); Donna Harrington-Lueker, "The Uneasy Coexistence of High Stakes and Developmental Practice," *The School Administrator* (January 2000); Frederick M. Hess and Frederick Brigham, "None of the Above," *American School Board Journal* (January 2000); Jeff Berger, "Does Top-Down, Standards-Based Reform Work?" *NASSP Bulletin* (January 2000); Peter Schrag, "High Stakes Are for Tomatoes," *The Atlantic Monthly* (August 2000); Georgia Hedrick, "Real Teachers Don't Test," *Educational Horizons* (Winter 2002); Dale DeCesare, "How High Are the Stakes in High-Stakes Testing?" *Principal* (January 2002); and Mary Ann Raywid, "Accountability: What's Worth Measuring?" *Phi Delta Kappan* (February 2002).

Although most of the focus is now on state mandates, proposals for national testing are still under consideration. Long a practice in many foreign countries, high-stakes national examinations in valued subject matter areas are an explosive topic in the United States. A sampling of opinion can be found in "Yes to National Tests," by Diane Ravitch, *Forbes* (May 5, 1997); "Getting Testy," *The New Republic* (September 29, 1997); and "National Tests Are Unnecessary and Harmful," by Monty Neill, *Educational Leadership* (March 1998).

Multiple articles on the standards and testing movement can be located in the May 1999 issue of *Phi Delta Kappan*, the Winter 1999 issue of *Kappa Delta Pi Record*, the February 2000 issue of *Educational Leadership*, the January 2001 issue of *NASSP Bulletin*, the January 2001 issue of *Principal Leadership*, the December 2001 issue of *The School Administrator*, the February 2002 issue of *Phi Delta Kappan*, and the Winter 2002 issue of *Kappa Delta Pi Record*.

ISSUE 10

Have Public Schools Failed Society?

YES: William J. Bennett et al., from "A Nation Still at Risk," *Policy Review* (July/August 1998)

NO: Forrest J. Troy, from "The Myth of Our Failed Education System," *The School Administrator* (September 1998)

ISSUE SUMMARY

YES: Former secretary of education William J. Bennett and 36 other leaders and scholars examine the state of public schooling on the 15th anniversary of the publication of the U.S. Department of Education report *A Nation at Risk* and issue a new manifesto for needed reforms.

NO: Veteran newspaper editor Forrest J. (Frosty) Troy counteracts the continued criticism of the public schools with a point-by-point presentation of facts.

The movement to set national goals and standards, initiated by governors and reinforced by both the Bush and Clinton administrations, reflects a widespread concern about the quality of American public education in general and the wide disparity in quality from state to state and community to community. In November 1996 a "report card" on the "Goals 2000" campaign—a plan in which educational goals to be accomplished nationally by the year 2000 were set—was released by a bipartisan federal panel. The report indicates that progress has been limited and that many states are having difficulty achieving some of the key goals of the effort. The report states that after six years of work the "overall national performance is virtually static."

A significant segment of the educational and political community has expressed disdain over the prospect of internal reform of the public schools. It is the contention of these critics that the "education establishment"—the U.S. Department of Education, the National Education Association (NEA), the American Federation of Teachers (AFT), and the teacher-training institutions—is either unwilling or incapable of improving on the status quo. Critics such as William J. Bennett, E. D. Hirsch, Jr., Chester E. Finn, Jr., Charles J. Sykes, and Cal Thomas contend that young Americans are not learning enough for their own or their nation's good, that international comparisons rank U.S. academic performance from the middle to the bottom year after year, and that many employers say that they cannot find people who have the necessary skills, knowledge, attitudes, and habits to do the work.

Finn, in "What to Do About Education," *Commentary* (October 1994), charges that the education profession is awash in bad ideas, holding to precepts such as these: There is really not much wrong with the public schools; whatever may be wrong is the fault of the larger society; competition is harmful; a child's sense of "self-esteem" counts more than what he knows; what children should learn depends on their race and ethnicity; students should never be grouped according to their ability or prior achievement; only graduates of teacher-training programs should be permitted in the classroom; and none but products of administrator-training programs should be allowed to lead schools. Hirsch, in *The Schools We Need and Why We Don't Have Them* (1996), charges "educationists" with disdaining alternatives to current practices. "Why," he asks, "do educators persist in advocating the very antifact, anti-rote-learning, antiverbal practices that have led to poor results?" He contends that would-be reformers who are not members of the educational community—parents, politicians, and business leaders—have become used to defeat.

There is evidence, however, that American public education has improved in recent decades and continues to do so. Some researchers have sounded hopeful notes and have discounted the naysayers. Stout defenses of the quality of the public schools can be found in Gerald W. Bracey's annual reports in *Phi Delta Kappan,* the U.S. Department of Education's *The Condition of Education* reports, and *The Manufactured Crisis: Myths, Fraud, and the Attack on America's Public Schools* by David C. Berliner and Bruce J. Biddle (1995). Two provocative articles on the topic are "Ten Years of Silver Bullets: Dissenting Thoughts on Education Reform," by Wade A. Carpenter, *Phi Delta Kappan* (January 2000) and "The Deep Structure of Schooling," by Barbara Benham Tye, *The Clearing House* (July/August 1998).

But there are those who say that only choice-driven competition will bring about substantial and lasting improvement. Some public school systems have initiated internal choice, and some have allowed the formation of charter schools, which are essentially independent public schools. Other communities have extended the concept into the realm of privatization and vouchers for use in private schools.

In the following selections, William J. Bennett and his associates lament the persistence of mediocre performance by America's schools and chart two strategies: (1) standards, assessments, and accountability, and (2) pluralism, competition, and choice. Journalist Forrest J. Troy pulls no punches in attacking the attackers of public schooling, but he also gives some advice to public school leaders.

A Nation Still at Risk

Fifteen years ago, the National Commission on Excellence in Education declared the United States a nation at risk. That distinguished citizens' panel admonished the American people that "the educational foundations of our society are presently being eroded by a rising tide of mediocrity that threatens our very future as a Nation and a people." This stark warning was heard across the land.

A decade and a half later, the risk posed by inadequate education has changed. Our nation today does not face imminent danger of economic decline or technological inferiority. Much about America is flourishing, at least for now, at least for a lot of people. Yet the state of our children's education is still far, very far, from what it ought to be. Unfortunately, the economic boom times have made many Americans indifferent to poor educational achievement. Too many express indifference, apathy, a shrug of the shoulders. Despite continuing indicators of inadequacy, and the risk that this poses to our future well-being, much of the public shrugs and says, "Whatever."

The data are compelling. We learned in February that American 12th-graders scored near the bottom on the recent Third International Math and Science Study (TIMSS): U.S. students placed 19th out of 21 developed nations in math and 16th out of 21 in science. Our advanced students did even worse, scoring dead last in physics. This evidence suggests that, compared to the rest of the industrialized world, our students lag seriously in critical subjects vital to our future. That's a national shame.

Today's high-school seniors had not even started school when the Excellence Commission's report was released. A whole generation of young Americans has passed through the education system in the years since. But many have passed through without learning what is needed. Since 1983, more than 10 million Americans have reached the 12th grade without having learned to read at a basic level. More than 20 million have reached their senior year unable to do basic math. Almost 25 million have reached 12th grade not knowing the essentials of U.S. history. And those are the young people who complete their senior year. In the same period, more than 6 million Americans dropped out of high school altogether. The numbers are even bleaker in minority communities. In 1996, 13 percent of all blacks aged 16 to 24 were not in school and did not hold

From William J. Bennett et al., "A Nation Still at Risk," *Policy Review* (July/August 1998). Copyright © 1998 by The Board of Trustees of the Leland Stanford Junior University. Reprinted by permission of *Policy Review*.

a diploma. Seventeen percent of first-generation Hispanics had dropped out of high school, including a tragic 44 percent of Hispanic immigrants in this age group. This is another lost generation. For them the risk is grave indeed.

To be sure, there have been gains during the past 15 years, many of them inspired by the Excellence Commission's clarion call. Dropout rates declined and college attendance rose. More high-school students are enrolling in more challenging academic courses. With more students taking more courses and staying in school longer, it is indeed puzzling that student achievement has remained largely flat and that enrollment in remedial college courses has risen to unprecedented levels.

The Risk Today

Contrary to what so many seem to think, this is no time for complacency. The risk posed to tomorrow's well-being by the sea of educational mediocrity that still engulfs us is acute. Large numbers of students remain at risk. Intellectually and morally, America's educational system is failing far too many people.

Academically, we fall off a cliff somewhere in the middle and upper grades. Internationally, U.S. youngsters hold their own at the elementary level but falter in the middle years and drop far behind in high school. We seem to be the only country in the world whose children fall farther behind the longer they stay in school. That is true of our advanced students and our so-called good schools, as well as those in the middle. Remediation is rampant in college, with some 30 percent of entering freshmen (including more than half at the sprawling California State University system) in need of remedial courses in reading, writing, and mathematics after arriving on campus. Employers report difficulty finding people to hire who have the skills, knowledge, habits, and attitudes they require for technologically sophisticated positions. Silicon Valley entrepreneurs press for higher immigration levels so they can recruit the qualified personnel they need. Though the pay they offer is excellent, the supply of competent U.S.-educated workers is too meager to fill the available jobs.

In the midst of our flourishing economy, we are re-creating a dual school system, separate and unequal, almost half a century after government-sanctioned segregation was declared unconstitutional. We face a widening and unacceptable chasm between good schools and bad, between those youngsters who get an adequate education and those who emerge from school barely able to read and write. Poor and minority children, by and large, go to worse schools, have less expected of them, are taught by less knowledgeable teachers, and have the least power to alter bad situations. Yet it's poor children who most need great schools.

If we continue to sustain this chasm between the educational haves and have-nots, our nation will face cultural, moral, and civic peril. During the past 30 years, we have witnessed a cheapening and coarsening of many facets of our lives. We see it, among other places, in the squalid fare on television and in the movies. Obviously the schools are not primarily responsible for this degradation of culture. But we should be able to rely on our schools to counter the worst aspects of popular culture, to fortify students with standards, judgment, and

character. Trashy American culture has spread worldwide; educational mediocrity has not. Other nations seem better equipped to resist the Hollywood
invasion than is the land where Hollywood is located.

Delusion and Indifference

Regrettably, some educators and commentators have responded to the persistence of mediocre performance by engaging in denial, self-delusion, and blame
shifting. Instead of acknowledging that there are real and urgent problems, they
deny that there are any problems at all. Some have urged complacency, assur-
ing parents in leafy suburbs that their own children are doing fine and urging
them to ignore the poor performance of our elite students on international
tests. Broad hints are dropped that, if there's a problem, it's confined to other
people's children in other communities. Yet when attention is focused on the
acute achievement problems of disadvantaged youngsters, many educators seem
to think that some boys and girls—especially those from the "other side of the
tracks"—just can't be expected to learn much.

Then, of course, there is the fantasy that America's education crisis is
a fraud, something invented by enemies of public schools. And there is the
worrisome conviction of millions of parents that, whatever may be ailing U.S.
education in general, "my kid's school is OK."

Now is no time for complacency. Such illusions and denials endanger the
nation's future and the future of today's children. Good education has become absolutely indispensable for economic success, both for individuals and
for American society. More so today than in 1983, the young person without a
solid education is doomed to a bleak future.

Good education is the great equalizer of American society. Horace Mann
termed it the "balance wheel of the social machinery," and that is even more
valid now. As we become more of a meritocracy the quality of one's education matters more. That creates both unprecedented opportunities for those
who once would have found the door barred—and huge new hurdles for those
burdened by inferior education.

America today faces a profound test of its commitment to equal educational opportunity. This is a test of whether we truly intend to educate all our
children or merely keep everyone in school for a certain number of years; of
whether we will settle for low levels of performance by most youngsters and
excellence only from an elite few. Perhaps America can continue to prosper
economically so long as only some of its citizens are well educated. But can we
be sure of that? Should we settle for so little? What about the wasted human
potential and blighted lives of those left behind?

Our nation's democratic institutions and founding principles assume that
we are a people capable of deliberating together. We must decide whether we
really care about the debilitating effects of mediocre schooling on the quality of our politics, our popular culture, our economy and our communities,
as dumbing-down infiltrates every aspect of society. Are we to be the land of
Jefferson and Lincoln or the land of Beavis and Butthead?

The Real Issue Is Power

The Excellence Commission had the right diagnosis but was vague—and perhaps a bit naïve—as to the cure. The commissioners trusted that good advice would be followed, that the system would somehow fix itself, and that top-down reforms would suffice. They spoke of "reforming our educational system in fundamental ways." But they did not offer a strategy of political or structural change to turn these reforms into reality. They underestimated, too, the resilience of the status quo and the strength of the interests wedded to it. As former commissioner (and Minnesota governor) Albert Quie says, "At that time I had no idea that the system was so reluctant to change."

The problem was not that the Excellence Commission had to content itself with words. (Those are the only tools at our disposal, too.) In fact, its stirring prose performed an important service. No, the problem was that the commission took the old ground rules for granted. In urging the education system to do more and better, it assumed that the system had the capacity and the will to change.

Alas, this was not true. Power over our education system has been increasingly concentrated in the hands of a few who don't really want things to change, not substantially, not in ways that would really matter. The education system's power brokers responded to the commission, but only a little. The commission asked for a yard, and the "stakeholders" gave an inch. Hence much of *A Nation at Risk*'s wise counsel went unheeded, and its sense of urgency has ebbed.

Today we understand that vast institutions don't change just because they should—especially when they enjoy monopolies. They change only when they must, only when their survival demands it. In other parts of American life, stodgy, self-interested monopolies are not tolerated. They have been busted up and alternatives created as we have realized that large bureaucratic structures are inherently inefficient and unproductive. The private sector figured this out decades ago. The countries of the former Soviet empire are grasping it. Even our federal government is trying to "reinvent" itself around principles of competition and choice. President Clinton has declared that "the era of Big Government is over." It should now be clear to all that the era of the Big Government monopoly in public education needs to end as well.

The fortunate among us continue to thrive within and around the existing education system, having learned how to use it, to bend its rules, and to sidestep its limitations. The well-to-do and powerful know how to coexist with the system, even to exploit it for the benefit of their children. They supplement it. They move in search of the best it has to offer. They pay for alternatives.

But millions of Americans—mainly the children of the poor and minorities —don't enjoy those options. They are stuck with what "the system" dishes out to them, and all too often they are stuck with the least qualified teachers, the most rigid bureaucratic structures, the fewest choices and the shoddiest quality. Those parents who yearn for something better for their children lack the power to make it happen. They lack the power to shape their own lives and those of their children.

Here is a question for our times: Why aren't we as outraged about this denial of Americans' educational rights as we once were about outright racial segregation?

The Next Civil Rights Frontier

Equal educational opportunity is the next great civil rights issue. We refer to the true equality of opportunity that results from providing every child with a first-rate primary and secondary education, and to the development of human potential that comes from meeting intellectual, social, and spiritual challenges. The educational gaps between advantaged and disadvantaged students are huge, handicapping poor children in their pursuit of higher education, good jobs, and a better life.

In today's schools, far too many disadvantaged and minority students are not being challenged. Far too many are left to fend for themselves when they need instruction and direction from highly qualified teachers. Far too many are passed from grade to grade, left to sink or swim. Far too many are advanced without even learning to read, though proven methods of teaching reading are now well-known. They are given shoddy imitations of real academic content, today's equivalent of Jim Crow math and back-of-the-bus science. When so little is expected and so little is done, such children are victims of failed public policy.

John Gardner asked in 1967 whether Americans "can be equal and excellent" at the same time. Three decades later, we have failed to answer that question with a "yes." We have some excellent schools—we obviously know how to create them—and yet we offer an excellent education only to some children. And that bleak truth is joined to another: Only some families have the power to shape their children's education.

This brings us to a fundamental if perhaps unpleasant reality: As a general rule, only those children whose parents have power end up with an excellent education.

The National Commission on Excellence in Education believed that this reality could be altered by asking the system to change. Today we know better. It can only be altered by shifting power away from the system. That is why education has become a civil rights issue. A "right," after all, is not something you beg the system for. If the system gets to decide whether you will receive it or not, it's not a right. It's only a right when it belongs to you and you have the power to exercise it as you see fit—when you are your own power broker.

Inside the Classroom

Fortunately, we know what works when it comes to good education. We know how to teach children to read. We know what a well-trained teacher does. We know how an outstanding principal leads. We know how to run outstanding schools. We have plenty of examples, including schools that succeed with extremely disadvantaged youngsters.

Immanuel Kant said, "The actual proves the possible." If it can happen in five schools, it can happen in five thousand. This truly is not rocket science. Nor is it a mystery. What is mysterious is why we continue to do what doesn't work. Why we continue to do palpable harm to our children.

Let us be clear: All schools should not be identical. There are healthy dis-agreements and legitimate differences on priorities. Some teachers like multi-age grouping. Others prefer traditional age-grades. Some parents want their children to sit quietly in rows while others want them to engage in hands-on "experiential learning." So be it. Ours is a big, diverse country. But with all its diversity, we should agree at least to do no harm, to recognize that some practices have been validated while others have not. People's tastes in houses vary, too, yet all residences must comply with the fire code. While differing in design and size and amenities, all provide shelter, warmth, and protection. In other words, all provide the basics.

Guiding Principles

A.   Public education—that is, the public's responsibility for the education of the rising generation—is one of the great strengths of American democracy. Note, however, that public education may be delivered and managed in a variety of ways. We do not equate public education with a standardized and hierarchical government bureaucracy, heavy on the regulation of inputs and processes and staffed exclusively by government employees. Today's public school, properly construed, is any school that is open to the public, paid for by the public, and accountable to public authorities for its results.

B.   The central issues today have to do with excellence for all our children, with high standards for all teachers and schools, with options for all families and educators, and with the effectiveness of the system as a whole. What should disturb us most about the latest international results is not that other countries' best students outstrip our best; it is that other countries have done far better at producing both excellence and equity than has the United States.

C.   A vast transfer of power is needed from producers to consumers. When it comes to education reform, the formulation of the Port Huron Statement (1962) was apt: "Power to the people." There must be an end to paternalism, the one-size-fits-all structure, and the condescending, government-knows-best attitude. Every family must have the opportunity to choose where its children go to school.

D.   To exercise their power wisely and make good decisions on behalf of their children, education's consumers must be well-informed about school quality, teacher qualifications, and much else, including, above all, the performance of their own children vis-à-vis high standards of academic achievement.

Strategies for Change

We urge two main renewal strategies, working in tandem:

I. Standards, Assessments and Accountability

Every student, school, and district must be expected to meet high standards of learning. Parents must be fully informed about the progress of their child and their child's school. District and state officials must reward success and have the capacity—and the obligation—to intervene in cases of failure.

II. Pluralism, Competition and Choice

We must be as open to alternatives in the delivery of education as we are firm about the knowledge and skills being delivered. Families and communities have different tastes and priorities, and educators have different strengths and passions. It is madness to continue acting as if one school model fits every situation and it is a sin to make a child attend a bad school if there's a better one across the street.

10 Breakthrough Changes for the 21st Century

1.   **America needs solid national academic standards and (voluntary) standards-based assessments,** shielded from government control, and independent of partisan politics, interest groups, and fads. (A strengthened National Assessment Governing Board would be the best way to accomplish this.) These should accompany and complement states' own challenging standards and tough accountability systems.

2.   In a free society, people must have the power to shape the decisions that affect their lives and the lives of their children. No decision is more important than where and how one is educated. **At minimum, every American child must have the right to attend the (redefined) public school of his choice.** Abolish school assignments based on home addresses. And let the public dollars to which they are entitled follow individual children to the schools they select. Most signers of this manifesto also believe strongly that this range of choices —especially for poor families—should include private and parochial schools as well as public schools of every description. But even those not ready to take that step—or awaiting a clearer resolution of its constitutionality—are united in their conviction that the present authoritarian system—we choose our words carefully—must go.

3.   **Every state needs a strong charter-school law,** the kind that confers true freedom and flexibility on individual schools, that provides every charter school with adequate resources, and that holds it strictly accountable for its results.

4.   More school choice must be accompanied by more choices worth making. **America needs to enlarge its supply of excellent schools.** One way to do

that is to welcome many more players into public education. Charter schools are not the whole story. We should also harness the ingenuity of private enterprise, of community organizations, of "private practice" teachers and other such education providers. Schools must be free to contract with such providers for services.

5.   Schools must not harm their pupils. They must eschew classroom methods that have been proven not to work. They must not force children into programs that their parents do not want. (Many parents, for example, have serious misgivings about bilingual education as commonly practiced.)

6.   Every child has the right to be taught by teachers who know their subjects well. It is educational malpractice that a third of high-school math teachers and two-fifths of science teachers neither majored nor minored in these subjects while in college. Nobody should be employed anywhere as a teacher who does not first pass a rigorous test of subject-matter knowledge and who cannot demonstrate their prowess in conveying what they know to children.

7.   One good way to boost the number of knowledgeable teachers is to throw open the classroom door to men and women who are well educated but have not gone through programs of "teacher education." A NASA scientist, IBM statistician or former state governor may not be traditionally "certified" to teach and yet may have a great deal to offer students. A retired military officer may make a gem of a middle-school principal. Today, Albert Einstein would not be able to teach physics in America's public-school classrooms. That is ridiculous. Alternative certification in all its variety should be welcomed, and for schools that are truly held accountable for results, certification should be abolished altogether. Colleges of education must lose their monopoly and compete in the marketplace; if what they offer is valuable, they will thrive.

8.   High pay for great educators—and no pay for incompetents. It is said that teaching in and leading schools doesn't pay enough to attract a sufficient number of well-educated and enterprising people into these vital roles. We agree. But the solution isn't across-the-board raises. The solution is sharply higher salaries for great educators—and no jobs at all for those who cannot do their jobs well. Why should the principal of a failing school retain a paycheck? Why shouldn't the head of a great school be generously rewarded? Why should salaries be divorced from evidence of effectiveness (including evidence that one's students are actually learning what one is teaching them)? Why should anyone be guaranteed permanent employment without regard to his or her performance? How can we expect school principals to be held accountable for results if they cannot decide whom to employ in their schools or how much to pay them?

9.   The classroom must be a sanctuary for serious teaching and learning of essential academic skills and knowledge. That means all available resources —time, people, money—must be focused on what happens in that classroom.

More of the education dollar should find its way into the classroom. Distractions and diversions must cease. Desirable-but-secondary missions must be relegated to other times and places. Impediments to order and discipline must be erased. And the plagues and temptations of modern life must be kept far from the classroom door. Nothing must be allowed to interfere with the ability of a knowledgeable teacher to impart solid content to youngsters who are ready and willing to learn it.

10.   Parents, parents, parents… and other caring adults. It is a fact that great schools can work miracles with children from miserable homes and awful neighborhoods. But it is also a fact that attentive parents (and extended families, friends, et cetera) are an irreplaceable asset. If they read and talk to their children and help them with their homework, schools are far better able to do their part. If good character is taught at home (and in religious institutions), the schools can concentrate on what they do best: conveying academic knowledge and skills.

Hope for the Next American Century

Good things are already happening here and there. Most of the reforms on our list can be seen operating someplace in America today. Charter schools are proliferating. Privately managed public schools have long waiting lists. Choices are spreading. Standards are being written and rewritten. The changes we advocate are beginning, and we expect them to spread because they make sense and serve children well. But they are still exceptions, fleas on the elephant's back. The elephant still has most of the power. And that, above all, is what must change during the next 15 years in ways that were unimaginable during the past 15. We must never again assume that the education system will respond to good advice. It will change only when power relationships change, particularly when all parents gain the power to decide where their children go to school.

Such changes are wrenching. No monopoly welcomes competition. No stodgy enterprise begs to be reformed. Resistance must be expected. Some pain must be tolerated. Consider the plight of Detroit's automakers in the 1980s. At about the same time the Excellence Commission was urging major changes on U.S. schools, the worldwide auto market was forcing them upon America's Big Three car manufacturers. Customers didn't want to buy expensive, gas-guzzling vehicles with doors that didn't fit. So they turned to reliable, inexpensive Asian and European imports. Detroit suffered mightily from the competition. Then it made the changes that it needed to make. Some of them were painful indeed. They entailed radical changes in job expectations, huge reductions in middle management, and fundamental shifts in manufacturing processes and corporate cultures. The auto industry would not have chosen to take this path, but it was compelled to change or disappear.

Still, resistance to structural changes and power shifts in education must be expected. Every recommendation we have made will be fought by the current system, whose spokesmen will claim that every suggested reform constitutes an

Table 1

Signatories of *A Nation Still at Risk*

Jeanne Allen President Center for Education Reform	**Howard Fuller** Director Institute for the Transformation of Learning, Marquette University	**Will Marshall*** President Progressive Policy Institute
Leslye Arsht Co-Founder Standards Work	**Carol Gambill** Math Teacher Sewickley, Penn.	**Deborah McGriff** Senior Vice President The Edison Project
William J. Bennett Co-Director Empower America	**Mike Gambill** Business Leader Sewickley, Penn.	**Michael Moe** Senior Managing Director Montgomery Securities
Randy Bos District Superintendent Waterloo, New York	**P. R. Gross** Biologist Falmouth, Mass.	**Paul Peterson** Professor of Government Harvard University
Stacey Boyd Founding Director, Academy of the Pacific Rim Charter Boston, Mass.	**Scott Hamilton** Assoc. Commissioner of Education Massachusetts	**Susan Pimentel** Co-Founder Standards Work
Frank Brogan State Commissioner of Education, Florida	**Eugene Hickok** Secretary of Education Pennsylvania	**Albert Quie** Former Governor of Minnesota Member Natl. Comm. On Excellence in Educ.
John Burkett Former Statistical Analyst Office of Educational Research and Improvement, U.S. Dept. of Ed.	**E.D. Hirsch** Professor of English University of Virginia	**Diane Ravitch** Senior Fellow Brookings Institution
Murray Dickman President Pennsylvania Manufacturers' Assn.	**William J. Hume** Chairman Center for Education Reform	**Nina Shokraii** Education Policy Analyst The Heritage Foundation
Dennis Doyle Senior Fellow Hudson Institute	**Raymond Jackson** President ATOP Academies Phoenix, Ariz.	**Jay Sommer** Former Teacher of the Year Member Natl. Comm. on Excellence in Educ.
Dwight Evans Member Pa. House of Representatives	**Lisa Graham Keegan** State Superintendent of Schools Arizona	**Leah Vukmir** Director Parents Raising Educational Standards in Schools
Willard Fair President The Urban League of Greater Miami	**Yvonne Larsen** Board President California State Board of Education Vice-chairman Natl. Comm. on Excellence in Educ.	**Herbert J. Walberg** Research Professor of Education University of Illinois at Chicago
Chester E. Finn Jr. President, Thomas B. Fordham Foundation	**Thaddeus S. Lott** Senior Project Manager Acres Homes Charter Schools Houston, Texas	
Rev. Floyd Flake Pastor Allen A.M.E. Cathedral and School Queens, N.Y.	**Robert Luddy** CEO Captive Aire Systems	

*Mr. Marshall dissents from that portion of recommendation #2 that would have public dollars flow to private and parochial schools on the same basis.

attack on public education. They will be wrong. What truly threatens public education is clinging to an ineffective status quo. What will save it are educators, parents, and other citizens who insist on reinvigorating and reinventing it.

The stakes could not be higher. What is at stake is America's ability to provide all its daughters and sons with necessary skills and knowledge, with environments for learning that are safe for children and teachers, with schools in which every teacher is excellent and learning is central. What is at stake is parents' confidence that their children's future will be bright thanks to the excellent education they are getting; taxpayers' confidence that the money they are spending on public education is well spent; employers' confidence that the typical graduate of the typical U.S. high school will be ready for the workplace; and our citizens' confidence that American education is among the best in the world.

But even more is at stake than our future prosperity. Despite this country's mostly admirable utilitarianism when it comes to education, good education is not just about readiness for the practical challenges of life. It is also about liberty and the pursuit of happiness. It is about preparation for moral, ethical, and civic challenges, for participation in a vibrant culture, for informed engagement in one's community, and for a richer quality of life for oneself and one's family. Test scores are important. But so, too, are standards and excellence in our society. The decisions we make about education are really decisions about the kind of country we want to be; the sort of society in which we want to raise our children; the future we want them to have; and even—and perhaps especially—about the content of their character and the architecture of their souls. In the last decade of this American Century, we must not be content with anything less than the best for all our children.

NO

Forrest J. Troy

The Myth of Our Failed Education System

On a return to earth, Dante almost certainly would establish a new rung in hell for those attempting to obliterate public education. It is the most lied-about, misreported story in America. Newsweekly magazines, mindless editorial pages, television newscasts, talk radio and televangelists malign public education with a ferocity usually reserved for serial killers.

Why? What is it about this 200-year-old institution that makes it a lightning rod? Is it the tool of gluttonous unions as depicted by Rush Limbaugh? Is public schooling the "place of darkness" that Jerry Falwell has termed it? Is it the total academic failure painted by two ex-secretaries of education, Republicans Lamar Alexander and William Bennett?

Name one other institution that flings open itself to all comers—a perfect microcosm of our nation. Every autumn the miracle of America takes place when the doors of those 87,000 schools are thrown open, welcoming the genius and slow learner, rich and poor, average and developmentally disabled. Among them are the loved and unloved, the washed and unwashed.

Those who savage the public schools tear at the heart of this country. Everything America is or ever hopes to be depends upon what happens to those 46.3 million students in public school classrooms.

Myths Versus Facts

I unashamedly speak for public education—warts and all—and have done so for 30 years, delivering more than 2,800 speeches. My remarks are not Pollyannish. Public education has serious problems in the inner cities, and I don't ignore that. I'm not in the self-esteem business.

I've spent 40 years as an award-winning journalist, including a Pulitzer Prize nomination, dealing with hard facts and how those facts are interpreted. But outside of the major cities and rural pockets of poverty, America has a superbly successful public school system—certainly among the best in the world.

Myth: Teachers teach only nine months so why do they bellyache about low salaries?

Fact: Repeated studies show this isn't true. If you count hours worked, the average teacher does in nine months what it takes regular 40-hour workers to do in 11.5 months.

Myth: American students score less well than kids in almost every other country.

Fact: This is the biggest canard of them all. America's smart kids are as smart or smarter than those in any other country. Test scores have recovered after a huge dip due to integration of public education. Separate was never equal.

Myth: Twenty-five per cent of students drop out, evidence of how ineffective public schools are.

Fact: More horse hockey. The dropout rate last year was 11 percent. Add to that a record-high graduation rate and a whopping 450,000 GEDs issued last year and America is among the best educated nations in the world.

Myth: We have students graduating from public schools who can't even read their diplomas.

Fact: You bet! They are among the nearly six million children in special education—most will never read well but they're getting their chance based on whatever gifts they bring to school. It's the best unreported story in America.

Myth: Unions are running the public schools.

Fact: Don't extrapolate to more than 14,400 school districts the mindless contracts (and overpaid janitors) in cities such as Cleveland, New York City or Chicago.

Myth: The PTA is a tool of teacher unions.

Fact: This had to be dreamed up by someone who never has been to a PTA meeting. I ought to know. I am not only a PTA veteran, but I hold the National PTA's Distinguished Service to Children Award.

Myth: Teachers are recruited from the dregs of college graduates.

Fact: Nearly half of the three million teachers in public schools have master's degrees. The political climate is so hateful toward public schools, a third quit within 10 years. Who can blame them? The committed stick, and most perform magnificently.

Myth: Public educators are afraid of competition. That's why they oppose charter schools and vouchers.

Fact: Only a nitwit public educator would favor vouchers, which suck funds from public school systems. Voucher is another way of spelling "segregation" —this time along class lines. Even the charter school movement is hardly the howling success predicted. Been to Arizona? Checked Michigan test scores?

Myth: Kids can't read today because schools don't exclusively use phonics.

Fact: America's 4th-grade readers just outperformed every country in the world except Finland, according to the National Assessment of Educational Progress. Phonics isn't the only way to learn to read. As any good reading teacher knows, this skill often requires a blend of whole language instruction with phonics.

Myth: Look how few American kids make it through college.

Fact: America is second only to Japan in the college graduation rate (by two percentage points). America exceeds every country in the world in graduate-level completion.

Myth: Entering test scores prove public schools don't adequately prepare students for college.

Fact: Any senior can take the SAT or the ACT. As many as 17 percent of those taking the SAT never had earned above a C in their classes. The College Board, which owns the SAT, decries constant misuse of test data by critics with an anti-public education agenda. The SAT score on reasoning just hit a 25-year high. Three out of four test takers this year scored higher than the national average. The ACT is at a five-year high. (My dream is to someday give the ACT exam to members of Congress!)

Myth: Today's students need to take the rigorous courses provided in the good old days.

Fact: I wish somebody who could talk slow enough would explain it to the likes of Rush Limbaugh, William F. Buckley or G. Gordon Liddy that there is a report entitled "The Condition of Education 1995" with 60 indicators related to preschool, elementary, secondary and postsecondary education. It revealed stunning improvement in public education. Between 1985–1995, the percentage of high school graduates taking core courses increased 47 percent. Critics who think schools are soft ought to check today's math, science and social studies texts. They make yesterday's stuff look like kindergarten.

Myth: Public schools locked God out of the classroom.

Fact: The U.S. Supreme Court banned sectarian prayer. Schools that have ignored that opinion have lost every single court case. Student prayer is not illegal —it happens every time there's a final exam.

Myth: Teachers are secular humanists.

Fact: Oh really? Public educators lead all other professions and occupations in teaching Sunday school, according to a survey published in *Parade* magazine.

Myth: Public schools don't teach values.

Fact: Define values. Nearly a third of students receive their only hot meal of the day in public schools. For thousands, the only hug they get is in public school. Teachers spend large sums of personal funds (average $400 last year) for things like workbooks and supplies. Thousands of teachers sponsor everything from drama to chess clubs on their own time, often without reimbursement.

Myth: The National Education Association and the American Federation of Teachers seek only higher salaries for less work.

Fact: The NEA and AFT spend huge sums of money on grants, scholarships and programs to support reform efforts and quality schooling initiatives. I have searched in vain for a list of positive programs financed by the critics.

Myth: School boards have outlived their usefulness. Parents ought to run the schools.

Fact: More than 77,000 school board members are parents and community leaders. Few are reimbursed for their time and selfless efforts.

Myth: There would be more money for schools were it not for overpaid administrators.

Fact: School administrators make a fraction of what they would earn running the same payroll and plant operation in the private sector.

Myth: We don't need school boards—they just get in the way.

Fact: Examples of waste, graft, corruption and illegalities already are emanating from charter schools, which have no comparable boards. School boards are designed to provide accountability, and they do. Check the voucher disaster in Cleveland.

Myth: Catholic schools do a better job with less money.

Fact: The average Catholic per-pupil cost of $3,200 compares with the $5,884 in public schools, but that's where the comparison ends. Public schools are required to provide regular education, vocational education, special education, counseling, dropout prevention, alternative education, attendance control, bilingual education, compensatory education, after-school athletics, regular student transportation, student activities, health and psychological programs, food services, security and violence prevention and much better employee benefits—such as a living wage and retirement programs.

Whom to Believe?

Who are you going to believe, the critics or the consumers? The annual Gallup education poll showed again that 65 percent of the parents who send 52 million children to public schools award those schools honors grades. But only 20 percent of those who have no connection with the schools grant them honors. They get their information from the popular media—the sorriest possible source. (A new Public Agenda poll reveals a 71 percent approval rating of public schools by patrons.)

Chester Finn, a former assistant secretary of education in charge of anti-public school propaganda, has the gall to write that parents should not believe what they personally experience. In other words, they are too dumb to know what a good school is. His motive? Finn is heavily invested in commercial privatization of public schools, writing the curriculum for the Edison Project, a privatization initiative. (To its shame, *Education Week* publishes him regularly without letting readers know of his financial connections.)

Why are public schools in the crosshairs when 90 percent of them are as good as any in the world? One reason is that major news media outlets are in the cities with the majority of failed schools. The blather from network news is almost always negative. Too many viewers with no firsthand knowledge extrapolate those conditions to all public schools. Add to this a heavy dose of racism, religious right fervor and nonstop right-wing slander on talk radio. Stir in 60 percent of adults with no connection with schools today in an environment of declining social and political cohesion, and you have a recipe for disaster.

Who Answers the Bell?

It's tough to be a teacher today. Every possible societal malfunction affects the classroom—drugs, alcohol, divorce, gangs and poverty.

According to the U.S. Department of Education, 46 million students attend 87,125 schools in 14,471 districts. Of that total, nearly six million have disabilities. They are educated at an average cost of $9,900, nearly twice the average spent on other students. More than 6.2 million are limited in their English proficiency with two million speaking no English. Two million are latchkey children. They go home to an empty house.

Nearly two million are abused and neglected. An estimated million kids suffer from the effects of lead poisoning, a leading cause of slow learning. More than 500,000 come from foster and institutional care. Thirty-thousand are products of fetal alcohol syndrome. Nearly 400,000 entering students are crack babies and children of other hard-core drug users.

More than half a million are homeless, coming from no permanent address. One in five students lives with a mother who did not finish high school. One in five kids under 18 (14.4 million) comes from abject poverty—with half showing up at public school hungry. More than half of poor children are white and live in rural and suburban areas.

Today's student body represents a challenge undreamed of by previous generations of educators.

Morale Busters

It's not unusual for an educator to wake up to a bashing on the "Today Show," to read another attack editorial in the morning newspaper, then hear motormouth Rush Limbaugh on the drive home trashing public schools. I have encountered thousands of angry and bewildered educators who want to fight back but don't know how.

The newsweeklies glory in spurious stories. Yet when good news is available, little is reported. When the International Math Olympiad was won by an all-public school cast, *Time* used a paragraph and didn't print the students' names.

Bob Dole described public education as an abject failure in a kickoff speech for his failed presidential campaign at a Milwaukee Catholic school.

("If education were a war, you'd be losing it. If it were a business, you would be driving it into bankruptcy. If it were a patient, it would be dying," he said.)

And who would consider Rush Limbaugh an education expert? He barely graduated from high school and was flunking out when he quit Southwestern Missouri State University. Yet *Family Circle* magazine invited him to produce a full page on how bad the public schools are! Grandma Troy was right—the higher a monkey climbs, the more you see of his ass. Limbaugh's ambition is to die in his own arms.

Religious Right Assault

The assault from radio and television evangelists is the hardest for educators to swallow. Pat Robertson's 700 Club is a nonstop critic, claiming that public schools are teaching a religion, or what he and others have dubbed secular humanism. What Robertson is really after is taxpayer-supported vouchers for Christian and parochial schools and home-schooled students. After he bowed out of his race for president, Robertson said he had it wrong—the way to take over the country was to start with school boards and legislative offices. On that score he's right.

Among this aggregation are TV's ubiquitous D. James Kennedy, the Old-Time Gospel Hour's Jerry Falwell, Focus on the Family's James Dobson, Jimmy Swaggart and several dozen radio and TV clones. They have favorite targets in the public schools: sex education ("Honey, they found you on a stump in the forest!"), school-to-work programs (send every kid to college, able or not) and multiculturalism (if you are not a white fundamentalist, your forefathers didn't exist).

They rage endlessly against condoms in the schools, yet fewer than two percent of schools even make condoms available. The Catholic hierarchy's chronic assaults are designed to pick up federal aid to religious schools via vouchers.

Critics include Phyllis Schlafly, who never spent a day of her life in a public school, yet she produces Eagle Forum reports stating that public education "is a form of child abuse." *Forbes* magazine relentlessly publishes ignorant stories designed for only one purpose—elimination of union affiliation for public educators. There are good unions and bad unions just as there are good magazines and *Forbes*.

Don't be surprised to learn how few educators, especially among three million classroom teachers, possess the ammunition necessary to refute the critics. Teaching is essentially a lonely profession—the classroom door closes and the entire day is spent with children, with only a short break for lunch. The evening is spent grading papers and working on lesson plans. Teachers know what's going on in their classroom and their school but few have the foggiest notion about the system of which they are a part.

Selling the Sizzle

The crisis, if there is one, does not reside in the typical U.S. classroom, and it doesn't infect a majority of students. Scientific acumen isn't needed to recognize that the bedrock of successful education is nurturing parents who play with their infants and read to their toddlers, who belong to the PTA and volunteer in the classroom; who send disciplined children to school. These are the same parents who support school bond issues, vote in school board elections and see education as an investment, not an expense.

If I could go one-on-one with every school administrator in America, my message would be simple: The failure isn't in the product but in the marketing. Or, as they say on Madison Avenue, "You don't sell the steak, you sell the sizzle." Public education's public relations are woefully inadequate. Here's how to merchandise the product:

- No. 1: Never let a newsletter or any other correspondence out of any school that doesn't contain at least one or more positive strokes—latest test scores, individual student and/or educator achievements, etc. (My facts have shown up in hundreds of school bulletins.)
- No. 2: A speaker's bureau is a must for civic clubs, chambers of commerce, etc. Civic organizations are the heartbeat of any community and they love to see and hear kids.
- No. 3: Create a committee on correspondence. Don't give the local news media, the critical letter writers or anyone else a free shot. Fight back with facts. Challenge the mistaken, the misinformed and the outright prevaricator while acknowledging honest criticism.

My grandmother was full of aphorisms. Here's my favorite:

> *Heretic, rebel, thing of doubt,*
> *He drew a circle that shut me out.*
> *But wit and I had the will to win*
> *We drew a larger circle that took him in.*

Ladies and gentlemen, start your drawings.

POSTSCRIPT

Have Public Schools Failed Society?

Failure or success? Research results present a mixed message and an unclear verdict. But regardless of the current evaluation, it is clear that reform is a continuing need in any social institution, especially in an institution that touches so many lives and has a direct impact on society and its economy. The questions for reformers are What most needs fixing? and How can the fixing be done best, and by whom?

Identification of reform targets are set forth in *Dumbing Down Our Kids: Why American Children Feel Good About Themselves But Can't Read, Write, or Add* by Charles J. Sykes (1995); *Poisoned Apple: The Bell-Curve Crisis and How Our Schools Create Mediocrity and Failure* by Betty Wallace and William Graves (1995); *The Things That Matter Most* by Cal Thomas (1994), particularly chapter 8, "The Promise of Progressive Education"; *Beyond the Classroom: Why School Reform Has Failed and What Parents Need to Do* by Laurence Steinberg (1995); and *Choosing Excellence: "Good Enough" Schools Are Not Good Enough* by John Merrow (2001).

Many constructive reform ideas may be found in *Horace's Hope* by Theodore R. Sizer (1996), in which the author discusses the many lessons he has learned from his work with reform-minded schools during the past decade; "Shifting the Target of Educational Reform," by William E. Klingele, *Educational Horizons* (Summer 1994); Deborah Meier's "How Our Schools Could Be," *Phi Delta Kappan* (January 1995); Benjamin R. Barber's "America Skips School: Why We Talk So Much About Education and Do So Little," *Harper's* (November 1993); "What General Motors Can Teach U.S. Schools About the Proper Role of Markets in Education Reform," by Richard J. Murnane and Frank Levy, *Phi Delta Kappan* (October 1996); and " 'A Light Feeling of Chaos': Educational Reform and Policy in the United States," by Karen Seashore Louis, *Daedalus* (Fall 1998).

Multiple articles may be found in the May 1996 issue of *The School Administrator* and the April 1999 issue of *NASSP Bulletin*. The February 17, 1997, issue of *The Nation* offers the symposium "Saving Public Education: Progressive Educators Explain What It Will Take to Get Beyond the Gimmicks." Also recommended are Stanley Pogrow's "Reforming the Wannabe Reformers: Why Education Reforms Almost Always End Up Making Things Worse," *Phi Delta Kappan* (June 1996); "Whose Schools? And What Should We Do With Them?" by John F. Covaleskie, *Educational Theory* (Fall 1997); "The Public School as Wasteland," by Lawrence Baines, Chris Muire, and Gregory Stanley, *Contemporary Education* (Winter 1999); Elliot W. Eisner, "What Does It Mean to Say a School Is Doing Well?" *Phi Delta Kappan* (January 2001); and James P. Comer, "Schools That Develop Children," *The American Prospect* (April 23, 2001).

School Choices

This pro-voucher site reports on choice plans and links to other sources.

http://www.schoolchoices.org

The Center for Education Reform

Here the Center for Education Reform provides information on charter schools, academic standards, and other topics.

http://edreform.com/pubs/charti.htm

Circle of Inclusion

This Web site offers materials, lessons, and methods for serving learners with disabilities in inclusive settings.

http://www.circleofinclusion.org

National Association for Bilingual Education

The National Association for Bilingual Education is exclusively concerned with the education of language-minority students in American schools.

http://www.nabe.org

Partnerships Against Violence Network

This site is a virtual library of information about violence and at-risk youth.

http://www.pavnet.org

ERIC Clearinghouse on Urban Education

This site offers manuals, articles, annotated bibliographies, and conference announcements in urban education.

http://eric-web.tc.columbia.edu

From Now On: The Educational Technology Journal

This site examines issues in integrating technology into the public schools.

http://www.fno.org

National Service-Learning Clearinghouse

This site provides information on service-learning topics.

http://www.servicelearning.org

PART 3

Current Specific Issues

*T*his section presents specific questions currently being probed and debated by educators, policymakers, scholars, and parents. In most cases these issues are grounded in the more basic questions explored in Parts 1 and 2.

- Are Vouchers an Appropriate Choice Mechanism?

- Can Charter Schools Revitalize Public Education?

- Have Public Schools Adequately Accommodated Religion?

- Is Full Inclusion of Disabled Students Desirable?

- Is Size Crucial to School Improvement?

- Should Bilingual Education Programs Be Abandoned?

- Does School Violence Warrant a Zero-Tolerance Policy?

- Can Self-Governing Schools Rescue Urban Education?

- Should Technology Lead the Quest for Better Schools?

- Is Mandatory Community Service Desirable and Legal?

- Should Alternative Teacher Training Be Encouraged?

ISSUE 11

Are Vouchers an Appropriate Choice Mechanism?

YES: Gary Rosen, from "Are School Vouchers Un-American?" *Commentary* (February 2000)

NO: National Education Association, from "School Vouchers: The Emerging Track Record," A Report of the National Education Association (January 2002)

ISSUE SUMMARY

YES: Gary Rosen, a *Commentary* editor, counters what he feels are cynical criticisms leveled by anti-voucher forces and makes the case for expanding voucher programs.

NO: The National Education Association, a major voucher foe, offers an array of research studies and reports to substantiate its position.

One of the more heated educational debates in recent years has been the one concerned with finding ways to provide parents and learners with a greater range of choices in schooling. Some people see the public school system as a monolithic structure that runs roughshod over individual inclinations and imposes a rigid social philosophy on its constituents. Others feel that the reduced quality of public education, particularly in large urban areas, demands that parents be given support in their quest for better learning environments. Still others agree with sociologist James S. Coleman's contention that "the greater the constraints imposed on school attendance—short of dictating place of residence and prohibiting attendance at private schools—the greater the educational gap between those who have the money to escape the constraints and those who do not."

Measures that emphasize freedom of choice abound and are often connected with desegregation and school reform goals. Some jurisdictions have developed a system of magnet schools to serve the dual purposes of equality and quality; some districts now allow parents to send their children to any public school under their control (given logistical constraints); and a few urban districts (notably Milwaukee, Wisconsin, and Cleveland, Ohio) are experimenting with funding plans to allow private school alternatives.

Two of the much-discussed ideas for providing funding for private school alternatives are tuition tax credits and voucher plans. The first, provided by the federal or state government, would expand the number of families able to send their children to the school of their choice by refunding part of the tuition cost. Voucher plans, first suggested in 1955 by conservative economist Milton Friedman, are designed to return tax monies to parents of school-aged children for tuition use in a variety of authorized public and private educational settings. Opponents of either approach take the position that such moves will turn the public schools into an enclave of the poor and will lead to further racial, socioeconomic class, and religious isolation. The question of church-state separation looms large in the minds of those who oppose these measures.

In his 1995 book *Dumbing Down Our Kids,* Charles J. Sykes raises a crucial point. He states, "The first step of meaningful reform is to recognize that saving our children is not the same as saving the public school system. That means changing our definition of 'public' education by seeing it as a commitment to provide all children with a quality education rather than as the perpetuation of a specific system of funding and bureaucratic organization." Voucher advocates build on this basic shift in the treatment of the concept "public," holding that something valued as a benefit to the public in general or some segment of the public does not have to be provided by a government-run facility. An existing example would be Catholic, Jewish, or Adventist hospitals, which are open to the public and are partially funded by public tax monies.

In a *Washington Post* opinion piece titled "Public Schools: Make Them Private" (February 19, 1995), Milton Friedman put forth the idea that "the most feasible way to bring about a gradual yet substantial transfer from government to private enterprise is to enact in each state a voucher system that enables parents to choose freely the schools their children attend." Other experts feel that such notions demolish the traditional democratic ideal of public schooling and run counter to prevailing interpretations of constitutional legality.

Gregory Shafer, in "The Myth of Competition and the Case Against School 'Choice,'" *The Humanist* (March/April 1999), says that "at the heart of the call for competition is an undying belief that the educational establishment has become bloated, lazy, and unresponsive to the parents who represent their constituency." He also contends that "one of the most disquieting and bizarre aspects of the school competition idea is its unabashed and monolithic adoration of business as a metaphor for success."

In the following selections, Gary Rosen examines in detail the voucher initiatives in Milwaukee, Cleveland, and Florida, and he critiques the liberal position against the movement. The National Education Association counters Rosen's argument with specific negative information on the three programs.

Gary Rosen  **YES**

Are School Vouchers Un-American?

$\mathbf{B}$y any measure, public education in America's cities is in deep trouble, and has been for some time. On any given day in Cleveland, almost one of every six students is likely not to show up. In Washington, D.C., a majority of tenth graders never finish high school. And in Los Angeles, school officials recently retreated from a plan to end the practice of "social promotion," realizing that it would have required holding back for a year more than half of the district's woefully unprepared students. Nor do things look any better in the aggregate. As *Education Week* concluded in a special report..., "Most fourth graders who live in U.S. cities can't read and understand a simple children's book, and most eighth graders can't use arithmetic to solve a practical problem."

The response to this dismal situation has taken many shapes in recent years, but none more radical—or more promising—than the idea of school vouchers. Though little more than a thought-experiment as recently as the late 1980's, vouchers are now being used in one form or another in every major American city, providing low-income families with scholarships or subsidies that allow them to send their children to private schools. Of these programs, the great majority are privately financed, currently sponsoring more than 50,000 students nationwide. Considerably more controversial, despite affecting just some 12,000 students, are the three state-funded programs now in operation. In Milwaukee, in Cleveland, and [most recently] in the state of Florida, qualifying families are using *public* dollars for *private* education, usually at religious schools.

For the teachers' unions, liberal interest groups, and Democratic politicians who are the most determined foes of vouchers, these programs are objectionable not so much for their scope—after all, the number of students involved is but a tiny fraction of the country's school population—as for the precedent they set and the unmistakable message they send. Whether public or private, today's voucher initiatives are an explicit rebuke to the failing inner-city public-school systems whose students are the chief beneficiaries of the new programs. As activists on all sides of the issue recognize, if these pilot programs succeed, it is far more likely that school choice for the poor will be transformed from a modest, mostly philanthropic experiment into a full-scale public policy.

And it does, in fact, appear that today's voucher programs are succeeding, at least from the perspective of the families taking part in them. Though isolating the deciding factor in improved test scores is a notoriously difficult business, studies by Harvard's Paul E. Peterson and other social scientists have found that students with vouchers perform at least as well—and often much better—than their peers in public schools.[1] Looking at the question from a different angle, John F. Witte of the University of Wisconsin reports that voucher recipients in Milwaukee have resisted the "normal pattern" of declining achievement among inner-city students, maintaining their test scores relative to national averages even as they enter higher grades. Every study has also found that parents who take advantage of vouchers are vastly more satisfied with the quality of their children's education, a sentiment based on everything from more rigorous homework assignments to better classroom discipline.

Unsurprisingly, given these results, interest in school choice has risen greatly over the last few years among inner-city families. One survey found that 85 percent of the urban poor now favor vouchers; another put support for the idea at 59 percent among blacks and 68 percent among Latinos. As if to prove these figures, when the Children's Scholarship Fund, the largest of the private voucher programs, recently announced its first national lottery for 40,000 scholarships, applications poured in from an astonishing 1.25 million children, all from low-income households. Such desperation, in the view of former Mayor Kurt Schmoke of Baltimore—one of a handful of black Democrats who have dissented from their party's line on education—makes the movement for school choice "part of an emerging new civil-rights battle."

This groundswell of grassroots support has created an increasingly uncomfortable situation for those committed to thwarting school choice. When a federal district judge suspended Cleveland's publicly financed voucher program [recently]—setting in motion a series of appeals that is still ongoing—local opinion turned sharply against him, with the *Cleveland Plain Dealer* branding him a "voucher vulture" for his "utter disregard for the needs of children across the city." Within days, the judge felt compelled to reverse his order, allowing the program to carry on, as it has continued to do even in the wake of his ruling... that it is unconstitutional. So, too, the leading groups in the antivoucher movement have been made to see the political awkwardness in taking a stand that so plainly defies the wishes of low-income families eager to improve the lot of their children.

Many of those making the case against school choice are now willing to concede—grudgingly—that the children who participate in these programs may benefit in some way. But, in their view, this is no compensation for the wider harm that vouchers threaten to do. A lucky few may be helped by the government's willingness to underwrite private education, but society as a whole, they insist, will inevitably suffer from a policy so contrary to our most fundamental civic principles and institutions. Indeed, if the most vociferous critics are to be believed, the idea of school vouchers is not just wrongheaded, it is positively un-American.

◦◦◦

The most frequently invoked argument on this score is that allowing public dollars to help support sectarian schools is unconstitutional on its face and strikes at the very heart of our tradition of religious freedom. As the American Civil Liberties Union puts it, "vouchers violate the bedrock principle of separation of church and state," forcing "all taxpayers to support religious beliefs and practices with which they may strongly disagree."

In a more strictly legal vein, voucher opponents point to a series of Supreme Court decisions during the 1970's rejecting various forms of government assistance to religious schools. The first and most important of these decisions, in the landmark case of *Lemon* v. *Kurtzman* (1971), set out the criteria the Court has used ever since to determine whether a given state action violates the First Amendment by "establishing" religion. Though the Justices themselves have never ruled on the narrow question of whether vouchers may be used for sectarian schools, several lower courts—including the federal district court in Cleveland—have concluded that such programs are unconstitutional under *Lemon* and its judicial progeny.

A second set of civic-minded objections to school choice has to do with the nation's historic commitment to public education. As a practical matter, opponents charge, government-financed vouchers invariably rob public schools of much-needed resources—not only scarce education dollars but also top students, since private schools exploit voucher programs by "skimming" or "cherry-picking" only the highest achievers. What such a policy amounts to, writes Sandra Feldman, president of the American Federation of Teachers (AFT), is "to hell with all the kids left behind."

Adding to this injustice, antivoucher spokesmen say, is the fact that citizens have virtually no way of knowing whether their tax dollars are being spent well by private schools. People for the American Way, a liberal interest group, warns that the schools receiving vouchers "lack basic standards of public accountability for their funds and management" and have resisted further regulation. Most damning are the problems experienced in Milwaukee, where several scandal-ridden private schools have closed in the middle of the academic year, leaving students and parents to fend for themselves.

Finally, the adversaries of vouchers contend, if private education expands at the expense of the public-school system, the shift will severely weaken America's democratic habits and ideals. Some predict that school choice will place government funds in the hands of extremists—critics warn of "Farrakhan" or "creationist" schools—or that it will serve, in the words of one representative of the NAACP [National Association for the Advancement of Colored People], as a "subterfuge for segregation."

But the broader concern is that the venerable tradition of the "common school"—ingrained in the national imagination by the experience of generations of successfully assimilated immigrants—will be abandoned in the rush to privatize. Reciting the Pledge of Allegiance in a classroom of diverse peers will give way, it is feared, to the (publicly supported) cultivation of narrow religious and ethnic interests, further damaging our already fragile sense of national identity.

As the National Education Association (NEA), the country's largest and most powerful teachers' union, has declared, "At a time when America is fractured by race, religion, and income, we can't afford to replace the one remaining unifying institution in the country with a system of private schools pursuing private agendas at taxpayer expense."

❦

Are the opponents right? Would the spread of school choice, whatever its benefits for a fortunate few, do grave harm to our common culture, and to the republic?

As far as the constitutional question goes, it is useful to start—as these discussions seldom do—with the actual text of the First Amendment, the relevant portion of which reads, "Congress shall make no law respecting an establishment of religion, or prohibiting the free exercise thereof." For most of American history, this language was taken to mean precisely what it says and what its 18th-century authors intended: that the federal government—and the federal government alone—has no authority over religion. The states, by contrast, could do as they wished in these matters, limited only by the protections for religious liberty enshrined in their own constitutions.

All this changed in the 1940's, when the Supreme Court decided through a bit of legal legerdemain that *every* level of American government was bound by the religion clauses of the First Amendment. Suddenly, the Court found itself having to rule on the constitutionality of a range of church-state relationships over which it previously had had no say, including the question of whether state and local governments could give aid to religious schools, as many of them had been doing for some time.

In the earliest of these cases, the Court showed some willingness to accommodate the practices that had grown up under the old federalism-based arrangement. Thus, the Justices gave their imprimatur to government assistance whose content was plainly secular, like textbooks and reimbursement for transportation. But by the early 1970's, this attitude had changed dramatically. In *Lemon*, the Court ruled that a secular purpose was not enough. In addition, no program aiding sectarian schools could have the "primary effect" of advancing religion or result in an "excessive entanglement" between church and state—a "test," as it turned out in several cases decided shortly thereafter, that effectively banned almost every form of state aid, including such seemingly innocent items as maps, instructional films, and laboratory equipment.

For the past two decades, the Supreme Court has struggled to make sense of these contradictory precedents. Though accepting the basic standard set by *Lemon*, the Justices have tried to apply it in a way that will not automatically find the "establishment" of religion in any program that somehow benefits a sectarian institution. In the most important of these cases—*Mueller* v. *Allen* (1983), *Witters* v. *Washington Department of Services for the Blind* (1986), *Zobrest* v. *Catalina Foothills School District* (1993), and *Agostini* v. *Felton* (1997)—the Court has upheld several different forms of public aid to students in religious schools. Such assistance is permissible, the Justices have ruled, when it comes about as part of a broader, religiously neutral program and when its benefits accrue to religious schools only indirectly, through the private decisions of individuals.

For school vouchers, the implications could not be clearer. As the highest state courts in both Wisconsin and Ohio have held, the programs currently operating in Milwaukee and Cleveland easily meet the requirements laid down by the Supreme Court: families may opt for a religious *or* a secular school, and the schools themselves receive public funds only as a result of these private choices. Even so strict a church-state separationist as Harvard Law School's Laurence Tribe admits that, "One would have to be awfully clumsy to write voucher legislation that could not pass constitutional scrutiny."

None of this has prevented a handful of judges from overturning publicly financed vouchers by invoking the Supreme Court's *Lemon*-era cases, but it is widely expected that the recent federal-court ruling against Cleveland's program will finally prompt the Justices to resolve the issue. If that decision falls to the current members of the Court—a big "if," to be sure, since several of them are likely to retire after the 2000 election—they are almost certain to find that school vouchers are perfectly compatible with the First Amendment.[2]

⋘❦⋙

Of course, the fact that vouchers are constitutional does not make them sound policy. Most Americans are understandably reluctant to see tax dollars spent to support religion, even indirectly. The exceptions to this rule—so commonplace today as to be uncontroversial—are various programs that let sectarian institutions use public funds to meet some obvious secular need: few object when a federal Pell grant allows a low-income college student to attend Notre Dame or Brigham Young, or when New York City subsidizes an Orthodox charity that provides kosher food to housebound elderly Jews.

School vouchers fall into precisely the same category. Yes, they may incidentally promote one or another religious creed, but their primary purpose is to improve the educational prospects of inner-city students trapped in our very worst public schools. Low-income parents who take advantage of vouchers know all this. Asked by researchers why they participate in the programs, they give reasons based overwhelmingly on academic concerns; religious considerations trail far behind. For them, school choice is above all a way to save their children's minds, not their souls.

As for the damage that vouchers would supposedly inflict on public schools, the arguments advanced by the teachers' unions and their allies are deeply disingenuous, if not dishonest. From a financial point of view, it is certainly true that public-school budgets are likely to decline as students leave for private institutions, taking some part of their per-pupil funding with them. But it is unclear why this should create any special hardship, since the schools would be losing money only for students whom they are no longer expected to educate. Moreover, because per-pupil support comes from both state and local funds, and vouchers tend to be financed exclusively with the state's share (and often not even all of that), affected public schools already get to keep much of the money earmarked for students who decide to enroll elsewhere—

receiving a bonus, in effect, for driving them away. In the 1996–97 school year, this dividend amounted in both Cleveland and Milwaukee to some $3,000 for each departing voucher student.

That the professed concern of the teachers' unions over the financial consequences of vouchers has little to do with the fate of students "left behind" was neatly demonstrated by the journalist Matthew Miller in a recent issue of the *Atlantic Monthly*. Interviewing Bob Chase, the president of the NEA, Miller proposed an experiment in which funding for education would be raised by 20 percent in several cities; every student would receive a voucher for his share of the newly enlarged budget, to be used as he and his parents saw fit. By this means, students who chose to remain in public schools would be guaranteed generous financial support. Chase rejected the idea outright—and did so again even when Miller suggested doubling or even tripling the amount of money. In their approach to vouchers, as to a host of other education reforms proposed in recent years—from giving principals more authority to fire incompetent teachers to expanding the number of independent and (usually) non-unionized "charter" schools—the one great imperative for both the NEA and the AFT has been to preserve the jobs of their members.

No less cynical is the charge that school choice serves only the most capable students, leaving the toughest cases for the public schools. As one study after another has confirmed, the children who use vouchers are hardly distinguishable from their peers, whether in terms of race, income, family background, or academic performance. Nor should this come as a surprise, since these programs do not seek out the most talented students (or, for that matter, allow participating private schools to do so), and are restricted to families that qualify for the federal school-lunch program or meet some other means test. In many cases, in fact, vouchers are used by the *worst*-performing students—for the commonsense reason that their parents are the ones most likely to be unhappy with the public schools.

The issue of accountability is somewhat more slippery. As one might expect, the private schools that accept vouchers vary in quality, and a few have been truly awful. By all reports, though, the vast majority are reasonably well managed and, more important, employ educators profoundly committed to their disadvantaged students; most work for a fraction of what their unionized public-school counterparts earn.

More to the point, like all private schools, these must comply with state regulations concerning health, safety, attendance, and the basic structure of the curriculum. In order to qualify for vouchers, they often must meet other requirements as well. In Milwaukee, such requirements run the gamut from nondiscrimination laws to accounting practices. Though this sort of regulation hardly ensures that the schools will be problem-free, it does hold them to a meaningful standard of fairness and professional competence.

When the critics of vouchers demand still *more* formal accountability, their intent is seldom benign. By attaching additional regulatory strings—

reporting requirements, elaborate administrative procedures, restrictions on single-sex programs or on using teachers uncertified by the state—they hope to drive away as many private schools as possible, threatening to erode what the AFT, in mock concern, calls their "cherished autonomy and independence." Opponents also understand that if the rules end up involving public officials too intimately in the operation of religious schools, courts will be likelier to throw out the whole program as an "excessive entanglement" of church and state. As Susan Mitchell of the Wisconsin Policy Research Institute observes, the campaign for further regulation of private schools is "part of a clear strategy to either kill choice or limit its growth."

Needless to say, no one would wish to see public funds wasted on schools that fail to educate or that just function as job services for those who run them. But legitimate as such concerns may be in the case of voucher programs, they apply with still greater force to the massively bureaucratized and patronage-riddled public-school systems of our big cities. After decades of abysmal performance, with no end in sight, how are *they* to be held accountable? For all the talk about the need to impose stricter oversight, private schools are already subject to a form of accountability that inner-city public-school officials almost never have to face: the possibility that dissatisfied families will simply decide to educate their children somewhere else.

In fact, one beneficial consequence of the school-choice programs now in existence is that they have begun to shake this complacency. After the philanthropist Virginia Gilder offered vouchers to every student at the worst elementary school in Albany, New York, local education officials rushed into action, hiring a new principal, sacking 20 percent of the school's teachers, and revamping its reading curriculum. In Florida, the schools whose poor records have made their students eligible for the state's voucher program have begun to "fight back," according to one newspaper report; they have introduced, among other things, after-school and Saturday tutoring, more classroom instruction in the basics, and home visits to parents in order to discourage truancy. Most impressive of all is the case of Milwaukee, where a reformist school board, strongly opposed by the teachers' union whose minions have long dominated school governance in the city, was elected last spring on a platform welcoming the competitive challenge posed by vouchers.

If school choice were implemented on a much grander scale—with full public funding for considerably more low-income families—there is ample reason to think that our inner-city public schools, far from suffering, might just begin to turn themselves around.

◦◉◦

As for the alarm sounded by critics about the destructive effect vouchers would have on America's democratic ethos, here too there has been much exaggeration, often of a self-serving nature. The fact is that our public schools, whatever their past glories, are not the engines for Americanization that they once were. On the other hand, private schools turn out to do a much better job these days at citizen education, perhaps because their generally more traditional bent has insulated them to some degree from the antipatriotic dictates of multiculturalism.

On the civics portion of the National Assessment of Educational Progress, the results of which were announced [in] November [1999], 80 percent of private-school seniors demonstrated basic "civic competency," as compared to just 63 percent of their public-school counterparts—roughly the same margin as prevailed in the scores for fourth and eighth graders as well. Significantly, the test measured both knowledge of government and civic disposition in the broadest sense, including the readiness of students to respect "individual worth and human dignity" and to assume "the personal, political, and economic responsibilities of a citizen."

Private schools also do better at approximating the ideal of the American "melting pot," as studies by Jay P. Greene of the Manhattan Institute have shown. Not only are they more racially integrated than public schools, but they are also home to more interracial friendships and less race-related fighting. As far as voucher programs go, rather than serving as a "subterfuge for segregation," they have usually allowed students to enter more racially mixed schools. This is because private schools in our big cities typically enroll students from different parts of the community, while public schools, even after— or perhaps because of—decades of forced busing, tend to reflect the ethnically homogeneous make-up of their neighborhoods.

What, finally, of the extremists who may use vouchers as a vehicle for antidemocratic creeds? It is safe to say that the most extreme of them are unlikely to tolerate the regulations that come along with vouchers, not least the almost universal requirement that schools accept any student interested in attending. But this is not to deny that some of the private schools taking part in voucher programs in inner cities do aim to cultivate narrower identities—identities that make many Americans, particularly of the prosperous, white, secular variety, deeply uneasy.

In an article for *City Journal*, Sol Stern visited one such school in Milwaukee, the Believers in Christ Christian Academy. The people running the school, he wrote, teach "the literalness of the Scriptures," and do not "separate their faith from their role as educators." The preoccupations of other voucher schools in Milwaukee are discussed in a new book by Mikel Holt, the editor of Wisconsin's largest African-American newspaper and a self-described "black nationalist."[3] Holt writes passionately about the need of black children for an "African-centered curriculum," one in which they will be constantly reminded that "their ancestors didn't mysteriously appear on Earth as slaves, but were creators of science and math and the arts."

Such educational philosophies can, admittedly, promote disquietingly false ideas. They can :also lead to Balkanization (or worse). Yet, they do not seem to preclude—and may even encourage—serious learning. As the founder of Believers in Christ told Stern, "We absolutely believe in our faith, but we also believe that there is a body of knowledge that our children must know in order to survive in the real world." For his part, Holt boasts that Afrocentric schools in Milwaukee are places where "disciplined, respectful" students can be found "performing advanced algebra" and "speaking the Queen's English." The bottom line with school choice, he emphasizes, is that it helps "solve the problem of an ill-prepared workforce."

Indeed, for all the civic *angst* displayed by the critics of vouchers, the most urgent threat to the health of our cities is not an excess of religiosity or even of ethnic self-assertion, however worrisome some of its manifestations. Rather, it is that an enormous and growing number of poor, mostly minority teenagers will continue to emerge from our urban public schools utterly lacking in the skills and habits they will need to find a place in the country's social and economic mainstream. Vouchers can help to reverse this cruel process of marginalization, both for the students who receive them and for those who remain in the public schools. What could be more democratic—or more American—than that?

◦◉◦

This brings us to perhaps the most peculiar feature of the current debate over vouchers: namely, how few liberals have embraced what is so quintessentially liberal a cause. After all, most middle-class Americans already have school choice: they possess the wherewithal either to pick communities where the public schools are good or to pay for private education, and they know how to make the most of public magnet schools and programs for the gifted. Only the less-well-off have to put up with whatever the local school bureaucracy sees fit to provide their children. As John E. Coons, a retired law professor at Berkeley and a long-ignored voucher advocate on the Left, has written, "The rich choose; the poor get conscripted."

But why so many liberals—and, by extension, the Democratic party—are so fiercely resistant to school choice is really no mystery. For decades now, an absolutist and completely ahistorical view of church-state separation has been a defining creed of the American Left. At the same time, and more understandably, liberals remain attached to a public-school system that has served the country well in the past and continues to do so in some ways today, especially in the suburbs. And then there are the teachers' unions, whose three million members stand to lose the most if vouchers succeed, and who are perhaps the most influential constituency in the Democratic party, having sent more delegates to the 1996 Democratic national convention than did the entire state of California.

Still, both politically and morally, the almost frankly reactionary character of the antivoucher position is growing less tenable by the day. While leading Republicans and conservatives speak out for the educational interests of the urban poor, liberal and Democratic standard-bearers continue to stonewall for a status quo that even they must admit is unacceptable—a stance no less embarrassing to the traditions of the Democratic party than to the democratic traditions of the country.

Notes

1. See Peterson's "A Report Card on School Choice," COMMENTARY, October 1997.

2. Whether vouchers are consistent with *state* constitutions is a separate question. Many states have so-called "Blaine amendments," passed during the anti-Catholic ferment of the late 19th century and explicitly intended to prevent public funds from reaching parochial schools. It is important to note that these restrictions came about largely as the result of a failed effort to pass such an amendment to the federal Constitution—further evidence, if any were needed, that until the middle of this century, the First Amendment was universally understood to pose no barrier to such aid. For a complete discussion of this constitutional history and its implications for the debate over vouchers, see Joseph P. Viteritti's invaluable new book, *Choosing Equality: School Choice, the Constitution, and Civil Society*. Brookings Institution Press.

3. *Not Yet "Free at Last": The Unfinished Business of the Civil Rights Movement—Our Battle for School Choice*. Institute for Contemporary Studies.

School Vouchers:
The Emerging Track Record

Proponents of private school tuition vouchers make a wide array of claims about their benefits. They claim that competition will spur public school improvement, vouchers will reduce the cost of education, students who get vouchers will show dramatic achievement gains, and vouchers are a success in most industrialized nations. None of this has happened.

Real evidence of how vouchers work now exists. Private school tuition vouchers began in Milwaukee, Wisconsin, beginning in 1990 and were followed by two other voucher plans in Cleveland, Ohio, and in the state of Florida. Private scholarship programs also have a clear track record.

Have vouchers had the impact predicted by some economists, education theorists, and others? Do the results argue for wider experiments or the adoption of broad-based vouchers? Following are some of the results.

Access

Vouchers fail to significantly expand choices for parents.

In the places where vouchers exist, access means a chance in a lottery. One's name is thrown into the hopper. If it is pulled out, the parent gets a chit good for use in a limited number of places. One might be able to use the voucher to pay private school tuition, if the school has space available and there are no other barriers—such as exclusions or preferences based on race, gender, ability, or other factors.

Vouchers are never likely to be widely available because they lack popular and political support. The August 2001 Gallup Poll for *Phi Delta Kappan* magazine found that "When given the specific choice, 71 percent of the general public would improve and strengthen existing public schools while just 27 percent would opt for vouchers, the alternative most frequently mentioned by public school critics." (http://www.pdkintl.org/kappan/k0109gal.htm)

Milwaukee
Wisconsin state law sets the cap for voucher participants at 15,000. And yet, only 10,739 students use them in 2001–02, less than 10 percent of the Milwaukee public schools enrollment. Some schools have declined to accept any voucher-bearing students; most of the rest have some exclusions or preferences based on ability, gender, religion, or race. Enrollment in public schools has increased from 78 percent to 80 percent of the school aged youth, according to a recent report published by voucher advocates (http://www.jsonline.com/news/Metro/jan02/14410.asp).

Cleveland
Less than 5 percent of Cleveland students use vouchers, about 4,195 students in 2001–02. About two-thirds of the Cleveland students who use vouchers never attended public schools. Vouchers in Cleveland are mostly rebates for families who were already sending their children to private schools. According to the *Akron Beacon Journal*, "rather than bring about a shift from public to private schools, the voucher program merely slowed an exodus from Cleveland's Catholic schools to the city's public schools." (December 14, 1999).

Florida
In the Florida "statewide" voucher plan, about 47 students participate in two schools in Pensacola in 2001–02. At least 93 percent of the schools in the state announced they would not accept any voucher students.

Student Achievement

Vouchers have failed to improve student achievement significantly or consistently for students who have moved from public to private schools.

Research on the impact vouchers [have] on student achievement is surrounded by enormous controversy, with questions about the motives of those conducting the research, the methods, and the sources of funding. According to *Time* magazine, "A study of private programs in New York, Washington, and Dayton, Ohio... showed a headline-grabbing 6.3% gain in test scores by African-American students who used vouchers. However, one of the research companies [Mathematica] that gathered data for [Paul] Peterson expressed concern about how he used the information, and called his study's findings premature." (*Time*, 10/9/00)

"Statistically significant" achievement gains for voucher students are negligible. The gains have not been consistent, they have been far below projections, and they give no compelling evidence to justify expanding vouchers.

Milwaukee
In 1990, Dr. John Witte of the University of Wisconsin was hired by the Wisconsin Department of Public Instruction to conduct an evaluation of all aspects of the Milwaukee Parental Choice Program. Witte and his colleagues released

annual reports during the first five years, before the legislature discontinued funding for the studies. Two other research groups reanalyzed the Witte data. Jay Greene, Paul Peterson, and Jiangtao Du conducted one of the studies; Cecilia Rouse conducted the other.

Among Witte's conclusions:

- Student achievement in the fourth year of the program, after controlling for prior achievement and demographic variables, *was not significantly different for voucher students than for other low-income Milwaukee public school students.*
- While voucher and public school students tested came from demographically similar families, "the families of the voucher children were better educated and more interested in their child's education, both before and after entering the program." (John Witte, et al., Fifth Year Report: Milwaukee Parental Choice Program, University of Wisconsin-Madison, 1995; Achievement Effects of the Milwaukee Voucher Program, University of Wisconsin-Madison, 1997)

The study conducted by Jay Greene, Paul Peterson, and Jiangtao Du concluded the Milwaukee voucher students outperformed public school students in math and reading. But the press release and the report itself were not the same. The research team found no statistically significant advantage for private school students in math in the first three years and in reading in the first four years. (The Effectiveness of School Choice in Milwaukee: A Secondary Analysis of Data from the Program's Evaluation, Harvard University, 1996)

Cecilia Rouse of Princeton University conducted a third analysis in an effort to clear up the disagreement between Peterson and Witte. Rouse found a statistically significant and positive effect in math achievement, but not in reading. She concluded: "these are average effects that do not necessarily mean all of the choice schools are 'better' than the Milwaukee public schools." (Cecilia E. Rouse, Private School Vouchers and Student Achievement: An Evaluation of the Milwaukee Parental Choice Program, Princeton University, 1997)

Cleveland

The Ohio Department of Education commissioned an evaluation of Cleveland's voucher program beginning in April 1997. Among the findings of Dr. Kim Metcalf, et al., at Indiana University:

- Voucher students had been achieving at higher levels than their public school peers prior to receiving the vouchers.
- After accounting for prior achievement and demographics, there were no significant differences in third-grade achievement between voucher students and their public school peers at the end of the first year, but significant and positive effects in language and, less clearly, in science, at the end of two.

- Students attending the two newly established private schools were achieving at significantly lower levels by the end of the second year than either their public school or private school peers.

A research group including Jay Greene and Paul Peterson conducted two additional studies of the Cleveland vouchers, including one that found "positive school choice effects in some subject domains among third grade students."

A balanced summary of all of the research on Cleveland and Milwaukee is provided in an article entitled "Free Market Policies and Public Education: What Is the Cost of Choice?" by Kim Metcalf and Polly Tait. http://www.pdkintl.org/kappan/kmet9909.htm.

Private Scholarships

In August 2000, Paul Peterson, et al., released their conclusions from a study of private scholarship programs in New York City, Washington, D.C., and Dayton, Ohio. Among their findings:

- In the three cities taken together, the overall test-score performance of African-American students who switched from public to private schools was higher after the first and second years.
- No statistically significant effects were observed for students from other ethnic groups who switched from public to private schools.

Within a matter of weeks, the company that gathered the data in New York called Peterson's findings premature. David Myers of Mathematica Policy Research noted that "students who were offered scholarships to attend private schools as part of one of the nation's largest private voucher programs performed about the same on standardized reading and mathematics tests as students who were not offered scholarships."

Further, the Mathematica analysis showed "no gains for Latino students in any grade, large and statistically significant gains for African American students who are now in 6th grade, and no impacts for African American students in the 3rd, 4th, or 5th grades," and concluded that "Because gains are so concentrated within this single group, one needs to be very cautious in setting policy based on the overall modest impacts on test scores." (Voucher Claims are Premature in New York City, David Myers, http://www.mathinc.com).

Three other significant analyses were concluded in 2001.

Kim Metcalf, director of the Indiana Center for Evaluation, conducted an analysis of student achievement in the Cleveland voucher plan covering the years 1998–2000 (http://www.indiana.edu/~iuice/forms/rprt_rqs.html). According to Metcalf, "Students' academic performance in each of the four areas [reading, language, mathematics, and total achievement] improved significantly from beginning first grade.... This was true for all students, independent of their scholarship status and suggests that students benefited significantly from their schooling, whether in private or public schools and whether they were scholarship, applicant/non-recipient, or non-applicant students."

In other words, students learn in public and private schools. Contrast those findings with the statements by critics, such as Clint Bolick of the Institute for Justice, who describes the Cleveland voucher as "a program designed to rescue economically disadvantaged children from a failing public school system."

The United States Government Accounting Office [GAO] released a study in August 2001, conducted for voucher supporter Senator Judd Gregg (R-NH) that looked at both publicly funded vouchers and private scholarship programs. According to the study, "The contract researcher teams for Cleveland and Milwaukee found little or no statistical significant differences in voucher students' achievement test scores compared to public school students, but other investigators found that voucher students did better in some subject areas tests."

Virtually all of the glowing reports published by Paul Peterson and others in praise of the student achievement benefits of vouchers have been funded by pro-voucher individuals and organizations, such as the Walton Foundation and Rose and Milton Friedman Foundation. Most of these studies did not fit GAO's standards for objectivity, including peer review.

In December 2001, The RAND research organization released a report entitled "Rhetoric Versus Reality: What We Know and What We Need to Know About Vouchers and Charter Schools." The study found that "Long-term effects on academic skills and attainment in both voucher and charter programs are as yet unexamined. Moreover, there is little information that would permit the effectiveness of vouchers and charters to be compared with other, more conventional reforms, such as class-size reduction, professional development, high-stakes accountability, and district-level interventions."

To some extent, their conclusions beg the question about the impact of vouchers. Pro-voucher advocates take credit for improvements in Milwaukee public schools, including class size reduction and enhanced professional development and Florida voucher advocates take credit for improvements in schools rated "F" for two consecutive years—with vouchers as a consequence. But, in fact, other school districts and states have had class size reductions and professional development enhancements with good effect—without the threat of vouchers, and school districts and states have had similar positive effects by strong accountability measures. In fact, the accountability legislation in Florida, pre-cursor to the voucher scheme, had the same impact. Schools designated as low-performing soon moved off the list with the right combination of attention and resources.

Accountability

States with private school vouchers have not provided safeguards to protect against fiscal irregularities or educational deficiencies.

Milwaukee
- Milwaukee voucher schools do not have to administer or report test results. The state eliminated all funding for student achievement data collection in 1995.

- About 40 percent of the costs of the Milwaukee vouchers ($11.5 million) represent payments to schools above the tuition costs charged other students. For 21 schools, about one-third of the total, the state pays between 200 and 400 percent of the tuition and fees charged other students.
- In 1999, the Metropolitan Milwaukee Fair Housing Council found that voucher schools violated state laws regarding open admissions and opt-outs for religious practices. At the beginning of the 2000-01 school year, all of those schools remained on the state's approved list.
- In the 1995–96 school year, four of the 18 voucher schools were shut down because of fraud, mismanagement, or negligence.
- Nine Milwaukee voucher schools have no accreditation, were not seeking accreditation, and administered no standardized tests, according to a recent state audit.
- In September 2000, one individual was just days away from receiving about $560,000 from the state to educate 130 students at an "Institute for Holistic Learning." The school director claimed he had to sign the application for some of the parents because they could not themselves, and he had told parents their children could stay at home and not be marked 'absent' because "technically they were still 'present'."

Cleveland
- An independent auditor hired by Ohio found almost $2 million in questionable expenses in the Cleveland voucher program in the first year. Of that, $1.4 million was spent for taxis to transport students —including $419,000 in over-billing by taxi companies charging for absent students.
- Five schools were able to collect about $1 million in vouchers prior to completing their applications process, resulting in schools with serious fire code violations, health hazards, inadequate curricula, and unqualified teachers. Three of the five schools remained in the program as of December 1999.
- The Islamic Academy of Arts and Sciences was allowed to operate for two years in a 110-year old building with no fire alarm or sprinkler system and lead-based paint eight times greater than the level considered safe. Eight of the 12 instructors did not have teaching licenses, and one had been convicted of first-degree murder. In 1999, more than one-half of the students for whom the school received voucher payments did not attend the school or did so for only part of the year.
- The Golden Christian Academy was found to be a "parent-run video school." Students watched recorded lessons given by an on-screen teacher. The video lessons and workbooks are provided by the Pensacola Christian Academy, which features a "faculty of master [video] teachers." The school remained eligible for vouchers, even after discovery of numerous violations of safety codes by the Cleveland Plain Dealer (7/10/99).

Florida
- At least 93 percent of the private schools in Florida refuse to accept any voucher students.
- The state assigns public schools a letter grade, A through F, based on students' test scores on the state standardized test. But private school students are not required to take the test, and therefore private schools are not rated. In short, there is no comparable way to discover if a private school is, in fact, better than the public school a student with a voucher leaves.

Costs of Vouchers

Vouchers end up costing taxpayers more—for administration and to pay the costs of students not formerly served in public schools.

Milwaukee
By 1998–99, about 6,000 Milwaukee students received vouchers worth about $5,000 each for a total cost of about $29 million. This created a net loss of $22 million to the public schools. ("Tax Funding for Private School Alternatives: The Financial Impact on Milwaukee Public Schools and Taxpayers," Institute for Wisconsin's Future, 1998)

Cleveland
For 2000–02, 3,900 Cleveland students received vouchers worth about $2,250 each at a cost of about $9 million. Additional transportation and administrative costs bring the total up to more than $10 million.

Private Scholarships
Even private scholarship programs can reduce funds available for public schools, especially when students use such scholarships initially but then return to public schools mid-year. A September 2000 study by Paul Peterson found that about half the students who received private scholarships in Dayton, Ohio, New York City, and Washington, DC, were back in the public schools by the second year of the program.

Edgewood School District in San Antonio, Texas, provides an illustration of the financial impact of private scholarships. More than 800 students used $4,000 scholarships to attend private and parochial schools—and the Edgewood district lost $5,800 for each student who left. Since students left from a wide array of schools and grades—and given the large number who returned to public schools the loss of $4.8 million caused numerous disruptions and diminutions in the quality of education for public school students.

Proposed Vouchers
A study of the California voucher proposal, Proposition 38 has found that vouchers would cost $3 billion annually by the fourth year—just to pay the costs of students who already attended private schools, regardless of income.

(Public Analysis for California Education, University of California at Berkeley and Stanford University, September 2000)

The Michigan voucher proposal would have cost up to $35 million a year to pay for vouchers in the seven school districts deemed eligible because of a high dropout rate. If a school district were determined to qualify for vouchers, the law made no distinction between students in public schools and those in private schools, and approximately 10,500 students attending private schools in those seven districts would have been eligible to receive vouchers.

Vouchers and School Improvement

The effects of competition on public schools are purely conjectural.

Milwaukee
Milwaukee took steps to raise standards for schools and expectations for students before vouchers were established. Alex Molnar of the University of Wisconsin at Milwaukee conducted a study of student achievement among regular public schools, voucher schools, and public schools that reduced class size and enhanced professional development (as part of the Student Achievement Guarantee in Education or SAGE program). Students in the SAGE schools outperformed their peers in private schools and other Milwaukee public schools.

Florida
Florida established a mechanism for determining low performing schools before the voucher plan was created. Under the School Improvement and Educational Accountability Act, 33 schools statewide were identified as "critically low achieving." After two years of concerted effort, including redesigning programs and increasing community involvement, all of those 33 schools came off the list.

Public schools throughout the nation are engaged in improvement efforts —all without the threat of vouchers or other competition. For teachers and others who work in the schools to meet the needs of children, school improvement has intrinsic rewards—beyond the financial punishments and rewards used in profit-making enterprises.

POSTSCRIPT

Are Vouchers an Appropriate Choice Mechanism?

V oucher plans have been challenged on the grounds of unconstitutionality (if sectarian schools are included) and as a threat to the public schools as democratic institutions. A number of serious legal and political questions have been raised during the discussion of this innovation, including the following:

- Do voucher programs "skim the cream" from the public school population?
- Does confining choice to the public sector shield government-run schools from authentic competition?
- Will unlimited school choice lead to the further balkanization of America?
- Is the Supreme Court's "child benefit" theory, used in earlier cases to allow public aid to religious schools, applicable to the argument over vouchers?
- Are the regulations imposed on religious schools that accept vouchers a matter of "excessive entanglement" of government and religion?

A book by Jerome J. Hanus and Peter W. Cookson, Jr., *Choosing Schools: Vouchers and American Education* (1996), addresses the issue of vouchers, as does Terry M. Moe's *Schools, Vouchers, and the American Public* (2001). And a flurry of journal articles have added a variety of opinions to the debate, including "The Empty Promise of School Vouchers," by Edd Doerr, *USA Today Magazine* (March 1997); "Vouchers for Religious Schools," by Denis P. Doyle, *The Public Interest* (Spring 1997); "The Voucher Debate," by Judith Brody Saks, *The American School Board Journal* (March 1997); "Teacher of the Year Gives Vouchers a Failing Grade," by Bob Peterson, *The Progressive* (April 1997); Martin Carnoy "Do School Vouchers Improve Student Performance?" *The American Prospect* (January 2001); Sheila Suess Kennedy, "Privatizing Education: The Politics of Vouchers," *Phi Delta Kappan* (February 2001); Jay P. Greene, "The Surprising Consensus on School Choice," *The Public Interest* (Summer 2001); Clark Robenstine, "Public Schooling, the Market Metaphor, and Parental Choice," *The Educational Forum* (Spring 2001); and Janet M. Ferguson, "Vouchers—An Illusion of Choice," *American School Board Journal* (January 2002).

Multiple articles on school choice may be found in *Education and Urban Society* (February 1995), *American School Board Journal* (July 1996), *Phi Delta Kappan* (September 1996), *Educational Leadership* (October 1996), and *Phi Delta Kappan* (September 1999).

ISSUE 12

Can Charter Schools Revitalize Public Education?

YES: Chester E. Finn, Jr., Bruno V. Manno, and Gregg Vanourek, from "The Radicalization of School Reform," *Society* (May/June 2001)

NO: Marc F. Bernstein, from "Why I'm Wary of Charter Schools," *The School Administrator* (August 1999)

ISSUE SUMMARY

YES: Former assistant secretaries of education Chester E. Finn, Jr., and Bruno V. Manno, along with Gregg Vanourek, vice president of the Charter School Division of the K12 education program, provide an update on the charter school movement, which, they contend, is reinventing public education.

NO: School superintendent Marc F. Bernstein sees increasing racial and social class segregation, church-state issues, and financial harm as outgrowths of the charter school movement.

The public education system as currently structured is archaic." So say Diane Ravitch and Joseph Viteritti in "A New Vision for City Schools," *The Public Interest* (Winter 1996). "Instead of a school system that attempts to impose uniform rules and regulations," they contend, "we need a system that is dynamic, diverse, performance-based, and accountable. The school system that we now have may have been right for the age in which it was created; it is not right for the twenty-first century."

Currently, the hottest idea for providing alternatives to the usual public school offering is the charter school movement. Charter schools, which receive funding from the public school system but operate with a good deal of autonomy regarding staffing, curriculum, and spending, began in Minnesota in 1991 through legislative action prompted by grassroots advocates. Charter schools have gained wide support, all the way up to the White House. In the 1998–1999 school year some 1,700 charter schools served about 350,000 students nationwide. The 2000–2001 year saw about 500 additional charters granted.

The movement has certainly brought variety to the school system menu and has expanded parental choice. Community groups, activists, and entrepreneurs seem to be clamoring for available charters for Core Knowledge schools, Paideia schools, fine arts academies, Afrocentric schools, schools for at-risk students and dropouts, technology schools, character education–based schools, job-training academies, and so on.

The National Commission on Governing America's Schools has recommended that every school become a charter school, which would bring an end to the era of centralized bureaucratic control of public school districts. The Sarasota County School District in Florida has already embarked on a decentralized organizational model offering a "100% School Choice Program" through newly conceived "conversion, deregulated, and commissioned schools."

There are obstacles to success, however, and indeed some have already failed. According to Alex Medler in "Charter Schools Are Here to Stay," *Principal* (March 1997), these obstacles include inadequate capital funding and facilities, cash flow and credit problems, regulations and paperwork, disputes with local school boards, and inadequate planning time. A recently released report by the Hudson Institute, *Charter Schools in Action,* indicates wide success in overcoming such obstacles.

Michael Kelly, in "Dangerous Minds," *The New Republic* (December 30, 1996), argues that in a pluralistic society public money is shared money to be used for shared values. He finds that too many of the charter schools are run by extremists who like the idea of using public money to support their ideological objectives. He cites the failed Marcus Garvey School in Washington, D.C., which spent $372,000 in public funds to bring an Afrocentric curriculum to 62 students. However, he notes that this case has not led to a wave of protests against the concept of charter schools.

In fact, *Washington Post* columnist William Raspberry recently declared that he finds himself slowly morphing into a supporter of charter schools and vouchers. "It isn't because I harbor any illusions that there is something magical about those alternatives," he explains. "It is because I am increasingly doubtful that the public schools can do (or at any rate *will* do) what is necessary to educate poor minority children."

An associated topic is privatization. This either involves turning public school management over to private companies, such as Educational Alternatives, Inc., or cooperating with entrepreneurs who want to develop low-cost private alternatives for students currently enrolled in public schools. The most talked-about of the latter is entrepreneur Chris Whittle's Edison Project, an attempt to build a nationwide network of innovative, for-profit schools.

In the following selections, Chester E. Finn, Jr., Bruno V. Manno, and Gregg Vanourek review the charter school movement's progress, seeing it as a potential fulfillment of the basic promise of American education. Contrarily, Marc F. Bernstein sounds a number of warning signals as the public rushes to embrace charter schools as a reform mechanism.

Chester E. Finn, Jr., Bruno V. Manno, and Gregg Vanourek

 **YES**

The Radicalization of School Reform

$\mathbf{M}$uch has changed in the education world since the United States was declared a "nation at risk" in 1983 by the National Commission on Excellence in Education. We've been reforming and reforming and reforming some more. In fact, "education reform" has itself become a growth industry, as we have devised a thousand innovations and spent billions to implement them. We have tinkered with class size, fiddled with graduation requirements, sought to end "social promotion," pushed technology into the schools, crafted new academic standards, revamped teacher training, bought different textbooks, and on and on.

Most of these alterations were launched with good will and the honest expectation that they would turn the situation around. But the problem with much of this reform churning is that the people who courageously addressed this issue in 1983 basically took for granted that the public school system as we knew it was the proper vehicle for making those changes and that its familiar machinery could produce better products if it were tuned up, adequately fueled and properly directed. In short, requisite changes would be made by school boards and superintendents, principals and teachers, federal and state education departments, and would be implemented either in time-honored system-wide fashion or through equally familiar "pilot" and "demonstration" programs.

Yet despite bushels of effort, barrels of decent intentions, and billions of dollars, most reform efforts have yielded meager dividends, with little changing for the better. Test scores are generally flat, and U.S. twelfth graders lag far behind their international counterparts in math and science, although our school expenditures are among the planet's highest. On the reports of the National Education Goals Panel which monitors progress toward the ambitious objectives set by President Bush and the governors in 1989, most years we see the number of arrows that point upward just about equaled by the number pointing down. Combining large budgets and weak performance, American schools can fairly be termed the least productive in the industrial world.

Many in the education establishment excuse the lack of progress by asserting that the reforms we've undertaken still haven't had time to gain traction, haven't been adequately funded, haven't been accompanied by enough "staff development," have been undermined by complacent parents or retrograde political leaders, and so forth. Others explain that families are deteriorating, poverty is spreading, morals are decaying, and it's not realistic to expect schools to do a better job until the whole society is overhauled. A few naysayers still insist that the "excellence movement" is itself unnecessary, that American schools are doing okay as is, and that the whole flap stems from a right-wing conspiracy to bring down public education by badmouthing it.

Our sense, however, is that the chief explanation for their failure is the essential incrementalism of many of these "reforms"—i.e., the conventional reforms of the past two decades don't fundamentally alter our approach to public education in America. They do not replace the basic institutional arrangements, shift power, or rewrite the ground rules. That is acceptable if one believes the old structures remain sound. But that is not how we read the evidence. We judge that the traditional delivery system of U.S. public education is obsolete.

This view echoes the late 1960s claim of the iconoclastic psychologist Kenneth B. Clark, whose study of the malign effects of school segregation was cited in the Supreme Court's landmark 1954 decision, *Brown v. Board of Education.* Clark called for "realistic, aggressive, and viable competitors" to the public school system that would strengthen "that which deserves to survive," arguing "that public education need not be identified with the present system of organization of public schools." To be sure, there are today some fine schools within the "regular" system and a number of exceptional ones on its periphery. But the system itself is failing because its basic mechanisms and structures *cannot* change in the ways needed to meet today's education needs and societal demands. Its many "stakeholders" and interest groups fight every significant alteration.

Outside the establishment's fortified citadels, however, an important breakthrough can be seen: widening awareness that the American primary and secondary education system as we know it not only needs radical improvement but also that genuine advances will be made only if we rewrite the system's ground rules, replace many of its assumptions, overturn its structures and transform its ancient power relationships. In other words, the present school enterprise is not just doing poorly; it's incapable of doing much better because it is intellectually misguided, ideologically wrong-headed, and organizationally dysfunctional. The spread of this awareness we term the radicalization of school reform.

At day's end, this radicalization defends the principle and function of public education while arguing for a top-to-bottom makeover of its ground rules and institutional practices. It rejects the Hobson's choice that has long paralyzed serious education reform: the choice between a moribund government-run system and the chimera of privatization. We are, in fact, seeing signs of a new view of education change, one that welcomes decentralized control, entrepreneurial management, and grassroots initiatives within a framework of publicly defined standards and accountability.

Charter schools are the most prominent manifestation of the radicalization of school reform (though publicly financed vouchers are the most controversial). In fact, charters are the liveliest reform in American education today. Connecticut Democratic Senator Joseph Lieberman writes:

> "School reform is no longer an option—it is a necessity. Competition from charter schools is the best way to motivate the ossified bureaucracies governing too many public schools. This grass-roots revolution seeks to reconnect public education with our most basic values: ingenuity, responsibility, and accountability."

Before these unconventional independent public schools of choice vaulted into the spotlight in the mid-1990s, education reform in the United States was nearing paralysis—stalemated by politics and interest groups, confused by the cacophony of a thousand fads and pet schemes working at cross purposes, and hobbled by most people's inability to imagine anything very different from the schools they had attended decades earlier. Enter charter schools in 1991, a seedling reform that grew into a robust tree, then a whole grove. The trees are still young, to be sure, and the grove attracts plenty of lightning strikes. But it is steadily expanding and mostly thriving.

Even if the charter forest doesn't come to dominate our education ecosystem, the idea behind it has powerful implications for the entire enterprise of public schooling. In what follows, we explain charter schools, provide an overview of their present status, account for where they came from, and conclude by describing their potential to renew and redefine U.S. public education.

What, Exactly, Is a Charter School?

Few outside the charter movement are clear about the definition of a charter school. A workable starting point is that a charter school is an "independent public school of choice, freed from rules but accountable for results." A charter school is a new species, a hybrid, with important similarities to traditional public schools, some of the prized attributes of private schools—and crucial differences from both familiar forms.

As a public school, a charter school is open to all who wish to attend it (i.e., without regard to race, religion, or academic ability); paid for with tax dollars (no tuition charges); and accountable for its results—indeed, for its very existence—to an authoritative public body (such as a state or local school board) as well as to those who enroll (and teach) in it.

Charter schools are also different from standard-issue public schools. Most can be distinguished by four key features: they can be created by almost anyone; they are exempt from most state and local regulations, essentially autonomous in their operations; they are attended by youngsters whose families choose them and staffed by educators who are also there by choice; and they are liable to be closed for not producing satisfactory results.

Charter schools resemble private schools in two important particulars. First, their independence. Although answerable to outside authorities for their results (far more than most private schools), they are free to produce those results as they think best. They are self-governing institutions. They, like private schools, have wide ranging control over their own curriculum, instruction, staffing, budget, internal organization, calendar, schedule, and much more. The second similarity is that they are schools of choice. Nobody is assigned to attend (or teach in) a charter school. Parents select them for their children, much as they would a private school, albeit with greater risk because the new charter school typically has no track record.

The "charter" itself is a formal, legal document, best viewed as a contract between those who propose to launch and run a school and the public body empowered to authorize and monitor such schools. In charter-speak, the former are "operators" and the latter are "sponsors."

A charter operator may be a group of parents, a team of teachers, an existing community organization such as a hospital, Boys and Girls Club, university or day care center, even (in several states) a private firm. School systems themselves can and occasionally do start charter schools. Sometimes an existing school seeks to secede from its local public system or, in a few jurisdictions, to convert from a tuition-charging non-sectarian private school to a tax-supported charter school. They apply for a charter and, if successful, are responsible for fulfilling its terms. The application spells out why the charter school is needed, how it will function, what results (academic and otherwise) are expected, and how these will be demonstrated. The operator may contract with someone else— including private companies or "education management organizations" (EMOs) —to manage the school, but the operator remains legally responsible to the sponsor.

The sponsor is ordinarily a state or local school board. In some states, public universities also have authority to issue charters, as do county school boards and city councils. If the sponsor deems an application solid, it will negotiate a more detailed charter (or contract) for a specified period of time, typically five years but sometimes as short as one or as long as fifteen.

During that period, the charter school has wide latitude to function as it sees fit. At least it does if its state enacted a strong charter law and did not hobble charter schools with too many of the constraints under which conventional public schools toil. Key features of the charter idea include waivers from most state and local regulations; fiscal and curricular autonomy; the ability to make its own personnel decisions; and responsibility for delivering the results that it pledged.

If a charter school succeeds, it can reasonably expect to get its charter renewed when the time comes. If it fails, it may be forced to shut down. And if it violates any of the unwaived laws, regulations, or community norms during the term of its charter, it may be shut down sooner.

Where Are We Today?

As of early 2001, there are about 2,100 charter schools, located in 34 states and the District of Columbia. Nearly 518,000 youngsters are enrolled in these schools, slightly more than 1 percent of U.S. public school students. Thirty-six states and the District of Columbia have enabling legislation for charter schools and several more are considering it. Fifty-nine charter schools have, for various reasons, ceased operation.

Future growth in the number of charter schools depends in considerable part on state legislation, especially whether limits on the number of charters that can be granted by charter sponsors remain in effect. There is a heated debate now underway in several states (e.g., Kansas, Michigan) over raising these caps, while other states (e.g., Alaska, California, Massachusetts, Texas) have already loosened them due to demand-side pressures. Clearly, the fuel for charter growth will have to come either from amending state laws to lift those caps or from states without real limits (such as Arizona and Texas) or with high limits (like California and New Jersey).

Largely due to these statutory constraints (not lack of interest or demand since 70 percent of all charter schools have waiting lists) charter schools are distributed unevenly. Eleven states account for over 80 percent of them. Arizona alone had 352 in 1999–00; there were 239 in California, 173 in Michigan, 167 in Texas, and 111 in Florida. A large proportion of charters is concentrated in the three states of Arizona, California, and Michigan, but that percentage decreased from 79 percent in 1995–96 to 45 percent in 1999–00.

Charter schools are found in all types of communities: cities, suburbs, and rural areas; industrial towns, deserts, and Indian reservations; ethnic neighborhoods, commuter towns, even in cyberspace. A tour of the charter landscape does not stop at the U.S. border as similar developments can be found around the world, including the United Kingdom, Canada, New Zealand, Australia, Brazil, Chile, and Pakistan.

Numerous cities across the United States have been profoundly affected by charter schools, and in a few we are beginning to glimpse what a system of public education based on the charter principles of autonomy, choice, and accountability might look like. In Washington, D.C. nearly 15 percent of public school students are now enrolled in charter schools; in Kansas City, Missouri, the total is 18 percent; and in Arizona, 4 percent of all youngsters are in charters —which comprise one-fifth of all the state's public schools.

Still, when compared with the vastness of American K–12 education, charters are a flea on the elephant's back, representing 2 percent of all public schools and less than 1 percent of total enrollments. There are about 15 times as many private schools as charter schools. But thus far, the number of charter schools exceeds voucher schools: as of spring 2000, there were only about 150 publicly funded voucher schools compared to nearly 2,000 charter schools.

Charter schools are much studied and intensively scrutinized, so a great deal is known about them. According to the major federal study of these schools, 72 percent of them are new schools, 18 percent are pre-existing district public schools that converted to charter status, and the remaining 10 percent are pre-existing private, non-sectarian schools that have converted. What's more, the percentage of newly created schools is increasing over time: 85 percent of charters opening in 1998–99 were newly created, compared with just over half of the schools that opened in 1994–95 and earlier. Moreover, most charter schools are relatively young—i.e., the average charter school at the end of 1999–2000 was less than three years old.

One can obtain ample information on charter enrollments, demographics, laws, curricula, founders, sponsors, staff, missions, funding, and facilities.

According to the Center for Education reform, over half of all charter schools are in urban districts, one-quarter have a back-to-basics curriculum, 40 percent serve dropouts or students at risk of dropping out, and one-quarter are geared to gifted and talented youth. About 10 percent of charter schools are managed by for-profit EMOs, such as Edison Schools, Advantage Schools, and Charter Schools USA.

Most charter schools are small. The federal study estimates their median enrollment at 137 students, compared to the 475-pupil public school average in 27 charter states. Almost two-thirds (65.2 percent) of charters enroll fewer than 200 students. (Just 17 percent of regular public schools are that small.) With small scale comes intimacy and familiarity that are often missing from the larger and more anonymous institutions of public education.

Unfortunately, some schools called "charter schools" are in fact Potemkin charters, displaying the façade but not the reality. So-called "weak" charter laws place constraints on schools' educational, financial, and operational autonomy—e.g., teacher certification requirements, uniform salary schedules, and collective-bargaining agreements. And many charter schools receive less than full per-pupil funding, with no allowance for facilities and other capital expenses. The upshot is that some charter schools are pale shadows of what they are meant to be.

Where Did Charter Schools Come From?

Most charter experts agree that the phrase "charter schools" was first used by the late Albert Shanker, longtime president of the American Federation of Teachers, in a 1988 speech to the National Press Club and a subsequent article. This is ironic, in view of the teacher unions' initial hostility and continuing skepticism to the charter movement. But it was not unusual for the brilliant and venturesome Shanker to suggest education reform concepts well in advance of their time.

Basing his vision on a school he had visited in Cologne, Germany, Shanker urged America to develop "a fundamentally different model of schooling that emerges when we rethink age-old assumptions—the kind of rethinking that is necessary to develop schools to reach the up to 80 percent of our youngsters who are failing in one way or another in the current system."

He contemplated an arrangement that would "enable any school or any group of teachers . . . within a school to develop a proposal for how they could better educate youngsters and then give them a 'charter' to implement that proposal." "All this," Shanker wrote, "would be voluntary."

> No teacher would have to participate and parents would choose whether or not to send their children to a charter school. . . . The school . . . would have to accept students who are representative of other students in the district or building in terms of ability and background. Charter schools also would have to conform to other civil rights guarantees. For its part, the school district would have to agree that so long as teachers continued to want to teach in the charter school and parents continued to send their children there and there was no precipitous decline in student achievement indicators, it would

maintain the school for at least 5–10 years. Perhaps at the end of that period, the school could be evaluated to see the extent to which it met its goals, and the charter could be extended or revoked.

Shanker was echoed in a 1989 article by Ray Budde called "Education by Charter." Then a Minnesota legislator named Ember Reichgott Junge resolved to launch this idea in her state, the first to pass charter school legislation in 1991.

Yet that scrap of history doesn't do justice to the many tributaries that fed into the charter idea, both in the education environment and the wider culture. Within the world of education, these ideas include the hunger for higher standards for students and teachers; the realization that education quality would be judged by its results rather than its inputs (e.g., per pupil spending or class size) and its compliance with rules; the impulse to create new and different school designs that meet the needs of today's families; and the movement to give families more choices of schools.

In addition to changes in the education realm, developments in other domains of U.S. society helped clear the path for charter schools. In the corporate sector, traditional bureaucratic arrangements were being restructured, dispensing with middle management and top-down control. In the public sector, the effort to reinvent government was spawned. Both these sectors moved in the direction of a "tight-loose" management strategy: tightly controlled with respect to their goals and standards—the results they must achieve, and the information by which performance is tracked—but loose as to the *means* by which those results get produced.

Besides transformations in education, business, and government, other societal changes helped create a hospitable climate for charter schools. Beginning in the 1960s, there was the broad liberalization of American culture, what political scientist Hugh Heclo grandly terms an "awakening... to a plurality of authenticities." Its elements have included, for better or worse, the decline of traditional authority, the exaltation of personal freedom, the rise of tolerance as a supreme value, and the spread of pluralism, multiculturalism, and diversity.

Accompanying these changes has been rekindled interest in the vitality of "civil society," with the civic order recognized as a third path—neither governmental nor strictly private—to meet human needs and solve community problems. Mediating institutions—e.g., churches, Neighborhood Watch groups, and organizations such as the Red Cross and the Girl Scouts—can help solve intractable social problems while strengthening community bonds.

These many tributaries have fed a river of change in public education, which we term "the radicalization of school reform." Charter schools are today's most prominent expression of that process. They change the emphasis from inputs to results by focusing on student achievement. They flip the structure from rule-bound hierarchy to decentralized flexibility by allowing individual schools to shape their own destinies. They constitute education's version of civil society, a hybrid that draws on the best of the public and private sectors. They introduce enterprise, competition, choice, community, and accountability into a weary system.

Reinventing America's Schools

We often think of charters as "reinventing public education." Traditionally, Americans have defined a public school as any school run by the government, managed by a superintendent and school board, staffed by public employees, and operated within a public-sector bureaucracy. "Public school" in this familiar sense is not very different from "public library," "public park," or "public housing" project.

Now consider a different definition: a public school is any school that is open to the public, paid for by the public, and accountable to public authorities for its results. So long as it satisfies those three criteria, it is a public school. Government need not run it. Indeed, it does not matter—for purposes of its "publicness"—who runs it, how it is staffed, or what its students do between 9 a.m. and 10 a.m. on Tuesdays.

Charter schools are the farthest-flung example today of a reinvented—a radicalized—public education. But it is important to bear in mind that they are part of a bigger idea: public education in which elected and appointed officials play a strategic rather than a functional role. Public support of schooling without governmental provision of schools.

What is the nature of the charter approach to radicalizing school reform? Some see the charter idea as a dangerous predator in the education ecosystem, one that will gradually consume and thereby destroy public education. But that isn't the only way to view this dynamic change.

Stephen Jay Gould's discussion of the "cropping principle" in evolution offers a different perspective. The conventional wisdom about the appearance of a new plant- or meat-eating animal—a "cropper"—into a territory is that it shrinks the number of species in the area. But science has found that in nature precisely the opposite occurs. The cropper actually tends to enrich, not decimate, the ecosystem. In Gould's words, "A well-cropped ecosystem is maximally diverse, with many species and few individuals of any single species. Stated another way, the introduction of a new level in the ecological pyramid tends to broaden the level below it." We believe this is the effect that the charter idea will have—indeed is beginning to have—on public education: enriching and broadening the entire ecosystem.

Charter enthusiasts and opponents both tend to depict these schools as a revolutionary change, a policy earthquake, an unprecedented and heretofore unimaginable innovation. The boosters seize on such colorful rhetoric because it dramatizes the historic significance of their crusade. Enemies deploy the same terminology for the opposite purpose: to slow this reform's spread by scaring people into seeing it as radical, risky, and unproven. Both groups tend to stand too close to the objects they are describing.

Viewed from a few inches away, charter schools *do* represent sharp changes in the customary patterns and practices of today's public school systems, especially the large ones. But with more perspective, we readily observe that charter schools embody three familiar and time-tested features of American education.

First, they are rooted in their communities, the true essence of local control of education, not unlike the village schools of the early 19th century and the one-room schoolhouses that could be found across the land through most of the 20th century. They are much like America's original public schools in their local autonomy, their rootedness in communities, their accountability to parents, and their need to generate revenues by attracting and retaining families. Creatures of civil society as much as agencies of government, charter schools would have raised no eyebrows on Alexis de Tocqueville.

Second, charter schools have cousins in the K-12 family. Their DNA looks much the same under the education microscope as that of lab schools, magnet schools, site-managed schools, and special focus schools (e.g., art, drama, science), not to mention private and home schools. Much the same, but not identical. The Bronx High School of Science is selective, while charter schools are not. Hillel Academy and the Sancta Maria Middle School teach religion, while charter schools cannot. The Urban Magnet School of the Arts was probably designed by a downtown bureaucracy and most likely has carefully managed ethnic ratios in its student body, whereas most charter schools do not. Yet the similarities outweigh the differences.

Third, these new schools reveal a classic American response to a problem, challenge, or opportunity: institutional innovation and adaptation. In that respect, they resemble community colleges, which came into being (and spread rapidly and fruitfully) to meet education needs that conventional universities could not accommodate. As an organizational form, then, charter schools are not revolutionary. They are part of what we are and always have been as a nation.

NO

Marc F. Bernstein

Why I'm Wary of Charter Schools

With its passage of the New York Charter Schools Act of 1998, New York...
became the 34th state to authorize or implement charter schools.

As a result, roughly two-thirds of the school districts nationwide now are
subject to an educational reform that has yet to prove its worth but has raised
the most serious practical and philosophical challenges to the viability of public
education in our country's history.

In New York, a charter school can be established through an application
submitted by teachers, parents, school administrators, community residents or
any combination thereof. Though charter schools are subject to the same health
and safety, civil rights and student assessment requirements of other public
schools, they are exempt from all other state regulations.

The Case for Charters

The case for charter schools is quite simple—the arguments typically revolve
around the alleged failure of the public schools. Though many have contested
the validity of these charges (educational researchers Gerald Bracey and David
Berliner prime among them), the news media, the political establishment and a
large segment of the public have become convinced that our schools are failing
to serve the children with whom they've been entrusted.

The 15-year diatribe, beginning with the *Nation at Risk* report in 1984,
has been translated in recent years into legislative action enabling students
to attend alternative charter schools paid for by the school districts that the
students would have otherwise attended. Charter schools, by law, are free of
most state mandates and are not obligated to conform to teacher union work
rules and hours.

Charter school proponents contend the freedom from state regulations
and collective bargaining constraints will yield significant advantages:

- Charter schools will permit and encourage a more creative approach to
  teaching and learning;
- Charter schools will establish models of educational reform for other
  schools in the same community;

- Charter schools will be more reflective of parent and community priorities through the alternative programs that cater to special interests and needs;
- Charter schools will operate in a more cost-effective manner; and
- Charter schools will be governed by boards consisting of parents, teachers and community members, making them more responsive than public schools.

Unrealized Gains

Not only have these benefits not accrued to most of the students attending existing charter schools, but charter school proponents neglect to address three overarching concerns regarding the potential consequences of this movement.

First, the public money used to fund charter schools must come from an existing source and that source is the budget of the public school district.

Second, charter school populations tend to be more homogeneous than most public schools in terms of ethnicity, religion or race. This homogeneity will have a Balkanizing effect when young children are most open to dealing with differences among people.

Third, the constitutional separation between school and religion will be compromised by people of goodwill (and others) who see opportunities to provide alternate education to children in need.

Before elaborating on these concerns, it is instructive to review the formal studies completed to date that have examined the progress of charter schools in fulfilling their stated goals. Charter school advocates, however, seem to show little or no interest in research data about charter schools.

The Case Not Made

In perhaps the most extensive study to date, "Beyond the Rhetoric of Charter School Reform: A Study of Ten California School Districts," researchers at UCLA, led by Professor Amy Stuart Wells, looked at 17 charter schools in 10 school districts. Their selection of districts were chosen for their diversity in order "to capture the range of experiences within this reform movement."

Among its 15 findings, the study concluded that California's charter schools have not lived up to proponents' claims. Four of the findings are most telling:

- California's charter schools, in most instances, are not yet being held accountable for enhanced academic achievement of their students;
- Charter schools exercise considerable control over the type of students they serve;
- The requirement that charter schools reflect the social/ethnic makeup of their districts has not been enforced;
- No mechanisms are in place for charter schools and regular public schools to learn from each other.

Moreover, the researchers found "no evidence that charter schools can do more with less" and that "regular public schools in districts with charter schools felt little to no pressure from the charter schools to change the way they do business." Thus, the UCLA study disputes in the strongest of terms that charter schools raise the academic achievement of their students in a more cost-effective manner and that nearby public schools will do a better job educating their children by adopting the innovations of the charter schools.

In a yearlong study of Michigan's charter school initiative, researchers at Western Michigan University concluded that charter schools may not be living up to their promise of educational innovation and more effective use of public money. The report, which was presented to the pro-charter state board of education . . . , characterized many charters as "cookie-cutter" schools run by for-profit companies and suggested that many administrators and charter school boards were ill-equipped to run a school.

These two studies are clear in their findings, yet the charter movement grows. If the spread of charter schools did not auger the most dangerous consequences, we could ignore it as yet another failed experiment in American education. But the risks here are too great, not only to America's public schools, but to our very society.

The gravest concerns fall into three categories: financial impact, Balkanization and religious intrusion.

Financial Harm

The most direct and immediate impact upon the public schools relates to financing. Money to operate the charter schools comes from the public schools, whether the financing mechanism be that (1) the public school draws a check to the charter; (2) the state forwards a proportion of what the public would have received to the charter; or (3) the state's discretionary resources that could have been used to improve the public schools are budgeted for charter schools.

Regardless of the process, public schools wind up with fewer dollars to improve the education of their students. Such reduced funding likely will lead to poorer academic results, which then will be used to strengthen the case that charter schools (or voucher programs) are the only recourse for failing public schools. Is this Orwellian in intent or merely ignorant in practice?

In New York, where I've worked as a superintendent for 13 years, the public schools are required to pay the charter schools the average operating expenditure per pupil as computed for the most recent school year based on the number of students the charter school claims it will serve in the forthcoming school year. When public school leaders suggested that their schools would be denied a disproportionate amount of money, charter school proponents (and legislators) responded that the money is merely following the student. As such, the public school would have the same percentage of money as students.

This simplistic argument totally ignores the economic concept of marginal cost. It costs less to educate the 24th student in the class than the initial 5, 10, 15 or 20. In my letter to the editor of *The New York Times* on this subject . . . , I wrote: "This means that if 10 students in each grade were to transfer to a charter school from a 1,000-student public elementary school, the public school would lose approximately $500,000. No teacher, custodian or secretary salaries can be eliminated as a result of the reduction in the number of students. However, the public school would have $500,000 less available to educate its remaining students."

Where is the public school to go to recoup this lost $500,000? There are but two choices—raise taxes or reduce programming. Either choice has serious consequences for public education. If we raise taxes, our taxpayers will be paying more to educate fewer students. They won't care to hear about the principle of marginal cost. They will see the public schools as inefficient and will scream for tax relief or increased accountability for the costly public schools. And, if we cut programming or classroom staffing, our parents will demand to know why we are shortchanging their children.

Clearly, the cost of educating some students is greater than it is for others. Few would question that it costs more to meet the needs of a child with disabilities or one who enters public school without speaking English. Research shows it is the knowledgeable parents who do their homework in terms of investigating alternatives to the public school. Therefore, charter schools are more likely to have a sufficient pool of "less costly" applicants leaving the public school with the more costly students to educate.

In addition to penalizing public schools by reducing operating funds, New York state will have fewer total dollars available for educating students.

One provision of the new charter school law requires the state to establish a fund to provide charter schools with loans for furniture, equipment and facilities. The reservoir of available state money is only so large. It can only drain in so many directions. Thus, public schools that are now required to meet higher academic standards will be told that the state lacks the resources to assist.

The only other source of revenue for the public schools is the local taxpayer. Of course, the alternative is to eliminate or cut back nonacademic offerings. Those programs most likely to be dropped or curtailed are those in art or music, the ones for which there is no bottom-line, quantitative assessment.

Either choice results in a no-win situation. We can alienate our taxpayers or we can jeopardize the support of our parents.

Moreover, citizens in this state have the opportunity to register their support or disagreement with a school district's educational program through their vote on the annual school budget. Inasmuch as the charter school's program is solely within the control of its board of directors, is there not a true gap between the public's right of the purse strings and the independence given to charter schools?

A Balkanizing Effect

Can separate be equal?

This question, we thought, had been answered in 1954 by the U.S. Supreme Court in *Brown vs. Board of Education* when racially segregated schools prevailed in parts of our country by the design of governmental entities.

Nearly a half century later, we now have a government-endorsed policy leading us back to that same situation. Surprisingly, charter schools seem to enjoy strong support among minority legislators and advocates, the same groups that rallied behind the Supreme Court's decision that "separate is not equal" in education.

This reversal may reflect the disenchantment of minority parents with America's inner-city schools, which serve the greatest percentage of minority students. For example, a recent poll by the Washington-based Joint Center for Political and Economic Studies reported that blacks are 11 percent less likely than whites to be satisfied with their local public schools.

Though charter school laws in most states attempt to address the matter of potential racial imbalancing, the charter schools nonetheless are becoming increasingly segregated. The Minnesota Charter Schools Evaluation, conducted in 1998 by the University of Minnesota, found that charter schools in that state typically enroll greater numbers of ethnic minorities than the regular schools in their home districts. Half of the charters have student populations that are more than 60 percent children of color.

In Michigan, a statewide study of charters by Western Michigan University identified a segregation pattern in which white children were opting out of local public schools. The percentage of minorities in charters declined by more than 22 percent between 1995 and 1998.

Two other detailed studies—one in North Carolina, the other in Arizona—concluded that their states' charter schools have become increasingly segregated by race. The North Carolina Office of Charter Schools found that 13 of 34 charter schools that opened in 1997 were disproportionately black, compared with their districts. And, the North Carolina Education Reform Foundation, which helps to start charter schools, says at least 9 of the 26 schools that opened last year violate the diversity clause.

Having anticipated the possibility of segregation, North Carolina's charter school law included a diversity clause requiring charter schools to "reasonably reflect" the demographics of their school districts. Even so, the opposite has occurred.

A study titled "Ethnic Segregation in Arizona Charter Schools," issued in January 1999 by Casey Cobb of University of New Hampshire and Gene Glass of Arizona State University, found that nearly half of the state's 215 charter schools (as of 1997) "exhibited evidence of substantial ethnic separation."

These studies describe but one type of segregation—racial—while the term Balkanization connotes the formal division of a geographic area along racial, ethnic and/or religious lines. How unfortunate it would be for our nation's communities to become more fractionalized than they already are.

The limited existing research points to this as a possible outcome as students' attendance is based upon factors other than the schools' academic performance, whether at the parents' choosing or the schools' selection.

America's public schools have as one of their primary goals to acculturate, sensitize and civilize our children to prepare them for their future roles in a democratic society. Will this goal be seriously compromised due to charter schools? I believe it was René Descartes who wrote that the chief cause of human error is to be found in the prejudices picked up in childhood.

Religious Intrusion

Following our state's adoption of a charter school law, New York City religious leaders began enthusiastically preparing themselves to establish charter schools. They already had access to classroom space, an extremely rare commodity, and a significant presence in their communities, which could only help in attracting students. Plus, the religious leaders have been persistent critics of the city's schools.

The most vocal of the clergy, the Rev. Floyd H. Flake of Queens, N.Y., a former U.S. congressman, argued for "skirt(ing) the constitutional barriers between church and state by offering religious instruction outside school hours."

This creative thinking is not limited to New York City. *Education Week* reported . . . that the Rev. Michael Pfleger, a pastor on Chicago's South Side, "has discussed shutting down St. Sabina (its parish school) and, in its place, opening a publicly funded charter school run by a nonprofit board, possibly with links to the parish or the Catholic archdiocese." Both Flake and Pfleger see charter schools as an opportunity to use public money to subsidize their educational and religious efforts.

The U.S. Constitution speaks loudly and clearly against religious intrusion into the public schools. In spite of Supreme Court cases defining the nature of permissible involvements, the issue is never truly resolved. Litigation involving charter schools inevitably will require the court to rule on charter schools' use of church property, the participation of religious leaders on charter school governing boards and the attendance of charter school students at home and afterschool religious education programs when the church's facilities are used to house the charter school.

The court's decisions will significantly affect public school finances and the influence religion will have upon children attending the nation's public schools, whether they are charter or regular public schools.

Constant Monitoring

Though charter schools have yet to prove their academic worth, they are rapidly increasing in number across the country. They provide choices to parents for their children's education and level the playing field between higher and lower socioeconomic classes. Charter schools lend a warm feeling that government is doing something to fix our failing schools by turning the capitalistic engine of competition loose upon the schools.

In reality, charter schools are denying public schools the financial resources they require to address the needs of an increasingly disparate student population. Our communities will be further divided along racial, religious and ethnic lines as children attend their schools of choice, opting to be with children of similar backgrounds. And the never-ending battle to maintain the separation of church and state will suffer another setback as public money moves in the direction of religious (charter) schools, where children receive religious instruction under the guise of attending charter schools.

As educational leaders committed to the values of public education, we must be wary of these unintended consequences. We must continually monitor charter schools' academic performance, use of public money for religious instruction and adherence to diversity provisions.

Undoubtedly, many policymakers have prejudged the success of the charter schools movement. But we must assume the duty to inform the public about this most serious challenge to public education. As part of a professional leadership organization and as career educators, we must monitor the performance of charters in our communities and communicate our concerns to legislators.

POSTSCRIPT

Can Charter Schools Revitalize Public Education?

Charter schools—are they a source of innovation, inspiration, and revitalization in public education or a drain on human and fiscal resources that will leave regular public schools weaker than ever? The debate has just begun, and preliminary results are just beginning to trickle in. But the air is filled with predictions, opinions, and pontifications.

Alex Molnar offers some scathing commentary on the charter school and privatization movements in his article "Charter Schools: The Smiling Face of Disinvestment," *Educational Leadership* (October 1996) and in his book *Giving Kids the Business: The Commercialization of America's Schools* (1996). A more positive assessment is delivered by Joe Nathan in his book *Charter Schools: Creating Hope and Opportunity for American Schools* (1996) and in his article "Heat and Light in the Charter School Movement," *Phi Delta Kappan* (March 1998). Further positive descriptions are provided in James N. Goenner's "Charter Schools: The Revitalization of Public Education," *Phi Delta Kappan* (September 1996) and James K. Glassman's "Class Acts," *Reason* (April 1998).

Additional sources of ideas include *How to Create Alternative, Magnet, and Charter Schools That Work* by Robert D. Barr and William H. Parrett (1997); "Homegrown," by Nathan Glazer, *The New Republic* (May 12, 1997); "Charter Schools: A Viable Public School Choice Option?" by Terry G. Geske et al., *Economics of Education Review* (February 1997); "A Closer Look at Charters," by Judith Brody Saks, *American School Board Journal* (January 1998); "Healthy Competition," by David Osborne, *The New Republic* (October 4, 1999); "Chinks in the Charter School Armor," by Tom Watkins, *American School Board Journal* (December 1999); and Seymour Sarason's *Charter Schools: Another Flawed Educational Reform* (1998).

Some recent provocative publications are Arthur Levine, "The Private Sector's Market Mentality," *The School Administrator* (May 2000); Bruce Fuller, ed., *Inside Charter Schools: The Paradox of Radical Decentralization* (2000); and Bruno V. Manno, "The Case Against Charter Schools," *The School Administrator* (May 2001), in which Manno responds to common complaints.

A few more articles worthy of note are "No Magic Bullet," *The American Teacher* (December 1997); "How to Revive America's Public Schools," *The World & I* (September 1997); and "School Reform—Charter Schools," *Harvard Law Review* (May 1997). Multiple articles may be found in *The School Administrator* (August 1999), *Education and Urban Society* (August 1999), and *Phi Delta Kappan* (March 2002).

ISSUE 13

Have Public Schools Adequately Accommodated Religion?

YES: Edd Doerr, from "Religion and Public Education," *Phi Delta Kappan* (November 1998)

NO: Warren A. Nord, from "The Relevance of Religion to the Curriculum," *The School Administrator* (January 1999)

ISSUE SUMMARY

YES: Edd Doerr, executive director of Americans for Religious Liberty, asserts that a fair balance between free exercise rights and the obligation of neutrality has been achieved in the public schools.

NO: Warren A. Nord, a professor of the philosophy of religion, contends that the schools are still too secular and that a place in the curriculum must be found for religion.

The religious grounding of early schooling in America certainly cannot be denied, nor can the history of religious influences on the conduct of governmental functions. For example, U.S. Supreme Court decisions in the early decades of the twentieth century allowed certain cooperative practices between public school systems and community religious groups. However, it must also be recognized that many students, parents, and taxpayer organizations were distressed by some of these accommodating policies. Legal action taken by or on the behalf of some of the offended parties led to Supreme Court restrictions on prayer and Bible reading in the public schools in the 1960s. Particularly notable were the decisions in *Engel v. Vitale* (1962), *Murray v. Curlett* (1963), and *School District of Abington Township v. Schempp* (1963). These decisions curtailed the use of public school time and facilities for ceremonial and devotional religious purposes, but they did not outlaw the discussion of religion or the use of religious materials in appropriate academic contexts.

During the 1970s and 1980s religious activists, led by the Reverend Jerry Falwell's Moral Majority, campaigned against what they perceived to be the tyranny of a public education establishment dominated by the philosophy of secular humanism. Efforts were made to include creationism in the science curriculum as an antidote to the theory of evolution and to legalize voluntary organized prayer in the public schools. Despite these efforts, the courts have generally disallowed the teaching of "creation science," have vetoed organized moments of "silent meditation," and have declared unconstitutional the practice of including prayers in graduation ceremonies. Religious groups gained at least one major victory in the 1980s with the passage of the Equal Access Act, federal legislation that guarantees access to public school facilities for students wishing to engage in religious activities during nonschool hours. The legislation, which has been challenged in some localities, has been upheld by the U.S. Supreme Court.

And the battles continue. Recently, Kansans attempted to remove the theory of evolution from the science curriculum, Texans have pressed for approval of student-led invocations at high school football games, Virginians have tested a new version of daily "meditation moments," and several states have allowed the posting of the Ten Commandments in public schools. In the wake of the Columbine High School massacre and mounting evidence of "moral decay" among American youth, the pressure for further accommodation of religion seems to be growing. In December 1999 President Bill Clinton issued new guidelines promoting stronger partnerships between religious institutions and public schools in local communities, particularly in the areas of school safety, discipline, and literacy. Some national groups, such as Americans United for Separation of Church and State and People for the American Way, raised questions about the vagueness of these guidelines and the absence of clear limits on the extent of involvement. Another type of accommodation involves the providing or lending of secular learning materials and computer equipment to religious schools. A *Washington Post* editorial, "Church-State Muddle" (December 6, 1999), poses this dilemma: To disallow such aid programs discriminates against schools because of their religious affiliations, but to uphold these programs validates public support for religious institutions.

Some sources that examine the current status of this ongoing struggle include Perry Glanzer, "Religion in Public Schools: In Search of Fairness," *Phi Delta Kappan* (November 1998); Oliver S. Thomas, "Legal Leeway on Church-State in School," *The School Administrator* (January 1999); Gilbert T. Sewall, "Religion Comes to School," and Thomas Lickona, "Religion and Character Education," *Phi Delta Kappan* (September 1999); and Charles C. Haynes, "Seeking Common Ground," *American School Board Journal* (February 2000).

In the first of the following selections, Edd Doerr reviews what is permitted and what is forbidden on the basis of some 50 years of Supreme Court rulings and expresses belief that accommodation has gone as far as it can. Warren A. Nord, in the second selection, asserts that the study of religious thought and influence has been marginalized in the curriculum and that public school students are systematically taught to think about the world in secular ways only.

Edd Doerr

 **YES**

Religion and Public Education

On 4 June 1998, the U.S. House of Representatives voted 224 to 203 for the so-called Religious Freedom Amendment, sponsored by Rep. Ernest Istook (R-Okla.) and more than 150 co-sponsors.[1] The measure fell well short of the two-thirds majority required to pass a constitutional amendment. In fact, the 52.4% vote dropped well below the 59.7% garnered on a similar proposal in 1971, the last time a school prayer amendment reached the House floor. The amendment's defeat is especially significant because it had strong backing from the House majority leadership and was the culmination of a massive four-year campaign led by televangelist Pat Robertson's Christian Coalition.

The Istook Amendment aroused strong opposition from education organizations, mainstream religious groups, and civil liberties organizations because it would have embroiled school districts and communities in prolonged, bitter, divisive conflicts over religious activities in the classroom or at graduations, athletic events, school assemblies, and other gatherings. In addition, the amendment's clause against "deny[ing] equal access to a benefit on account of religion" would have cleared the way for massive tax support of sectarian schools and other institutions. Opponents of the amendment correctly worried that it would weaken or wreck the First Amendment, taking the first major bite out of the Bill of Rights since its ratification in 1791.

Two weeks before the vote on the amendment, the U.S. Commission on Civil Rights held the first of three projected hearings on "Schools and Religion." Most of the 16 experts who spoke at the hearing (including this writer, I must disclose) agreed that the relevant Supreme Court rulings and other developments have pretty much brought public education into line with the religious neutrality required by the First Amendment and the increasingly pluralistic nature of our society. A fair balance has been established between the free exercise rights of students and the constitutional obligation of neutrality.

The speakers attributed the current reasonably satisfactory situation to 50 years of appropriate Supreme Court rulings plus two specific developments: passage by Congress in 1984 of the Equal Access Law, which allows student-

From Edd Doerr, "Religion and Public Education," *Phi Delta Kappan* (November 1998). Copyright © 1998 by Phi Delta Kappa International, Inc. Reprinted by permission of Phi Delta Kappa International, Inc., and the author.

initiated religious groups or other groups not related to the curriculum to meet, without school sponsorship, during noninstructional time; and the U.S. Department of Education's issuance in August 1995 of guidelines on "Religious Expression in Public Schools."

A minority of speakers at the heating cited anecdotes about alleged violations of students' religious freedom. These turned out to be either exaggerations or cases of mistakes by teachers or administrators that were easily remedied by a phone call or letter. The occasional violations of student rights, like "man bites dog" stories, are few and far between and certainly do not point to any need to amend the Constitution.

Julie Underwood, general counsel designate for the National School Boards Association (NSBA), told the hearing that inquiries to the NSBA about what is or is not permitted in public schools declined almost to the vanishing point once the "Religious Expression in Public Schools" guidelines were published.

The guidelines grew out of a document titled "Religion in the Public Schools: A Joint Statement of Current Law," issued in April 1995 by a broad coalition of 36 religious and civil liberties groups.[2] The statement declared that the Constitution "permits much private religious activity in and around the public schools and does not turn the schools into religion-free zones." The statement went on to detail what is and is not permissible in the schools.

On 12 July 1995, President Clinton discussed these issues in a major address at—appropriately—James Madison High School in northern Virginia and announced that he was directing the secretary of education, in consultation with the attorney general, to issue advisory guidelines to every public school district in the country. This was done in August.

In his weekly radio address of 30 May 1998, anticipating the June 4 House debate and vote on the Istook Amendment, the President again addressed the issue and announced that the guidelines, updated slightly, were being reissued and sent to every district. This effort undoubtedly helped to sway the House vote.

The guidelines, based on 50 years of court rulings (from the 1948 *McCollum* decision to the present), on common sense, and on a healthy respect for American religious diversity, have proved useful to school boards, administrators, teachers, students, parents, and religious leaders. Following is a brief summary.

Permitted

"Purely private religious speech by students"; nondisruptive individual or group prayer, grace before meals, religious literature reading; student speech about religion or anything else, including that intended to persuade, so long as it stops short of harassment; private baccalaureate services; teaching *about* religion; inclusion by students of religious matter in written or oral assignments where not inappropriate; student distribution of religious literature on the same terms as other material not related to school curricula or activities; some degree of right to excusal from lessons objectionable on religious or conscientious grounds, subject to applicable state laws; off-campus released time or dismissed time for religious instruction; teaching civic values; student-initiated "Equal Access" religious groups of secondary students during noninstructional time.

Prohibited

School endorsement of any religious activity or doctrine; coerced participation in religious activity; engaging in or leading student religious activity by teachers, coaches, or officials acting as advisors to student groups; allowing harassment of or religious imposition on "captive audiences"; observing holidays as religious events or promoting such observance; imposing restrictions on religious expression more stringent than those on nonreligious expression; allowing religious instruction by outsiders on school premises during the school day.

Required

"Official neutrality regarding religious activity."

In reissuing the guidelines, Secretary Riley urged school districts to use them or to develop their own, preferably in cooperation with parents, teachers, and the "broader community." He recommended that principals, administrators, teachers, schools of education, prospective teachers, parents, and students all become familiar with them.

As President Clinton declared in his May 30 address, "Since we've issued these guidelines, appropriate religious activity has flourished in our schools, and there has apparently been a substantial decline in the contentious argument and litigation that has accompanied this issue for too long."

As good and useful as the guidelines are, there remain three areas in which problems continue: proselytizing by adults in public schools, music programs that fall short of the desired neutrality, and teaching appropriately about religion.

There are conservative evangelists, such as Jerry Johnston and the Rev. Jerry Falwell, who have described public schools as "mission fields." In communities from coast to coast, proselytizers from well-financed national organizations, such as Campus Crusade and Young Life, and volunteer "youth pastors" from local congregations have operated in public schools for years. They use a variety of techniques: presenting assembly programs featuring "role model" athletes, getting permission from school officials to contact students one-on-one in cafeterias and hallways, volunteering as unpaid teaching aides, and using substance abuse lectures or assemblies to gain access to students. It is not uncommon for these activities to have the tacit approval of local school authorities. Needless to say, these operations tend to take place more often in smaller, more religiously homogeneous communities than in larger, more pluralistic ones.

Religious music in the public school curriculum, in student concerts and theatrical productions, and at graduation ceremonies has long been a thorny issue. As Secretary Riley's 1995 and 1998 guidelines and court rulings have made clear, schools may offer instruction about religion, but they must remain religiously neutral and may not formally celebrate religious special days. What then about religious music, which looms large in the history of music?

As a vocal and instrumental musician in high school and college and as an amateur adult musician in both secular and religious musical groups, I feel qualified to address this issue. There should be no objection to the inclusion of religious music in the academic study of music and in vocal and instrumental performances, as long as the pieces are selected primarily for their musical or historical value, as long as the program is not predominantly religious, and as long as the principal purpose and effect of the inclusion is secular. Thus there should be no objection to inclusion in a school production of religious music by Bach or Aaron Copland's arrangements of such 19th-century songs as "Simple Gifts" or "Let Us Gather by the River." What constitutes "musical or historical value" is, of course, a matter of judgment and controversy among musicians and scholars, so there can be no simple formula for resolving all conflicts.

Certain activities should clearly be prohibited. Public school choral or instrumental ensembles should not be used to provide music for church services or celebrations, though a school ensemble might perform a secular music program in a church or synagogue as part of that congregation's series of secular concerts open to the public and not held in conjunction with a worship service. Sectarian hymns should not be included in graduation ceremonies; a Utah case dealing with that subject has been turned down for Supreme Court review. Students enrolled in music programs for credit should not be compelled to participate in performances that are not primarily religiously neutral.

As for teaching *about* religion, while one can agree with the Supreme Court that public schools may, and perhaps should, alleviate ignorance in this area in a fair, balanced, objective, neutral, academic way, getting from theory to practice is far from easy. The difficulties should be obvious. Teachers are very seldom adequately trained to teach about religion. There are no really suitable textbooks on the market. Educators and experts on religion are nowhere near agreement on precisely what ought to be taught, how much should be taught and at what grade levels, and whether such material should be integrated into social studies classes, when appropriate, or offered in separate courses, possibly electives. And those who complain most about the relative absence of religion from the curriculum seem to be less interested in neutral academic study than in narrower sectarian teaching.

Textbooks and schools tend to slight religion not out of hostility toward religion but because of low demand, lack of time (if you add something to the curriculum, what do you take out to make room for it?), lack of suitable materials, and fear of giving offense or generating unpleasant controversy.

The following questions hint at the complexity of the subject. Should teaching about religion deal only with the bright side of it and not with the dark side (religious wars, controversies, bigotry, persecutions, and so on)? Should instruction deal only with religions within the U.S., or should it include religions throughout the world? Should it be critical or uncritical? Should all religious traditions be covered or only some? Should the teaching deal only with sacred books—and, if so, which ones and which translations? How should change and development in all religions be dealt with?

To be more specific, should we teach only about the Pilgrims and the first Thanksgiving, or also about the Salem witch trials and the execution of Quakers? Should schools mention only the Protestant settlers in British North America or also deal with French Catholic missionaries in Canada, Michigan, and Indiana and with the Spanish Catholics and secret Jews in our Southwest? Should we mention that Martin Luther King was a Baptist minister but ignore the large number of clergy who defended slavery and then segregation on Biblical grounds?

Should teaching about religion cover such topics as the evolution of Christianity and its divisions, the Crusades, the Inquisition, the religious wars after the Reformation, the long history of anti-Semitism and other forms of murderous bigotry, the role of religion in social and international tensions (as in Ireland, in the former Yugoslavia, and in India and Pakistan), the development in the U.S. of religious liberty and church/state separation, denominations and religions founded in the U.S., controversies over women's rights and reproductive rights, or newer religious movements?

The probability that attempts to teach about religion will go horribly wrong should caution public schools to make haste very slowly in this area. In my opinion, other curricular inadequacies—less controversial ones, such as those in the fields of science, social studies, foreign languages, and word literature—should be remedied before we tackle the thorniest subject of all.

And let us not forget that the American landscape has no shortage of houses of worship, which generally include religious education as one of their main functions. Nothing prevents these institutions from providing all the teaching about religion they might desire.

The late Supreme Court Justice William Brennan summed up the constitutional ideal rather neatly in his concurring opinion in *Abington Township S.D. v. Schempp*, the 1963 school prayer case: "It is implicit in the history and character of American public education that the public schools serve a uniquely public function: the training of American citizens in an atmosphere free of parochial, divisive, or separatist influence of any sort—an atmosphere in which children may assimilate a heritage common to all American groups and religions. This is a heritage neither theistic nor atheistic, but simply civic and patriotic."

Notes

1. Text of H.J. Res. 78, Rep. Ernest Istook's Religious Freedom Amendment: "To secure the people's right to acknowledge God according to the dictates of conscience: Neither the United States nor any State shall establish any official religion, but the people's right to pray and to recognize their religious beliefs, heritage, or traditions on public property, including schools, shall not be infringed. Neither the United States nor any State shall require any person to join in prayer or other religious activity, prescribe school prayers, discriminate against religion, or deny equal access to a benefit on account of religion."

2. Copies of the statement are available free of charge from Americans for Religious Liberty, P.O. Box 6656, Silver Spring, MD 20916.

NO

Warren A. Nord

The Relevance of Religion to the Curriculum

For some time now, public school administrators have been on the front lines of our culture wars over religion and education—and I expect it would be music to their ears to hear that peace accords have been signed.

Unfortunately, the causes of war are deep-seated. Peace is not around the corner.

At the same time, however, it is also easy to overstate the extent of the hostilities. At least at the national level—but also in many communities across America—a large measure of common ground has been found. The leaders of most major national educational, religious and civil liberties organizations agree about the basic principles that should govern the role of religion and public schools. No doubt we don't agree about everything, but we agree about a lot.

For example, in 1988, a group of 17 major religious and educational organizations—the American Jewish Congress and the Islamic Society of North America, the National Association of Evangelicals and the National Council of Churches, the National Education Association and American Federation of Teachers, the National School Boards Association and AASA among them—endorsed a statement of principles that describes the importance of religion in the public school curriculum.

The statement, in part, says this: "Because religion plays significant roles in history and society, study about religion is essential to understanding both the nation and the world. Omission of facts about religion can give students the false impression that the religious life of humankind is insignificant or unimportant. Failure to understand even the basic symbols, practices and concepts of the various religions makes much of history, literature, art and contemporary life unintelligible."

A Profound Problem

As a result of this (and other "common ground" statements) it is no longer controversial to assert that the study of religion has a legitimate and important place in the public school curriculum.

Where in the curriculum? In practice, the study of religion has been relegated almost entirely to history texts and courses, for it is widely assumed that religion is irrelevant to every other subject in the curriculum—that is, to understanding the world here and now.

This is a deeply controversial assumption, however. A profoundly important educational problem lingers here, one that is almost completely ignored by educators.

Let me put it this way. Several ways exist for making sense of the world here and now. Many Americans accept one or another religious interpretation of reality; others accept one or another secular interpretation. We don't agree—and the differences among us often cut deeply.

Yet public schools systematically teach students to think about the world in secular ways only. They don't even bother to inform them about religious alternatives—apart from distant history. That is, public schooling discriminates against religious ways of making sense of the world. This is no minor problem.

An Economic Argument

To get some sense of what's at issue, let's consider economics.

One can think about the economic domain of life in various ways. Scriptural texts in all religious traditions address questions of justice and morality, poverty and wealth, work and stewardship, for example. A vast body of 20th century literature in moral theology deals with economic issues. Indeed, most mainline denominations and ecumenical agencies have official statements on justice and economics. What's common to all of this literature is the claim that the economic domain of life cannot be understood apart from religion.

Needless to say, this claim is not to be found in economics textbooks. Indeed, if we put end to end all the references to religion in the 10 high school economics texts I've reviewed in the past few years, they would add up to about two pages—out of 4,400 pages combined (and all of the references are to premodern times). There is but a single reference to religion—a passing mention in a section on taxation and non-profit organizations—in the 47 pages of the new national content standards in economics. Moreover, the textbooks and the standards say virtually nothing about the problems that are the major concern of theologians—problems relating to poverty, justice, our consumer culture, the Third World, human dignity and the meaningfulness of work.

The problem isn't just that the texts ignore religion and those economic problems of most concern to theologians. A part of the problem is what the texts do teach—that is, neoclassical economic theory. According to the texts, economics is a science, people are essentially self-interested utility-maximizers, the economic realm is one of competition for scarce resources, values are personal preferences and value judgments are matters of cost-benefit analysis. Of course, no religious tradition accepts this understanding of human nature, society, economics and values.

That is, the texts and standards demoralize and secularize economics.

An Appalling Claim

To be sure, they aren't explicitly hostile to religion; rather they ignore it. But in some ways this is worse than explicit hostility, for students remain unaware of the fact that there are tensions and conflicts between their religious traditions and what they are taught about economics.

In fact, the texts and the standards give students no sense that what they are learning is controversial. Indeed, the national economics standards make it a matter of principle that students be kept in the dark about alternatives to neoclassical theory. As the editors put it in their introduction, the standards were developed to convey a single conception of economics, the "majority paradigm" or neoclassical model of economic behavior. For, they argue, to include "strongly held minority views of economic processes [would only risk] confusing and frustrating teachers and students who are then left with the responsibility of sorting the qualifications and alternatives without a sufficient foundation to do so."

This is an appalling statement. It means, in effect, that students should be indoctrinated; they should be given no critical perspective on neoclassical economic theory.

The problem with the economics texts and standards is but one aspect of the much larger problem that cuts across the curriculum, for in every course students are taught to think in secular ways that often (though certainly not always) conflict with religious alternatives. And this is always done uncritically.

Even in history courses, students learn to think about historical meaning and causation in exclusively secular ways in spite of the fact that Judaism, Christianity and Islam all hold that God acts in history, that there is a religious meaning to history. True, they learn a few facts about religion, but they learn to think about history in secular categories.

Nurturing Secularity

Outside of history courses and literature courses that use historical literature, religion is rarely even mentioned, but even on those rare occasions when it is, the intellectual context is secular. As a result, public education nurtures a secular mentality. This marginalizes religion from our cultural and intellectual life and contributes powerfully to the secularization of our culture.

Ignoring religious ways of thinking about the world is a problem for three important reasons.

It is profoundly illiberal.

Here, of course, I'm not using the term "liberal" to refer to the left wing of the Democratic Party. A liberal education is a broad education, one that provides students with the perspective to think critically about the world and their lives. A good liberal education should introduce students—at least older students—

to the major ways humankind has developed for making sense of the world and their lives. Some of those ways of thinking and living are religious and it is illiberal to leave them out of the discussion. Indeed, it may well constitute indoctrination—secular indoctrination.

We indoctrinate students when we uncritically initiate them into one way of thinking and systematically ignore the alternatives. Indeed, if students are to be able to think critically about the secular ways of understanding the world that pervade the curriculum, they must understand something about the religious alternatives.

It is politically unjust.

Public schools must take the public seriously. But religious parents are now, in effect, educationally disenfranchised. Their ways of thinking and living aren't taken seriously.

Consider an analogy. A generation ago textbooks and curricula said virtually nothing about women, blacks and members of minority subcultures. Hardly anyone would now say that that was fair or just. We now—most of us —realize this was a form of discrimination, of educational disenfranchisement. And so it is with religious subcultures (though, ironically, the multicultural movement has been almost entirely silent about religion).

It is unconstitutional.

It is, of course, uncontroversial that it is constitutionally permissible to teach about religion in public schools when done properly. No Supreme Court justice has ever held otherwise. But I want to make a stronger argument.

The court has been clear that public schools must be neutral in matters of religion—in two senses. Schools must be neutral among religions (they can't favor Protestants over Catholics or Christians over Jews), and they must be neutral between religion and nonreligion. Schools can't promote religion. They can't proselytize. They can't conduct religious exercises.

Of course, neutrality is a two-edged sword. Just as schools can't favor religion over nonreligion, neither can they favor nonreligion over religion. As Justice Hugo Black put it in the seminal 1947 *Everson* ruling, "State power is no more to be used so as to handicap religions than it is to favor them."

Similarly, in his majority opinion in *Abington v. Schempp* in 1963, Justice Tom Clark wrote that schools can't favor "those who believe in no religion over those who do believe." And in a concurring opinion, Justice Arthur Goldberg warned that an "untutored devotion to the concept of neutrality [can lead to a] pervasive devotion to the secular and a passive, or even active, hostility to the religious."

Of course this is just what has happened. An untutored, naïve conception of neutrality has led educators to look for a smoking gun, an explicit hostility to religion, when the hostility has been philosophically rather more subtle— though no less substantial for that.

The only way to be neutral when all ground is contested ground is to be fair to the alternatives. That is, given the Supreme Court's longstanding interpretation of the Establishment Clause, public schools must require the study of religion if they require the study of disciplines that cumulatively lead to a pervasive devotion to the secular—as they do.

Classroom Practices

So how can we be fair? What would a good education look like? Here I can only skim the surface—and refer readers to *Taking Religion Seriously Across the Curriculum,* in which Charles Haynes and I chart what needs to be done in some detail.

Obviously a great deal depends on the age of students. In elementary schools students should learn something of the relatively uncontroversial aspects of different religions—their traditions, holidays, symbols and a little about religious histories, for example. As students mature, they should be initiated into that conversation about truth and goodness that constitutes a good liberal education. Here a two-prong approach is required.

First, students should learn something about religious ways of thinking about any subject that is religiously controversial in the relevant courses. So, for example, a biology text should include a chapter in which scientific ways of understanding nature was contrasted with religious alternatives. Students should learn that the relationship of religion and science is controversial, and that while they will learn what most biologists believe to be the truth about nature, not everyone agrees.

Indeed, every text and course should provide students with historical and philosophical perspective on the subject at hand, establishing connections and tensions with other disciplines and domains of the culture, including religion.

This is not a balanced-treatment or equal-time requirement. Biology courses should continue to be biology courses and economics courses should continue to be economics courses. In any case, given their competence and training, biology and economics teachers are not likely to be prepared to deal with a variety of religious ways of approaching their subject. At most, they can provide a minimal fairness.

A robust fairness is possible only if students are required to study religious as well as secular ways of making sense of the world in some depth, in courses devoted to the study of religion.

A good liberal education should require at least one year-long high school course in religious studies (with other courses, I would hope, available as electives). The primary goal of such a course should be to provide students with a sufficiently intensive exposure to religious ways of thinking and living to enable them to actually understand religion (rather than simply know a few facts about religion). It should expose students to scriptural texts, but it also should use more recent primary sources that enable students to understand how contemporary theologians and writers within different traditions think about those subjects in the curriculum—morality, sexuality, history, nature, psychology and the economic world—that they will be taught to interpret in secular categories in their other courses.

Of course, if religion courses are to be offered, there must be teachers competent to teach them. Religious studies must become a certifiable field in public education, and new courses must not be offered or required until competent teachers are available.

Indeed, all teachers must have a much clearer sense of how religion relates to the curriculum and, more particularly, to their respective subjects. Major reforms in teacher education are necessary—as is a new generation of textbooks sensitive to religion.

Some educators will find it unrealistic to expect such reforms. Of course several decades ago textbooks and curricula said little about women and minority cultures. Several decades ago, few universities had departments of religious studies. Now multicultural education is commonplace and most universities have departments of religious studies. Things change.

Stemming an Exodus

No doubt some educators will find these proposals controversial, but they will [be] shortsighted if they do. Leaving religion out of the curriculum is also controversial. Indeed, because public schools don't take religion seriously many religious parents have deserted them and, if the Supreme Court upholds the legality of vouchers, as they may well do, the exodus will be much greater.

In the long run, the least controversial position is the one that takes everyone seriously. If public schools are to survive our culture wars, they must be built on common ground. But there can be no common ground when religious voices are left out of the curricular conversation.

It is religious conservatives, of course, who are most critical of public schooling—and the most likely to leave. But my argument is that public schooling doesn't take any religion seriously. It marginalizes all religion—liberal as well as conservative, Catholic as well as Protestant, Jewish, Muslim and Buddhist as well as Christian. Indeed, it contributes a great deal to the secularization of American culture—and this should concern any religious person.

But, in the end, this shouldn't concern religious people only. Religion should be included in the curriculum for three very powerful secular reasons. The lack of serious study of religion in public education is illiberal, unjust and unconstitutional.

POSTSCRIPT

Have Public Schools Adequately Accommodated Religion?

Of all the groundless, hurtful attacks on public education, none is more painful than the charge that public schools are 'godless institutions of secular humanism.' ... The public school day may not start with a Hail Mary or an Our Father, a mantra or a blood sacrifice, but public education does more of God's work for children every day than any other institution in America—and that includes the churches." So says journalist Frosty Troy in "Far From 'Godless' Institutions," *The School Administrator* (March 2000).

For more moderate positions on the issue, see Rachael Kessler, "Nourishing Students in Secular Schools," *Educational Leadership* (December 1998/January 1999) and two articles in the December 1998 *American School Board Journal*, Jerry Cammarata's "We Haven't Got a Prayer" and Benjamin Dowling-Sendor's "Protecting Religious Vitality."

More recent opinions include the following: Charles A. Rohn, "Plenty of Religious Expression in Public Schools," *The School Administrator* (June 2000); Kenneth T. Murray and Craig S. Evans, "U.S. Supreme Court Revisits School Prayer," *NASSP Bulletin* (December 2000); Ralph D. Mawdsley, "Let Us Pray?" *Principal Leadership* (April 2001); Martha M. McCarthy, "Religious Influences in Public Education: Political and Judicial Developments," *The Educational Forum* (Spring 2001); and Michael H. Romanowski, "Is School Prayer the Answer?" *The Educational Forum* (Winter 2002).

Perhaps a reasonable summation of the total situation was provided by Charles C. Haynes in the *American School Board Journal* article cited in the issue introduction:

> The vast majority of educators are caring, dedicated professionals who want nothing more than to uphold the rights of all students and to address issues of religion and values with fairness and respect. But their training has left them ill-prepared to tackle religious-liberty questions or to teach substantively about religion in the curriculum, and they don't feel support from school boards and administrators to do so. Many school districts, in fact, have few or no policies concerning religion because school administrators and board members are often reluctant to address the underlying problems before a crisis erupts. Ironically, this avoidance is precisely what causes conflicts and lawsuits—either because religion is being ignored or because it is being improperly promoted by school officials.

ISSUE 14

Is Full Inclusion of Disabled Students Desirable?

YES: Jean B. Arnold and Harold W. Dodge, from "Room for All," *American School Board Journal* (October 1994)

NO: Karen Agne, from "The Dismantling of the Great American Public School," *Educational Horizons* (Spring 1998)

ISSUE SUMMARY

YES: Attorney Jean B. Arnold and school superintendent Harold W. Dodge discuss the federal Individuals with Disabilities Education Act and argue that its implementation can benefit all students.

NO: Assistant professor of education Karen Agne argues that legislation to include students with all sorts of disabilities has had mostly negative effects and contributes to the exodus from public schools.

T he Education for All Handicapped Children Act of 1975 (Public Law 94–142), which mandated that schools provide free public education to all students with disabilities, is an excellent example of how federal influence can translate social policy into practical alterations of public school procedures at the local level. With this act, the general social policy of equalizing educational opportunity and the specific social policy of ensuring that young people with various physical, mental, and emotional disabilities are constructively served by tax dollars were brought together in a law designed to provide persons with disabilities the same services and opportunities as nondisabled individuals. Legislation of such delicate matters does not ensure success, however. Although most people applaud the intentions of the act, some people find the expense ill-proportioned, and others feel that the federal mandate is unnecessary and heavy-handed.

Some of the main elements of the 1975 legislation were that all learners between the ages of 3 and 21 with handicaps—defined as students who are hearing impaired, visually impaired, physically disabled, emotionally disturbed, mentally retarded, or who have special learning disabilities—would be provided a free public education, that each of these students would have an individualized education program jointly developed by the school and the parents, that each student would be placed in the least restrictive learning environment appropriate to him or her, and that parents would have approval rights in placement decisions.

The 1990 version of the original law, the Individuals with Disabilities Education Act (IDEA), has spawned an "inclusive schools" movement, whose supporters recommend that *no* students be assigned to special classrooms or segregated wings of public schools. According to advocates of the act, "The inclusion option signifies the end of labeling and separate classes but not the end of necessary supports and services" for all students needing them.

The primary justification for inclusion, or "mainstreaming," has traditionally resided in the belief that disabled children have a right to and can benefit from inclusion in a regular educational environment whenever possible. French sociologist Emile Durkheim felt that attachment and belonging were essential to human development. If this is the case, then integration of young people with disabilities into regular classrooms and into other areas of social intercourse—as opposed to keeping them isolated in special classrooms—would seem to be highly desirable.

Douglas Fuchs and Lynn S. Fuchs, in "Inclusive Schools Movement and the Radicalization of Special Education Reform," *Exceptional Children* (February 1994), pose this question: How likely is the "inclusive schools" movement to bring special education and general education into synergistic alignment? One viewpoint comes from a five-year government study released in 1994, which found that special-needs students who spend all their time in regular classrooms fail more frequently than those who spend only some. This report, along with the American Federation of Teachers' call for an end to the practice of seeking all-day inclusion for every child, no matter how medically fragile or emotionally disturbed, have helped to keep the issue boiling.

Abigail Thernstrom, in "Courting Disaster in the Schools," *The Public Interest* (Summer 1999), contends that the rights of the disabled stipulated under IDEA have made discipline a "nightmare." The 1997 amendments to IDEA, however, expanded the school's alternatives for dealing with disruptive special needs student. Such students can be suspended for 10 days (or more in some cases); can be placed in an alternative setting for up to 45 days, even over a parent's objection; and can be kept out of the regular classroom for an additional 45 days after a special hearing.

In the selections that follow, Jean B. Arnold and Harold W. Dodge direct specific suggestions toward school board policymakers for complying with the requirements and intentions of the current law regarding full inclusion, and they argue that quality inclusion programs and services for students with disabilities will be beneficial to all students. Karen Agne contends that the inclusion of emotionally disturbed and intellectually unfit students in regular classes robs other students of needed attention, robs teachers of their sanity, and does not serve the special needs students effectively.

Jean B. Arnold and Harold W. Dodge  **YES**

Room for All

Few topics ignite more controversy among educators these days than full inclusion of disabled youngsters in regular classrooms. Part of the reason is that many people don't understand—or wrongly understand—what's required under the law.

One of the greatest myths is that full inclusion obligates a public school district to educate *every* student with a disability in a regular classroom for the *entire* school day. Full inclusion doesn't mean that. It means students with disabilities might be placed in a regular education classroom on a full-time basis, but, if appropriate and necessary, they still can be "pulled out" for special instruction or related services.

That is what Congress originally intended in adopting the statutory provision of the Individuals with Disabilities Education Act (IDEA) concerning placement in the "least restrictive environment appropriate." But many educators have been implementing the concept backward.

Here's what we mean: School officials might decide to place Johnny, a 6-year-old Down's syndrome child with an IQ of 45, in a classroom for the trainable mentally retarded as soon as his parents enroll him in school. They might later determine Johnny can be "mainstreamed" with regular education students for art, music, and lunch.

Actually, the way the law reads, Johnny should be placed in a regular classroom first, along with appropriate supplemental aids and services to assist him in that setting. If Johnny isn't benefiting from the education he receives in that setting, then the district should consider more restrictive and segregated options or settings that would enable him to get a good education, but still remain in his regular classroom as much as possible.

In some cases, even this scenario is not appropriate, and the student needs a more segregated environment, but the determination must be made on a case-by-case basis for each child. And it should begin with the idea of placement in a regular classroom and only then move to the more restricted setting—not vice versa.

Placement

For school boards, understanding inclusion—and what's legally required of your schools in educating disabled students—begins with understanding certain key legal concepts surrounding inclusion, as well as the findings in significant court cases.

The first legal concept to be familiar with is *placement*. Simply defined, placement is the setting in which the disabled child receives instruction. It is *not* the curriculum or program provided the student.

Both IDEA and case law indicate that you should heed certain points when deciding a child's placement:

- If possible, you should place a disabled child in a regular education classroom in the public school the child would attend if he or she had no disability. The deciding factor: whether, given the nature or severity of the child's disability, appropriate goals and objectives for the child can be achieved in a regular classroom, with or without the use of supplemental aids and services. The child's individualized education program, or IEP, determines the appropriate goals and objectives for that child.
- If you rule out the regular classroom for a specific child, you must select an alternative placement from a continuum of settings and arrangements (arrayed from least restrictive to most restrictive) maintained by the school system. The continuum might include, for example, resource-room instruction, a self-contained classroom, or even a private placement. You must select the placement in which the appropriate education goals for the child can be achieved with the fewest restrictions possible.
- Even when you rule out primary placement in the regular education environment, the disabled child must be educated with, and allowed to interact with, other children to the maximum extent appropriate to the needs of the disabled child.
- Placement decisions must be made at least annually by a group of people who consider broad-based, documented information about the child. These people must know the child and understand the evaluation data and the placement alternatives. At a minimum, the school representatives on the committee should include an educator who is knowledgeable about the student's disability, the student's teacher, and a special education supervisor.

Least-Restrictive Environment

Another essential item for you and your school board colleagues to understand is *least restrictive environment,* or LRE. According to IDEA, "Each public agency shall insure: (1) That to the maximum extent appropriate, handicapped children, including children in public or private institutions or other care facilities, are educated with children who are not handicapped, and (2) That special classes, separate schooling, or other removal of handicapped children from the regular educational environment occurs only when the nature or severity of the handicap is such that education in regular classes with the use of supplementary aids and services cannot be achieved satisfactorily." (34 C.F.R. 300.550 [b].)

Note that the law doesn't prohibit separate classes and separate schools; it merely requires they be filled on the basis of student need—not administrative convenience.

The leading court case in defining least restrictive environment is *Daniel R.R. v. State Board of Education* (1989). This case established several questions your district can use to decide whether a disabled child can be educated satisfactorily in the regular classroom. Before removing any child from the regular education classroom, your district should weigh its answers to each of these questions:

1. Have you taken steps to accommodate children with disabilities in regular education?   IDEA requires school districts to provide supplementary aids and services and to modify the regular education program in an effort to mainstream children with disabilities. Examples of these modifications include shortened assignments, note-taking assistance, visual aids, oral tests, and frequent breaks. The modifications should be geared to each disabled child's individual needs. If you make no effort to accommodate children with disabilities in the regular education classroom, you violate the law.

2. Are your district's efforts to accommodate the child in regular education sufficient or token?   A school district's efforts to supplement and modify regular education so disabled children can participate must amount to more than "mere token gestures," according to the ruling in *Daniel R.R.* The IDEA requirement for accommodating disabled children in regular education is broad. But, the ruling says, a school district need not provide "every conceivable supplementary aid or service" to assist disabled children in regular education. Furthermore, regular education instructors are not required to devote all or even most of their time to one disabled child to the detriment of the entire class.

A district also is not required to modify the regular education program beyond recognition. As the court held in *Daniel R.R.:* "[M]ainstreaming would be pointless if we forced instructors to modify the regular education curriculum to the extent that the handicapped child is not required to learn any of the skills normally taught in regular education." Such extensive modifications would result in special education being taught in a regular education classroom.

3. Will the child benefit educationally from regular education?   Another factor to consider is whether the child is capable of benefiting from regular education. Central to this question is whether the child can achieve the "essential elements" of the regular education curriculum.

You must consider both the nature and severity of the child's handicap as well as the curriculum and goals of the regular education class in determining educational benefit. However, a disabled child cannot be expected to achieve on a par with children who don't have disabilities before being permitted to attend the regular education classroom. Furthermore, you must remember that academic achievement is not the only purpose of mainstreaming. Allowing the child to be with children who aren't disabled can be beneficial in itself.

4. What will be the child's overall educational experience in the mainstreamed environment? Just because a child can receive only minimal academic benefit from regular education doesn't mean the child automatically should be excluded from regular education. You must consider the child's overall educational experience in the mainstreamed environment, balancing the benefits of regular and special education. Children who can't comprehend many of the essential elements of a lesson might still receive great benefit from their nondisabled peers, who serve as language and behavior models.

On the other hand, some children might become frustrated by their inability to succeed in the regular education classroom. If this frustration outweighs any benefit received from regular education, mainstreaming might prove detrimental to the child. Similarly, other children might need more structure than is available in the regular education setting. Your district must determine whether mainstreaming would be more beneficial or detrimental to the disabled child, considering both academic and social benefit.

5. What effect does the disabled child's presence have on the regular classroom environment? In determining the LRE, consider whether the child's presence in a regular education classroom adversely affects the education other children are receiving. First, determine whether the child engages in disruptive behavior that negatively affects the other children. Second, determine whether the disabled child requires so much of the teacher's attention that the teacher is forced to ignore the other children. If the teacher spends so much time with the disabled child that the rest of the class suffers, then the child should be educated in a special education classroom.

If you determine the child cannot be educated full time in the regular education classroom, you still have a duty to mainstream the child to the maximum extent appropriate. For instance, if regular academic classes are not appropriate for a given disabled child, the district could mainstream the child for nonacademic classes and activities, such as gym, recess, music, art, or lunch.

In short, placement in regular education is not an "all-or-nothing" proposition. Rather, school districts are required to offer a continuum of services for disabled children. A disabled child should be mainstreamed in regular education for as much of the time as is appropriate. Rarely will total exclusion from children without disabilities be deemed appropriate.

Beyond the Legal Requirements

Regardless of what IDEA says, the issue of whether students with disabilities can or should be served in regular education settings will continue to be debated and decided in the legal arena. Even so, the real issues are not legal; they are based in tradition, values, and beliefs. An increased understanding of how inclusion works, when implemented under the law, will help shape those traditions, values, and beliefs and will help school boards like yours design and put into practice high-quality inclusive programs and educational services for their students with disabilities.

Such services, however, can't be mandated or created without the contributions of teachers, administrators, and parents. Your board can try to reduce the number of potential problems or pitfalls by providing technical assistance for teachers and by finding activities that build consensus between staff and parents and provide information and education for everyone. Also, your district can attempt to learn from the successful experiences of other school districts.

A compelling case for inclusion does exist, supported by research, school statistics, and informal observations about inclusive programs presently in place. The biggest benefit will come when disabled students feel they "belong" with the regular-education children, rather than being segregated in separate classes or separate schools. As Sen. Robert T. Stafford, the Republican senator from Vermont and one of the bill's primary sponsors, said on the final days of passage of the Education of All Handicapped Children Act, the precursor of IDEA, these extraordinary children want only to lead ordinary lives.

NO

Karen Agne

The Dismantling of the Great American Public School

Everybody's talking about it. Public education, rarely a topic of discussion unless teachers are on strike or tax referendums proposed, is now under review everywhere people gather. The same concerns are being voiced in the checkout line, the dentist's office, the shopping mall. So prevalent is this topic that it's not necessary to take a formal survey to get the data. Just listen and take notes.

> "We took our kids out of public school and put them in Catholic school, and we're not even Catholic. The teacher was taking half the morning to get around to the 'regular' kids."
>
> "I'm staying home now to teach my kids. They weren't learning anything at school. We have a Home-Schooling Mothers group. Do you want to join?"
>
> "We had to move because that school had no program for our child; he's accelerated."
>
> "I'm not a teacher, but I'm home schooling. I got tired of hearing my child cry and complain every day about going to school. She was bored silly."
>
> "I don't want to be teaching. It's hard work and I'm afraid I might not be doing it right, but at least he gets individual attention now."
>
> "Public schools are just for kids with problems."

What happened? How did it all slip away while we weren't looking? "How could this be happening in this country?" parents want to know. In a word, inclusion happened. What does inclusion mean? Take a look:

A kindergarten teacher attempts to explain directions to the tiny charges seated on the rug before her. But a child with Down syndrome, focused on her own agenda, remains the center of attention as she crawls about pinching the bottoms of each child she reaches.

Ear-piercing screams come from a third-grade classroom where a behaviorally disabled child is expressing her displeasure at not being first to observe the science artifact being passed amongst her classmates. Her exhausted teacher says, "Oh, this happens every day. I have to call for help to watch my class while I take her out." The eight-year-old child refuses to walk and continues her high-pitched screams, punching and kicking at her teacher, as she is carried bodily down the hall. Returning, the teacher offers, "They'll just bring her right back in here and we'll go through this again. This year I just pray to get through each day."

Several children talk or play together in one corner while classmates read or write. "What are they doing?" I ask. "Oh, they don't understand what we're working on," replies the teacher. "I'm told they're supposed to be here. I've tried, but I don't know what to do with them. An aide comes in for half an hour." This scene is repeated throughout the various classrooms of schools in several counties I've observed.

In some elementary schools teachers team up to get through the day. A disruptive, emotionally disturbed child is sent to sit in the other classroom to "calm down," after which time he may return to his assigned classroom. "This helps give the other children a little break from him," the teachers explain.

A special education teacher shares that she is paid to "teach" one student all year. At eleven years of age, this brain-damaged child is confined to a wheelchair. He cannot speak, he must be fed and diapered, and he "has never, in the three years that I've worked with him, ever demonstrated evidence of understanding anything," she explains. But this child is mandated by law to receive regular classroom time. This means that he is wheeled into a classroom each day. Every twenty minutes he begins gasping and must be suctioned to prevent choking. His specially trained teacher says, "I hate having to take him in there. Where's the benefit? He understands nothing. The other kids are frightened by his constant choking, and they can't just ignore the suctioning procedure. I worry about how much of their learning is lost. I worry that he's being used. But if anyone protests, the parents just holler 'Hearing! Hearing!' So there's nothing anyone can do." This single child is granted more than $140,000 per year to meet his special needs.

What I have related here is but a sampling of many such scenarios I have witnessed. How prevalent must this tendency be throughout the country? No one will speak of it, to avoid reproach as cruel, inhuman, or uncaring. The approach described here can hardly be considered advantageous to either the special needs students or their classmates, let alone their teachers. As a result, concerned parents around the country are quietly taking their "unchallenged" children out of our public schools.

While disquieted parents express their disappointment regarding the state of the public school, few ever utter a word suggesting that children with special needs be sent elsewhere, to other rooms or buildings. They lament only that the present approach, with everyone in the same group for academic activities, isn't working for all students; that, indeed, the majority of schoolchildren is falling behind.

Liberty and justice for all, in today's schools, has come to mean that everyone of the same age shall be lumped together in the same classroom, with the same teacher, regardless of a multitude of mental, emotional, and physical needs and requirements.

By analogy, if a horticulturist were to provide the same amount and type of food, water, soil, and light to every one of the hundreds of plants in her care, easily half would not survive. Moreover, it would surely require many years for the same professional to acquire enough varied knowledge and skill to ensure that each plant will survive, much less thrive.

Now, if every ten months each gardener's stock was replaced with a collection of completely new and different plants, only then would his task begin to compare even slightly with that of today's professional teacher. And the hopeful survivor in her care is of significantly deeper complexity; whose survival, yea, whose desired advancement, is of monumental importance in comparison.

Yet regular in-service teachers, already overtaxed and underpaid, are expected to take on even more responsibility and to educate themselves for the expertise necessary to care for these new special needs. Although special education teachers receive years of training and experience designed to prepare them for working with children of diverse learning needs, most regular classroom teachers receive none. Some new in-service recruits may have taken a three-hour course, suggested or required in their preparation. But, as many colleges of education adjust requirements to include a course in special education—a Band-Aid approach to the problem—countless teachers express resentment.

"If I had wanted to teach special education I would have trained for it. I'm not cut out for that. It takes a certain type of person. This isn't fair to me or to the special students assigned to my classroom."

But, wait a minute—if teachers and parents are so opposed to what's happening in public schools, who's responsible for these changes? How did this happen? Who or what, is to blame? And why is nothing being done about it?

How about P.L. 94-142, or IDEA, the well-known mainstreaming law? Heralded by social scientists and inclusion advocates as an educational equalizer, this "one size fits all approach"[1] is anything but equal. It has systematically removed the individual attention required by the most needy few, while simultaneously denying it to the mainstream majority of students. So, why has this faulty approach remained on the education scene? Because it's cheap! Politicians love it. Supporting this movement makes them appear benevolent but allows them to move funding, for which education is in dire need, to more popular, vote-procuring issues. No need to hire the quantity of specialists required to maintain settings in which student-teacher ratios used to be no more than eight to one. No press to provide accelerated programs for gifted students, for we're pretending that all students are gifted these days. No, these requisites no longer mesh with the "one size fits all" plan.

In spite of studies reported by the U.S. Department of Education showing that students with disabilities included in the regular classroom fail more often than do those taught in special settings,[2] proponents continue to press for inclusion. They urge modifying teaching methods and beliefs in ways designed to camouflage the problems and shoehorn all students into one "equal" mold. Some of these changes include the following:

- Knowledge of facts is not important.
- Students needn't know correct grammar, spelling, or punctuation to graduate.
- Memorization, multiple-choice exams, rewards, and competition are all old-fashioned.

- Ability grouping (except for athletics) must be eliminated.
- Honor rolls, advanced or honor classes, valedictorian, and salutatorian recognition must be eliminated.
- Assign group rather than individual grades.
- Use portfolios for "authentic" assessment.
- Raise standards, but don't use tests to detect mastery.
- Cooperative learning should be practiced 80 percent of the time in the classroom.
- Peer tutoring should be encouraged.
- Disruption in classrooms reflects teacher failure.
- Acceleration robs students of "normal" socialization.
- All students are gifted.[3]

A majority of these ideas are being parroted by educationists, 17 percent of whom have never been a classroom teacher and 51 percent of whom have not been a K–12 teacher in more than sixteen years.[4]

A look at our present school system reflects an anti-intellectual society, forged by a misguided, synthetic egalitarianism. The most able students in our society are being taught to devalue their abilities and also themselves. In many cases they are taught little else in today's schools.

Bumper stickers read, "My athlete can beat up your honor student!" Able students purposely underachieve in order to avoid labels like "geek," "nerd," and "dweeb." It's great to be a superior athlete but not even okay to be a superior scholar in an institution established to disseminate learning. Something is wrong with this picture.

A capable student finally drops out of public school, finding no peers, no appropriate programs, and no superintendent who will permit grade acceleration. Cause for great concern? Yes, but when this student can then proceed to pass college entrance exams and be accepted into several college programs without a high school degree, something is definitely amiss in our formula for assessment and decision-making. Clearly, this is not equal educational opportunity, for there is nothing so unequal as equal educational treatment of students with diverse abilities.

When we permit a few educationists to promote the overuse of certain methods as "best for all students"—when in fact these methods (cooperative learning, peer tutoring) obviously exploit the ablest students and systematically prevent their progress—we establish serious consequences in our schools.

But when the Office of Gifted and Talented is eliminated; only two cents of every dollar for K–12 education is allotted to serve our most promising students; honors classes are dismantled; and a state rules that only disabled students may receive funding for special education; our public school system, yea, our society is dangerously compromised.[5]

Until we come to realize that education can never be equal unless each student is allowed and enabled to progress at his own highest rate, our efforts to reform our public school system will continue to fail. In our urgency to reform we seem to have fallen into a common trap produced by myopic vision. We can see only one way—either-or. This eliminates the possibility of a flexible middle, a healthy balance that permits commitment to all needs, however diverse.

For instance, regarding the inclusionists' list, much benefit may be afforded memorization capabilities. The fact that all children cannot commit certain information to memory, however, should not dictate eliminating that challenge for others. Many professions depend on rote memorization capability. Indeed, daily life may be enhanced by one's memorized information, selected thoughts, and ideas. There is a special feeling of security that comes with "owning" information. Students love participation in theatrical production, a wonderful way to practice memorization. The activity of brain calisthenics can be fun and rewarding.

Portfolios are not even a good, let alone "best," form of assessment, as Vermont discovered. Several years after the state adopted portfolio assessment, its schools were able to manage only 33 percent reliability.[6] That's because portfolios by nature are purely subjective, making them seriously unreliable for overall assessment purposes. Additionally, they are extremely time-consuming for students and teachers alike, while requiring enormous storage space, a luxury lacking in most schools.

"Authentic assessment," like "inclusion," sounds nice and appears more benevolent, but its purpose is to resolve one of the major problems of inclusion. Many included students cannot pass basic skills tests. But performance-based assessment methods are impractical for large-scale assessment and are not supported by many educational evaluation experts. Major concerns include the neglected issues of reliability and validity, the lack of consensus of how this form of assessment should be used, its ineffectiveness in complex subject areas, and the fear that reliance on such an approach reduces motivation for capable students. A common conclusion of educational psychometricians is that "authentic assessment is a fad that will be of only historical interest" in years to come.[7]

Multiple choice and standardized exams, on the other hand, although highly reliable and useful for determining mastery of basic skills, are certainly inadequate for measuring all human capabilities, especially those deemed most important, such as creativity and high-level problem solving. Shouldn't these factors serve to inform us that both methods are necessary for the most efficient and effective evaluation?

Cooperative learning, which may promote motivation for some students, enhanced socialization, and just plain fun in the classroom, is essential for many learning projects and endeavors. Although currently touted as some great panacea, it's hardly new. Effective teachers have always relied on student grouping, teams, squads, and the like for selected classroom purposes. Too much reliance on group learning, "discovery" methods, and peer teaching, however, can become counterproductive. Misinformation and unnecessary remediation may rob precious learning time. Teachers need to direct as well as facilitate. Students need individual study and on-task time. Each student must also be encouraged to seek her own directions, interests, and challenge levels.

Clearly, none of the various notions, methods, and ideas on the foregoing list of "inclusion-ordered" approaches is, by itself, effective. Each must be varied with the "old-fashioned" methods to ensure "best for all" learning. There must be a balance to serve students of all types and abilities equally.

Students must have some experience with others of like ability. Identical age grouping assumes that all students of the same age can learn together adequately. Yet one common definition of a gifted student is a comprehension level two chronological years beyond his same-age peers. When a child reads at three, circling alphabet letters in kindergarten is clearly not a challenge. When she relishes multiplication computer games at home, we must be prepared to ask more of her than to count to ten. We dare not pretend that there is no such thing as a gifted student or that all children are gifted.

Learners must also have time for individual study. Assigned seats placed in rows may well signal emphasis on control rather than learning, but occasionally this arrangement is perfect for the discerning teacher's purpose. Successful education for all requires appropriate individual challenge and remediation, as well as caring interaction and socialization among students. Most important of all is the teacher/student relationship, which is diminished when teachers must devote excessive time to many children with multiple needs. With distance-learning access on the rise, the opportunity for one-to-one interaction between each learner and her teacher becomes all the more crucial. A healthy mentoring relationship between the teacher and the student has always been and remains a pivotal factor for education excellence.

Successful schools must be prepared to offer all these approaches in order to serve all learners equally. It is not about either-or. People are not designed for either-or treatment. Incredibly, miraculously varied in their needs and capabilities, they also require an education with techniques and methods that can fulfill these unparalleled individual distinctions.

Such an education requires much support, much expertise, varied and multiple personnel needs, and therefore, enormous monetary backing. How much are our children worth? How much is our future worth? How can a nation that currently enjoys such increased prosperity afford not to invest in its children? There can be no either-or. All children must be served.

It is possible to build a great public school system, great because it offers everything needed for all its students; those who learn less easily, those who excel, and all those in between. But we can never achieve this ideal state until fanatical inclusionists and overzealous egalitarians allow a complete portrayal of our students, including encouraging and enabling the very highest capabilities among us.

In a poignant article, the father of a physically handicapped child afflicted with the rare Cornelia de Lange syndrome pleaded,

> The advocates of full inclusion speak glibly of giving teachers training necessary to cope with the immense variety of challenges which handicapped children bring to the classroom. No amount of training could prepare a regular teacher for Mark. The requisite expertise and commitment are found only among teachers who have chosen to specialize in the handicapped. Special education is by no means the unmitigated disaster its critics charge. The drive to ditch this flawed program in favor of a radical alternative will almost certainly result in just such a disaster. One can only hope that we

will not repeat the pattern of sabotaging our genuine achievements in the pursuit of worthy-sounding but deeply wrongheaded ideas.[8]

Notes

1. Albert Shanker, "Full Inclusion Is Neither Free Nor Appropriate," *Educational Leadership* (December/January 1995).

2. Lynn Schnailberg, "E.D. Report Documents 'Full Inclusion' Trend," *Education Week,* 19 October 1994, 17, 19.

3. Robert Slavin, "Cooperative Learning and the Cooperative School," *Educational Leadership* 45, no. 3 (1987): 7–13; Ellen D. Fiedler, Richard E. Lange, and Susan Winebrenner, *Roeper Review* 16 (1993): 4–7; and John Goodlad and Thomas Lovitt, *Integrating General and Special Education* (New York: Merrill, 1993), 171–201.

4. Public Agenda, a nonpartisan, nonprofit organization, *Different Drummers: How Teachers of Teachers View Public Education,* an opinion poll comparing ideas of the general public, in-service teachers, and teacher educators, (New York: October 1997).

5. Ellen Winner, *Gifted Children: Myths and Realities* (New York: Basic Books, 1996) and Karen Diegmueller, "Gifted Programs Not a Right, Connecticut Court Rules," *Education Week,* 30 March 1994, 8.

6. Koretz et al., *RAND Corporation* (1992) studied the Vermont statewide assessment program. Average reliability coefficients ranged from .33 to .43. If the reliability of test scores is under .50, there is no differentiation in the performance of an individual student from the overall average performance of students. See also James Popham, *Classroom Assessment: What Teachers Need to Know* (Boston: Allyn and Bacon, 1995), 171–173 and Blaine Worthen, Walter Borg, and Karl White, *Measurement and Evaluation in the Schools* (New York: Longman, 1993), 441–442.

7. Thomas Brooks and Sandra Pakes, "Policy, National Testing, and the Psychological Corporation," *Measurement and Evaluation in Counseling and Development* 26 (1993): 54–58; James S. Terwilliger, "Semantics, Psychometrics, and Assessment Reform: A Close Look at 'Authentic' Tests," ERIC Document Reproduction Service #ED397123, 1996; and Louis Janda, *Psychological Testing: Theory and Applications* (Boston: Allyn and Bacon, 1998), 375.

8. Arch Puddington, "Life with Mark," *American Educator* (1996): 36–41.

POSTSCRIPT

Is Full Inclusion of Disabled Students Desirable?

One wit has stated that P.L. 94–142 was really a "full employment act for lawyers." Indeed, there has been much litigation regarding the identification, classification, placement, and specialized treatment of disabled children since the introduction of the 1975 act.

The 1992 ruling in *Greer v. Rome City School District* permitted the parents to place their child, who has Down's syndrome, in a regular classroom with supplementary services. Also, the decision in *Sacramento City Unified School District v. Holland* (1994) allowed a girl with an IQ of 44 to be placed in a regular classroom full time, in accordance with her parents' wishes (the school system had wanted the student to split her time equally between regular and special education classes). These cases demonstrate that although the aspect of the law stipulating parental involvement in the development of individual education programs can invite cooperation, it can also lead to conflict.

Teacher attitude becomes a crucial component in the success or failure of placements of disabled students in regular classrooms. Some articles addressing this and related matters are "Willingness of Regular and Special Educators to Teach Students With Handicaps," by Karen Derk Gans, *Exceptional Children* (October 1987) and Lynn Miller, "The Regular Education Initiative and School Reform: Lessons From the Mainstream," *Remedial and Special Education* (May–June 1990).

Other noteworthy articles are "Disruptive Disabled Kids: Inclusion Confusion," by Diane Brockett, *School Board News* (October 1994) and multiple articles in *Theory Into Practice* (Winter 1996), *Educational Leadership* (December 1994/January 1995 and February 1996), *Phi Delta Kappan* (December 1995 and October 1996), *Kappa Delta Pi Record* (Winter 1998), and *NASSP Bulletin* (February 2000). Also see Philip Ferguson and Dianne Ferguson, "The Future of Inclusive Educational Practice," *Childhood Education* (Mid-Summer 1998); Susan G. Clark, "The Principal, Discipline, and the IDEA," *NASSP Bulletin* (November 1999); and Jean Mueth Dayton, "Discipline Procedures for Students With Disabilities," *The Clearing House* (January/February 2000).

Of special interest are David Aloyzy Zera and Roy Maynard Seitsinger, "The Oppression of Inclusion," *Educational Horizons* (Fall 2000); Shireen Pavri and Richard Luftig, "The Social Face of Inclusive Education," *Preventing School Failure* (Fall 2000); Nathan L. Essex, "Americans With Disabilities: Are They Losing Ground?" *The Clearing House* (January/February 2002); and Lewis M. Andrews, "More Choices for Disabled Kids," *Policy Review* (April & May 2002).

ISSUE 15

Is Size Crucial to School Improvement?

YES: Patricia A. Wasley, from "Small Classes, Small Schools: The Time Is Now," *Educational Leadership* (February 2002)

NO: Kirk A. Johnson, from "The Downside to Small Class Policies," *Educational Leadership* (February 2002)

ISSUE SUMMARY

YES: Education dean Patricia A. Wasley contends that schools and classrooms must be small if they are to be places where students' personal and learning needs are met.

NO: Policy analyst Kirk A. Johnson, of the Heritage Foundation, argues that while small scale is a popular concept when it comes to class size, the cost is not justified by research findings.

In the early days of American urban public schooling, local authorities, faced with increasing numbers of immigrant children, resorted to "monitorial schools" (based on a British model spawned by the Industrial Revolution) in which one teacher, abetted by monitors, could teach a class of 300 or more students. While this approach may have been expedient at the time, the twentieth century has seen a growing campaign for reduced class sizes at all levels of education.

Another historical trend was the movement toward consolidation of rural and small-town schools. From over 114,000 one-room elementary schools in 1940 to almost none in 1980, and from over 50,000 school districts in the 1950s to about 16,000 in the 1980s, the trend was obviously toward large schools. According to Robert L. Hampel, in "Historical Perspectives on Small Schools," *Phi Delta Kappan* (January 2002), the dominant beliefs were that large schools offer more opportunities for students, attract better teachers and administrators, and counteract provincialism. Since the 1980s, however, there has been a backlash against these beliefs, and advocates of small schools have joined small class proponents in exerting pressure on local, state, and federal authorities to fund size reductions.

While school size reduction has been handled primarily through internal reorganization such as schools-within-schools, the federal government, more than half the states, and countless districts have devised class-size reduction programs. As Jeremy D. Finn points out in "Small Classes in American Schools: Research, Practice, and Politics," *Phi Delta Kappan* (March 2002), the U.S. Department of Education, in an effort to reduce the size of classes in poor urban school districts, has paid the salaries of 29,000 new teachers, and in California alone 28,000 new teachers were hired in the first three years of a statewide class-size reduction initiative. Finn warns, however, that both federal and state efforts have been slowed by the recent economic instability and the shift in priorities brought about by the September 11 attacks.

In "Personalization: Making Every School a Small School," *Principal Leadership* (February 2002), Tom Vander Ark contends that small schools—a benefit enjoyed by affluent private school communities for 200 years—must be brought to inner-city areas to counter the crippling effects of poverty. He cites a Chicago study showing that more personalized small schools can improve attendance, achievement, graduation rates, safety, parent involvement, staff satisfaction, and community engagement. The small learning community strategy includes the forming of houses, academies, school-within-a-school programs, and small autonomous schools.

Positive notes on small classes are sounded by Anke Halbach et al. in "Class Size Reduction: From Promise to Practice," *Educational Leadership* (March 2001), who report on Wisconsin's Student Achievement Guarantee in Education (SAGE) begun in 1996. The program, reducing pupil-teacher ratios to 15 to 1 in disadvantaged K–3 classrooms, was shown to reduce discipline problems, increase instructional time and time for individualization, and support greater flexibility in learning activities. Similarly, Charles M. Achilles, Jeremy D. Finn, and Helen Pate-Bain, in "Measuring Class Size: Let Me Count the Ways," *Educational Leadership* (February 2002), report on positive results in Tennessee's Student Teacher Achievement Ratio (STAR) experiment begun in the 1980s. Contrarily, Eric A. Hanushek, in a recent Fordham Foundation report, "The Evidence on Class Size," maintains that student achievement will be unaffected by class size reductions and that the most noticeable result will be a dramatic increase in the costs of schooling.

In the following selections, Patricia A. Wasley draws on research and personal experience to make the case for small classes and small schools, whereas Kirk A. Johnson cites evidence showing little or no relationship between class size and achievement.

Patricia A. Wasley

 **YES**

Small Classes, Small Schools:
The Time Is Now

For many years, educators have debated the effects of class size and school size on student learning. The class size debate centers on the number of students a teacher can work with effectively in any given class period. The school size issue focuses on whether smaller schools encourage optimal student learning and development—and how small a "small school" must be to produce such effects.

... To frame the [issue], I want to pose a series of questions:

- Why have issues of class and school size gained prominence?
- What does the research say?
- What does my experience lead me to believe about the impact of class and school size on teaching and learning?

Why Are Class and School Size Important?

Issues of class size and school size have resurfaced as important school improvement ideas for a variety of reasons. First, the standards movement has encouraged the resurgence of the class size and school size debates. All U.S. states but one have academic standards in place. Of those states with standards, 36 use or plan to use test results to make high-stakes decisions about students. Standards enable educators and the public to clarify what they believe students should know and be able to do before the students leave school.

The standards movement has highlighted the fact that schools are largely inequitable places. Students in schools with large populations of disadvantaged students perform least well on standardized assessments. Evidence also suggests that these schools often have the least-experienced teachers (NCTAF, 1996; Roza, 2001). In effect, having standards in place emphasizes that standards are necessary but insufficient in themselves to improve student performance. Unless we change students' learning opportunities, especially for students who are ill-served by their schools, standards alone are unlikely to influence student learning. Educators and policymakers are looking for strategies that will enable students to succeed on the new assessments (thereby supporting the standards movement) and, more important, that will enhance students' learning opportunities. Small classes and small schools may be two such strategies.

Second, class size and school size issues have resurfaced because of the increasing consensus among educators and the public that all students can learn. When I began teaching in the early 1970s, teachers generally accepted the notion that some students had an exceptional aptitude for learning and others did not. At that time, my colleagues and I believed that as long as one-fourth of the students in a class performed exceptionally well and another half of the class did reasonably well, we were fulfilling our responsibilities as educators—even if one-fourth of the students in a class failed to learn at an acceptable level. We had been taught that the normal distribution of scores (the "bell curve") was what teachers should aim for and what we should accept as reasonable evidence of accomplishment. In the ensuing years, cognitive scientists, neurological biologists, and educators determined that all students have the capacity to learn. This new, convincing research means that no student should be left behind in the learning process. Educators need to examine all approaches to schooling to determine which strategies are most likely to return gains for students who typically have not done well in schools. Proponents of reduced class size and school size suggest that these factors contribute to the success of a broader swath of learners.

Third, following the events of September 11, educators have a renewed appreciation for the importance of the basic freedoms we enjoy and the advantages that a democracy provides its citizens. We know that a democratic citizenry must value differences among its participants. Schools should strive to develop in students the skills that they need to examine their differences productively and to coexist peacefully while protecting basic freedoms for all (Goodlad, Soder, & Sirotnik, 1990). Schools also have a central responsibility for helping students learn the basic skills of productive citizenry. Both class size and school size influence whether teachers are able to engage students in meaningful discussions of these issues and to help them build these crucial citizenship skills.

Renewed interest in class size and school size is broad-based and nationwide. The Bill & Melinda Gates Foundation has dedicated more than $250 million to reducing the size of U.S. high schools. The U.S. Department of Education has committed $125 million to fund small-school initiatives. In Boston, Chicago, and New York, small-school initiatives are under way. Small-school collaboratives, designed to support the change from comprehensive high schools to smaller learning communities, are springing up everywhere and include New Visions for Learning in New York, the Small Schools Workshop in Chicago (Illinois), the Small Schools Project in Seattle (Washington), and the Bay Area Coalition of Essential Schools in Oakland (California).

Lawmakers in Kentucky, California, Georgia, and Washington have passed legislation to reduce class sizes, believing that teachers will be better able to help all students meet the standards when the teacher-student ratio is substantially reduced.

What Does Research Tell Us?

The United States has had large schools for a relatively short period of time. Until the middle of the 20th century, most U.S. schools were small. In 1930, 262,000 U.S. public schools served 26 million students; by 1999, approximately 90,000 U.S. public schools served about 47 million students (National Center for Education Statistics, 1999). Responding to the recommendations of the Committee of Ten in 1894 and the authors of the Conant Report in 1959, proponents of the school consolidation movement suggested that schools would be more efficient and effective if they were larger. Single plants housing 500–2,000 students presumably could offer greater variety in subject matter, would provide teachers with the opportunity to track their students according to ability, and might put less strain on community resources (Wasley & Fine, 2000).

Research conducted on the validity of the assertions favoring large schools has suggested that less-advantaged students end up in the largest classes, with the least-experienced teachers and the least-engaging curriculum and instructional strategies (Oakes, 1987; Wheelock, 1992). Further research suggests that schools are organized more for purposes of maintaining control than for promoting learning (McNeil, 1988).

Powell (1996) examined independent schools in the United States and learned that private preparatory schools value both small school and small class size as necessary conditions for student success. In 1998, the average private school class size was 16.6 at the elementary level and 11.6 at the high school level. By contrast, the average class size was 18.6 in public elementary schools and 14.2 in public high schools (National Center for Education Statistics, 1999).[1]

Powell also determined that independent elementary schools tend to be small and independent high schools tend to be even smaller—in contrast to public schools, which tend to increase in size as the students they serve get older. In *The Power of Their Ideas,* Meier (1995) suggests that we abandon adolescents just at the time when they most often need to be in the company of trusted adults. . . .

What Has My Experience Taught Me?

Over the years, I have taught students at nearly every level, from 3rd grade through graduate school. As a researcher, I have spent time gathering data on students at every level from preschool through 12th grade. My teaching and research experiences have provided me with data that convince me that both small classes and small schools are crucial to a teacher's ability to succeed with students.

One of my earliest teaching experiences was in a large comprehensive high school in Australia that included grades 7–10. I had more than 40 students in each of seven classes each day. During my second year, I taught Ray Campano. He was a quiet 10th grader who wasn't doing well in English. His parents, aware of his academic weaknesses, came to see me early in the first term. They asked that I keep them informed of the homework required and let them know if Ray was in danger of failing. They wanted to help and were supportive of my efforts on their son's behalf. In the ensuing weeks, I kept track of Ray's progress, but I gradually paid less attention to him. He was pleasant and quiet and well behaved, but there were other students in the class who were not. Other students demanded that I give them individual attention because they wanted to excel. These two groups of students—the rebellious and the demanding—absorbed most of my time, while Ray quietly slipped out of my attention. To be sure, I saw him each day and recorded whether his work was coming in, but I neglected to examine his performance in the midst of competing demands to plan, grade papers, and work with the needier or more demanding students.

When midterm reports came due, I was horrified to realize that I had neglected to keep my eye on Ray's performance, which was less than satisfactory. I met with his parents and explained that I had not kept my end of our bargain. They were angry—and rightly so—but they were fair. Ray's mother asked to come to class for a week to see what was going on. At the end of that week, she said that she thought the work I asked the students to do was appropriate and that I was relatively well organized and focused. Nevertheless, she couldn't imagine how a teacher could manage anything more than a cursory relationship with any given student in so large a classroom. Mrs. Campano confirmed my own experience, which suggested that really knowing all 40 students in each of seven classes was impossible. Despite parental involvement and teachers' good intentions, it is easy for students to get lost in large classes and in large schools.

As Dean of Bank Street College of Education in New York City several years ago, I team-taught 5th and 6th graders in the College's School for Children. We were looking for a course of study that would engage the students in making some contribution to the local community while simultaneously building their reading, computer, writing, and observation skills. After long deliberation and engagement in a number of exploratory activities, our 5th and 6th graders decided that they would tutor younger students in a neighborhood public school. One of the students cried, "How are we supposed to teach reading? We're only kids. We just learned to read ourselves a few years ago!" A heated discussion ensued, during which one of the girls ran up to the chalkboard and said, "I know. Let's map how each of us learned to read."

The students made a chart of how old they were, where they were (home or school), with whom they were engaged in a reading activity, and what activity they were engaged in at the precise moment that they understood that they could read. Seventeen students in the classroom generated 14 different approaches to learning to read. I suggested that the students pick several of the most commonly used approaches and organize a seminar on each approach so that they could learn several methods for working with their reading buddies. They looked at me as if either I had lost my mind or I hadn't been listening. "We can't learn just three approaches, or we'll never learn to help all these kids learn to read! If we needed a bunch of different approaches to learn to read, why wouldn't they?"

This experience reinforced my belief that different students learn differently and that teachers need to build a repertoire of instructional strategies to reach individual students. Small class size is integral to this individualization:

Teachers should be responsible for a smaller number of students so that they can get to know each student and his or her learning preferences. It takes time to get to know one's students and to individualize the learning experience, and doing so requires concentration. In a classroom with a large number of students, such attention simply isn't an option.

Colleagues and I recently conducted a study of small schools in Chicago. Part of our time was spent in a small school-within-a-school with eight teachers. Because they were few, they could meet together every day for an hour, work toward common agreements and understandings, and accept shared responsibility for their students. They discussed the curriculum in all subjects, agreed on instructional approaches, and tried to build as much coherence in the curriculum as they could manage. In the larger school, which had some 70 faculty members, a common agenda simply wasn't possible.

The school-within-a-school teachers spent an enormous amount of time talking about their 300 students. They argued about students, challenged one another to see individual students differently, and agreed to work together to communicate to students that math or English or science was important for everyone. By the end of the first year, students in the smaller school-within-a-school had outperformed their peers on a number of measures: More of the smaller-school students had stayed in school, completed their courses, and received higher grades than had students in the host school. For example, between September 1998 and September 1999, approximately 11.1 percent of school-within-a-school students dropped out of school. By contrast, about 19.8 percent of their host-school peers dropped out during the same period (Wasley et al., 2000).

When we asked the school-within-a-school students why they thought they had achieved such results, they said that their teachers "dog us every day. They're relentless. They call our parents. They really care whether we get our work done. There's no hiding in this school!"

The time is ripe for educators to make the case for what research suggests and what our own experience has been telling us for years: Students do best in places where they can't slip through the cracks, where they are known by their teachers, and where their improved learning becomes the collective mission of a number of trusted adults. We have the resources to ensure that every student gets a good education, and we know what conditions best support their success. It is time to do what is right.

Note

1. The low average class size of public high schools obscures the fact that upper division courses in math and science and Advanced Placement courses are typically smaller, whereas many lower-track courses have more than 30 students.

NO

Kirk A. Johnson

The Downside to Small Class Policies

From the attention and financial support given to class size reduction by politicians and the public, one might assume that research has shown small class size to be essential to positive academic outcomes. In fiscal year 2000, the U.S. Congress allocated $1.3 billion for the class size reduction provision of the Elementary and Secondary Education Act (ESEA). During the Clinton administration, class size received a great deal of attention through proposals to pump large sums of money into efforts to increase the number of teachers in public elementary schools, thereby decreasing the ratio of students to teachers (The White House, 2000).

Proponents of class size reduction claim that small classes result in fewer discipline problems and allow teachers more time for instruction and individual attention and more flexibility in instructional strategies (Halbach, Ehrle, Zahorik, & Molnar, 2001).

Do small classes make a different in the academic achievement of elementary school students? Are class size reduction programs uniformly positive, or does a downside exist to hiring and placing more teachers in U.S. public schools?

The California Experience

In 1995, California enacted one of the broadest-reaching laws for ensuring small classes in the early grades. Strong bipartisan approval of the class size reduction measure in the California legislature reflected broad support among constituents for reducing class sizes. The program has been wildly popular over its short lifetime, but it has faced substantial obstacles to success.

California's class size reduction program has suffered from a lack of qualified teachers to fill classrooms. More or less simultaneously, nearly all elementary schools in the state demanded more teachers, and some schools—typically suburban—attracted far more teaching applicants than did those in the inner city.

A consortium of researchers from RAND, the American Institutes for Research (AIR), Policy Analysis for California Education (PACE), EdSource, and WestEd analyzed the effects of California's class size reduction initiative and

From Kirk A. Johnson, "The Downside to Small Class Policies," *Educational Leadership* (February 2002). Copyright © 2002 by The Association for Supervision and Curriculum Development. Reprinted by permission of The Association for Supervision and Curriculum Development; permission conveyed via Copyright Clearance Center, Inc.

outlined two basic problems. First, K–3 classes that remained large were "concentrated in districts serving high percentages of minority, low-income, or English learner (EL) students" (Stecher & Bohrnstedt, 2000, p. x). Second,

> the average qualifications (that is, education, credentials, and experience) of California teachers declined during the past three years for all grade levels, but the declines were worst in elementary schools.... Schools serving low-income, minority, or EL students continued to have fewer well-qualified teachers than did other schools. (p. x)

Do Students Learn More in Small Classes?

Clearly, if billions of dollars are to be spent on reducing class size, tangible evidence should exist that students benefit academically from such initiatives. As yet, evidence of the efficacy of class size reduction is mixed at best.

One of the most frequently cited reports on class size is Mosteller's (1995) analysis of the Project STAR study of elementary school students in Tennessee. Mosteller found a significant difference in achievement between students in classes of 13–17 students per teacher and those in classes of 22–25.

University of Rochester economist Eric Hanushek, however, questioned Mosteller's results, noting that "the bulk of evidence . . . points to no systematic effects of class size reductions within the relevant policy range" (1999, p. 144). In other words, no serious policy change on a large scale could decrease class size enough to make a difference.

The current class size reduction debate often ignores the fact that class sizes have been dropping slowly but steadily in the United States over the course of many years. In 1970, U.S. public schools averaged 22.3 students per teacher; by the late 1990s, however, they averaged about 17 students per teacher—a result of a combination of demographic trends and conscious policy decisions to lower pupil-teacher ratios (U.S. Census Bureau, 1999).

Local and programmatic changes in class size can be illustrative, but does research indicate that, on a national level, students in small classes experience academic achievement gains superior to those of their peers in large classes?

The National Assessment of Educational Progress

The most useful database for analyzing whether small classes lead to better academic achievement is the National Assessment of Educational Progress (NAEP). First administered in 1969, the NAEP measures the academic achievement of 4th, 8th, and 12th graders in a variety of fields, including reading, writing, mathematics, science, geography, civics, and the arts. Students take the math and reading tests alternately every two years. For example, students were assessed in reading in 1998; they were tested in math in 1996 and 2000.

The NAEP is actually two tests: a nationally administered test and a state-administered test. More than 40 states participate in the separate state samples used to gauge achievement within those jurisdictions.

In addition to test scores in the subject area, the NAEP includes an assortment of background information on the students taking the exam, their main subject-area teacher, and their school administrator. Background information includes students' television viewing habits, students' computer usage at home and at school, teacher tenure and certification, family socioeconomic status, basic demographics, and school characteristics. By including this information in their assessment of the NAEP data, researchers can gain insight into the factors that might explain differences in NAEP scores found among students.

Results From the Center for Data Analysis

A study from the Center for Data Analysis at the Heritage Foundation examined the 1998 NAEP national reading data to determine whether students in small classes achieve better than students in large classes (Johnson, 2000). Researchers assessed students' academic achievement in reading by analyzing assessment scores as well as six factors from the background information collected by the NAEP: class size, race and ethnicity, parents' education attainment, the availability of reading materials in the home, free or reduced-price lunch participation, and gender.

Class size   The amount of time that a teacher can spend with each student appears to be important in the learning process. To address class size, the Center for Data Analysis study compared students in small classes (those with 20 or fewer students per teacher) with students in large classes (at least 31 students per teacher).

Race and ethnicity   Because significant differences exist in academic achievement among ethnic groups, the variables of race and ethnicity were included in the analysis.

Parents' education   Research indicates that the education attainment of a child's parents is a good predictor of that child's academic achievement. Because the education level of one parent is often highly correlated with that of the other parent, only a single variable was included in the analysis.

The availability of reading materials in the home   The presence of books, magazines, encyclopedias, and newspapers generally indicates a dedication to learning in the household. Researchers have determined that these reading materials are important aspects of the home environment (Coleman, Hoffer, & Kilgore, 1982). Essentially, the presence of such reading materials in the home is correlated with higher student achievement. The analysis thus included a variable controlling for the number of these four types of reading materials found at home.

Free and reduced-price lunch participation   Income is often a key predictor of academic achievement because low-income families seldom have the resources to purchase extra study materials or tutorial classes that may help their children perform better in school. Although the NAEP does not collect data on household income, it does collect data on participation in the free and reduced-price school lunch program.

Gender Although data on male-female achievement gaps are inconsistent, empirical research suggests that girls tend to perform better in reading and writing subjects, whereas boys perform better in more analytical subjects such as math and science.

After controlling for all these factors, researchers found that the difference in reading achievement on the 1998 NAEP reading assessment between students in small classes and students in large classes were statistically insignificant. That is, across the United Sates, students in small classes did no better on average than those in large classes, assuming otherwise identical circumstances.

Such results should give policymakers pause and provoke them to consider whether the rush to hire more teachers is worth the cost and is in the best interest of students. In terms of raising achievement, reducing class size does not guarantee success.

When Irwin Kurz became the principal of Public School 161 in Brooklyn, New York, well over a decade ago, the schools' test scores ranked in the bottom 25th percentile of schools in Brooklyn's 17th District. Today, P.S. 161 ranks as the best school in the district and 40th of 674 elementary schools in New York City, even though a majority of its students are poor. The pupil-teacher ratio at P.S. 161 is 35 to 1, but the teachers make neither class size, nor poverty, nor anything else an excuse for poor performance. As Kurz likes to say, "better to have one good teacher than two crummy teachers any day."

References

Coleman, J., Hoffer, T., & Kilgore, S. (1982). *High school achievement.* New York: BasicBooks.

Halbach, A., Ehrle, K., Zahorik, J., & Molnar, A. (2001, March). Class size reduction: From promise to practice. *Educational Leadership, 58*(6), 32–35.

Hanushek, E. (1999). Some findings from an independent investigation of the Tennessee STAR experiment and from other investigations of class size effects. *Educational Evaluation & Policy Analysis, 21*(2), 143–164.

Johnson, K. (2000, June 9). *Do small classes influence academic achievement? What the National Assessment of Educational Progress shows* (CDA Report No. 00-07). Washington, DC: Heritage Foundation.

Mosteller, F. (1995). The Tennessee study of class size in the early school grades. *The Future of Children, 5*(2), 113–127.

Stecher, B., & Bohrnstedt, G. (Eds.). (2000). *Class size reduction in California: The 1998-99 evaluation findings.* Sacramento: California Department of Education.

U.S. Census Bureau. (1999). *Statistical abstract of the United States.* Washington, DC: Government Printing Office.

The White House (2000, May 4). President Clinton highlights education reform agenda with roundtable on what works [Press release].

POSTSCRIPT

Is Size Crucial to School Improvement?

Eric Hanushek, a professor of economics and public policy and Hoover Institution fellow, has asserted in various publications that extensive statistical investigations show no relationship between class size and student performance, that the modest gains shown during Tennessee's STAR experiment were only in kindergartens, and that there is no firm foundation for pouring huge amounts of money into class size reduction on a nationwide basis. Others have raised questions about the validity of some of the statistics cited by researchers on both sides of the issue, arguing that pupil-teacher ratio is an administrative figure not reflective of actual class size figures. According to some analysts, the approximate difference between the two figures on a nationwide basis is 10 (if a school's pupil-teacher ratio is 17 to 1, then its teachers will average about 27 students per class).

The benefits of small schools have been more clearly demonstrated by researchers in major urban areas. Most of these schools develop a unique culture that nourishes interpersonal relationships and constructively interacts with the surrounding community. But there are many barriers to be overcome. Wasley and Richard J. Lear, in "Small Schools, Real Gains," *Educational Leadership* (March 2001), for example, cite these barriers: the tightly woven structure of high schools makes real change difficult, some small schools try too hard to act like large schools, the focus is too often on short-term goals, and many educators lack a clear image of what a small school can be.

When such barriers are successfully overcome, the resulting connectedness that the small school fosters can have a positive effect on student behavior. A recent federally funded survey, the National Study of Adolescent Health, showed that students who attend small junior and senior high schools are less likely to engage in violence, drug use, and early sexual activities, with the primary causative factor being a sense of connectedness to their teachers and to their fellow students.

Other slants on these combined issues can be found in Anne Reynolds, "Less Is More: What Teachers Say About Decreasing Class Size and Increasing Learning," *American School Board Journal* (September 2001); Craig Howley and Robert Bickel, "The Influence of Scale: Small Schools Make a Big Difference for Children of Poor Families," *American School Board Journal* (March 2002); Mary Anne Raywid, "The Policy Environments of Small Schools and Schools-Within-Schools," *Educational Leadership* (February 2002); and 10 articles on "Small Learning Communities" in *Principal Leadership* (February 2002).

ISSUE 16

Should Bilingual Education Programs Be Abandoned?

YES: Rosalie Pedalino Porter, from "The Politics of Bilingual Education," *Society* (September/October 1997)

NO: Richard Rothstein, from "Bilingual Education: The Controversy," *Phi Delta Kappan* (May 1998)

ISSUE SUMMARY

YES: Rosalie Pedalino Porter, director of the Research in English Acquisition and Development Institute, offers a close examination of the major research studies and concludes that there is no consistent support for transitional bilingual education programs.

NO: Richard Rothstein, a research associate of the Economic Policy Institute, reviews the history of bilingual education and argues that, although many problems currently exist, there is no compelling reason to abandon these programs.

The issue of accommodating non-English-speaking immigrants by means of a bilingual education program has been controversial since the late 1960s. Events of the past decades have brought about one of the largest influxes of immigrants to the United States in the nation's history. And the disadvantages that non-English-speaking children and their parents experience during the childrens' years of formal schooling has received considerable attention from educators, policymakers, and the popular press.

Efforts to modify this type of social and developmental disadvantage have appeared in the form of bilingual education programs initiated at the local level and supported by federal funding. Approaches implemented include direct academic instruction in the primary language and the provision of language tutors under the English for Speakers of Other Languages (ESOL) program. Research evaluation of these efforts has produced varied results and has given rise to controversy over the efficacy of the programs themselves and the social and political intentions served by them.

A political movement at the national and state levels to establish English as the official language of the United States has gained support in recent years.

Supporters of this movement feel that the bilingual approach will lead to the kind of linguistic division that has torn Canada apart.

Perhaps sharing some of the concerns of the "official English" advocates, increasing numbers of educators seem to be tilting in the direction of the immersion approach. In *Forked Tongue: The Politics of Bilingual Education* (1990), Rosalie Pedalino Porter, a teacher and researcher in the field of bilingual education for over 15 years, issues an indictment of the policies and programs that have been prevalent. One of her central recommendations is that "limited-English children must be placed with specially trained teachers in a program in which these students will be immersed in the English language, in which they have as much contact as possible with English speakers, and in which school subjects, not just social conversations, are the focus of the English-language lessons from kindergarten through twelfth grade."

Amado M. Padilla of Stanford University has examined the rationale behind "official English" and has also reviewed the effectiveness of bilingual education programs (see "English Only vs. Bilingual Education: Ensuring a Language-Competent Society," *Journal of Education,* Spring 1991). Padilla concludes that "the debate about how to assist linguistic minority children should focus on new educational technologies and *not* just on the effectiveness of bilingual education or whether bilingualism detracts from loyalty to this country."

Recent treatments of the problem, prompted by state initiatives and congressional bills, include "English *Über Alles,*" *The Nation* (September 29, 1997); "Ingles, Si," by Jorge Amselle, *National Review* (September 30, 1996); and "Should English Be the Law?" by Robert D. King, *The Atlantic Monthly* (April 1997), in which the author contends that proponents of "official English" are tearing the nation apart. Another provocative portrayal of the dilemma is presented in Laurie Olsen's "Learning English and Learning America: Immigrants in the Center of a Storm," *Theory Into Practice* (Autumn 2000).

Linguistics professor Donaldo Macedo, in "English Only: The Tongue-Tying of America," *Journal of Education* (Spring 1991), maintains that the conservative ideology that propels the movement against bilingual education fails to recognize the need to prepare students for the multicultural world of the twenty-first century and relegates the immigrant population to the margins of society.

In the first of the selections that follow, Rosalie Pedalino Porter exposes the political assumptions behind governmental efforts to help non-English-speaking schoolchildren gain language competency. She finds the "politically correct" native-language instruction approach to be mired in a record of poor results. In the second selection, Richard Rothstein looks at the complexities of the problem, cites historical precedents and modern research findings, and makes a plea for removing the debate from the political realm.

Rosalie Pedalino Porter

 **YES**

The Politics of Bilingual Education

In the United States, the efforts being made and the money being invested in the special programs to help immigrant, migrant, and refugee school children who do not speak English when they enter U.S. schools is still largely misguided. The current population of limited-English students is being treated in ways that earlier immigrant groups were not. The politically righteous assumption is that these students cannot learn English quickly and must be taught all their school subjects in their native language for three to seven years while having the English language introduced gradually. Twenty-seven years of classroom experience with this education policy and a growing body of research show no benefits for native-language teaching either in better learning of English or better learning of school subjects. These facts have hardly dented the armor of the true believers in the bilingual education bureaucracy.

Yet some changes and improvements have occurred in this most contentious area of public education. Research reports contribute additional evidence on the poor results of native-language instruction as the superior road to English-language competency for classroom work. But the successful results from programs emphasizing intensive English are beginning to appear, now that some small measure of funding is being allocated to these so-called alternative model programs.

All too often, it remains almost impossible to voice criticism of bilingual education programs without being pilloried as a hater of foreigners and foreign languages and of contributing to the anti-immigrant climate. Another area in which little positive change has occurred in the past few years is in reducing the established power of state education departments to impose education mandates on local school districts. The power of the bilingual education bureaucracy has hardly diminished, even in states like California where the state bilingual education law expired in 1987. However, there are counterforces opposing the seemingly settled idea that native-language programs are the single best solution for limited-English students, and these challenges are growing at the local school level.

Updating the Research

The basic questions posed in the early years of bilingual education still have not found clear-cut answers. Are there measurable benefits for limited-English students when they are taught in their native language for a period of time, both in their learning of the English language for academic achievement and in their mastery of school subjects? Has a clear advantage emerged for a particular pedagogy among the best-known models—transitional bilingual education, English as a Second Language [ESL], structured immersion, two-way, dual immersion, or developmental bilingual programs? There is no more consensus on the answers to these questions than there was five years ago. However, there is growing evidence of an almost total lack of accountability in states that have invested most heavily in bilingual education for the past fifteen or twenty years and have not collected data or evaluated programs to produce answers to the questions raised above. The research that has been published in recent years includes a study by the General Accounting Office, the ALEC [American Legislative Council] Study, a review of the El Paso Bilingual Immersion Project, a longitudinal study of bilingual students in New York, a report of a two-year study of California's bilingual education programs, and a report of a state commission on Massachusetts's bilingual education.

The GAO Study

Every year since the late 1970s, the school enrollment of limited-English students has increased at a faster rate than the rest of the school population, and the costs of special programs nationwide are beginning to be tallied. The U.S. General Accounting Office (GAO) published a study in January 1994 titled *Limited-English Proficiency: A Growing and Costly Educational Challenge Facing Many School Districts* at the request of the Senate Committee on Labor and Human Resources. The GAO study provides an overview of the serious problems confronting U.S. public schools in meeting the needs of limited-English students, new demographics on where these students are concentrated, and a detailed description of five representative school districts with rapidly growing limited-English proficient (LEP) populations.

Briefly, the GAO report highlights these problems in the five districts that are common to all public schools with LEP students:

- Immigrant students are almost 100 percent non-English speaking on arrival in the U.S.
- LEP students arrive at different times during the school year, which causes upheavals in classrooms and educational programs.
- Some high school students have not been schooled in their native lands and lack literacy skills in any language.
- There is a high level of family poverty and transiency and a low level of parental involvement in students' education.
- There is an acute shortage of bilingual teachers and of textbooks and assessment instruments in the native languages.

The information gathered by the GAO study is valuable to educators, researchers, and policy makers. An alarming fact reported in this study is mentioned only in passing and never explained: *Immigrant children account for only 43 percent of the limited-English students in our schools.* Who, then, make up the other 57 percent and why are such large numbers of native-born children classified as limited- or non-English proficient and placed in native-language instruction programs? In a private conversation with one of the GAO regional managers, I was unable to get an explanation for the high percentage of native-born students classified as limited-English. I was told that the GAO had not found an agreed upon definition of what a "limited-English person" is and that they have included in this category children who speak English but who may not read and write it well enough for schoolwork. In that case, there surely are a large number of students who are wrongly enrolled in programs where they are being taught in another language when what they urgently need is remedial help in reading and writing in English. . . .

The ALEC Study

The ALEC Study makes a bold attempt to unravel the mysteries of exactly how many students are served by special programs that aim to remove the language barrier to an equal education, what kinds of programs they are enrolled in, where these students are concentrated—by state—and how much is actually being spent in this special effort. As a former school administrator, I know firsthand that it is quite possible to account for special costs. In the Newton, Massachusetts, public schools annual budget there is an account for bilingual/ESL programs that covers all the costs incurred for the LEP students: teachers, teacher aides, books, materials, transportation, and administration. One knew what was spent each year, over and above the school costs for general education, and in Newton this averaged about $1,000 per student per year for LEP students. Not all school districts keep such information, and it is not collected consistently by all state education departments because this is not required by the federal government.

Analyzing data from the National Center for Education Statistics, the Office of Bilingual Education and Minority Languages Affairs (OBEMLA), and various other federal and state sources, the ALEC study synthesizes the data to arrive at these conclusions for the 1991–1992 school year:

- On average, all federal funding for education amounts to 6 percent; state and local sources provide roughly 47 percent each.
- Federal funding for bilingual education, $101 million in 1991 and $116 million in 1992, was mostly allocated to native-language instruction programs, giving only 20–30 percent to ESL programs.
- There were 2.3 million limited-English students enrolled in U.S. public schools while only 1.9 million were enrolled in any special language program, leaving 450,000 LEP students without any special language help.

- Of the 1.9 million students in special programs, 60 percent were enrolled in bilingual programs, 22 percent in ESL, and 18 percent in a category labeled "unknown" because states could not describe their special language programs.
- Candidly explaining the difficulties of collecting strictly accurate data, the costs of programs for LEP students are estimated to be $5.5 billion (56 percent) for bilingual programs, $1.9 billion (20 percent) for ESL, and $2.4 billion (24 percent) for unknown programs, totaling $9.9 billion for 1991–1992.
- Projecting that increases in enrollments in 1993 would be the same as recent increases, spending on special language programs would amount to $12 billion in 1993.

The ALEC study draws some tenable conclusions from the data summarized above while it admits that the approximate cost figures may be over- and underestimations of what is actually spent. Both federal and state agencies do give preference to native-language instruction programs over ESL in funding decisions by a wide margin, even though "there is no conclusive research that demonstrates the educational superiority of bilingual education over ESL." Even if the ALEC cost estimates were overestimated, this is only one of several recent reports that point out the widespread lack of accountability in bilingual education. Twenty-seven years of heavy investment in mainly bilingual programs has not produced exact data on how much these programs cost or how successful they are in realizing their goals in student achievement. . . .

The El Paso Bilingual Immersion Project

In 1992, the Institute for Research in English Acquisition and Development (READ) published a monograph by Russell Gersten, John Woodward, and Susan Schneider on the final results of the seven-year longitudinal study of the Bilingual Immersion Project; the results were summarized by Gersten and Woodward in *The Elementary School Journal* in 1995. This evaluation clearly demonstrates advantages for the immersion approach over the transitional bilingual education (TBE) model.

- The Iowa Test of Basic Skills (in English) results for grades 4 and 5 do show superior performance in all academic areas for students in the immersion program over students in the transitional bilingual program.
- By grade 6, 99 percent of immersion students were mainstreamed; at end of 7th grade, 35 percent of TBE students are still in the bilingual program.
- Well-designed bilingual immersion leads to more rapid, more successful, and increased integration of Latino students into the mainstream, with no detrimental effects in any area of achievement for students who took part in this program. The increased integration may lead to

a decrease in high school dropout rates among Hispanic students. Subsequent research is needed to explore the possibility of this effect of immersion programs.

- The major strengths of the bilingual immersion program are its use of contemporary thinking on language acquisition and literacy development and its relatively stress-free approach to the rapid learning of English in the primary grades.
- Teacher questionnaires revealed much greater satisfaction with the early, systematic teaching of English in the immersion program than with the slow introduction of English in the bilingual program.
- Student interviews indicated no significant differences in reactions to the two programs. No evidence emerged, from students, parents, or teachers, that native-language teaching produces a higher level of self-esteem or that early immersion in a second language is more stressful, two of the common beliefs promoted by bilingual education advocates.

Research such as that conducted in El Paso is invaluable in the ongoing debate on program effectiveness. Because the comparison was made between two radically different teaching methods in the same school district with the same population of limited-English students, this study provides incontrovertible proof of the benefits to students of early second-language learning. More recently, the New York City public schools published a report that threw a metaphorical bombshell into the bilingual education camp.

The New York Study

Educational Progress of Students in Bilingual and ESL Programs: A Longitudinal Study, 1990–1994, was published in October 1994 by the Board of Education of the City of New York. New York City invested $300 million in 1993 in bilingual programs where the instruction was given in Spanish, Chinese, Haitian Creole, Russian, Korean, Vietnamese, French, Greek, Arabic, and Bengali—an investment that was not only misguided but harmful to the student beneficiaries, as the results of the longitudinal study show.

The New York City study is important because, like the El Paso study, it examines student achievement in basically different programs in large, urban school districts and because it charts student progress over a period of years. The criteria of student success measured included number of years served in a special language program before exiting to a mainstream classroom, reading level in English, and performance in math. The two groups of limited-English students whose achievement was monitored were (1) Spanish speakers and speakers of Haitian Creole who were enrolled in bilingual classrooms where they received mostly native-language instruction in reading, writing, and school subjects, with brief English-language lessons, (2) students from Russian, Korean, and Chinese language backgrounds who were placed in ESL classes where all instruction is provided through a special English-language curriculum. The study included children who entered school in fall 1990: 11,320 entering kindergarten, 2,053 entering 1st grade, 841 entering 2nd grade, 797 entering 3rd grade, 754 entering 6th grade, and 1,366 entering 9th grade.

As any disinterested observer might have anticipated, there is strong evidence showing that the earlier a second language is introduced, the more rapidly it is learned for academic purposes. Surprising? Not at all, but it flies in the face of the received wisdom of Jim Cummins's theories that were developed, after the fact, to justify bilingual education: the facilitation theory and the threshold hypothesis. With appropriate teaching, children can learn a new language quickly and can learn subject matter taught *in* that language. Reading and writing skills can be mastered, and math can be learned successfully in a second language; here are the proofs from thousands of New York City schoolchildren.

The most riveting outcome of this research reported in the New York study is the fact that "at all grade levels, students served in ESL-only programs exited their programs faster than those served in bilingual programs." The three-year exit rates were as follows: For ESL-only programs, the exit rates were 79.3 percent, 67.5 percent, and 32.7 percent for students who entered school in grades kindergarten, 2, and 6, respectively; for bilingual programs, the exit rates were 51.5 percent, 22.1 percent, and 6.9 percent, respectively.

The three-year exit rates for LEP students who entered kindergarten from different language groups, whether they were in ESL or bilingual programs, [were] reported as follows: 91.8 percent for Korean, 87.4 percent for Russian, 82.6 percent for Chinese, 58.7 percent for Haitian Creole, and 50.6 percent for Spanish.

Differences among language groups remained steady even for students entering the New York schools in the higher grades. Critics of the study, including Luis O. Reyes of the New York City School Board, allege that Korean, Russian, and Chinese background students are from middle-class families and that the social class difference invalidates the study. Socioeconomic data is not reported in the study. We do not know how many of the children in any of the language groups are from poor, working-class, or middle-class families, and we should not make unwarranted assumptions. One could hazard a guess that most immigrant, migrant, and refugee children attending the New York City public schools do not come from affluent families. The undeniable facts are that children from Spanish and Haitian Creole speaking families are mostly funneled into bilingual classrooms, and children from other language groups are mostly assigned to ESL classrooms. I firmly believe that the type of schooling these children receive makes a large difference in their ability to achieve at their own personal best. I believe, even more firmly, that Haitian and Latino children would succeed in mastering English-language skills better and faster and, therefore, join their English-speaking peers in mainstream classes much sooner than is now the case *if they were given the same opportunity given to Russian, Korean, and Chinese students.*

Exiting the special program classrooms more expeditiously is not only a cost consideration but a matter of integration and opportunity. Remaining in substantially segregated bilingual classrooms for several years does not equip students to compete in the broader life of the school and community—in fact it has the opposite effect....

The California Study and Others

... New York City's willingness actually to monitor the progress of LEP students and report the results to the public is much to be praised when we survey the lack of accountability in other parts of the country. The State of California, with 1.2 million limited-English students (43 percent of all LEP students in the United States) and a twenty-year history of involvement with bilingual education, commissioned an evaluation of educational programs for these students. *Meeting the Challenge of Language Diversity: An Evaluation of Programs for Pupils with Limited Proficiency in English,* the published report of a two-year study, 1990–1992, shows generally poor results for bilingual education programs in California and essentially evades the legislature's requirement that it provide "information to determine which model for educating LEP pupils is most effective and cost effective."

Major findings of this study are the following:

1. California public schools do not have valid assessments of the performance for students with limited proficiency in English. Therefore, *the state and the public cannot hold schools accountable for LEP students achieving high levels of performance* (emphasis added).
2. Many schools do not reclassify students (that is, move them from the bilingual programs with appropriate skills to work in mainstream classrooms), keeping them in native-language classrooms well beyond the time when they are fluent in English. "It is not surprising that many students may wait years to be formally retested for program exit and that many others may never be reclassified, going on to the middle school still bearing the LEP label."
3. Junior and senior high school LEP students do not have access to core academic subjects through Sheltered English or ESL. Long stays in bilingual programs in elementary schools delay the effective learning of the English-language literacy skills that are so important for secondary school work.

Meeting the Challenge presents a bleak picture of the disappointing results of twenty years of bilingual education in California. When the Chacon-Moscone Bilingual Bicultural Act of 1976 expired in 1987, the California State Department of Education sent notification to each school district that the intent of the act would still be promoted by state regulations, principally, "that the primary goal of all [bilingual] programs is, as effectively and efficiently as possible, to develop in each child fluency in English." *Meeting the Challenge* fails to tell us how or if this goal is being properly met but offers a variety of excuses for not fulfilling its mission. The weaknesses in this giant instructional system for limited-English students—one out of every five students in California—are of huge proportions. The fact that the State Department of Education has allowed school districts to evade their responsibility to assess and report on student progress shows an unconscionable lack of accountability by this powerful bureaucracy. If we cannot hold the schools responsible for program outcomes after twenty years, then perhaps the responsibility for this failure rests squarely on the state agency that has forcefully promoted the bilingual education policy.

California's high school dropout rates reported in June 1995 amounted to a statewide average of 5 percent per year, or a four-year average of 20 percent of students leaving school before graduation. Discouraging as that seems, the dropout rate for Latino students statewide is even higher—28 percent, compared to 10 percent for Asian students and 12 percent for white students. The four-year dropout rate for the Los Angeles Unified School District, the district enrolling the highest percentage of LEP students in the state, is a shocking 43.6 percent.

In 1993 the Los Angeles Unified School District embarked on a plan to improve its bilingual education programs, partly through expanded teacher training in the native languages of the students (actually, in Spanish only). Clearly, the increased emphasis on native-language instruction has not had any positive effect on the dropout rates for LEP students in the Los Angeles schools. The latest Los Angeles figures on dropout rates by ethnic breakdown, as reported by the State Department of Education in October 1994 for the 1993–1994 school year, are 44.4 percent for Hispanic students, *three-fourths of whom are enrolled in bilingual classes in the district.* ...

Massachusetts Revisited

Ironically, the Commonwealth of Massachusetts, which passed the first state law mandating native-language teaching in 1971, Chapter 71-A, has an even more dismal record than California in the area of public accountability. Efforts to reform the Transitional Bilingual Education law have been successfully resisted, even though there can hardly be one legislator who has any documented proof·for the effectiveness of bilingual education in Massachusetts. A state commission was appointed by Governor Weld to survey the status of bilingual education in the state, and in December 1994 it reported this conclusion:

> We do not know, on the basis of measured outcomes, whether TBE programs in Massachusetts produce good results or poor results. There are no comprehensive data that evaluate the performance of TBE pupils compared with pupils from other groups. This specialized program which accounts for 5% of all pupils in Massachusetts public schools and 17% of all pupils in Boston public schools is not held separately accountable for its performance.

Apparently, the commission has recommended that the state department of education develop new guidelines on accountability as soon as suitable tests are developed. As a veteran Massachusetts educator who has seen many a set of "guidelines" arrive with a flourish and disappear without a trace, I reserve judgment on the latest pronouncements.

Massachusetts probably leads the country in zany educational experiments. I reported earlier on the Cape Verdean project to try to encourage the use of a nonstandard dialect as the classroom language of instruction. The Boston public school system, in its infinite wisdom, now maintains a K–12 bilingual program in Kriolu, a dialect of Portuguese spoken in the Cape Verde Islands that has no alphabet, no written language, and no books. Massachusetts is thought to be the only place in the world to have schoolrooms in which Kriolu is the language of instruction, with Kriolu programs in Boston, Brockton, and New Bedford schools. Portuguese is the official language of education in Cape Verde.

Aside from the minor matters of alphabets, a written language, or books, there are these exquisite complications. Cape Verdean students may speak one of many dialects and not understand Kriolu, as explained by a science teacher in the Dearborn School, Boston, who says: "Sometimes a student gets upset because he's not understanding the Fogo dialect so you have to go back and help him in Kriolu or Portuguese." Communication between the schools and Cape Verdean parents is not improved either. Massachusetts law requires that all paperwork be sent to parents in the student's native language. A teacher at the Condon School, Eileen Fonseca, says it frustrates parents to receive a notice written in Kriolu: "When we send home report cards and matriculation papers in Kriolu, parents complain. This is new to them. They have to have it read three times, or they just ask for Portuguese or English, often so it can be read to them by family or friends." One parent made this comment: "They sent me a letter apparently to tell me something. I never understood what it was trying to say. I called to say that if the intent of the letter is to communicate, it would be better in Portuguese."

The Kriolu Caper makes an amusing, now-I've-heard-everything anecdote, but the enormity of such folly in education policy is no laughing matter. This program neither helps students learn the language or acquire the literacy skills necessary for school achievement, nor does it facilitate communication between school and family. What it does do is foster resentment in the Cape Verdean community, which does not feel respected or understood, a situation similar to the misguided attempt to make black English the language of instruction for African-American schoolchildren two decades ago. The Peoples Republic of Massachusetts is in serious need of a reality check.

Let me conclude with the review of a chapter in *The Emperor Has No Clothes: Bilingual Education in Massachusetts* by Christine Rossell and Keith Baker that summarizes the major studies on the effectiveness of bilingual education and analyzes those studies that are methodologically acceptable.

Social science research in education is, at best, an approximation of true scientific research. Schoolchildren cannot be isolated in laboratory test tubes and studied under pristine conditions, controlling for minute variables. In the area of bilingual education research, the quality of the product is generally acknowledged to be especially low. The elements of a scientifically valid evaluation of a special effort must include, at the minimum:

- random assignment of subjects to avoid self-selection bias
- a control group to compare with the group receiving the special program (treatment)
- pretesting to establish that students in different groups are starting with the same traits—i.e., that all are limited or non-English speakers— or statistical adjustments to account for pre-treatment differences
- posttesting to determine the effect of different treatments

- assurance that one group does not receive extra benefits, aside from the difference in treatments, such as after-school programs or a longer school day.

In the area of bilingual education research, there is the added problem that the label is applied to a range of educational varieties, from the classic model, in which native language instruction is given 80–90 percent of the school day, to the other extreme, in which the teacher may use a word or two of another language on occasion. This complicates the work of analyzing the effects of bilingual programs.

Rossell and Baker read over five hundred studies, three hundred of which were program evaluations. The authors found seventy-two methodologically acceptable studies, that is, studies that show the effect of transitional bilingual education on English-language learning, reading, and mathematics, compared to (1) "submersion" or doing nothing, (2) English as a Second Language, (3) structured immersion in English, and (4) maintenance bilingual education. The authors' overall finding, which is of crucial importance as this is the most current, comprehensive analysis of the research, is that *"there is still . . . no consistent research support for transitional bilingual education as a superior instructional practice for improving the English language achievement of limited-English-proficient children"* (emphasis added).

Bilingual Education: The Controversy

Bilingual education, a preferred strategy for the last 20 years, aims to teach academic subjects to immigrant children in their native languages (most of-ten Spanish), while slowly and simultaneously adding English instruction.[1] In theory, the children don't fall behind in other subjects while they are learning English. When they are fluent in English, they can then "transition" to English instruction in academic subjects at the grade level of their peers. Further, the theory goes, teaching immigrants in their native language values their family and community culture and reinforces their sense of self-worth, thus making their academic success more likely.

In contrast, bilingual education's critics tell the following, quite differ-ent, story. In the early 20th century, public schools assimilated immigrants to American culture and imparted workplace skills essential for upward mobility. Children were immersed in English instruction and, when forced to "sink or swim," they swam. Today, however, separatist (usually Hispanic) community leaders and their liberal supporters, opposed to assimilation, want Spanish in-struction to preserve native culture and traditions. This is especially dangerous because the proximity of Mexico and the possibility of returning home give today's immigrants the option of "keeping a foot in both camps"—an option not available to previous immigrants who were forced to assimilate. Today's attempts to preserve immigrants' native languages and cultures will not only balkanize the American melting pot but hurt the children upon whom bilin-gual education is imposed because their failure to learn English well will leave them unprepared for the workplace. Bilingual education supporters may claim that it aims to teach English, but high dropout rates for immigrant children and low rates of transition to full English instruction prove that, even if educators' intentions are genuine, the program is a failure.

The English First Foundation, a lobbying group bent on abolishing bilin-gual education, states that most Americans "have ancestors who learned English the same way: in classrooms where English was the only language used for all learning activities."[2] According to 1996 Republican Presidential nominee Bob Dole, the teaching of English to immigrants is what "we have done . . . since our founding to speed the melting of our melting pot. . . . We must stop the practice of multilingual education as a means of instilling ethnic pride, or as a therapy

From Richard Rothstein, "Bilingual Education: The Controversy," *Phi Delta Kappan* (May 1998). Adapted from *The Way We Were?* (Century Foundation Press, 1998). Copyright © 1998 by The Century Foundation, Inc. Reprinted by permission.

for low self-esteem, or out of elitist guilt over a culture built on the traditions of the West."[3]

Speaker of the House Newt Gingrich chimed in as well:

> If people had wanted to remain immersed in their old culture, they could have done so without coming to America.... Bilingualism keeps people actively tied to their old language and habits and maximizes the cost of the transition to becoming American.... The only viable alternative for the American underclass is American civilization. Without English as a common language, there is no such civilization.[4]

This viewpoint has commonsense appeal, but it has little foundation in reality.

Bilingual Education: The History

Despite proximity to their homeland, Mexican Americans are no more likely to reverse migrate than were Europeans in the early 20th century. One-third of the immigrants who came here between 1908 and 1924 eventually abandoned America and returned home.[5]

What's more, the immigrants who remained did not succeed in school by learning English. During the last great wave of immigration, from 1880 to 1915, very few Americans succeeded in school, immigrants least of all. By 1930, it was still the case that half of all American 14- to 17-year-olds either didn't make it to high school or dropped out before graduating. The median number of school years completed was 10.

Far from succeeding by immersing themselves in English, immigrant groups did much worse than the native-born, and some immigrant groups did much worse than others. The poorest performers were Italians. According to a 1911 federal immigration commission report, in Boston, Chicago, and New York 80% of native white children in the seventh grade stayed in school another year, but only 58% of Southern Italian children, 62% of Polish children, and 74% of Russian Jewish children did so. Of those who made it to eighth grade, 58% of the native whites went on to high school, but only 23% of the Southern Italians did so. In New York, 54% of native-born eighth-graders made it to ninth grade, but only 34% of foreign-born eighth-graders did so.[6]

A later study showed that the lack of success of immigrants relative to the native-born continued into high school. In 1931, only 11% of the Italian students who entered high school graduated (compared to an estimated graduation rate of over 40% for all students). This was a much bigger native/immigrant gap than we have today.

While we have no achievement tests from that earlier period by which to evaluate relative student performance, I.Q. tests were administered frequently. Test after test in the 1920s found that Italian immigrant students had an average I.Q. of about 85, compared to an average for native-born students of about 102. The poor academic achievement of these Italian Americans led to high rates of "retardation"—that is, being held back and not promoted (this was the origin of the pejorative use of the term "retarded").

A survey of New York City's retarded students (liberally defined so that a child had to be 9 years old to be considered retarded in the first grade, 10 years old in the second grade, and so on), found that 19% of native-born students were retarded in 1908, compared to 36% of Italian students. The federal immigration commission found that the retardation rate of children of non-English-speaking immigrants was about 60% higher than that of children of immigrants from English-speaking countries.[7] The challenge of educating Italian immigrant children was so severe that New York established its first special education classes to confront it. A 1921 survey disclosed that half of all (what we now call) "learning disabled" special education children in New York schools had Italian-born fathers.[8]

As these data show—and as is the case today—some groups did better than others, both for cultural reasons and because of the influence of other socio-economic factors on student achievement. If Italian children did worse, Eastern European Jewish children did better. This is not surprising in light of what we now know about the powerful influence of background characteristics on academic success. In 1910, 32% of Southern Italian adult males in American cities were unskilled manual laborers, but only one-half of 1% of Russian Jewish males were unskilled. Thirty-four percent of the Jews were merchants, while only 13% of the Italians were. In New York City, the average annual income of a Russian Jewish head-of-household in 1910 was $813; a Southern Italian head-of-household averaged $688.[9]

But even with these relative economic advantages, the notion that Jewish immigrant children assimilated through sink-or-swim English-only education is a nostalgic and dangerous myth. In 1910, there were 191,000 Jewish children in the New York City schools; only 6,000 were in high school, and the overwhelming majority of these students dropped out before graduating. As the Jewish writer Irving Howe put it, after reviewing New York school documents describing the difficulties of "Americanizing" immigrant children from 1910 to 1914, "To read the reports of the school superintendents is to grow impatient with later sentimentalists who would have us suppose that all or most Jewish children burned with zeal for the life of the mind."[10] There may have been relatively more such students among the Jewish immigrants than in other immigrant communities, Howe noted, but they were still a minority.

Immersing immigrants in an English-language school program has been effective—usually by the third generation. On the whole, immigrant children spoke their native language; members of the second generation (immigrants' native-born children) were bilingual, but not sufficiently fluent in English to excel in school; members of the third generation were fluent in English and began to acquire college educations. For some groups (e.g., Greek Americans), the pattern more often took four generations; for others (e.g., Eastern European Jews), many in the second generation may have entered college.

This history is not a mere curiosity, because those who advocate against bilingual education today often claim that we know how to educate immigrant children because we've done it before. However, if we've never successfully educated the first or even second generation of children from peasant or unskilled immigrant families, we are dealing with an unprecedented task, and history can't guide us.

To understand the uniqueness of our current challenge, compare the enormous—by contemporary standards—dropout rate of New York City Jewish students in 1910 with that of Mexican students in the Los Angeles school district today. Like New York in 1910, Los Angeles now is burdened with a rising tide of immigrants. In 1996, there were 103,000 Hispanic students in grades 9–12 in Los Angeles (out of the city's total K–12 Hispanic population of 390,000). Hispanic high school students were about 26% of the total Hispanic student population in Los Angeles in 1996,[11] compared to 3% for Jews in New York in 1910 (only 6,000 high school students out of 191,000 total Jewish enrollment). In Los Angeles today, 74% of Mexican-born youths between the ages of 15 and 17 are still in high school; 88% of Hispanic youths from other countries are still in attendance.[12] More than 70% of Hispanic immigrants who came to the United States prior to their sophomore year actually complete high school (compared to a 94% high school completion rate for whites and a 92% rate for blacks).[13] English immersion programs for Jews early in this century (and certainly similar programs for Italians) cannot teach us anything that would help improve on today's immigrant achievement or school completion, much of which may be attributable to bilingual education programs, even if imperfectly administered.

If the notion is misleading that English immersion led previous generations of immigrants to academic success, so too is the claim that bilingual education repudiates the assimilationist approach of previous immigrants. In reality, today's Hispanics are not the first to seek bicultural assimilation. Some 19th- and early 20th-century European immigrants also fought for and won the right to bilingual education in the public schools.[14] Native-language instruction was absent from 1920 until the mid-1960s only because a fierce anti-German (and then anti-immigrant) reaction after World War I succeeded in banishing it from American classrooms. Even foreign-language instruction for native-born students was banned in most places. If Chicago's Bismarck Hotel found it necessary to rename itself the "Mark Twain," it should not be surprising that bilingual education programs were also abolished.

Before World War I, immigrant groups often pressed public schools to teach children in their native language. The success of these groups depended more on whether adult immigrant activists had political power than on a pedagogical consensus. The immigrants' objective, as it is today, was to preserve a fragment of ethnic identity in children for whom the pull of American culture seemed dangerously irresistible. In this, they were supported by many influential educators. William Harris, the school superintendent in St. Louis and later U.S. commissioner of education, argued for bilingual education in the 1870s, stating that "national memories and aspirations, family traditions, customs and habits, moral and religious observances cannot be suddenly removed or changed without disastrously weakening the personality." Harris established the first "kindergarten" in America, taught solely in German, to give immigrant students a head start in the St. Louis schools.[15]

Nineteenth-century immigrant parents were often split over the desirability of bilingual education, as immigrant parents are split today. Many recognized that children were more likely to succeed if schools' use of the native language validated the culture of the home. But others felt that their children's education would be furthered if they learned in English only.

The first bilingual public school in New York City was established in 1837 to prepare German-speaking children for eventual participation in regular English schools. The initial rule was that children could remain in German-language instruction only for 12 months, after which they would transfer to a regular school. But the German teacher resisted this rule, believing that, before transferring, the children needed more than the limited English fluency they had acquired after a year of German instruction. The record is unclear about how often the rule was stretched.

Many immigrant children, not just Germans, did not attend school at all if they could not have classes in their native language. In his 1840 address to the New York legislature, Gov. William Seward (later Lincoln's secretary of state) explained that the importance of attracting immigrants to school—and of keeping them there—motivated his advocacy of expanded native-language instruction: "I do not hesitate to recommend the establishment of schools in which [immigrant children] may be instructed by teachers speaking the same language with themselves." Only by so doing, Gov. Seward insisted, could we "qualify... [them] for the high responsibilities of citizenship."

Buoyed by Seward's endorsement, Italian parents in New York City demanded a native-language school as well, and in 1843 the Public School Society established a committee to determine whether one should be established. The committee recommended against an Italian-language school, claiming the Italian community was itself divided. "Information has been obtained," the committee stated, "that the more intelligent class of Italians do not desire such a school, and that, like most [but not, apparently, all] of the better class of Germans, they would prefer that those of their countrymen who come here with good intentions should be Americanized as speedily as possible."[16]

Bilingual education, though sometimes controversial, was found nationwide. In Pennsylvania, German Lutheran churches established parochial schools when public schools would not teach in German; in 1838, Pennsylvania law converted these German schools to public schools. Then, in 1852, a state public school regulation specified that "if any considerable number of Germans desire to have their children instructed in their own language, their wishes should be gratified."[17]

In 1866, succumbing to pressure from politically powerful German immigrants, the Chicago Board of Education decided to establish a German-language school in each area of the city where 150 parents asked for it. By 1892 the board had hired 242 German-language teachers to teach 35,000 German-speaking children, one-fourth of Chicago's total public school enrollment. In 1870, a public school established in Denver, Colorado, was taught entirely in German. An 1872 Oregon law permitted German-language public schools to be established in Portland whenever 100 voters petitioned for such a school. Maryland, Iowa, Indiana, Kentucky, Ohio, and Minnesota also had bilingual education laws, either statewide or applying only to cities with large immigrant populations. In Nebraska, enabling legislation for bilingual education was enacted for the benefit of German immigrant children as late as 1913.[18]

There was considerable variation in how these programs arranged what we now call the "transition" to English. In St. Louis, Harris' system introduced English gradually, beginning in the first grade. The 1888 report of the Missouri supervisor of public instruction stated that "in some districts the schools are taught in German for a certain number of months and then in English, while in others German is used part of the day and English the rest. Some of the teachers are barely able to speak the English language." Ohio's 1870 rules provided that the lower grades in German-language public schools should be bilingual (half the instructional time in grades 1 through 4 could be in German), but in grades 5 through 8 native-language instruction had to be reduced to one hour a day. Baltimore permitted public schools in the upper grades to teach art and music in German only, but geography, history, and science had to be taught in both English and German. In some midwestern communities, there was resistance to any English instruction: an 1846 Wisconsin law insisted that public schools in Milwaukee must at least teach English (as a foreign language) as one academic subject.[19]

While Germans were most effective in demanding public support for native-language instruction, others were also successful. In Texas in the late 19th century, there were seven Czech-language schools supported by the state school fund. In California, a desire by the majority to segregate Chinese children seemed to play more of a role than demands by the Chinese community for separate education. San Francisco established a Chinese-language school in 1885; the city later established segregated Indian, Mongolian, and Japanese schools.[20]

San Francisco's German, Italian, and French immigrants, on the other hand, were taught in their native languages in regular public schools. Here, bilingual education was a strategy designed to lure immigrant children into public schools from parochial schools where they learned no English at all. According to San Francisco's school superintendent in 1871, only if offered native-language instruction could immigrant children be brought into public schools, where, "under the care of American teachers," they could be "molded in the true form of American citizenship."[21]

Support for bilingual education was rarely unanimous or consistent. In San Francisco, the election of an "anti-immigrant" Republican school board majority in 1873 led to the abolition of schools in which French and German had been the primary languages of instruction and to the firing of all French- and German-speaking teachers. After protests by the immigrant community, bilingual schools were reestablished in 1874. In 1877, the California legislature enacted a prohibition of bilingual education, but the governor declined to sign it. William Harris' bilingual system in St. Louis was dismantled in 1888, after redistricting split the German vote and the Irish won a school board majority.[22]

In 1889, Republican Gov. William Hoard of Wisconsin sponsored legislation to ban primary-language instruction in public and private schools, claiming the support of German immigrant parents. The *Milwaukee Sentinel* published a front-page story about "a German in Sheboygan County... who

sent his children away to school in order that they might learn English." The father, reported the *Sentinel,* complained that "in the public schools of the town, German teachers, who... did not know English... had been employed...,
[and] he felt it essential to the welfare of his children, who expected to remain citizens of this country, to know English."[23]

But both the newspaper and Wisconsin's Republican politicians had misjudged the immigrants' sentiments. In response to the anti-bilingual law, enraged German Americans (who had previously supported Republican candidates) mobilized to turn the statehouse over to Democrats and to convert the state's 7-to-2 Republican majority in Congress to a Democratic majority of 8-to-1. The Democrats promptly repealed the anti-bilingual education law.

An almost identical series of events took place in Illinois, where formerly Republican German American voters mobilized in both East St. Louis and Chicago to elect a liberal Democrat, Peter Altgeld, governor in 1890, largely because of his bilingual school language policy. These upheavals in two previously safe Republican states played an important role in the election of Democrat Grover Cleveland as President in 1892. Nonetheless, the controversy continued, and in 1893 the *Chicago Tribune* began a new campaign against German-language instruction. In a compromise later that year, German instruction was abolished in the primary grades but retained in the upper grades, while Chicago's mayor promised German Americans a veto over future school board appointments to ensure that erosion of primary-language instruction would not continue.[24]

But these controversies ended with World War I. Six months after the armistice, the Ohio legislature, spurred by Gov. James Cox, who was to be the Democratic Presidential candidate in 1920, banned all German from the state's elementary schools. The language posed "a distinct menace to Americanism," Cox insisted. The *New York Times* editorialized in 1919 that, although some parents "want German to be taught [because it] pleases their pride..., it does not do their children any good." Within the following year, 15 states in which native-language instruction had flourished adopted laws requiring that all teaching be in English. By 1923, 35 states had done so.[25] Only when Nebraska went so far as to ban native-language instruction in parochial as well as public schools did the Supreme Court, in 1923, strike down an English-only law.[26]

During the next 30 years, bilingual instruction had its ups and downs, even where English was not the native language. In 1950, Louisiana first required English, not French, to be the language of public school instruction. In the Southwest, where teaching in Spanish had long been common, the practice continued in some places and was abolished in others. Tucson established a bilingual teaching program in 1923, and Burbank established one in 1931. New Mexico operated bilingual schools throughout most of the 20th century, up until the 1950s. The state even required the teaching of Spanish to English-speaking children in elementary school. But in 1918, Texas made teaching in Spanish a crime, and, while the law was not consistently enforced (especially along the Mexican border), as recently as 1973 a Texas teacher was indicted for not teaching history in English.[27] In the same year, Texas reversed itself and adopted bilingual education as its strategy.

When bilingual education began to reemerge in the 1970s—spurred by a Supreme Court finding that schools without special provisions for educating language-minority children were not providing equal education—the nation's memory of these precedents had been erased. Today many Americans blithely repeat the myth that, until the recent emergence of separatist minority activists and their liberal supporters, the nation had always immersed its immigrant children in nothing but English and this method had proved its effectiveness.

Bilingual Education: Mixed Evidence

This mixed history, however, does not prove that bilingual education is effective, any more so than English immersion or intense English-language instruction. To an unbiased layperson, the arguments of both advocates and opponents of bilingual education seem to make sense. On the one hand, it's reasonable to insist that children who don't speak English continue their education in a language they understand in history, literature, math, and science, while they learn English. It's also reasonable to expect, however, that this might make it too tempting to defer English-language instruction. Moreover, the best way to do something difficult—e.g., making the transition to English—is simply to do it without delay. It makes sense to acknowledge that children may adapt better to school if the school's culture is not in conflict with that of the home. But some immigrant parents may be more intent on preserving native culture for their children than are the children themselves.

Modern research findings on bilingual education are mixed. As with all educational research, it is so difficult to control for complex background factors that affect academic outcomes that no single study is ultimately satisfying. Bilingual education advocates point to case studies of primary-language programs in Calexico, California; Rock Point, Arizona; Santa Fe, New Mexico; New Haven, Connecticut; and elsewhere that show that children advance further in both English and other academic subjects when native-language instruction is used and the transition to English is very gradual. Opponents point to case studies in Redwood City and Berkeley, California; in Fairfax, Virginia; and elsewhere that prove that immersion in English or rapid and intensive English instruction is most effective.[28] Overall, the conflicting evidence from these case studies does not suggest that abolition of bilingual education or even the substitution of parental choice for pedagogical expertise in determining whether bilingual approaches should be used would improve things much.

The problem is especially complex because not only economic factors but also generational variation apparently affects the achievement of immigrant youths. In 1936, the principal of a high school in New York City that enrolled large numbers of Italian immigrants wrote:

> The problem of juvenile delinquency... baffles all the forces of organized society.... The highest rate of delinquency is characteristic of immigrant communities.... The delinquent is usually the American-born child of

foreign-born parents, not the immigrant himself. Delinquency, then, is fundamentally a second-generation problem. This intensifies the responsibility of the school.[29]

The same is true today. The challenge now facing immigrant educators is that academic achievement for second-generation Hispanic and Asian children is often below that of children who arrive in the U.S. as immigrants themselves.[30] Many of these children of the second generation seem to speak English, but they are fully fluent in neither English nor their home language. Many of their parents, frustrated that their own ambition has not been transmitted to their children, may become convinced that only English immersion will set their children straight, while others seek bilingual solutions to prevent the corruption of American culture from dampening their children's ambition.

In the absence of persuasive evidence, the issue has become politicized. In a country as large as ours, with as varied experience, there is virtually no limit to the anecdotes and symbols that can be invoked as substitutes for evidence.

Opponents of bilingual education promote Hispanic parents to the media when they claim they want their children to learn English without bilingual support; the clear implication is that only liberal ideologues and separatists support native-language instruction. These claims, like those circulated by the *Milwaukee Sentinel* a century ago, may not reflect the feelings of most parents. And the technology of teaching a new language to immigrant children is complex; both bilingual education advocates and opponents claim their goal is full English literacy as rapidly as possible. But there's no reason to expect that politicized parent groups are the best judges of language acquisition research.

There are also successful adult immigrants who brag of their English fluency, acquired either with or without bilingual education. As always, such anecdotal evidence should be treated with caution. Richard Rodriguez' autobiography, *Hunger of Memory*, describes his successful education in an English-only environment. But Rodriguez, unlike most immigrants, was raised in a predominantly English-speaking neighborhood and was the only Spanish speaker in his class.[31] His experience may be relevant for some immigrants, but not relevant for many others.

Whichever method is, in fact, more effective for most immigrant children, there will be many for whom the other method worked well. It may be the case that immigrant children's social and economic background characteristics should affect the pedagogy chosen. Even if some Russian Jewish immigrants did not require bilingual education to graduate from high school, perhaps Italians would have progressed more rapidly if they'd had access to bilingual instruction. Today, the fact that some (though not all) Asian immigrants seem to progress rapidly in school without native-language support provides no relevant evidence about whether this model can work well for Mexican or Caribbean children, especially those low on the ladder of socioeconomic status and those whose parents have little education. Nor does it tell us much about what the best pedagogy would be for Asians who generally do less well in school, such as Hmong, Laotian, and Cambodian children.[32]

It is certain, however, that the American "melting pot" has never been endangered by pluralist efforts to preserve native languages and cultures.

Bilingual instruction has never interfered with the powerful assimilationist influences that overwhelm all children whose parents migrate here. And this is equally true of Spanish-speaking children today.

After the last 20 years of bilingual education throughout America, Spanish-speaking children continue to assimilate. From 1972 to 1995, despite rapidly accelerating immigration (more Hispanic youths are first-generation immigrants today than 20 years ago), the Hispanic high school completion rate has crept upward (from 66% to 70%). Hispanic high school graduates who enroll in college jumped from 45% to 54% (for non-Hispanic whites, it's now 64%). And the number of Hispanic high school graduates who subsequently complete four years of college jumped from 11% to 16% (for non-Hispanic whites, it's now 34%).[33] A study of the five-county area surrounding Los Angeles, the most immigrant-affected community in the nation, found that from 1980 to 1990, the share of U.S.-born Hispanics in professional occupations grew from 7% to 9%, the share in executive positions grew from 7% to 10%, and the share in other administrative and technical jobs grew from 24% to 26%.[34] Overall, 55% of U.S.-born Hispanics are in occupations for which a good education is a necessity, in an area where bilingual education has been practiced for the last generation.

Perhaps we can do better. Perhaps we would do better with less bilingual education. But perhaps not. All we can say for sure is that the data reveal no apparent crisis, and the system for immigrant education with which we've been muddling through, with all its problems, does not seem to be in a state of collapse.

The best thing that could happen to the bilingual education debate would be to remove it from the political realm. Sound-bite pedagogy is no cure for the complex interaction of social, economic, and instructional factors that determine the outcomes of contemporary American schools.

Notes

1. Technically, "bilingual education" refers to all programs designed to give any support to non-English-speaking children, including programs whose main focus is immersion in English-speaking classrooms. In public debate, however, the term generally refers to only one such program, "transitional bilingual education (TBE)," in which native-language instruction in academic subjects is given to non-English speakers. In this article, I use the term in its nontechnical sense to refer only to "TBE" programs.

2. Web site, English First Foundation: http://englishfirst.org.

3. Mark Pitsch, "Dole Takes Aim at 'Elitist' History Standards," *Education Week,* 13 September 1995, p. 18.

4. Newt Gingrich, *To Renew America* (New York: HarperCollins, 1995), pp. 161–62.

5. Irving Howe, *World of Our Fathers* (New York: Simon and Schuster, 1983), p. 58.

6. Michael R. Olneck and Marvin Lazerson, "The School Achievement of Immigrant Children: 1900–1930," *History of Education Quarterly,* Winter 1974, pp. 453–82, Tables 3, 5, 6.

7. David K. Cohen, "Immigrants and the Schools," *Review of Educational Research,* vol. 40, 1970, pp. 13–27.

8. Seymour B. Sarason and John Doris, *Educational Handicap, Public Policy, and Social History* (New York: Free Press, 1979), pp. 155–56, 340–51.

9. Olneck and Lazerson, Tables 11 and 12.

10. Howe, pp. 277–78.

11. *Fall 1995 Preliminary Ethnic Survey* (Los Angeles: Information Technology Division, Los Angeles Unified School District, Publication No. 124, 1996).

12. Georges Vernez and Allan Abrahamse, *How Immigrants Fare in U.S. Education* (Santa Monica, Calif.: RAND Corporation, 1996), Table 3.2.

13. These figures are not strictly comparable; estimates are based on data in Vernez and Abrahamse, Table 4.2, and in National Center for Education Statistics, *Dropout Rates in the United States: 1995* (Washington, D.C.: Office of Educational Research and Improvement, U.S. Department of Education, NCES 97–473, 1997), Table 9.

14. Native-language instruction in public schools was also common in the Southwest, particularly in Texas, New Mexico, and Arizona, which were formerly part of Mexico and whose native populations, not their immigrants, were originally Spanish-speaking Mexicans. It was also common in Louisiana, where French-language public schools were established well after the Louisiana Purchase to preserve native French culture.

15. Diego Castellanos, *The Best of Two Worlds: Bilingual-Bicultural Education in the United States* (Trenton: New Jersey State Department of Education, CN 500, 1983), pp. 23–25.

16. Sarason and Doris, pp. 180–81, 194.

17. Heinz Kloss, *The American Bilingual Tradition* (Rowley, Mass.: Newbury House, 1977), pp. 149–50.

18. Ibid., pp. 61, 86, 180; Castellanos, p. 19; and Mary J. Herrick, *The Chicago Schools: A Social and Political History* (Beverly Hills, Calif.: Sage, 1971), p. 61.

19. Kloss, pp. 69, 86, 158–59, 190; and Castellanos, pp. 24–25.

20. Kloss, pp. 177–78, 184.

21. Castellanos, p. 23; and Paul E. Peterson, *The Politics of School Reform, 1870–1940* (Chicago: University of Chicago Press, 1985), p. 55.

22. Peterson, pp. 55–56; Castellanos, p. 25; and James Crawford, *Bilingual Education: History, Politics, Theory, and Practice* (Trenton, N.J.: Crane Publishing Company, 1989), p. 22.

23. "The School Question," *Milwaukee Sentinel,* 27 November 1889.

24. Herrick, p. 61; Kloss, p. 89; Peterson, pp. 10, 58; William F. Whyte, "The Bennett Law Campaign in Wisconsin," *Wisconsin Magazine of History,* vol. 10, 1927, pp. 363–90; and Bernard Mehl, "Educational Criticism: Past and Present," *Progressive Education,* March 1953, p. 154.

25. Crawford, pp. 23–24; and David Tyack, "Constructing Difference: Historical Reflections on Schooling and Social Diversity," *Teachers College Record,* Fall 1993, p. 15.

26. *Meyer v. Nebraska,* 262 US 390 (1923).

27. Castellanos, pp. 43, 49; Crawford, p. 26; and idem, *Hold Your Tongue* (Reading, Mass.: Addison-Wesley, 1992), p. 72.

28. See, for example, Rudolph Troike, "Research Evidence for the Effectiveness of Bilingual Education," *NABE Journal,* vol. 3, 1978, pp. 13–24; *The Bilingual Education Handbook: Designing Instruction for LEP Students* (Sacramento: California Department of Education, 1990), p. 13; Iris Rotberg, "Some Legal and Research Considerations in Establishing Federal Bilingual Policy in Bilingual Education," *Harvard Educational Review,* May 1982, pp. 158–59; and Rosalie Pedalino Porter,

Forked Tongue: The Politics of Bilingual Education (New York: Basic Books, 1990) p. 141.

29. Leonard Covello, "A High School and Its Immigrant Community—A Challenge and an Opportunity," *Journal of Educational Sociology,* February 1936, p. 334.

30. Ruben G. Rumbaut, "The New Californians: Research Findings on the Educational Progress of Immigrant Children," in idem and Wayne Cornelius, eds., *California's Immigrant Children: Theory, Research, and Implications for Educational Policy* (San Diego: Center for U.S.–Mexican Studies, University of California, 1995).

31. For a discussion of Rodriguez as prototype, see Stephen D. Krashen, *Under Attack: The Case Against Bilingual Education* (Culver City, Calif.: Language Education Associates, 1996), p. 19.

32. Rumbaut, Table 2.6.

33. *Dropout Rates in the United States: 1995,* Table A–37; and National Center for Education Statistics, *The Condition of Education 1997* (Washington, D.C.: U.S. Department of Education, NCES 97–388, 1997), Indicators 8, 22.

34. Gregory Rodriguez, *The Emerging Latino Middle Class* (Malibu, Calif.: Pepperdine University Institute for Public Policy, 1996), Figure 22.

POSTSCRIPT

Should Bilingual Education Programs Be Abandoned?

Research comparing the effectiveness of the several approaches to helping linguistically disadvantaged students remains inconclusive. At the same time, the effort is clouded by the political agendas of those who champion first-language instruction and those who insist on some version of the immersion strategy. Politics and emotional commitments aside, what must be placed first on the agenda are the needs of the students and the value of native language in a child's progress through school.

Some books to note are Jane Miller's *Many Voices: Bilingualism, Culture and Education* (1983), which includes a research review; Kenji Hakuta's *Mirror of Language: The Debate on Bilingualism* (1986); *Bilingual Education: A Sourcebook* by Alba N. Ambert and Sarah E. Melendez (1985); *Sink or Swim: The Politics of Bilingual Education* by Colman B. Stein, Jr. (1986); and *Teaching Other People's Children: Literacy and Learning in a Bilingual Classroom* by Cynthia Ballenger (1999). Thomas Weyr's book *Hispanic U.S.A.: Breaking the Melting Pot* (1988) presents a detailed plan of action in light of the prediction that "by the year 2000 as many people in the U.S. will be speaking Spanish as they will English."

A number of pertinent articles may be found in the March 1989 issue of *The American School Board Journal,* the March 1988 issue of *The English Journal,* the Summer 1988 issue of *Equity and Excellence*, and the Autumn 2000 issue of *Theory Into Practice*. Some especially provocative articles are "Bilingual Education: A Barrier to Achievement," by Nicholas Sanchez, *Bilingual Education* (December 1987); " 'Official English': Fear or Foresight?" by Nancy Bane, *America* (December 17, 1988); and "The Language of Power," by Yolanda T. DeMola, *America* (April 22, 1989).

More recent articles include David Hill's "English Spoken Here," *Teacher Magazine* (January 1998); Jerry Cammarata's "Tongue-Tied," *American School Board Journal* (June 1997); and Glenn Garvin's "Loco, Completamente Loco," *Reason* (January 1998). Donaldo Macedo offers a wide-ranging critique of current educational practices in "Literacy for Stupidification: The Pedagogy of Big Lies," *Harvard Educational Review* (Summer 1993). Also see his book *Literacies of Power: What Americans Are Not Allowed to Know* (1994).

Of especial note are "Americanization and the Schools," by E. D. Hirsch, Jr., *The Clearing House* (January/February 1999) and Lynn W. Zimmerman's "Bilingual Education as a Manifestation of an Ethic of Caring" and Gail L. Thompson's "The Real Deal on Bilingual Education," *Educational Horizons* (Winter 2000).

ISSUE 17

Does School Violence Warrant a Zero-Tolerance Policy?

YES: Albert Shanker, from "Restoring the Connection Between Behavior and Consequences," *Vital Speeches of the Day* (May 15, 1995)

NO: Pedro A. Noguera, from "The Critical State of Violence Prevention," *The School Administrator* (February 1996)

ISSUE SUMMARY

YES: Albert Shanker, president of the American Federation of Teachers (AFT), advocates a "get tough" policy for dealing with violent and disruptive students in order to send a clear message that all students are responsible for their own behavior.

NO: Professor of education Pedro A. Noguera maintains that the AFT's zero-tolerance stance and other "armed camp" attitudes fail to deal with the heart of the problem and do not build an atmosphere of trust.

$\mathbf{B}$eyond basic classroom discipline and general civility lies the more serious realm of violence in schools: unpredictable acts of violence against students and teachers and what Jackson Toby refers to as everyday school violence fueled by a disorderly educational and social atmosphere. Toby, in "Everyday School Violence: How Disorder Fuels It," *American Educator* (Winter 1993/1994), states, "The concept of 'school disorder' suggests that schools, like families, also vary in their cohesiveness and effectiveness. What school disorder means in concrete terms is that one or both of two departures from normality exists: A significant proportion of students do not seem to recognize the legitimacy of the rules governing the school's operation and therefore violate them frequently; and/or a significant proportion of students defy the authority of teachers and other staff members charged with enforcing the rules." Toby and other experts feel that teachers lost much of their authority, especially in inner-city high schools, during the 1960s and 1970s when school systems stopped standing behind teachers' disciplinary actions and many teachers became afraid of confronting aggressive student behavior.

A 1978 report to Congress by the National Institute of Education, *Violent Schools—Safe Schools,* documented widespread incidents of theft, assaults, weapon possession, vandalism, rape, and drug use in America's schools. These findings helped lead to the current period of security guards, metal detectors, book bag searches, locker raids, and pursuit of armed teenagers in school halls. "Zero tolerance" has emerged as a rallying cry of the 1990s—zero tolerance for any weapons in school (handguns, semiautomatics, knives, and, in a few cases, fingernail files) and zero tolerance for any drugs in school (crack cocaine, pot, alcohol, and, in some cases, Midol or Tylenol).

These measures have sparked a heated debate over the conflict between students' rights and the need to protect students and professionals from violence. We pride ourselves on being a tolerant society, but it has become obvious that new lines must be drawn. Daniel Patrick Moynihan, senior senator from New York, in "Defining Deviancy Down," *The American Scholar* (Winter 1993), contends that we have become accustomed to alarming levels of criminal and destructive behavior and that the absence of meaningful punishment for those who commit violent acts reinforces the belief that violence is an appropriate way to settle disputes among members of society.

Congressional passage of the Gun-Free Schools Act in 1994 placed an automatic one-year expulsion on weapon-carrying students and demanded referral of offenders to the criminal justice or juvenile delinquency system after due process procedures are carried out. According to Kathleen Vail, in "Ground Zero," *American School Board Journal* (June 1995), some child advocates, educators, and parents feel that such zero-tolerance policies do not allow enough room for exceptions, especially when young children are involved. There is also a concern that get-tough measures weaken the implementation of conflict-resolution strategies aimed at uncovering deeper explanations of aggressive behavior.

A flurry of articles on school violence has appeared in recent years. Among the best are Jackson Toby's "Getting Serious About School Discipline," *The Public Interest* (Fall 1998); "The Dark Side of Zero Tolerance," by Russ Skiba and Reece Peterson, *Phi Delta Kappan* (January 1999); Abigail Thernstrom's "Courting Disorder in the Schools," *The Public Interest* (Summer 1999); Michael Easterbrook's "Taking Aim at Violence," *Psychology Today* (July/August 1999); "Zero Tolerance for Zero Tolerance," by Richard L. Curwin and Allen N. Mendler, *Phi Delta Kappan* (October 1999); W. Michael Martin's "Does Zero Mean Zero?" *American School Board Journal* (March 2000); and two articles on the controversial practice of profiling potentially violent students in *The School Administrator* (February 2000).

The American Federation of Teachers (AFT) has strongly supported zero-tolerance policies. In the first of the following selections, the late Albert Shanker, former AFT president, makes the case for tough measures to restore safety and confidence in the public schools and thereby stem the exodus of concerned parents. In the second selection, Pedro A. Noguera questions the effectiveness of such measures and offers alternatives that he feels would better address the causes of violence and the social factors that contribute to it.

Albert Shanker  **YES**

Restoring the Connection Between Behavior and Consequences

I can't think of a more important topic.... [T]here have been and will be a number of conferences on this issue. I can assure you, all of the other conferences resemble each other, and this one will be very different. It will have a very different point of view.

We have had, over the last decade or more, a national debate on the issue of school quality. And there is a national consensus that we need to do a lot better. We are probably doing better than we used to, but we're not doing as well as other industrial countries. And in order to do well, we are going to have to do some of the things that those other countries are doing, such as develop high standards, assessments related to those standards, and a system of consequences so that teachers and youngsters and parents know that school counts. School makes a difference, whether it's getting a job or getting into a college or getting into a training program.

We're well on the way. It's going to take time, but we're on the way to bringing about the improvement that we need. But you can have a wonderful curriculum and terrific assessments and you can state that there are consequences out there but none of this is going to do much good in terms of providing youngsters with an education if we don't meet certain basic obvious conditions. And those conditions are simply that you have to have schools that are safe and classrooms where there is sufficient order so that the curriculum means something. Without that, all of this stuff is nonsense. You can deliver a terrific curriculum, but if youngsters are throwing things, cursing and yelling and punching each other, then the curriculum doesn't mean anything in that classroom. The agenda is quite different.

And so we have a very interesting phenomenon. We have members of Congress and governors and state legislators talking about choice and vouchers and charter schools, and you know what the big incentive is for those issues. Parents are not really pushing for these things, except in conditions where their children seem to be unsafe or in conditions where they can't learn. And then they say, well, look, if you can't straighten things out here, then give me a chance to take my youngster somewhere else. And so we're about to put in place a ridiculous situation. We're going to create a system of choice and vouchers, so that 98 percent of the kids who behave can go someplace and be safe. And we're going to leave the two percent who are violent and disruptive to take over the schools. Now, isn't it ridiculous to move 98 percent of the kids, when all you have to do is move two or three percent of them and the other 98 percent would be absolutely fine?

Now this is a problem which has a number of aspects and I want to talk about them. First, there is, of course, the problem of extreme danger, where we are dealing with violence or guns or drugs within the school. And, as we look to the schools, what we find is that the schools seem to be unable to handle this. We had headlines here in DC... saying that the mayor and school officials say they don't know what else to do. In other words, they've done everything that they can, and the guns, and the knives, and the drugs are still there. So, it just happens that they have actually said it, but that is, in fact, how many school administrators and school boards across the country behave. They treat violence as a fact of life, that's what society is like, and they just go through a couple of ritual efforts to try to show that they're doing something. But, basically they give up.

What we have is what amounts to a very high level of tolerance of this type of activity. Now, of course, the violence and the guns and the drugs have to be distinguished from another type of activity. This other type isn't deadly in the sense that you are going to read tomorrow morning that some youngster was stabbed or shot. And that's the whole question of just plain out-and-out disruption: the youngster who is constantly yelling, cursing, jumping, fighting, doing all sorts of things, so that most of the time the other students in the class and the teacher is devoted, not to the academic mission of the schools, but to figuring out how to contain this individual. And in this area, we have an even higher tolerance than we do in the area of violence, where occasionally youngsters are suspended or removed for periods of time....

Last year when Congress was debating the Goals 2000 education program, there were an awful lot of people who said, you know, in addition to having different kinds of content standards—what you should learn—and performance standards—how good is good enough—you ought to have opportunity-to-learn standards. It's not fair to hold kids to these standards unless they've had certain advantages. It's not fair, if one kid has had early childhood education and one hasn't, to hold them to the same standard. It's not fair, if at this school they don't have any textbooks or the textbooks are 15 years old, and in that school they have the most modern books. It's not fair, if in this school they've got computers, and in that school kids have never seen a computer.

Well, I submit to you that if you want to talk about opportunity-to-learn standards, there are a lot of kids who've made it without the most up-to-date textbooks. It's better if you have them. There are a lot of kids who've made it without early childhood education. It's a lot better if you've got it, and we're for that. Throughout history, people have learned without computers, but it's better if you've got them. But nobody has ever learned if they were in a classroom with one or two kids who took up 90 percent of the time through disruption, violence, or threats of violence. You deprive children of an opportunity to learn if you do not first provide an orderly situation within the classroom and within the school. That comes ahead of all of these other things.

Now, I said that this conference was going to be different from every conference that I've been to and every conference that I've read about. I have a report here that was sent to me by John Cole [President of the Texas Federation of Teachers], who went to The Scholastic Annual Summit on Youth Violence on October 17 [1994]. I'm not going to read the whole thing, but I'll just read enough that you get the flavor of what these other conferences are like:

> "So start with the concept that the real victims of violence are those unfortunate individuals who have been led into lives of crime by the failure of society to provide them with hope for a meaningful life. Following that logic, one must conclude that society has not done enough for these children and that we must find ways to salvage their lives. Schools must work patiently with these individuals offering them different avenues out of this situation. As an institution charged with responsibility for education, schools must have programs to identify those who are embarking on a life of crime and violence and lift them out of the snares into which they have fallen. Society, meanwhile, should be more forgiving of the sins of these poor creatures, who through no real fault of their own are the victims of racism and economic injustice.
>
> "Again and again and again, panelists pointed out that the young people we are talking about, to paraphrase Rodney Dangerfield, 'don't get no respect.' The experts assured us that young people take up weapons, commit acts of violence, and abuse drugs because this enables them to obtain respect from their peers. I found myself thinking that we aid and abet this behavior when we bend over backwards to accommodate those young people who have bought into this philosophy. By lavishing attention on them, we may even encourage a spread of that behavior. Many of these programs are well meaning but counterproductive.
>
> "I don't want to condemn this conference as a waste of time. Obviously, we do need programs to work with these young people, and we should try to salvage as many as we can. However, we must somehow come to grips with the idea that individuals have responsibility for their own actions. If we assume that society is to blame for all of the problems these young people have, may we then assume that society must develop solutions that take care of these young people's problems? We take away from each individual the responsibility for his or her own life. Once the individual assumes that he or she has lost control of his own destiny, that individual has no difficulty in justifying any act because he or she feels no responsibility for the consequences."

Now with that philosophy, the idea is not that we want to be punitive or nasty, but essentially schools must teach not only English and mathematics and reading and writing and history, but also teach that there are ways of behaving in society that are unacceptable. And when we sit back and tolerate certain types of behavior, we are teaching youngsters that certain types of behavior are acceptable, which eventually will end up with their being in jail or in poverty for the rest of their lives. We are not doing our jobs as teachers. And the system is not doing its job, if we send youngsters the message that this is tolerable behavior within society....

All we ask of our schools is that they behave in the same way that a caring and intelligent parent would behave with respect to their own children. I doubt very much, if you had a youngster who was a fire bug or a youngster who used weapons, whether you would say, well, I owe it to this youngster to trust him with my other children to show him that I'm not separating him out or treating him differently. Or I'm going to raise his self-esteem by allowing him to do these things. All of these nutty things that we talk about in school, we would not do. So the starting point of this conference, which is different from all of the others, is that I hope that you people join with me in a sense of outrage that we have a system that is willing to sacrifice the overwhelming majority of children for a handful. And not do any good for that handful either. And we need to start with that outrage, because without that we're not going to change this system.

That outrage is there among parents. That outrage was partly expressed in the recent election as people's anger at the way government was working. Why can't government do things in some sort of common sense way? And this is one of the issues that's out there. Now, what are some of the things that enter into this? Well, part of it is that some people think of schools as sort of custodial institutions. Where are we going to put the kids? Put them here. Or they think the school's job is mostly socialization. Eventually troubled kids will grow up or grow out of this, and they're better off with other youngsters than they are separated. Of course, people who take that point of view are totally ignoring the fact that the central role of schools, the one that we will be held accountable for, is student academic achievement. We know the test scores are bad. And we know that our students are not learning as much as youngsters in other countries. So we can't just say we know we are way behind, but, boy, are we good custodians. Look at how socialized these youngsters are.

People are paying for education and they want youngsters who are going to be able to be employed and get decent jobs. We want youngsters who are going to be as well off or in better shape than we are, just as most of us are with respect to our parents and grandparents. And the academic function is the one that's neglected. The academic function is the one that's destroyed in this notion that our job is mainly custodial.

So our central position is that we have to be tough on these issues, and we have to be tough because basically we are defending the right of children to an education. And those who insist on allowing violence and disruptive behavior in the school are destroying the right to an education for the overwhelming majority of youngsters within our schools.

Two years ago or three years ago, I was in Texas at a convention of the Texas Federation of Teachers. I didn't know this was going to happen, but either just before I got there or while I was there, there was a press conference on a position the convention adopted, and they used the phrase "zero tolerance." They said that with respect to certain types of dangerous activities in schools, there would be zero tolerance. These things are not acceptable and there are going to be consequences. There might be suspension, there might be expulsion, or there might be something else, but nevertheless, consequences will be clear. Well, that got picked up by radio, television, legislators. I was listening to a governor the other night at the National Governors Association, who stood up and came out for zero tolerance. It is a phrase which has caught on and is sweeping the country.

I hope it is one that all of you will bring back to your communities and your states, that there are certain types of activities that we will not tolerate. We will not teach youngsters bad lessons, and we're going to start very early. When a youngster does something that is terribly wrong, and all of the other youngsters are sure that something is going to happen to him because he did something wrong, we had better make sure that we fulfill the expectations of all those other youngsters that something's going to happen. And they're all going to say, "Thank God, I didn't do a terrible thing like that or I would be out there, and something would be happening to me." That is the beginning of a sense of doing something right, as against doing wrong.

And we have to deal with this notion that society is responsible, social conditions are responsible. The AFT does not take second place to anybody in fighting for decent conditions for adults and for youngsters and for minorities and for groups that have been oppressed. We're not in a state of denial; we're not saying that things have been wonderful. But when your kids come home and say "I'm doing these terrible things because of these conditions," if you're a good parent, you'll say, "That's no excuse." You are going to do things right, because you don't want your youngster to end up as a criminal or in some sort of horrible position....

Now what should schools do? Schools should have codes of conduct. These codes can be developed through collective bargaining or they can be mandated in legislation. I don't think it would be a bad idea to have state legislation that every school system needs to have a code of discipline that is very clear, not a fuzzy sort of thing, something that says these things are not to be done and if this happens, these are the consequences. A very clear connection between behavior and consequences. And it might even say that, if there is a legitimate complaint from a group of parents or a group of teachers or a group of students that clearly shows the school district doesn't have such a code or isn't enforcing it, there would be some sort of financial penalty against the district for failing to provide a decent education by allowing this type of violence and disruption to continue.

Taxpayers are sending money into the district so that the kids can have an education, and if that district then destroys the education by allowing one or two youngsters to wipe out all of the effects that money is supposed to produce, what the hell is the point of sending the money? If you allow these youngsters to so disrupt that education, you might as well save the money. So there's a reason for states to do this. And, by the way, I think that you'll find a receptive audience, because the notion of individuals taking responsibility for their actions is one of the things fueling the political anger in this country—that we have a lot of laws which help people to become irresponsible or encourage them not to take responsibility for their own actions.

Now, enforcement is very important. For every crime, so to speak, there ought to be a punishment. I don't like very much judgment to be used, because once you allow judgment to be used, punishments will be more severe for some kids than for others and you will get unfairness. You will get prejudice. The way to make sure that this is done fairly and is not done in a prejudiced way is to say, look, we don't care if you're white or Hispanic or African-American or whether you're a recent immigrant or this or that, for this infraction, this is what happens. We don't have a different sanction depending upon whether we like you a little more or a little less. That's how fairness would be ensured, and I think it's very important that we insist on that....

One of the big problems is school administrators. School administrators are concerned that, if there are a large number of reports of disruptions and violence in their schools, their reputations will suffer. They like to say they have none of those problems in their schools. Now, how do you prove that you have none of these problems in your school? Very simple. Just tell the teachers that if they report it, it's because they are ineffective teachers. If you tell that to one or two teachers, you will certainly have a school that has very little disruption or violence reported. You may have plenty of disruption and violence. So, in many places we have this gag rule. It's not written, but it's very well understood.

As a teacher, I myself faced this. Each time I reported something like this, I was told that if I knew how to motivate the students properly, this wouldn't happen. It's pretty universal. It wasn't just one district or just my principal. It's almost all of them. Therefore, I think that we ought to seek laws that require a full and honest reporting of incidents of violence and extreme disruption. And that would mean that, if an administrator goes around telling you to shut up or threatening you so that you're not free to report, I think that there ought to be penalties. Unless we know the extent of this problem, we're never going to deal with it adequately.

Of course, parents know what the extent of it is. What is the number one problem? It's the problem of violence and order in the schools. They know it. The second big problem and obstacle we face is, what's going to happen if you put the kid out on the streets? It reminds me of a big campaign in New York City to get crime off the streets, and pretty soon they were very successful. They had lots of policemen on the streets, and they drove the criminals away. The criminals went into the subways. Then they had a campaign about crime in the subways, and they drove them back up into the streets. So the business community, parents, and others will say, you can't just throw a kid out and put them on the streets. That's no good. But you could place some conditions on it. To return to school, students would have to bring with them a parent or some other grown-up or relative responsible for them. There is a list of ways in which we might handle it. But we can't say that we're going to wait until we build new schools, or build new class-rooms, or have new facilities. The first thing you do is separate out the youngster who is a danger to the other youngsters.

Now, let me give an example. And I think it's one that's pretty close. We know that, when we arrest adults who have committed crimes and we jail them, jail will most likely not help those who are jailed. I don't think it does, and I don't think most people do. However, most of us are pretty glad when someone who has committed a pretty bad crime is jailed. Not because it's going to do that person any good, but because that person won't be around to do the same thing for the next ten or fifteen years. And for the separation of youngsters who are destroying the education of others, the justification is the same. I'm not sure that we can devise programs that will reach those youngsters that will help them. We should try. But our first obligation is to never destroy the education of the twenty or twenty-five or thirty because you have an obligation to one. Especially when there's no evidence that you're doing anything for that one by keeping him there.

Now, another big obstacle is legal problems. These are expensive and time-consuming. If a youngster gets a lawyer and goes to court, the principal or some other figure of authority from the school, usually has to go to court. They might sit a whole day and by the end of the first day, they decide not to hear it. And they come a second day, and maybe it's held over again. It might take three or four days for each youngster. So if you've got a decent-sized school, even if you're dealing with only two or three percent of the youngsters, you could spend your full time in court, instead of being in school. Well, I wouldn't want to do that if I were the principal of the school. And then what does the court do when you're all finished? The court says, well, we don't have any better place to put him, so send him right back. So, that's why a lot of teachers wouldn't report it, because nothing happens anyway. You go through all of this, you spend all of that time and money, and when you're all finished, you're right back where you started. So we need to change what happens with respect to the court, and we have two ideas that we're going to explore that have not been done before.

One of the things we need to do is see whether we can get parents, teachers, and even perhaps high school students to intervene in these cases and say, we want to come before the judge to present evidence about what the consequences are for the other children. When you go to court now, you have the lawyer for the board of education, the lawyer for the youngster, and the youngster. And the youngster, well, he's just a kid and his lawyer says, "This poor child has all of these problems," and the judge is looking down at this poor youngster. You know who is not there? The other 25 youngsters to say, this guy beats me up every day. If I do my homework, I get beat up on the way to school because he doesn't want me to do my homework. So instead of first having this one child standing there saying, "Poor me, let me back in school, they have kicked me out, they have done terrible things to me," you also have some of the victims there saying, "Hey, what about us?" You'll get a much fairer consideration if the judge is able to look at both sides, instead of just hearing the bureaucrat from the board of education. None of these board of education lawyers that I've met talk about the other students. They talk about the right of the board of education under the law to do thus, and so what you have is a humane judge who's thinking of the bureaucrat talking about the rights of the board of education as against the child. I think we need to balance that.

Now, there's a second thing we are going to explore. We are all familiar with the fact that most of our labor contracts have a provision for grievance procedures. And part of that grievance procedure is arbitration. Now, you can take an arbitration award to court and try to appeal it, but it's very, very difficult to get a court to overthrow an arbitrator's award. Why? Because the court says, look, you had your day, you went to the arbitrator and you presented all your arguments, the other side presented all their arguments. In order for me to look into that arbitration and turn it over, you're going to have to prove to me that something in this arbitration was so terrible that we have to prove that the arbitrator was absolutely partial or that he broke the law. You've got to prove something outrageous. Otherwise, the judge is going to say, "You've had your day in court."

Now, why can't school districts establish a fair, inexpensive, due-process arbitration procedure for youngsters who are violent or disruptive? So that when the youngster goes to court, they can say, "Hey, we've had this procedure. We've had witnesses on both sides, and here was the determination. And, really, you shouldn't get into this stuff unless you can show that these people are terribly prejudiced or totally incompetent or something else." In other words, we don't have to use the court. We could create a separate school judicial system that had expertise and knowledge about what the impact is on students and teachers and the whole system of these kinds of decisions. Arbitration is a much cheaper, much faster system, especially if you have an expedited arbitration system. There is a system in the American Arbitration Association of expedited arbitration that says how many briefs you're allowed to write and how much time each side can take, and all of that. So we have a legal team and we're going to explore the notion of getting this stuff out of the courts and creating a system that is inexpensive and fair to the youngster and fair to the other youngsters in the school.

Now, let me point out that a lot of the tolerance for bad behavior is about to change, because we are about to have stakes attached to student academic outcomes. In other words, in the near future, we are going to have a situation where, if you don't make it up to this point, then you can't be admitted into college. Or if you don't make it here, then you will not get certified for a certain type of employment. But in Chapter I schools, this is going to start very soon. There is a provision in the new Chapter One, now called Title I, and very soon, if Title I schools do not show a substantial progress for students, the school's going to be punished. And one of the punishments is reconstitution of the school. The school will be closed down, teachers will go elsewhere, students will go elsewhere, and the school will open up with a new student body, slowly rebuild. That's one of the punishments. There are other punishments as well. So if you've got a bunch of these disruptive youngsters that prevent you from teaching and the other students from learning, it won't be like yesterday, where nobody seems to care, the kids are all going to get promoted anyway and they can all go to college, because there are no standards. There are no stakes.

Now, for the first time, there will be stakes. The teachers will know. The parents will know, hey, this school's going to close. I'm going to have to find a way of getting my kid to some other school because of the lack of learning that comes from this disruption. Teachers are going to say, hey, I'm not going to have my job in this school a couple of years from now because they're going to shut it down. I don't know what the rules are, what happens to these teachers, whether other schools have to take them or not. But we are entering a period where there will be consequences and parents and teachers are going to be a lot more concerned about achievement.

Now, one of the other issues that has stood in the way of doing something here is a very difficult one to talk about in our society, and that's the issue of race. And whenever the topic of suspension or expulsion comes up, there's always the question of race. Cincinnati is a good example. The union there negotiated a good discipline code as part of a desegregation suit. And the question was raised, "Well, is there a disparate impact, with more minority kids being suspended than others?" And who are the teachers who are suspending them? Do you have more white teachers suspending African-American kids?

Our position on that is very clear. In any given school, you may have more white kids with infractions or you may have more African-American kids, or you may have more Hispanic kids. We don't know. I don't think anybody knows. But we handle that by saying, "Whatever your crime is and whoever you are, you're going to get exactly the same punishment." If we do that, I'm sure that the number who will be punished will end up being very, very small. Because, as a young kid, if you see that there is a consequence, you will change your behavior. . . .

Now we have another very big problem, and we're going to try to deal with this in legislation. Under legislation that deals with disabled youngsters, we have two different standards. Namely, if a youngster in this class is not disabled and commits an infraction, you can do whatever is in that discipline code for that youngster. But if the youngster is disabled and is in that same class (for instance, the youngster might have a speech defect), you can't suspend that youngster while all of the proceedings are going on because that's a change in placement. It might take you a year-and-a-half in court, and meanwhile that youngster who is engaged in some threatening or dangerous behavior has to stay there. This makes no sense. We have a lot of support in the Congress on this, and we think we have a good chance of changing this. . . .

Well, that's the whole picture. And to return to the theme at the beginning, we have a cry for choice, a cry for vouchers, a cry for charters. It's not really a cry for these things. People really want their own schools, and they want their kids to go to those schools, and they want those schools to be safe and orderly for their youngsters.

It is insane to set up a system where we move 98 percent of our kids away from the two percent who are dangerous, instead of moving the two percent away from the 98 percent who are OK. We need to have discipline codes, we need to have a new legal system, we need to have one standard for all students. We need to have a system where we don't have to wait for a year or a year-and-a-half after a student has perpetrated some terrible and atrocious crime before that student is removed for the safety of the other students. How are we going to do this? We are going to do this, first of all, by talking to our colleagues within the schools. Our polls show that the overwhelming majority accepts these views.

The support of African-American parents for the removal of violent youngsters and disruptive students is higher than any other group within our society. Now very often when youngsters are removed, it's because some parents group or some committee starts shouting and making noise, and the school system can't resist that. Now I think that it's time for us to turn to business groups, it's time for us to turn to parents' groups. When youngsters commit such acts, and when they've had a fair due-process within the system, we need to have a system of public support, just as we have in the community when someone commits a terrible crime. People say, send that person to jail, don't send him back to us. We need to have a lot of decent people within our communities, when you have youngsters who are destroying the education of all the others, who will stand up and say, "Look, we don't want to punish this kid, but for the sake of our children, you're going to have to keep that one away, until that one is ready to come back and live in a decent way in society with all of the other youngsters."

I'm sure that if we take this back to our communities, and if we work on it, the appeal will be obvious. It's common sense. And we will save our schools and we will do something which will give us the basis for providing a decent education for all of our children.

 **NO**

The Critical State of Violence Prevention

The problem of violence in schools, like the related problem of violence in society, has become one of the most pressing educational issues in the United States. In many school districts, concerns about violence have surpassed academic achievement as the highest priority for reform and intervention.

Public clamorings over the need for something to be done about school violence has brought the issue to a critical juncture. The threat of violence constitutes a fundamental violation of the social contract between school and community. If effective measures to address the problem are not taken soon, support for public education could be irreparably jeopardized.

Across the country, school districts have adopted various "get tough" measures to address school violence. I believe sound reasons exist to question the effectiveness of these measures and present alternative strategies that have proven successful in reducing the incidence of school violence.

Getting Tough

Not surprisingly, the search for solutions to school violence has generated a package of remedies that closely resemble those used in society to combat the threat of violence and crime.

Some popular measures include the installation of metal detectors at school entrances to prevent students from bringing weapons on to school grounds; the enactment of "zero tolerance" policies (advocated by the American Federation of Teachers and other groups), which require the automatic removal of students (through suspension, expulsion, or transfer) who perpetrate acts of violence; and the use of armed security guards to patrol and monitor student behavior while school is in session.

Accompanying the implementation of such measures has been a tendency of school officials to treat violent incidents, and sometimes non-violent incidents as well, as criminal offenses to be handled by law enforcement officials and the courts, rather than by school personnel. Forced to do something about a growing problem, many politicians and school officials have attempted to quell the tide of violence by converting schools into prison-like facilities.

Yet despite the tough talk and punitive actions, little reason for optimism exists given the track record of these methods and the persistence of violence in schools. For example, despite spending more than $28 million during the 1980s for the installation of metal detectors at public schools in New York City, crime and violence continue to be a major concern. In fact, while teachers and parents are increasingly frustrated about the problem, the mayor and school board were locked last fall in an angry debate over who should bear the blame for the problem. Recently, at a high school in Richmond, Calif., two students were shot at a school despite the presence of metal detectors. In several states, the failure of public schools to curtail violence has been cited as a primary factor influencing public support for school vouchers and school choice proposals.

Misleading Picture

Two main problems exist with "get tough" measures:

- they don't address the causes of school violence, and
- they don't help us understand why schools have become increasingly vulnerable to its occurrence.

As evidence that something is being done about school violence, school officials often point to statistics related to the number of weapons confiscated and the number of students who have been suspended, expelled, or arrested for violent reasons. Such data are used to demonstrate that valiant efforts are being undertaken to reduce the incidence of violence.

The compilation of such data is important because it creates the impression that something is being done even if the problem persists. It also plays an important role in rationalizing the expenditure of resources on school safety—allocations that often result in the elimination of other educational programs and services.

For parents and students who live with the reality of violence and who must contend daily with the threat of physical harm, such data does little to allay fears. When engaging in what were once ordinary activities—such as walking through the halls between classes or playing sports after school—evokes such extreme paranoia as to no longer seem feasible, news that arrests or suspensions have increased provides little reassurance.

Moreover, recognition is growing that many measures used to deter violence have little if any impact on the problem. Suspending students who do not attend school regularly does little to deter poor behavior.

Even at schools where administrators manage to keep the site safe through additional security, victory over violence cannot be declared if kids fight or are attacked on their way to and from school. In such cases, the limited safety provided at the site does little to reduce the fears and anxieties of parents or students.

Quantifying Symbols

Not long ago, I attended a meeting with school officials from an urban district on the West coast. We were reviewing data on the incidence of violence from the past year and discussing what could be done to further reduce violence.

After seeing the disciplinary reports, I jokingly remarked: "Here's some good news, homicides are down 100 percent from last year." To my amazement, an administrator replied: "Yes, the news isn't all bad. Some of our efforts are beginning to pay off."

What surprised me about the comment was his apparent belief that since no murders had occurred at any school in the district at the midpoint of the school year (compared to two during the previous year), there was reason for hope and optimism. I found it hard to believe that district administrators, who generally have little regular contact with school sites, could accept a statistical analysis as evidence that the schools had in fact become safer.

Yet within the context of the fight against violence, symbols such as crime statistics take on great significance, even though they may have little bearing upon the actual occurrence of violence or how safe people feel. Pressed to demonstrate to the public that efforts taken to reduce violence are effective, school districts often pursue one of two strategies: either they present statistics quantifing the results of their efforts, or they go to great lengths to suppress information altogether hoping that the community will perceive no news as good news.

Metal detectors, barbed wire fences, armed guards and police officers, and principals wielding baseball bats as they patrol the halls are all symbols of tough action. However, most students realize that a person who wants to bring a weapon to school can get it into a building without being discovered by a metal detector and that it is highly unlikely that any principal will hit a student with a baseball bat. Still, the symbols persist lest the truth be known that those responsible really don't have a clue about what to do to stem the tide of violence.

Overcoming Fear

To understand why violence has become rampant and how a climate of fear and intimidation has come gradually to be the norm in so many urban schools, we must examine the relationships that are fostered between young people and adults at most schools.

Criminologist Alan Wilson has pointed out that only two ways exist to control behavior and deter crime: (1) by relying on police officers and the courts or (2) by promoting collective morals and sanctions. Any society that comes to rely exclusively on the former to enforce safety is doomed for there will never be enough police officers to go around.

Increasingly, our society, and now our schools, have looked to the police and the courts for answers because we have given up on the possibility that collective morality and sanctions could be effective.

While police officers, security guards, and administrators generally assume primary responsibility for managing and enforcing school discipline, in most cases, teachers make the first referral in the discipline process, and therefore have tremendous influence in determining who receives discipline and why.

In my work with urban schools, the most frequent concern I hear from teachers is that they have trouble disciplining and controlling their students. This problem is particularly true in schools at which the majority of students are black and the majority of teachers are white. Though I don't believe the problem is primarily racial, I do believe racial differences add to the difficulty of dealing with this issue.

Having taught in urban public schools, I am familiar with what classroom teachers are up against. Order and safety are essential requisites to an environment where teaching and learning can occur. However, when I conduct workshops about safety in schools I try to shift the focus of discussion away from discipline to discussion about what teachers know about their students. I do this because I have found that teachers who lack familiarity with their students' lives outside of school are more likely to misunderstand and fear them.

Widening Gulf

The gulf in experience between teacher and student, which is typical in many urban schools, contributes to the problem of violence in schools. Too often, teachers and administrators will fill the knowledge void with stereotypes about their students and the community in which they live. These stereotypes may be based upon what they have read or seen in the news media or what they have picked up indirectly from stories told to them by children.

Lacking another source of information, many teachers begin to fear the children they teach because to some they seem to embody the less-than-civilized images associated with people who reside in the inner city. Fear invariably influences interaction between teachers/administrators and students.

Though it may never be stated, students often can tell when adults fear them, and many will use this to undermine their teachers' authority in the classroom or elsewhere at school.

This is not to say that violence in schools is an imagined problem. However, school violence is a problem exacerbated by fear. A teacher who fears the students that she or he teaches is more likely to resort to discipline when challenged or to ignore the challenge in the hope that she or he will be left alone. Rather than handling a classroom disruption on their own, they are more likely to request assistance from those responsible for handling discipline. They also are less likely to reach out to students in ways that make teaching less impersonal.

Likewise, students who know their teachers fear them are less likely to show respect and more likely to be insolent and insubordinate. When fear is at the center of student-teacher interactions, good teaching becomes almost impossible, and concerns about safety and control take precedence over concerns about teaching and learning.

Alternative Approaches

In critiquing the approaches to discipline that are most widely practiced in the country today, I in no way want to belittle the fact that many classroom teachers and students have become victims of violence and deserve the right to work and attend school in safety. In many schools, violence is real, and the fear that it produces is understandable.

Still, I am struck by the fact that even when I visit schools that have a notorious reputation for the prevalence of violence, I can find at least one classroom where teachers are working effectively with students and where fear is not an obstacle to dialogue and even friendship. While other teachers within the school may be preoccupied with managing the behavior of their students (an endeavor at which they are seldom successful), I have seen the same students enter other classrooms willing to learn and comply with the instructions of their teachers.

Many of these "exceptional" teachers have found ways to cross the borders that separate them from their students. For such teachers, differences based on race, class, or age are unable to prevent them from establishing rapport with their students. Consistently, when I have asked students in interviews what is it that makes a particular teacher special and worthy of respect, the students cite three characteristics these teachers share: firmness, compassion, and an interesting, engaging and challenging style of teaching.

Of course, even a teacher who is perceived as exceptional by students can be a victim of violence because of its increasingly random occurrence. However, such teachers and administrators are less likely to allow fear to paralyze them in their work with students.

The fact that teachers and administrators who possess what the French sociologist Emile Durkheim described as "moral authority" tend to be so few in number compels me to ask why. Are fewer exceptional individuals going into teaching, or is there something about the structure and culture of schools that propagates and reproduces the destructive interpersonal dynamics that are so prevalent?

My experience in schools leads me to believe it is the latter. The vast majority of teachers and administrators whom I meet seem genuinely concerned about their students and sincerely desire to be effective at what they do. Even those who have become cynical and bitter as a result of enduring years of ungratifying work in underfunded public schools generally strike me as people who would prefer more humane interactions with their students.

Social Control

What stands in the way of better relations between teachers and students? And how has it happened that fear and distrust characterize those relations rather than compassion and respect?

My answer to these questions focuses on the legacy of social control that continues to dominate the educational agenda and profoundly influences the structure and culture of schools. So many schools are preoccupied with controlling their students or with ensuring safety that they have lost sight of the fact that schools are supposed to be centers of learning where children receive intellectual and psychological nurturing.

The few safe urban schools I have visited share several characteristics: they are small and attempt to treat students as individuals; they bridge the gap between school and community by involving parents and community residents in the school in a society of mutually supportive relationships; they create a physical environment that is aesthetically pleasant; and they focus less energy on enforcing rules than on developing relationships between adults and students to foster trust and personal accountability.

I have visited urban schools that have found ways to effectively address the problem of violence without relying on coercion or excessive forms of control.

At one middle school in West Oakland, rather than hiring a large man to work as security guard, a grandmother from the surrounding community was hired to monitor students. Instead of using physical intimidation to carry out her duties, this woman greets children with hugs, a smile, and words of encouragement. When some form of punishment is needed, she admonishes the children to behave themselves because she expects better behavior from them. Without relying on force she can break up any fight or handle any disruptive student. She also facilitates dialogue between parents and teachers, often serving as a mediator who helps both parties overcome distrust and resentment to find common ground.

I know of a continuation high school where the principal was able to close the campus at lunch time without installing a fence or some other security apparatus. Concerned that too many students were not returning to campus after lunch, he asked the students for suggestions about what should be done to address the problem.

The students suggested that the school develop a student-managed store and dining area so it no longer would be necessary for them to leave for meals. Without erecting a fence, the school is now officially a closed campus, and at lunch time, students, teachers, and administrators can be seen eating together at the student-operated cafe.

Efforts such as these are effective at addressing the potential for violence because they are based on the assumption that students will respond favorably to humane treatment. When the threat of removal is used as a form of discipline, it is most effective when students genuinely desire to attend school. Public health researchers have called attention to the fact that environmental conditions can either promote or deter violent behavior.

Improving the aesthetic character of schools by including art in the design of schools or making space available within schools for student-run gardens or greenhouses can make schools more pleasant and attractive. Similarly, the divide that separates urban schools from the communities in which schools are located can be overcome by encouraging adults who live within the community to volunteer or, if possible, to be employed as tutors or even teachers, mentors, and coaches.

Undoubtedly, if we can increase the presence of individuals who possess moral authority in the eyes of children, this too will help in reducing the threat of violence at school.

Intrinsic Desires

Ultimately, the promotion of safe schools cannot be separated from the goal of producing schools where children learn. To do so only takes us further down the path of creating prison-like institutions that bring greater control, but do not create an atmosphere of safety and trust.

Those of us who seek to create safe learning environments at our schools must recognize that urban youth today are not passive or compliant and will not be easily controlled. Rather than pursuing that goal we must devise new strategies for providing an education that is perceived as meaningful and relevant and that begins to tap into the intrinsic desire of all individuals to obtain greater personal fulfillment.

Anything short of this will leave us mired in a situation that grows increasingly depressing and dangerous each day.

POSTSCRIPT

Does School Violence Warrant a Zero-Tolerance Policy?

How can the aggressive drive be harnessed so that it provides young people with the energy to live productively in American society rather than being unleashed in the form of violence? This question is posed by Lorraine B. Wallach in "Violence and Aggression in Today's Schools" in the Spring 1996 issue of *Educational Horizons*. Wallach contends that "children who accumulate an overload of anger, hate, or jealousy or feel worthless are more likely to be violent, particularly when these feelings are combined with poor inner controls." The building of internal controls and the channeling of normal aggressiveness must begin, of course, in the home and at the presecondary levels of schooling.

Related articles of interest include "What to Do About the Children," by William J. Bennett, *Commentary* (March 1995), in which the author discusses the governmental role in dealing with crime, immorality, and uncivilized behavior; "Waging Peace in Our Schools: Beginning With the Children," by Linda Lanteiri, *Phi Delta Kappan* (January 1995); and "Ganging Up on Gangs," by Reginald Leon Green and Roger L. Miller, *American School Board Journal* (September 1996). An excellent array of articles may be found in *The School Administrator* (February 1996); the *NASSP Bulletin* (April 1996); and the *Harvard Educational Review* (Summer 1995), which features Janie V. Ward on cultivating a morality of care, Pedro A. Noguera on violence prevention, and interviews with Noam Chomsky and Peggy Charren. Students who will soon enter the teaching profession may also profit from reading *Safe Schools: A Handbook for Practitioners*, which was released in 1994 by the National Association of Secondary School Principals.

Other commentary on the problem may be found in Nancy Day's book *Violence in Schools: Learning in Fear* (1996); Jeanne Wright's "Discipline and Order in the Classroom," *Current* (July–August 1997); and multiple articles in the Summer 1999 issue of *American Educator*, the February 2000 issue of *The School Administrator*, and the March 2000 issue of *NASSP Bulletin*.

Other articles of interest are Roger W. Ashford, "Can Zero Tolerance Keep Our Schools Safe?" *Principal* (November 2000); Charlene M. Alexander, "Helping School Counselors Cope With Violence," *USA Today Magazine* (January 2002); Reece L. Peterson and Russell Skiba, "Creating School Climates That Prevent School Violence," *The Clearing House* (January/February 2001); Cherry Henault, "Zero Tolerance in Schools," *Journal of Law and Education* (July 2001); Catherine Seipp, "Asthma Attack: When 'Zero Tolerance' Collides With Children's Health," *Reason* (April 2002); and Jean Hannon, "No Time for Time Out," *Kappa Delta Pi Record* (Spring 2002).

ISSUE 18

Can Self-Governing Schools Rescue Urban Education?

YES: Deborah Meier, from "Can the Odds Be Changed?" *Phi Delta Kappan* (January 1998)

NO: Emeral A. Crosby, from "Urban Schools: Forced to Fail," *Phi Delta Kappan* (December 1999)

ISSUE SUMMARY

YES: Deborah Meier, a leading urban educator, contends that decaying public schools in large cities can be rejuvenated by the proliferation of self-governing exemplary schools that are given encouragement by the system.

NO: High school principal Emeral A. Crosby, while sharing many of Meier's hopes, maintains that only a powerful political force and a massive infusion of funds can halt the downward spiral of urban school quality.

In 1991 Jonathan Kozol graphically portrayed the prevailing conditions in inner-city public schools in his book *Savage Inequalities: Children in America's Schools.* The book provided a guided tour of dilapidated buildings, outdated equipment, disheartened teachers, and understimulated students. Kozol's quest for equalization of funding for urban schools began with his 1967 book *Death at an Early Age,* which described the deterioration of poverty-area schools in Boston, Massachusetts.

Has what Gene Maeroff depicted as "Withered Hopes, Stillborn Dreams: The Dismal Panorama of Urban Schools," in *Phi Delta Kappan* (1991), been altered since Kozol made the public more aware of the situation? According to Gary Rosen, in "Are School Vouchers Un-American?" *Commentary* (February 2000),

> By any measure, public education in America's cities is in deep trouble.... On any given day in Cleveland, almost one of every six students is likely not to show up. In Washington, D.C., a majority of tenth graders never finish high school. And in Los Angeles, school officials recently retreated from a

plan to end the practice of "social promotion," realizing that it would have required holding back for a year more than half of the district's woefully unprepared students.

Rosen advocates following the lead of Milwaukee, Wisconsin, and Cleveland, Ohio, in moving toward voucher plans for poverty-area students, which would allow public funds to be used for private education, sometimes at religious schools. A Florida voucher plan designed for that purpose, however, was recently shelved by court action. Matthew Miller, in "A Bold Experiment to Fix City Schools," *The Atlantic Monthly* (July 1999), states, "A political stand-off has kept vouchers unavailable to nearly 99 percent of urban schoolchildren. Bill Clinton and most leading Democrats oppose them, saying we should fix existing public schools, not drain money from the system." Miller suggests an expanded voucher plan experiment that would provide all poverty-level students with vouchers while simultaneously increasing federal funding for existing inner-city public schools.

Joseph P. Viteritti, in "A Way Out: School Choice and Educational Opportunity," *Brookings Review* (Fall 1999), contends that

> the demand for choice, especially among minorities and the poor, is high. We know this from the size and composition of the waiting lists of applicants who have expressed interest in existing voucher programs, charter schools, and private scholarship initiatives. Even charter schools that do not specifically target poor children tend to attract a disproportionate number of minorities who see them as an escape route from failing schools.

Beyond the voucher and charter school solutions, which are presently limited in scope and often mired in controversy, there are some other rays of hope. Michael Casserly, executive director of Great City Schools, in "Urban Public Schools on the Comeback," *Principal* (January 1999), cites evidence of increased student achievement, lower dropout rates, higher daily attendance, and increased percentages of students taking college entrance exams. The School Reform Demonstration Program has been funded by Congress to develop exemplary schools in order to stimulate reform dissemination. The U.S. Department of Education has released a study entitled *Hope for Urban Education* describing nine poverty-area elementary schools that have fashioned dramatic turnarounds in the past five years. The Success for All program attacks problems involved in the development of literacy. The Children's Scholarship Fund offers some 40,000 scholarships in nearly 50 locales. And Deborah Meier's practical accomplishments in East Harlem continue to inspire other urban educators.

But deep-rooted barriers still exist. The history of political and economic exploitation in inner cities is chronicled by Jean Anyon in *Ghetto Schooling: A Political Economy of Educational Reform* (1997). And Martin Haberman offers a realistic appraisal of the problem in "The Anti-Learning Curriculum of Urban Schools," *Kappa Delta Pi Record* (Spring 1997 and Winter 1999).

In the selections that follow, Meier and Emeral A. Crosby each draw upon their vast experience with urban schools to arrive at somewhat contrary views of what is needed to avert complete disaster.

Deborah Meier

 **YES**

Can the Odds Be Changed?

There are numerous stories of schools that have been successful with students who would otherwise count among society's failures. However, such school successes rarely set the stage for Big Reform agendas. These one-of-a-kind schools flicker brightly. A few manage to survive by avoiding the public's attention or by serving powerful constituents; the rest gradually burn out. Can we change that? Can we make the exceptions the norm?

The Search for Silver Bullets

To the vast majority of serious policy makers, the existing exemplary schools offer no important lessons. Most policy makers define *systemic* so that it applies only to the kinds of solutions that can be more or less simultaneously prescribed for all schools, irrespective of particulars. Solutions, in short, that seek to improve schooling by taking away the already too limited formal powers of those closest to the students. Examples range from more prescriptive curricula to new, more centralized testing systems; fiscal rewards and penalties; or changed school governance bodies.

School-level folks are as skeptical about the capacity of any of these top-down recipes to make a significant impact on the minds of teachers or children as policy-level folks are about the idiosyncratic bottom-up ones. Practitioners —in classrooms and central offices—know at heart that "this too shall pass" or can be gotten around or overcome. They wait out the innovators. Policy makers work overtime to come up with ways to circumvent such resistance. The more things change, the more they stay the same.

This is a climate that encourages impatience: enough's enough! If we can't do a better job of marrying top-down and bottom-up reform, we're probably in for big trouble. Giving up on the new thought that all children can learn to use their minds well is hard, especially for those of us who know firsthand that schools as designed are hardly suited to the job and that vastly more children could be well-educated if we came up with a better design. We've "tasted" it. It seems both so near and so far. Perhaps if we posed the problem differently, the oddball schools might offer us systemic answers. The Annenberg Challenge gave a substantial boost to a wave of projects around the country that were, on the one hand, fueled by the growing interest in vouchers and charters but that sought on the other hand a response more compatible with public education and equity concerns. By seeking a solution to the systemic through looking at the particular, different possibilities became thinkable.

Good schools are filled with particulars—including particular human beings. And it is these human beings that lie at their heart, that explain their surprising successes. In fact, it is these particulars that inspire the passions of those involved and draw upon the best in each. Rather than ignore such schools because their solutions lie in unreplicable individuals or circumstances, it's precisely such unreplicability that should be celebrated. Maybe what these "special" schools demonstrate is that *every school must have the power and the responsibility to select and design its own particulars* and thus to surround all young people with powerful adults who are in a position to act on their behalf in open and publicly responsible ways. That may be the "silver bullet."

Will grown-ups all jump at the chance to be such responsible adults? Of course not. Most have never been asked to have their own wonderful ideas, much less to take responsibility for them. Many will be leery because along with the freedom to design their own particulars must come new responsibilities for defending the outcomes. But the resultant practice, responsible citizenship, is not only a good means for running a good school but also the central aim of public schooling. How convenient.

In designing a way to make it easier to invent powerful and responsible schools, we can stack the deck in favor of good schooling, so that great schools are more likely, good schools become ordinary practice, and poor schools are more quickly exposed and dealt with. This effort will require us to learn how to make judgments about schools with standards in mind, but not with a standardized ruler in hand. For too long we've acted as though, in the name of standards, we have to treat students and teachers as interchangeable parts. Nothing could be worse for standards, and nothing would be more unnecessary.

We already know some of the common features of exemplary schools —public or private—that serve ordinary and extraordinary children well. For example:

Smallness.   It helps if schools are of a reasonable size, small enough for faculty members to sit around a table and iron things (such as standards) out, for everyone to be known well by everyone else, and for schools and families to collaborate face-to-face over time. Small enough so that children belong to the same community as the adults in their lives instead of being abandoned in adultless subcultures. Small enough to both feel safe and be safe. Small enough so that phony data can easily be detected by any interested participant. Small enough so that the people most involved can never say they weren't consulted.

Self-governance.   It helps if those most directly involved have sufficient autonomy over critical decisions. Only then will it be fair to hold people accountable for the impact of their decisions. This will entail creating democratic adult communities that have the power to make decisions about staffing, leadership, and the full use of their budget, as well as about the particulars of scheduling, curriculum, pedagogy, and assessment.

Choice.   It helps if there are sufficient choices available for parents, students, and teachers so that schools can afford to be different from one another—to have their own definite characters, special emphases, and styles of operating that appeal to some but not all. Responsibility flows more naturally from willing and informed parties. (If schools are small, they can share big old buildings, and choices can be easily available.)

These three qualities—schools that are small enough in size, sufficiently self-governing, and self-chosen—offer a good beginning. They won't in themselves solve anything, although together they could help solve everything.

Two different historic endeavors in New York City—the 22-year experiment with schools of choice in District 4 and the Alternative High School Division's 12-year effort that created dozens of small alternatives, came together in the 1990s to challenge "business as usual." These ventures caught the public's fancy, stimulating a movement on behalf of small schools of choice for all ages and types of students. The genie was out of the bottle and hard to put back. The idea of small alternative schools attracted the attention of families who did not see themselves as "at risk." Word of mouth suggested that students in these schools matched their counterparts academically and surpassed them on many critical dimensions: college attendance, work preparedness, and ability to perform socially valued tasks. They were also achieving improved scores on typical academic assessments. The research community gradually confirmed such impressions. The studies suggest that such schools provide for the possibility of a community powerful enough to be compelling to young people—a club worth joining.

The skeptics say it still can't work en masse. Whether we create another 100 or 200 small schools of choice—some starting from scratch, others carved out of existing schools—they can't be built to last. Everyone agrees that, under present circumstances, such schools have a limited future. The reformers argue, however, that "present circumstances" are not engraved in stone.

Why Exceptions Can't Become the Norm

Without deep-seated changes in the system that surrounds these small schools of choice, history suggests that the critics will be right: most will water down their innovations or give up altogether. As their numbers increase, so, oddly enough, does their vulnerability. This is one case in which there may not be more safety in numbers. For one thing, these maverick schools tax the capacities of the existing institutions—both the formal system and the godfatherly individuals and organizations that spring up to provide nurturance and cover. Second, as their numbers increase, they're more noticeable. This visibility, in turn, creates new demands to bring them into compliance. Their mainstream counterparts ask why the mavericks are allowed to "get away" with this or that. Who do they think they are? Third, as new roadblocks appear, which require new Herculean responses, school folks begin to complain of weariness—the original fire in the belly that fueled the pioneering spirit begins to wane. Doing the new and the old at the same time seems more and more unfair, an imposition rather than an opportunity.

The existing system is simply not designed to support such oddball entities. It believes in its mission of control and orderliness. The people who operate the present system do not see themselves in the business of trying to best match teacher to job, child to school. Nor could they do so if they wanted. Instead, whenever they look at a problem, they've been trained to seek, first and foremost, ways to solve it by rule. If it's not good for everyone, it's not good for anyone. To make exceptions smacks of favoritism and inefficiency. Each exception must thus be defended over and over again. How else can we hold everyone accountable?

The results of such rule-boundedness are well-documented—above all by such thoughtful critics of public education as John Chubb and Terry Moe. (We all know that the expression "to work to the rule" describes a form of job sabotage.) Except for small enclaves within the large institution, in which special constituencies carve out their own intimate subschools (the ones designed for the top students or for the most vulnerable), the school as a whole remains remarkably anonymous and unchangeable, the model of a nonlearning institution. But there is an alternative. It means changing the "circumstances" so that those three magic bullets described earlier—small, self-governing schools of choice—can be in the mainstream, not on the sidelines, of the system.

If nearly all good schools in the private sector share these three characteristics, why can't we offer them publicly for all children? Because, it's said, it's not politically feasible when public monies are at stake. If that's the nub of the argument, then we should either roll over and admit defeat or make it politically feasible. That means inventing a system of accountability for public funds and aiming for educational results that don't require bad educational practice. It's as simple—and every bit as hard—as that.

Changing the Present Circumstances

Small, self-governing schools of choice could be encouraged to flourish, grow like Topsy, spread like weeds, if we built our system *for them,* not them for our system. To create highly personalized schools, however, we have to be willing to shift both our practices and our mindset cautiously and relentlessly over many years. Present practice isn't inevitable. What we have, after all, is a human invention that's only a hundred years old. But just because it's one of those newfangled ideas that doesn't work doesn't mean it will fade away naturally. In fact, it's got a tenacious hold. But our current practice is not the inevitable product of our human nature. In fact, it's peculiarly in conflict with our humanity and with everything we know about rearing the young.

Until the *relationships* between all the people—parents and teachers—responsible for raising our children are changed, changing the parts (curriculum, pedagogy, or assessment) won't matter very much. But it's precisely because, in the long run, these professional "details" matter a great deal that we need to create a system of schooling that allows us to spend our time and energy honing them, close to home. As Theodore Sizer wisely said when Central Park East Secondary School was started, "Keep it simple, so that you can focus on what will always remain complex the mind of each individual learner and the subject matter we're trying to help her master." Schools have been doing the reverse for far too long.

We shouldn't declare all schools independent tomorrow. We shouldn't remove all rules and regulations by fiat. We shouldn't even downsize all schools by fiat. Until we have more parents clamoring for change, more teachers with the skill and confidence to try out new approaches, and more living examples of schools that are both independent and accountable, we need to keep our ambitions in check. We're aiming at a change that sticks, not another fad.

On the immediate agenda, for example, is creating a series of large-scale pilot "laboratories" to see how it might work if we let the existing idiosyncratic schools, with their already eager stalwarts, officially break loose and be different. Add to them all those interested in staffing new schools to replace the worst of our current enterprises. Then we'll need a lean master contract between these schools, the union, the city, and the state—a contract coveting the most basic obligations as well as those unwaivable local, state, and federal rules pertaining to health, safety, and equity. If those on the sidelines can sit back and watch, not rush in, as the pioneers develop their own answers—including mistaken ones—then we'll learn something. The present system of schooling and accountability is chock-full of mistakes, after all, not to mention disasters that are perpetuated year after year. Of course we're accustomed to them, so we barely notice. This time, let's notice the mistakes and the disasters—with equal charity. As a way of noticing, let's honor forms of accountability that support rather than sabotage the very qualities such independence is trying to achieve: accountability through the responsible exercise of collective human judgment.

The "magic" three—smallness, self-governance, and choice—provide some of the necessary basic ingredients for more responsible individual schools and thus for more accountability. Smallness creates self-knowledge, self-governance allows for a range of voices now often missing, and choice permits disgruntled parents and teachers to vote with their feet. But while these three elements appear to undercut some of the pressure for more and more external accountability, there's a strong argument for adding several other ingredients that will support the development of a more responsible community of schools. Not just because it's politically smart—but because without a powerful system of public accountability, good individual schools can too easily become stuck in routines, parochial, smug, and secretive. Even tyrannical. Smallness, for example, makes it harder to hide from the impact of bad leadership as well as good leadership.

There are several forms of public accountability that are not only compatible with but actually supportive of school-based initiatives. One way to improve the odds, compatible with the three magic bullets, is to increase constituents' voices about the work not only of their own schools but also of other people's schools in terms of student outcomes, equity, and fiscal integrity. Experience suggests that networks of schools can offer us an opportunity to have the best of both worlds: individuality and close external accountability. We need ways to hold schools up to a mirror and ask, "Is this what you meant to be doing?" We need to tackle professional myopia and defensiveness. We assume that schoolchildren learn by being exposed to criticism, but we have not transferred that to the way teachers and schools learn. For this to happen, we need to create instruments that are consistent with the very quality that led us to propose small schools in the first place: responsiveness to often nonstandard ways of maintaining high standards. What strong democratic schooling needs are new forms of horizontal accountability focused on the collective work of the school.

The first step involves creating stronger internal accountability systems, such as those pioneered at Central Park East Secondary School, Urban Academy, University Heights, and International High School, which use both peers and external critics—college faculty members, parents, community members, and other high school teachers—to examine their students' work. It's the job of the teachers, for example, to grade their own students and to determine when they meet schoolwide standards—a task too few schools take seriously today. But the teachers, in turn, need to be publicly accountable for such judgments—both to their internal constituents and to the larger public.

At the next step, schools must answer to one another for the quality of their work. Through the creation of networks of sister schools, not uncommon in private schooling, we can learn how to look at one another's work as critical friends. Such networks can also serve to make up for any problems of scale, if schools choose to use them in that way. Schools that provide feedback on the work of sister schools are creating built-in professional development tools, as well as a powerful form of parent and community education. There is nothing better for one's own learning curve than to formally observe and give support to others.

Third, networks need "cooler," noncollegial audiences to answer to. For this we need formal review panels—public auditors—composed of both critical friends and more distanced and skeptical publics, to attest to the credibility of the networks and the work of their schools. It is such bodies that must demand convincing evidence that the network of schools under review is doing its job, is on the right track, and is acting responsibly. Such review panels must ultimately be responsible to the larger, democratically chosen public authorities.

And finally, everyone—teachers, parents, assessors, legislators, and the public—needs a shared body of credible information (actual student work as well as statistical data) as evidence on which to build reflections and judgments. These are the essentials for creating public credibility, but they are also the essentials for producing good schools. The task of these varied groups of observers—the school's immediate community, the networkers, and the external review panels—is not to find the "one right answer" but to push those closest to the action to act with greater enlightenment.

This is no idle dream. In New York City in 1995, with the support of funds from the Annenberg Challenge, nearly 100 small schools broke themselves down into more than 20 such self-chosen networks and began the work of shared support and accountability. More of these schools were in the works within a year. Simultaneously, a system of review panels to accredit such networks and to maintain audits of their work was being developed, as was a system for collecting credible and accessible data. In return, both the union and the city agreed to negotiate new freedoms and greater flexibility. The largest city in the land was on the brink of the biggest experiment on the potential of smallness. But New York City's inability to keep the same chancellor for more than a few years soon put the more risky and experimental aspects of the project on the back burner.

On a smaller scale, also with support from Annenberg, Boston launched a similar approach—called pilot schools—and throughout the country at other Annenberg sites comparable efforts were begun. Not surprisingly, system folks are always tempted by apparently easier solutions that do not change the locus of power and are simpler to implement—at least on paper.

We periodically imagine that we can avoid the messiness of human judgments and create a foolproof automatic system to make everyone good or smart or intelligent. At least, we pretend to believe it is possible. Then we get upset at the bureaucracy it inevitably spawns. But if juries of our peers will do for deciding life-and-death matters of law, why not juries of our peers to decide life-and-death matters of education? As Winston Churchill once said about democracy itself, nothing could be more flawed—except all the alternatives. Of course, juries need guidelines, a body of precedents, rules of procedure, evidence, and the requirement to reach a publicly shared decision. This will not come easily or overnight, and, like democracy itself, such an approach rests on restoring levels of mutual trust we seem inclined to abandon altogether—to our peril.

The criterion we need to keep at the forefront of our minds is clear: How will this or that policy affect the intelligent and responsible behavior of the people closest to the students (as well as the students themselves)? That's the litmus test. Creating forms of governance and accountability that are mindful first and foremost of their impact on effective relationships between teachers, children, and families will not be an easy task. It may not even show up as a blip on next year's test scores. But shortcuts that bypass such relationships are inefficient.

If we do it right, we might in the process help create responsible and caring communities that are more powerful than those adultless subcultures that dominate far too many of our children's lives and that endanger our larger common community. The problem we face is, after all, more than "academic."

NO

Emeral A. Crosby

Urban Schools: Forced to Fail

Is there anyone who doesn't recall the famous opening sentence of *A Tale of Two Cities*? "It was the best of times, it was the worst of times, it was the age of wisdom, it was the age of foolishness, it was the epoch of belief, it was the epoch of incredulity, it was the season of Light, it was the season of Darkness, it was the spring of hope, it was the winter of despair, we had everything before us, we had nothing before us...."

Such a string of seeming contradictions applies to the late-20th-century world, in which more people have more money than ever before, yet there is more grinding poverty than ever before in isolated rural areas and in the slums of our cities. Affluence exists side by side with deprivation. More young people graduate from high school, yet more young people are classified as dropouts. Good education coexists with miseducation. While there is more security, there is more uncertainty.

For those of us who work in schools, it is also the best of times and the worst of times. Our urban schools, once the pride of our nation, are now a source of controversy and inequity. We have watched with dismay their descent into confusion and failure. Time and space do not permit a thorough discussion of all the factors that bear down on urban schools. However, in this article I will deal with several of the factors that I believe are forcing urban schools to fail.

The Bureaucracy

The decision-making process in urban schools contributes to their failure. But first let me try to define that process broadly. According to many observers, the "decision process" by which both government and private corporations are run in America is a group process. It is not individual ability that determines success in our society; it is the efficient operation of the decision-making process, which is the sum of accumulated information and the skills of a group. The only implication we can safely draw from this fact is that the process has worked for government, private enterprise, education, unions, medicine. No single person or committee can govern these mammoth domains. The "leader" depends on the actions of others, and his actions are dictated to some extent by subordinates who are considered "specialists." This is how a bureaucracy operates.

And that is how things work in America. But making decisions in this way is not always in the best interests of the majority of citizens.

The settling of the American colonies offers an early example of the decision-making process. When the oppression of the controlling powers of 17th-century Europe became too burdensome for the powerless colonists, many fled to the colonial "suburbs"—the new frontiers of America. Flight was their strategy for solving the problems of taxation, inadequate housing, legal injustices, and unemployment.

Flight and the displacement of other people became a pattern in America, but it is a pattern that was determined by the decision of the group. For example, the colonial settlers had to displace the Native Americans in order to establish themselves in new territories. The Native Americans were forced to move on to less desirable areas, to what amounted to ghettos created by the people who displaced them. This policy could be carried out with a clear conscience as long as the Native Americans were considered "different"—barbarians, savages, inferiors, not humans. Of course, no one person made such judgments or decisions. They were made through myriad individual decisions of all members of the group. In this way, everyone and no one was responsible for the outcome.

Such a system continues to operate to this day. The decision-making process is itself an institution, and urban schools are deeply rooted in the decision-making process. To go against it is to be a noncomformist, to act against the group, which amounts to a kind of heresy that can bring misfortune to the offender.

This decision-making process can be described as "bureaucratic." Bureaucracy operates when decisions require that all information be moved upward from one level of specialists to another through a management hierarchy whose multiple levels often distort the nature of the information. Although the bureaucracy is composed of people (aided by computers), it is not controlled by individuals. It is self-generating, self-regulating, and self-perpetuating.

Because the decision-making process is what drives the institution or the organization, the bureaucracy is quite powerful. Because it is an anonymous and faceless collective, it is difficult to control, sidestep, or subvert. Because it seeks to perpetuate itself and its processes, it frequently serves as the brakes that bring innovation and change to a halt.

How does this bear upon the urban schools? They are run by institutional bureaucracies that resist change. Yet the urban schools must change in response to the growing complexities and demands of our society that have made the existing networks and organizational structures obsolete. When the bureaucracy blocks meaningful change, it is inevitable that the urban schools will fail a large number of their clients, the students.

Buildings and Sites

Environment affects learning. We can surely agree on that, but we have yet to measure the magnitude of the role that environment plays in learning—both in aiding it and in hindering it.

While curriculum, school organization, and communication technology undergo significant changes, school buildings themselves are often too old to accommodate to these changes. Many urban schools are well over 50 years old and designed to provide an environment different from what we need today. Often located in the oldest parts of the city, many of these buildings are in violation of modern fire codes and are hazards to safety. The plumbing is obsolete; asbestos insulation poses health problems; lead poisoning from paint and soil has a negative impact on student learning and the brain development of young children. Furthermore, these buildings cannot accommodate the activities, the equipment, and the materials that new programs and modern technology demand.

These old buildings are hard to heat in winter, and they retain heat in the summer. They require constant renovation, but they can never be properly updated to meet the needs of modern students. Even when their condition is not especially dilapidated, their appearance is often oppressive. And research has shown that such oppressive, unattractive surroundings are detrimental to the learning process.

Costly as it is, remodeling offers one solution. But, once again, the process of decision making gets in the way. Of course, flight is still one solution to the problem of these ancient, inadequate structures. Build somewhere else. Build on the periphery of the city or in the suburbs.

When an existing urban school is remodeled or replaced, its architecture often doesn't meet the real needs of the school community. The physical plant often works against successfully housing the thousands of students who attend the urban school. Elementary schools, built for smaller populations, often cram a thousand students into a small building, while large high schools must accommodate up to 3,000 students in a single building. Handling the volume of students entering, passing through the halls, and exiting the building is a tremendous problem. What's more, the lack of a campus means that many interscholastic and intramural activities—such as soccer, softball, and tennis—cannot be offered.

Planners and decision makers do not often consider the importance of environment to the inhabitants of school structures. When it is possible to do significant remodeling and upgrading of an urban school to create a positive educational environment, the needs of the inhabitants of these buildings must be considered. We must ask and answer some basic questions: What should happen in the urban school? How can the environment of an urban school be planned so that desired behaviors and educational goals can be accomplished? Unless sensible and realistic actions result from answering such questions, the physical environment of urban schools becomes just one more factor in the process of failure.

Overload

Most people agree that the central goal of the public schools is to teach students to read, write, and compute. Urban schools today simply have too many other things to accomplish under too many unfavorable conditions. The urban school is no longer merely an academic institution; it is also a social and welfare institution. Among the necessary services it provides are recreation, cultural growth, emotional development, basic health care, food service, voter registration, draft registration, driver education, sex education, employment service, immunization, and the collection of census data. The urban school is, in effect, like a government of a small city. Yet the added responsibilities have come without any administrative or structural change and without the addition of essential personnel. Problems increase, but the means to solve them are not available.

Too much responsibility without the means to carry it out overloads the urban schools. Students come to see their educational experiences in these institutions as if they were looking through the small end of a telescope: their experiences appear artificial, remote, unreal, and irrelevant.

When the system cannot afford to fulfill its responsibilities—already enormous—the solution is often to cut "nonbasic" school programs rather than to reduce the burden of the outer layers of the organization. Because of the power and influence of those people who have positions in the outer organization, the programs cut tend to be the very enrichment programs that children in urban areas need to make use of their basic education. These programs, too important to appear on the list of superfluous classes, include remedial reading, remedial math, guidance counseling, school newspaper, the media center, art, music, and any extracurricular activities that might have survived the last round of cuts. For indifferent students who often come to school unwillingly and reluctantly, these courses—last to be added, first to go—can offer inspiration and a reason to learn.

Unless the organization of education is restructured to handle the additional demands placed on schools, the urban schools will continue to fail large numbers of their clients.

A New Population

"What the best and wisest parent wants for his own child," John Dewey remarked in 1899, "that must the community want for all of its children. Any other idea for our schools is narrow and unlovely; acted upon, it destroys our democracy." Our democracy is in peril because the community is not providing the best education it can for its poor and urban youngsters. Too often minority students and poor students are not provided with the intellectual skills and the academic knowledge needed to earn a decent living and to participate fully in the economic, social, and political life of the community.

Our urban schools were not designed for their present clients. The urban school population changed radically after World War II. Prior to that time, the urban school population included large numbers of white and middle-class students, with even a smattering of the children of the wealthy. Today, this population consists largely of minorities: immigrants, African Americans, and the poor.

In the early 1950s the exodus of the white middle and upper classes from the cities was as dramatic and sudden as the departure of Moses and his people from Egypt. But, once again, this flight was the secondary result of the decision-making process in two areas: the development of the interstate highway system, which made commuting more convenient, and the creation of federal mortgage programs, which financed suburban housing construction. The advertising industry reinforced the desirability of migrating to the suburbs. Automobiles were shown being driven through beautiful suburbs, not through city streets. Children were seen running in from lush green lawns for their Campbell's soup, their Kraft macaroni, or their Cheracol cough syrup. They weren't shown coming in from the city streets where they had been playing basketball so that their mothers could wash their shirts in Tide or give them Kool-Aid from the refrigerator in their middle-class kitchens.

Another development that shifted the demographics was the rapid mechanization of farms, which displaced many rural people and sent them to the cities and their children to urban schools.

The new wave of immigration of the last 25 years from Hispanic countries, from the Middle East, and from Asian countries has washed over the urban schools like a tidal wave, bringing with it additional challenges, this time cultural and linguistic.

As the total population of major cities decreases, the school population decreases as well. But at the same time, the minority population of urban schools increases, and the duties and problems that come with the new population are overwhelming to the institution. There is the need for food and sanitation and for keeping records and storing supplies. There are demands for safety and surveillance, including fire rules and drills and protection against intrusion, robbery, assault, and vandalism. And there are gangs and the problems that come with drugs. Special education is the fastest-growing element in the urban schools. And it is an element for which urban schools are poorly prepared.

Delinquent behavior is too mild a term to describe a problem that can be devastating for urban schools. In the high schools, for example, there is a kind of anarchy or civil war that is more serious than most people outside the schools realize. Students are angry young people, and they question every rule. Students commit acts of defiance that are astonishing in their destructive effect on the population and the institution.

In the face of this multitude of problems, those in authority react with stricter punishments, armed hallway guards, metal detectors, and forms of repression meant to stem the tide. The rules become more mechanical, rigid, and impersonal. The students are known by their I.D. numbers, and the personalities of teachers are effaced by the need to maintain order at great cost to everyone in the school.

I can barely touch on the causes of delinquent behavior in this article. However, as far as the schools are concerned, the following deficiencies are key to delinquent behavior:

- The education being offered is not meaningfully related to the real world—the world of employment and changing social conditions.
- The school does not present itself as a model of the pluralistic society. Students are grouped according to ability, race, and economic class. The school isolates and excludes when inclusion is its reason for being.
- The school often fails to prepare young people for mature life. Students learn through imitation, but they do not have the models of behavior that will benefit them in the future. Consequently, they remain children. Above all, in this bureaucratic institution, students must be allowed to develop personal responsibility and have opportunities for decision making as part of their preparation for adult life.

When school experience is irrelevant to life experience and to employment opportunities, it contributes heavily to dropout rates. When the school organization isolates and excludes according to ability, race, or economic class, it denies young people the opportunity for meaningful interaction with all segments of society. The resulting alienation lies at the heart of delinquency. The system is a machine that is not equal to its task, and it forces the urban schools to fail.

Cost of Security

Imagine the high school as a giant marketplace where consuming and selling occurs every day. In the course of a day, the student purchases food, school supplies, tickets for school events, and items sold for fund-raising. Money is exchanged as a matter of course in a relatively unguarded atmosphere.

Imagine also the young entrepreneur who attends the urban school. What does he see? A free flow of money that is unprotected except by teachers, and those teachers already have more than enough to do. He sees no barriers to taking clothes, shoes, or jackets from his peers. He sees few restraints on the sale of illegal drugs and narcotics. He sees the marketplace, filled with goods for the taking, as a source of income for himself.

Elsewhere—in fact, everywhere else—security measures have been taken to deal with the criminal element that pervades the larger marketplace that we call our society. Security personnel are included in the operating budgets of supermarkets, banks, parking lots, service stations, laundromats, restaurants, and department stores. Security has been a fact of life everywhere except in the marketplace of the school.

When it becomes obvious that the exchange of money demanded protection for the consumer—the high school client, who is still a child and in the care of the adults who staff the school—the first line of defense was the teacher. Put teachers on hall duty. Put teachers in the lunchroom. Then, when they have expended enough psychic energy to exhaust themselves, send them back to the classroom, where they are expected to provide meaningful and challenging instruction in math, science, history, and English.

It never did work, and it isn't working today. It takes away from the teacher preparation time and refueling time. Professionals, who are being paid professional wages, are doing the work of security personnel. In terms of dollars alone, that is an expensive mistake.

Today, even when teachers are used to staff the halls and lunchrooms, at least 10% of every urban school budget is set aside for security-related measures: security personnel, metal detectors, replacement of stolen property. The equivalent of an entire police precinct has been created to serve the security needs of urban schools, and that means more expense for patrol cars, officers, supervisors, and uniforms, as well as coverage for special events and board meetings.

In the last two decades, the decision makers in urban school districts have recognized that the schools need the same level of security as any other agency in the community. After all, aren't our students our most precious commodity? But perhaps that doesn't include urban students, because allocations from the state for education do not allow for security expenses. Therefore, the urban schools have to use some of their classroom allocations for security. It turns out that security eats up from 10% to 12% of their budgets.

What does this mean in terms of dollars? An urban district with a budget of $500 million or more must subtract at least $50 million from its classroom budget, which includes teachers' salaries. In many cases, the costs of security for urban school districts exceed the total budget for many smaller municipalities, and the security force of an urban school often outnumbers the entire police force of small towns.

When we talk about the costs of security in urban schools, we are talking about numbers with a lot of zeroes. And we can't even count all the costs. The hidden expenses of security cannot be calculated. Indeed, it might be too frightening if we examined the costs any further than we have here.

The Professional Staff

Given the new populations in our urban schools, the number of professional staff members is not the result of any general shortage in the supply of teachers. In suburban communities that surround large, urban districts, the ratio of professional personnel to students is higher than in urban districts. Where the need is greatest, the supply is smallest. The higher salaries, better working conditions, and better recruiting methods of the suburban districts are magnets that draw personnel away from the urban districts.

The teacher turnover rate in the urban schools is much higher than in the suburban schools and in other more stable communities. The result is that urban schools, especially those in the inner cities, are often staffed largely by newly hired or uncertified teachers. Teachers who have remained in the urban schools through the traumatic and radical changes of the last three decades are in need of retraining and of rethinking their roles as educators. These teachers, who were trained to teach students from middle-class families and who often come from middle-class families themselves, now find themselves engulfed by minority students, immigrants, and other students from low-income families—students whose values and experiences are very different from their own. Teachers who are unaware of these differences or who are alienated from the norms of their students are often unable to communicate with or understand them. Retraining for these teachers, while essential, is not generally available.

The staffing of urban schools has also been affected by the shift of populations from city to suburbs. Many teachers who have remained in urban schools no longer live in the city where they work but have moved to the suburbs. This is the first step in the disengagement of urban teachers from the urban situation. The teachers withdraw themselves from the community of the students, and the only result can be a growing reluctance to be a part of that community in any way except to earn a paycheck. It is a form of disloyalty to the students. This withdrawal and this disloyalty cannot be cured by a program or a workshop. Yet those are the cures now being offered.

On the other side of the ledger, teachers are forced to fail by the bureaucracy of the decision makers. The loyal teachers experience what can only be called disloyalty on the part of the system, which withdraws from its teachers. The system is reluctant to reward teachers for their devotion to students. The system disengages itself from the classroom, the teacher's workstation, by not providing adequate support in the form of supplies and encouragement. Teachers suffer from a lack of psychic nurturing, and they are virtually alone in the classroom, without adult support.

Indeed, teaching, as it is now practiced in urban schools, is the most isolated of the professions. Some nonurban districts have begun to move toward cooperative teaching, team teaching, and common planning. The professional isolation of the urban teachers must end as well.

One severe ramification of this isolation is that talented teachers do not have the opportunity to pass their talents and expertise on to others. Their skill dies in their classrooms—and, with every teacher retirement, a vacuum is created. Experienced teachers have gotten that way by learning from their mistakes over many years. Sharing the fruits of their experience—the successes and the failures—could help new teachers avoid making the same mistakes. Moreover, it could inspire new teachers to reach the best in themselves. The teacher training institutions have not placed sufficient emphasis on preparing new teachers to work in schools that serve minority students. There are no lucrative college scholarships for prospective teachers, as there are in athletics. Nor are there significant bonuses offered for those who will teach in urban schools. Teacher candidates are not offered courses designed to familiarize them with the history and the culture of their potential students, much less with their learning problems and their psychology. Teachers who are already part of the school organization are generally not provided with inservice training to make them more effective in their classrooms. The current practices of awarding bonuses and scholarships, making personnel assignments, and offering inservice training must be changed.

Every time teachers serve on hall duty or lunchroom duty, their talents are being misused. Teachers could be tutoring students or mentoring other teachers. They could be conferencing, sharing, and doing observations. But urban teachers are denied professional renewal during the course of the school day. The only time they can engage in professional activities is after school—after they have already taught five classes and performed many other mentally and physically exhausting duties. At the end of the day, their minds are not fresh, their energy is low, they are fatigued, and their spirits are depleted. How much professional renewal can we expect? Such abuse of teacher talent is a crime against the profession, but its ultimate victims are the students. When teachers are forced to fail, then the urban schools themselves are forced to fail.

Lack of Political Courage

Revolutions that benefit society rather than destroy the good in it require revolutionary methods and processes. To date, urban school problems have been handled in an ad hoc and inefficient manner. Confusion about goals is matched by lack of commitment to the real cure for educational ills. Indeed, the resistance to change is strong because many people benefit from the status quo in urban education: owners of ghetto housing and small businesses, privileged white workers protected from minority competition, and all those who gain when society's dirty work is done cheaply by others.

But the changes that assault our urban schools are producing a cultural revolution that will spread throughout the entire education community in time. Brought about by vandalism, drug abuse, poverty and unemployment, and changing sexual mores, this revolution could be as significant as any past revolution, whether it be political, religious, military, industrial, or technological. Existing structures are being undermined by immigration, racial integration, freedom schools, court decisions, vouchers and charters, and school takeovers. We have no way of successfully predicting the extent of the changes that the future might bring.

But the current pseudo-revolution that is benefiting no one is called "restructuring the urban school." The social engineers want to rebuild urban education on a shaky foundation; they want to build pyramids on an eroding base of sand. They think, for example, that they can mandate parent involvement with people whose time is totally consumed in a struggle to survive. These social engineers want full participation in the school from parents who lack the means to do what they want to do for their children.

A number of generalizations can be made about minority education in the United States, and they apply in particular to urban schools, where most members of minority groups are educated. First, substantial minority deprivation does exist, along with exploitation and segregation. Second, these types of discrimination are endemic to the form of internal colonialism that has been developed in this country. Third, they continue because important segments of white society profit from such arrangements; therefore, while significant social and educational legislation has been enacted, there is only token enforcement.

Fourth, political influence follows economic power, and those with vested interests use their power to resist progressive reforms in education. Indeed, when there is change—either for the sake of appearance or as a result of popular pressure—educational programs are set up in a manner that ensures failure. For example, a special program may be funded for only one year, or an inconsequential appendage may be added to a program. Significant and long-lasting reforms are nearly impossible to bring about because our national priorities are set so as to preclude meaningful change.

There are some things that urban educators never talk about in public. Urban educators are silent when the bureaucracy mandates better student attendance. The problem is bigger than the school, and it is beyond the school's power to solve it. Urban educators know some things about the lives of the people in the communities they serve. They know that the poorest of the poor live farthest from the school. They know that it is dangerous to walk the city streets on dark mornings—or even in broad daylight. They know that an automobile is still a luxury among the very poor. And, in case no one else has noted, urban educators know that city transportation is just not available.

Urban educators shake their heads over the cures proposed for the ills of the public school system: the creation of charter schools or magnet schools or the implementation of vouchers. Tear down the old system and start again—but only in urban areas. Although criticism is leveled against all public schools, the remedies are to be applied only to the *urban* public schools. Suburban school districts have sufficient funds and political support to reach their educational goals. Only an educational heretic would propose the purposeful demolition of an affluent suburban school system. Yet this very demolition is what is being offered as a cure for the ills of urban schools. Only an urban bureaucracy would support such a notion.

By their very nature, institutions resist change. Institutions are power, and power concedes to nothing but greater power. If the urban schools are to offer their population of minority children access to the American dream, a powerful political force must move into the educational arena to represent their cause. The alternative is complete failure and the destruction of urban schools.

For urban schools, it is now "the season of light" and "the season of darkness." We have "everything before us," we have "nothing before us." We are going to succeed, or we will surely fail what rests in our charge—the urban schools and the children who attend them.

POSTSCRIPT

Can Self-Governing Schools Rescue Urban Education?

Rethinking the relationship between private goods and the common good is a first step toward a more adequate response to urban poverty in the United States. So says David Hollenbach in "The Common Good and Urban Poverty," *America* (June 5–12, 1999), and this theme trails through the central issue discussed here and the multiple subissues involved. These subissues include inequities in public school funding, the dropout problem, the racial and ethnic gaps in student achievement, the participation of parents in school improvement, the struggle to attain adequate literacy, the quality of inner-city Catholic schools, and the survival of gifted students in urban public schools.

A wealth of material addresses these many related problems. Particularly recommended books are *Fixing Urban Schools* edited by Paul T. Hill and Mary Beth Celio (1998); Gene I. Maeroff's *Altered Destinies: Making Life Better for Schoolchildren in Need* (1998); Joseph P. Viteritti's *Choosing Equality: School Choice, the Constitution, and Civil Society* (1999); Miles Corwin's *And Still We Rise: The Trials and Triumphs of Twelve Gifted Inner-City High School Students* (2000); and Samuel Casey Carter, *No Excuses: Lessons From Twenty-One High-Performing High-Poverty Schools* (2000).

Articles of especial note include Evelyn Hanssen's "A White Teacher Reflects on Institutional Racism," *Phi Delta Kappan* (May 1998); "Lessons Learned," *The New Republic* (October 4, 1999); Bruce R. Joyce's "The Great Literacy Problem and Success for All," *Phi Delta Kappan* (October 1999); Robin Cooper's "Urban School Reform From a Student-of-Color Perspective," *Urban Education* (January 2000); Ronald J. Sider's "Making Schools Work for the Rich and the Poor," *The Christian Century* (August 25, 1999); Richard Nadler's "Low Class: How Progressive Education Hurts the Poor and Minorities," *National Review* (December 21, 1998); "Why Do At-Risk Students Thrive in Catholic Schools?" by Nina H. Shokraii, *USA Today Magazine* (May 1998); "Dropout Prevention: A Case for Enhanced Early Literacy Efforts," *The Clearing House* (January 1999); Henry Duvall, "Big City Schools: Struggling to Be the Best," *Principal* (September 2001); Joyce Baldwin, "Meeting the Challenge of the Urban High School," *Carnegie Reporter* (Spring 2001); Martin Haberman, "Urban Schools: Day Camps or Custodial Centers?" *Phi Delta Kappan* (November 2000); and Arthur E. Wise and Marsha Levine, "The Ten-Step Solution," *Education Week* (February 27, 2002).

Multiple articles can be found in the November 1998 issue of *Education and Urban Society,* the November/December 1999 issue of *The Clearing House,* and the December 1999 issue of *Phi Delta Kappan.*

ISSUE 19

Should Technology Lead the Quest for Better Schools?

YES: Barbara Means, from "Technology Use in Tomorrow's Schools," *Educational Leadership* (December 2000/January 2001)

NO: Jane M. Healy, from "The Mad Dash to Compute," *The School Administrator* (April 1999)

ISSUE SUMMARY

YES: Barbara Means, codirector of the Center for Technology in Learning at SRI International, explores the roots of educational technology and paints an optimistic picture of its future impact on meaningful learning.

NO: Jane M. Healy, an educational psychologist, raises serious questions about the long-term ramifications of technology use in schools.

The schools have not always used or responded to new media constructively, so it is crucial that media experts help teachers, administrators, and curriculum designers carve out appropriate strategies for dealing with new technologies. Some experts—while seeing many exciting possibilities in computer-based instruction, particularly in the realm of individualization and self-pacing—caution that we need far more sophisticated understanding of the processes of learning, human motivation, and factors involved in concentration. Others fear the controlling force of computer programs because it could lead to the diminution of the spontaneity and instinctive responses of the learner. The ultimate effect of the new technology could be a complete transformation of learning and the conception of organized education—but similar predictions were made with the advent of television and even radio.

In 1984 MIT professor Seymour Papert predicted, "There won't be schools in the future; I think that the computer will blow up the school." But Larry Cuban, in "Revolutions That Fizzled," *The Washington Post* (October 27, 1996), warns that the persistent urge to reengineer the schools has continually failed to transform teaching practices. Papert, writing in the same issue, counters that the computer makes possible John Dewey's depiction of learning through experimentation and exposure to the real world of social experience. Computer enthusiasts Jim Cummins of New York University and Dennis Sayers of the Ontario Institute for Studies in Education, in their 1996 book *Brave New Schools*, urge heavy investment in an Internet-wired nationwide school system.

On the negative side, Richard P. Lookatch, in "The Ill-Considered Dash to Technology," *The School Administrator* (April 1996), warns that "hardware hucksters have found K–12 schools to be open landfills for outdated central processing units, while software pushers find technology-zealous media specialists ideal targets for software, much of which ultimately ends up in a storage cabinet because it is either too frustrating, too complicated, or too poorly correlated to the curriculum." His position is that educational media offer no unique benefits and may well lead to inequity, lower standards, and wasted financial resources.

In "The Emperor's New Computer: A Critical Look at Our Appetite for Computer Technology," *Journal of Teacher Education* (May–June 1996), David Pepi and Geoffrey Schuerman pose several crucial questions, including the following:

- Is technology an effective catalyst for educational reform?
- Are past, current, and anticipated uses of technology consistent with contemporary theories of learning?
- Is using computers synonymous with good teaching?
- Does technology promote critical thinking?
- Does technology build cooperation?
- How much information can we tolerate?

In considering responses to such questions, the authors draw on Neil Postman's 1993 book *Technopoly*, in which "technopoly" is defined as a culture in which all aspects of human life must find meaning in terms of the current technology and in which there is no tolerance of alternative worldviews. It is Postman's opinion that we are moving toward that culture.

Books addressing the issue include Nicholas Negroponte's *Being Digital* (1995); Janet W. Schofield's *Computers and Classroom Culture* (1995); Sherry Turkle's *Life on the Screen: Identity in the Age of the Internet* (1995); Jane M. Healy's *Failure to Connect* (1998); Frederick Bennett's *Computers as Tutors: Solving the Crisis in Education* (1999); Clifford Stoll's *High Tech Heretic* (1999); Andrea A. DiSessa's *Changing Minds: Computers, Learning, and Literacy* (2000); Larry Cuban's *Oversold and Underused* (2001); and Seymour Papert's *The Connected Family* (1996). In his book, Papert states, "Despite frequent predictions that a technological revolution in education is imminent, school remains in essential respects very much what it has always been, and what changes have occurred (for better or for worse) cannot be attributed to technology."

The opinions that follow pit Barbara Means, who explains the grounds of her enthusiasm for technology, against Jane M. Healy, who explores the trade-offs involved in technology use.

Barbara Means

 **YES**

Technology Use in Tomorrow's Schools

Students and teachers have increasing access to almost limitless amounts of information on the World Wide Web. In addition, the trend toward using such general-purpose application packages as word processing, spreadsheet, and database software for school assignments has grown considerably since the 1980s. Nearly 50 percent of teachers in a recent national survey, for example, had required word processing during the previous school year (Becker, 1999). Students also are increasingly involved in building Web pages and multimedia presentations to show their solutions to problems or to demonstrate what they have learned in their research. Educators are using network technology to support collaborations—locally and at great distances—among students, experts, and teachers. The percentage of classrooms participating in network-based collaborations is still relatively small, however.

Despite great strides in incorporating technology into U.S. schools, we still fall short of providing a seamless, convenient, robust, and reliable technology support structure for all students and teachers. Today's desktop computers and Internet usages are not the educational ideal (Roschelle, Hoadley, Pea, Gordin, & Means, in press). Many educators lament the relative paucity of up-to-date computers and network connections in classrooms, but a look into almost any classroom with a sizable number of computers reveals all kinds of problems related to the computers' size, weight, shape, and requirements for multiple cords and wires. Similarly, today's World Wide Web is disorganized, of uneven quality, and overrun with advertising. In too many cases, students and teachers are either not using the technology available to them or are using technology to accomplish tasks that could be done offline more quickly and with less effort extraneous to the learning content (Healy, 1998).

Nevertheless, our experience with the less-than-ideal technological infrastructure available in today's schools suggests important directions for the 21st century. The insights gained from these experiences, coupled with advances in research on human learning and the technological improvements that can be expected in the coming decade, give rise to cautious optimism concerning technology's role in the schools of tomorrow.

The Roots of Educational Technology

Mastery learning approaches dominated the early days of computer use to teach academic subjects, with skills and subject matter broken down into byte-sized bits for discrete skill practice or knowledge transmission. These efforts to teach content through computers were supplemented by courses in computer literacy and, at the high school level, computer programming.

In the late 1980s, these practices gave way to an emphasis on incorporating general-purpose technology tools, such as word processors and spreadsheets, into learning in the academic content areas. General office applications became more common in the classroom than software explicitly designed for instructional purposes. The emphasis on adopting general tools for educational purposes received a further boost from the rise of the World Wide Web and search engines for locating Web sites on almost any topic. Such slogans as *connecting the classroom to the world* and *the world at your fingertips* reflect today's emphasis on access to a much broader information base through the Web.

Although classrooms continue to lag behind the business and entertainment sectors in terms of capitalizing on network technologies, the rate of increase in Internet access within U.S. schools during the final decade of the 20th century was phenomenal. In 1990, few U.S. schools had Internet connections, and many of these were low-speed, dial-up modem connections from a single computer. By 1994, the percentage of schools with Internet access was significant—35 percent—and by 1999, the percentage had risen to 95 percent. As with computers, we stopped counting school connections and started looking at the availability of Internet access within individual classrooms.

In 1994, only 3 percent of U.S. classrooms had Internet access. In 1996, President Clinton announced a set of national educational technology goals, including providing Internet access to every classroom in the United States. By 1997, the proportion of connected classrooms had grown to 27 percent. Sixty-three percent of U.S. public school classrooms had Internet access by 1999, according to National Center for Education Statistics data (2000), resulting in part from the E-rate—the telecommunications discount to schools and libraries passed in 1996.

Technology for Meaningful Learning

As access to technology grows, educators must decide how best to use it. *How People Learn,* a recent report from the National Research Council (Bransford, Brown, & Cocking, 1999), applies principles from research on human learning to issues of education. The report explores the potential of technology to provide the conditions that research indicates are conducive to meaningful learning: real-world contexts for learning; connections to outside experts; visualization and analysis tools; scaffolds for problem solving; and opportunities for feedback, reflection, and revision.

A few examples illustrate how technology can provide these capabilities. The Global Learning and Observations to Benefit the Environment (GLOBE) program helps elementary and secondary school students learn science by involving them in real scientific investigations, such as measuring soil and water quality. Students follow detailed data collection protocols for measuring characteristics of their local atmosphere, soil, and vegetation. Using GLOBE Internet data-entry forms, thousands of students submit data to a central archive, where it is combined with data from other schools to develop visualizations—a data map showing measured values and their geographic locations—that are posted on the Web. The scientists who developed the data collection protocols and depend on the students' data for their research visit classrooms, exchange e-mail with students, and participate with students in scheduled Web chats (Means and Coleman, 2000).

Hands-On Universe, a program of the University of California at Berkeley's Lawrence Hall of Science, gives students the opportunity to use image processing software to investigate images from a network of automated telescopes. Automated telescopes now capture many more images from outer space than professional astronomers have time to analyze. Hands-On Universe enlists students to review images from space and to help search for supernovas and asteroids as they acquire astronomy concepts and research skills. Hands-On Universe lets students use the same kinds of software tools as scientists, albeit with more user-friendly interfaces, to examine and classify downloaded images. Hands-On Universe students have discovered a previously unknown supernova and published their work in a scientific journal.

Teachers have also found advantages in using technology supports for student collaboration within their own schools and classrooms. Knowledge Forum —formerly Computer-Supported Intentional Learning Environments (CSILE)— for example, provides a communal database, with text and graphics capabilities. Students create text and graphics "nodes" about the topic they are studying, labeling their contributions by the kind of thinking represented: "my theory for now" or "what we need to learn about next." Other students can search and comment on these nodes. With teacher support, students can use Knowledge Forum to share information and feedback, to accumulate knowledge over time, and to exercise collaboration skills. The communal hypermedia database provides a record of students' thoughts and electronic conversations over time (Scardamalia & Bereiter, 1996), allowing teachers to browse the database to review their students' emerging understanding of key concepts and their interaction skills (Means & Olson, 1999).

ThinkerTools software, another visualization and analysis tool, helps middle school students learn about velocity and acceleration. Students begin with what the program developers call "scaffolded inquiry activities"—problems, games, and experiments that help students understand motion, first in one direction and then in two directions. As students progress, they are exposed to more complex simulations, culminating in their learning of the principles underlying Newtonian mechanics. In a carefully controlled study, middle school students who had used ThinkerTools outperformed high school physics students in their ability to apply principles of Newtonian mechanics to real-world situations (White & Frederiksen, 1998).

Although such examples of technology-enhanced learning activities are prominent in the education literature, they do not represent mainstream educational practice in the United States. A national survey of 4,100 teachers found that in the 1997–98 school year, the most commonly assigned use of technology was still word processing—required by nearly 50 percent of the teachers (Becker, 1999). Thirty-five percent of the teachers asked students to use CD-ROMS for research. Internet research or information gathering was the third most common teacher-directed student use of computers. Nearly 30 percent of all the teachers—and more than 70 percent of the teachers with high-speed Internet connections in their classrooms—had their students conduct Internet research (Becker, 1999). Internet assignments had become slightly more common than games and software drills, which 29 percent of the teachers had assigned. Interactive uses of the Internet were relatively infrequent. Only 7 percent of the teachers reported having their students use e-mail three times or more during the school year and even fewer had their students work with students at a distance in cross-classroom projects.

What's Next?

Despite their relative scarcity, such uses of technology and learning principles in carefully designed instructional activities foretell future innovations that are likely to have the advantage of much more seamless, unobtrusive technology supports. Today's desktop computers and the networks they run on offer a huge array of potential uses—everything from keeping track of student grades to supporting the manipulation of digitized images—but they are bulky, expensive, and awkward to use in a classroom.

Many technology trend watchers believe that the 21st century will see a move away from such strong reliance on general-purpose computing devices toward lower-cost, portable, hand-held devices, often connected through global networks and tailored for specific applications (Norman, 1998). Major equipment manufacturers are investing in wireless technologies, wireless personal area networking has emerged, and the popularity of both hand-held computing devices and cell phones is growing rapidly. Nowhere is the potential impact of these trends greater than in our nation's schools.

Students could carry and use lightweight, low-cost learning appliances rugged enough to fit in their backpacks as they move from class to class, school to home, or between school-based and community-based learning settings. When used with wireless networks, high-powered servers, and teacher workstations, these low-cost devices are likely to provide more narrow but more effective functionality than today's desktop computers and to be much easier to use. Computing and networking will be taken for granted as part of the school environment. Teacher workstations will be able to exchange information with student devices and with school- or district-level servers. Complex, memory-hogging programs can reside on servers and be pulled down to local computers or appliances on an as-needed basis.

Tomorrow's Classroom

Given the possibilities of new technologies, what might tomorrow's classroom look like? A MathPad, for example, might be an educational appliance—smaller and lighter than today's hand-held devices, with capability for stylus input, display, and mathematical calculations and graphing. Such devices might feature short-range radio communication capabilities linking the hand-held device to other hands-helds or to another computing device, such as a teacher workstation, a share-board display system, or sensors built into the environment.

Given this emerging technology infrastructure, we can envision such educational activities as the following. Middle school students in an environmental science class monitor local haze using a sun photometer to measure attenuation of sunlight caused by haze, smoke, and smog. Seven small groups of students take their photometer readings at their school's softball field each day at noon, and the readings are automatically sent to their MathPads. The students' MathPads contain a template for displaying the readings of all seven groups, so the students can send their readings to one another.

Upon returning to the classroom, one group transmits the completed template for today's readings to the class's share-board computer, and the teacher begins a class review and discussion of the data on the wall-sized display. The teacher and students call up software that incorporates prompts to help them judge the reasonableness of the measurements the student groups have taken. The teacher plots each group's reading on a graph showing measurements over the last six months as a point of departure for discussing the distinction between accuracy and precision.

The teacher then introduces the next assignment: work in small groups to investigate haze data from their own and other schools. Controlling the display from her workstation, the teacher connects through the Internet to the online Haze Project database and reminds the students of the contents of the database and strategies for navigating the database Web site. To make sure they know how to read the data tables, the teacher asks several comprehension questions, having students submit answers with their MathPads and checking the students' responses on her workstation to make sure no one is lost. She directs students to return to their small groups to explore the data archive before deciding on a research question for a project that will take them several weeks and culminate in presentations for their class and submission of their work to the Haze Project's online student journal. Students may choose to collaborate with students at other schools through e-mail and real-time online discussions using software that allows them to share and manipulate data graphs.

As in today's GLOBE and Hands-on Universe projects, the Haze Project students of tomorrow participate in the real-world context of ongoing scientific investigation. Connections to a larger world become second nature. The students' data and analyses are part of much larger projects with real stakeholders. Students contribute to and learn from a community of investigators. Visualization and analysis tools on the students' MathPads and the teacher's workstation help the students see patterns in their data. Prompts built into the data-recording software scaffold students' efforts to check the reasonableness of the data they have collected. The technology also supports access to similar data sets and conferencing with others involved in the Haze Project, two activities that provide opportunities for reflection, analysis, and revision. The teacher's ability to exchange information with individual student MathPads lets students receive quick feedback on their lines of reasoning and allows the teacher to adjust instruction to meet students' needs.

In terms of the technology itself, a combination of small quantities of expensive equipment (one or a few central workstations for each classroom and a top-notch display facility) and large numbers of inexpensive devices (such as the MathPads themselves) is likely to be more cost-effective than current technology expenditures. The most challenging technical requirement is that of compatibility so that different pieces of equipment can communicate.

Challenges Ahead

Is this scenario realistic? One could easily predict a very different impact of technology on education. The increasing availability of Web-based alternative learning resources coincides with a decline in public confidence in the efficacy of schools and increasing interest in alternatives, such as voucher programs, charter schools, and homeschooling. Over the next two decades, public schools will likely have to compete for resources and for students—not only with private schools and homeschooling options—but with Internet-based alternatives as well. I doubt that brick-and-mortar schools will become obsolete, if only for their utility as places for students to spend their time, but they will become one among many kinds of organizations offering formally organized, distributed learning.

The increased pressure of competition should stimulate schools to improve. Schools that incorporate the technology of the future can offer the best combination of traditional face-to-face instruction—role modeling, socialization, and morale building—and projected benefits of learning with new technologies: increased participation in systems of distributed learning that engage broader communities, learning-enhancing representations of concepts and data, a restructuring of teaching and learning roles, and more meaningful assessment practices.

My vision for educational technology use is at least as dependent on improvements in teacher preparation and professional development around pedagogy, content, and assessment practices as it is on technological advances. My vision is technologically feasible—the question is whether our education system, and society in general, will support and promote the policies, resources, and practices needed to make it a reality.

References

Becker, H. J. (1999). *Internet use by teachers: Conditions of professional use and teacher-directed student use.* Irvine, CA: Center for Research on Information Technology and Organizations.

Bransford, J. D., Brown, A. L., & Cocking, R. R. (Eds.). (1999). *How people learn: Brain, mind, experience, and school.* Washington, DC: National Academy Press.

Healy, J. (1998). *Failure to connect: How computers affect our children's minds—for better and worse.* New York: Simon & Schuster.

Means, B., & Coleman, E. (2000). Technology supports for student participation in science investigations. In M. J. Jacobson & R. B. Kozma (Eds.), *Innovations in science and mathematics education* (pp. 287–319). Mahwah, NJ: Erlbaum.

Means, B., & Olson, K. (1999). Technology's role in student-centered classrooms. In H. Walberg & H. Waxman (Eds.), *New directions for teaching practice and research* (pp. 297–319). Berkeley, CA: McCutchan.

National Center for Education Statistics. (2000). *Internet access in U.S. public schools and classrooms: 1994–1999.* (NCES No. 2000086). Washington, DC: U.S. Government Printing Office.

Norman, D. A. (1998). *The invisible computer: Why good products can fail, the personal computer is so complex, and information appliances are the solution.* Cambridge, MA: MIT Press.

Roschelle, J., Hoadley, C., Pea, R. Gordin, D., & Means, B. (in press). Changing how and what children learn in school with computer-based technologies. *The Future of Children.*

Scardamalia, M., & Bereiter, C. (1996, November). Engaging students in a knowledge society. *Educational Leadership, 54*(3), 6–10.

White, B. Y., & Frederiksen, J. R. (1998). Inquiry, modeling, and metacognition: Making science accessible to all students. *Cognition and Science, 16,* 90–91.

NO

Jane M. Healy

The Mad Dash to Compute

Ifeel as if we're being swept down this enormous river—we don't know where we're going or why, but we're caught in the current. I think we should stop and take a look before it's too late."

This comment about the use of technology in schools was voiced plaintively by an assistant superintendent from Long Island, N.Y. It was typical of many I collected recently in a three-year investigation of our heavily hyped technological revolution.

Having started this saga as a wide-eyed advocate for educational computing, I now must admit that the school official was right. New technologies hold enormous potential for education, but before any more money is wasted, we must pause and ask some pointed questions that have been bypassed in today's climate of competitive technophilia ("My district's hard drives are bigger than yours!").

Educators, who are seen as one of the ripest growth markets in hardware, software and Internet sales, have been carefully targeted by an industry that understandably wants to convince us that its products will solve all our problems. (Did you ever previously see multiple double-page ads in *Education Week* for any educational product? Have you been offered "free" equipment—that eventually demands as much upkeep and fiscal lifeblood as the man-eating plant in "Little Shop of Horrors?"). The advertising's thrust to both educators and parents is that you should invest in as much technology as early as possible or students will be left hopelessly behind. The parents, failing to appreciate the nonsense inherent in this assumption, in turn put additional pressure on schools to "get with the program."

As educators, we should have the wit to evaluate these pressures, resist public opinion and shun manipulative marketing. It also becomes our obligation to interpret to the public what we know is really good for kids. Yet three major issues are being largely overlooked as we rush to capture the trend. I will call them (1) trade-offs, (2) developmental questions and (3) winners in the long run?

From Jane M. Healy, "The Mad Dash to Compute," *The School Administrator* (April 1999). Copyright © 1999 by The American Association of School Administrators. Reprinted by permission.

The Trade-Offs

During my recent research, which involved visits to dozens of elementary and secondary schools across the United States, I was invited to observe the flagship elementary school of a district that prides itself on the scope of its technology budget. Yet I had difficulty finding students using computers. Many expensive machines were sitting idle (and becoming increasingly obsolete) in classrooms where teachers have not learned to incorporate them into daily lessons. ("When they break, I just don't get them repaired," one 1st-grade teacher confided.)

Finally, in the computer lab, I found 32 5th-grade students lined up at two rows of machines and confronted the following scenario: The technology coordinator—technologically adept but with virtually no background in either teaching or curriculum development—explains that this group comes four times a week to practice reading and math skills. Many students are below grade level in basic skills.

I randomly select a position behind Raoul, who was using a math software program. The director, now occupied in fixing a computer that eager young fingers have crashed, hastily reminds the students to enter the program at the correct level for their ability, but I begin to suspect something is amiss when Raoul effortlessly solves a few simple addition problems and then happily accepts his reward—a series of smash-and-blast games in which he manages to demolish a sizeable number of aliens before he is electronically corralled into another series of computations. Groaning slightly, he quickly solves these problems and segues expertly into the next space battle.

By the time I move on, Raoul has spent many more minutes zapping aliens than he has in doing math. My teacher's soul cringes at the thought of important learning time squandered. I also wonder if what we are really teaching Raoul is that he should choose easy problems so he can play longer or that the only reason to use his brain even slightly is to be granted—by an automaton over which he has no personal control—some mindless fun as a reward. I wonder who selected this software or if any overall plan dictates the implementation of this expensive gadgetry.

Moreover, this computer lab, like so many others, has been morphed from a music room. In this school system, cutbacks in arts, physical education and even textbooks are used to beef up technology budgets.

The trade-offs inherent in this all-too-typical situation should be troubling to all of us:

- *Haste and pressure for electronic glitz.* These should not replace a carefully designed plan based on sound educational practice. Grafting technology onto schools without good curriculum or excellent teaching guarantees failure. First things first.
- *Money on hardware, software and networks instead of essential teacher education.* Informed estimates suggest it takes five years of ongoing in-service training before teachers can fully integrate computer uses into lesson plans. They must also have solid technical support so that instructional time is not spent repairing machines.

- *Technology coordinators without adequate preparation in education.* Rather, the key instructional decisions should be made by teachers who are adept in linking computer use to significant aspects of curriculum. "The 3rd-graders made T-shirts in computer lab today," one techie boasted during one of my school visits. "Why?" I asked. "Well, we can—and besides, the kids just loved it." If this sort of justification prevails in your schools, don't be surprised if your test scores start to drop!

- *Cuts in vital areas used to finance technology purchases.* Computers, which have as yet demonstrated questionable effects on student learning, must not be bought at the expense of proven staples of mental development, such as art, music, drama, debate, physical education, text literacy, manipulatives and hands-on learning aids. One teacher in a Western state told me her district "could be IBM for all the technology we have," yet she was refused money to purchase a set of paperback literature books for her classroom. Why? "The money had all been spent on the machines," she sighed.

- *Pie-in-the-sky assumptions.* Don't be mislead by claims that computers, instead of proven interventions, will remediate basic skills. Many of today's youngsters need solid, hands-on remediation in reading and math delivered by teachers trained in established programs such as Reading Recovery. Don't forget that those "proven studies" about the impact of electronic learning systems and their cost effectiveness were financed by people with products to sell.

- *Installing computers instead of reducing class size.* To my surprise, I found that good technology use is actually more teacher intensive than traditional instruction and works best with smaller classes! Research also is beginning to show the skill/drill software that manages learning for large groups actually may limit students' achievement once the novelty wears off. We need good, objective long-range data before committing money and growing minds to such programs.

- *Funding electronic glitz instead of quality early childhood programs.* Again, we must weigh a large expense of unproven value against proven upstream prevention of academic and social problems. Ironically, estimated costs for connecting all classrooms to the Internet also could provide every child with an adequate preschool program.

- *Time wasted vs. productive learning.* Without good planning and supervision, youngsters tend to use even the best educational programs for mindless fun rather than meaningful learning. Moreover, if you do not have a district policy on selecting software, implement one today. Poorly selected "edutainment" and drill-and-practice programs actually can depress academic gains, whereas well-implemented simulations and conceptually driven programs may improve learning—if a good teacher is in charge.

Engaged Learning

Consider a different scenario that I observed at a middle school in a suburban school district. A small group of 12-year-olds eagerly surround a computer terminal but don't complain about the slightly fuzzy image. They are too busy following the action on the screen where a disheveled-looking young man in bicycling clothes stands in a jungle talking earnestly with someone in a bush jacket who appears to be a scientist.

One of the students giggles, pokes another and attempts a whispered comment, but he is rapidly silenced. "Shush, Damon. Don't be such a jerk. We can't hear!" hisses his neighbor.

What has inspired such serious academic purpose among these kids? They and their teacher are involved in directing (along with others around the globe) a three-month bicycle expedition, manned by a team of cyclists and scientists, through the jungles of Central America in search of lost Mayan civilizations. At the moment, they are debating the possibility of sending the team through a difficult, untravelled jungle track to a special site. How fast can they ride? How far? What obstacles will they encounter? What are the odds of success? What plans must be made?

Like others in a new breed of simulations, this activity uses on-line and satellite phone communications to establish real-time links between students around the world and the adventurers. Because students' votes actually determine the course of the journey, they must problem-solve right along with the scientists. To acquire the necessary knowledge, the class also has plunged into a variety of real-life, hands-on learning: history, archaeology, visual arts, math (e.g., Mayans calculated in base 20), science of flora and fauna, Mayan poetry, building a miniature rain forest, reading the daily journals of the adventurers, researching, developing theories and debating about why the civilization collapsed.

This example is only one of many powerful supplements to a well-planned curriculum. New technologies can be used wisely—or they can be a costly impediment to educational quality. As you debate the trade-offs of your technology choices, you might keep these questions in mind:

1. What can this particular technology do that cannot be accomplished by other less expensive or more proven methods?
2. What will we gain—and what will we lose?
3. How can we sell wise educational decisions to a public foolishly buying the message that computers are a magic bullet for education?

Developmental Questions

A question too rarely considered is what effect extended computer use will have on children's developing bodies and brains. Moreover, it is imperative to ask at what age this technology should really be introduced. My observations have convinced me that normally developing children under age seven are better off without today's computers and software. Technology funds should be first allocated to middle and high schools where computer-assisted learning is much more effective and age-appropriate.

- *Physical effects*: Too little is known about technology's physical effects on digitized youngsters, but troubling evidence of problems resulting from computer use include: vision (e.g., nearsightedness), postural and orthopedic complaints (e.g., neck and back problems; carpal tunnel syndrome), the controversial effects of electromagnetic radiation emitted from the backs and sides of machines and even the rare possibility of seizures triggered by some types of visual displays. Administrators should be on top of this.

  Nonetheless, I found a woeful disregard in schools of even the basic safety rules mandated for the adult workplace. Clear guidelines exist, and before you consign all your 3rd-graders to laptops you would be wise to check the suggestions out.
- *Brain effects:* In terms of what happens to children's cognitive, social and emotional development as a function of computer use, even less is known. The brain is significantly influenced by whatever media we choose for education, and poor choices now may well result in poor thinkers in the next generation.

In my book, *Failure to Connect,* I trace the course of brain development with technology use in mind, and one thing is clear. Computers can either help or hurt the process. For younger children, too much electronic stimulation can become addictive, replacing important experiences during critical periods of development: physical exploration, imaginative play, language, socialization and quiet time for developing attention and inner motivation. For children of any age, improper software choices can disrupt language development, attention, social skills and motivation to use the mind in effortful ways. (The next time you see a classroom of students motivated by computer use, be sure to question whether they are motivated to think and learn—or simply to play with the machines.)

By mid-elementary school, students can start to capitalize on the multimedia and abstract-symbolic capabilities of computers—if an effective teacher is present to guide the learning. For middle and high school students, new technologies can make difficult concepts (e.g., ratio, velocity) more accessible and provide new windows into visual reasoning, creativity and the challenges of research. Yet the first step must still be the filtering process: What is worthwhile in support of the curriculum, and what is merely flashy? Districts that take this job seriously and gear computer use to students' developmental needs are beginning to show real benefits from technology use.

Winners in the Long Run

"Kids need computers to prepare them for the future."

Like so many advertising slogans, this one bears closer examination. First, learning to use a computer today is a poor guarantee of a student's future, since workplace equipment will have changed dramatically for all but our oldest students. Moreover, because so much current use is harming rather than helping students' brain power and learning habits, the computer "have-nots" today actually may end up as the "haves" when future success is parcelled out.

But even more important is the question of what skills will really prepare today's students for the future. Surely the next decades will be ones of rapid change where old answers don't always work, where employers demand communication and human relations skills as well as the ability to think incisively and imagine creative solutions to unforeseen problems. Many of today's computer applications offer poor preparation for such abilities.

One skill of critical importance in a technological future is symbolic analysis, with reading and writing the common entry point. Yet while cyberspace may be filled with words, "a growing portion of the American population will not be able to use, understand or benefit from those words," contend Daniel Burstein and David Kline in their book, *Road Warriors*. "Some of these people may be digitally literate, in that they feel at home with joysticks and remote controls and are perfectly capable of absorbing the sights and sounds of multimedia entertainment. But if you are not functionally literate, your chances of getting a significant piece of the cyberspace pie are slim, even if you have access to it."

Our future workers also will need other abstract-symbolic skills. As the creation of wealth moves farther and farther away from raw materials and hands-on labor, successful workers will need to synthesize information, juggle abstract numbers and acquire multiple-symbol systems in foreign languages, math or the arts; they will also need a familiarity with new digital languages and images. As software design improves, computers will doubtless help with such preparation, but the key will continue to lie in the quality of the teachers who plan, mediate and interpret a thoughtful curriculum.

The future also will favor those who have learned how to learn, who can respond flexibly and creatively to challenges and master new skills. At the moment, the computer is a shallow and pedantic companion for such a journey. We should think long and carefully about whether our purpose is to be trendy or to prepare students to be intelligent, reasoning human beings whose skills extend far beyond droid-like button clicking.

If we ourselves cannot think critically about the hard sell vs. the real business of schooling, we can hardly expect our students to do so.

POSTSCRIPT

Should Technology Lead the Quest for Better Schools?

Afew years ago educational reformer John I. Goodlad declared that "school" should be considered a concept rather than a place and that this formulation would seem to be an appropriate keynote for education in the twenty-first century. Certainly, advocates of computerization and global networking would be comfortable with the idea. But today, as more school systems are being "wired," questions of initial cost, hardware obsolescence, variable availability, software quality and appropriateness, teacher reluctance, and productive utilization remain to be discussed and resolved.

Help in exploring these and related questions may be found in Gary Kidd's "Using the Internet as a School," *The Educational Forum* (Spring 1996); "Unfilled Promises," by Jane McDonald, William Lynch, and Greg Kearsley, *The American School Board Journal* (July 1996); Frederick Bennett's *Computers as Tutors* (1999); Leon Botstein's "A Brave New World?" *The School Administrator* (March 2001); Craig A. Cunningham's "Improving Our Nation's Schools Through Computers and Connectivity," *Brookings Review* (Winter 2001); R. W. Burniske's "When Computer Literacy Goes Too Far," *Phi Delta Kappan* (March 2001); and Frederick Bennett's "The Future of Computer Technology in K-12 Education," *Phi Delta Kappan* (April 2002). The April 1996 issue of *The School Administrator* contains a number of articles on such topics as Internet access and technology's usefulness in the inclusion of disabled students. Other journal issues devoted to the controversy include *Educational Leadership* (November 1997), *Thrust for Educational Leadership* (May 1997), *Contemporary Education* (Winter 1997), *NASSP Bulletin* (November 1997), *Theory Into Practice* (Winter 1998), *The School Administrator* (April 1999), *NASSP Bulletin* (May 1999 and September 1999), *Principal* (January 2000), *The Futurist* (March–April 2000), *Educational Leadership* (October 2000), *Kappa Delta Pi Record* (Fall 2000), *American Educator* (Fall 2001), *The School Administrator* (October 2001), and *NASSP Bulletin* (November 2001).

Finally, educational psychologist Richard P. Lookatch has argued that multimedia use in school offers students the opportunity to interact with the images behind a glass screen, but the looming danger is that it replaces students' interaction with each other and their environment.

ISSUE 20

Is Mandatory Community Service Desirable and Legal?

YES: James C. Kielsmeier, from "A Time to Serve, a Time to Learn: Service-Learning and the Promise of Democracy," *Phi Delta Kappan* (May 2000)

NO: Institute for Justice, from "'Compulsory Volunteering': Constitutional Challenges to Mandatory Community Service," *Litigation Backgrounder* (1994)

ISSUE SUMMARY

YES: James C. Kielsmeier, president of the National Youth Leadership Council, depicts service-learning as a crucial component for citizenship and a fulfillment of John Dewey's "involvement in real-world activities" goal.

NO: The Institute for Justice, a nonprofit, public-interest law center in Washington, D.C., argues that government-mandated service is unconstitutional and negates the spirit of voluntarism.

In recent years governmental action at the state and national levels has aimed to generate altruism among America's youth through programs of community service. State and local policymakers have added new high school graduation requirements that stipulate the completion of a given number of community service hours. At the federal level, Congress has passed the National and Community Service Trust Act of 1993 (P.L. 103–82), a reauthorization of P.L. 101–610, passed in 1990, and the Domestic Volunteer Service Act. The new legislation, which was strongly promoted by President Bill Clinton, established the Corporation for National and Community Service "to engage Americans of all ages and backgrounds in community-based service" in order to deal with the nation's "education, human, public safety, and environmental needs" while fostering civic responsibility and providing educational opportunity for those who make a substantial contribution to service. Although participation is not compulsory, the federal effort is being driven by the same principles that are animating the more binding state and local programs. The administration of

George W. Bush has extended and expanded the federal effort with the USA Freedom Corps and subsidiary units.

Supporters of state-mandated community service echo the Aristotelian sentiment "We become just by doing just acts." Kathleen Kennedy Townsend, executive director of the Maryland Student Service Alliance, contends that "required service is the best strategy for graduating smart, thoughtful, and committed citizens. Without a requirement whether a student becomes involved in service activities depends on happenstance. With a requirement all young people will learn that they can be effective and powerful, that they can solve problems, and that helping others can be enjoyable." Roland MacNichol, a teacher, contends that service learning is "the right thing to do in helping make our schools thoughtful, caring places with strong belief systems based on service and on young people making a difference."

The movement, however, is not without its detractors. Williamson Evers, for example, argues that students who are not up to grade level in math should not be spending time in a mandatory service program, that a "service learning" program gives teachers a license to instill partisan doctrines, and that the movement is "a chintzy way for politicians to get cheap labor out of young people." Evers further argues that the program's coercion aspect takes the spirit of generosity out of service.

Lawsuits stemming from mandatory service programs have been initiated in a number of localities, including Chapel Hill, North Carolina; Mamaroneck, New York; and Bethlehem, Pennsylvania. The legal challengers have held that mandatory, uncompensated service violates the constitutional prohibition against involuntary servitude and that the policy intrudes improperly on parental responsibility. On October 8, 1996, the U.S. Supreme Court ruled on the Mamaroneck case. Rejecting the "involuntary servitude" argument, the Court found that the school system's requirement of 40 hours of community service for high school graduation was constitutionally valid.

Harry C. Boyte, director of Project Public Life, argues that community service programs, which are widely touted as the cure for young people's political apathy, in fact teach little about the art of participation in public life. In "Learning to Serve," *American School Board Journal* (November 2000), Lottie L. Joiner raises questions about the activities students choose to meet service requirements.

Other views on the issue are expressed in a variety of articles in the October 1997 *NASSP Bulletin* and the Summer 1997 *Theory Into Practice,* as well as in "Learning Through Community Service Is Political," by Bird L. Jones, Robert W. Maloy, and Charlotte M. Steen, *Equity and Excellence in Education* (September 1996) and "Service Learning: Facilitating Learning and Character Development," by Shelly Schaefer Hinck and Mary Ellen Brandell, *NASSP Bulletin* (October 1999).

In the following selections, James C. Kielsmeier details the organizations and activities that he feels make service-learning valuable and necessary. The Institute for Justice, which has provided legal support for those who have challenged the constitutionality of mandatory service programs, maintains that the decision to serve others is not a choice that should be made by the state.

James C. Kielsmeier  **YES**

A Time to Serve, a Time to Learn

A new partner has stepped boldly forward to help shoulder the burden of improving schools and communities. That partner is the young people themselves. And service-learning, a way of teaching and learning that engages students in active service tied to curriculum, can transform the idealism of youth into a powerful force for educational change and democratic renewal.

At every level of schooling, youth participation in service is at an all-time high. Distrustful of politicians and adversarial politics, young people are the vanguard of a new politics of participation and voluntary service. Fueled largely by renewed interest in national service and citizenship, the service-learning movement demands nothing less than reconceptualizing the role of young people in modern democratic societies, particularly in the context of schooling.

By engaging actively as citizens, students today shed the passive mantle of dependence for the more active roles of contribution and influence. Because students involved in service-learning are expected to solve tangible problems and share responsibility for teaching, they discover for themselves key elements that are largely missing in the school reform debate: meaning and purpose. Service-learning also challenges the existing roles of teachers, parents, and other members of communities by demanding new levels of involvement and shared responsibility.

Voting With Their Feet

The growing commitment of young people to contribute voluntarily to larger issues through service is well documented. In 1995, Independent Sector reported that 59% of teenagers volunteered an estimated 3.5 hours per week and that a staggering 93% of those who volunteered did so when asked.[1] These figures are comparable to the findings of the 1996 National Household Education Survey, conducted by the U.S. Department of Education's Office of Educational Research and Improvement, which found that 49% of students in grades 6 to 12 in public and private schools participated in community service during the 1995–96 school year. Of the students volunteering, 86% were in schools that endorsed volunteer service by requiring participation or by arranging the opportunities.

From James C. Kielsmeier, "A Time to Serve, a Time to Learn: Service-Learning and the Promise of Democracy," *Phi Delta Kappan* (May 2000). Copyright © 2000 by Phi Delta Kappa International, Inc. Reprinted by permission. Some references omitted.

Moreover, there was little difference between the participation rates of those required to serve and those who chose to do so. "The most important factor was whether schools arranged participation in community service."[2] In other words, if students understood that they were needed and were asked to help, they volunteered.

A follow-up survey on community service and service-learning, conducted by the U.S. Department of Education in 1999 and co-sponsored by the Corporation for National Service, found that 83% of high schools offered some type of community service. Overall, 64% of K–12 public and private schools had students participating in service that was recognized or arranged by the school. Once again, this survey found that, if the schools asked, the students responded. These findings contrast sharply with those of a 1984 survey of community service in high schools, conducted at the University of Wisconsin, which found that only 27% of all high schools, public and private, offered community-service options to students.[3]

Since 1966, an annual nationwide survey of freshmen has been conducted by the Higher Education Research Institute at UCLA. It regularly measures the level of service activity in high school, as reported by freshmen newly arrived on college campuses. The 1999 survey reported that 75.3% of freshmen, the highest figure ever, reported having been involved in community service in their senior year of high school, up from 74.2% in 1998. In 1997, 73.1% of incoming freshmen reported having volunteered in high school, while in 1989 just 62% said they had volunteered. The survey results show that more and more students are volunteering, even though only 21.3% of them attended high schools that require community service for graduation. According to the study's director, Linda Sax, "These findings suggest that the majority of students who engage in volunteer work do so of their own volition."[4]

College students surveyed by the Mellman Group in 1999 about their current involvement in service reported a high level of volunteer activity on campus; 73% indicated doing service in the areas of helping the homeless, teaching, the environment, and health care. However, the students' enthusiasm for service was not matched by equal enthusiasm for traditional politics. According to a news story on the survey, "They found more immediate rewards from volunteering than in political activity."[5] Another 1999 study, this one conducted by the Boys and Girls Clubs of America, reported that only 10% of the 13- to 18-year-olds who were questioned believed that "engaging in the political system is an effective way to make change."[6]

Creative educators find a link between the burgeoning of youth service and the largely dormant principles of progressive education and project-based learning that were espoused by such educators as John Dewey, Jerome Bruner, and Ralph Tyler.[7] Clearly the conceptual roots of service-learning can be found in the progressive tradition and in its constructivist kin. But the movement has gained new impetus from the evolving idea of nonmilitary national service and from the creation by the Bush Administration of the Commission on National and Community Service in 1990, followed by the Clinton Administration's creation of the Corporation for National Service (CNS).

Citizen Service

The 1990 National and Community Service Act redefined federally supported national service by including school-based service-learning along with funding for full-time service. The inclusion of a school-based component resulted from a compromise by Sen. Edward Kennedy (D-Mass.) and Sen. David Durenberger (R-Minn.). In Minnesota, Vermont, Maryland, Massachusetts, and Pennsylvania, state service-learning initiatives were already taking form. Thus Sen. Durenberger pressed for funds for service-learning, based on advocacy by Minnesotans. Sen. Kennedy later noted that "service-learning should be a central component of current efforts to reform education."[8]

In a similar effort to include service-learning provisions in 1993 legislation, Sen. Durenberger said, "In fact, the ultimate purpose of this bill is to make every community in America a classroom and an environment in which the talents and energies of our youngest citizens can be fully engaged and fully appreciated."[9]

Although within the CNS service-learning has been overshadowed by AmeriCorps, since 1993 funding of approximately $40 million per year and President Clinton's rock-solid support for CNS have created a relatively stable base for school-based service-learning. Funds are allotted, based on population, to officers of the Learn and Serve America program in departments of education in every state, and the states then dispense the resources competitively. This consistent state involvement has raised awareness of and generated additional funding for service-learning.

Fostering active citizenship among young people is by far the most commonly mentioned rationale for service-learning. Support for this view has been strengthened by the decline among young people in some indices of citizenship, particularly voting rates. Just 32% of 18- to 24-year-olds voted in the 1996 election, while 67% of people over 65 went to the polls. Voting rates for young adults have declined steadily since 1972, when 18-year-olds got the right to vote. By contrast, nearly 75% of young adults volunteered in the last two years.[10]

There are consistent reports that service-learning has had short-term impacts on the civic attitudes of students, but these results have faded over time, causing Brandeis University researcher Alan Melchior to note, "Put simply, there is little evidence that short-term, one-time involvement in even a well-designed service-learning program is likely to produce substantial long-term benefits."[11]

When the National Youth Leadership Council (NYLC) was just forming some 15 years ago, we banked heavily on a highly experiential residential camp experience to prepare high school students to engage in service when they returned home. For some students, the experience was life changing, but for most, like the students studied by the Brandeis team, there was not much lasting impact. This disappointing message came from students who found little receptivity to their ideas back in their home schools. This recognition started NYLC on the road to linking the service experience to school reform through staff development, curriculum design, and advocacy for state and national service integrated in the schools.

National service today is not a single federal program but a national purpose that starts with service-learning in school and ties in with community-based youth development organizations and with higher education. Opportunities for a year or more of full-time service, such as AmeriCorps, then lead to a series of adult volunteer options.

If the CNS seeks to accomplish its mission of inculcating an ethic of service into the fabric of American life, it must carefully examine and upgrade the resources and direction it provides its department of service-learning. Indeed, it is only through K–12 education that all citizens can be reached—and reached during a most formative period of their lives. For example, approximately half of the 20,000 AmeriCorps members work with school-age youngsters. Most tutor or supervise students during parts of the day when teachers are not involved in instruction. Why not equip AmeriCorps members to be service-learning coordinators and so seek to replicate an ethic of service in the young people with whom they work?

A highly effective development in linking national service and education is a joint declaration on the relationship between service and learning, signed originally in 1995 by Secretary of Education Richard Riley and Eli Segal, then CEO of the CNS. *The Declaration of Principles* was reaffirmed in 1999 by Secretary Riley and the current CEO of the CNS, Harris Wofford.... This well-developed rationale can be the basis for similar connections between the worlds of service and of learning at the state and local levels.

Notable initiatives in the private sector also support service-learning as an instrument for developing active citizens. In 1999 the W. K. Kellogg Foundation began a four-year, $13-million investment to infuse service-learning into K–12 education. A multidimensional effort, Learning In Deed consists of demonstration projects in five states, a national commission, a network of collaborating organizations, and a research group. This latest Kellogg initiative builds on the foundation's record over the past 11 years of investing more than $23 million in service-learning. A major partner in the Kellogg initiative is the Compact for Learning and Citizenship (CLC), a project of the Education Commission of the States. The CLC is a membership organization of state and local superintendents who are committed to supporting service-learning through policy initiatives.

Education Common

A compelling and particularly hopeful dimension of today's service-learning movement is its reach into all sectors of American society. Student-driven and locally flavored service-learning is a coalescing force for the cornucopia of American ethnic, spiritual, and cultural diversity. It offers a pathway of knowing and being that touches students of every background. Along with the progressive heirs of [John] Dewey, who brought their innovative insights largely from a European American perspective, there is a new wave of service-learning leaders of every heritage who shape current practice and theory.[12]

For example, when a group of eighth-graders from the Academy of Science and Foreign Language Middle School in Huntsville, Alabama, were touring the Maple Hill Cemetery, their questions brought the tour to a complete halt.

After hearing thorough biographical descriptions of the many important 19th-century citizens of Huntsville who were buried in the cemetery, the students asked if any of them were African American.[13] The guide did not know, and the answer, discovered later, was that this beautifully maintained resting place for Civil War veterans, former governors, and other upstanding individuals was for "whites only."

After the cemetery episode, the students and teachers of the Academy, an NYLC "Generator School,"[14] set off on a journey to discover where Huntsville's African Americans from the last century were buried. Along the way, they learned a great deal more. They found Glenwood Cemetery, a resting place for African Americans, in a deplorable state, with unmarked graves, vandalized headstones, and poorly kept records. They also found an equally unrecorded larger history that would have remained forgotten had not students and teachers launched a project that has changed the community.

Teachers at the Academy responded to the interest of students and found answers to many questions, including one that is left out of most classrooms: "What are we going to do about it?" The answer to that question was the creation of the Alabama African American History Project and a dazzling array of community contributions and learning experiences.

Students subsequently led the restoration of Glenwood Cemetery, raising funds to replace or repair 166 headstones. They also saw to it that the state placed an official registry sign at the cemetery. Math classes platted the previously unmapped site, using resources donated by the University of Alabama. The students' concern about the neglect of Glenwood Cemetery led them to ask state legislators to change a state law that related to preservation of cemeteries. This project, now tied to government classes, is still under way.

The young people "scoured court records; city council minutes; deeds, marriage certificates, and wills; family inventories; and *The Negro Gazette*, a locally published newspaper from the 1800s. They also listened to and recorded oral histories."[15] Curricular materials developed by the middle-schoolers from original historical sources are now the basis of a third-grade social studies unit about the history of Huntsville. Over the years, the students have also published several books based on their research on prominent African Americans of the area.

Joel Gabre, a seventh-grader, took a particular interest in the life of John Thomas Moore, an African American veteran of the Union Army from Huntsville. Moore had received a dishonorable discharge at the close of the war through an apparent administrative error. Joel met with Moore's grandson, Lawrence Jacobs, age 83, who had tried and failed to reverse the ruling on his grandfather. At last report, Joel is still working on the project, petitioning officials in Washington to clear the name of John Thomas Moore.

Teachers and students from the Academy present their findings annually at state and national conferences. This year they presented their work with a group of educators from Harvard University at the National Service-Learning Conference in Providence, Rhode Island. What's more, students want similar opportunities through service-learning when they reach high school, according to Ollye Conley, principal of the Academy. "They pulled the principal of Lee

High School aside" at orientation and asked if they could continue with the service-learning approach they had used at the Academy.[16] According to Conley, at the request of Lee High School, the Academy will consult next year with the high school about starting a service-learning program there. The support for questioning and critical thinking that began at Maple Hill Cemetery could well continue for the middle-schoolers as they begin their high school careers—and perhaps for some time beyond that.

Service-learning is the equivalent of an "education common"—a pedagogical meeting place whose origins and principles are shared by a wide range of American and international cultural communities. The eighth-graders from Huntsville who reclaimed the desolated cemeteries in order to honor their forebears are active citizens today. So too are the sons and daughters of Northern European descent from Hill City, Minnesota, who interviewed local military veterans in preparation for building a community memorial.[17] Similarly, students in Hudson, Massachusetts, within miles of Walden Pond, evoke the transcendental musings of Thoreau as they help preserve a wetland,[18] while children of the Acoma Pueblo, New Mexico, integrate modern ecology with ancestral agricultural practices.[19] Service-learning is a particularly American way of learning, embracing democratic practices and the dignity of all members of the learning community.

Quality Practice

The service-learning of today has new leadership and is driven by a multicultural point of view and by a movement toward national "citizen service." With its new-found visibility, the bars of expectation and accountability have been raised. Moreover, the dismissive comment that service-learning has become a mile wide but just an inch deep strikes a note of truth. While the route to education reform through service-learning is evolving, it nonetheless has a few "north star" principles for guidance. The path to sustainability, according to the recently convened Kellogg Foundation Learning In Deed stakeholders' group, must include emphasis on well-defined practice, staff development, preservice training for teachers, and better research.

If the movement toward service-learning is to maintain the highest standards of practice and grow in a sustainable fashion, it must forgo the strategy of blanket expansion through mandated service requirements and other top-down approaches. But such a policy will require patience. Moreover, the acceleration of service-learning participation from an estimated 81,000 high school students in 1984 to 2.9 million in 1999 is real[20] and suggests a pattern of growth that could threaten sustainability if staff development does not keep pace. New research reveals a close association between achieving intended results and adherence to standards.[21] Hands-on, site-based, student-centered service-learning demands a high level of teacher investment and administrative support: it's not for every class or for every school.

Just what does constitute effective practice? Are teachers and schools prepared to take service-learning seriously by viewing young people as contributors to teaching and learning? Let's consider these questions as we listen to students and their teachers.

Coolly clinical, Andrea (not her real name) looked me in the eye across the conference table with the unqualified authority of an expert. "Fetal Alcohol Syndrome (FAS) and Fetal Alcohol Effect (FAE) are the number-one causes of mental retardation and completely preventable," she carefully explained. "They have warning labels on beer bottles, but nobody reads them. I know I didn't."

Andrea isn't a health professional; she has more compelling credentials for teaching me and others about the effects of alcohol on unborn and nursing children. Andrea is a 16-year-old mother and a member of an instructional team of peers who last fall made presentations on the impact of and prevention strategies for FAS/FAE to more than 15 student groups throughout a two-county area near Minneapolis. Andrea's class of 20 students volunteered to take on a variety of roles in delivering their health program: in addition to giving the presentations, they created brochures using desktop publishing and promoted their project through public service announcements in English and Spanish on local radio stations.

The teacher and a public health nurse, who team-teach the class, reported that more than three-quarters of the young mothers in this special high school admit to having used either drugs or alcohol at the time of conception. They had no idea of the potential impact alcohol could have on their children. According to the students I spoke with, the same is true of the high school students they encounter during presentations. "They listen to us," emphasized Carmen, a soft-spoken young woman who also made the radio announcements in Spanish, her first language. "And I'm not drinking again. It's not worth it," she volunteered matter-of-factly.

Fortunately, the lead teacher at the school had taken a graduate course on service-learning at the University of Minnesota, where she saw how hands-on learning with a giving dimension could be linked to well-defined learning objectives. The students earned English, science, and government credits as they wrote, researched, and presented their insights to small classes, full gymnasiums, and even larger radio audiences. Reflection activities included papers and discussion, as well as personal portfolios based on Minnesota's new performance-based assessment requirements.

Service-learning starts with the presupposition that the primary purpose of education can no longer be socialization, standardization, and synchronization—the shaping of students into clearly defined roles for a predictable future. Rather, in a world marked by pluralism, uncertainty, and variability, we need to move from the idea of students as receptacles, merely receiving deposits of information from teachers, to students as creators, disseminators, and implementers of knowledge.[22] What we need are learning communities in which participants both learn and teach, lead and serve. Students as teachers! Adults as learners![23] Service-learning is a philosophy of education that acknowledges that students who are actively building a health unit around a highly charged personal issue are much more likely to delve deeply into content than those merely doing textbook exercises.

Service-learning appeals to educators as a credible method of teaching because it addresses the need for students to achieve academically and personally in a project-based way that can be a terrific motivator.[24] The levels of student involvement and learning through service have a great deal to do with students' desire to contribute and whether or not they have a voice in selecting the project. The Minnesota students, for example, had a choice of several roles, including writing a brochure, editing the video version of their FAS/FAE presentation, or filling several other needs.

We have come to understand that students are more invested in their learning and so more likely to learn when they understand that their service or public work is authentic, has substance over time, and can be understood in the context of academic or civic content.[25] In other words, the act of service is perceived to be "real," not a simulation or "feel-good" act of charity that primarily benefits the student. Instead, the contribution is necessary and requires a high level of personal investment; it becomes a conscious act of citizenship.[26]

The fetal alcohol service-learning unit was neither a casual encounter with a topic nor a one-time "service project." These young mothers, struggling with a tangle of personal issues and diminished societal expectations, were fighting to be heard, to contribute where they were deeply invested emotionally: in the health of children.

As students enter classrooms to teach other students, as they research their past and make contributions to history, as they bring visibility and change to an environmental issue, they are citizens today—not just the promise of tomorrow.

References

1. *America's Teenage Volunteers* (Washington, D.C.: Independent Sector, 1996).
2. See National Center for Education Statistics, *Statistical Analysis Report: Student Participation in Community Service Activity* (Washington, D.C.: U.S. Department of Education, 1997), p. 28.
3. National Center for Education Statistics, *Statistics in Brief: Service-Learning and Community Service in K-12 Public Schools* (Washington, D.C.: U.S. Department of Education, September 1999); and Fred M. Newmann and Robert A. Rutter, "A Profile of High School Community Service Programs," *Educational Leadership*, December 1985/January 1986, pp. 64–71.
4. Linda J. Sax et al., *The American Freshman: National Norms for Fall 1999* (Los Angeles: Higher Education Research Institute, UCLA, 1999), Press Summary, p. 2.
5. Adam Clymer, "College Students Not Drawn to Politics," *New York Times*, 11 January 2000.
6. *Youth Today: What Teens Tell Teens, Bridge to Next Century Survey* (Atlanta, Ga.: Boys and Girls Clubs of America, February 2000), p. 11.
7. Dan Conrad and Diane Hedin, "School-Based Community Service: What We Know from Research and Theory," *Phi Delta Kappan*, June 1991, pp. 743–49; and Richard J. Kraft, "Service-Learning: An Introduction to Its Theory, Practice, and Effects," *Education and Urban Society*, February 1996, pp. 131–35.
8. Sen. Edward M. Kennedy, "National Service and Education for Citizenship," *Phi Delta Kappan*, June 1991, p. 772.
9. Sen. David Durenberger, "Service-Learning Act of 1993," *Congressional Record*, 30 March 1993.
10. Lori Lessner, "Most Young Adults Turned Off to Politics, Don't Bother to Vote," *St. Paul Pioneer Press*, 30 January 2000, p. 3-A.

11. Alan Melchior, "Impact on Youth and Communities," *State Education Leader*, Fall 1999, p. 6.
12. McClellan Hall, "Gadugi: A Model of Service-Learning for Native American Communities," *Phi Delta Kappan*, June 1991, pp. 754–57; and Wokie Weah, Verna Cornelia Simmons, and McClellan Hall, "Service-Learning and Multicultural/ Multiethnic Perspectives," *Phi Delta Kappan*, May 2000, pp. 673–75.
13. Olleye B. Conley, National Service-Learning Leader School Application, Academy for Science and Foreign Language, Huntsville, Ala., 3 February 2000, p. 2.
14. Sandra Montgomery and Deborah West, "The Alabama African American History Project," *The Generator*, Winter 2000, p. 9.
15. Conley, p. 3.
16. Interview with Olleye B. Conley, 28 February 2000.
17. Personal correspondence with Lin Benson, 25 February 2000.
18. Sheldon Berman, "Integrating Service-Learning with School Culture," *Service-Learning Network*, Constitutional Rights Foundation, Los Angeles, Calif., Spring 1999, pp. 1–5.
19. *Essential Elements of Service-Learning* (St. Paul: National Service-Learning Cooperative, National Youth Leadership Council, April 1998).
20. Robert Shumer, *The Status of Service-Learning in the United States* (St. Paul: National Service-Learning Clearinghouse, University of Minnesota, 1999).
21. *Essential Elements of Service-Learning*.
22. Ruthanne Kurth-Schai, "The Roles of Youth in Society: A Reconceptualization," *Educational Forum*, Winter 1988, pp. 113–32.
23. Michelle Collay et al., *Learning Circles: Creating Conditions for Professional Development* (Thousand Oaks, Calif.: Corwin Press, 1998), pp. 31–61; and Paulo Freire, *Pedagogy of the Oppressed* (New York: Seabury Press, 1973).
24. National Center for Education Statistics, *Statistics in Brief*, p. 10.
25. Peter Scales and Dale A. Blyth, "Effects of Service-Learning on Youth: What We Know and What We Need to Know," *The Generator*, Winter 1997, pp. 6–9.
26. Harry C. Boyte and Nan Skelton, "The Legacy of Public Work: Educating for Citizenship," *Educational Leadership*, February 1997, pp. 12–17.

Institute for Justice

"Compulsory Volunteering": Constitutional Challenges to Mandatory Community Service

Introduction

Ninth-grader Aric Herndon of Chapel Hill, North Carolina will soon receive his Eagle Scout award. He faithfully serves the Chapel Hill community through his work on Scout-sponsored projects and merit badge requirements.

But Aric may not graduate from high school—not because of any academic failings, but because he does not conform to the Chapel Hill School District's ideal of model citizenship. The community service that Aric performs for the Boy Scouts does not qualify for credit under the school district's new mandatory community service program. In the school district's judgment, since Aric receives an independent "benefit" from his service, such as an award or merit badge, the work does not rise to the level of "true" and selfless community service.

The Chapel Hill School District's twisted logic exemplifies the growing number of public schools around the country that require community service as a condition of graduation. Approximately 21 percent of public schools surveyed impose some type of community service requirement while an additional 10 percent will implement programs in the next year.[1] Like many other mandatory community service plans, the Chapel Hill program requires high school students to "serve" 50 hours in the community as a condition of graduation. The work must be performed after school hours, on weekends, or over summer vacation, and the students cannot receive compensation for their services.

Rye Neck High School in Mamaroneck, New York similarly conditions the receipt of a high school diploma on students performing 40 hours of labor in the community. Daniel Immediato, a student at Rye Neck, currently does not perform community service as defined by the school. Although Daniel does not object to helping others, he instead works as a lifeguard at a public pool and contributes to the modest earnings of the family. Daniel's lifeguarding, while

From Institute for Justice, " 'Compulsory Volunteering': Constitutional Challenges to Mandatory Community Service," *Litigation Backgrounder* (1994). Copyright © 1994 by The Institute for Justice. Reprinted by permission.

certainly a service to the community, does not count toward the community service requirement since he receives compensation for his work.

Regardless of whether Aric or Daniel's community service qualified for credit, the students and their parents believe that the decision to serve others must come from within, not through government edict. The parents fundamentally object to their sons being forced to participate in a government-created program intended to inculcate a sense of obligation to the community. So they have joined other families in challenging the constitutionality of mandatory community service.

On April 19, 1994, the Institute for Justice will file two lawsuits challenging mandatory community service for public high school students in Chapel Hill and Mamaroneck as a violation of constitutional rights.

The issue of mandatory community service raises important and fundamental questions about the obligations of individuals in a free society to serve others and the role of the government in determining what individuals owe to the "community." The question of whether students can be drafted into a government-mandated community service program goes directly to the heart of the Institute for Justice's commitment to individual liberty and to the principle that voluntarism, not government coercion, is the basis of a free society.

The National Fight Against Mandatory Community Service

Mandatory community service was first challenged in a lawsuit filed in 1990 by the Steirer and Moralis families in Bethlehem, Pennsylvania.[2] Lynn Steirer pioneered the fight against mandatory community service. An avid volunteer and now a senior at Liberty High School in Bethlehem, Lynn compellingly captures the unintended consequences of coerced community service: "People should volunteer because they want to, not because of a government threat. So many kids who do this treat it like a joke; they do the minimum to get the credit."[3]

The lawsuit was unsuccessful in the lower courts and last summer, when the families' resources were exhausted, the Institute for Justice took on their case. The Institute filed a petition for certiorari in the U.S. Supreme Court, which declined to hear the case. This result was not surprising as the Court often lets issues ripen for several years in multiple court cases before addressing them.

The Third Circuit Court of Appeal's ruling in the *Steirer* case emboldened school districts nationwide. More and more school districts now condition the receipt of a high school diploma on students performing community service. And students are not the only targets for the "mandatory volunteering" juggernaut. The Tulsa, Oklahoma school district, citing the *Steirer* opinion as authority, wants to adopt a community service requirement not only for students, but for their parents as well. Under the proposed plan, if the parents do not perform the service, the students do not graduate.

Many community service advocates view mandatory programs as necessary to counter what they perceive as excessive selfishness and materialism in young people today. Recent polls, however, debunk the myth of selfish and lazy youths: a surprising six out of ten 12- to 17-year-olds volunteer their time to others.[4] This outpouring of good will and voluntarism on the part of today's youth counts for naught among community service proponents. Kathleen Kennedy Townsend, one of the most outspoken advocates of the first state-wide service program in Maryland, declared, "You don't choose to do good unless you learn to do good. A lot of people who are forced to do something learn to like it."[5]

In 1993, Maryland imposed the first statewide community service requirement, covering nearly 200,000 public high school students. Much public discussion and debate surrounded the adoption of Maryland's program. Indeed, all but one of Maryland's local school districts adamantly opposed the state-wide program. Because of the outcry by the public and school officials alike, the state board of education granted local schools broad discretion to craft their own programs. As a result, the local school districts in Maryland do not aggressively enforce this new graduation requirement.

Even with local school officials' unenthusiastic acceptance and enforcement of mandatory community service, the Maryland program already exhibits one of the most disturbing aspects of school-sponsored community service: the increasing politicization of programs and service opportunities. The Maryland program teaches that political activism is the highest form of community service.[6] Even the promotional posters for community service produced by the Maryland Department of Education demonstrate the overt emphasis upon political action as a means of solving community problems. One poster depicts a student climbing the mountain of community service. On each layer of the mountain is a type of community service. At the pinnacle of the mountain, above such service as caring for the sick and the aged, rests the form of service Maryland deems most important: lobbying. Another poster shows students in the service program demonstrating outside Maryland's capital for greater public education funding.

Unlike the heated controversy surrounding the Maryland program, the Chapel Hill School District unceremoniously imposed its mandatory community service requirement with little fanfare and seemingly no public discussion. The school district merely notified parents of this great expansion of government power through a letter sent at the beginning of the 1993–94 school year. However, two families in Chapel Hill refused to accept the school district's new intrusion into their lives and have instead joined in a constitutional challenge to mandatory community service.

Several years ago, the Rye Neck School District in Mamaroneck, New York imposed community service after many far wealthier school districts in Westchester County adopted service requirements. Compulsory community service typically exists in public schools with privileged children from wealthy families. Families in Rye Neck, however, have more modest incomes and struggle to provide a good education for their children. Also, many students in Rye Neck, including the Institute's clients, work part-time after school and contribute to the family income. Not surprisingly, these families want their children to concentrate on their studies, rather than be subjected to experiments requiring children to engage in out-of-school activities the authorities deem good for them.

The Institute's new challenges to mandatory community service aim to prevent the dilemma now confronting Bethlehem students Lynn Steirer and David Moralis as their senior year draws to a close. They must either participate in a program that violates their fundamental beliefs about the nature of helping others, or not receive a crucial stepping stone to success in life: a high school diploma. No student should have to face this Hobson's choice in the future.

Litigation Strategy

The Institute challenges the Chapel Hill and Rye Neck coerced service programs under the 13th Amendment's guarantee against involuntary servitude and the Ninth and 14th Amendment rights to parental liberty and due process of law.... While a 13th Amendment claim was raised in the Bethlehem case, a 14th Amendment challenge to mandatory community service has thus far not been presented to a court. With the filing of these lawsuits in the Fourth and Second U.S. Circuit Courts of Appeal, the Institute seeks a "circuit split" among the federal appellate courts, thereby increasing the chances of Supreme Court review.

It is widely known that the 13th Amendment banned the institution of slavery throughout the United States. However, the amendment also prohibits "involuntary servitude," except as punishment for a crime. While slavery involves the ownership and complete control of one individual by another, the U.S. Supreme Court defines involuntary servitude as a "condition of enforced compulsory service of one to another."[7] Mandatory community service programs fit this definition by requiring students to work for others against their will without compensation. The requirement for providing free labor to others, either organizations or individuals, distinguishes service programs from other mandatory school activities, such as gym classes, chemistry labs, and so on.

The Third Circuit Court of Appeals in the *Steirer* case virtually admitted that the program constituted a textbook definition of servitude. However, the court decided to ignore the constitutional text and instead opted for a "contextual" approach to the 13th Amendment. Furthermore, the court held that even if the program was a form of servitude, it was not "involuntary" because students had the "option" of quitting school, going to a private school, or receiving their G.E.D. Logically, this ruling means that the 13th Amendment has no applicability to the public school setting. Under the court's reasoning, public schools could require any type of student labor, from building a new addition to the school to mowing the lawns of school board members, and the students could not raise a claim under the 13th Amendment because they could always leave the public schools. The Institute's new challenges to coerced community service place this unprecedented holding directly at issue.

The 14th Amendment guarantees to parents the right to direct and control the upbringing and education of their children. The U.S. Supreme Court recognized this important right in two landmark U.S. Supreme Court cases: *Meyer v. Nebraska*[8] and *Pierce v. Society of Sisters*.[9] The Court held in those cases that certain "ideas touching the relation of the individual and the state [are] wholly different from those upon which our institutions rest" and do "violence to both the letter and spirit of the Constitution."[10] The decision to help others under our system of law has always been left to the conscience of the individual and to the moral education of children by parents. Programs that require service to others are foreign to the relationship between the individual and the state under the U.S. Constitution and the *Meyer* and *Pierce* cases.

Courts have consistently held that in public schools, mere exposure to ideas or beliefs with which parents disagree does not normally give rise to a constitutional violation.[11] However, when public schools require students to *act* on the basis of those values or beliefs, especially outside of the public school setting, constitutional limits apply. For instance, while public schools can teach the values of thrift and the importance of saving money, could schools require students as a condition of graduation to save a certain percentage of any money they earned? To stress the importance of abstinence to students, could schools require them to sign a pledge stating that they will remain virgins until they graduate? To underscore the importance of participating in our democratic system, could schools condition graduation on proof that students voted in the first election in which they were eligible?

All of the above-described programs would no doubt raise very serious constitutional concerns since in each instance the government intrudes into areas that have always been left to the private domain of individuals and to the relationship between parents and their children. Moreover, mandatory community service programs require students to act in programs that directly clash with their parents' fundamental belief that the decision to help others must be a voluntary one and cannot be imposed by the state.

Under the *Meyer* and *Pierce* cases, intrusion by the government into the relationship between parent and child requires a showing of a compelling state interest. In the mandatory community service context, the government must demonstrate that the programs are justified by such compelling interests. This task will be made difficult for the government by the lack of empirical studies showing mandatory community service programs having any serious educational value, especially when compared to the harm coercive programs do to recognized parental rights. Indeed, a 1991 survey of community service programs concluded that "much of the initiative for school-based service comes from policy makers and politicians—not educators."[12]

The Institute's litigation team in these lawsuits is headed by staff attorney Scott G. Bullock. Local counsel for the challenge in Chapel Hill, North Carolina is Robert H. Edmunds, Jr., former U.S. Attorney for the Middle District of North Carolina, and a partner at the Greensboro law firm of Stern, Graham & Klepfer, L.L.P. Local counsel for the Mamaroneck challenge is Lance Gotko, an attorney in New York.

Conclusion

People across the political spectrum share the desire to build strong and interconnected communities. But the hallmark of community is voluntarism.

Too many people today confuse the ideal of community with what government officials deem the community's interest. In today's highly regulated society, individuals endure many government intrusions into their lives. By filing lawsuits that will have nationwide ramifications, families in Chapel Hill and Mamaroneck draw a line and proclaim that certain decisions, especially the decision to serve others, must be between an individual and his conscience, not the individual and the state. Through this principled stand, the families reinforce institutions that unquestionably build well-functioning communities: true voluntarism and private charitable efforts.

Notes

1. Gordon Cawelti, *High School Restructuring: A National Study,* Educational Research Service, pp. 32–35 (1994).

2. The court opinions are reported in *Steirer v. Bethlehem Area School District,* 987 F.2d 989 (3rd Cir. 1993) and 789 F. Supp. 1337 (E.D. Pa. 1992).

3. Michael Winerip, "Required Volunteerism: School Programs Tested," *The New York Times,* Sept. 23, 1993.

4. "Schools Shouldn't Force Community Service," *USA Today,* Sept. 15, 1993.

5. Aaron Epstein, "Forced Community Service Likened to Slavery," *Phil. Inquirer,* Sept. 3, 1993.

6. For an enlightening article on the workings of the Maryland program, *see* Mark Parenti, "Lobbying School," *Reason,* pp. 56–57 (April 1994).

7. *Hodges v. United States,* 203 U.S. 1, 16 (1906).

8. 262 U.S. 390 (1923).

9. 268 U.S. 510 (1925).

10. *Meyer,* 262 U.S. at 401-02.

11. *See,* for example, *Mozert v. Hawkins County Board of Education,* 827 F.2d 1058 (6th Cir. 1987).

12. Dan Conrad & Diane Hedin, "School-Based Community Service: What We Know From Research and Theory," *Phi Delta Kappan,* p. 744 (June 1991).

POSTSCRIPT

Is Mandatory Community Service Desirable and Legal?

The Civilian Conservation Corps, the National Youth Conservation Corps, the Peace Corps, Volunteers in Service to America (VISTA), and AmeriCorps, an action group sponsored by the Corporation for National and Community Service, all attest to the success of federal efforts to kindle and reward altruism and idealism. However, the manifestation of this effort at the state and local levels has become far more controversial since "voluntary" service has evolved into "required." In addition to the organizations mentioned above, many advocacy groups support the community service movement, including Youth Service America, the Points of Light Foundation, the National Center for Service Learning in Early Adolescence, and the Community Service Learning Center. But the central questions remain: Can bureaucratically run volunteer programs fulfill their intentions? And can community service be a legal requirement for high school graduation?

Books that address the first of these related questions include Donald J. Eberly, ed., *National Youth Service: A Democratic Institution for the Twenty-First Century* (1990); *National Service: Pro and Con* edited by Williamson M. Evers (1990); *A Call to Civic Service* by Charles C. Moskos (1988); and E. B. Gorham, *National Service, Citizenship, and Political Education* (1992). Theme issues of journals addressing many aspects of the total controversy include *Phi Delta Kappan* (June 1991), *Social Policy* (Fall 1993), *Equity and Excellence in Education* (September 1993), *Educational Horizons* (Summer 1999), and *The School Administrator* (August 2000).

Some interesting articles, most of them supportive of community service, are "Making a Difference: Students and Community Service," by Derek Bok and Frank Newman, *Change* (July–August 1992); "School-Based Community Service Programs: An Imperative for Effective Schools," by Harry Silcox, *NASSP Bulletin* (February 1993); and Deborah Hirsch, "Politics Through Action: Student Service and Activism in the '90s," *Change* (September–October 1993).

Somewhat more critical perspectives are offered in Harry C. Boyte, "Community Service and Civic Education," *Phi Delta Kappan* (June 1991); Jonathan Schorr, "Class Action: What Clinton's National Service Program Could Learn from 'Teach America,' " *Phi Delta Kappan* (December 1993); and "National Service and the Ideal of Community: A Commentary on *What You Can Do for Your Country*," *Journal of Education Policy* (May–June 1994). For a thorough review of the issue, see the report of the Education Commission of the States, "Mandatory Community Service: Citizenship Education or Involuntary Servitude?" (1999).

ISSUE 21

Should Alternative Teacher Training Be Encouraged?

YES: Robert Holland, from "How to Build a Better Teacher," *Policy Review* (April & May 2001)

NO: Linda Darling-Hammond, from "How Teacher Education Matters," *Journal of Teacher Education* (May/June 2000)

ISSUE SUMMARY

YES: Public policy researcher Robert Holland argues that current certification programs are inadequate, especially given the growing shortage of teachers.

NO: Educational professor Linda Darling-Hammond offers evidence of failure among alternative programs and responds to criticism of standard professional preparation.

T he quality and appropriateness of teacher preparation programs have long been topics of discussion in academic and professional circles, as well as in the media. From the appraisals by educators James Bryant Conant, Sterling Mc-Murrin, and James Koerner in the 1960s to recent critiques by James Coleman, Ernest Boyer, John I. Goodlad, and William J. Bennett, the education of future teachers has consistently been under careful scrutiny. Rita Kramer called for the closing of all schools of education in her 1991 book *Ed School Follies: The Miseducation of America's Teachers*. Education dean Donald J. Stedman, in "Re-inventing the Schools of Education," *Vital Speeches of the Day* (April 15, 1991), recommended a serious restructuring of teacher preparation to replace the current bureaucratic rigidity with a flexible interdisciplinary approach.

In 1985 the Carnegie Forum released its agenda for wide-ranging improvements, and the American Association of Colleges of Teacher Education published *A Call for Change in Teacher Education*. Of greater impact was the formation of the Holmes Group by deans of education schools at almost all of the leading universities in the country. In 1986 a report released by this organization entitled *Tomorrow's Teachers* called for a stronger preparation in the liberal arts and academic majors and for moving teacher certification courses to the master's degree level. A National Board of Professional Standards was established in 1987, offering the prospect of a higher level of certification and status enhancement for teachers. In 1995 the Holmes Group, in *Tomorrow's Schools of Education*, supported the concept of professional development schools run jointly by universities and public school systems and fueled by applied research. A firm message was sent: "Reform—or get out of business!"

While many internal reforms have been carried out in the past two decades, pressures from the outside for alternatives to the usual paths of entry into the profession have been steadily building. Frederick M. Hess, in "Break the Link," *Education Next* (Spring 2002), contends that anyone who has not completed the specified training is unsuited to enter a classroom and must be prohibited from applying for a job, regardless of any other qualifications. About 10 years ago, Wendy Kopp launched Teach for America in an attempt to bring bright and dedicated teacher candidates into disadvantaged schools by providing an abbreviated training program. In her 2001 book *One Day All Children... The Unlikely Triumph of Teach for America and What I Learned Along the Way*, she explains the program and offers a self-appraisal.

The growing undersupply of teachers has created more urgent calls for change. The 1998 report of the National Center for Education Information, *Alternative Teacher Certification—An Overview*, documents the evolution of alternative routes and the rapid growth in the number of individuals pursuing them. Articles that examine this issue include Linda Darling-Hammond, "The Challenge of Staffing Our Schools," *Educational Leadership* (May 2001); Mary E. Diez, "The Certification Connection," *Education Next* (Spring 2002); Arthur E. Wise, "Creating a High-Quality Teaching Force," *Educational Leadership* (December 2000–January 2001); and Richard M. Ingersoll, "Holes in the Teacher Supply Bucket," *The School Administrator* (March 2002).

In the following selection, Robert Holland reviews the criticism of traditional teacher certification programs, critiques the profession's attempts at internal reform, and suggests a "value-added" approach. In the second selection, Darling-Hammond presents evidence that internal reforms have strengthened the programs and that alternatives such as Teach for America are woefully inadequate.

Robert Holland  **YES**

How to Build a Better Teacher

American schools need more teachers. American schools need better teachers. Practically everyone with a stake in the education debate agrees with those two premises. However, there is sharp disagreement as to whether more regulation or less is the way to go.

The differences of perspective begin over just how vital to transmitting knowledge a teacher is. No one is more certain about the overriding importance of a teacher in a child's academic progress than Tennessee statistician William Sanders, who has developed a value-added instrument that might revolutionize how good teachers are found and rewarded for productive careers. Speaking before the metropolitan school board in Nashville in January [2001], Sanders risked friendly fire when he disputed the connection much of the education world makes between poverty and low student performance: "Of all the factors we study—class size, ethnicity, location, poverty—they all pale to triviality in the face of teacher effectiveness."

That flies in the face of a widespread conviction in the education world that poverty is such a powerful depressant on learning that even the greatest teachers may only partially overcome its effects. As Diane Ravitch documents in her recent book *Left Back* (Simon & Schuster), education "progressives" long have believed that many children shouldn't be pushed to absorb knowledge beyond their limited innate capacities; that they are better off with teachers who help them get in touch with their feelings and find a socially useful niche.

But Sanders has volumes of data to back up his contention. While at the University of Tennessee, he developed a sophisticated longitudinal measurement called "value-added assessment" that pinpoints how effective each district, school, and teacher has been in raising individual students' achievement over time. His complex formula factors out demographic variables that often make comparisons problematic. Among other things, he found that students unlucky enough to have a succession of poor teachers are virtually doomed to the education cellar. Three consecutive years of first quintile (least effective) teachers in Grades 3 to 5 yield math scores from the thirty-fifth to forty-fifth percentile. Conversely, three straight years of fifth quintile teachers result in scores at the eighty-fifth to ninety-fifth percentile.

The state of Tennessee began using value-added assessment in its public schools in 1992, and Sanders is in demand in many other states where legislators are considering importing the system. The "No Excuses" schools identified by an ongoing Heritage Foundation project—high-poverty schools where outstanding pupil achievement defies stereotypes about race and poverty—buttress Sanders' contention that the quality of teaching is what matters most. Consider, for instance, Frederick Douglass Academy, a public school in central Harlem that has a student population 80 percent black and 19 percent Hispanic. The *New York Times* recently reported that all of Frederick Douglass's students passed a new, rigorous English Regents exam last year, and 96 percent passed the math Regents. The Grades 6-12 school ranks among the top 10 schools in New York City in reading and math, despite having class sizes of 30 to 34.

And what makes the difference? "Committed teachers," said principal Gregory M. Hodge—teachers, he said, who come to work early, stay late, and call parents if children don't show up for extra tutoring. The disciplined yet caring climate for learning set by Hodge and principals of other No Excuses schools also is due much credit.

Those who believe in deregulation of teacher licensing see in value-added assessment a potential breakthrough. Principals (like Hodge) could hire and evaluate their teachers not necessarily on the basis of credit-hours amassed in professional schools of education but in terms of objective differences instructors make when actually placed before classrooms of children. The Thomas B. Fordham Foundation published in April 1999 a manifesto on teacher quality that argues strongly for a "results-based accountability system," disaggregated by teacher, along the lines of what Sanders has devised.

However, much of the education establishment—those in and around education school faculties nationwide, the professional development specialists at teacher unions and associations, state and local boards of education, and education specialists in much of the foundation world—takes a very different view. They argue that what is needed is much more centralized control of teacher preparation and licensing to ensure that teachers are better and more uniformly qualified when they enter the classroom. They propose to ensure this by placing professional licensing under the aegis of a single accreditation body, one that would be controlled to a great extent by the teachers themselves—or, more precisely, their national unions.

Which side prevails in this dispute over how to get the best teachers into schools—the Sanders model of ongoing evaluation of effectiveness or the establishment preference for centralized credentialing—may tell us more than anything else about the quality of instruction American pupils and their parents can expect from their schools for a generation. This is the key battleground in public education today.

Teacher Certification: A Primer

The one point on which both camps agree is that the existing system of teacher certification badly needs reform. Hence, a brief survey of that system may be helpful. Currently, state departments of education and collegiate schools of education are the gatekeepers to teaching careers in America's public schools. This is a collaboration dedicated to the use of government power to standardize and centralize education, or, in the economists' term, "regulatory capture." Government licensing agencies that are charged with protecting the public interest are effectively controlled by the interests—in this case, the teacher-trainers—they are supposed to be regulating.

As a result, an aspiring teacher typically must complete a state-approved program of teacher education that is heavy on how-to-teach or pedagogical courses. All 50 states require new teachers to obtain a bachelor's degree, and all 50 require course work in pedagogy. In some states, the teacher's degree must be in education, while other states require an academic major but specify that within that degree there must be a considerable number of education courses (about a semester's worth) and also a period of student teaching (another semester). In addition, many teacher colleges tack on additional training requirements, so that fulfilling requirements for the study of pedagogy can consume well over a year of college. Most states require prospective teachers to pass one or more subject-area tests, but these often ask for regurgitation of nostrums taught by education professors.

Critics of the schools of pedagogy are legion. Seventy years ago, H.L. Mencken (never one to mince words) asserted that most pedagogues "have trained themselves to swallow any imaginable fad or folly, and always with enthusiasm. The schools reek with this puerile nonsense."

In the early 1990s, Rita Kramer took a nationwide tour of leading schools of education, from Teachers College at Columbia to the University of Washington, and reported in *Ed School Follies* on the intellectual emptiness of teacher preparation—hours spent on how to teach Tootles the Locomotive with the proper attitude, but precious little depth in history, mathematics, science, or literature. Recently Heather Mac Donald took a close look at ed schools for *City Journal* and summed up teacher educators' dogma in the phrase "Anything But Knowledge." She found teachers of teachers still holding fast to the doctrine laid out in 1925 by Teachers College icon William Heard Kilpatrick: Schools should instill "critical thinking" in children instead of teaching them facts and figures, which (he surmised) they could always look up for themselves as they became "lifelong learners." Today, Teachers College mandates courses in multicultural diversity and has students act out ways to "usurp the existing power structure."

Jerry Jesness, a special education teacher in a south Texas elementary school, observes that "every profession has its gatekeepers, the college professors who not only teach, but also sift out the slow, the lazy, and the mediocre, those unfit to practice the profession for which they are preparing. One must have intelligence, drive, and stamina, especially to get through schools of engineering, law, or medicine.

"In colleges of education, the reverse seems to be the case. After a few weeks of Ed 101, the students most possessed of those qualities begin to slip away. By the time education students begin their semester of student teaching, the best and brightest have already defected to other disciplines. Colleges and departments of education separate the wheat from the chaff, but unlike those of the other disciplines, they then throw away the wheat."

The current system does allow for a semblance of public accountability. At least in theory, citizens—by their votes for governors and state legislators, and in some states, the state education boards and superintendents of public instruction—can pressure education bureaucrats to adopt more sensible rules for preparing and employing teachers. One state in which the political process has recently yielded reform is Georgia, where Democratic Gov. Roy Barnes last year won legislative approval for eliminating seniority-based teacher tenure.

At the center of the school of thought that believes tighter national regulation is key to reform is a foundation-funded entity called the National Commission on Teaching and America's Future (NCTAF). NCTAF is the latest incarnation of a Carnegie Corporation commission—the first was the 1986 Carnegie Task Force on Teaching as a Profession—advocating a centralized, national system of teacher licensing controlled by private organizations with stakes in the process. With North Carolina Gov. James Hunt as its chairman and Stanford education professor Linda Darling-Hammond as its director, NCTAF issued its report, "What Matters Most: Teaching for America's Future," in 1996. (The Rockefeller Foundation joined Carnegie in bankrolling the commission.) NCTAF, which stayed active to lobby for its proposals, drew raves in the press for its "action agenda" to reform the training and certifying of teachers. Little ink went toward exploring the deeper implications of nationalizing control of teaching.

NCTAF called for, among other things:

- Mandatory accreditation by an organization called the National Council for Accreditation of Teacher Education (NCATE) of all teacher-training programs in the country.
- National Board for Professional Teaching Standards (NBPTS) certification of more than 100,000 "master" teachers.
- Formation of "independent" professional boards in each state to set policies on teacher preparation, testing, and licensing, in tune with the nationalized policy.

In December 1999, Linda Darling-Hammond forcefully stated the case for the pro-regulatory proposition that education credentials do make a difference. "It stands to reason," she wrote, "that student learning should be enhanced by the efforts of teachers who are more knowledgeable in their field and are skillful at teaching it to others. Substantial evidence from prior reform efforts indicates that changes in course taking, curriculum content, testing, or textbooks make little difference if teachers do not know how to use these tools well and how to diagnose their students' learning needs."

The Union Interest

The National Education Association [NEA], the nation's largest teacher union, has emerged as a leading advocate of the NCTAF model of "reforming" the system by stripping control of teacher certification from the state departments of education. The NEA touts this as "professionalization," meaning self-regulation by teachers or benign-sounding "peer review." But critics dispute how much rank-and-file teachers would be empowered. Education Consumers Clearinghouse founder John Stone, a professor of education at East Tennessee State University, believes "the parties serving up these bold proposals represent the interests that have governed teacher training and licensure all along. Since publication of *A Nation at Risk* in 1983, teacher training and licensure have undergone repeated rewrites, none of which has produced any noticeable improvements in schooling."

The NEA likes the idea of all teachers having to graduate from a teacher-training program certified by NCATE. This is perhaps unsurprising, given that NCATE has been tightly linked to the NEA since the former's founding in 1954. NCATE's director, Arthur E. Wise, also heads the NEA's 31-year-old nonprofit subsidiary, the National Foundation for the Improvement of Education. Meanwhile, NEA president Robert F. Chase chairs the Executive Committee of NCATE. Furthermore, Wise sat on the national commission, NCTAF, that would grant NCATE control of all teacher accreditation that it has not been able to gain on a voluntary basis over the past 40 years.

An important link in the pro-regulatory reformers' plan is the National Board for Professional Teaching Standards (NBPTS), an outgrowth of the 1986 Carnegie report. NBPTS subsequently received Carnegie Corporation outlays of several million dollars. In the 1990s, the federal government also began subsidizing the NBPTS heavily, at the urging of President Clinton. The board is a key element in today's strategy to centralize control of the gates to teaching. The privately operated NBPTS confers national certification on teachers who submit portfolios (videotapes of the teaching, lesson plans, samples of student work) for evaluation. The teachers also must pay a $2,300 application fee, but sometimes their school boards pay it for them.

The NBPTS purports to identify excellence through this process, but economists Dale Ballou of the University of Massachusetts and Michael Podgursky of the University of Missouri—who called "professionalization" into question after careful analysis—point out that there has been no evidence to show that students of NBPTS-certified teachers learn any more than students of other teachers. Researchers at the Consortium for Policy Studies at the University of Wisconsin at Madison recently found that NBPTS-certified teachers tend to become more reflective about their teaching, but their principals found it difficult to link any improvements in student achievement to the teachers' national certification.

From the perspective of economists Ballou and Podgursky, "The activities over which the profession seeks control—accreditation of teacher education programs and teacher licensing—are well-recognized means of restricting supply," which puts upward pressure on salaries. They add there can be no doubt that teacher unions see the professionalization movement "as a means to increase salaries." For further evidence of how tightly linked some of the regulatory reform is, consider that NEA president Chase serves as a member of NCTAF, which seeks to greatly augment the powers of NCATE, on which Chase is a major power —and all this would confer more economic muscle on the NEA.

NCTAF was remarkably successful using the rhetoric of reform to persuade business leaders and the media that its program actually was a "scathing indictment" of the system for training and certifying teachers. The *New Republic* begged to differ: "Forcing teachers," the journal's editors commented, "to attend NCATE certification programs that douse them with pedagogical blather (NCATE's 'vision of quality' seeks to promote 'equity' and 'diversity' but says nothing about academic achievement) will likely scare off math and science specialists in droves."

The NEA stepped up its campaign in spring 2000. Chase and his associates unveiled revised NCATE standards for accreditation at a Washington news conference. NCATE stated that schools of education it accredits will have to meet "rigorous new performance-based standards" in order to win NCATE accreditation.

By focusing on "candidate performance," said NCATE president Wise, the "standards represent a revolution in teacher preparation." But skeptics wonder how "revolutionary" it is to assess candidates largely according to videotaped activities, portfolios of projects, personal journals, or their compatibility with a team. That's the emphasis of the NBPTS, but portfolio assessment relies heavily on subjective judgment, as opposed to testing a teacher's knowledge of the subject being taught.

"In spite of claims to the contrary," notes Podgursky, "at present there exists no reliable evidence indicating whether or not graduates of NCATE-accredited teacher training programs are better teachers." Although several states have responded by mandating NCATE accreditation, Podgursky added, "mandatory accreditation would almost certainly restrict the supply of teachers and exacerbate teacher shortages, yet its effect on the teacher quality pool is uncertain. It may also stifle promising state-level experiments with alternative teacher certification and the entry of new teacher-training institutions into the market."

For his part, Wise claims: "As more institutions meet NCATE's national professional standards, more qualified teacher candidates will be available, since candidates from accredited institutions pass licensing examinations at a higher rate than do those from unaccredited institutions or those with no teacher preparation." Wise based that assertion on a recent Educational Testing Service (ETS) study of the rates at which teacher candidates pass the Praxis II licensing exams. However, the same study shows that the SAT and ACT scores of NCATE graduates who passed licensing exams are lower than those of non-NCATE peers. In addition, Podgursky observed that the released ETS data are so flawed as to make any comparisons problematic. For instance, 14 percent of the sample of Praxis II test-takers never enrolled in a teacher-training program—yet the researchers sorted them into NCATE categories based on the colleges they attended. The study also failed to take into account wide variations in how states test prospective teachers.

The new standards condense NCATE's 1995 version of standards from 20 categories into six. Examiners will look at teacher-candidates' knowledge, skills, and "dispositions"; the school's assessment system; the inclusion of field experience and clinical practice; the institution's devotion to "diversity"; how faculty model "best practices"; and unit governance, including the wise use of information technology.

Actually, notes Professor Stone, the "new" standards implement mostly old ideas about teaching from existing standards. As for the portfolios, classroom observations, and emphasis on Praxis II, "performance on these various assessments reflects nothing more than a grasp of the same old faulty teaching practices that education professors have been espousing right along."

Most parents—the primary consumers of education—want schools to stress academic achievement, as studies by the nonpartisan Public Agenda have shown. However, as Public Agenda's surveys also reveal, many education professors believe "best practice" is a teacher not teaching, but facilitating in the progressive tradition, while children construct their own meaning, an approach called constructivism. "Social justice" is valued more highly than achievement. Arguably, that's the approach NCATE accreditation would enshrine.

As Podgursky and Ballou note in a recent Brookings Institution paper, public education already is a regulated monopoly. In most school districts, parents have little or no choice of their children's schools or teachers. In addition, unlike in medicine or other service markets, education consumers lack the protection of antitrust or malpractice lawsuits. Within this structure, the teacher unions already exercise enormous economic power as their well-organized affiliates bargain with fragmented local school boards.

If, next, teacher unions win control of the gates to teaching through their domination of such organizations as NCATE, they arguably would possess "market power not enjoyed by producers or unions in any major industry in our economy." That would not bode well for efforts to expand consumer choice and to get fresh blood into the teaching profession. Moreover, when a monopoly can restrict supply, prices will rise—in this case, teacher salaries. That would fulfill a primary objective of the teacher unions, but without any guarantee of increased quality.

Another Approach

What kind of persons might be attracted to teaching were the doors to teaching careers open to people with a wide variety of backgrounds that didn't necessarily include sitting through hundreds of hours of education courses, whether NCATE-accredited or not? Suppose principals could hire their own teaching staffs without having to follow the credits-hours prescribed by education bureaucracies?

Well, there would be more teachers like Scott (Taki) Sidley, who taught English at T.C. Williams High School in Alexandria, Va., the past three years, but ran athwart the state bureaucracy's insistence that he take additional prescribed courses in order to be "certified." In a piece of Sunday commentary in the *Washington Post* (June 25, 2000), long-time teacher Patrick Welsh lamented the "bureaucratic narrow-mindedness" that pushes people like Sidley out of teaching.

Welsh noted that Sidley, a University of Virginia graduate who has served in the Peace Corps, won acclaim from students and parents and was considered "one of our [T.C. Williams'] finest teachers." But he must leave the young people he was teaching so well because he lacks on his resume 30 credit-hours that regulators insist he must have—one being a low-level composition course, even though he took 48 graduate hours in creative writing at U.Va. and the university exempted him from introductory composition because of his Advanced Placement English score in high school.

Many young teachers like Sidley, Welsh notes, "see the petty adherence to the certification rules as symptomatic of a pervasive problem." For an alternative vision, he quoted Dave Keener, head of the school's science department and the 1998 Virginia winner of the Presidential Award for Excellence in Science and Mathematics Teaching: "The process of getting the best has to be streamlined. Individual high schools should be given the power to advertise positions and do their own recruiting.... Principals, with advice of teachers, should be able to do all the hiring on the spot without having to get approval from the central office, which often takes weeks. De-emphasize the education courses. Once we get the kind of people we want, we could train them in the schools."

That's the sensible approach that one kind of education reform, the charter school, facilitates. Organizers of charter schools—often teachers with a common vision—receive waivers from certification and other bureaucratic rules. In exchange for independence, they agree to be accountable for academic results. Many charter schools freely hire teachers who know their subjects but haven't been through the education-school mill. Only a small fraction of charter school teachers choose to belong to the national teacher unions.

In its 1996 report, NCTAF gave the impression with its sharp attack on the current state-controlled certification system that it wanted a thorough-going reform that would bring bright young teachers into the classroom. But as Professors Ballou and Podgursky observe, NCTAF focuses not on recruiting more talented individuals but on beefing up the system of teacher training—and shifting its control from political bodies to organizations, like NCATE, that may also reflect private agendas, such as the NEA'S.

There are a few small-scale programs designed to deepen the pool of teaching talent by going outside the certification routine. One is Teach for America, which places liberal arts graduates in high-need urban and rural districts. Another is Troops to Teachers, which assists retiring military personnel in becoming teachers. In both instances, the newly minted teachers obtain provisional certification and then work toward obtaining enough professional education credits to gain full certification.

New Jersey is one state that has taken seriously the desirability of offering alternative routes to teaching. In 1984, the state reduced the number of education courses required for traditional certification, while putting new teachers under the tutelage of a mentor teacher. At the same time, it allowed teachers to recruit liberal arts graduates who hadn't been through education schools at all. These teachers were also put under the supervision of a mentor. They would get on-the-job training in applied teaching. The new approach has resulted in higher scores on licensing tests, a lower attrition rate, and a more diverse teaching force, notes former New Jersey Education Commissioner Leo Klagholz in a Fordham Foundation paper.

Such programs are fine as far as they go—but they don't go nearly far enough nationwide. Strict regulation of K-12 teaching has yielded pervasive mediocrity. It is time to deregulate and to emphasize results. Instead of screening teachers according to courses taken and degrees earned, school administrations should free principals to hire the most intellectually promising material —English majors to teach English, history majors to teach history—and then let the schools assimilate them in the nitty-gritty of preparing lesson plans and monitoring lunchrooms.

Value-Added Assessment

The quest for reform based on proof of good teaching brings us back to William Sanders and the Tennessee Value-Added Assessment System (TVAAS), which generates annual reports of gains in student achievement produced by each teacher, school, and school district. Progress is broken down by core subject, and gains are compared to national, state, and local benchmarks.

Professor John Stone explains the significance of using such a system:

> By comparing each student's current achievement to his or her past performance and aggregating the results, value-added assessment statistically isolates the impact of individual teachers, schools, and school systems on the average progress of the students for which they are responsible. Not incidentally, value-added assessment can also be used by education's decision-makers to isolate and assess the effectiveness of everything from the latest curricular innovations, to the preparedness of novice teachers, to the quality of the programs in which teachers were trained.

Here, in short, is a real-world way to assess the performance of teachers—as opposed to the paperwork realm of NCATE, which deems credentials and licensure hoops to be the equivalent of quality assurance.

The most thoroughgoing reform of teacher licensing and hiring could come through a combination of the New Jersey and Tennessee approaches. Schools could hire teachers with liberal-arts educations and/or valuable working-world experiences, then give them on-the-job mentoring, and finally evaluate their teaching prowess according to a value-added assessment.

It's known from Sanders's research, the No Excuses schools, and plain common sense that teachers make a profound difference in students' lives. Deregulated teacher hiring combined with value-added assessment could bring an infusion of fresh talent into teaching and provide a basis for rewarding those teachers who do the most to help children learn. Such a system also could quickly identify teachers who needed extra training, or those who ought to be pursuing a different line of work. Such a change would deserve to be called reform; mandatory accreditation locking in the status quo in teaching preparation does not.

Three days into his administration, President George W. Bush unveiled an accountability plan for federal education spending that sparked hope for a fresh approach to bringing good teachers to K–12 schools. He proposed that Congress revise Title II of the Elementary and Secondary Education Act so that school districts can come up with alternative ways to certify teachers. And he would reserve a chunk of funding for grants to states that develop systems to measure teacher effectiveness according to student academic achievement.

That's value-added, and it may turn out to be the most significant education tool since chalk.

How Teacher Education Matters

O ver the past decade, public dissatisfaction with schools has included dissatisfaction with teacher education. Education schools have been variously criticized as ineffective in preparing teachers for their work, unresponsive to new demands, remote from practice, and barriers to the recruitment of bright college students into teaching. In more than 40 states, policy makers have enacted alternative routes to teacher certification to create pathways into teaching other than those provided by traditional 4-year undergraduate teacher education programs. Whereas some of these are carefully structured postbaccalaureate programs, others are little more than emergency hiring options. Upon his election in 1988, President Bush's only education proposal was the encouragement of alternative teacher certification. In 1995, Newt Gingrich proposed the elimination of teacher certification rules as his major education initiative. In 1999, Chester Finn and the Thomas B. Fordham Foundation issued a manifesto arguing against teacher education requirements as a "barrier" to entering teaching.

Voices of dissatisfaction have been raised from within the profession as well (Goodlad, 1990; Holmes Group, 1986). These voices, however, have urged the redesign of teacher education to strengthen its knowledge base, its connections to both practice and theory, and its capacity to support the development of powerful teaching. Proposals at the far ends of this continuum stand in stark contrast to one another. One approach would replace university-based preparation with on-the-job training that focuses on the pragmatics of teaching, whereas the other would expand professional training to prepare teachers for more adaptive, knowledge-based practice, while simultaneously tackling the redesign of schools and teaching. Which of these routes holds the most promise? What are the implications for teachers' capacities, and, most important, for the education of children?

Although the debates on these questions have been largely ideological, there is a growing body of empirical evidence about the outcomes of different approaches to teacher education and recruitment. This research suggests that the extent and quality of teacher education matter for teachers' effectiveness, perhaps now even more than before. The expectations that schools teach a much more diverse group of students to much higher standards create much

From Linda Darling-Hammond, "How Teacher Education Matters," *Journal of Teacher Education*, vol. 51, no. 3 (May/June 2000). Copyright © 2000 by The American Association of Colleges for Teacher Education. Reprinted by permission of Corwin Press, Inc., a Sage Publications Company.

greater demands on teachers. Teaching for problem solving, invention, and application of knowledge requires teachers with deep and flexible knowledge of subject matter who understand how to represent ideas in powerful ways [and] can organize a productive learning process for students who start with different levels and kinds of prior knowledge, assess how and what students are learning, and adapt instruction to different learning approaches.

Do Education Schools Help Teachers Learn?

Even if one agrees that there are desirable knowledge and skills for teaching, many people believe that anyone can teach, or, at least, that knowing a subject is enough to allow one to teach it well. Others believe that teaching is best learned, to the extent that it can be learned at all, by trial and error on the job. The evidence strongly suggests otherwise. Reviews of research over the past 30 years have concluded that even with the shortcomings of current teacher education and licensing, fully prepared and certified teachers are generally better rated and more successful with students than teachers without this preparation (Ashton & Crocker, 1986; Evertson, Hawley, & Zlotnik, 1985; Greenberg, 1983; Haberman, 1984; Olsen, 1985).

In fields ranging from mathematics and science to vocational education, reading, elementary education, and early childhood education, researchers have found that teachers who have greater knowledge of teaching and learning are more highly rated and are more effective with students, especially at tasks requiring higher order thinking and problem solving. (For a review of this literature, see Darling-Hammond, 1996b). Interestingly, whereas subject-matter knowledge is often found to be an important factor in teaching effectiveness, it appears that its relationship to teaching performance is curvilinear; that is, it exerts a positive effect up to a threshold level and then tapers off in influence. Furthermore, measures of pedagogical knowledge, including knowledge of learning, teaching methods, and curriculum, are more frequently found to influence teaching performance and often exert even stronger effects than subject-matter knowledge (Ashton & Crocker, 1986; Begle & Geeslin, 1972; Byrne, 1983; Evertson et al., 1985; Ferguson & Womack, 1993; Guyton & Farokhi, 1987; Monk, 1994; Perkes, 1967–1968). It seems logical that pedagogical skill would interact with subject matter knowledge to bolster or undermine teacher performance. As Byrne (1983) suggests,

> insofar as a teacher's knowledge provides the basis for his or her effectiveness, the most relevant knowledge will be that which concerns the particular topic being taught and the relevant pedagogical strategies for teaching it to the particular types of pupils to whom it will be taught. (p. 14)

Meanwhile, studies of teachers admitted with less than full preparation find that recruits tend to be less satisfied with their training and have greater difficulties planning curriculum, teaching, managing the classroom, and diagnosing students' learning needs. They are less able to adapt their instruction to promote student learning and less likely to see it as their job to do so, blaming students if their teaching is not effective. Principals and colleagues rate these teachers less highly on their instructional skills, and they leave teaching at higher-than-average rates. Most important is that their students learn less, especially in areas such as reading, writing, and mathematics, which are critical to later school success (Darling-Hammond, 1999b).

Illustrating these findings, Gomez and Grobe's (1990) study of the performance of alternate certification (AC) candidates in Dallas, who receive a few weeks of summer training before they assume full teaching responsibilities, found that their performance was much more uneven than that of traditionally trained entrants who had equivalent scores on the state's subject matter exams. From 2 to 16 times as many AC recruits were rated "poor" on each teaching factor evaluated, and their students showed significantly lower achievement gains in language arts and writing.

Perhaps it is not surprising that alternate route teachers from short-term programs report less satisfaction with their preparation and less commitment to remaining in teaching than other recruits (Darling-Hammond, Hudson, & Kirby, 1989; Lutz & Hutton, 1989). Problems resulting from inadequate preparation headed the list of complaints of the 20% of Los Angeles AC candidates who quit before they completed their summer training programs in 1984 and 1985, as well as many of those who remained but voiced dissatisfaction (Wright, McKibbon, & Walton, 1987). Stoddart's (1992) analysis reveals that 53% of these recruits had left teaching within the first 6 years of program operation. Among AC candidates in Dallas, only half successfully "graduated" to become full-fledged teachers after their first year as interns. Only 40% said that they planned to stay in teaching, as compared to 72% of traditionally trained recruits (Lutz & Hutton, 1989).

Even very intelligent people who are enthusiastic about teaching find that they cannot easily succeed without preparation, especially if they are assigned to work with children who most need skillful teaching. The best-publicized program founded on this idea is Teach for America (TFA), created to recruit bright college graduates to disadvantaged schools en route to careers in other professions. If anyone could prove the claim that teachers are born and not made, these bright eager students might have been the ones to do it. Yet, four separate evaluations found that TFA's 3-to-8-week summer training program did not prepare candidates adequately (Grady, Collins, & Grady, 1991; Popkewitz, 1995; Roth, 1993; Texas Education Agency, 1993), despite the intelligence and enthusiasm of many of the recruits. Many recruits knew that their success—and that of their students—had been compromised by their lack of access to the knowledge needed to teach. Yale University graduate Schorr (1993) was one of many to raise this concern:

> I—perhaps like most TFAers—harbored dreams of liberating my students from public school mediocrity and offering them as good an education as I had received. But I was not ready.... As bad as it was for me, it was worse for the students. Many of mine ... took long steps on the path toward dropping out.... I was not a successful teacher and the loss to the students was real and large. (pp. 317–318)

These feelings contribute to the program's high attrition rate. Even though many recruits report that they initially entered the program with the intention of exploring teaching as a career, many also indicate that they left in discouragement because they felt unsuccessful. TFA statistics show that of those who started in 1990, 58% had left before the third year, a 2-year attrition rate nearly three times the national average for new teachers. The Maryland State Department of Education found that 62% of corps members who started in Baltimore in 1992 left within 2 years.

Aside from high attrition, studies of short-term alternative programs have also noted that what little pedagogical training they provide tends to focus on generic teaching skills rather than subject-specific pedagogy, on singular techniques rather than a range of methods, and on specific, immediate advice rather than research or theory (Bliss, 1992; Stoddart, 1992; Zumwalt, 1990).

The lack of traditional coursework and student teaching in these programs are generally supposed to be compensated for by intensive mentoring and supervision in the initial months of full-time teaching. Ironically, however, most studies have found that promised mentors did not often materialize (Darling-Hammond, 1992).

Unfortunately, the least well-prepared recruits are disproportionately assigned to teach the least advantaged students in high-minority and low-income schools (National Commission on Teaching and America's Future [NCTAF], 1996). In the aggregate, this can make a substantial difference in what children learn. Recent multivariate studies of student achievement at the school and district level have found a substantial influence of teachers' qualifications on what students learn. Ferguson's (1991) analysis of Texas school districts found that teachers' expertise, including their scores on a licensing examination measuring basic skills and teaching knowledge; master's degrees' and experience accounted for more of the interdistrict variation in students' reading and mathematics achievement in grades 1 through 11 than student socioeconomic status. The effects were so strong, and the variations in teacher expertise so great, that after controlling for socioeconomic status, the large disparities in achievement between Black and White students were almost entirely accounted for by differences in the qualifications of their teachers. This finding contravenes the common presumption that students' school achievement is largely a function of their socioeconomic status and that school variables make little difference in educational outcomes.

A more recent Texas study (Fuller, 1999) found that students in districts with greater proportions of fully licensed teachers were significantly more likely to pass the Texas state achievement tests after controlling for student socioeconomic status, school wealth, and teacher experience. Similar to this, a North Carolina study (Strauss & Sawyer, 1986) found that teachers' average scores on the National Teacher Examinations measuring subject matter and teaching knowledge had a large effect on students' pass rates on the state competency examinations. A 1% increase in teacher quality (as measured by NTE scores) was associated with a 3% to 5% decline in the percentage of students failing the exam.

A recent school-level analysis of mathematics test performance in California high schools (Fetler, 1999) found a strong negative relationship between average student scores and the percentage of teachers on emergency certificates, after controlling for student poverty rates. Another California study found that across all income levels, elementary students' reading achievement is strongly related to the proportions of fully trained and certified teachers (Los Angeles County Office of Education, 1999), much more so than to the proportion of beginners in the school. The study concluded that "this supports the finding that differing test scores are a teacher training issue and not merely due to new teachers' lack of classroom experience."

Responses to Critiques of Traditional Teacher Education

Lest schools of education become sanguine, however, there are grounds for concern about traditional preparation programs as well. The often-repeated critiques of traditional teacher education programs include the pressure of inadequate time within a 4-year undergraduate degree, which makes it hard to learn enough about both subject matter and pedagogy; the fragmentation of content and pedagogical coursework and the divide between university- and school-based training; the weak content of many courses that pass on folklore instead of systematically developed knowledge; the lack of adequate clinical training; and the lack of resources in many education programs that serve as "cash cows" for their universities, which perpetuates much of the above.

Over the past decade, many schools of education and school districts have begun to change these conditions. Stimulated by the efforts of the Holmes Group and the National Network for Educational Renewal, more than 300 schools of education have created programs that extend beyond the confines of the traditional 4-year bachelor's degree program, thus allowing more extensive study of the disciplines to be taught along with education coursework that is integrated with more extensive clinical training in schools. Some are 1- or 2-year graduate programs that serve recent graduates or midcareer recruits. Others are 5-year models that allow an extended program of preparation for prospective teachers who enter teacher education during their undergraduate years. In either case, because the 5th year allows students to devote their energies exclusively to the task of preparing to teach, such programs allow for year-long school-based clinical experiences that are woven together with coursework on learning and teaching.

Many of these programs have joined with local school districts to create professional development schools where novices' clinical preparation can be more purposefully structured. Like teaching hospitals in medicine, these schools aim to provide sites for state-of-the-art practice that are also organized to support the training of new professionals, extend the professional development of veteran teachers, and sponsor collaborative research and inquiry. These approaches resemble reforms in teacher education abroad. Countries such as Germany, Belgium, France, and Luxembourg have long required from 2 to 3 years of graduate-level study in addition to an undergraduate degree for prospective teachers, including an intensively supervised internship in a school affiliated with the university.

A number of recent studies have found that graduates of extended programs (typically 5-year programs) are not only more satisfied with their preparation, they are viewed by their colleagues, principals, and cooperating teachers as better prepared, are as effective with students as much more experienced teachers, and are much more likely to enter and stay in teaching than their peers prepared in traditional 4-year programs (Andrew, 1990; Andrew & Schwab, 1995; Arch, 1989; Denton & Peters, 1988; Dyal, 1993; Shin, 1994). In fact, the entry and retention rates of these programs are so much higher than those of 4-year programs—which are, in turn, much higher than short-term alternative programs—that it is actually less expensive to prepare career teachers in this way once the costs of preparation, recruitment, induction, and replacement due to attrition are taken into account (Darling-Hammond, 1999a).

These new programs typically engage prospective teachers in studying research and conducting their own inquiries through cases, action research, and the development of structured portfolios about practice. They envision the professional teacher as one who learns from teaching rather than one who has finished learning how to teach, and the job of teacher education as developing the capacity to inquire sensitively and systematically into the nature of learning and the effects of teaching. This is an approach to knowledge production like the one that Dewey (1929) sought, one that aims to empower teachers with greater understanding of complex situations rather than to control them with simplistic formulas or cookie-cutter routines for teaching:

> Command of scientific methods and systematized subject matter liberates individuals; it enables them to see new problems, devise new procedures, and in general, makes for diversification rather than for set uniformity. (p. 12)

> This knowledge and understanding render (the teacher's) practice more intelligent, more flexible, and better adapted to deal effectively with concrete phenomena or practice.... Seeing more relations he sees more possibilities, more opportunities. His ability to judge being enriched, he has a wider range of alternatives to select from in dealing with individual situations. (pp. 20–21)

Dewey's notion of knowledge for teaching is one that features inquiry into problems of practice as the basis for professional judgment grounded in both theoretical and practical knowledge. If teachers investigate the effects of their teaching on students' learning, and if they study what others have learned, they come to understand teaching to be an inherently nonroutine endeavor. They become sensitive to variation and more aware of what works for what purposes in what situations. Access to contingent knowledge allows them to become more thoughtful decision makers.

Training in inquiry also helps teachers learn how to look at the world from multiple perspectives, including those of students whose experiences are quite different from their own, and to use this knowledge in developing pedagogies that can reach diverse learners. Learning to reach out to students, those who are difficult to know as well as those who are easy to know, requires boundary crossing, the ability to elicit knowledge of others, and to understand it when it is offered. As Delpit (1995) notes, "We all interpret behaviors, information, and situations through our own cultural lenses; these lenses operate involuntarily, below the level of conscious awareness, making it seem that our own view is simply 'the way it is' " (p. 1512). Good teachers must develop an awareness of their perspectives and how these can be enlarged to avoid a "communicentric bias" (Gordon, 1990), which limits their understanding of those whom they teach.

Developing the ability to see beyond one's own perspective, to put oneself in the shoes of the learner and to understand the meaning of that experience in terms of learning, is perhaps the most important role of universities in the preparation of teachers. One of the great flaws of the "bright person myth" of teaching is that it presumes that anyone can teach what he or she knows to anyone else. However, people who have never studied teaching or learning often have a very difficult time understanding how to convey material that they themselves learned effortlessly and almost subconsciously. When others do not learn merely by being told, the intuitive teacher often becomes frustrated and powerless to proceed. This frequently leads to resentment of students for not validating the untrained teacher's efforts. Furthermore, individuals who have had no powerful teacher education intervention often maintain a single cognitive and cultural perspective that makes it difficult for them to understand the experiences, perceptions, and knowledge bases that deeply influence the approaches to learning of students who are different from themselves. The capacity to understand another is not innate; it is developed through study, reflection, guided experience, and inquiry.

Among the tools teacher educators increasingly use for this purpose are inquiries that engage prospective teachers in investigating learning and the lives of learners and evaluating the many different outcomes of teaching. These include prospective teachers conducting case studies of children while studying development and learning, thus coming to better understand the children' thinking and experiences; conducting community studies that investigate local neighborhoods in ways that illuminate culture, customs, and life experiences of different groups of people; conducting investigations of student learning, like the National Board for Professional Teaching Standards' student learning commentaries that evaluate artifacts of the learning of 3 diverse students over time; assembling portfolios that use artifacts of teaching and learning to analyze the effects of practice; and pursuing problem-based inquiries that seek to identify problems of practice and understand them through action research coupled with reviews of others' research. These tools allow the application of theoretical principles to problems in specific contexts while appropriately complicating efforts to draw generalizations about practice. A small but growing body of research suggests that such strategies can help teachers understand more deeply the many variables that influence their work. For example, in the case of cases and portfolios that require teachers to examine student learning in relation to their teaching, teachers claim that the process of engaging in such analysis ultimately enriches their ability to understand the effects of their actions and helps them better meet the needs of diverse students. (For a review of this literature, see Darling-Hammond and Snyder, in press.) One of the ways in which this occurs is through the process of trying to view teaching and classroom events from the perspectives of the students who experience them. As teachers look beyond their own actions to appreciate the understandings and experiences of their students, and evaluate these in light of their self-developed knowledge of individual learners and their professional knowledge of factors influencing development and learning, they grow wiser about the many ways in which learning and teaching interact.

A commitment to open inquiry, the enlargement of perspectives, and the crossing of boundaries are critical features of the ideal of university education. In fact, the basis of the very earliest universities was that they tried to bring together scholars from all over the known world. They sought to create ways to share diverse perspectives from various geographic areas, cultures, and disciplines as the basis for developing knowledge and finding truth. If universities are to continue to make the important contribution to the education of teachers that they can make, they need to pursue these ideals of knowledge building and truth finding by creating a genuine praxis between ideas and experiences, by honoring practice in conjunction with reflection and research, and by helping teachers reach beyond their personal boundaries to appreciate the perspectives of those whom they would teach.

References

Andrew, M. (1990). The differences between graduates of four-year and five-year teacher preparation programs. *Journal of Teacher Education, 41,* 45–51.

Andrew, M., & Schwab, R. L. (1995). Has reform in teacher education influenced teacher performance? An outcome assessment of graduates of eleven teacher education programs. *Action in Teacher Education, 17,* 43–53.

Arch, E. C. (1989, April). *Comparison of student attainment of teaching competence in traditional preservice and fifth-year master of arts in teaching programs.* Paper presented at the annual meeting of the American Educational Research Association, San Francisco.

Ashton, P., & Crocker, L. (1986). Does teacher certification make a difference? *Florida Journal of Teacher Education, 3,* 73–83.

Begle, E. G., & Geeslin, W. (1972). *Teacher effectiveness in mathematics instruction.* (National Longitudinal Study of Mathematical Abilities Reports No. 28). Washington, DC: Mathematical Association of America and National Council of Teachers of Mathematics.

Bliss, T. (1992). Alternate certification in Connecticut: Reshaping the profession. *Peabody Journal of Education, 67*(3), 35–54.

Byrne. (1983). *Teacher knowledge and teacher effectiveness: A literature review, theoretical analysis, and discussion of research strategy.* Paper presented at the meeting of the Northeastern Educational Research Association, Ellenville, NY.

Darling-Hammond, L. (1992). Teaching and knowledge: Policy issues posed by alternative certification for teachers. *Peabody Journal of Education, 67*(3), 123–154.

Darling-Hammond, L. 1999a). *Solving the dilemmas of teacher supply, demand, and standards: How we can ensure a competent, caring, and qualified teacher for every child.* New York: National Commission on Teaching and America's Future.

Darling-Hammond, L. (1999b). *Teaching quality and student achievement: A review of state policy evidence.* Seattle, WA: Center for the Study of Teaching and Policy, University of Washington.

Darling-Hammond, L., Hudson, L., & Kirby, S. (1989). *Redesigning teacher education: Opening the door for new recruits to science and mathematics teaching.* Santa Monica, CA: RAND.

Darling-Hammond, L., & Snyder, J. (in press). Authentic assessment of teaching in context. *Journal of Teaching and Teacher Education.*

Denton, J. J., & Peters, W. H. (1988). *Program assessment report: Curriculum evaluation of a non-traditional program for certifying teachers.* College Station, TX: Texas A & M University.

Dewey, J. (1929). *The sources of a science of education.* New York: Horace Liveright.

Dyal, A. B. (1993). *An exploratory study to determine principals' perceptions concerning the effectiveness of a fifth-year preparation program.* Paper presented at the annual meeting of the Mid-South Educational Research Association, New Orleans, LA.

Evertson, C., Hawley, W., & Zlotnick, M. (1985). Making a difference in educational quality through teacher education. *Journal of Teacher Education, 36*(3), 2–12.

Ferguson, R. F. (1991). Paying for public education: New evidence on how and why money matters. *Harvard Journal on Legislation, 28*(2), 465–498.

Ferguson, P., & Womack, S. T. (1993). The impact of subject matter and education coursework on teaching performance. *Journal of Teacher Education, 44*(1), 55–63.

Fetler, M. (1999, March 24). High school staff characteristics and mathematics test results. *Education Policy Analysis Archives, 7* [Online]. Available: http://epaa.asu.edu.

Fuller, E. J. (1999). *Does teacher certification matter? A comparison of TAAS performance in 1997 between schools with low and high percentages of certified teachers.* Austin: Charles A. Dana Center, University of Texas at Austin.

Gomez, D. L., & Grobe, R. P. (1990, April). *Three years of alternative certification in Dallas: Where are we?* Paper presented at the Annual Meeting of the American Educational Research Association, Boston.

Goodlad, J. (1990). *Teachers for our nation's schools.* San Francisco: Jossey-Bass.

Gordon, E. W. (1990). Coping with communicentric bias in knowledge production in the social sciences. *Educational Researcher, 19.*

Grady, M. P., Collins, P., & Grady, E. L. (1991). *Teach for America 1991 Summer Institute evaluation report.* Unpublished manuscript.

Greenberg, J. D. (1983). The case for teacher education: Open and shut. *Journal of Teacher Education, 34*(4), 2–5.

Guyton, E., & Farokhi, E. (1987, September–October). Relationships among academic performance, basic skills, subject matter knowledge and teaching skills of teacher education graduates. *Journal of Teacher Education, 37*–42.

Haberman, M. (1984, September). *An Evaluation of the rationale for required teacher education: Beginning teachers with or without teacher preparation.* Paper prepared for the National Commission on Excellence in Teacher Education, University of Wisconsin-Milwaukee.

Holmes Group. (1996). *Tomorrow's teachers: A report of the Holmes Group.* East Lansing, MI: Author.

Los Angeles County Office Of Education. (1999).

Lutz, F. W., & Hutton, J. B. (1989). Alternative teacher certification: Its policy implications for classroom and personnel practice. *Educational Evaluation and Policy Analysis, 11*(3), 237–254.

Monk, D. H. (1994). Subject matter preparation of secondary mathematics and science teachers and student achievement. *Economics of Education Review, 13*(2), 125–145.

National Commission on Teaching and America's Future. (1996). *What matters most: Teaching for America's future.* NY: Author.

Olsen, D. G. (1985). The quality of prospective teachers: Education vs. noneducation graduates. *Journal of Teacher Education, 36*(5), 56–59.

Perkes, V. A. (1967–1968). Junior high school science teacher preparation, teaching behavior, and student achievement. *Journal of Research in Science Teaching, 6*(4), 121–126.

Popkewitz, T. S. (1995). Policy, knowledge, and power: Some issues for the study of educational reform. In P. Cookson & B. Schneider (Eds.), *Transforming schools: Trends, dilemmas and prospects.* Garland Press.

Roth, R. A. (1993). *Teach for America 1993 summer institute: Program review.* Unpublished report.

Schorr, J. (1993, December). Class action: What Clinton's National Service Program could learn from "Teach for America." *Phi Delta Kappan,* 315–318.

Shin, H.-S. (1994). *Estimating future teacher supply: An application of survival analysis.* Paper presented at the annual meeting of the American Educational Research Association, New Orleans, LA.

Strauss, R. P., & Sawyer, E. A. (1986). Some new evidence on teacher and student competencies. *Economics of Education Review, 5*(1), 41–48.

Stoddart, T. (1992). An alternative route to teacher certification: Preliminary findings from the Los Angeles Unified School District Intern Program. *Peabody Journal of Education, 67*(3).

Texas Education Agency. (1993). Teach for American visiting team report. Meeting minutes of Texas State Board of Education Meeting (Appendix B), Austin.

Wright, D. P., McKibbon, M. & Walton, P. (1987). *The effectiveness of the teacher trainee program: An alternate route into teaching in California.* Sacramento: California Commission on Teacher Credentialing.

Zumwalt, K. (1990). Alternate routes to teaching: Three alternative approaches. New York: Teachers College, Columbia University.

POSTSCRIPT

Should Alternative Teacher Training Be Encouraged?

The present shortage of teachers, which has brought about the admission of college graduates without indoctrination in "methods," is an opportunity not to be missed. Liberal arts majors, if their courses were truly liberal, will be free of crippling ideas about how to teach.

— Jacques Barzun

This sentiment, of course, is in direct contrast to Darling-Hammond's position expressed in *The Right to Learn* (1997): "Many people sincerely believe that anyone can teach, or, at least, that knowing a subject is enough to allow one to teach it well. Others believe that teaching is best learned, to the extent that it can be learned at all, by trial and error on the job. The evidence, however, strongly suggests otherwise."

Further argumentation on this basic issue can be found in the following sources: Chester E. Finn, Jr., and Kathleen Madigan, "Removing Barriers for Teacher Candidates," *Educational Leadership* (May 2001); Carol Tell, "Making Room for Alternative Routes," *Educational Leadership* (May 2001); David C. Berliner, "A Personal Response to Those Who Bash Teacher Education," *Journal of Teacher Education* (November/December 2000); and Susan Moore Johnson, "Can Professional Certification for Teachers Reshape Teaching as a Career?" *Phi Delta Kappan* (January 2001).

Articles related to the Wendy Kopp alternative include Molly Ness, "Lessons of a First-Year Teacher," *Phi Delta Kappan* (May 2001); Sara Mosle, "Mrs. Ed: Teach for America's Misguided Critics," *The New Republic* (January 23, 1995); and Margaret Raymond and Stephen Fletcher, "The Teach for America Evolution," *Education Next* (Spring 2002).

Special theme issues may be found in *Educational Horizons* (Fall 1999 and Spring 2000), *Kappa Delta Pi Record* (Spring 2000), *The School Administrator* (January 2001), *Educational Leadership* (March 2002), and *Education Next* (Spring 2002).

In the midst of all of this wrangling about the components and length of teacher preparation, perhaps what is needed is a reconceptualization of teaching as a career. We need to address what is needed before entry into the profession, what is needed in the formative stages of the developing professional, and, most important, what is needed in the various fulfillment stages along the path to retirement and beyond.

Contributors to This Volume

EDITOR

JAMES WM. NOLL has retired from his professorial position in the College of Education at the University of Maryland in College Park, Maryland, where he taught philosophy of education and chaired the Social Foundations of Education unit. He has been affiliated with the American Educational Studies Association, the National Society for the Study of Education, the Association for Supervision and Curriculum Development, and the World Future Society. He received a B.A. in English and history from the University of Wisconsin–Milwaukee, an M.S. in educational administration from the University of Wisconsin, and a Ph.D. in philosophy of education from the University of Chicago. His articles have appeared in several education journals, and he is coauthor, with Sam P. Kelly, of *Foundations of Education in America: An Anthology of Major Thought and Significant Actions* (Harper & Row, 1970). He also has served as editor and editorial board member for McGraw-Hill/Dushkin's *Annual Editions: Education* series.

STAFF

Theodore Knight   List Manager
David Brackley   Senior Developmental Editor
Juliana Gribbins   Developmental Editor
Rose Gleich   Administrative Assistant
Brenda S. Filley   Director of Production/Design
Juliana Arbo   Typesetting Supervisor
Diane Barker   Proofreader
Richard Tietjen   Publishing Systems Manager
Larry Killian   Copier Coordinator

AUTHORS

MORTIMER J. ADLER (1902–2001), during a long and distinguished career, taught philosophy at the University of Chicago, served on the board of the *Encyclopedia Britannica,* founded the Institute for Philosophical Research and the Aspen Institute, and coedited the *Great Books of the Western World.* His books include *Six Great Ideas* (1981), *Mind Over Matter* (1990), and an autobiography, *Philosopher at Large* (1977).

KAREN AGNE is an assistant professor of education in the Center for Educational Studies and Services at the State University of New York at Plattsburgh and director of the Adirondack Advocacy for Gifted Education. She is a 20-year veteran of the Illinois public schools, where she served as a specialist in programs for gifted students.

JEAN B. ARNOLD is an attorney with the law firm McGuire, Woods, Battle, and Boothe in Charlottesville, Virginia.

WILLIAM J. BENNETT, codirector of Empower America, served as U.S. secretary of education in the Reagan administration and as chairman of the National Endowment for the Humanities in the George Bush administration. His most recent books are *The Educated Child,* coauthored with Chester E. Finn, Jr., and John T. E. Cribb, Jr. (1999), and *Why We Fight: Moral Clarity and the War on Terrorism* (2002).

MARC F. BERNSTEIN is superintendent of the Bellmore-Merrick Central High School District in North Merrick, New York.

JACQUELINE GRENNON BROOKS is an associate professor in the Professional Education Program and director of the Science Education Program at the State University of New York at Stony Brook. She is nationally known for her work in teacher training and development.

MARTIN G. BROOKS is superintendent of the Valley Stream Central High School District in New York. He is coauthor, with Jacqueline Grennon Brooks, of *In Search of Understanding: A Case for Constructivist Classrooms* (1993).

R. FREEMAN BUTTS is the William F. Russell Professor Emeritus in the Foundations of Education at Columbia University's Teachers College in New York City. His books include *The Civic Mission in Educational Reform: Perspectives for the Public and the Profession* (1989) and *In the First Person Singular: The Foundations of Education* (1993).

ROBERT L. CORD is the University Distinguished Professor of Political Science at Northeastern University in Boston, Massachusetts. He is the author of several books and articles about the U.S. Constitution, including *Separation of Church and State: Historical Fact and Current Fiction* (1988), which has been cited in numerous constitutional law books and in U.S. Supreme Court opinions.

EMERAL A. CROSBY is principal of Pershing High School in Detroit, Michigan. He served on the National Commission on Excellence in Education that produced the 1983 *A Nation at Risk* report, at which time he was principal of Northern High School in Detroit.

LINDA DARLING-HAMMOND is the Charles E. Ducommun Professor of Education at Stanford University and executive director of the National Commission on Teaching and America's Future. She has also been codirector of the National Center for Restructuring Education, Schools, and Teaching. Among her publications is *The Right to Learn: A Blueprint for Creating Schools That Work* (1997).

JOHN DEWEY (1859–1952) was a philosopher and a leader in the field of education. He taught at the University of Michigan, the University of Chicago (where he founded a laboratory school to test his ideas), and Columbia University (where he spawned the progressive education movement). His writings had a profound impact on the fields of philosophy, educational theory, educational psychology, and political science. Among his many books are *The School and Society* (1899) and *Democracy and Education* (1916).

HAROLD W. DODGE is superintendent of the Mobile County Public Schools in Alabama. He previously served as superintendent of schools in Cumberland County, Virginia.

EDD DOERR is executive director of Americans for Religious Liberty in Silver Spring, Maryland. He is also a columnist for *The Humanist* and the author of *The Case Against School Vouchers* (1996).

THOMAS J. FAMULARO is operations manager for Bowne Financial Printers in Secaucus, New Jersey. He is a former English instructor at the City University of New York.

CHESTER E. FINN, JR., is president of the Thomas B. Fordham Foundation and a senior fellow at the Manhattan Institute. He served as assistant U.S. secretary of education from 1985 to 1988, and he was a member of the National Assessment Governing Board from 1988 to 1996.

JANE M. HEALY is an educational psychologist specializing in brain research applications. She is the author of *Failure to Connect: How Computers Affect Our Children's Minds—For Better and Worse* (1998).

ROBERT HOLLAND is a senior fellow of the Lexington Institute in Arlington, Virginia. A journalist, he served as op-ed page editor for the Richmond, Virginia, *Times-Dispatch.*

JOHN HOLT (1923–1985) was an educator and a critic of public schooling. He authored several influential books on education, including *How Children Fail* (1964) and *Instead of Education: Ways to Help People Do Things Better* (1976).

NINA HURWITZ was a high school teacher in Westchester County, New York, for 23 years. She and her husband, Sol, have written many articles on education and student health care.

SOL HURWITZ is an education consultant and a freelance writer. He has also served as a board member of the Albert Shanker Institute.

ROBERT M. HUTCHINS (1879–1977) was chancellor of the University of Chicago, cocompiler of *The Great Books of the Western World,* and director of the Center for the Study of Democratic Institutions. Among his books are *The Higher Learning in America* (1936) and *University of Utopia* (1964).

INSTITUTE FOR JUSTICE is a nonprofit public interest law center in Washington, D.C., that seeks to promote a free and responsible society.

KIRK A. JOHNSON is a senior policy analyst at the Center for Data Analysis at the Heritage Foundation in Washington, D.C. He was previously affiliated with the Center for Economic Studies at the U.S. Census Bureau.

JAMES C. KIELSMEIER is founder and president of the National Youth Leadership Council in St. Paul, Minnesota. He also founded the Center for Experiential Education and Service-Learning at the University of Minnesota.

ALFIE KOHN writes and lectures widely on education and human behavior. His books include *Punished by Rewards* (1993), *Beyond Discipline: From Compliance to Community* (1996), *The Schools Our Children Deserve* (1999), and *The Case Against Standardized Testing* (2000).

THOMAS LICKONA, a developmental psychologist, is a professor of education at the State University of New York at Cortland and director of the Center for the Fourth and Fifth Rs (Respect and Responsibility). He is on the board of the Character Education Partnership, and he is the author of *Educating for Character* (1991).

HORACE MANN (1796–1859), a lawyer and a politician, served as secretary of the Massachusetts State Board of Education for 12 years. He was instrumental in bringing about publicly supported common schools in the United States. His writings include *Lectures on Education* (1855) and *A Few Thoughts on the Powers and Duties of Woman* (1853).

BRUNO V. MANNO is a senior program associate with the Annie E. Casey Foundation and a former U.S. assistant secretary of education.

BARBARA MEANS is an educational psychologist and codirector of the Center for Technology in Learning at SRI International in Menlo Park, California.

DEBORAH MEIER is cofounder and vice-chair of the Coalition of Essential Schools and developer of the Central Park East public elementary and secondary schools in East Harlem. Her work has won her a MacArthur Award. She is the author of *The Power of Their Ideas: Lessons for America From a Small School in Harlem* (1996).

NATIONAL EDUCATION ASSOCIATION is the largest and oldest professional organization for teachers and school administrators. Founded in 1857, it is headquartered in Washington, D.C., and currently has over 2.5 million members in over 13,000 local communities.

SONIA NIETO is a professor of language, literacy, and culture at the University of Massachusetts, Amherst. She is the author of *The Light in Their Eyes: Creating Multicultural Learning Communities* (1999) and *Affirming Diversity: The Sociopolitical Context of Multicultural Education,* 3rd ed. (2000).

PEDRO A. NOGUERA is the Judith K. Dimon Professor in Communities and Schools in the Harvard School of Education. He previously served as professor of education at the University of California, Berkeley. His research focuses on social and economic forces on urban schooling, and he writes articles on race relations and youth violence.

WARREN A. NORD is director of the Program in the Humanities and Human Values and teaches philosophy of religion at the University of North Carolina, Chapel Hill. He is the author of *Religion and American Education* (1995) and coauthor, with Charles Haynes, of *Taking Religion Seriously Across the Curriculum* (1998).

DANIEL H. PINK is a contributing editor at *Fast Company* magazine. He has written articles on technology, economic transformation, and the future for *New Republic,* the *New York Times,* and the *Washington Post.* He is a former White House speechwriter for Vice President Al Gore.

ROSALIE PEDALINO PORTER is chairman of the board and acting director of the Research in English Acquisition and Development (READ) Institute in Amherst, Massachusetts. She served in bilingual and English as a Second Language programs in the Newton, Massachusetts, public schools for 10 years, and she has lectured widely on the subject of bilingualism. She is the author of *Forked Tongue: The Politics of Bilingual Education* (1996).

CARL R. ROGERS (1902–1987), a noted psychologist and educator, taught at the University of Chicago and the University of Wisconsin–Madison. He introduced the client-directed approach to psychotherapy in 1942, and he was the first psychologist to record and transcribe therapy sessions verbatim. He authored *On Becoming a Person* (1972), among many other influential works.

GARY ROSEN is an associate editor of *Commentary* magazine and the author of *American Compact: James Madison and the Problem of Founding* (1999). He is a former senior editor of the Manhatttan Institute's *City Journal.*

ANDREW ROTHERHAM is director of educational policy at the Progressive Policy Institute in Washington, D.C. He also served as director of the institute's 21st Century Schools Project and has been a White House adviser.

RICHARD ROTHSTEIN is a research associate at the Economic Policy Institute in Washington, D.C., a senior correspondent for *The American Prospect,* a national education columnist for the *New York Times,* and an adjunct professor of public policy at Occidental College. He is the author of *The Way We Were? Debunking the Myth of America's Declining Schools* (1998).

ALBERT SHANKER (1928–1997) was president of the American Federation of Teachers in Washington, D.C., which gave teachers a union alternative to National Education Association membership. A leader in the educational reform movement, he was the first labor leader elected to the National Academy of Education. His Sunday *New York Times* column "Where We Stand" brought educational issues to a wide audience.

B. F. SKINNER (1904–1990), a noted psychologist and influential exponent of behaviorism, held the William James Chair in the Department of Psychology at Harvard University. His major works include *About Behaviorism* (1976) and *Reflections on Behaviorism and Society* (1978). His most widely read book is *Walden Two* (1948).

LISA SNELL is director of the Education and Child Welfare Program at the Reason Public Policy Institute. She is a monthly columnist for the institute's *Privatization Watch,* and she has worked on public policy issues for the Institute for Justice.

FORREST J. (FROSTY) TROY is editor of *The Oklahoma Observer* and the author of many articles on controversial issues in education. He has received the National Friend of Education Award and the First Amendment Award.

GREGG VANOUREK is vice president of the Charter School Division at K12 in McLean, Virginia.

PATRICIA A. WASLEY is dean of the College of Education at the University of Washington in Seattle, Washington, and former dean of the Graduate School of Education at the Bank Street College of Education.

Index

On the Internet ...

Pay-for-Performance and Merit Pay

This site of the National Council on Teacher Quality is a good place to begin exploring the topic of merit pay for teachers.

http://www.nctq.org/issues/merit.html

Student Voices: School Vouchers

This site, maintained by New York City Student Voices, provides numerous links to news and journal articles on various aspects of the school voucher issue, including the controversies surrounding recent Supreme Court rulings.

http://student-voices.org/newyork/links/vouchers.php3

PART 4

Bonus Issues

*T*he two debates presented in this part represent issues that have become especially contentious since the publication of the 12th edition of this book. They are particularly important in that they are shaping public policy that is being considered today. The first issue focuses on one of today's most controversial proposals for school reform: performance-based merit pay for teachers. The second debate stems from the 2002 Supreme Court decision regarding Cleveland's school voucher program.

- Can Merit Pay Accelerate School Improvement?

- Has the Supreme Court Reconfigured American Education?

ISSUE 22

Can Merit Pay Accelerate School Improvement?

YES: Steven Malanga, from "Why Merit Pay Will Improve Teaching," *City Journal* (Summer 2001)

NO: Al Ramirez, from "How Merit Pay Undermines Education," *Educational Leadership* (February 2001)

ISSUE SUMMARY

YES: Steven Malanga, a senior fellow of the Manhattan Institute, draws on examples from the corporate world and from public school systems in Cincinnati, Iowa, and Denver to make his case for performance-based merit pay for teachers.

NO: Associate professor of education Al Ramirez contends that merit pay programs misconstrue human motivation and devalue the work of teachers.

The issue of merit pay, or pay-for-performance, for teachers is certainly not new, but as Steven Malanga, one of the combatants presented in the pairing offered here, says, it is "one of the bitterest controversies in today's school reform debate." The current push to improve public education, particularly in impoverished areas, and to hold individual schools more accountable for achieving desired results has rekindled the argument over merit pay as a replacement for a reward system based primarily on seniority and earned course credits.

Although some forms of merit plans were widely used in the early part of the twentieth century, the economic depression of the 1930s prompted conversions to uniform pay scales. Teachers' unions, which gained strength throughout the remainder of the century, were not supportive of incentive pay schemes. They expressed doubts about the fairness of various evaluation methods and concerns about possible threats to collegiality and the standardization of teaching practices. Since the 1980s, and particularly since the passage of the "No Child Left Behind" legislation, pressure for an accountability system containing specific rewards for teachers and schools that meet desired outcomes has vastly increased.

The matter of how to appropriately and fairly evaluate teacher performance remains a major stumbling block in the adoption of merit pay plans. Local socioeconomic factors and the unevenness of support structures among school systems and states add complexity to the process. According to Sandra McCollum, in "How Merit Pay Improves Education," *Educational Leadership* (February 2001), merit pay programs are often discontinued because of one or more of the following reasons: they are unfairly implemented, teachers' unions refuse to endorse them, they create poor teacher morale, legislators who support them leave office, and they are simply too costly and difficult to administer.

An economist's view is offered by Darius Lakdawalla in "Quantity Over Quality," *Education Next* (Fall 2002). He contends that schools have been hiring more teachers in an effort to reduce class sizes but have not been rewarding them for quality performance. In the past few decades, serious opportunities outside teaching have opened up, and school systems have not risen to challenge the competition. The problem of retaining and attracting top-quality teachers is addressed in Marge Scherer, "Improving the Quality of the Teaching Force: A Conversation With David C. Berliner," *Educational Leadership* (May 2001). Berliner states that 7 of 23 nations surveyed exceed the United States in starting salaries for teachers and that 9 of 21 nations exceed the United States in top teacher salaries. In the realm of pay, status, and working conditions, says Berliner, "The U.S. is saying to its educators that they are not really important; if we thought they were important, we'd pay them a larger share of our gross domestic product, as other nations do." Yet Berliner is also worried that a merit pay plan based primarily on student achievement could lead to teachers' doing the wrong thing in their classrooms—cheating and narrowing the curriculum.

Some guidelines for the fair evaluation of teacher performance are put forth by Thomas R. Hoerr in "A Case for Merit Pay," *Phi Delta Kappan* (December 1998). In Hoerr's view, there must be trust between the administration and the faculty, judgments must be treated with confidentiality, there must be recognition that both what is valued and how it is measured will vary by context, and teachers who do not perform satisfactorily and do not respond to supportive intervention should not be rehired. Getting rid of ineffective teachers, however, is so arduous and expensive that many school systems do not attempt it. So says Peter Schweizer in "Firing Offenses," *National Review* (August 17, 1998). He analyzes the companion issue of teacher tenure, a system that was originally designed to protect the best teachers from wrongful termination but that Schweizer says now protects the worst teachers from rightful termination.

In the following selections, Steven Malanga argues that merit pay is essential to meaningful teacher evaluation and school improvement, while Al Ramirez contends that merit pay is a misguided policy with numerous unintended consequences.

Steven Malanga

 **YES**

Why Merit Pay Will Improve Teaching

One of the bitterest controversies in today's school-reform debate is merit pay—rewarding teachers not for seniority and the number of ed-school credits they've piled up, as public schools have done since the early 1920s, but for what they actually achieve in the classroom. Education reformers argue that merit pay will give encouragement to good teachers and drive away bad ones, and thus improve under-performing public schools. But most teachers' unions adamantly oppose the idea. We don't have reliable means to measure a teacher's classroom performance, the unions charge, so merit plans will inevitably result in supervisor bias and favoritism: "Just too many cliques in the system," one teacher typically complains in a recent survey.

Nowhere is the incentives debate raging more fiercely than in New York City, where teachers' contract negotiations have been at an impasse for months. Mayor Rudolph Giuliani has demanded that merit pay for individual teachers be part of any deal; the teachers' union response (at least so far): fuhgeddaboudit.

Missing from the argument, though, are lessons from the private sector, where sophisticated, effective performance-based compensation has been *de rigueur* since the 1980s—part and parcel, experts believe, of corporate America's hugely successful restructuring. Also ignored are experiments with comprehensive merit-pay plans that are under way in a few innovative school districts across the country—districts burdened with much less political resistance than Gotham.

✲❦✲

To get a sense of what merit pay could do for the public schools, consider the benefits it has showered on American industry over the last two decades. Before the eighties, merit pay in U.S. firms—if it existed at all—was pretty simple: the boss gave you a fat bonus if you (or your unit) met sales or production goals. But as international economic competition pummeled them in the early 1980s, U.S. corporations, desperate to regain their competitiveness, began to experiment with measuring individual worker performance. They established pay incentives to improve it in formerly hard-to-measure categories of output and in previously intangible areas like customer service or product quality. Of course, the bottom line was still the bottom line, but these intangibles, companies now reasoned, mattered to the long-term economic health of the firm, even if they didn't show up right away in the quarter-by-quarter numbers.

Familiar today, the new performance criteria—and the multi-faceted compensation plans built on their foundation—were strikingly original at the time. Retailers hired "mystery" shoppers to check out how employees treated customers, and based salaries, in part, on what they found. Businesses built into sales contracts "integrity" clauses that gauged not just how many widgets an employee sold but how long clients stuck with him. Banks remunerated loan officers not just for the lending they brought in but for the long-term quality of their loan portfolios. Some auto dealers tied part of salesmen's pay to how customers rated them in follow-up surveys. Companies combined these kinds of individualized incentives with rewards for everybody if the whole firm did well. Airlines, for example, gave the entire crew bonuses if the fleet's on-time performance improved.

Predictably, when U.S. businesses first introduced these innovations, workers grumbled, especially in heavily unionized industries like auto manufacturing, where any change threatened cushy labor arrangements. "They said that you couldn't measure some things, that the pay systems were too subjective, that supervisors were too subjective—in short, everything that teachers today are saying," observes Alan Johnson, a New York–based compensation consultant. Many efforts stumbled at first, too, and companies had to discard or overhaul them. Creating effective programs, it became clear, would not be an overnight fix. "Even today, with all we know, it takes three years to start up an effective incentive-pay program," cautions Martha Glantz, a compensation expert with Buck Consultants in Manhattan. "You can spend the first year just deciding what the company's goals and missions are, and collecting the data."

But American firms, needing to change or perish, forged ahead, winning over employees who liked the challenge of incentive pay and, through trial and error, developing pay plans that worked. By the mid-1990s, half of all major American corporations used such incentives. "It's no longer credible to say you can't measure something or that the only thing you can measure is a simple output," says Johnson. Merit pay played a crucial role, most observers believe, in generating the zooming productivity gains and superior product quality that American firms began recording in the late 1980s and that have been central to the nation's economic prosperity ever since.

⋘◉⋙

The public education monopoly has long resisted merit pay with the same ferocity with which private-sector workers at first greeted it. Opponents have constantly invoked previous attempts that failed—though their only examples have been two experiments that are over 100 years old, and another from the 1960s, before modern notions of performance pay emerged. The conventional wisdom among educators had long been that any attempt to pin down exactly what makes for good teaching, let alone measure and reward it fairly, was doomed to fail. "There was a general feeling that you were either gifted as a teacher or you weren't, and that good teaching wasn't something you could define," says Charlotte Danielson, an expert on teaching at the Educational Testing Service in New Jersey. As a last-ditch defense, some educators even argued that factors outside school, especially a student's socioeconomic and family situation, had a much greater impact on student performance than teachers did, so that using merit pay based on student performance to promote good teaching, even if it could be defined, wasn't fair. The unasked question was why teachers should ever receive salary hikes if what they do doesn't matter.

Over the last decade, these views have utterly collapsed, undermining the intellectual case—weak as it was—against merit pay. A key figure has been University of Tennessee statistician William Sanders, who discovered how to measure a teacher's effect on student performance. Rather than try to filter out the myriad sociological influences on pupils, a nearly impossible task, Sanders used complex statistical methods to chart the progress of students against themselves over the course of a school year and measure how much "value" different teachers added. Now called the Tennessee Value-Added Assessment System, Sanders's approach proved what every parent already knew: not only did teachers matter, but some were lots better than others. Other education experts, including Danielson, author of several popular books on pedagogy, developed widely accepted criteria to judge good teaching, which put paid to the absurd notion that it was too elusive to define.

⚜

If the 1990s helped re-establish the centrality of teaching in the education debate, however, that victory hasn't melted away the teachers' unions' political opposition to merit pay. Even so, a small number of school systems across the country, under intense pressure from parents, politicians, and administrators to improve student performance, have turned to merit pay to promote better teaching. And, after some give-and-take, they've managed to get the teachers' unions on board.

Cincinnati's public school system, the first to experiment with performance incentives, persuaded its teachers' union in 1997 to do a test run of merit pay. Two years later, a ten-school pilot program, designed by administrators and teachers, got under way. Essential to union support was the pilot's proposed use of peers to evaluate teachers. "The peer evaluators, who have no stake in how teachers are judged, are important to the perception of the fairness of the system," observes Kathleen Ware, associate superintendent of Cincinnati schools. Using Danielson's criteria of good teaching—they include class preparation and clarity of presentation—the principals and peer evaluators devoted 20 to 30 hours to assessing every teacher in the ten chosen schools. Based on how they scored, teachers then wound up in one of five salary categories, with "novices" making the least money and "accomplished" teachers the most.

The pilot proved successful. A majority of teachers involved found it fair and judged the standards used as appropriate for the whole school district. The city's board of education adopted it in the spring of 2000, and, in a subsequent election, union members signed on. Teachers will go through evaluations every five years, though those looking to move up quickly can request an appraisal after just two years. New teachers and one-fifth of all experienced teachers [had] evaluations done [in 2001], but no one [started] getting paid under the new system until 2002.

Unfortunately, Cincinnati's new program doesn't directly use student test scores in its evaluations. Bringing in scores would have generated too much union hostility for the plan to gain acceptance, reports school superintendent Steven Adamowski. And in all likelihood, tying pay solely to test scores is a bad idea; nobody would call meritorious a teacher who boosted scores but left his students psychological wrecks because of his bullying. Yet leaving tests out altogether also makes no sense. After all, what better way to determine how well students are doing—the only reason for the concern over teaching quality in the first place—than test scores? Cincinnati's program recognizes this implicitly. The district will monitor test results of students whose teachers score the highest ratings. If those students don't show substantial improvement, school officials will toughen the program's standards. In addition, the district will rely on student tests to award bonuses to all teachers in a school whose kids take big strides.

⌒◉⌒

One major benefit of merit systems is that they enable schools to pay teachers —especially young and ambitious teachers—fatter salaries. That's the overriding rationale behind Iowa's new incentives program, enacted by the state legislature to keep better-paying nearby states from spiriting away top teachers. The state has anted up $40 million for salary increases, but, in a program similar to Cincinnati's, Iowa will now evaluate teachers thoroughly to make sure the extra dough goes only to the good classroom performers, not the duds. "We believe this system will help us retain the best people by re-professionalizing teaching," enthuses John Forsyth, chief executive of the Des Moines–based Wellmark Blue Cross and Blue Shield. Forsyth helped the state dream up the new system, looking to the market for inspiration. "We know good teachers make a difference," he continues, "and we're going to pay those who do make a difference." How much more reasonable this is than the New York union's claim that, because a few city teachers jump to higher-paying suburban schools each year, all teachers —the good and the bad alike—need equal raises to make them stay.

In Iowa's new system, good teachers will now be able to reach higher salary levels much earlier in their careers than before. "The private pay consultants who looked at our old seniority system thought it must have been designed specifically to keep teacher pay low and save school districts money," says Ted Stilwill, director of Iowa's Department of Education. "The only way for teachers to get paid more under that system was for them to stick it out for years." As in Cincinnati, union opposition means that Iowa won't rely on test scores to evaluate teachers—at least not directly. But in addition to paying teachers based on their performance evaluations, the state will also offer modest yearly bonuses to all teachers in a school whose students do well on standardized tests, with the biggest bonuses going to the school's best instructors, rather than all teachers getting equal rewards.

Helping to develop Iowa's plan has been an eye-opener for the state's education chief. "Private-sector compensation experts taught me that businesses use pay as a way of getting everyone to follow common goals," Stilwill says. "Being in the public sector most of my life, I never understood that."

⋅⟨⊙⟩⋅

Though Cincinnati and Iowa have skirted the controversy of using student test scores, Denver is confronting it head-on. The city has launched two pilot plans that link pay directly to scores. One pilot program uses student scores in standardized tests of basic skills; another relies on scores in specific subjects. Principals and teachers agree at the beginning of the school year on what kinds of improvements in test scores they'll shoot for and then face evaluation at the end of the year to see if they've met their goals. Denver is also instituting a third merit-pay pilot program that instructs teachers in the principles of good teaching and then evaluates their teaching skills and rewards them accordingly. Denver will later measure how their students perform on tests to see if its criteria for good teaching really produce results. Through these experiments, Denver hopes to figure out what motivates teachers best and what works best for students.

Denver's teachers' union, surprisingly, has contributed mightily to developing the pilots; the head of the project's design team, Brad Jupp, is a union negotiator. He says the union is participating because the demand to make schools more accountable is so intense that teachers would rather help create performance systems than have them imposed from above. "If you believe that your union members are doing a good job—and we do—then you want a system that accurately measures that," says Jupp.

Experiences from the private sector suggest that it will take several years before these imaginative programs work out all their kinks. In the meantime, controversy will dog the new programs. Critics will pounce on their every mistake as evidence that paying teachers for performance is a bad idea. And unions are likely to push for watered-down plans in order to deflect criticism without giving up too much.

This last is exactly what's happening in New York. The teachers' union has offered the mayor a compromise: pay *every* teacher in a school or district a bonus if the school's or district's test scores rise. A trial run of such a system, supported by Gotham's business community, is under way in two urban districts; other states, including California and Georgia, already have school-based bonuses.

But group bonuses will never substitute adequately for true performance pay, compensation experts believe, since they don't single out good and bad teachers. All they're likely to do is to frustrate first-rate teachers working in schools with mediocre staffs. "If you have four workers doing well in a unit that is not otherwise performing, over time those four will leave the company and go somewhere that they can be rewarded for their superior work," says consultant Glantz. And since schoolwide bonuses don't put any pay at risk—poor performance doesn't mean less money—they won't help rid schools of lousy teachers either. By contrast, teachers who score poorly in, say, Cincinnati, now find themselves shunted into the lowest salary level, discouraging them from sticking around. Mayor Giuliani, rightly, has rejected the union's offer.

Of course, smaller cities like Cincinnati are far removed from the we-don't-do-windows union obstructionism of a New York or a Los Angeles. For 15 years, Cincinnati's teachers' union has accepted some kind of peer evaluation of teachers; it's easily one of the nation's most flexible teachers' unions. Unions in New York and Los Angeles, conversely, have fought almost every education reform tooth and nail. Last year in Los Angeles, thousands of teachers ferociously protested against a proposed merit-pay plan, eventually killing it. Moreover, in the current public school monopoly, there's nothing really comparable to the outside economic pressure that forced American industry to develop its merit programs—one more argument for school choice.

Without individualized merit pay, teacher evaluations will remain perfunctory at best. Today, New York principals fail less than 1 percent of all teachers in annual evaluations. New York hopes to get principals to crack down on bad teaching by rewarding them financially when their schools do well. That will eliminate one of the main objections to teacher merit pay—that it leads to supervisor favoritism: even if a principal hates an effective teacher's guts, he's not going to want to lose someone who's helping him sweeten his own salary. But until teachers are part of any performance-pay system, the impact of such innovations will be severely limited—and students will continue to get shortchanged, regardless of how much their teachers take to the bank.

Al Ramirez

 **NO**

How Merit Pay Undermines Education

P roposals for merit pay, including pay-for-performance, continue to surface as policymakers search for ways to motivate administrators and teachers to be more effective—and to make educators do what policymakers want them to do. These types of remuneration plans are different from paying a teacher extra for taking on additional duties, such as running an after-school computer laboratory or serving as a mentor or master teacher. Instead, these merit pay policies give individual employees extra compensation, above and beyond the base salary, for work and contributions that exceed some pre-established criteria. These criteria often include achieving higher student test scores on standardized tests.

Carrots and Sticks

Why can't teachers and administrators be "incentivized" like aluminum-siding salespeople? Not all lawyers in a legal firm take home the same annual salary and bonuses, so why can't policymakers for public education find a way to pay similar classifications of employees different rates of pay on the basis of their job performance? Professional sports teams pay their players on the basis of their performance and perceived potential value to the team, so why can't school districts do the same?

But do compensation decisions really reflect employees' contributions? As Rosabeth Moss Kanter (1987) points out, "Status, not contribution, has traditionally been the basis for the numbers on employees' paychecks. Pay has reflected where jobs rank in the corporation hierarchy—not what comes out of them" (p. 60). Despite centuries of experience with employee compensation plans, status still wins out over contribution. Contrast the pay of corporate CEOs in the United States, some of whom earn more than 600 times as much as their typical non-management employees, to the much smaller differential between the pay of employees and CEOs in Europe and Japan. Do American corporate boards know something about compensation plans that their foreign competitors don't?

In fact, the seemingly logical link between employee production and compensation is often debatable and highly subjective. We can understand why new

From Al Ramirez, "How Merit Pay Undermines Education," *Educational Leadership,* vol. 58, no. 5 (February 2001), pp. 16–20. Copyright © 2001 by ASCD. Reprinted by permission of The Association for Supervision and Curriculum Development.

approaches to determining pay are so difficult to establish in public school districts today if we look at the historical development of educators' most common compensation approach—uniform salary schedules with steps and lanes. This compensation system rewards professionals for their years of experience on the job and level of educational attainment. Incentives are structured to encourage teachers and some administrators to remain loyal to the school district and to improve their skills and knowledge by pursuing additional training, usually by attending approved workshops and courses or earning graduate degrees.

In the ideal situation, this system rewards a teacher or principal who, for example, participates in a workshop, typically on his or her own time, about the educational uses of computers. This employee is building on a knowledge base and thus is able to make a greater contribution to the school district's mission to prepare students for success in our democratic society. In theory, this compensation system motivates employees to get better at their jobs. Critics argue that the theory behind this system doesn't hold up. They point to the lack of linkage between the incentive system and outcomes in schools and classrooms. They also challenge the abuses in such systems, where employees are rewarded for taking courses in wok cooking or given graduate credit by diploma mills for signing up for the walking tour of downtown Los Angeles.

But the tenacious attachment to this system has deep roots. In the past, policy leaders set up teacher compensation systems according to criteria that they felt were justified and appropriate, and boards of education, city councils, and other similar deliberative bodies used democratic means to arrive at pay policies. Nonetheless, some of these decisions look strange to us today. Consider the Chicago school system in the early 1900s. As the school system matured, policymakers moved to standardize the employee compensation system. One of the components of their system was a substantial pay differential between male and female employees (Peterson, 1985), and the gender pay differential continued even when women started to assume administrative roles. At the beginning of the 20th century, pay differentials in Atlanta, Georgia, were based on race. Although the African American community had managed to secure minimal services from the Atlanta school board, the dual system of education determined that African American and white teachers would not have the same rate of pay (Peterson, 1985). History has demonstrated that governing bodies are capable of establishing unfair practices. The legacy of such compensation systems in public education has been to elevate one criterion—fairness—as the paramount consideration in all pay decisions.

Logic would dictate that a teacher's years of experience in the classroom and level of educational attainment are somewhat related to the academic performance of students. In theory, a first-year chemistry teacher fresh out of college is not as effective with high school students as is a 10-year veteran with a master's degree in science teaching or organic chemistry. But critics counter that empirical evidence doesn't support such logic. They assert that a teacher's training is irrelevant and that experience counts for nothing. What matters, they say, are the results a teacher gets with students; outcomes, not inputs, should determine rewards. Using an outcome-based criterion, they claim, is the only fair approach to rewarding teachers.

Educators point out that such proposals for output-based compensation are not fair, reverting once again to the fairness issue. How can teachers be held accountable for school conditions that they cannot control? Unless all inputs are equalized for all teachers and administrators, how can policymakers judge the value of the outcome? Educators further argue that their jobs involve more than teaching academic subjects and often extend beyond the measurable —for example, consoling a child whose parents are going through a divorce or advising a student about options for college.

Understanding Human Motivation

The problem with both the input-reward system and the outcome-reward system is that they ignore the basic dynamics of what motivates human beings. The approach of focusing on fairness above all else has inhibited the contribution of some members of the group—for example, those with exceptional abilities who may not fit the mold. In contrast, the outcome-centered motivation system devalues the significance of an individual's contribution and oversimplifies the role of the educator. Neither system considers the body of research related to the psychology of human motivation.

Consider the work of Frederick Herzberg (1987) and his studies of employee motivation. He and his colleagues identified a series of more than 3,000 items that either motivated workers or diminished employees' enthusiasm for their jobs. The "satisfiers" and "dissatisfiers" will surprise policymakers who view money as the sole motivator on the job. Organizational policy and administrative procedures, supervisory practices, employee-employer relations, working conditions, and salary proved to have greater potential to be dissatisfiers than satisfiers. These dissatisfiers are important and need the attention of employers. But the satisfiers—the motivators that are essential to spurring performance to higher levels—included achievement on the job, recognition for one's contribution or for a job well done, the work itself, job responsibility, opportunities for career advancement, and professional growth.

Abraham Maslow's (1970) study of human motivation should also inform policymakers who are intent on lighting a fire under professional educators. Maslow bases his theory on a hierarchy of needs to which all humans respond. This hierarchy ascends from basic needs (water, shelter, and food) to complex needs (advancement, growth, and achievement). Money, benefits, and job security appear at the lower end of the hierarchy. Merit pay systems that attempt to use money alone as a lever for improvement are more likely to cause educators who have other employment options to leave the school district than to strive for the desired results of their supervisors.

William Glasser (1997) presents an articulate explanation of human motivation through his Choice Theory. Glasser points out that all people are motivated to meet their needs for belonging to groups, maintaining a sense of self-efficacy or power, and having fun. These are natural and intrinsic needs that humans are driven to meet. When institutions use extrinsic motivation devices to manipulate their members, they often divert their members from meeting these intrinsic human needs. The frustration and anger that often result are destructive to the organization. Ill-conceived reward systems that diminish employee loyalty and increase resentment toward management can cause incalculable productivity losses in organizations. Here again, money alone does not work as a motivator.

Perhaps no one has been more eloquent than the late W. Edwards Deming (1993) in addressing the destructive nature of extrinsic reward systems

> that squeeze out from an individual, over his lifetime, his innate intrinsic motivation, self-esteem, dignity. They build into him fear, self-defense, extrinsic motivation. We have been destroying our people, from toddlers on through the university, and on the job. (p. 124)

According to Deming, the forces of destruction include grade rankings; merit systems, particularly ones that categorize people; contrived competition among people within organizations; schemes for incentive pay and pay-for-performance; and numerical goals, targets, and quotas—without any guidelines on how to achieve them. These forces suboptimize the system and cause humiliation, resentment, and fear. Using such approaches also shifts the burden to produce results from management to the employees. Deming asserts that such practices belie the fact that more than 90 percent of the organization's outcomes are the result of the leadership and governance structure of the organization and not the effort of individual workers who work in the system.

Extrinsic reward systems create the illusion of employer control but at the expense of the full involvement and commitment of dedicated, enthusiastic employees. Extrinsic reward systems divert resources and energy from what is much more likely to move the organization to higher levels of performance. They discard the most valuable resources in the organization: the brainpower, problem-solving ability, and innovative thinking that every employee brings to the job.

Dud Silver Bullets

A growing number of legislators, governors, mayors, superintendents, school board members, and business people advocate programs for merit pay or pay-for-performance. Their good intentions to make schools better often lead them to quick-fix solutions and seemingly obvious, but wrong, answers. Perhaps one of the biggest ironies encountered by school leaders is the ill-informed advice they receive, often unsolicited, from business leaders who proffer "real-world" solutions—like merit pay—to fix school problems. These business leaders are ignorant of the research literature that does not support such practices; ironically, these findings often come out of business leaders' own university-based business colleges. In some cases, unfortunately, the political leaders know better but cannot resist the temptation to scapegoat the less powerful members of the organization—teachers—and pander to an ignorant public and news media. And in the worst cases, leaders are so cynical about the public education system that they blame and punish employees as a way of diverting attention from the real, and typically more costly, issues confronting the schools.

Donald Campbell, Kathleen Campbell, and Ho-Beng Chia (1998) conducted a thorough investigation of merit pay systems. They concluded that pay-for-performance programs raise problematic issues related to measurement, performance appraisal and feedback, and the desirability of the rewards. For example, questions arise about the validity either of the instrument used to measure performance or the nature of the work. Attempts to address these issues through training or better measures fall short. Additionally, the researchers found that employees tend to reject most or all of the evaluation systems, regardless of what adjustments are made. Money, the key factor in such systems, is usually in short supply, so the potential impact of rewards is minimal and does not outweigh the negative effects of the merit pay system. Finally, the authors conclude that the implementation of merit pay systems becomes unwieldy, contributes to mission drift, and often leads to unintended consequences, such as enormous pay differentials between subordinates and supervisors, or the ignoring of work assignments that do not earn consideration for merit.

Questions to Ask

Policymakers and school leaders are supposed to make changes that improve the education systems for which they are responsible. The penchant to move to action and make sweeping changes without proper policy analysis and policy development techniques contributes to the dysfunction of many school systems. The one-step-forward-two-steps-back method of creating education policy, so common today, is certainly irresponsible, if not unethical. Flashy or feel-good policies make the system worse. Policymakers, leaders, and deliberative bodies that are interested in investigating the value of merit pay systems should ask themselves these questions:

- Do I understand the nature of human motivation? Why have our teachers and administrators chosen to work in our school district? It is often difficult to tap into the employee's motivation for employment, and some appraisal and reward systems may even reduce enthusiasm for the job and productivity.
- Can a school district be run like a business? Do business practices readily transfer to a publicly held organization run by highly trained professionals with an educational mission? Do the culture and structure of a school district support or deter the use of business-like evaluation and merit systems?
- Is this evaluation and reward system fair? How would I feel if my employer instituted such a program at my job? Fairness in the design and implementation of appraisal and reward systems is both crucial and complex. The fairness issue will permeate any proposed system and must apply to the employee, the appraiser, the organization, and the organizational stakeholders, including students, parents, and taxpayers.

- Can my organization find an evaluation and compensation system that is not excessively burdensome and that operates effectively? Do I understand that some important job functions may not be measurable? Do I understand that some elaborate evaluation systems may distract staff from their duties?
- Have I explored the unintended consequences of a new system? Organization leaders must be careful about what is rewarded in a merit pay system—because they will get it! Have I considered what won't get done because it doesn't count for merit pay? The goal is to move forward, not to suboptimize the organization.
- Am I clear about whom to reward? This central question must be part of policymakers' considerations. Will the system reward individuals or teams? Enterprises that are highly collaborative should be cautious about setting compensation systems in motion that promote destructive competition.

A candid discussion of these questions among policymakers, school leaders, and stakeholders will go a long way toward forming sound education policy. Employee evaluation and reward systems are complicated matters that require thoughtful deliberation. They have the potential to be as destructive as they are constructive. Our schools are too important to operate with misguided policies.

References

Campbell, D. J., Campbell, K. M., & Chia, H. B. (1998). Merit pay, performance appraisal, and individual motivation: An analysis and alternative. *Human Resources Management, 37*(2), 131–146.

Deming, W. E. (1993). *The new economics for industry, government, education.* Cambridge, MA: Massachusetts Institute of Technology Center for Advanced Engineering Study.

Glasser, W. (1997). A new look at school failure and school success. *Phi Delta Kappan, 78*(8), 596–602.

Herzberg, F. (1987). One more time: How do you motivate employees? *Harvard Business Review, 65,* 109–120.

Kanter, R. M. (1987, March/April). Attack on pay. *Harvard Business Review, 65,* 60–67.

Maslow, A. H. (1970). *Motivation and Personality.* New York: Harper & Row.

Peterson, P. E. (1985). *The politics of school reform, 1870–1940.* Chicago: University of Chicago Press.

POSTSCRIPT

Can Merit Pay Accelerate School Improvement?

After the Soviet Union's challenge to America's technological superiority manifested itself in the late 1950s, financial incentives were given to present and recruited teachers of math and science under a federal initiative. Currently, the "crisis" focus is on underperforming public schools located primarily in districts with high percentages of minority students. Some critics have made the argument that a maximum federal effort should be directed at schools with the greatest need in order to close the existing achievement gaps. This idea is elaborated upon by Cynthia D. Prince in "Attracting Well-Qualified Teachers to Struggling Schools," *American Educator* (Winter 2002). "Today," she explains, "both the ATF [American Federation of Teachers] and the NEA [National Education Association] favor offering locally-developed financial incentives to qualified teachers who choose to work in hard-to-staff schools."

In "The Teacher Shortage: A Case of Wrong Diagnosis and Wrong Prescription," *NASSP Bulletin* (June 2002), Richard M. Ingersoll offers an analysis of reasons why large numbers of qualified teachers are departing their jobs for reasons other than retirement. In "Why Are Experienced Teachers Leaving the Profession?" *Phi Delta Kappan* (September 2002), Barbara Benham Tye and Lisa O'Brien report on their survey of teachers who have already left the profession and those who are considering leaving. They found that those who had left ranked the pressure of increased accountability (high-stakes testing and standards) as the number one reason. Salary considerations ranked seventh. Of those who were considering leaving, however, salary considerations ranked first.

A stinging indictment of merit pay can be found in Maurice Holt's "Performance Pay for Teachers: The Standards Movement's Last Stand?" *Phi Delta Kappan* (December 2001). In it, Holt states, "Having done their best to demoralize schools and give the phrase 'testing to destruction' a new meaning, there's one last aspect of civilized education that the Standardistos have in their sights: the sense of trust and cooperation among teachers." Their ammunition: "competitive salary structures."

Further resources on the topic of merit pay for teachers include Lawrence Hardy, "What's a Teacher Worth?" *American School Board Journal* (August 2002); Allan Odden, "New and Better Forms of Teacher Compensation Are Possible," *Phi Delta Kappan* (January 2000); Cynthia D. Prince, "Higher Pay in Hard-to-Staff Schools: The Case for Financial Incentives," *The School Administrator* (June 2002); and Allan Odden, Dale Ballou, and Michael Podgursky, "Defining Merit," *Education Matters* (Spring 2001).

ISSUE 23

Has the Supreme Court Reconfigured American Education?

YES: Charles L. Glenn, from "Fanatical Secularism," *Education Next* (Winter 2003)

NO: Paul E. Peterson, from "Victory for Vouchers?" *Commentary* (September 2002)

ISSUE SUMMARY

YES: Professor of education Charles L. Glenn argues that the Supreme Court's decision in *Zelman v. Simmons-Harris* is an immediate antidote to the public school's secularist philosophy.

NO: Professor of government Paul E. Peterson, while welcoming the decision, contends that the barricades against widespread use of vouchers in religious schools will postpone any lasting effects.

In June 2002 the U.S. Supreme Court released its decision of *Zelman v. Simmons-Harris,* which dealt with Ohio's Pilot Project Scholarship Program. This program provides tuition vouchers to certain students in the Cleveland Public School District who wish to transfer from their assigned public school to a participating school of their choosing. The available choices include public schools in adjacent school districts, nonreligious private schools, and religious private schools. Controversy over this program stemmed from the fact that in the 1999–2000 school year, 96 percent of the Cleveland students who were receiving vouchers were enrolled in schools with religious affiliations. Ohio taxpayers (Doris Simmons-Harris et al.) sued state school officials (Superintendent Susan Tave Zelman et al.) to enjoin the program on the grounds that it violated the establishment clause of the U.S. Constitution, which mandates separation of church and state.

The Supreme Court found (by a 5–4 vote) that Ohio's voucher program does not offend the establishment clause, thereby reversing lower courts' judgments that the program is unconstitutional. The majority opinion–delivered by Chief Justice William H. Rehnquist–stated that the program was enacted for the valid secular purpose of providing educational assistance to poor children in a demonstrably failing public school system; that government aid reaches religious institutions only by way of the deliberate choices of individual recipients; and that the only preference in the program is for low-income families, who receive greater assistance and have priority for admission. In dissent, Justice John Paul Stevens queried, "Is a law that authorizes the use of public funds to pay for the indoctrination of thousands of children in particular religious faiths a 'law respecting an establishment of religion' within the meaning of the First Amendment?" He stated, "The voluntary character of the private choice to prefer a parochial education over an education in the public school system seems to me quite irrelevant to the question whether the government's choice to pay for religious indoctrination is Constitutionally permissible. Whenever we remove a brick from the wall that we designed to separate religion and government, we increase the risk of religious strife and weaken the foundation of our democracy."

The history of the Cleveland voucher program and the litigation surrounding it is summarized by Joseph P. Viteritti in "Vouchers on Trial," *Education Next* (Summer 2002). Begun in 1995, the program allows about 4,000 low-income students to attend private schools with up to $2,250 in public support. Since parochial schools were the only nonpublic schools with tuition rates low enough to accommodate voucher students, opponents maintained that the program was indeed an incentive to attend these schools.

Dan D. Goldhaber and Eric R. Eide, in "What Do We Know (and Need to Know) About the Impact of School Choice Reforms on Disadvantaged Students?" *Harvard Educational Review* (Summer 2002), examine empirical evidence and find that school choice programs have little clear-cut impact on either students in the programs or those who remain in their assigned public schools. They do cite evidence that there is greater support for vouchers among African Americans, however. Frederick M. Hess and Patrick J. McGuinn, in "Muffled by the Din: Competitive Noneffects of the Cleveland Voucher Program," *Teachers College Record* (June 2002), contend that the political and legal ambiguity about Cleveland's voucher program dampened the willingness of parochial and independent schools to expand their capacity to receive voucher students. These schools saw voucher programs as a minor threat as far as competitive pressure for reform is concerned. Perhaps the *Zelman* decision will convert this symbolic threat into a true reform movement.

In the following selections, Charles L. Glenn portrays the *Zelman* decision as a harbinger of the emergence of faith-based alternatives to the public school establishment's rampant secularism. Paul E. Peterson admits that *Zelman* is a welcome addition to the pro-voucher arsenal, but he expresses concern about establishment backlash and, even more so, governmental encroachment on religious schools' independence.

Charles L. Glenn

 **YES**

Fanatical Secularism

The Supreme Court's majority opinion in the Cleveland voucher case, *Zelman v. Simmons-Harris,* was of course the most newsworthy aspect of the decision, but the dissents were no less revealing. In about 500 words, Justice Stevens managed to use the word "indoctrination" four times and "religious strife" twice. Likewise, Justice Breyer's dissent begins and ends with warnings of "religiously based social conflict" resulting from allowing parents to use public funding to send their children to sectarian schools. Today it is a little startling to encounter these echoes of Justice Black's 1968 dissent in *Board of Education v. Allen,* in which he warned:

> The same powerful sectarian religious propagandists who have succeeded in securing passage of the present law to help religious schools carry on their sectarian religious purposes can and doubtless will continue their propaganda, looking toward complete domination and supremacy of their particular brand of religion.... The First Amendment's prohibition against governmental establishment of religion was written on the assumption that state aid to religion and religious schools generates discord, disharmony, hatred, and strife among our people, and that any government that supplies such aids is to that extent a tyranny.... The Court's affirmance here bodes nothing but evil to religious peace in this country.

Although the Supreme Court's decision in *Allen* has left no detectable sign of "disharmony, hatred, and strife among our people," the dissenting justices in the Cleveland case seem to believe that the only way to avoid "indoctrination" and religious warfare is to educate children in government-run schools (even though most industrialized countries provide support to religious schools. Concerns over deep entanglements between government and religion have of course haunted the nation from its very beginning. But in the education realm, the sheer hostility toward religious schools is not just a matter of separating church from state. It in part reflects and derives from the self-image of many educators, who like to think of themselves as having been specially anointed to decide what is in the best interest of children. Faith-based schools, they assume, are in the business of "indoctrinating" their pupils, while public schools are by definition committed to critical thinking and to the emancipation of their pupils' minds from the darkness of received opinions, even those of their own parents.

What I have elsewhere called "the myth of the common school" is a deeply held view with tremendous political resonance, first articulated in the 1830s by Horace Mann and his allies. This myth insists that enlightenment is the exclusive province of public schools, which are thus the crucible of American life and character in a way that schools independent of government could never be.

The actual working out of this powerful idea in the 19th and early 20th centuries was not altogether benign. It included, for example, systematically denying that there were a number of ways to be a good American. Nor was the common school ideal ever fully realized, even in its New England home. Segregation by social class persisted, and black pupils were unofficially segregated in much of the North and West and officially segregated in all of the South. Even the famed "steamer classes" that served immigrant children in the cities of the East and Midwest often did not keep them in school beyond the first year or two.

Nonetheless, the myth of the "common school" deserves credit for many of the accomplishments of public education in this country. It articulated a coherent vision of the American character and of an America-in-process, and it made both convincingly attractive. In recent decades, however, this hopeful myth has been transmuted into an establishment ideology that borrows much of the language and the positive associations of the common school to serve a bureaucratized, monopolistic system that is increasingly unresponsive to what parents want for their children.

The Enlightenment Mission

In *The Myth of the Common School* (1988), a historical account of how the ideology of state schooling emerged, I traced the myth's development in 19th century France, the Netherlands, and the United States. To a great extent the myth was informed by a bias against orthodox religion, often in the name of what was considered a "higher and purer" form of Christianity stripped of "superstitious" elements such as an emphasis on sin and salvation, in favor of a purified morality and faith in progress. State-sponsored schooling was intended to replace religious particularism (whether Catholic or Calvinist) as well as local loyalties and norms with an emerging national identity and culture.

Enlightenment in this form was experienced by many as oppressive rather than liberating. In place of the convictions that had given meaning and direction, and often color and excitement, to their lives, people were offered a diffuse array of platitudes, a bloodless "secular faith" without power to shape moral obligation or to give direction to a life. The effect was to set people free for a new and more oppressive bondage, unrestrained by the custom and ceremony from which, as the Irish poet William Butler Yeats reminded us, innocence and beauty come to enrich our lives.

This political account of the development of public education continues to be helpful in understanding present-day conflicts in Western democracies. If we recognize that the attempt to achieve a government monopoly on schooling was intended to serve political purposes during a period of nation-building, we can see that this monopoly is no longer appropriate—if it ever was.

The case for charter schools, vouchers, and other forms of "marketized" education rests not only on educational performance but also on the claims of freedom of conscience. Parents have a fundamental right—written into the various international covenants protecting human rights—to choose the schooling that will shape their children's understanding of the world. But a right isn't really a right if it can't be exercised. Families who can't afford tuition at a private school or a move to the suburbs should still be able to make choices regarding their children's education.

There is, in other words, a strong argument against attempts by government to use schooling to achieve political or cultural change—or stability, for that matter. John Stuart Mill gave this argument definitive form in 1859, writing:

> All that has been said of the importance of individuality of character, and diversity in opinions and modes of conduct, involves, as of the same unspeakable importance, diversity of education. A general State education is a mere contrivance for moulding people to be exactly like one another; and as the mould in which it casts them is that which pleases the predominant power in the government... in proportion as it is efficient and successful, it establishes a despotism over the mind, leading by natural tendency to one over the body.

The same point was made in a lapidary phrase by the U.S. Supreme Court in its 1925 *Pierce v. Society of Sisters* decision: "the child is not the mere creature of the State."

But does this leave nothing to be said for the role of schools in fostering the qualities of civic virtue on which, all moralists agree, the meaningful exercise of freedom depends? Put another way, does a commitment to limiting government's role in the education realm also require that schools refrain from seeking to form the character and worldview of their pupils? This is one of the central dilemmas of a republican form of government, at least in its contemporary form of limited state power. While republics pledge to respect the freedom of their citizens, they also depend on the voluntary adherence of those citizens to often complex norms of civic life. As a result, as Montesquieu pointed out, "It is in republican government that the full power of education is needed." The citizens of a republic must be virtuous since they govern themselves.

Jean-Jacques Rousseau wrote that the teacher must choose whether he will make a man or a citizen. The choice is not so stark, but it is nevertheless real. The state may seek to mold citizens on a particular pattern, but citizens in a free society surely have a right not to be molded, in their opinions and character, by the state. The child is not the mere creature of the state.

Emancipating the Mind

Any account of the tensions between the educational goals of government and of families must consider the third side of the triangle: how teachers and other educators have understood their mission. It is easy to assume that public school teachers line up on the side of the "state project" in education, while teachers in faith-based and other nonstate schools line up on the side of parents. But the reality is much more complex. Indeed, the simple state-versus-parents dichotomy fails to do justice to many educators' perception of themselves as emancipators of the minds of their students.

As noted, education theorists have long contrasted the emancipatory role of the public school with the "indoctrination" they attribute to religious schools. This strikes a note with tremendous cultural resonance. "Emancipation," Jacques Barzun tells us, is "the modern theme par excellence." The most influential of contemporary educators like to think of themselves as liberators of the minds of their pupils rather than as conveyors of "dead" information, such as the traditions of Western culture.

As a result, those who set the pace in the world of American education, and those who follow their lead, look down on the teachers, parents, and policymakers who do not share this understanding of the teacher's mission. Leadership for American education has increasingly been provided by big-city and state superintendents, professors of education, and officials of the education associations and teacher unions who see little need to respond to the uninformed views of the general public and of parents. This was illustrated by a 1997 Public Agenda survey of "teachers of teachers," professors in teacher-training institutions. Of the 900 professors surveyed, 79 percent agreed that "the general public has outmoded and mistaken beliefs about what good teaching means." They considered communication with parents important, but not in order to learn what education parents wanted for their children. Parents were to be "educated or reeducated about how learning ought to happen in today's classroom."

The professors of education surveyed were convinced, for example, that "the intellectual process of searching and struggling to learn is far more important... than whether or not students ultimately master a particular set of facts." Sixty percent of them called for less memorization in classrooms, with one professor in Boston insisting that it was "politically dangerous... when students have to memorize and spout back." By contrast, according to another Public Agenda study, 86 percent of the public and 73 percent of teachers want students to memorize the multiplication tables and to learn to do math by hand before using calculators.

These are not purely technical questions; they reflect assumptions about the very nature of education. The professors are expressing one form of the "cosmopolitan" values that have been promoted by American schooling over the past century. This perspective has made the exclusion of religion from the public schools seem not a matter of political convenience or respect for societal diversity, but essential to the mission of education. It is also a sign of intellectual laziness. Teaching facts requires knowledge, which is acquired through rigorous study and research. All it takes to teach values is the ability to spout your own beliefs and prejudices.

Platonic Education

The marks of this condescension can be found in the various controversies that swirl around public schooling. State-imposed curriculum frameworks and standardized tests are condemned as distractions from the teaching of "critical thinking." Lecturing is rejected as an unsound practice because it wrongly assumes that the teacher holds some authority. Nor should the teacher stress right and wrong solutions to the problems that she poses; what is important is the pupil's engagement with the search for an answer. This self-censorship on the part of teachers is even more important when it comes to sex education, where talk of "character" and "virtue" is deeply suspect.

So much is this set of attitudes—the priority of "liberation" or "emancipation" as the central metaphor for the teacher's work—taken for granted among American educators that the higher performance of pupils in other countries on international tests in math and science is often dismissed as reflecting other countries' inappropriate stress on drill and memorization. The possibility that a stress on rich curriculum content can result in lively, engaged classrooms is seldom credited. American pupils may not know as much, we are told, but they know how to think and to solve problems creatively.

This complacent assumption rests on a fundamental misunderstanding. Mental "emancipation" can be a very good thing, of course, when it removes the chains of misinformation and when it arouses a thirst for the truth that can be satisfied only by hard, honest mental effort. This is the traditional justification for a "liberal" education.

The classic description of such an emancipation is Plato's parable of prisoners in an underground cavern, convinced that the shadows on the wall are the only reality. One of the prisoners, in a process that Plato explicitly calls an analogy for education, is freed from his chains and brought to a state, literally, of enlightenment.

Plato makes it clear, though, that it is not enough to loose the chains; the prisoner must be forced to turn toward the light and compelled to venture out of the cavern. Only gradually can he bear the light of day, and only after much experience can he look directly at the source of light and truth. Even the gifted youth who are being groomed for leadership, we are told elsewhere in *The Republic,* should not be exposed to the pleasures and rigors of the search for truth through argument until they have mastered the disciplines of music and gymnastics and have matured through responsibility. Otherwise, Plato warns, they will just play with ideas, without any solid foundation or useful result.

While Plato stressed the laborious acquisition of knowledge and understanding as the means to enlightenment, our impatient age has preferred to think of the emancipation to be achieved through education as simply the removal of the chains of illusion (conventional morality and traditional religious worldviews) without the discipline of seeking truth or the confidence that there is truth to be found.

Critical thinking and creative problem-solving are certainly among the primary goals of a good education, but they are not developed casually in the course of an undirected exploration. Nor should we assume that there is an innate human propensity to rise to that challenge. Most of us are intellectually lazy about large spheres of the world around us. For every person who really wants to know how an automobile engine works, there must be a dozen of us who are content if it starts reliably when we turn the key. This is not necessarily bad. Life would be impossible if we could not take much around us for granted, and even new discoveries rest on the discoveries of others that we do not have to repeat.

Deconstructivism

This is the fundamental wrong-headedness of another classic description of education, Rousseau's Emile. Raised in isolation, denied the use of books and of direct instruction by his tutor, Emile is expected to learn by following his natural inclinations and responding to situations that his tutor secretly creates for him. The boy, Rousseau tells us, "instructs himself so much the better because he sees nowhere the intention to instruct him." His tutor "ought to give no precepts at all; he ought to make them be discovered."

Here is the authentic note of much current pedagogical advice. The article of faith widely held among educators, especially those who have themselves benefited from the most sophisticated education, is that the teacher should never impose anything on his students, nor suggest to them that there are fixed truths that are worth learning or seeking to discover. Instead he should closely observe the interests of his students and create situations in which they are challenged to use those interests as opportunities for learning. In responding to these challenges, the students will "construct" solutions and even meanings that are uniquely their own and will thus be more deeply and validly learned than any that might be suggested by the teacher or by the wider culture and tradition. In the process, students will become autonomous human beings, not the mere creatures of their culture, and will develop capacities of critical judgment that will enable them to participate in creating—"constructing"—a better world.

According to a recent account of "constructivism" in the 2000 yearbook of the National Society for the Study of Education:

> There is to be no notion of correct solution, no external standard of right or wrong. As long as a student's solution to a problem achieves a viable goal, it has to be credited. Nor can relevant educational goals be set externally; they are only to be encountered by the student... the constructivistic teacher is to make do without any concept of objective truth or falsehood.

"Even if it were possible to educate children in this way," philosopher Roger Scruton has written, "one thing is certain: that each generation would know less than the one before.... And that, of course, is Rousseau's underlying intention—not to liberate the child, but to destroy all intellectual authority, apart from that which resides in the self." As a result, Emile "is the least free of children, hampered at every point in his search for information," and "one can read *Emile* not as a treatise on education, but as a treatise against education." Rousseau's pupil could arrive at a quite incorrect understanding of many natural and social phenomena by relying naively on his experience alone.

Why should we concern ourselves with what Rousseau wrote almost two-and-a-half centuries ago—or indeed with what Plato wrote long before that? Because education is an enterprise, more perhaps than any other save religion, that is shaped by how we choose to think about it.

There is another tradition of thinking about education. It is expressed in the Hebrew scriptures and Jewish practice: "Why do we do these things?" The Passover questions are answered with a story about the experience of a people, a story that has sustained them and given moral direction and meaning to their lives. Does being taught a tradition and taught within a tradition prevent questioning? Of course not; it provides the content that makes questioning fruitful. It can also be found in the classical Greek concept of *paideia* as, in Michael Oakeshott's words, a "serious and orderly initiation into an intellectual, imaginative, moral and emotional inheritance."

"The knowledge-centered teacher," Scruton points out, "is in the business of passing on what he knows—ensuring, in other words, that his knowledge does not die with him." The teacher who loves his subject and cares about his students is concerned that the rising generation not know less than the one that preceded it.

Emancipation is among the elements of a good education; it can help to prepare the way for the exercise of freedom by removing barriers, but it does not of itself make a man or woman free. Education that supports individual freedom and a free society is induction into a culture, not as a straitjacket but as the context of meanings and restraints that make the exercise of real freedom possible. As Philip Rieff has noted, "A culture must communicate ideals... those distinctions between right actions and wrong that unite men and permit them the fundamental pleasure of agreement. Culture is another name for a design of motives directing the self outward, toward those communal purposes in which alone the self can be realized and satisfied."

It is for this reason that structural reforms supporting freedom and diversity in education are not enough; they must be paired with a willingness to confront the much more difficult issue of the purposes, the means, and the content of a good education. Diversity and choice must be paired with common standards, and the content of these must be rich and meaningful. This will require an effort for which the schooling we have received in recent decades almost unfits us, to rediscover and give new life and conviction to those elements of history and culture, the virtues, achievements, and consolations, that have at all times shaped and sustained civilization. This is not a plea for a narrowly Western nostalgia trip, but rather an insistence that only a recovery of the permanent things, of humanity's highest accomplishments, can serve as the basis for a worthy education.

Such a happy outcome would be helped along if opponents of school vouchers would refrain from scare tactics based on unfounded stereotypes about faith-based schooling. Schools that teach in ways shown to be harmful to children should be shut down, but the debate over how to organize a pluralistic education system is not helped by worst-case scenarios. Many Western democracies have faced this challenge successfully, finding an appropriate balance between the autonomy of schools and public accountability, and we can do so too, now that the Supreme Court majority has decided in favor of educational freedom.

Paul E. Peterson

 **NO**

Victory for Vouchers?

In the most anticipated decision of its recent term, the Supreme Court ruled, in the case of *Zelman* v. *Simmons-Harris,* that the school-voucher program in Cleveland, Ohio did not violate the Constitution's ban on the "establishment" of religion. Opponents of vouchers—i.e., the use of public funds to help families pay tuition at private schools, including religious schools—were predictably disappointed, but pledged to fight on. As Senator Edward M. Kennedy declared, "Vouchers may be constitutional," but "that doesn't make them good policy."

The policy's sympathizers, needless to say, saw the ruling in a different light. President Bush used the occasion of the Supreme Court's decision to issue a full-throated endorsement of vouchers. *Zelman,* he told a gathering in Cleveland, did more than remove a constitutional cloud; it was a "historic" turning point in how Americans think about education. In 1954, in *Brown* v. *Board of Education,* the Court had ruled that the country could not have two sets of schools, "one for African-Americans and one for whites." Now, he continued, in ruling as it did in the Cleveland case, the Court was affirming a similar principle, proclaiming that "our nation will not accept one education system for those who can afford to send their children to a school of their choice and one for those who can't." *Zelman,* according to the President, is *Brown* all over again.

But is it?

⋅⟨⟩⋅

Publicly funded school vouchers got their start in Milwaukee, Wisconsin in 1990. Established at the urging of local black leaders and Wisconsin Governor Tommy Thompson (now the Secretary of Health and Human Services), the program was originally restricted to secular private schools and included fewer than a thousand needy students. To accommodate growing demand, religious schools were later allowed to participate, an arrangement declared constitutional in 1998 by the Wisconsin Supreme Court. The Milwaukee program now provides a voucher worth up to $5,785 to over 10,000 students, amounting to more than 15 percent of the school system's eligible population.

In 1999, at the behest of Governor Jeb Bush, Florida also established a publicly funded voucher program, aimed at students attending public schools that failed to meet state standards. Though just two schools and fewer than a hundred students have participated in the program thus far, ten other schools, with thousands of students, will be eligible to participate this fall. (The Florida program is also noteworthy because it served as a model for the voucher-like federal scholarship program advocated by George W. Bush during the 2000 presidential campaign—a program subsequently abandoned by the administration in its push for an education bill.)

Though the Milwaukee and Florida programs had until recently received the most public attention, it was the program in Cleveland—the country's only other publicly funded voucher program of any size[1]—That won the opponents of vouchers their day before the Supreme Court. The Cleveland program is relatively small, providing a maximum of $2,250 a year to each of roughly 4,000 students. Parents use the vouchers overwhelmingly for religious schools, which in recent years have enrolled over 90 percent of the program's participants. This, according to lawyers for the teachers' unions, the most powerful foe of vouchers, constituted an obvious violation of the separation between church and state. And they prevailed twice in federal court, winning decisions at the trial and appellate level against Susan Zelman, Ohio's superintendent of public instruction and the official responsible for administering the Cleveland program.

But the five more conservative members of the Supreme Court were not persuaded. In his opinion for the majority in *Zelman*, Chief Justice William Rehnquist pointed to three well-known precedents—*Mueller* (1983), *Witters* (1986), and *Zobrest* (1993)—in which the Court had allowed government funds to flow to religious schools. What these cases had in common, he wrote, and what they shared with the Cleveland voucher program, was that public money reached the schools "only as a result of the genuine and independent choices of private individuals." Under Cleveland's program, families were in no way coerced to send their children to religious schools; they had a range of state-funded options, including secular private schools, charter schools, magnet schools, and traditional public schools. Considered in this wider context, the voucher program was, Rehnquist concluded, "entirely neutral with respect to religion."

The dissenters in *Zelman*, led by Justice David Souter, challenged the majority's reading of the relevant precedents—especially of *Nyquist* (1973), a ruling that struck down a New York State program giving aid to religious schools—and suggested that the choice in Cleveland between religion and non-religion was a mere legal fiction. They saved their most pointed objections, however, for what they saw as the likely social consequences of the ruling. The Court, Souter wrote, was promoting "divisiveness" by asking secular taxpayers to support, for example, the teaching of "Muslim views on the differential treatment of the sexes," or by asking Muslim-Americans to pay "for the endorsement of the religious Zionism taught in many religious Jewish schools." Justice Stephen Breyer suggested that the decision would spark "a struggle of sect against sect," and Justice John Paul Stevens wondered if the majority had considered the lessons of other nations' experience around the world, including "the impact of religious strife... on the decisions of neighbors in the Balkans, Northern Ireland, and the Middle East to mistrust one another."

⚜

If judicial rhetoric is all that counts, the dissenters in *Zelman* had the better of it. In the majority opinion, by contrast, there is very little that rises to the level of *Brown's* often-cited language about the demands of American equality. Even observers pleased by the ruling were disappointed that the majority's opinion did not go much beyond showing how the facts of the case fit past precedents; no ringing declarations are to be found in Chief Justice Rehnquist's cautious prose.

Only in the concurrences written by two of the Justices does one get a sense of the wider issues at stake. Responding to the worries of the dissenters, Justice Sandra Day O'Connor pointed out that taxpayer dollars have long flowed to various religious institutions—through Pell Grants to denominational colleges and universities; through child-care subsidies that can be used at churches, synagogues, and other religious institutions; through direct aid to parochial schools for transportation, textbooks, and other materials; and, indirectly, through the tax code, which gives special breaks to the faithful. If government aid to religious institutions were such a problem, she suggested, wouldn't American society be torn already by sectarian strife?

What Justice O'Connor failed to answer was the dissenters' obvious disquiet—one shared these days by many Americans—at the prospect of public money going to support the teaching of extremist religious creeds. This is a reasonable concern—though it is hardly clear, as the Justices themselves might have argued, that the best tool for conquering intolerance born of religious zeal is for the government to impose secular enlightenment. The U.S. has achieved religious peace not by depending upon school-based indoctrination of any stripe but by ensuring that the members of all creeds have access to the democratic process and a robust private sphere in which to meet their particular needs.

As an educational matter, several well-designed studies have shown that students who attend private schools in the U.S. are not only just as tolerant of others as their public-school peers but are also *more* engaged in political and community life. Catholic schools have a particularly outstanding record, probably because for more than a century American Catholics have felt compelled to teach democratic values as proof of their patriotism. There are obviously extremist outliers among, for instance, some of the American *madrassas* discovered by journalists since September 11, but there is no reason to doubt that most of the country's religious schools are attempting to prove that they, too, can create good citizens.

As for *Brown* itself, only Justice Clarence Thomas, in his own stirring concurrence, pointed to it as an explicit precedent, quoting Frederick Douglass to argue that today's inner-city public-school systems "deny emancipation to urban minority students." As he observed,

> The failure to provide education to poor urban children perpetuates a vicious cycle of poverty, dependence, criminality, and alienation that continues for the remainder of their lives. If society cannot end racial discrimination, at least it can arm minorities with the education to defend themselves from some of discrimination's effects.

For Justice Thomas—as for President Bush, whose own remarks were undoubtedly influenced by these passages—vouchers are a civil-rights issue; they promise not to intensify religious strife, as the Court's dissenters would have it, but to help heal the country's most enduring social divide.

⋘◉⋙

Whether *Zelman* can in fact meet these high expectations remains very much to be seen. *Brown,* in principle, was self-enacting. Neither state legislatures nor local school boards could defy the ruling without running afoul of the law. George Wallace, Bull Connor, and many other Southern politicians were willing to do just that, but in the end, federal authorities imposed the Supreme Court's decision on the vested interests that opposed it.

Zelman is different. Though it keeps existing voucher programs intact, it does not compel the formation of new ones. Here the barricades to change remain extraordinarily high.

Public opinion does not pose the most serious obstacle; indeed, on this issue it is highly uncertain. Pollsters can get either pro-voucher or anti-voucher majorities simply by tinkering with the working of their questions and the order in which they are asked. Nor, despite greater exposure for the issue, have the public's views evolved much in recent years; questions asked in 1996 generated basically the same results in 2001.

Vouchers suffer from graver problems among members of the political class. Whether in Congress or at the state level, substantial bipartisan support is usually necessary to get a piece of legislation through the various committees, past a vote in two chambers, and signed into law. For vouchers, such support has never materialized. Whatever the private opinions of Democrats, for most of them, it is political suicide to support vouchers publicly. Teachers' unions have long placed vouchers at the top of their legislative kill list, and they are a key Democratic constituency, providing the party with both substantial financing and election-day shock troops.

Nor can voucher proponents rely on whole-hearted support from the GOP. Most Republicans, especially social conservatives and libertarians who have read their Milton Friedman, support vouchers in principle. Still, an idea whose primary appeal is to black Americans, the most faithful of all Democratic voting blocs, is a hard sell among the Republican rank-and-file. Vouchers simply do not have much resonance with well-heeled suburbanites who already have a range of educational choices. When vouchers came up as state ballot questions in both California and Michigan two years ago, most Republican politicians found a way to dodge the issue—and the proposals lost badly.

Even if this political situation were to change, most states have constitutional restrictions of their own that may be invoked to scuttle attempts to provide vouchers for use at religious schools. Many of these provisions are so-called "Blaine" amendments, dating to the 19th century, when James Blaine, a Senator from Maine and a Republican presidential candidate, sought to win the anti-immigrant vote by campaigning to deny public funds to Catholic schools. (Blaine is perhaps most famous for describing the Democrats as the party of "Rum, Romanism, and Rebellion.") In its classic version, the Blaine amendment read as follows:

> No money raised by taxation for the support of public schools, or derived from any public fund therefore, nor any public lands devoted thereto, shall ever be under the control of any religious sect; nor shall any money so raised or lands so devoted be divided between religious sects or denominations.

In a number of cases, state courts have interpreted Blaine amendments to mean nothing more than what is required, according to the Supreme Court, by the establishment clause of the First Amendment. On this view, vouchers are safe—but not every state judge necessarily shares this view. Such language may prove to be a hurdle for the voucher program in Florida, where a trial court has now ruled that the law violates the state constitution. Depending on what finally happens at the state level, the Supreme Court may in time be asked to decide whether, on account of their nativist and anti-Catholic origins, the Blaine amendments themselves are unconstitutional.

◦◦◦

However much these practical differences may separate *Zelman* from *Brown*, one powerful similarity remains: like the Court's famed ruling against segregation in the schools, the decision to allow vouchers means much more for black students and their families than for other Americans.

For decades, and despite a host of compensatory reforms the sizable gap in educational performance between blacks and whites has remained roughly the same. According to the National Assessment of Educational Progress, black eighth graders continue to score about four grade levels below their white peers on standardized tests. Nor is this gap likely to close as long as we have, in President Bush's words, "one education system for those who can afford to send their children to a school of their choice and one for those who can't."

When parents choose a neighborhood or town in which to live, they also select, often quite self-consciously, a school for their children. That is why various Internet services now provide buyers—and real-estate agents—with detailed test-score data and other information about school districts and even individual schools. But there is a catch: the mobility that makes these choices possible costs money. It is no accident that children lucky enough to be born into privilege also attend the nation's best schools.

African-Americans are often the losers in this arrangement. Holding less financial equity, and still facing discrimination in the housing market, they choose from a limited set of housing options. As a result, their children are more likely to attend the worst public schools. Richer, whiter districts rarely extend anything more than a few token slots to low-income minority students outside their communities.

It is thus unsurprising that blacks have benefited most when school choice has been expanded. In multi-year evaluations of private voucher programs in New York City, Washington, D.C., and Dayton, Ohio, my colleagues and I found that African-American students, when given the chance to attend private schools, scored significantly higher on standardized tests than comparable students who remained in the public schools. In New York, where the estimates are most precise, those who switched from public to private schools scored, after three years, roughly 9 percentage points higher on math and reading tests than their public-school peers, a difference of about two grade levels. If reproduced nationwide, this result would cut almost in half the black-white test-score gap. (Interestingly, there is no evidence that vouchers have improved the academic performance of students from other ethnic groups. In my own research, they had no impact, positive or negative, on the test scores of either whites in Dayton or Hispanics in New York City.)

These findings about the especially positive effects of private schools on African-American students are hardly isolated. One review of the literature, conducted by the Princeton economist Cecilia Rouse, concludes that even though (once again) it is difficult to discern positive benefits for white students, "Catholic schools generate higher test scores for African-Americans." Another, done by Jeffrey Grogger and Derek Neal, economists from the University of Wisconsin and the University of Chicago, finds little in the way of detectable gains for whites but concludes that "urban minorities in Catholic schools fare much better than similar students in public schools."

No less important, in light of concerns about the effect of vouchers on students "left behind," is that school choice also seems to improve the performance of students who remain in the *public* schools. The best data from Milwaukee show strong advances in test scores since the voucher program was put into place there ten years ago, especially at public schools in those low-income neighborhoods where the voucher option was available. As observers in Milwaukee have noted, it was only in the wake of the voucher program's expansion that the public-school system there began to adopt a series of apparently successful reforms.

We do not know precisely what accounts for the gains that black students have made by switching to private schools. The answer is certainly not money, since the private schools they attend are usually low-budget, no-frills operations. The most striking difference, according to my own research, lies in the general educational environment: the parents of these students who reported being much more satisfied with everything from the curriculum, homework, and teacher quality to how the schools communicate with the parents themselves. The classes tend to be smaller, they say, and there is less fighting, cheating, racial conflict, or destruction of property.

ぐ◎ぐ

That vouchers can produce such results has been known for some time. The question now is whether the ruling in *Zelman* will have any impact on what the public and politicians think about the issue. If nothing else, the Court's authoritative pronouncement on the constitutionality of vouchers has already conferred new legitimacy on them. Newspaper editors and talk-show hosts have been forced to give the idea more respect, and political opponents cannot dismiss it so easily.

Still, the key to change lies within the black community, and especially with parents, who increasingly know that private schools provide a better education for their children. A 1998 poll by Public Agenda, a nonpartisan research group, found that 72 percent of African-American parents supported vouchers, as opposed to just 59 percent of white parents. A poll conducted two years later by the Joint Center for Political and Economic Studies had similar results, with just under half of the overall adult population supporting vouchers but 57 percent of African-American adults favoring the idea. Perhaps more to the point, blacks constituted nearly half of all the applicants for the 40,000 privately funded vouchers offered nationwide by the Children's Scholarship Fund in 1999, even though they comprised only about a quarter of the eligible population.

Even in the face of such numbers, it is too much to expect that men like Jesse Jackson and Al Sharpton will reconsider their virulent opposition to vouchers; their political tendencies are too well defined. But pressure to support school vouchers is building among black parents, and black leaders will have to act. Howard Fuller, the former superintendent of Milwaukee's public-school system, has formed the Black Alliance for Educational Options, a pro-voucher group that has mounted an effective public-relations campaign and is making waves in civil-rights circles. And young politicians like Cory Booker in Newark have begun to challenge their old-line, machine-style elders, using vouchers as a key dividing point. Responding to these currents—and to the decision in *Zelman*—the city council of Camden, composed entirely of black and Hispanic Democrats, passed a unanimous resolution in July urging the state of New Jersey to establish a voucher program for the city's dysfunctional public schools. Such examples are sure to multiply.

Not even the Supreme Court, it should be recognized, can make educational change come quickly in America. Though *Brown* was handed down in 1954, it took more than a decade before major civil-rights legislation was enacted; Southern schools were not substantially desegregated until the 1970's. Anyone writing about *Brown* ten years after its passage might have concluded that the decision was almost meaningless.

The same may be said about *Zelman* on its tenth anniversary. Perhaps the safest prediction is that, in four or five decades, American education will have been altered dramatically, in ways we cannot anticipate, by the parental demand for greater choice—a demand codified in *Zelman*. Many battles will be fought and lost along the way, to be sure, but the victories will accumulate, because choice, once won, is seldom conceded.

Note

1. New York City, Washington, D.C., and numerous other cities have well-developed *private* voucher programs designed to help low-income families; these currently serve over 50,000 students.

POSTSCRIPT

Has the Supreme Court Reconfigured American Education?

In "Privatizing Education: The Politics of Vouchers," *Phi Delta Kappan* (February 2001), Sheila Suess Kennedy identifies the partisans in the voucher wars. Pro-voucher groups include pro-market libertarians, business organizations, the Christian Right, and the Catholic Church. The anti-voucher side includes the education establishment (teachers' unions, in particular), civil libertarians, church/state separationists, and official African American organizations. Regarding this last group, Michael Leo Owens, in "Why Blacks Support Vouchers," *The School Administrator* (June 2002), states that although urban black America favors school vouchers, its leaders do not. He cites a 1999 survey showing that 68 percent of blacks favor vouchers whereas a similar percentage of black state and local officials do not support voucher plans. Apparently, despite their shortcomings, vouchers offer hope to poor families whose children are trapped in the nation's worst schools. On the contrary, Benjamin O. Canada, in "Black Leadership and Vouchers," *The School Administrator* (June 2002), contends that vouchers cannot systematically expand educational opportunities for blacks—they are a hoax.

Clearly, the *Zelman* decision has rekindled the debate about breaking up the government monopoly in schooling and giving parents and children new options. So say Lawrence W. Reed and Joseph P. Overton in "The Future of School Choice," *USA Today* (January 2003), who assert, "The empowerment and transformation of parents into active agents is the foundation of educational choice theory." Reed and Overton further contend that the Supreme Court's momentous decision has opened the door to improving schools through the power of choice and competition. In time, they say, it will be seen as a pivotal ruling in the restoration of American education.

In contrast, Peterson's concerns are echoed in Steven Menashi's "The Church-State Tangle: School Choice and Religious Autonomy," *Policy Review* (August & September 2002), in which the author worries that "if voucher laws saddle private schools with the same regulatory regime that now hampers the public education system, school choice will prove an iatrogenic aggravation of the educational crisis." He further contends that "school choice is doomed to fail if it does not include religious schools.... [But] at the same time, a school choice program that forces schools to compromise their religious missions and to accept government oversight in admissions and curriculum is ultimately self-defeating." Menashi's position is that the Court has answered the establishment clause question with the principle of private choice, yet all the precedent about excessive entanglement remains.

For further slants on the issue, see the April 2002 issue of *Educational Leadership* and the Winter 2001 issue of *Education Next*.